A SOCIAL AND RELIGIOUS HISTORY OF THE JEWS

Late Middle Ages and Era of European Expansion
1200–1650

VOLUME XIV

CATHOLIC RESTORATION AND WARS OF RELIGION

A SOCIAL
AND RELIGIOUS
HISTORY OF
THE JEWS

By SALO WITTMAYER BARON

Second Edition, Revised and Enlarged

Late Middle Ages and Era of European Expansion
1200–1650

VOLUME XIV

CATHOLIC RESTORATION AND WARS OF RELIGION

Columbia University Press
New York and London *1969*

The Jewish Publication Society of America
Philadelphia *5730*

CONTENTS

A SOCIAL AND RELIGIOUS HISTORY OF THE JEWS

PUBLISHED VOLUMES

Late Middle Ages and Era of European Expansion

CATHOLIC RESTORATION
AND WARS OF RELIGION

LIX

CATHOLIC REFORM

R EACTION in the Catholic camp to the reformatory trends was immediate and strong. It grew in power and violence when the Catholic world realized that the new reformers were becoming increasingly militant and separatist. At first the Protestant leaders had merely taken up the cry for ecclesiastical reform *within* the Church, a cry which had been heard all over Europe for more than a century, and which had brought forth the two great reform Councils of Constance (1411–18) and Basel (1431–49). Even Luther's famous Ninety-Five Theses of 1517 were fully in line with Catholic precedents; they did not appear to many contemporaries as a major revolutionary move, although they were considered sufficiently "subversive" for the ecclesiastical establishment to initiate some repressive measures. In time, however, Protestantism gathered enough strength to attack the existing order and to create independent religious sects. Ultimately, the Catholic leaders resorted to military force. As a result western and central Europe became embroiled in those protracted Wars of Religion which, culminating in the Thirty Years' War of 1618–48, helped to reshape the face of the Western world and particularly its religious and cultural structure.

Even less than the Reformation can one precisely date the Counter Reformation, or Catholic Restoration. Movements of this type grow slowly and assume ever vaster proportions. Hence it is left to the more or less arbitrary decision of individual scholars which particular event they wish to take as their starting point. For our purposes it will suffice to treat the period of 1517–64 as the heroic era of the Protestant Reformation led by Luther, Zwingli, and Calvin, and that of 1540–1650 as the era of Catholic consolidation, initiated by the Jesuit Order and the Council of Trent, and followed by the Wars of Religion. The outcome was the permanent denominational divisions within Western Christendom. Together with the simultaneous political and socioeconomic changes these ideological conflicts deeply affected the destinies of European Jewry.[1]

PRELIMINARY EFFORTS

From the outset, the Councils of Constance and Basel had been weakened by their division into national groupings which not only cherished their own regional customs and outlooks but also often tried to defend their countries' national interests. As we recall, Constance treated even the Hussite schism as a "minor matter" and left it to the German army to take care of that significant socioreligious revolution. In general, the contrast between the fifteenth-century popes and councils and Innocent III and the Fourth Lateran Council is startling. While in the thirteenth century the Church had held the initiative and had been a prime factor in shaping the development of most European nations, two centuries later the papal organs as a rule merely reacted to various national pressures and largely followed the direction of political leaders. True, the great "Turkish menace," especially after the fall of Constantinople in 1453, might have reunited the entire Catholic *corpus mysticum* including the long-separated Eastern Churches. For a moment it indeed looked as if the two branches of Christianity would close ranks before the Ottoman onslaught. In this respect Eugenius IV and his Council of Ferrara-Florence (1438–42) had a great historic opportunity for healing the centuries-old breach. But they bungled it, mainly because the nationalist conflicts within Europe overshadowed the long-range needs for solidarity. Ultimately, the major European potentates, including Maximilian I, the doge of Venice, and particularly Francis I, actually sought support from Turkey against their Christian enemies. Nor were the popes consistent in calling for an anti-Ottoman crusade; at times they themselves took part in the game of power politics on the Turkish side.[2]

It is small wonder, then, that in the Jewish question, too, the Church had lost its preeminent position of leadership. If the late medieval ecumenical councils occasionally took up problems raised by the presence of Jews in Christian society, they almost invariably rehashed, with but minor modifications, the long-accepted approaches and decisions of their more creative predecessors. Whatever innovations were introduced into Christian-Jewish relations stemmed largely from provincial leaders, while the Church universal merely nodded its approval or, at the most, voiced weak disapproval. It certainly was a Church divided against itself which tolerated the excesses of Spanish rulers and churchmen in their anti-Jewish policies during the quarter century after the massacres of 1391. Even after Martin V reestablished some order in the treatment of Jews, the Papacy was not always able to control its own anti-Jewish representatives abroad. Though acting as a papal legate, St. John Capistrano responded much more to the rising tide of German Jew-baiting than to the responsibility of upholding the traditional ecclesiastical checks and balances. Later Sixtus IV put up but a token resistance to the establishment of the Spanish Inquisition, in the main dictated by the exigencies of Spain's national policy. If papal resistance was more sustained and effective against similar Portuguese demands, this was owing more to tactical pressures and counterpressures in Rome than to any deeply thought-out ecclesiastical principles.

Similarly, the Church was too slow in perceiving the strength and implications of the forces transforming medieval feudalism into modern capitalism. Not only did the Papacy allow the continued predominance of feudal landownership in her own Pontifical States until late in the sixteenth century, it also completely lacked comprehension of the vital role played by the credit system in the new economy. That is why it failed to moderate the anti-Jewish attacks connected with the late fifteenth-century movement for the establishment of the *monti di pietà*. Outwardly appealing to the charitable instincts of pious Christians, this movement, sponsored by such churchmen as Bernardino da Feltre, helped to make Jews expendable and thus paved the way for their total elimination from many parts of the Apennine Peninsula. Finally, after long hesitation Leo X, dedicated humanist though he was, condemned his fellow humanist Johannes Reuchlin for defending the Talmud, although, as a devotee of ancient cultures, he had himself shown interest in having that classic of Judaism printed for general use in Rome and Venice. If the Turkish menace inspired his successor, Clement VII, to enter into negotiations with that extraordinary pair of Jewish spokesmen David Reubeni and Solomon Molkho, the Papacy showed little strength in saving their lives when they were caught in the inquisitorial net in the 1530s.[3]

Nor were the ecclesiastical leaders sufficiently alert to respond quickly to the Lutheran challenge. Not until Leo X's aforementioned bull of 1520 ordering the suppression of Luther's works, and the reformer's countermove in publicly burning that bull, did they realize the seriousness of the situation. In fact, the papal reaction evoked an instantaneous international response. Luther's works were speedily burned in public bonfires arranged in various parts of Germany and in Venice, Naples, and Cambridge. In London such an auto-da-fé was staged, on May 12, 1521, by Cardinal Thomas Wolsey, archbishop of Canterbury, in the presence of a large crowd and many foreign ambassadors, the king being absent only because of illness. The Paris Parlement soon thereafter decreed that the mere possession of Luther's writings made one liable to fine or imprisonment. At the same time the dramatic proceedings of the Diet of Worms, where Luther refused to retract when ordered to do so by Charles V, and his escape under the protection of German princes and nobles heightened the tensions. And yet, a well-informed leader like Cardinal Girolamo Aleandro (Aleander), while serving as a papal legate at that Diet, could find no better explanation for the spread of heretical movements than the alleged influence exercised by unreliable New Christians. Although the charge of Jewish instigation to heresy had been a permanent accompaniment of Christian sectarian struggles from ancient times and had no more validity now than a similar censure uttered at the condemnation of John Huss at the Council of Constance, this accusation was now aimed at a group of Christians of Jewish descent who allegedly were, so to say, boring from within. There may have been some truth in the rumor that Jews and New Christians helped to disseminate Luther's works, including his pro-Jewish pamphlet of 1523, in French and Spanish intellectual circles. However, Aleandro's sweeping denunciation was supported by no more valid evidence than had been Charles V's (or rather, as Spanish King, Charles I's) similar assertion in his aforementioned letter of 1519 to Pope Leo X. More significantly, after 1547 the Papacy accepted, however reluctantly, Archbishop

Silíceo's parallel contention justifying his newly enacted Toledan "statute of purity." The popes must have realized that the racialist principle underlying that statute ran counter to the entire tradition of the Church universal and that it would ultimately hamper its missionary program. Yet Rome meekly surrendered, in this as in other areas, to the nationalist demands of certain Church provinces backed by strong political power.[4]

Ideologically, too, the first answers of Catholic leaders to Protestant attacks did not go beyond a reiteration of long-accepted Catholic teachings. Confronted with the insistence by Wyclif and Huss, and the even more vigorous emphasis by Luther, Zwingli, and Calvin, on the *sola Scriptura* as the decisive source of Christian truth, Cardinal Cajetan (Tommaso de Vio) could adduce no stronger arguments than to contend that authentic Church tradition is a necessary prerequisite for the understanding of, and hence also a source coordinate with, the words of Scripture. For a while the reformers themselves still believed in the unbroken continuity of the Catholic tradition and professed to be merely seeking remedies for certain shortcomings within the Church's body politic. As late as 1541 Cardinal Gasparo Contarini could still hope to bring all parties assembled in Ratisbon to agree on a common platform. However, by that time, the growing radicalism of the Protestant movement had unavoidably bred warring camps of believers, each of which invoked its own interpretation of Scripture without reference to traditional exegesis.[5]

In the meantime Luther's theses had been violently denounced, in 1518, by Johann Maier von Eck, who soon became the chief Catholic apologist in German lands. Eck branded Luther a Hussite and challenged him to a debate, which took place in Leipzig in June and July 1519. (Luther was assisted by Andreas Bodenstein von Carlstadt.) To the end of his life in 1543, Eck consistently combated the Reformation, orally and in writing. One of his pamphlets, the *Enchiridion locorum communium adversus Lutherum,* published in 1525, appeared in 46 editions within half a century. Jews did not come out unscathed from the debate. True, in his early years Eck had controverted some of the doctrines propagated by his former teacher Ulrich Zasius in *De parvulis Judaeorum.* But because he was a well-informed, if frequently crude and highly inflated, controversialist and took issue with almost anything published in the Protestant camp, he also assailed in 1541 the anonymous repudiation of the blood libel (written by Andreas Osiander) and strongly insisted on the Jews' need of Christian blood. A learned theologian who in any debate paraded a vast array of quotations from the patristic and canonistic literatures (many of them apparently taken from contemporary anthologies), Eck must have been aware of the consistent denial of that accusation by popes and emperors. Yet in his polemical ruthlessness he totally ignored that part of the official Catholic tradition and lumped together Jews and Protestants as the Church's great enemies, who had to be fought with all means, fair and foul. His polemics set the tone for many other Catholic apologists, including Johannes Cochlaeus (Dobeneck) of Frankfort, whose challenge to a debate had been rejected by the Wittenberg reformer in 1521. Cochlaeus' fine humanist training did not prevent him from descending to the depths of personal vituperation. Nevertheless his image of Luther was to influence the outlook of Catholic theologians and historians in later generations. Unlike Eck, however, he did not allow his anti-Protestantism to translate itself into an equally rabid anti-Judaism.[6]

Catholic counteraction on a large scale, however, came only after the countries outside the Holy Roman Empire began to feel seriously threatened. In the Empire the Reformation almost immediately became entangled in domestic power politics, which greatly distorted its socioreligious message. Even Charles V, a devout Catholic and soon the main supporter of the Counter Reformation, for a time wished to make use of the new movement to keep the Papacy, France, and his domestic rivals in check. But when the Protestant preachments began appealing to a number of influential leaders, including some Marranos, in France, Italy, and Spain, the Catholic world felt sufficiently endangered to embark upon a counteroffensive. No longer satisfied with mere apologetical dialogues, it undertook to combat the new doctrines with both the force of arms and its own internal rejuvenation. One of the main instruments of that counteraction was the newly organized Society of Jesus, whose members also performed signal services as leaders in the comprehensive internal reforms adopted by the ecumenical Council of Trent.

JESUIT ORDER

In St. Ignatius of Loyola (1491–1556), Luther, Zwingli, and Calvin found their worthy counterpart. By coincidence, Loyola and Calvin (who at that time was still a humanist scholar rather than reformer) met in 1533 at the College of St. Barbe in Paris. The young Spanish nobleman had grown up amidst the reign of terror established by the Inquisition, whose victim he almost became at a critical moment. At first he conducted himself like a typical young soldier and bon vivant, but he was soon converted to mystical Catholicism and began leading an exemplary life. Before long he embarked on a missionary pilgrimage to Jersualem; but he was dissuaded from remaining there by the local Franciscans, who feared that his impetuosity in converting Muslims would embroil them in difficulties with the Turkish authorities. Through his studies at the Universities of Alcalá, Salamanca, and Paris, his numerous visits to Rome, and a life of self-imposed penury and suffering, he gathered experiences and insights which prepared him well for his great, historic role. He finally succeeded in assembling around him a band of devoted disciples and associates, out of which emerged the Society of Jesus, given grudging recognition by Pope Paul III in 1540. Harking back to his earlier training as a soldier, and emulating, in part, the militant Spanish brotherhoods of his youth, he gave the new "Company" a quasi-military organization, based upon unquestioning obedience to superiors but at the same time stressing individual responsibility. In time, this rigorous discipline helped the Society to become, particularly through its brilliant educational efforts within and outside Christendom, a leading power in shaping the destinies of Catholicism, not only in the Western world but all over the globe. As early as 1547, Loyola wrote to Joannes Alphonso de Polanco that "here in Rome, especially among the few who fail to see the truth, we have the reputation of striving to rule the world." [7]

From the outset the Society, deeply dedicated to its missionary ideals, wished to convert Jews, as well as Muslims, heretics, and pagans. Although originating in Spain, where all *conversos* lived under a cloud of suspicion and where purity of non-Jewish descent increasingly became a prerequisite to admission to many fields of endeavor, the Order decided to treat even newly converted Jews on a par with Old Christians. After establishing their headquarters in Rome, Loyola and his immediate associates considered the general provisions of canon law much more authoritative than the excessive strictness of the Spanish Inquisition. "Perhaps no founder of an Order," admiringly observes L. Cristiani, "carries on him a greater imprint of his century, his race, his family origins; yet he [Loyola] has placed himself better than anyone else on the plane of universality, as well as eternity." From the beginning the Society opened its membership to converts meeting the rigid qualifications of piety and character demanded from all novices. Loyola himself did not hesitate to admit, in 1552, one of Elijah Levita's grandsons, then twenty-two years old. Giovanni Battista Eliano (Salomone Romano) at first followed in his grandfather's footsteps and taught Hebrew and Arabic at the newly founded Collegio Romano. In this capacity he played a rather sinister role in the then heatedly debated censorship of Hebrew books. He subsequently turned foreign missionary and spent many years in the Middle East spreading Catholic teachings among Copts and Maronites.[8]

More complicated was the problem of admission of descendants of Spanish *conversos*, who formed a separate class in the Iberian population. It is, therefore, doubly remarkable that, in choosing his closest collaborators, Loyola either did not care to investigate their Jewish ancestry or knowingly disregarded it. His secretary and constant assistant, Joannes Alphonso de Polanco, and his most distinguished associate, Diego (Jaime or Jacobus) Laynez (Lainez), generally considered the cofounder and chief organizer of the Society, were known to be of Jewish descent. This "blemish" did not hinder Loyola from sending Laynez to Sicily in 1548 on a visitational journey, the first such tour recorded in the history of the Order, a supervisory and centralizing method which was to contribute greatly in later years to the Jesuits' international cohesiveness and efficiency. Laynez was also sent, under papal auspices, to the Council of Trent, where he played a most prominent role. Two years after the founder's death the Society elected Laynez as its second general (1558–64). (Rumor had it that, after Paul IV's demise in 1559, this known New Christian was seriously considered as a candidate for the papal tiara.) During his tenure of office the New Christian friar was one of the intellectual leaders of the Counter Reformation. For one example, in 1562 he addressed a lengthy memorandum to Queen Mother Catherine de Médicis of France, advising her how best to combat the spreading Protestant "heresy." His major counsel was to refuse permission for the erection of any kind of sectarian church, arguing:

We have an example of such a move in the Jews and Saracens who had been ordered to leave Spain unless they became converted to Christianity. Up to the present a large number of those who remained behind have persevered in their infidelity despite their baptism. Yet because they were not left in possession of synagogues and mosques, some of them have from day to day become sincere converts and have turned out to be good Christians. For man is by nature inclined toward religion. When he is not permitted to practice that which he prefers, he finally embraces another faith, in order not to live without any religion.

Evidently, Laynez was not sufficiently informed about the secret forms of Marrano worship in private homes. Nor did he realize how decidedly secondary synagogue buildings had been in the traditional system of Jewish worship, which merely required the presence in any place of ten adult male Jews to perform congregational services equivalent to those performed in the most elaborate structures. On the other hand, he had a profound knowledge of Catholic theology and canon law and was able to make significant contributions to the deliberations at the closing sessions of the Council of Trent in 1562–63. He successfully intervened at a particularly critical moment when a raging controversy over the independent rights of bishops versus papal supremacy almost threatened to break up the Council. In his speech of October 20, 1562, he allayed the conflict (which reappeared under a different guise in the recent Second Vatican Council), by suggesting the so-called Laynez formula, according to which each bishop was to be considered basically sovereign in his diocese by virtue of his ordination and the ensuing *potestas ordinis*. However, to exercise his authority, he required the additional *potestas jurisdictionis,* which only the pope could confer upon him.[9]

Nor is it at all surprising that the first Jesuit to wear a cardinal's hat was Francisco de Toledo, another scion of Spanish converts.

Even enemies conceded Francisco's vast learning and enormous capacity for work. But they often criticized his policies. They accused him, for instance, of delaying Robert Bellarmine's appointment as cardinal, so that he himself could become the first Jesuit to achieve that rank. His style of preaching was likewise controversial. It was highly appreciated by Popes Gregory XIII and Sixtus V, in whose presence he often delivered sermons, but it was detested by the philosopher Giordano Bruno. Bruno actually contrasted Toledo's sermons with those of a "Hebrew" preacher (probably the convert Andrea del Monte) whom he admired "for his eloquence and still more for his knowledge." [10]

The aloofness of Loyola and his friends toward the Holy Office may be explained partially by their own experiences with the Inquisition. On several occasions their peculiar piety and good works, their asceticism, occasionally even their strange dress, sufficed for the Inquisition to put them behind bars. They thus learned firsthand of the proneness of informers to submit wrong denunciations to the Holy Office and of the unreliability of many of its witnesses. Once haled before the Inquisition, moreover, even if acquitted, a defendant carried with him a stigma to the end of his life, as happened indeed to Loyola himself after he had inspired Paul III to found in Rome a House of Catechumens for the conversion of Italian Jews (by the bull *Illius, qui pro Dominici* of February 19, 1543). With Loyola's cooperation, the pope appointed Don Giovanni da Torano, rector of one of the Roman churches, to direct the new archconfraternity charged with the supervision of all such institutions. Don Giovanni almost immediately turned upon his benefactor and, in 1547, submitted a lengthy denunciation of the Jesuits to the pope. He invoked the three or four (really five) inquisitorial prosecutions of Jesuit leaders as evidence that they were heretics propagating false doctrines in their sermons and frequently violating canon law. According to him, Loyola had dismissed some members because they had failed to reveal secrets entrusted to them under the seal of confession, while Polanco had tried to persuade a lady censured by her father confessor to transfer her confessions to a Jesuit priest. These accusations carried little weight with the pope and merely led to the banishment of the accuser. Nonetheless, they must have illustrated to the Society's leaders the type of rumor-mongering which underlay much of the evidence gathered for the inquisitorial trials.[11]

Having been away from his country for many years, Loyola thus repudiated his homeland's prejudices as criteria for his new international organization. According to his devoted disciple and biographer Pedro de Ribadeneira, at a dinner discussion about the "blemish" of Jewish ancestry St. Ignatius expressed the wish that he had been of Jewish descent and thereby a blood relative of Jesus and Mary. "He spoke these words with so deep an emotion that his eyes filled with tears." True, as a realist he wrote at the end of 1545 to his close associate Peter Faber (de Lefèvre): "The Society must pay heed and try to be helpful to everyone; for this reason its members must be free of any blemish which might impede their fruitful activity." But he added that even such blemishes could be overcome by saintly behavior, great talent, or other useful attributes, and urged Faber in each case to use his discretion. A few years later, however, he sharply repudiated the strictures of Archbishop Juan Martínez Silíceo of Toledo against the Society's admitting pupils of the late Juan de Ávila, a New Christian. (We recall the storm unleashed by the archbishop's "statute of purity" of 1547.) Loyola replied: "There is no question about our considering his wishes and altering our constitution to conform with his ordinances. Let him mind his own business." When, in 1553, a conflict broke out in the Spanish branch of the Society between two distinguished *alumbrado* professors and the provincial, however, Loyola dictated the following more guarded reply to Antonio de Araoz (August 14, 1553):

Our Father cannot be convinced that we will serve God by not accepting New Christians. But he believes that one ought to employ great caution with respect to such candidates. If it is thought there that, on account of the attitude of the Court or the king, one ought not to admit them, you may send them here [to Rome], provided they can be put to some use, as has been written to you on previous occasions. Here one does not so carefully investigate an individual's race [*raça*], so long as he is an able person, just as noble parentage does not suffice if the other requirements are lacking.

Two years later (February 20, 1555) he suggested to the Portuguese leader Jacobus Miro (Mirón) that, subject to royal consent, they might persuade New Christian members to change their names and residences in order to escape detection.[12]

After Loyola's death, Laynez even more pointedly rejected these "imaginary prejudices," although he, too, admitted that one necessarily had to make some concessions in certain provinces. From the outset he faced some opposition at the very headquarters of the Society. Most formidable was that of Nicholas Alonso (called Bobadilla from his place of birth), seconded by the Frenchman Ponce Cogordan. A learned theologian and a member of the founding group, Bobadilla was a serious adversary. Generally an extremist—his bitter opposition to the so-called Augsburg Interim of June 1548, which had sought to establish a modicum of religious peace in the Empire, had earned him a decree of banishment from Augsburg by the Catholic Ferdinand I—he spoke out in 1558 against Laynez' candidacy, just as he had often criticized Loyola's autocratic regime. Characteristically, however, he toned down the objections relating to Laynez' ancestry, perhaps because he knew that many Spanish nobles were related to the Jesuit leader and that some of Laynez' brothers and nephews had joined the Order. Instead he emphasized the new general's lack of prudence and organizational ability, virtues in which, on the contrary, Laynez happened to excel. Curiously, the man who saved the latter's reputation and position of leadership was Cardinal Michele Ghislieri (later Pope Pius V), to whom Paul IV entrusted the investigation of the controversy. Although the pope had not been friendly to Loyola and the Jesuits, and Ghislieri himself, a rigid inquisitor, was anything but sympathetic to persons of New Christian descent, Ghislieri yielded to the majority opinion within the Society, represented by the revered Jerome Nadal, one of Loyola's closest collaborators, and persuaded the pope to dismiss all charges against Laynez. Little did any of these men anticipate that in 1614 the Society's historian, Francesco Sacchini, would evoke a stormy reaction on the Iberian Peninsula because he included in his narrative a reference to Laynez' Jewish parentage. In 1622 the Spanish fathers actually demanded the suppression of that passage, which they claimed would cast opprobrium on the whole Society. But the Society's Italian general, Mutius

Vitelleschi (1615–45), roundly rejected that demand, and pointed out that Laynez' Jewish descent was an historical fact.[13]

Before long, however, these Iberian prejudices made themselves effectively felt. When after the death of the third general, Francisco Borgia, in 1573, a new leader was to be elected, the obvious choice was Polanco. But King Sebastian of Portugal as well as Cardinal Infante Henry successfully intervened with Pope Gregory XIII to prevent the election of another New Christian or, as Henry added, "any other candidate apparently favored by the New Christians." Such interference by foreign states is not at all surprising when one considers how deeply the elections of new popes had become enmeshed in the European power struggles. The opposition to Polanco was further strengthened by certain inner disturbances allegedly caused by a few New Christian members. Thereupon the pope forced the Society to elect the Flemish member Everard Mercurian. Dissensions during the latter's administration (1573–81) and the long regime of the fifth general, Claude Acquaviva (1581–1615), led to a considerable deterioration in the Jesuits' internal discipline and external prestige. The controversy over racial purity doubtless accelerated the decline in the quality of leadership which, in the Jesuit Order as often elsewhere, followed upon the demise of the creative pioneers. "The cynic might say," observes Christopher Hollis, "that the great difference between the Jesuits of the first generation and those of the second was that the first Jesuits had not, in youth, received a Jesuit training, and that the Jesuit training is admirably fitted to produce men who will obey, but not well suited to produce men who can command." Whatever one thinks of the merits of this generalization, it is obvious that the new leaders displayed less fortitude and skill in resisting Spain's political pressure with respect to *limpieza* than had their predecessors. After many efforts to settle the problem of descent, including a temporary resolution in 1593 which barred all descendants of Jews and Moors from membership, the Sixth General Congregation of 1608 finally adopted the rather vague constitutional provision forbidding the admission of candidates whose ancestors included notoriously dishonorable persons. The investigation was not to go back beyond the fifth generation and it was to be conducted with great secrecy in order not to cast aspersion on the candidates' relatives. In this form the constitution remained binding on the Society for more than two centuries. In practice some generals went much further, however, and, in their replies to inquiries, often disqualified candidates of known Jewish ancestry up to the sixteenth generation, "even if that parentage included two cardinals." The first breach in this exclusivist policy was made by Pope Leo XIII, who in 1886 gave a wholesale dispensation to persons of Jewish descent on the distaff side. But not until 1923 did the Twenty-Seventh General Congregation extend Leo XIII's ruling to male ancestors, who were to be investigated only up to the fourth generation; the new rule also permitted further individual dispensations by the officiating general.[14]

In general, notwithstanding Loyola's great mystical fervor (his works were to inspire many devout Catholics to the present day) and Laynez' profound theological learning (which never achieved its definitive formulation in a *Summa*, long planned by him), the Society's basic religious outlook did not substantially depart from the dominant doctrines of the medieval Church. Even more conservative was the Jesuit attitude to professing Jews and the Old Testament. Working hand in hand with Paul III, Loyola and his associates opposed the forcible conversion of Jews, but greatly encouraged voluntary converts. For this purpose they took the initiative in establishing houses of catechumens. Probably in cooperation with them Paul III had issued, on March 21, 1542, the bull *Cupientes Judaeos*, which repeated the old canonical insistence that neophytes retain all their property except for profits derived from usury. Local authorities were requested to extend to them full rights of citizenship on a par with born Christians. Yet taking cognizance of the complaints of the Spanish clergy, a provision was inserted forbidding new converts to marry within their own group, to perform Jewish ceremonies, or to bury their dead according to Jewish rites.[15]

Unavoidably, the enthusiastic educational and missionary campaigns led by Jesuits in many lands, which so greatly aided the Church in its counteroffensive against the Protestant Reformation, also set the Society on a collision course with many local Jewish communities. Upon the admission of Jesuits to the duchy of Mantua in 1584, for example, Duke Guglielmo Gonzaga established their headquarters in the church of San Salvatore, which happened to be located in the very midst of the Jewish street, not yet declared a formal ghetto. The Mantuan Jews strongly resented the presence there of ardent missionaries, while many Jesuits themselves felt uncomfortable in such exclusively Jewish surroundings. An agreement was therefore speedily reached: the Jewish community paid the Jesuits 3,500 gold scudi to enable them to move to another street. The church was closed down (even its doors facing the Jewish quarter were locked up permanently), only a caretaker being left on the premises. Needless to say, this physical removal did not prevent the Jesuits from pursuing their missionary activities among Jews, which here, as elsewhere, gave rise to some troublesome incidents. In time difficulties multiplied, as the Society became increasingly permeated by an anti-Jewish animus, as well as embroiled in domestic partisan strifes and international power politics. It ultimately became a thorn in the flesh to many rulers, which fact led to its suppression in various Catholic countries during the eighteenth century. Among the first signs of retreat from the founders' idealistic approach was the gradual acceptance of Iberian racism by the Society's leadership under General Acquaviva and his successors.[16]

COUNCIL OF TRENT

Jesuit leaders also played a great role in the momentous Council of Trent (1545–63). This council had had to be forced upon the Papacy by Charles V and other Catholic princes, since the popes, taught by the experiences of the fifteenth-century reform councils, viewed with suspicion any demand for another ecumenical gathering. In 1459 Pius II had actually threatened to excommunicate any person appealing for such a council. Despite the intervening Fifth Lateran Council under Julius II and Leo X (1512–17), the Papacy consented to the Tridentine meetings with great reluctance. It rightly felt, at least before 1530, that the emperor was more interested in the inner reforms of the Church than in the repression of heresy, in the *causa reformationis* rather than in the *causa fidei*. Later on, Paul III and his successors watched the proceedings at Trent with great care, and in the end, by fine maneuvering, succeeded in making the Council a pliant instrument of their own policies. On the whole, the three major assemblies (1545–47, 1551–52, 1562–63) dealt with basic problems, both dogmatic and organizational, and had a permanent salutary effect upon the destinies of Roman Catholicism. They did not deal with the Jewish question as such, however, evidently because it was assumed that the existing canon law had made sufficient provisions for it.

Before the convocation of the Council, to be sure, some churchmen urged a reconsideration of the entire position of Jews in the Christian world. In his *Miscellanies,* submitted to Pope Paul III in June 1543, Bishop Friedrich Nausea (Gran) of Vienna demanded that, among the existing abuses to be remedied, should be the toleration theretofore extended by popes to "the most perfidious Jews, the most confirmed enemies of the name of the Christian Church." The bishop was particularly aroused by the tacit toleration of some Christian Judaizers among the popes' own subjects. However, Nausea's comprehensive memorandum included such a devastating critique of the Church and its organs, from the Papacy down, as well as of the secular princes, that it was completely ignored by the Council. In general, despite the pope's accommodation of Charles V's wishes to have the Council meet in a locale under imperial control, the attendance of German, including Austrian, prelates, was always very slight. Much more representative of the wishes of the dominant conciliar group was an early plea by Girolamo Aleandro, who, having often served as a papal legate in Germany and elsewhere, was quite familiar with the general European theological and diplomatic situation. In his memorandum of 1537, Aleandro attacked "the Protestant wolves," but he advocated ignoring the non-Christian peoples. "They should be left to the justice and judgment of the supreme God, just as the Jews should be committed to the care of the One God." He merely expressed the hope that some day they, too, would be converted. As a result, Jews were hardly mentioned in the Council sessions, except in occasional stereotyped references to ancient Hebrews. For example, when five days after the opening session, of

December 13, 1545, Geronimo (Hieronymus) ab Oleastro, one of three Dominicans representing Portugal, delivered a public oration in which he expressed his king's high hopes for the Council's accomplishments, he found no better parallel than the rejoicing of the ancient Jews at Ezra's convocation and reading of the Law. Similarly, in a debate of June 18, 1562, over the differences of opinion regarding the Eucharist, the Spanish theologian Joannes Villetta claimed that such deviations had "never been committed in any Hebrew churches" except by those who wished to suffuse their tradition with Hellenism. Naturally, such homilies had little bearing on contemporary Jewish affairs. Not much more significant was the casual reference to Jews in the "Decree on Justification," adopted at the first session of the Council, on January 13, 1547. Insisting on the universality of sin, the Council declared that "not even the Jews by the very letter of the law of Moses were able to be liberated or to rise therefrom," and that Christ had been sent to both Jews and Gentiles to redeem them from that curse. This had long been an accepted article of faith in the Church, and its restatement by the Council had little effect on Judeo-Christian relations.[17]

Only one point on the Council's agenda appeared prejudicial to Jewish interests. After resuming its deliberations in 1562, the Council appointed, before the second session (the eighteenth of the entire Council) of February 26, a commission charged with compiling a new Index of Prohibited Books and proposing a set of guidelines for future censorship. This work was to replace the excessively rigid Index hastily promulgated by Paul IV. Clearly, a conciliar decision against the Talmud and other rabbinic works might indeed have had serious consequences for the publication and dissemination of Hebrew letters throughout the Catholic world.

News about these deliberations reached Italian Jews, and the Mantuan community, in particular, tried to stave off the impending calamity. That Mantua, rather than Rome, appeared in the forefront was doubtless owing to its special contacts with Cardinal Ercole Gonzaga (brother of the reigning Mantuan duke, Federico I), who had been delegated by Pius IV to serve as the chief presiding officer of the Council. Highly influential in Church circles, Ercole had received an extensive humanist training under the direction of his enlightened and tolerant mother, Isabella d'Este. He had been the leading candidate for the papal tiara after Paul IV's death, and only a coalition of the Farnese and Carafa factions prevented him from being elected. His opposition to Paul IV's policies and tactics must have been strengthened by Cardinal Carlo Carafa's machinations on that occasion. In him the Mantuan Jewish delegates doubtless found an attentive listener, especially in connection with the censorship of Hebrew books. Independently, Jews also approached the newly appointed Archbishop Anton Brus von Müglitz of Prague, who, throughout the proceedings, served as chairman of the Index Commission. Ultimately, that Commission was also charged with the preparation of several other important conciliar (and postconciliar) documents. The Jewish petition was presented by Jacob de Bonaventura, who asked the Council that its members

out of their general kindness and special grace order that that book [the Talmud] be carefully inspected and examined by the Council's censors but that they refrain from absolutely condemning it, since it is so indispensable to them [the Jews], and since many supreme pontiffs had on many occasions clearly and expressly permitted its use during their regimes. If, however, some matters should be found in it which appear prejudicial to the Christian religion, these could be deleted entirely; expurgated of such matters, the book should be allowed to be printed. In this fashion it could be owned and studied by everybody, without offense. Since the performance of this task [of expurgation] might not only require much work but also entail expenses, the said Jacob wishes specifically to be held responsible both for that outlay and for seeing to it that the book, in the form graciously allowed and permitted by the illustrious and most reverend doctors, be correctly published. He is prepared to accomplish and execute all that under whatever obligation or penalty they might impose upon him.

This petition is not dated. But Jacob received a discouraging reply, a copy of which Archbishop Brus forwarded to Emperor Ferdinand I on February 3, 1563.[18]

Brus' own role in these negotiations is not clear. He was not only chairman of the eighteen-member Index Commission, one of the Council's most important "congregations," which held its meetings at his residence, but also the emperor's main spokesman (*orator Caesareus*) and, as such, the chief representative of the Empire at the Council. On one occasion, when he wished to resign from his very arduous post on the Commission, he was dissuaded by Ferdinand I. He seems to have had but few previous contacts with Jews. For five years he had served as bishop of Vienna, at a time when the Habsburg capital had no organized Jewish community and only sporadic Jewish visitors. He came to Prague, on Ferdinand's recommendation, because he had greatly impressed the emperor with his knowledge and oratory. But hardly had he arrived there, at the end of 1561, when he had to leave for Trent, in January 1562. During April and May of 1563 he spent a few weeks in the Bohemian capital, but again he may have had no opportunity to discuss the problem of rabbinic letters with any Bohemian Jewish acquaintances. As a good Catholic traditionalist he had accompanied his February report to Ferdinand with a lengthy list of anti-Christian passages, "fables, and blasphemies, myriads of which are found in the Talmud," undoubtedly excerpted for him by some theologians attending the Council. Those churchmen may simply have copied these strictures from the older literature or from more recent accusations such as those presented by the convert Alessandro Franceschi da Foligno. Nevertheless, Brus seems to have taken a moderately liberal stand on the censorship of the Talmud and, probably upon his return to Prague, he received from the elders of the Jewish community a letter of "immortal thanks." With evident exaggeration they wrote that they had heard "that your Eminence has often fought with all your strength for the restitution of the Talmud and any other well-corrected work [*alioque correctissimo*]." [19]

During the Commission's deliberations some members had suggested that the Jews be made to submit a complete Latin translation of the Talmud. But the Jewish representatives rightly expostulated that such an undertaking "was not only very difficult but almost impossible, because of the large size of the work, the absence of qualified people, and for various other reasons." They suggested that the matter be left to the discretation of the pope and his officials, a stance supported by the papal legates in their report of February 22, 1563, to Carlo Borromeo, the papal secretary of state. Since the Council continued its deliberations about the Index down to its last session of December 4, 1563, the Mantuan community did not cease efforts to influence it, although Cardinal Gonzaga passed away on March 2 of that year. On October 19 (Marḥeshvan 2, 5324), the Mantuan elders elected a committee of five members, which dispatched two delegates, Samuel b. Moses Casis and Solomon b. Ḥayyim, to "the awesome Council in Trent" and ten days later provided them with the following instructions: They were first to try to persuade the Council not to concern itself with Hebrew books at all but to leave the final decision to the pope (the regnant Pope Pius IV happened to be fairly friendly to Jews). Should that prove unobtainable, they were to endeavor to limit the prohibition to the Talmud and, if denied on this score too, they were to seek a resolution allowing the future use of all Hebrew books after a rigid examination by censors designated by the Council. In any case the delegates were not to concede that Jews would give up studying the Talmud or any other Hebrew book, nor were they generally to make any commitments in behalf of their constituents. Finally, neither delegate should act without the prior consent of his colleague. The envoys were also provided with letters of recommendation, including one addressed by Duchess Eleanora of Mantua, daughter of Emperor Ferdinand I, to Pedro González de Mendoza. This influential Salamanca bishop commented thereon in his diary (under October 26–27, 1563): "I wished she would engage me in a more honest undertaking than in defending a cause held by them [the delegates] to be most pernicious and most injurious to our religion. [Alonso] Tostado [bishop of Ávila; died in 1455, whose tombstone had extolled him thus: 'Here lies the world's marvel able to discuss all that can be known'] had declared the Talmud of the Jews to be worse than Mohammed's *Al-Qur'an.*" Yet the bishop apparently could not entirely refuse to cooperate.[20]

Whether or not the Jewish representations had any effect on the Index Commission, the outcome of the deliberations proved relatively favorable. Because the Council was preoccupied with weighty last-moment decisions (complicated by both international tensions and the pope's severe illness) and had to steer clear of conflicting diplomatic pressures from the major Catholic powers, it adjourned on December 4, 1563, leaving several important items, such as the composition of an official catechism, missal, and breviary, as well as the Index, to the pope's final determination. It submitted to Pius IV transcripts of its deliberations on all these subjects, although the pope was by no means to be bound by them. Even the official conciliar canons required the pope's formal confirmation before they became binding on the Catholic Church. In the case of the Index Pius acted speedily. While the catechism, breviary, and missal did not appear until 1566, 1568, and 1570, respectively—all issued by his successor, Pius V—the Index was ready for publication less than four months after the Council's adjournment. Based on the ten general propositions elaborated in Trent, it was promulgated by the bull *Dominici gregis* on March 24, 1564. As published in Venice, 1564, "with the rules prepared by the Fathers of the Tridentine Council," the Index included the general prohibition of the Talmud, with "its glosses, annotations, interpretations, and expositions." But it added, "If these should be published without the title 'Talmud' and without insults and calumnies against the Christian religion they shall be tolerated." [21]

Characteristic of the Jews' general satisfaction with the outcome is the following comment of a contemporary Hebrew chronicler:

Cardinal Ercole Gonzaga, the cardinal of Mantua, served as their [the Council's] president and the pope's plenipotentiary. They [the delegates] came together from the four corners of the earth and also spoke about the sacred writings. They permitted them to us only under the condition that nothing would be printed therein against their faith. Under this condition they also allowed [publication of] the Babylonian Talmud, subject only to a change of its name. It was indeed printed in Basel under the title of "Six Orders."

This relative success of the Jewish delegation was the more remarkable since, in contrast to the situation at the Councils of Constance and Basel, there were in Trent no local Jews who could exert any influence on the assembled prelates and ambassadors. By a fortunate coincidence neither Paul IV nor Pius V was in office at the time of these conciliar deliberations, whereas Paul III, Julius III, and Pius IV were far less hostile to their Jewish subjects. However, even antagonistic Pius V followed the lead of the Council in including in his *Catechism* of 1566 a restatement of the Church's interpretation of ancient Israelitic history, which recognized Israel's ancient claim to "chosen peoplehood." More importantly, referring to the crucifixion of Jesus, this new authoritative statement stressed the fact that Jesus "offered Himself not involuntarily or by compulsion, but of His own free will," and insisted that

in this guilt are involved all those who fall frequently into sin; for, as our sins consigned Christ the Lord to the death of the cross, most certainly those who wallow in sin and iniquity crucify to themselves again the Son of God, as far as in them lies, and make a mockery of Him. This guilt seems the more enormous in us than in the Jews, since according to the testimony of the same Apostle [Paul]: "If they had known it, they would never have crucified the Lord of glory" [I Cor. 2:8], while we, on the contrary, professing to know Him, yet denying Him by our actions, seem in some sort to lay violent hands on Him.

In this formulation the statement could have counteracted, or at least mitigated, the widespread accusation of Jewish responsibility for Christ-killing. But there is no evidence that Jews—or more tolerant Catholic apologists better familiar with their official catechism—ever made use of that doctrine for the defense of modern Jewry, until the entire issue became the subject of lengthy debates at the recent Second Vatican Council.[22]

By confirming, despite some opposition, the canons adopted in all twenty-five sessions of the three assemblies held since 1545, the Council itself (followed by the approving papal bull of January 26, 1564) presented the Catholic world with an official restatement of many basic doctrines and organizational forms, particularly those most vigorously attacked by the Reformers. These resolutions have remained the Church's authoritative guidelines for four centuries. Most of the debates, in which Laynez and Salmerón consistently espoused the traditionalist point of view against Cardinal Girolamo Seripando and others who sought to liberalize certain teachings and practices, impinged little on Jews and Judaism. Certainly, the restatement of the nature and validity of Christian sacraments did not affect Jews, except perhaps in so far as the controversial doctrine of the Eucharist may have helped to stem accusations of alleged Jewish desecration of the host. Nor was the definitive restatement of the laws governing marriage of any concern to Jews until the period of Emancipation, when they became a serious obstacle to intermarriage. At most, the compromise sponsored by Laynez concerning the independent rights of bishops could serve as an occasional local counterbalance if excessively intolerant policies were pursued by individual popes. On the whole, however, the record showed that the central organs of the Church had more consistently adhered to the long-established blend of toleration and discrimination than had the local or regional churchmen, who were more subject to the varying sociopolitical pressures of their respective environments.

More serious may have appeared at first glance Laynez' espousal of an antiusury resolution and his six suggested remedies. However, his praise of the *monti di pietà* had, by that time, lost much of its poignancy. Laynez himself merely expressed the hope that, "with God's help, the evil of usury would be reduced, if not entirely, at least to a large extent." Certainly, it was too late for the Council to try, in any significant way, to stem the evolution of the capitalist credit system. Similarly, the reaffirmation of the exclusive authority of the Vulgate as interpreted by the medieval Church had few immediate effects on Jewish Bible studies, although it may have somewhat impeded the further progress of Catholic Hebraism, which had been nurtured by intensive study of the Hebrew Bible. In this pursuit Protestant scholars now speedily outpaced their Catholic counterparts. In general, it is still debatable whether the Council's comprehensive reformulation of Catholic doctrine and ecclesiastical organization initiated a completely new phase of Catholicism or merely renewed the Church's pristine purity, a question which was the subject of an extended discussion between the outstanding seventeenth-century thinkers Gottfried Wilhelm Leibniz and Jacques Bénigne Bossuet. In any case the Council evidently regarded the Jewish question as of relatively minor importance and did not devote to it as much consideration as had the Third and Fourth Lateran Councils or the Councils of Constance and Basel. In the long run, nevertheless, by lending new strength and direction to the Catholic Restoration and the general revival of religious zeal, it indirectly contributed to the growth of intolerance toward all unbelievers, including Jews.[23]

NEW PAPAL LEADERSHIP

Whatever one may think of the "innovations" of the Tridentine Council, there is no question about the radically changed outlook on the Jewish question of many popes during the second half of the sixteenth century. The Catholic Church, now on the defensive, mounted a counteroffensive to eradicate the growing "heresies." In the process the Papacy reestablished its position as the central international institution of the Catholic world. Although it frequently collided with the national interests and biases of individual Catholic countries, it did hold up the banner of religious and organizational universalism, which ultimately assured its victory in Italy, Spain, France, Poland, and beyond. In its struggle against the Reformation, however, the Church heard the frequent objection, now even more articulate and widespread than in the Middle Ages, that it prosecuted to death Christian sectarians believing in Christ and the Trinity, while it simultaneously offered protection to infidels like the Jews. It is small wonder, then, that in this gigantic conflict, as in other periods of aroused religious fanaticism, Jews became the victimized bystanders.

Paul III's pontificate (1534–49) marked a transitional stage. A scion of the distinguished Farnese family, the pope was both a worldly humanist-politician and a dedicated churchman. Deeply embroiled in the power politics of his time, he nevertheless pursued a course of moderate Church reform and thus sought to counteract the rising tide of the Reformation. Even before ascending to the throne of St. Peter he, in contrast to other leading churchmen, favored the idea of an ecumenical council, but, because of the bickering among the great powers over timing, location, and other details, he had had to wait eleven years before he could convoke the Council of Trent in 1545.

Similar contradictions characterized the pope's Jewish policies. On the one hand, like his immediate predecessors he extended considerable privileges to distinguished Jewish physicians, some of whom he allowed to reside at his own court. Following in Leo X's footsteps, he permitted the Jewish savant Jacob Mantino to dedicate to him a Latin translation of Averroës' Paraphrase of Plato's *Republic* and, in 1539, he even established a sort of ten-year "copyright" for that work. Nor did he object when Elijah and Joshua, sons of Solomon Corcos and members of the "Aragonese" congregation, opened a banking house in Rome on June 11, 1537; subsequently, together with twenty-one other Jewish bankers, they negotiated an agreement with their Christian colleagues. Paul banned the nightly performance of a Passion play at the Colosseum because the aroused spectators were prone, on leaving the performance, to attack Jewish passers-by. Early in his reign (February 10, 1535) he also conferred upon the Jews of the Romagna and the Exarchate of Ravenna extensive privileges similar to those long enjoyed by their coreligionists of the Marches. The ledgers of Jewish firms were to be given full credence on a par with those of Christian firms; *bona fide* acquisitions of stolen goods could be nullified only after full compensation for the purchasers' investments; nonpublic work on Christian holidays was not to be interfered with; convictions of Jewish defendants could be secured only by the testimony of two trustworthy witnesses owning property valued at 100 scudi or more; and so forth. At the same time the preparation and sale of meat prepared in a Jewish fashion was not to be impeded. "Nor were they [the Jews] to be subject to, or obliged to obey, any inquisitor, except for paying him his due according to custom." Not surprisingly, after five years in office Paul was accused by Jacopo Sadoleto, bishop of Carpentras, of excessively favoring his Jewish subjects. Demanding the expulsion of Jews from Avignon, Sadoleto wrote to Cardinal Alessandro Farnese on July 4, 1539:

How can one view a man who, for the love of religion, persecutes the Lutherans in his country while he tolerates the Jews there in such a fashion? Does he merely tolerate them? No, he promotes them and grants them decorations and honors. Never have Christians received so many favors, privileges, and concessions from a pope as have the Jews during these years of Paul III's pontificate.

Similar reproaches were voiced by Farnese himself and others.[24]

On the other hand, the progress of the Protestant Reformation made the pope aware of the dangerous growth of religious dissent. In censuring Charles V, on August 24, 1544, for the concessions he had made to the Protestants at the Diet of Spires, Paul exhorted the emperor to follow the example of Constantine, Theodosius, and Charlemagne, rather than that of the rebels against established ecclesiastical authority, from Korah to Frederick II, all of whom had paid dearly for their defiance. He also stressed the miserable fate of both the Jews and the Greeks, two once-flourishing nations who were severely suffering in retribution for their repudiation of the Church. These new challenges forced Paul to embark upon many internal reforms of the Church and to establish institutions which in time tended seriously to undermine the status of Roman Jewry. By promoting the new militant orders of Theatines and Jesuits he set in motion forces which were bound to increase popular hostility toward all religious dissidents. After long hesitation, we recall, he yielded to the Portuguese pressures and sanctioned the establishment of a Portuguese Inquisition along Spanish lines. If he hoped to mitigate this concession by his breve of 1537 ordering the inquisitors to treat all accused mildly, he must have been quickly disabused. Five years later his legate in Portugal had to intervene directly to secure freedom for 1,800 Marranos. In 1547–48 Paul totally surrendered to the blandishments of the Portuguese envoy, Balthasar de Faria, and the harsh threats of the Carmelite Bishop Balthasar de Limpo, and gave free reign to the Portuguese Inquisition. Guided in part by his self-interested quest to secure the substantial revenues from the bishopric of Viseu for his grandson Cardinal Alessandro Farnese, the pope no longer insisted that for a year all Portuguese New Christians be permitted to leave the country for any but an infidel land. In this connection he had to endure such implacable harangues as that addressed to him by Limpo: "What difference does it make whether they go to infidel countries or to Italy? They come to be circumcised in Ancona, at Ferrara, or at Venice, and from there they go on to Turkey. They have the pontifical privilege of not being asked whether they are Jews." Moreover, in 1542 the pope himself established a Spanish-type Inquisition in the Papal States. The numerous privileges Paul issued to individual Jewish doctors and bankers, as well as his exemption of Jewish artisans from the authority of competing Christian guilds, were in part counterbalanced by his establishment in 1539 of the first *monte di pietà* in Rome. Similarly, his original provision that Jews should not be forced to listen to missionary sermons was controverted by his bull *Cupientes Judaeos* of March 21, 1542, safeguarding extensive rights for neophytes, and by the foundation a year later of the House of Catechumens designed to accommodate prospective converts, male and female in separate sections. Most significantly, it was he who, despite his worldly preoccupations and excessive nepotism, laid the foundation for the Catholic Counter Reformation, with its calamitous consequences for all dissidents, including Jews.[25]

Such reform tendencies were soon combined with considerable hostility toward Jews and Judaism. This became, indeed, a keynote of the briefer pontificate of Julius III (1550–55). Julius, who as Cardinal Giovanni del Monte had presided over the first session of the Council of Trent (during which the casually antagonistic references to Judaism were made in the aforementioned preamble to the Decree on Justification), convoked the second session in 1551–52. Of more immediate interest to Jews was his bull *Pastoris aeterni vices* of August 31, 1554, which imposed upon all synagogues (then numbering 115) of the Papal States an annual tax of 10 ducats each for the maintenance of the Roman House of Catechumens. Following the thirteenth-century English precedent, this impost thus added insult to injury by forcing Jews to support an institution aimed at promoting apostasy from Judaism. The House soon began harboring a number of hostile informers and *agents-provocateurs* who, for many generations, were to help envenom all Judeo-Christian relations in Rome and the provinces. It doubtless was a denunciation from such a source which led the newly functioning Inquisition to condemn a Franciscan friar, Corneglio da Montalcino, for his conversion to Judaism; he was burned at the stake on September 4, 1553.

Even more serious were the effects of Julius III's approval of the Inquisition's drastic action against the Talmud. Curiously, the Papacy had long abandoned its opposition to rabbinic letters, and Leo X had actually welcomed the publication, by Daniel Bomberg, of the first complete edition of the Babylonian Talmud. Yet now the commercial rivalry between two other famous Venetian publishers, Marcantonio Giustiniani and Alvisi Bragadini, led to mutual recriminations that the other party was publishing rabbinic writings offensive to Christianity, recriminations which were eagerly supported by some of Rome's informed converts. Under the guidance of Grand-Inquisitor Gian Pietro Carafa (later Pope Paul IV) the Roman Holy Office issued on September (August) 12, 1553, a decree demanding that Jews deliver within three days all copies of both the Palestinian and Babylonian Talmudim to the local inquisitors or other episcopal officials. This order was to apply to inhabitants "of any of the Christian cities or lands." Jews were also forbidden, under the sanction of the confiscation of all their goods, to hold, copy, or print such books, or to import them from Muslim lands. To assure the implementation of this prohibition the decree promised informers a reward of one-quarter of the fine. On the other hand, any Christian, particularly any churchman, who would aid and abet Jews in keeping, copying, or printing talmudic works or would himself read them was to be subject to automatic excommunication *latae sententiae* and other penalties provided by law for protectors of heretics. As a result, thousands of valuable printed volumes and manuscripts of rabbinic classics, including many posttalmudic Hebrew writings, were burned in public bonfires in Rome's Campo de' Fiori. This action was greeted with dismay, not only by Jews, but also by many humanists familiar with rabbinic letters. For instance, the greatly admired Hebraist Andreas Masius, who had not only received many accolades from fellow scholars but was also highly regarded in court circles (he was mentioned as a likely successor to Gerhard Weltvyck as imperial councilor, and was to play a considerable role in the preparation of the royally sponsored Bible published by the Plantin firm), was deeply chagrined by the papal action. Having been in correspondence with the Roman Jewish scholars Elijah b. Menaḥem and Immanuel b. Yekutiel of Nola, and having from time to time acquired through them precious rabbinic and kabbalistic manuscripts, Masius expressed his sense of shock over this "criminal decision regarding the Talmud." Addressing himself to Cardinal Sebastiano Pighini, auditor of the papal *Rota,* he added:

Whenever I think about it, I feel deeply pained over your ill-advised sentence. It was passed on the basis of an accusation by two men prompted by pure greed and the testimony of two Jewish Christians— if they merit that designation—hired by these two hostile Venetian book dealers. It will accrue to the eternal shame of the Apostolic See.

All protests remained ineffective, however, in the upsurge of religious intolerance which soon engulfed other Italian communities as well.[26]

Regrettably, we have no statistical information about the number of Hebrew books destroyed in 1553–54. True, in his *Mishnat hakhamin* (The Lore of the Wise), published in Altona-Wandsbek, 1733, Moses b. Jacob Ḥagiz claimed that 3,328 volumes printed in Venice alone had been burned during that time. But, emphasizing the ultimate inefficacy of the papal decree, he pointed out that no less than 16,000 volumes of the Talmud's Venice editions had previously circulated among the Italian Jews, "quite apart from those printed in Turkey and other countries outside the pope's jurisdiction." On their part, the Avignon rabbis tried to stave off the destruction of Hebrew books, not only by bribing some officials but also by telling Cardinal Alessandro Farnese, then on a papal mission, that the Talmud antedated Christianity by some two thousand years. They evidently had in mind the Oral Law codified in the Talmud, which according to their tradition had been revealed to Moses on Sinai. We shall see, moreover, that while this inquisitorial decree caused many difficulties for the Italian Jewish communities, it was almost entirely disobeyed in other Catholic countries, including the Catholic parts of the Holy Roman Empire. The immediate Jewish reaction and the introduction of precensorship of Hebrew books by the synods of Italian communities in Ferrara in 1554 were likewise limited largely to the Italian area. There, however, the Ferrara compromise remained in operation for several generations.[27]

Compared with this sharp attack on the fundamental sources of Jewish learning, which, if implemented in all Catholic countries as was expected, would have seriously undermined the subsequent progress of Jewish studies, the numerous concessions granted by Julius III to Jewish doctors and bankers in the Papal States mattered very little. He intervened, for instance, in favor of a Jewish physician who, in 1554, was to receive his medical degree from the University of Pisa. Like many of his predecessors, the often ailing pope defied the old canonical prohibition and placed himself under the care of Jewish physicians, including the famous Amatus Lusitanus. More significantly, on June 8, 1551, he controverted John Duns Scotus, Ulrich Zasius, and others, and expressly forbade bishops and all other persons, lay or ecclesiastical, to remove Jewish children from the custody of their parents. "They shall not dare to baptize them [such children] in any fashion against the provisions of the holy canons." Any cleric performing such an illegal rite was to be suspended from office and fined 1,000 ducats. In general, however, the foundations were laid during the early 1550s for an unprecedented reversal of the Papacy's traditionally balanced attitude not only to Jewish residents of the Pontifical States but also to Judaism as a religion and to the Jewish people throughout Western Christendom.[28]

Nor was Julius' successor, Marcellus II, able to undo the harm caused by the outlawry of the Talmud. Although an interested Hebraist and a promoter of humanistic arts and letters, this fine administrator reigned too short a time to bring about any substantial changes in the papal policies. During the three weeks of his regime (April 9 to May 1, 1555) he could show only that he intended to stop the prevailing nepotism. We cannot even tell what part he took in uncovering a plot which had raised the specter of a dangerous Blood Accusation in the papal capital. A genuine bibliophile, Marcellus undoubtedly deplored the wholesale destruction of precious Hebrew books, but he died before he could revert to the more moderate administrative methods of his mentor, Paul III. He seems, however, to have set in motion a reconsideration of the indiscriminate condemnation of all Hebrew works. A Jewish delegation headed by R. Joseph of Arli successfully argued that many Hebrew books contained nothing to which the Church might conceivably object; it found support in a favorable report by the learned Hebraist Bishop Sacristo. Thereupon a plenary session of the Inquisition issued on May 4, 1554, three days after Marcellus' death, a "clarification" of the old order which was rightly hailed by the Italian Jewish public as offering considerable freedom for the pursuit of traditional Jewish studies. However, the pope's personal role in these negotiations is unclear. Hence even Hebrew contemporaries describing his regime were far from unanimous as to whether to praise or to condemn him.[29]

INQUISITORS WEARING TIARAS

The great turning point came under the reign of Gian Pietro Carafa, who was raised to the See of St. Peter at the age of seventy-nine, under the name of Paul IV (1555–59). He himself claimed that "he had never done a kindness to anyone and he did not know how it was that the cardinals had chosen him—that it must be God who made popes." This feeling of being an instrument of the divine will did not prevent him, however, from pursuing the nepotistic policies of some of his worst predecessors and from entrusting the management of all public affairs to his unworthy nephews Cardinal Carlo and Duke Giovanni Carafa. The new pope brought with him to Rome not only the intolerant spirit of his Neapolitan homeland but also a great admiration for the Spanish Inquisition, acquired while he served as papal nuncio and close adviser of Ferdinand the Catholic in Madrid from 1515 on. Subsequently, Pope Adrian VI, Spain's former inquisitor, called him to Rome. As grand-inquisitor under Julius III Carafa had already shown, despite his modicum of humanistic training in Greek, Latin, and Hebrew letters, an extreme zeal in prosecuting anything that smacked of heresy. As pope he intensified this policy of repression. Commenting on the operations of the Roman Holy Office since its establishment under Paul III, Cardinal Girolamo (Hieronymus) Seripando, the relatively liberal prior-general of the Augustinian Order and, from 1560 on, a reluctant member of the inquisitorial court, observed: "At first, this tribunal, in consonance with the pope's [Paul III's] inclinations, was moderate and mild, but later, as a result of the increase in its members and authority it became imbued with Carafa's excessive severity. It was believed that no more terrible and awesome verdicts were passed anywhere in the world." Carafa's attack on the Talmud and rabbinic literature was not an isolated phenomenon. Apart from the Church's traditional hostility to rabbinic letters, the inquisitor-pope may have been told by Jewish converts that, if he succeeded in diverting the Jews' intellectual interests from talmudic to kabbalistic studies, he might facilitate the Christian mission among them. This issue was, indeed, to become the subject of heated debates among the contemporary Italian rabbis. But in his Counter Reformation zeal, Paul IV did not even spare some outstanding secular works written by contemporary Christian authors. An example of his persecution mania was the new Index of prohibited books which he issued in 1557 and, in revised form, in 1559. It included in its outlawry such distinguished classics as Lodovico

Ariosto's *Orlando Furioso* and *Cento novelle antiche,* which from the religious standpoint were perfectly innocuous. This Index was rejected as too hasty and severe even by the conservative Jesuit Peter Canisius (later canonized), and it had to be replaced by that debated at the Tridentine Council several years later.[30]

Understandably, Jews were much perturbed to see the moving spirit behind the outlawry of the Talmud become their sovereign. To them he always remained essentially the cofounder, together with St. Gaetano da Thiene, of the militant Order of the Theatines, organized in 1524 for the purpose of combating the heresies spreading throughout Italy. As their resentment grew in the face of Paul's hostile legislation, the Jews readily used their traditional *gematria* in equating "Theatino" with "Haman," since both names had the same numerical value of ninety-five in their Hebrew letters. Their fears proved far from unfounded. Less than two months after assuming office Paul IV enacted his sharply discriminatory bull *Cum nimis absurdum* of July 14, 1555, which marked a reversal of the traditional papal policies toward the Roman Jews. The preamble reflected the pope's hatred of his Jewish subjects. He wrote:

It is both absurd and inappropriate that Jews, whom their own guilt has condemned to perpetual serfdom, should prove so ungrateful to the Christians under the pretext that the latter's piety would accept them and allow them to live among Christians. For mercy they pay back with insults, and in lieu of the subjection they owe the Christians, they arrogate to themselves dominion. We have received information that their insolence has gone so far in our capital city of Rome and in several other cities, villages, and localities of the Holy Roman Church that they not only venture to live mixed with the Christians, even in the vicinity of churches, without any distinction in their attire, but they also dare to rent houses in the choicer streets and squares of those cities, villages, and localities. They also acquire and own real estate, employ wet-nurses, maids, and other Christian servants, and commit many other acts to the shame and contempt of the Christian name.

To stave off these alleged social and religious evils the bull emphasized the segregationist policies of the Church with unprecedented vigor. Apart from prohibiting employment of Christian servants by Jews and ordering the latter to wear badges without any subterfuge, it forbade Christians to address any Jew as "sir," prohibited any work in public during Christian holidays, and made social intercourse between Jews and Christians very difficult. For this purpose it established, for the first time, obligatory Jewish quarters in Rome and the other papal cities, and outlawed the maintenance of more than one synagogue in any locality. While similar ordinances had been issued in many Christian lands before, the papal capital itself had theretofore allowed Jews to live in various sections of the city and to possess no fewer than nine or ten synagogues. All but one were now to be destroyed or transformed into churches. Another grave innovation consisted in the bull's discriminatory economic regulations. Even Jewish money-lenders, theretofore treated with great restraint, were now told that they must not charge interest except for full months of indebtedness, must wait eighteen months before disposing of pledges, and must deliver any surplus from such sales to the borrowers. Jewish physicians were not to attend Christian patients, "even if they were called and requested." Most importantly, Jews were not to own any real estate nor to engage in ordinary commerce except in secondhand goods.[31]

Unlike many earlier ordinances, moreover, this bull was quickly put into effect. The Roman ghetto, which was to achieve great notoriety in the following generations, was erected within two weeks of its promulgation, and soon thereafter was surrounded with a wall. After a century of easy-going Renaissance ways of life, Roman Jewry also viewed with dismay the harsh reimposition of the badge. One of its members, David Ascoli, wrote a Latin pamphlet arguing against the entire institution on scholarly grounds. Another Jew of standing in the community disrespectfully commented that the badge was mainly intended to serve as a new source of papal revenue. The retribution was swift and decisive: Ascoli was imprisoned, the other offender was publicly flogged.[32]

Even more shocking to Jews was Paul IV's sudden prosecution of the Anconitan Marranos in 1556. It is frequently assumed that September 1557 marks the turning point in the pope's policies, with the main emphasis now being placed on Church reforms, rather than on the international power struggle. But one may date the change back to April 1556, to that trial and execution of the Marranos, in which ideology prevailed over political and economic considerations. To be sure, as early as 1498 Alexander VI had formally suppressed the newly arisen community of Spanish New Christians in Rome, and in 1513 Julius II had again ordered the arrest of a number of secret Judaizers. Yet none of these defendants was executed. All along, the administration stood passively by whenever new groups of Marranos immigrated into the Papal States from the Iberian Peninsula or southern Italy. Because of the special importance of the Ancona harbor for Rome's Levantine trade, Paul III in 1535 enacted a special privilege for that city's Jewish residents, who, it was widely suspected, included quite a few relapsed converts. He may have tried thereby to appease that city, whose rebellious mood before its annexation in 1532 had found expression in the popular adage, "If Ancona were to be incorporated into the Pontifical States, there would be an uprising every week." On the other hand, the tacit toleration of Marranos in Rome and other papal cities had caused some adverse comment in parts of the Catholic world. In the early sessions of the Council of Trent, Bishop Balthasar de Limpo of Oporto voiced his country's astonishment over the papal actions in first encouraging the Portuguese Crown to allow the free emigration of Marranos and subsequently admitting some of them to the Pontifical States, where they more or less publicly reverted to Judaism. He also put, as we recall, this embarrassing question to Paul III in person, with his customary harshness. Such protests, even when supported by the mighty Charles V, went unheeded, however. Because of the great economic benefits of Jewish and Marrano trade with the Levant, both Ancona's city council and the papal officials shut their eyes to the New Christians' religious deviations. Even Julius III, under whose administration the Inquisition set in motion the burning of Hebrew books, nevertheless confirmed in 1553 all concessions theretofore granted to the Ancona community. In extending full freedom of trade to new settlers stemming from all nations and faiths, the pope specifically included the New Christians. He also confirmed the local Anconitan compact (of November 8, 1549) with the Jews, which assured the newcomers that none would "be subject to any inquest concerning his faith" by any ecclesiastic, except the pope in person, and that in the latter case the accused would be granted at least one year's freedom to depart.[33]

In thus reaffirming Paul III's original privilege, Julius may have been aware of Paul's rationale that the Marranos had never been true Christians, since they or their fathers had been forced to adopt Christianity against their will. This evidently also was the understanding of the Venetian envoy in Rome, Bernardino Navagero, in his report home of September 23, 1555. R. Joseph b. David ibn Leb of Salonica (who was to play a significant role in the ensuing controversy) was, therefore, not guilty of a gross overstatement when he wrote that Paul IV's predecessor had allowed the Ancona Marranos to return to Judaism "for the Christianity they had been forced to adopt in Portugal was involuntary." For some four months Paul, or his nephew, Cardinal Carlo Carafa, seems to have acquiesced in this interpretation. But on October 1, 1555, the pope changed his mind and revoked all earlier concessions to relapsed converts. On February 4, 1556, the papal administrator, Sebastian Portico di Lucca, archbishop of Ragusa, applying to Ancona the provisions of the bull *Cum nimis absurdum,* established a ghetto for Ancona Jewry. Finally, some four weeks later (April 30, 1556) Paul specifically ordered the prosecution of all "apostates," even if under severe torture they still denied that they had been baptized, lived as Christians, performed Christian rituals, or received ecclesiastical sacraments. The pope argued that it was a generally known fact that for some sixty years no Jew would have been allowed to live in Portugal unless he had been baptized and lived in a Christian fashion. By 1556, of course, the large majority of the Portuguese New Christians had been born and bred under the new law.[34]

It is small wonder, then, that this sudden reversal of papal policy, followed by the burning of twenty-four Anconitan Marranos (in addition to one who committed suicide) in May 1556, caused a great outcry in the Jewish world. Accustomed as Jews were to hearing about far more sanguinary autos-da-fé in Spain, this breach of privileges enacted by Paul IV's predecessors, which had had all the earmarks of mutually binding contractual obligations, called forth reprisals from Jewish leaders. Doña Gracia Mendesia and her son-in-law, Don Joseph Nasi, who had already attained a position of eminence in Constantinople, had been maintaining close commercial relations with Italy, in part channeled through the port of Ancona. The House of Mendes now tried to help some local agents directly affected by the new persecution. Their former family physician, Amatus Lusitanus, who interveningly had also attended some of the lay and ecclesiastical leaders of Ancona, succeeded in fleeing to Pesaro and subsequently settled in Salonica. But many others, in addition to the executed, suffered severely. If twenty-seven Marranos "reconciled" by the Inquisition and condemned to galley slavery in Malta, escaped before reaching their destination, scores of other refugees were seized by pirates in the Adriatic Sea and sold into slavery in Apulia. The reaction of the sixteenth-century Turkish Jews to these events was no longer as docile as that of their medieval ancestors, who had taken martyrdom in their stride. Among them were former Marranos who had attained positions of trust and influence in Gentile circles while still outwardly professing Christianity. They were affected not only by their neighbors' religious beliefs, manners, and speech but also by their political outlook and social conduct. Not surprisingly, many of these less tradition-bound men viewed direct political and economic retribution as the only appropriate answer to the sudden papal provocation, unprecedented though it might have been in the annals of Jewish history.[35]

The initiative came from some Marrano refugees. After failing to save themselves by bribing the papal commissioner, Johannes Vicentius Falangonius, who pocketed the large douceur of 16,000 ducats and absconded with it to Genoa, many left Ancona for the neighboring harbor city of Pesaro, some thirty-seven miles away. They persuaded the lukewarm Duke Guidobaldo II of Urbino to grant them extensive privileges for settlement in Pesaro and promised him, in return, to divert to that port most of Ancona's Levant trade. In order to fulfill that pledge they appealed to their coreligionists in Salonica and Constantinople to initiate a large-scale boycott of Ancona and to order even ships already under way to unload in the Pesaro harbor. Under the leadership of the House of Mendes, the Turkish Jews responded promptly and, after brief negotiations, proclaimed a boycott on all shipments to Ancona for eight months. At its expiration, coinciding with the Passover holidays, this boycott, couched in the terms of a rabbinic excommunication, was to be reviewed by a large and representative assembly of Turkish Jewish leaders. Its immediate effects are reflected in the plaintive letter addressed, as early as August 10, 1556, by Ancona's city council to the pope, which claimed that "unless the goodness of Your Holiness will help us, this city . . . will remain abandoned and derelict. It will become something like a burg or a village . . . [in lieu of] a city which used to be as full of business and traffic as any other noble city of Italy." [36]

Doña Gracia and Don Joseph went further. They persuaded the sultan to lodge a personal protest with the pope, as well as with the city council of Ancona. At that stage of international relations, as today (though not in the nineteenth century), it did not suffice to present merely humanitarian arguments. A country trying to intervene in the inner affairs of another sovereign state had to invoke some semblance of legitimate self-interest. This was indeed the tenor of the letter addressed on March 9, 1556, by Suleiman the Magnificent to Paul IV through the mediation of Baron Pierre Cachard, secretary of the French embassy in Constantinople. Cachard personally brought that letter to Rome. The sultan wrote:

When you shall have received My Divine and Imperial Seal, which will be presented to you, you must know that certain persons of the race of the Jews have informed My Elevated and Sublime Porte that, whereas certain subjects and tributaries of Ours have gone to your territories to traffic, and especially to Ancona, their goods and property have been seized at your command. This seizure has resulted in the loss by Our Treasury of the amount of 400,000 ducats, over and above the damage caused to Our subjects, who have been ruined and cannot meet their obligations to Our said Treasury arising from the customs duties and commerce of Our ports, of which they are in charge. We therefore request Your Holiness, that by virtue of this Our universal and illustrious Seal, which will be brought to you by Secretary Cachard, a man in the service of the Most High and Magnanimous King, Prince of Princes of the said generation of the Messiah Jesus, His Most Christian Majesty, the king of France, our very dear friend, you will be pleased to set free our above-mentioned . . . subjects, with all the property which they had and owned. In this way they may be able to satisfy their debts, and the above-mentioned customs officials will no longer have an excuse for their failure to pay by virtue of the arrest of the said prisoners. By so doing, you will give Us occasion to treat in friendly fashion your subjects and the other Christians who traffic in these parts.

This epistle, with its implicit threat of Turkish reprisals, was reinforced by a personal letter from the French ambassador to the pope's then all-powerful nephew Carlo Carafa. The stubborn pope, however, replied on June 1, 1556, with his usual vehemence. He now became, if anything, a more confirmed religious bigot. Having become involved in a long-enduring struggle with Spain, the Church's main protector against the advance of the Reformation, he told the Venetian ambassador, Bernardino Navagero, that the Spaniards were all "heretics, schismatics, accursed by God, the offspring of Jews and Moors, the scum of the earth." A few months later, on learning that one of his nephews had adopted Calvinism in Geneva, the pope told Navagero, that even if his own "father had been a heretic, We would personally have carried the lumber to burn him." To such an extent had Paul IV forgotten the requirement of *clementia catholica,* which had once forced, as we recall, a cleric to seek a special papal dispensation precisely for having as a youth carried lumber to the pyre of a relapsed Jewish convert.[37]

The intervention of the French officials is the more remarkable as the House of Mendes had earlier had difficulties in trying to collect debts owed it by the French king, Henry II. We shall see that the firm later had to resort to drastic means, again with the aid of the Porte, to secure payment. Ironically, Don Joseph thus indirectly aided the Spanish Habsburgs, Paul IV's most hated antagonists. His own anti-Spanish stance later earned him the bitter enmity of Philip II. In a coded message of 1569 Philip declared Joseph "the person who most consistently promotes and stimulates [in Constantinople] actions detrimental to all of Christendom and to Our dominions. He also maintains an important intelligence service at this Court and in other parts of My kingdoms. Hence it would be of great advantage to have him in our hands." Philip was actually prepared to enter a secret conspiracy to secure the capture of the Jewish statesman, alive if at all possible, but dead if necessary. This scheme failed, but it underscored the great influence exerted by Don Joseph in the international power politics of that period. However, in 1556 he still was a relative newcomer to the shores of the Bosporus, and even with the support of Doña Gracia (one of the *grandes dames* of the Renaissance era, greatly revered in Jewish circles as a patroness of Jewish scholars) he was unable to secure the unanimous backing of the Turkish Jewish communal leaders, which was indispensable for an effective boycott.[38]

Not surprisingly, the boycott ultimately failed, since it ran counter to basic political and economic factors. Pesaro's harbor was much inferior to that of Ancona, and some of the first ships diverted to it had difficulty in landing. Its overland communications and its distribution system for Levantine wares likewise left much to be desired. Moreover, while the Marrano exiles established in Pesaro might benefit from the boycott, the Jews remaining in Ancona were bound to suffer. Their community, which then looked back to three centuries of important cultural and business history, anticipated with trepidation not only the diminution in its long-established trade but also some retaliation from the aroused papal regime. Going beyond their immediate interests, they feared that papal reprisals might also severely affect other Jewish communities in the Papal States, if not in all Christendom.

Partisans of the Ancona Jews exaggerated these difficulties by claiming that Pesaro was at that time afflicted by a plague, and justly pointed out that Duke Guidobaldo was anything but a reliable friend of Jews. They cited a recent incident in which the duke's brother, together with other young malefactors, had with impunity attacked the local synagogue. The chief opponent of the boycott, the Constantinople rabbi Joshua Soncino, wrote of that attack, "Because of our numerous sins they dragged out the scroll of the Law and tore it; they took a pig, clad it in the scroll's mantle, and placed it in the ark." The proponents of the boycott, on the other hand, warned that, if disillusioned, the duke might hand over the Marrano refugees to the Inquisition. These arguments were part of a heated legalistic debate carried on in rabbinic responsa. Although the proponents were headed by the distinguished rabbinic leader Joseph ibn Leb, supported by the great Palestinian authorities Joseph b. Ephraim Karo and Moses b. Joseph di

Trani (the Elder), the Turkish community was sufficiently confused to prevent any united and sustained effort. Some merchants, particularly those of Anatolian Brusa, preferred to do business with Ancona, and they received enough support from Soncino and other rabbis to disregard the boycott, particularly after the expiration of its original term in the spring of 1557. In time even the House of Mendes had to acknowledge defeat. Doña Gracia must have been doubly irked when soon thereafter the pope's inquisitor-general, Cardinal Antonio Michele Ghislieri (later Pope Pius V), persuaded the liberal Duke Ercole d'Este of Ferrara to destroy all copies of Jacob da Fano's work containing his elegy on the Ancona martyrs. The press which had printed the elegy and which had once enjoyed Gracia's personal patronage during her stay in Ferrara was peremptorily shut down. By 1558 Duke Guidobaldo expelled all the now unwelcome Marranos from Pesaro. Thus petered out the first major international effort of modern Jewish communities to combat anti-Jewish persecutions on a higher political and economic plane. The much-vaunted Jewish solidarity revealed itself in its total impotence when confronted by the need of concerted political action, as contrasted with the Jews' traditional passive, if often even more heroic, resistance.[39]

Characteristic of the opposition's views was Joshua Soncino's remarkable statement that "more serious" than the auto-da-fé of the Ancona Marranos was the prank of the youthful offenders in Pesaro. To explain his evaluation of an attack on Jewish implements of worship as graver than the martyrdom of twenty-four (together with the suicide, twenty-five) persons and the affliction of scores of others who were condemned to slavery or forced into exile, Soncino added, "There is no greater insult to all of Israel [than the Pesaro misdeed], for it is the custom in any locality of the whole world to respect the scrolls of the Law." From another angle, the contemporary chronicler Joseph ha-Kohen expressed great admiration for Doña Gracia and devoted two pages to the sufferings of the condemned Marranos in Ancona and their repercussions in Pesaro, but he had no more than three lines to spare for the sultan's diplomatic intervention. Even Benjamin Neḥemiah b. Elnathan (Netanael-Diodato), whose chronicle of the days of Paul IV described the Ancona persecutions (of which he had been an eyewitness) in great length and even tried to sketch their international background, hardly mentioned the Turkish Jews' boycott. Himself a victim of Paul's ruthless policies, which soon extended to his own community of Civitanova, he could offer only the traditional Jewish self-blame in explanation of these tragedies. He wrote:

Because of our numerous sins he [the pope] succeeded in trampling under his feet the remnant of Israel living in exile under his reign, for the Lord had been contemplating its numerous sins and His heart had turned to hating His people. The Jews' behavior had become overbearing in exile because they relied on their wealth while they lived securely in their beautiful dwellings, courts, and palaces, everyone going to his vineyard or field and carrying his gold and silver with him. But they forgot the Lord and did not set aside time for study; because of their wealth they neglected the Torah.[40]

UNPRECEDENTED REJECTION

Roman Jewry received a relatively brief respite after Paul IV's demise, when there was a sharp reaction against the excesses of his administration among both the Roman populace and the cardinals. Amidst general rejoicing, the populace dismantled the deceased pontiff's statue, put a yellow Jewish hat on its head, and rolled it through the streets, with street urchins running after it and shouting, "Papa giudeo, Papa giudeo." The mob also freed all political and religious prisoners and burned down the building housing the Inquisition. This act called forth Monsignor Pietro Carnesecchi's observation, "The Holy Office has died the same death it had used to inflict on others, that is, by burning." Ultimately, Carlo and Giovanni Carafa were sentenced for the murder of Giovanni's wife and were executed, an action much more extreme than the then customary discharge of relatives of the preceding pope from the high offices they held under the regnant nepotistic system. Such a turnover, as observed in the mid-seventeenth century by Theodor Almeyden, Dutch advocate and adviser of Innocent X, was generally expected, at least since the days of Alexander VI and Julius II. It resembled the American practice of having a large number of higher officials "walk the plank" at every major change in party control of the administration. But it did not usually entail any loss of life. After Paul IV's death, however, there was for a time widespread anarchy, stemmed only by the election of a new pope, Giovanni Angelo de' Medici (not of the famous Florentine family), who assumed the name of Pius IV (1559–65).[41]

The new pope, temperamentally the antithesis of his predecessor, saw no conflict between the welfare of his Church and a more humane treatment of Jews. With respect to the Inquisition, too, he demanded that in its proceedings justice be tempered with mercy and that "the iniquity of malicious calumnies to the detriment of the faithful and [resulting in] general scandal be discontinued." Pius IV publicly enunciated these guidelines on March 13, 1560, while acquitting Cardinal Giovanni Morone of the accusation of heresy, for which he had been prosecuted by Carafa ever since 1551 and which, incidentally, had helped Carafa to remove a potential competitor for the papal tiara. From the outset Pius promised many alleviations to his Jewish subjects and even intervened with Ferdinand I in behalf of the Jews of Bohemia. He also tried to mitigate the severe economic hardships imposed upon his Jewish subjects by the bull *Cum nimis absurdum.* The sudden forced liquidation of Jewish houses and shops outside the ghetto had, according to Paul IV's own admission, made prices tumble to but a fifth of the original value. The immediate effects on the general Roman economy, too, were so severe that Paul himself had to issue certain "interpretations" which took the edge off his earlier provisions. Rome's supreme court, the *Rota,* added further modifications in favor of Jews. Now, without formally revoking the old bull, Pius IV "clarified" it for the Roman Jews on February 27, 1562, "since you have been in many ways annoyed and disturbed by the interpretation of those decrees much beyond the intention of Our said predecessor." The new regulation allowed Jews to acquire real estate up to the value of 1,500 ducats in other Roman quarters and outside the city. The pope also permitted them to open shops in the vicinity of the ghetto, though these stores were not to do business on Sundays and Christian holidays—a good precaution for the security of the Jews as well. At night the shopkeepers were to return to their quarter. At the same time Pius upheld his predecessor's insistence that only deeds and ledgers written in

Italian and in Latin script could be produced as evidence against Christian customers or debtors. Once again, the official "interpreters" went further and allowed Jewish businessmen to open shops on the Piazzas Colonna and San Marco, located in the city's most fashionable districts. With respect to the Talmud, the new Index, as debated at the Tridentine Council (which was constantly and firmly controlled by Pius IV and his legates) and as finally promulgated by Pius, included the aforementioned compromise solution, which appeared satisfactory to both sides. However, the new pope did not revoke his predecessor's orders relating to the ghetto or the badge, both of which remained permanent fixtures of Roman Jewish life under all Counter Reformation popes.[42]

Unfortunately for the Jews, the growing consolidation of the Protestant Reformation and internal disorders in the Papal States made the popes ever more uneasy. Almost every new pope reversed the Jewish policies of his predecessor. The gentle, statesmanlike Pius IV was succeeded by the ascetically rigid Antonio Michele Ghislieri, who had been appointed inquisitor-general by Paul IV and now was to reign as pope for over six years, under the name of Pius V (1566–72). The new pope's extraordinary zeal in upholding the purity of Catholic dogma and his rigorous persecution of infidels were to earn him canonization in 1712.

Immediately after his elevation (on January 7, 1566) Pius V suspended the theretofore customary homage publicly rendered by the Roman Jewish community to its new sovereign. Tommaso Manriquez, Master of the Apostolic Palace, issued a general prohibition against Jews acquiring books without a special license (January 19, 1566). Evidently, Jews were suspected of handling not only Hebrew texts but also vernacular works outlawed by the Inquisition. In the following months the papal organs enacted one restriction after another. On April 19, 1566, the pope renewed Paul IV's prohibitions "notwithstanding the privileges and concessions" granted them by his own immediate predecessor, Pius IV. "We order that all these [1555] provisions be strictly observed in the future, not only in the lands and possessions subjected to Us but also in all other places." Pius V also specifically forbade any new "interpretations" of his own decree. Of course, life proved stronger than theory, and the *Rota* once again had to allow Jews to display their wares outside the ghetto, a papal official explaining that otherwise Christians of high standing might have to go to the ghetto to acquire (or sell) such merchandise. Clearly, since the Jews' trade was now limited largely to secondhand goods, they had to be allowed to deal in clothes discarded by the aristocracy and hierarchy. In May the pope ordered that the public markets be held on Saturdays, not Wednesdays, and thus effectively barred Jews. Pius disregarded all pleas for mercy, even that presented to him by an unnamed Christian petitioner on August 13, 1566, who argued that only by good examples, rather than by force, could the Jews (as well as the courtesans whom the puritanical pope also tried to reform) be taught to mend their ways. Five months later the pope repeated the prohibition against Jewish ownership of real estate and threatened the confiscation, for the benefit of the *monte di pietà* and the House of Catechumens, of all such property acquired by Jews under the names of Christian straw men. Finally, in two decrees of 1567 and 1568 Pius completely outlawed all moneylending at interest. The Christian debtors in the Comtat Venaissin were informed by the authorities in August 1568 that they need not pay anything on loans due to Jews for more than ten years, and that they should settle debts of more recent vintage with a discount of 50 percent. So determined was the new papal administration to rehabilitate the memory of Paul IV that the Inquisition instituted in 1568 a lengthy prosecution of one Niccolò Franco because, immediately after Paul's death, he had dared to publish a pamphlet attacking the pope and his nephews. The trial ended after two years with Franco's execution.[43]

At the same time Pius and his officials combined the carrot with the stick in trying to induce Jews to adopt Christianity. On one occasion (in June 1566) they staged with much fanfare the public baptism of two Jewish adults and three children, the pope personally conducting the service and five cardinals acting as godfathers to the respective converts. Pius also readily approved Philip II's ruling that a cleric, son of a Genoese Christian father and a Spanish mother of Jewish descent, be excluded from any office at the Cathedral of Toledo in consonance with its "statute of purity" of 1547. Of course, approval of the Toledan statute did not necessarily imply enthusiastic acceptance of the excesses of the Spanish Inquisition. In fact, on October 25, 1569, the Spanish ambassador, Juan de Zuñiga, submitted to the pope a detailed memorandum complaining that, "for some years past the Pontifical Curia had denigrated and reduced the preeminence, prerogatives, and authority of the Spanish Holy Office." Nor did Pius refrain from entertaining friendly relations with New Christian Jesuit fathers, including Francisco de Toledo, whose diplomatic skill Pius and his successors often enlisted for important negotiations in behalf of the anti-Ottoman "Holy League." This is but another illustration of the line drawn by the Papacy between the treatment of New Christians in Rome and that on the Iberian Peninsula. Himself a former inquisitor, Pius V followed Paul IV's lead in reestablishing the Roman Holy Office as one of the Papacy's most authoritative organs; he attended many of its meetings and cosigned many of its decrees. Autos-da-fé became frequent spectacles in Rome and usually attracted large crowds. If few Marranos are recorded among the victims, this was probably owing more to their conscious avoidance of the States of the Church than to any inquisitorial leniency. The one Marrano among the fourteen defendants to appear in the first auto of June 23, 1566, was also sentenced for having undergone circumcision in order to marry a Jewish woman, although he still had a wife living in Spain. Not surprisingly, the Roman populace quickly sensed the new turn in papal policies. Its attacks on Jews began to multiply so alarmingly that, as early as April 10, 1566, the pope himself had to issue a special prohibition of assaults on Jews, under the sanction of flogging. Nevertheless, Jewish life became increasingly unbearable and in 1567 Jews began leaving the country en masse. Three hundred lent a willing ear to Don Joseph Nasi's call and embarked for the new Jewish colony around Tiberias. In its pathetic letter to Venetian coreligionists, the small community of Cori in the Campagna likewise expressed its readiness to proceed there in an organized fashion.[44]

All these measures were but preliminaries to nearly total exclusion. Anticipating the pope, the local authorities chased the Jews out of Palestrina and Ravenna in 1568, although the latter city had played a noteworthy role in Jewish history for more than a millennium. Finally, Pius V took a step unprecedented in the annals of papal-Jewish relations by proclaiming (in his bull *Hebraeorum gens sola* of February 26, 1569) a general banishment of Jews from the States of the Church in both Italy and France. After three months any Jew remaining in the provinces was to lose his property and be "condemned to perpetual servitude." (Evidently the legislator realized here the distinction between real slavery and the perpetual serfdom which had theoretically long been the normal status of Jews under the Church.) In justification, the pope advanced a whole array of accusations against Jewish behavior, ranging from excessive usuries ruinous to the population, to the practice of magic arts, and the procuring of "honest" Christian women for sinners of all kinds. The pope exempted only the cities of Rome and Ancona, where Jews were allowed to remain because the papal authorities could more closely supervise them there and because their presence greatly facilitated trade relations with the Levant. In Avignon both Archbishop Feliciano and the city elders argued against the banishment of Jews, the archbishop pointing out that Jews had been extending much-needed credit to local Catholics fighting the Huguenots. The pope replied that the bishop of Carpentras had, on the contrary, stated that no legislative act of recent years had given so much satisfaction to the local population. According to the populace, lightning which on September 24, 1569 had struck the Jewish quarter in Carpentras and killed nine persons was testimony of the divine wrath aroused by Jewish usury. A telling argument, however, was advanced by the Treasury, desirous of collecting large tax arrears from the Jews of the whole Comtat Venaissin before their departure. A first extension of six months proved insufficient and was followed by further extensions; despite nine successive summonses from the papal authorities, these delays lasted long enough for the decree to sink into oblivion after the death of Pius V on May 1, 1572.[45]

Jews of the Italian possessions were less fortunate. All the provincial communities, including the old and populous one of Bologna, were totally uprooted. No less than 108 synagogues were confiscated and either transformed into churches or closed. The Jewish cemetery in Bologna was handed over to the neighboring convent of St. Peter the Martyr, the sisters being allowed to remove or destroy the tombstones, to exhume the bodies, and otherwise to do with the property "as they pleased." The pope made his objective clear: "We thus wish to deprive the Hebrews of all hope of retaining at any future time a place in that city where either living persons might reside or the dead be buried." At the same time Pius ordered the pope's two remaining Italian communities of Rome and Ancona to keep up the full Jewish payments for the maintenance of the Roman Houses of Catechumens. In addition, they had to assume the burden of supporting the large number of expellees from the provinces. This task was but slightly alleviated by contributions from other Italian communities, such as Mantua, which also had to accommodate numerous refugees in their own midst. Pius had to make the exceptional concession, however, of enlarging Rome's Jewish quarter, established by Paul IV, so as to accommodate some of the exiles streaming into the capital. Yet it goes without saying that he continued Paul's harsh policies with respect to the censorship of Jewish books and the prosecution of suspected Marranos. Remarkably, however, as pointed out by Isaiah Sonne, Pius V's decree of banishment of 1569 seems to have made a less immediate impression on the Jewish public and inspired fewer poets to write dirges than had the burning of the twenty-four Marranos in Ancona thirteen years before. It appears that the sixteenth-century Jews had become so deeply imbued with the idea of their exilic instability and the right of every sovereign to withdraw his toleration from them at a moment's notice that they accepted their fate plaintively but without loud protests.[46]

FROM GREGORY XIII TO CLEMENT VIII

Jews of the Papal States had never before experienced such a large-scale expulsion, nor had they faced even a threat of banishment since the reign of John XXII two and a half centuries before, if then. Yet they learned from their other European coreligionists how to "roll with the wave" and felt confident that this storm, too, would pass after a few years. That is why the community of Ancona at first refused to assume the increased fiscal burden imposed on it by Pius V for the maintenance of the Houses of Catechumens. When in 1581 it was finally forced by the protests of Roman Jewry not only to participate in these payments but also to settle the intervening arrears at once, it stipulated that, as soon as other communities were reestablished in the States of the Church, they would have to share that responsibility. In fact, the decree of expulsion, then still being implemented, was officially sidetracked under the new popes, Gregory XIII (1572–85) and Sixtus V (1585–90).

True, an overzealous cardinal, Benedetto Lomellini, who had banished the Jews from Anagni, vowed as late as 1582 that "so long as I administer this land, I shall not tolerate the arrival here of another [Jew]." Nonetheless, without formally revoking Pius V's decree, Gregory resisted repeated efforts of the authorities of the Comtat, supported by his own secretary of state, Tolomeo Galli, to suppress Jewish immigration to that region. In 1580 he intervened in favor of some Jewish travelers who had been captured by Maltese Knights in expectation of high ransom. A year later he renewed Paul III's decree of 1543, granting Jewish transients, especially in Ancona, full protection for themselves and their property. He even appealed to all authorities not to impede their journeys to Africa or the Holy Land. On learning that some soldiers had attacked the Jewish quarter and had been repelled by the Jewish inhabitants only with difficulty, Gregory removed the troops from the city and later threatened anyone loitering in the ghetto's vicinity with capital punishment. He also permitted Jews to lend money at an interest rate of up to 24 percent. All the same, from 1577 on he rigidly enforced the compulsory attendance of Jews at Christian conversionist sermons. On September 1, 1584, Gregory devoted a special bull, *Sancta Mater ecclesia,* to this subject. He wrote:

We order all patriarchs, archbishops, bishops, and other prelates of churches, even those honorably distinguished as cardinals, to institute in all their cities, lands, and localities in which a sizable number of Jews reside and form a synagogue . . . such sermons and lectures . . . by qualified persons, wherever possible expert in Hebrew. [These men] should expound the Old Testament Scripture, especially those sections of the books of Moses and the Prophets which Jews recite on those particular Sabbaths, and explain them according to the interpretation of the Church Fathers and the true meaning given them by the Catholic Church. . . . [They should, in particular, controvert] the false interpretations of the Holy Scriptures by the rabbis, who have corrupted their literal meaning with fables, lies, and various subterfuges, and still continue to corrupt and deprave them.

To be sure, this sweeping order, addressed to the entire Catholic world, was but halfheartedly and sporadically executed outside the papal realm. But in the States of the Church it enjoyed immediate and long-lasting acceptance, for it was in line with the establishment, by St. Philip Neri, of courses at the Roman Congregation of the Oratory for the instruction of outstanding Roman laymen in the fundamentals of Christianity, which helped to bring about the revival of genuine Catholic feeling in the capital. Similar institutes were soon founded in other Italian localities. Gregory and Neri readily supported such converts as Andrea del Monte (formerly Joseph Sarfati), who had received his new family name at his baptism by Julius III (Giovanni del Monte). He not only was an effective missionary among Jews but in 1574 also delivered sermons at the Oratory to Christian laymen. Nor did he hesitate to publish two Hebrew polemical tracts, addressed to Jewish readers, in which he argued for the correctness of the Christian messianic doctrine. In short, Gregory hoped to achieve through these less drastic measures that wholesale conversion of Jews which had escaped the grasp of his more ruthless predecessor.[47]

On one occasion Gregory himself underscored the difference between his and Pius V's regime. In the preamble to his bull *Antiqua Iudaeorum improbitas* of July 1, 1581, he almost boasted of the fact that Jews, "dispersed through all regions of the world and subjected to perpetual servitude have in no area been treated with greater clemency than in Christian lands, and particularly in the lap of Apostolic piety." Ironically, this pasage introduced a series of provisions intended to broaden the authority of the Inquisition over professing Jews. While disclaiming any wish to interfere in the internal affairs of the Jewish community (whose autonomy he himself had reaffirmed in his breve of January 10, 1577) and even invoking the ancient principle enunciated in the First Epistle to the Corinthians—"For what have I to do to judge them also that are without?"—he reopened questions which had long since appeared to be adjusted by mutual agreement. He harked back to the postulates of the fourteenth-century grand-inquisitor Nicholas Eymeric and decreed that thenceforth inquisitors should have jurisdiction over professing Jews who violated principles common to Judaism and Christianity, adored the devil, possessed prohibited books, or employed Christian servants. In the July 1, 1581 decree the pope also ordered the Jews to submit all their Hebrew books to the papal censor within ten days for renewed scrutiny. Anyone subsequently found in possession of a Hebrew work, even if it had been previously expurgated, was to be severely punished. Shortly before, Gregory also renewed the prohibition against Jewish physicians attending non-Jewish patients in any Christian country. He also sanctioned the staging of public autos-da-fé. In 1578 seven Marranos were executed; five years later two Portuguese and two Spanish New Christians were condemned respectively for judaizing and for abetting Christian heresies. Among the victims of the Inquisition was the saintly Joseph Saralvo, whose readiness to suffer martyrdom was extolled by contemporary Hebrew poets. In 1581 Gregory also advised the Republic of Genoa not to admit any New Christians except after a very careful investigation of their conduct. Yet, these trials and tribulations did not prevent a contemporary Hebrew chronicler from contrasting Gregory's regime with that of his predecessor and calling the new pope "a good and learned man" in whose days "the remnant of Israel dwelled in peace and righteousness." [48]

Many of the abiguities of Gregory XIII's reign were temporarily resolved under the brief but energetic regime of Sixtus V, "indisputably the greatest pope that the Church has had for 300 years" (Ludwig Pastor). In his major bull *Christiana pietas* of October 22, 1586, Sixtus formally abrogated Pius V's decree of expulsion, and sweepingly provided in Article 2:

We generally provide that any Jew of whatever sex, rank, condition, and status shall from now on be able at his will to come and work throughout the States of the Church. He may dwell in cities, large castles, and the lands of these States, except for villages and hamlets, and live in accordance with the present provisions. They [the Jews] may freely engage in any craft, occupation, trade, and business of grain, produce, wine, agistment of cattle, and sowing of grain. Similarly, they may enter into partnerships with Christians and maintain relations of familiarity and friendship with them on the aforementioned occasions, making use of the crafts, offices, professions, and manual labor of Christians while paying them for their honest and rightful merchandise. In particular Christian butchers shall be obliged to provide them with meat, according to the customs in Ancona and other places, at prices paid by Christians. They are not to be allowed, however, to employ Christian servants, male or female, nor to cause those Christians to do things prohibited them by papal legislation.

Article 3 stated that Jews should be allotted housing at the customary rents. This provision laid the foundations for the famous *jus di gazagà,* or permanent tenant protection for the inmates of the ghetto. The bull concluded with a sweeping amnesty, along the lines once granted by Leo X, which guaranteed the Jews full immunity from prosecution for past crimes, except murder, counterfeiting of currency, rebellion, and sacrilege. These economic concessions were part of the pope's plan to increase the resources of the Papal States and Treasury so that they might serve the Holy See in its ambitious international undertakings. For this purpose he also enacted strict laws against disturbances of public order, particularly against crimes on public roads.[49]

This growing stability was, of course, very favorable to Jewish resettlement, as well as to the expansion of Jewish trade. Marranos still were very fearful of living in the papal possessions, where four new inquisitorial tribunals were established in 1585–88, although the Inquisition condemned but few culprits to death during Sixtus' reign, and hardly any for "judaizing." But professing Jews now rapidly increased in both number and affluence. Sixtus actually forbade the Maltese Hospitalers to extort any ransom whatsoever from Jewish captives. To encourage agriculture and industry he entered into a compact with a Venetian Jew, Magino (Meir) di Gabriele, to stimulate the planting of mulberry trees throughout the States of the Church and to utilize their yields twice a year for silk production of a special kind. In return Magino was granted on June 4, 1587, a sixty-year monopoly to exploit his method of production and the right to live with his family outside the ghetto. In the following year the pope extended to Magino the further exclusive privilege of polishing mirrors and crystal objects with a special vegetable oil fabricated by him. As a token of his gratitude Magino presented the pope with a brief

Italian tract in the form of a dialogue describing his approach to silk production, and prefaced by a dedicatory Hebrew poem extolling the pontiff. In all such economic planning, including the traditional sale of offices, which even that relatively incorruptible pope could not avoid, Sixtus was assisted by a Portuguese New Christian, Giovanni Lopez. As a result, the state Treasury accumulated within the short span of four years the substantial amount of 4,000,000 scudi in cash, which is doubly remarkable as Sixtus was one of the city's most prominent and generous builders who enriched Rome with a number of magnificent architectural and artistic monuments. Not unjustifiedly, he was styled the "creator of modern Rome" and an expert "urbanist" whose architectural and engineering ideas still are suggestive for Rome's municipal planning today. Nor did Sixtus hesitate to entrust his health to Jewish physicians.[50]

Remarkably, thus assured of personal security and freedom of movement and trade, the Roman Jews evinced immediate interest in securing a formal revocation of the ban on rabbinic books and, if possible, an outright permit to reprint an expurgated version of the Talmud. A general permission for Jews "to possess all expurgated Hebrew books," with special reference to the discussions at the Council of Trent and Pius IV's order, was indeed included in the bull of 1586 (Art. 4). But the formal authorization for the reprinting of the Talmud became the subject of protracted negotiations. In appealing for assistance to other Italian Jewish communities the Roman Jewish elders wrote on July 20, 1590, "Since you have done so much in preventing the threatened expulsion, how much more should you do for the preservation of our holy books, 'for that is thy life and the length of thy days' [Deut. 30:20]." This letter referred to the campaign conducted by several North-Italian communities which had met in Padua soon after the election of Sixtus V in 1585. The assembled representatives of communities from the duchies of Milan, Piedmont, Mantua, Ferrara, and Padua had indeed successfully sought both the revocation of the decree of expulsion and freedom of transit for Jews. Although partially secured under Gregory XIII, these residential and travel rights were not fully spelled out until Sixtus' bull of 1586. The Paduan conference now appointed a committee with headquarters in Cremona to direct the joint efforts also with respect to repealing the censorship of rabbinic works. The committee dispatched an envoy, Bezalel Massarani, to Rome and provided him with ample funds (up to 10,000 scudi) to conduct negotiations with the papal Index Commission.[51]

Revision of the vast "sea of the Talmud" created major difficulties, however. Neither the Council of Trent nor Pius IV had specified the passages and phrases which they wished to see deleted or modified; they left the extent and method of the prescribed expurgation entirely open. After some deliberation the papal Commission demanded merely that such equivocal terms as *goy, nokhri, 'arel, min,* or *'obed abodah zarah* (Gentile, stranger, uncircumcised person, heretic, or worshiper of foreign gods; our text transliterates these words phonetically, as they were pronounced by most Roman Jews, as *goi, nocri, ghorel, min* and *goved ghavoda zara'*) should be replaced by *'obed kokhabim u-mazzalot* (worshiper of stars and celestial bodies) and the like, so as to avoid their being mistaken as referring to Christians. An unnamed memorialist, probably representing an influential conservative faction among the cardinals, opposed such substitutions, however, arguing that "your eminences thus wish to leave unchanged the perverted commentaries of the Hebrews, which are their ruination. With these interpretations the rabbis cover up all the places where Christ appears in the Law and the Prophets, and thereby keep under their absolute control [*tyrannigiati*] the eyes and ears of the miserable people and the simpletons, who thus neither wish nor are able to see and hear the truth." He insisted upon the total uprooting of all such weeds from "the talmudic garden of Satan, the paradise of Hebrews, revered by them as the gospels of the talmudic Antichrist." Because of these differences of opinion, it was finally decided to leave the expurgation to the Jews themselves, who were to submit revised copies for approval to the experts of the papal Commission, aided by converts of its own choice. Interveningly, Massarani and his associates found a publisher who was ready to print the Talmud in Rome, provided the Jewish communities would underwrite a minimum of 700 sets at 14 scudi each. To avoid further delays the communities of Mantua and Ferrara assumed that obligation, too. Unfortunately, these plans went awry when Sixtus passed away, on August 27, 1590. Moreover, even if this edition of the Talmud had seen the light of day, it probably would have shared the fate of the Bible text sponsored by Sixtus, which in 1592 was suppressed by Clement VIII.[52]

Once again the pendulum of toleration swung away from the Jews. Of the three short-term administrations (between September 1590 and December 1591 three pontiffs were elected and died), that of Gregory XIV was most likely to continue the tolerant policies of Sixtus V. In fact, some Ferrara Jews, who seemed to have been helpful to the pope before his election, entertained great hopes that finally the Talmud project would be brought to fruition. However, Gregory passed away after a pontificate of but ten months. He was followed (after the two-month reign of Innocent IX) by Clement VIII, who held the tiara for over thirteen years (1592–1605). A well-informed student of the period explains the vagaries of Clement's regime by his "physical ailments, his obsessive quest for changes in locale, his undisciplined piety, and his profligacy, however unintentional." During the first year of his reign, this pro-Spanish pontiff merely tightened up existing anti-Jewish commercial and segregationist provisions. His bull of February 28, 1592, was specifically addressed only to Avignon and the Comtat Venaissin. But on February 25, 1593, he again ordered all Jews of the Papal States, except the residents of Rome, Ancona, and Avignon, to leave the country, offering for the exception the old rationale that Jewish commerce was needed in these three major centers and that Jews could be more closely supervised there and be made "to temper their malefactions." Christian missionaries could also more readily persuade them to abandon their ancestral faith. Three days later Clement ordered the delivery of all Hebrew works in Rome to the Roman Inquisition within ten days, and elsewhere in the States of the Church within two months. His bull Cum Hebraeorum malitia is unusually harsh in both tone and content. Its preamble justifies the hostile action by "the Jews' malice, which from day to day invents new fraudulent methods of disseminating pernicious volumes and impious, as well as plainly detestable, books long since condemned." Referring especially to the outlawry of the Talmud by many popes from Gregory IX to Gregory XIII, Clement continued:

We forbid the Jewish communities and individuals living in any part of the Christian world to hold any impious talmudic books or manuscripts, which have frequently been condemned. [The same holds true] for the utterly foolish kabbalistic and other nefarious works prohibited and condemned by Our predecessors, as well as for any commentaries, tracts, volumes, and writings, whether composed in Hebrew or in any other language, published or yet to be published, which tacitly or expressly contain heretical or erroneous statements against the Holy Scriptures of the Old Law and Testament.

This prohibition is noteworthy, not only by its broad sweep and its inclusion of kabbalistic works, long considered protrinitarian by Christian Hebraists, but also by its vague outlawry of *implied* heretical teachings against the Old Testament. Nor was prior expurgation of incriminated texts or the securing of specific licenses from ecclesiastical censors to be admitted as a legitimate excuse. If, on the petition of the Roman Jewish community, the terminal date for surrendering their books was extended to the end of May, the pope used this occasion to remind the Jews that the possession of such books had been forbidden "in perpetuity." However, in practice, the growingly rigid papal censorship was now aimed at Protestant, rather than Jewish, letters. The papal Commission in charge of the Index, before which the Jewish community pleaded that most Hebrew commentaries were completely innocuous from the Christian standpoint, decided in 1596 to outlaw only the rabbinically inspired commentaries written by the Protestant Hebraists Paul Fagius and Conrad Pellikan. The decree of expulsion of 1593 was likewise modified on July 2, when Jews engaged in business were allowed "to dwell, trade, and negotiate, so long as they do not establish a permanent domicile," in any locality of the Papal States. Eight months later Clement even renewed Paul III's privilege for the Turkish Jews arriving in Ancona, including exemption from all taxes and tolls. It appears that the original decree remained a dead letter in both the Italian and the French possessions of the Papacy.[53]

From then on papal censorship of Hebrew books became much more orderly; only books formally placed on the Index were burned in a public auto-da-fé in 1601. True, anti-Jewish enactments often were aggravated by administrative ordinances. For instance, the Roman governor Cardinal Girolamo Rusticucci not

only prohibited Jews of the States of the Church from living outside their assigned quarters without a special permit from the car-
dinal-vicar of Rome or the provincial holy offices, he also forbade
them to visit the capital for Jewish holiday services, under the severe penalty of the confiscation of their property and the closing
of the offending synagogues. He also outlawed Jewish sales of ritually slaughtered meat to Christians (1592) and, in a curious
reversal of the former policy of encouraging Jewish conversions by
contacts with catechumens, he forbade Jews to come within thirty
ells of the latter's houses, under the sanction of three lashes for
each transgression. Any attempt to persuade a prospective neophyte to remain a Jew was punishable by galley slavery. At the
same time, however, to stem the frequent insults and beatings of
Jewish passers-by on Roman streets, another governor, Annibale
Rucellai, though originally a protégé of the intolerant Pope Paul
IV, in 1595 threatened any assailant of a Jew with three lashes
and a fine of 200 scudi. This ordinance was confirmed in quick
succession in 1596, 1602, 1604, 1605, 1609, 1615, 1616, 1620, 1621,
1628, 1630, 1632, 1634, and several times thereafter. Its very repetition demonstrated its inefficacy in putting "an end to the gross
pleasantries and scandalous vexations of which the Jews have become the victims." In his bull Cum ex iniuncto of January 11,
1598, Clement sharply condemned the exclusion from ordination
of any New Christians of Jewish parentage "beyond the second degree on the father's side and beyond the first degree on the mother's side." Also, the pope approved, however reluctantly, the
suggestions submitted by the financially hard-pressed administration of Philip III of Spain to grant a general amnesty to the Span-
ish-Portugese Marranos. We shall see that these negotiations between the Crown and the papal nuncio, extending over the years
1602–1605, offered the Iberian New Christians a welcome, if
costly, reprieve from inquisitorial prosecutions. More remarkably,
Clement did not hesitate to initiate, in 1604, proceedings for the
beatification of the famous mystic Theresa de Jesús, although
these were not to be successfully concluded until ten years later,
under Paul V. From the outset, moreover, Clement allowed another New Christian, the Jesuit Cardinal Francisco de Toledo, to
play a leading role in the revision of the authorized text of the

Vulgate, prepared under the direction of Sixtus V. The final product, the so-called Sixto-Clementine version—the notes on which, according to their modern analyst, offer "a fine illustration of Toledo's learning and are still of value today"—has held a commanding position in Catholic biblical scholarship until the twentieth century. Because of such conflicting attitudes and regulations, partly explainable by the pope's poor health and ensuing reliance on subordinates, many Roman Jews became involved in endless litigations, both civil and criminal. Even the unfriendly pope was, therefore, persuaded to follow earlier precedents and, a few months before his death, he granted the Jews a general immunity from prosecution for any crime, except murder, counterfeiting of currency, lèse-majesté, rebellion, and sacrilege (June 5, 1604).[54]

FROM PAUL V TO INNOCENT X

After the stormy ups and down of 1555–1604 the Jewries of the States of the Church, in both Italy and France, settled down to a relatively stable life in the following half century. The three major popes of that period, Paul V (1605–1621), Urban VIII (1623–44), and Innocent X (1644–55), were no eager innovators. Preoccupied with complicated international relations during the Thirty Years' War, its preliminaries and aftermath, they evinced little interest in upsetting the existing system at home. Even Paul V, who, like Paul IV and Pius V, came to the Holy See directly from the Roman Inquisition, on which he had served during the preceding two years (1603–1605), did not wish to upset the existing tenuous balance. He and his successors concentrated on continuing the progress of the Counter Reformation and on regaining some of the Church's lost position in France, the Holy Roman Empire, and Poland, rather than on altering the basic status of their Jewish subjects.[55]

On the whole, therefore, the first half of the seventeenth century, though bringing many miseries to Jews under the pontifical scepter, saw them living in growing numbers in the major papal cities, under the old assumption (now less clearly articulated) that they must be maintained to the end of days. At times the Roman Jews succeeded, in a typical medieval fashion, in securing from the authorities a sweeping "amnesty" for all crimes except *lèse-majesté*, homicide, and counterfeiting. Such a decree was once again issued by the Cardinal Camerlingo M. A. Gozzadini on September 5, 1622; it even threatened officials disregarding that order with a fine of 1,000 ducats and other penalties. Nor was there any deviation from the principle, restated by Julius III, that Jews should be converted by persuasion, not by force. As late as 1639, the public was also reminded of Julius III's bull prohibiting the baptism of Jewish children without parental consent, under the sanction of a fine of 1,000 ducats and suspension from office. True, persuasion was now given a broader meaning than before. A 1604 decree provided that "a Jewish infant, baptized by its nurse without the knowledge of his father, shall not be restored to the father. It was decided that he be considered duly baptized and the father held responsible for his support." In 1613 a wealthy Roman Jew was ordered to continue to support his baptized daughter. When in 1639 a three-year-old girl was converted without her parents' knowledge, the baptizing woman was merely warned not to do it again. Papal officials often tried to shield converted husbands who illegally infringed on the dowry rights of their unconverted wives. Some jurists even excused converts from the duty of restoring previous usurious gains to identifiable debtors, although at least one traditional-minded theologian protested that even the pope had no right to grant a dispensation from that long-accepted canonical obligation.[56]

Conversions were to be promoted by the forced attendance at missionary sermons. Originally ordained by Nicholas III in 1278, this procedure was reintroduced in 1577 by Gregory XIII under the influence of Andrea del Monte. In 1586 Sixtus V reduced the sessions to six times a year, but seven years later Clement VIII restored weekly meetings, which persisted with minor changes until 1847. The entire Roman community, both men and women, even children over twelve, had to appear in relays at a designated place and attentively listen to the preachers, absenteeism being severely punished. After hearing such a conversionist sermon (probably by Andrea del Monte) in 1581 at the church of Santa Trinità de' Monti, Michel de Montaigne commented, "He is amazingly versed in the deep learning and the various languages essential to the performance of his task." Two years later Gregory founded a special school for missionary preachers to Jews. Even after several decades, the weekly spectacle of a mass of Jews gathering at a Christian chapel aroused anti-Jewish feelings among the populace, and a sharp papal order was required to protect the listeners returning home against molestation by rowdies (1620). Fathers and employers were made responsible for the acts of gamins under their tutelage and were threatened with severe punishment on the word of a Jewish accuser, "without further testimony." [57]

Oral presentations of this kind were supported by a host of polemical tracts, including the two aforementioned Hebrew pamphlets by Andrea del Monte. Among the leading controversialists in the days of Clement VIII was Tommaso Campanella, who achieved fame in the Catholic world especially by his utopia, *City of the Sun* (1602), modeled after Thomas More's classic. Campanella also wrote *Per la conversione degli Ebrei,* a tract which, despite its relatively moderate language, vigorously attacked Judaism and extolled the virtues of conversion to Christianity. Papal missionary efforts were also aided by the establishment in 1622 of a new administrative department, the *Congregatio de Propaganda fide,* whose world-wide range of activities helped to unify the disparate local undertakings. Its importance was emphasized soon thereafter by a leading official. After Urban VIII's demise in 1644, the *Congregatio's* secretary, Francesco Ingoli, discoursed on the tasks confronting the new pope. He insisted that, because of its function in the saving of souls, the *Congregatio* would have to be treated by the new head of the Church "with the esteem it merits, and he will have to concentrate on it more than on any other matter." Most galling to many Jews were the imposts placed upon their communities for the support of the missionary preachers and their assistants, as well as for the maintenance of the Houses of Catechumens. The latter institutions harbored many Jew-baiters who made a specialty of distorting the Jewish tradition before the Christian public and of embroiling their former coreligionists in constant difficulties with the papal regime. Some prominent Jews were enticed to relinquish their faith by spectacular baptismal ceremonies, sometimes performed by the popes in person while cardinals or other grandees served as the converts' godfathers. Since a newly baptized person often assumed his sponsor's name (Del Monte from Julius III, Buoncompagni from Gregory XIII, and so on), he and his descendants were often mistaken for members of the Roman aristocracy or for relatives of high Church dignitaries.[58]

As a result of all these pressures quite a few Roman Jews, adults as well as minors, underwent conversion. We do not have statistical data for the earlier periods, but records after 1634 show some deceleration of the trend. Without indicating his source, Ettore Natali reports that in the 66 years from 1634 to 1700, 1,195 Jews were baptized, or about 18 per year, whereas in the following 90 years the number of converts totaled 1,237, an annual average of less than 14. The percentage may have been higher during the period of 1555–1634, when the Counter Reformation élan and anti-Jewish persecutions were at their height.[59]

Offensive weapons of this type were supplemented by the Church's defensive measures, particularly papal censorship and the Inquisition. True, Paul IV's excesses were not repeated even under the pontificate of the no less zealous Pius V, himself likewise a former grand-inquisitor. Sixtus V, though he had in his youth also served in an inquisitorial capacity, appears to have been quite lenient toward Jewish religious peccadillos. Perhaps forewarned by Paul IV's much-deplored burning of the Ancona New Christians, most Marranos now steered clear of the papal areas, while professing Jews did not have much to fear of the inquisitorial investigations, except with respect to book-burning. Not that the popes in any way undermined the authority of the Inquisition. It was, in fact, under Paul V's administration that Prospero Farinacci published, in 1613, his authoritative treatise "On Heresy" as Part IV of his comprehensive work on criminal law. Not only did the pope accept the author's dedication, but the Master of the Apostolic Palace praised its teachings "as most useful to all theologians and jurists and, what may be considered even more significant, as extremely helpful to the courts of the Holy Inquisition." Provided also with special licenses from the emperor and the king of France, this work was reprinted in Frankfort and Venice in 1618, 1620, and 1632, and was widely employed in the study and practice of canon law. Yet few Marranos were burned during that period; among them Abraham del Porto, in 1641. As a minor concession to Rome's Jewish community, jurisdiction over its cemetery as well as over the Jews' sexual relations with Gentiles was withdrawn from the Inquisition and transferred to other ecclesiastical organs (1624–25). This change of venue, needless to say, did not save a Roman Jewish mistress of the son of the duke of Parma from being burned in 1628. In general, the Inquisition's main victims now became the few Protestants caught in its net, and liberal Italians whose philosophic or scientific endeavors did not meet with the Church's approval. Among these martyrs were no lesser personalities than Giordano Bruno and Galileo Galilei. The censorship of Hebrew books proceeded along customary lines. Although there was no relaxation of its rigidity even under Paul V, who evinced considerable interest in the promotion of the study of Oriental languages, neither was there any major repetition of the sixteenth-century calamities. There was some gradual diminution of penalties for the reading and possession of prohibited books, so that on December 30, 1622, Gregory XV felt impelled to issue a special bull revoking all such concessions. At the same time, however, the deep reorientation of the Catholic *Weltanschauung* brought forth several distinguished thinkers and saints who, through their work, gave Catholicism a new dimension and at least partially redeemed the excesses of their more political- and organizational-minded leaders. Next to the Jesuits, it was the Dominican Order which carried on its traditional function of serving as the torch-bearer of Catholic thought and culture. Some members of both orders now followed the example set by the humanists and utilized the Hebrew Kabbalah for their apologetic purposes.[60]

More conservative as the Papacy had become in religious and intellectual matters, it did not wholeheartedly try to stem the tide of modern economic progress. Feudalism had long been declining in the Papal States, and new semicapitalistic enterprises were springing up all over the land. However, in Jewish affairs reiterated efforts were made to maintain, even to revive, the medieval legislative heritage. The prohibition against Jews selling objects of Christian worship, such as crosses and paintings of saints, was repeated in quick succession in 1613, 1626, 1654, and 1659. Nor were Jews allowed to accept such objects as pledges for loans (1614). More significantly, the Papacy now tightened up the long-standing, but often ineffectual, prohibition against Christians using the services of Jewish physicians (1608, 1631). In 1636 the papal Inquisition rejected the renewal of a license for the Jewish physician Guglielmo Portaleone (in Hebrew, Benjamin b. David Mi-Sha'ar Aryeh) of Mantua. Although the dukes of Mantua had with papal consent employed physicians from that family for several generations, they were now informed that licenses earlier granted by cardinals had not necessarily been enacted by apostolic authority and definitely had no validity beyond the original beneficiary's lifetime. The papal congregation further wrote that

they have carefully considered that matter, since it is very unseemly for faithful Christians to avail themselves of the work of a people so infidel and inimical to the Christian name. This is particularly the case in any work which can be much better performed by Christian physicians. It is doubly inappropriate for princes, who, as defenders and executors of the sacred canons, ought to see to it that these be observed in their states; certainly, the princes ought not to set for their subjects an example of violating them. The practice of medicine generates too much intercourse with both patients and other members of the household; intercourse leads to friendship, friendship to protection, and from the protection of Jews there arises at least some scandal, even if there is no direct contamination [in religious convictions].

This sharp reversal of the old papal permissiveness, long applied at the Roman court itself, can best be explained by the growing competition of qualified Christian doctors, who considered all Christian patients their special preserve.[61]

Similarly, a new interpretation restricting all Jewish commerce to secondhand goods was the result of competitive pressures from Christian merchants. If in 1547 the Roman Jewish artisans had made a compact with their Christian colleagues to reduce competition, the latter were now able to compete with fewer restraints. At one point, in 1592, Cardinal Geronimo (Hieronymus) Rusticucci, as governor of Rome, tried to extend the prohibition of trading in new clothing to Jewish tailors sewing clothes for customers. However, it was not always easy to distinguish between tailoring on new and that on secondhand clothing. Because of the legal restrictions, Jewish traders and workers refined the technique of invisible mending, for which the Roman dialect coined the new term *rinacciare*. Moreover, when some Christian tailors complained to the *Rota* against Jewish violations, that tribunal, always more liberal in interpreting laws concerning Jews, decided that this commercial prohibition should not be expanded to handicrafts, the main source of Jewish livelihood. In 1621 the *Rota* went even further. Since the local law upheld the medieval system of debt bondage, it was decided that Christian claimants must support imprisoned Jewish debtors during their prison terms, just as Jewish creditors had to take care of their imprisoned Christian debtors. On this occasion the tribunal enunciated the general principle that Roman Jews lived under Roman civil law and that, barring specific exceptions stated in the legislation, civil relationships between Jews and Christians must be judged on the basis of equality before the law. Under this ruling the manual arts remained the major source of income for the Roman Jewish masses, which is also attested by a document of 1726.[62]

More remarkably, despite the fire and brimstone showered by preachers, apologists, and even papal legislators on "Jewish usury" —the anti-Jewish literature on this issue now proliferated throughout Italy in an unprecedented degree—the Jews were continually encouraged to provide credit for the "needy" population, more or less in the traditional fashion. Pius IV and others fully realized that Christian usurers, by employing ingenious subterfuges (Laynez described some of their methods in a special tract), were charging more exorbitant rates than Jews; they thus were a greater menace to both the welfare of the population and the observance of canon law. Hence the maximum interest rate of 18 percent, to which Jewish moneylenders were legally restricted, as well as the various protective regulations governing pledges and the property rights of borrowers, did not seriously interfere with Jewish banking. Even Pius V and Clement VIII, who banished the Jews from all provincial communities, stressed Jewish usefulness in commerce as the reason for keeping them in the major cities. With this euphemism the popes were able also to cover the real role which Jewish credit played in the papal economy. The late sixteenth and early seventeenth centuries witnessed, indeed, a renaissance of Jewish banking throughout the States of the Church.

Endowed with protective papal privileges, Jewish bankers started businesses in one locality after another, as they had done in the halcyon days of the fifteenth century when their northward expansion from Rome had only begun. The intervening establishment of *monti di pietà* (in Rome, in 1539) was no serious obstacle. In fact, some of these institutions, which had started as purely charitable enterprises, gradually developed into regular commercial banks. Paul V expressly permitted the Roman *monte* to grant loans on the nobles' estates, and in 1660 Queen Christina of Sweden pledged pieces of her jewelry with it for a loan of 20,000 scudi. On two occasions, in 1595 and 1647, Rome's Jewish community itself, in dire need of funds to meet the heavy demands by the papal Treasury, borrowed substantial amounts from that charitable loan bank, paying a handsome fee to the authorities for permission to do so. But Jewish communities had long preferred to negotiate loans with outsiders, rather than with Jewish bankers, who could not lawfully charge interest to Jewish institutions and, on the other hand, could not afford to invest any sizable portion of their limited cash resources in interest-free loans. If two Jewish credit arrangements *absque fructibus* were recorded by a Roman notary, these were exceptions confirming the rule that loans negotiated by Jews before the local notaries bore the usual interest charge of 18 percent.[63]

On the whole, the Jews of Rome, Ancona, and Avignon thus resumed, after a while, their traditional occupations and modes of living. They grew accustomed to the greater hostility of their Christian neighbors and the insecurity resulting from vacillating papal policies. After moving into the ghetto, they also evinced a growing solidarity in the face of danger and developed increasingly effective communal controls. Although Italians of both faiths had long been used to living in crowded quarters, particularly in a city like Rome with its rapidly increasing population, the narrowly confined Roman ghetto, despite its repeated enlargements, proved totally inadequate. The community and, following it, the papal administration were forced to resort to the extraordinary measure of protecting the tenants by the so-called *jus di gazagà,* formally instituted by Clement VIII in 1604. As early as 1660, it may be noted, the hereditary rights in a portion of such a protected tenancy were considered a safe investment. The banker Giuseppe di Elia Toscano provided in his will of that date that his *jus di gazagà* in Rome, along with some real estate shares in Florence and his banking privilege in the area of Lugo, should not be disposed of by the executors of his will, "except perhaps in the case that the sale price might be used for reinvestment in some other objects, equally or more useful and safe." The main outlines of the evolution of this remarkable institution have been mentioned above; it will have to be considered again more fully in connection with the internal life of the Jewish community. But at least during the first several generations Jews found life in the ghetto quite bearable; it discouraged neither immigration from other communities nor the natural growth of their own numbers. What Marcello Alberini had written about Rome during the 1520s continued to be true in the following century as well: "Clearly, only a minority of these people are Romans, for here, the common domicile of the world, all nations take refuge." According to the best available estimates, Rome's population, totaling some 97,000 in 1592, embraced no less than 3,500 Jews, making the community one of the largest in Christian Europe. If the ghetto subsequently became a veritable slum, this was primarily the result of the continued growth of population, which almost quadrupled in the course of the seventeenth century.[64]

REDEFINING OLD PRINCIPLES

The Roman ghetto was an innovation of the Counter Reformation. In many ways so were the Roman Inquisition along Spanish lines, the strict censorship of Hebrew books, the compulsory attendance at missionary sermons for Jews, and the *monte di pietà*. Radical departures from earlier practices were the two expulsions of Jews from the States of the Church (save the three major cities) enacted by Pius V in 1569 and, more halfheartedly, by Clement VIII in 1593. But, from the standpoint of world Jewish history, as well as of the established traditions of the medieval Church, all these actions were *vieux jeu*. Jews had long been used to expulsions, which indeed had reached their climax in the half century before the onset of the Counter Reformation around 1540. The institutional innovations were but variations of the old themes of segregation and discrimination which, even in their details, had long been sponsored by churchmen in various Catholic lands, if not in the Pontifical States.

On the Jewish question the Catholic Restoration was far less direct and all-embracing than in most other areas of Catholic life and thought. The great Tridentine Council, which reformulated the fundamentals of the Catholic faith and reestablished the organizational patterns of ecclesiastical life on fairly permanent foundations, had little to say on the Jewish issue. It dealt only tangentially with the problem of censorship of Hebrew works, as part of the preparation of a new Index of Prohibited Books. Even that task was not completed by the Council, and its implementation was left to the Papacy, which, dependent upon the temper of individual popes and changing sociopolitical circumstances in the following decades, revealed many almost fitful inconsistencies, quite unusual within the otherwise steady continuity of papal policy. The old and new religious orders betrayed the traditional monastic animosity toward Jews and Judaism, which had always exceeded that of the central organs of the Church. The Theatine Order, especially in the person of its cofounder Paul IV, pursued a militant policy toward all "infidels." Even the more subtle and influential Jesuit Order, notwithstanding its deep indebtedness to its New Christian cofounders, soon swung into the anti-Jewish camp and, through pervasive indoctrination in its far-flung educational system, became a source of difficulties for Jewish communities in many lands. With their usual adroitness, however, the Jesuit leaders avoided too direct a break with the Church's past traditions and, especially in the areas controlled by Spain and Portugal, often became the exponents of a more liberal policy, at least with respect to *limpieza*.

Curiously, in this matter, too, the Papacy gradually yielded to the pressures emanating from Spain, then Catholicism's foremost political and military defender. It not only approved various discriminatory statutes against New Christians on the Iberian Peninsula and in the New World, but, in a decree of 1611, it provided that in Rome, too, "persons of Jewish descent shall not be admitted to canonicates of cathedrals, dignities in brotherhoods [*collegiatis*], and offices entrusted with the care of souls." Little did the papal advisers realize that they were thereby defeating the very purpose of the compulsory sermons and other missionary activities among Jews. Whatever justification such a provision may have had in Spain, with its large mass of *conversos,* it had little bearing on conditions in Rome. But the inquisitorial contagion blinded even many reasonable persons and made them adopt racial measures running counter to the fundamentals of universalist Christianity.[65]

Nonetheless, even in the harsh clime of the Wars of Religion, the Church upheld the old principle that to the end of days Jews must be tolerated as a distinct group within the Christian world. At times the papal organs in both Rome and Avignon publicly proclaimed the rule that Jews were to be treated as *cives Romani.* We recall the *Rota's* decision that, except in the case of specific legal restrictions, the Jews should be treated as equals before civil law. There were, of course, many breaches in the application of these general principles. The very combination of toleration with segregation and discrimination had always led to conflicting interpretations and still more frequent diversities in practice. Nor was there any way of avoiding arbitrary acts by persons in positions of power, from the highest ecclesiastical dignitaries to the lowest clerics or fiscals of the Inquisition. But Jews had become inured to living dangerously, a condition partly remedied by their economic indispensability to the Treasuries and society at large, as well as by a variety of tactical means which they had learned to employ.

In short, the Catholic Restoration, which had started with the threatening autos-da-fé of both the Talmud and the Ancona Marranos and was climaxed by the expulsion of Jews from most areas of the Pontifical States, thus passed without uprooting the Jewish communities in most Catholic lands. In fact, North-Central Italy, the hereditary possessions of the Austrian Habsburgs, and particularly Poland-Lithuania now witnessed an upsurge of Jewish cultural endeavor which outstripped anything achieved in those areas by the late medieval Jews. Before long the Jewish people (at least in the guise of New Christians) established itself in the West-European and American lands still dominated by the Catholic

Church. In time, to be sure, the Jewries of Protestant countries waxed greater in economic and cultural power than did their co-religionists in Catholic territories. But this was owing primarily to the general historical trends, especially the modern capitalist evolution and the world-wide European expansion, which lent pre-eminence to the British Isles, Holland, and Northern Germany, at the expense of the leadership previously held by Italians and Spaniards. The French alone among the Catholic nations were able to hold their own for some time. But even they ultimately lost much of their universal influence when compared with their Anglo-Saxon counterparts. One certainly cannot blame the Catholic Restoration for the ultimate shift of the center of gravity of the Jewish people from Catholic to Protestant areas, a shift which took many centuries of northern growth and the simultaneous toning down of anti-Jewish features of the Protestant Reformation.

LX

ITALIAN CONFORMITY

PAPAL INITIATIVES brought to fruition in the Catholic Restoration received an immediate response in other Italian areas. There the reformatory trends, though quite noticeable in the Late Middle Ages and the early sixteenth century, were less vigorous than in the Holy Roman Empire and northern Europe, where they had been strongly nurtured by local nationalist springs. The Italian states, or at least some of their intellectual leaders, looked to the Papacy as the main symbol of Italian unity. Hence whatever differences prevailed between them and the Papal See (outside the purely theological and ritualistic domains, which generally lacked mass appeal) related to details rather than to basic principles.

Certainly, Italy had relatively few causes for complaints such as had been voiced by German diets in their long sequence of gravamina. Nor did it have a counterpart to the French Gallican movement, which, while closely adhering to the Catholic tradition, nevertheless gave rise to anti-Roman and hence also to reformatory postulates going beyond those adopted by the Reform Councils of Constance and Basel. Even Spain, the staunchest pillar of the Catholic Restoration, could not completely give up its quest for unhampered sovereignty in some religious facets of its internal life. Trying to combine absolute religious conformity regulated by the Inquisition with an equally absolutist governmental structure supported by a powerful army and growing bureaucracy, it brooked little interference even from the Papacy. As the main politicomilitary defender of the Counter Reformation, it often took the initiative in the ideological combat as well. From the international viewpoint, the independence of the Italian republics and principalities was far more seriously threatened by the external powers of the Austro-Spanish Habsburgs and the French than by their home-grown Papacy.

For all these reasons most Italian states were prone to follow the papal leadership in the Jewish question. True, there was sufficient diversity of interests and local conditions for the states to react differently from one another. But from the outset, the Counter Reformation, particularly at the Council of Trent, was a predominantly Italian enterprise. In general, the similarities among the respective areas greatly exceeded the dissimilarities. Any diversity between regions stemmed largely from their previous history as analyzed in our earlier volumes. We need not stress the geographic divisions here, therefore, but rather offer a more systematic survey of the major changes brought about in the life of Italian Jewry by the progress of the Catholic Restoration, without being oblivious of the important chronological as well as topographic disparities manifest in the period before 1650.

SHRINKING SETTLEMENT AREAS

Typical of the new Counter Reformation approach was the letter demanding the suppression of the Talmud sent by the Roman Inquisition on September 16, 1553, to Cosimo I of Florence.

The great diligence [the inquisitors wrote] already employed by Your Excellency, because of your zeal for religion, the protection of the Holy Faith, and the chastisement of heretics, assures us that in any similar case we need but point out to you the necessary remedies. Therefore without any array of persuasive arguments we let you know that, for the honor of His Divine Majesty, the salvation of many people, and in fulfillment of the duties of our office, we have been forced to condemn, let burn, and prohibit by rigorous edicts many Hebrew books entitled Talmud which contain most atrocious impieties against God, against moral living, and against Christ and His faith. To permit the circulation of such books is to consent and favor the abominable blasphemies found therein, according to the testimony of the rabbis themselves.

The inquisitors demanded that Florence emulate the Roman example and destroy all books of this type. Similar exhortations were dispatched by the Inquisition to other Italian states. They were followed up by letters addressed by the popes themselves, especially Paul IV and Pius V, and by diplomatic interventions of papal nuncios in various capitals. Such pressures were doubly effective whenever an Italian ruler wished to enlist papal support for his own political schemes. For instance, Pius V's harsh decree banishing Jews from the Papal States in 1569 found a responsive echo in Cosimo I, who was at that time seeking to secure from the Papacy the new title of Grand Duke of Tuscany. At a crucial moment in the negotiations, Pius is said to have declared, "We cannot refuse anything in Our power to a prince who . . . [sets] an example of love and obedience toward Us and the Holy See." Regardless of his personal attitude toward Jews, therefore, Cosimo was ready to comply with any papal request in return for the new dignity for himself and his descendants, a goal he achieved in December 1569.[1]

Other princes played a more independent role. Although, as a rule, few state or local authorities ventured overtly to defy the will of the popes, they often failed to carry it out. Only Duke Guidobaldo II of Urbino, as we saw, tried, in 1556, to benefit from Paul IV's difficulties by attracting refugees from Ancona to his harbor of Pesaro. Disappointed with the commercial results of this move, however, he expelled the new arrivals in 1558. There was some policy relaxation after the demise of Paul IV, when the Urbino ambassador in Rome reported with much glee the public contumely to which the pope's statue was exposed. Urbino actually opened its gates to the Roman Jewish refugees of 1569, but with the same inconsistency expelled them a year later. These vicissitudes did not prevent the Jewish communities of Pesaro, Senigallia, and, to a lesser extent, the capital itself from holding their own, numerically and economically, although the duchy as a whole was rapidly declining. In 1628 Pesaro's Jewish population consisted of 76 families (including those of 19 bankers) comprising 610 souls (in a total population of some 8,000 persons) and that of Urbino embraced 370 persons (including 8 banking families), while that of Senigallia had 25 families with less than 200 souls. There also were a number of lesser communities throughout the duchy. For instance, in 1628, 21 Jews lived among 1,370 Christians in Montebaroccio, near Pesaro. The situation became critical, however, after the abdication of Duke Francesco Maria II della Rovere in 1627, when the entire duchy was reincorporated into the Papal States, greatly accelerating the decline of the Jewish population. Following the pattern introduced in the States of the Church, a decree of 1634 eliminated the lesser settlements and concentrated all Jews in newly established formal ghettos in the three larger communities. By 1656, it is estimated, Pesaro embraced only 506 Jews, or some 20 percent less than thirty years earlier. Curiously, Senigallia now outstripped its sister communities and by the end of the century it more than trebled its Jewish population, while the Jewry of Urbino by 1718 lost almost half its members, and Pesaro barely kept its size despite the influx of many Jews from the provinces.[2]

Urbino and its adjacent localities dramatically illustrated the growing insecurity of sojourn of most Italian Jews. The majority, admitted on temporary *condottas,* knew that these "treaties," even if renewed decade after decade, might expire at the next due date and that banishment would automatically follow. Only in a few areas, such as the Papal States, were Jews able to live somewhat more securely, since their privileges, particularly as formulated in the bull *Sicut Judaeis,* had long been renewed by successive popes. That is why Pius V's unprecedented decree of expulsion in 1569 made a deep impression upon the Jewish public in and outside the Pontifical States. It was made more, rather than less, menacing by Pius' argument, later repeated by Clement VIII, that Jews should be allowed to live in Rome and Ancona for commercial reasons. Not a word was mentioned here about the Church's traditional position concerning the function of Jews as witnesses for the Christian tradition and the need for their preservation to the end of days. Of course, with the rise of the Renaissance schools of philological criticism and the growing knowledge of ancient cultures, this argument lost much of its cogency. Moreover, Christianity as such, if not Catholicism, was too well established and generally accepted as a fact of life to require any such "testimony." Yet to keen-minded readers, the omission of that standardized formula could indicate that the Papacy was veering away from the moderate Augustinian-Thomistic position to the almost total intolerance of a Duns Scotus. The fact that even Bologna, which had a well-grounded reputation of independence—a popular adage had it that the Bolognese obeyed papal ordinances "for twenty-nine days less a month"—completely eliminated her large and affluent Jewry in 1569 served as a distinct warning. The city had even handed over the Jewish cemetery to a neighboring nunnery, while the interred remains were removed to another burial ground in a small locality under the reign of the House of Este. If the subsequent reversals by the popes somewhat dispelled Jewish fears of total elimination, and the intolerant Scotist doctrine allowing for forcible conversion, particularly of Jewish children, never became regnant in the canonistic literature, nevertheless much room was left for genuine apprehension that other Italian states might follow Pius V's exclusivist policy. Settlement in new localities, on the other hand, was often hampered by the simultaneous appearance of large groups of refugees from the papal provinces. These new arrivals were rarely welcomed by the local population, since the need for the petty Jewish loan banks had been greatly reduced by the spread of charitable *monti di pietà*.[3]

Instability as the keynote of Jewish life was well illustrated even in one of the most progressive Italian states, the Florentine Republic. With the restoration of Medicean rule in 1530, Jews hoped to enjoy a prolonged period of tranquillity. They doubtless lulled themselves into the same feeling of complacency which then characterized the entire Florentine population. The first years of Duke Cosimo I's regime (1537–74) seemed to confirm these optimistic expectations. Through his wife, Eleonora, daughter of the Neapolitan viceroy, Don Pedro de Toledo, Cosimo became acquainted with Benvenida Abravanel, widow of Samuel Abravanel, who had served as leader of the Neapolitan Jewry in its declining years. Even after both ladies had separated (Benvenida settled in Ferrara after the expulsion of the Jews from Naples in 1541), the duchess continued to call her Jewish friend "mother" and consulted her on numerous occasions. Now Benvenida's son Jacob opened a bank in Florence and brought with him a number of Jews. He also introduced to the duke a "Greek" Jew of Damascus, Servadio (probably the equivalent of the Hebrew name Obadiah), who before long negotiated an agreement with the Florentine authorities to strengthen trade relations between the duchy and the Ottoman Empire. Although addressed to "Greeks, Turks, Moors, Hebrews, Aggiumi [Egyptians?], Armenians, and Persians," all of whom were invited to settle in Florence, Cosimo's charter of June 16, 1551, was aimed principally at Levantine Jewish merchants. For this purpose the duke extended to them not only commercial privileges and the permission to erect synagogues with a papal license but also complete immunity for crimes committed and debts incurred before their arrival in Florence. Although its purpose was not spelled out, this immunity was clearly intended to safeguard the rights of some earlier New Christians who had reverted to Judaism in Turkey. Any action against the new settlers, the Charter assured them, "shall be speedily revoked, notwithstanding any contrary provision." Nonetheless, within three years Cosimo, prompted by political and dynastic, rather than religious, considerations, meekly surrendered to papal demands and ordered the confiscation and burning of rabbinic works as instituted by the Roman Inquisition. Finally, he followed Pius V's lead, expelled all his Jewish subjects from the provincial communities, and confined them to the two ducal capitals of Florence and Siena. These decrees of October 3, 1570, and December 19, 1571, respectively, even disregarded the clear commitments made by the government to many Jewish bankers, whose compacts were not to expire for a number of years. At the same time formal ghettos were established in both major centers and were provided with protective provisions modeled after those interveningly enacted in Rome.[4]

Sometimes banishment was the result of warfare, as in the case of the Jews of the Venetian Republic on two occasions in the sixteenth century. When the League of Cambrai, consisting of the Habsburgs, the French, the Papacy, and several Italian states, "ganged up" in 1509 against the Republic and occupied, with much bloodshed and destruction, most of its possessions on the Italian mainland, the Jews were totally eliminated from Verona and Treviso. In Padua the possessions of the numerous Jewish bankers were removed—ironically, together with those of the rivaling *monte di pietà*—to a location near the University. This move was intended to protect the rights of borrowers and to prevent the destruction or theft of their pledges held by the creditors, but it did not forestall postwar controversies concerning pledges lost or the size of debts still outstanding. Jews also had to leave the Venetian suburb of Mestre, which was almost wholly destroyed by the conquerors. Although much of that devastation was wrought by the Austrian troops or, as in Treviso, by the pro-Habsburg faction in the local population, Jews did not evince any strong anti-Habsburg feelings. Perhaps some of them remembered Maximilian I's benefactions, as in 1491 when he had forced the Venetian authorities to admit his Jewish factor, Samuel di Marele (perhaps Me-Arli or di Arli), to residence, exempt him from wearing a badge, allow him to bear arms, and permit him to appear in public accompanied by two valets. Even more directly they doubtless appreciated the protective decree issued by the Austrian commander on June 5, 1509, in behalf of the Jews of Bassano, Castelfranco, Asolo, and Cittadella. Jews must have reciprocated in a way to inspire an unfriendly Venetian observer to declare five months later that "many very wealthy Jews [of these localities] were all rebels." If many of these misfortunes affected non-Jews as well, and both groups generally recovered in the following years, the Jews alone were repeatedly threatened by the Venetian rulers' announced refusal to renew their residential rights. On the other hand, a great many of the refugees from the mainland secured a strong foothold in Venice. They could not be dislodged by the authorities, who valued both their commercial contributions and their taxes (in addition to an annual tax of 10,000 ducats and the payment of many other imposts, they contributed no less than 60,000 ducats in loans to the Treasury during the short span of thirteen years from 1503 to 1516). The Venetian authorities finally compromised and allowed Jews to live in their newly founded ghetto, which bestowed its name on the entire institution (1516).[5]

The most dangerous situation arose in 1571, when Venice became embroiled in a war with the Ottoman Empire; the conflict was, with some exaggeration, attributed to the influence of Don Joseph Nasi (the former João Miguez) on Sultan Selim II (1566–74), often denigrated in the West as a "drunkard and Jew boy." Rumor had it that the Sultan had promised that, upon achieving his immediate war objective of conquering Cyprus, he would elevate Don Joseph to the kingship of that important island under Turkish suzerainty. Even before the Turkish invasion of Cyprus, the Venetian populace ascribed to Don Joseph's agents a major act of sabotage. On September 13, 1569, a terrific explosion and fire in the famed Venetian Arsenal destroyed several galleys and much war materiel and, it was widely believed, greatly weakened the Republic's defenses. As usual the local Jews were blamed for the machinations of their foreign coreligionist, who had indeed long harbored a personal grievance against the City of the Lagoons for the mistreatment he and his aunt, Doña Gracia Mendesia, had suffered there before they settled in Constantinople in 1553–54. In retaliation, the Venetian Senate decided, in December, 1571, to banish all Jews from the country.

Two months after the famous battle of Lepanto on October 7, 1571, when the allies, Venice, the Austro-Spanish Habsburgs, and the Papacy vanquished the Turkish navy (amidst the general rejoicing the Venetian authorities freed all prisoners), the Senate decreed that, in recognition of the divine aid in that victory, "the enemies of the faith" should be forced to leave the country (December 14). The Senate respected its treaty obligations sufficiently, however, not to proceed with the implementation of its decree before the expiration of the existing Jewish privileges two years later. In the meantime calmer counsels prevailed. The Venetian envoy in Constantinople, Marcantonio Barbaro, warned the home authorities that the Porte might adopt severe reprisals against Venetian citizens in the Middle East. Barbaro also reported that the Jewish rival of Don Joseph, the physician Solomon Ashkenazi, who had long maintained friendly relations with the successive Venetian envoys, was known to favor peace with the doge. In the end Solomon indeed helped to conclude a peace treaty with Venice, on March 7, 1573. Peace brought with it the repeal of the Jews' banishment, a repeal formally proclaimed by the Senate on July 7 after an affirmative vote of 104:69, with 7 abstentions. This was the last episode of its kind in the Republic's history. In fact, in 1574 Ashkenazi arrived in Venice as a Turkish ambassador, and one can easily imagine the great impression made upon the local Jews by the ceremonious reception their country extended to this influential Turkish diplomat, who happened to be a native of neighboring Udine and at that time still had brothers and nephews in Verona and Oderzo. Ashkenazi appeared on September 3, 1574, at a session of the Council of Ten, which in due form passed a vote of thanks to the Jewish leader for all his efforts in behalf of the Republic. In recognition thereof the Council gave him a galley for the transportation of "forty cases of clothing," some of which belonged to the French ambassador at the Porte, Jacques de Germigny. On its part the Venetian Jewish community solemnly greeted the distinguished visitor with a special ode composed in his honor and with prayers invoking divine blessings upon him and recited in the Levantine synagogue in a form usually reserved for a reigning monarch. The memory of his visit was sufficiently persistent for the authorities to extend a fine welcome also to his son Nathan, when he arrived in Venice in 1604.[6]

This change in Venetian policies carried over to some of the mainland territories. In Padua, for example, the authorities allowed the Jews in 1583 to establish a new cemetery, freed them in 1587 from forced attendance at missionary sermons, and in 1619 reiterated the prohibition against converting Jewish minors without parental consent. If in 1600–1602 a ghetto was erected there and in Verona, this was done in full cooperation with the Jewish community. We need not attribute the change in policies mainly to a growing sense of justice in the leading circles of the Venetian Republic. It certainly did not interfere with the expulsions of Jews from some provincial communities, such as Brescia in 1563 and Treviso in 1509 and 1590. Nor was Venetian Jewry ever allowed completely to forget its state of insecurity. Time and again it was reminded by its own preachers and chroniclers of its earlier sufferings as a warning for the future. Two anonymous compilations of this kind, written respectively at the end of the sixteenth and the middle of the seventeenth century, are representative of the literature intended for recitation on the Ninth of Ab. They offer classic examples of the "lachrymose conception of Jewish history," as well as of the Jews' traditional penchant for self-accusation. As usual, the authors assigned the main responsibility for the sufferings of their people to its sinful way of life. Needless to say, this facile interpretation, however effectively used for internal homiletical purposes, did not tell the entire story. Despite such recurrent manifestations of religious intolerance, both popular and official, however, the central authorities of the Republic began, from about 1583 on, consciously to attract new Jewish settlers from the Iberian Peninsula, notwithstanding the newcomers' rather obvious "apostasy" from the Christian faith. In 1647 and thereafter, the government constantly reconfirmed the *condotta* for these so-called Ponentine (western) Jews, along with those from the Levant. Before long these "westerners" began to dominate the entire community, including its Italo-German and Levantine segments, in both culture and wealth, if not in numbers. Although the government reserved to itself the right to cancel the privileges with but eighteen months' notice, it never exercised that right, and in the following generations the Venetian Jews of all three categories were allowed undisturbedly to pursue their peaceful careers.[7]

Most temperamental was the behavior of the authorities of the old commercial and banking center of Genoa. Not having been allowed to strike roots in the Republic during the Late Middle Ages, the Jews could not establish permanent settlements of any significant size there in the early modern period. Ruled by a powerful patrician class, which was constantly at loggerheads with both the landed nobility and the artisan groups, the city could not completely withstand the inroads of the Waldensian and, in the 1440s, the Hussite "heresies," but it successfully resisted any influx of Jews. Not even the arrival in 1492 of a downtrodden group of Spanish exiles, whose lamentable appearance, as we recall, aroused the compassion of onlookers, moved the rulers to grant them the right of sojourn beyond a limited time. Only a few venturesome individuals seem to have settled there and weathered the violent anti-Jewish harangues of Bernardino da Feltre, who appeared in Genoa in the same year. But they soon became the butt of domestic party politics. In 1515 Doge Ottaviano Fregoso issued a decree of banishment, which was revoked in the following year, when his opponent, Antoniotto II Adorno, called back the handful of persons who were willing to take their chances. Among these returnees seems to have been Joshua b. Meir, father of the famous chronicler Joseph ha-Kohen, to whose recital we owe much of our information concerning the Jewish misfortunes of the time. Before long, however, Joseph himself became the victim of another decree of expulsion, promulgated on April 6, 1550. He settled in neighboring Ovada and later in Voltaggio, where he practiced medicine. But the career of the Jews in the Genoese provinces, too, was cut short by another, more comprehensive decree of 1567. If a number of these exiles were allowed to return in 1569 and live in the city on the basis of a *condotta* renewable every five or six years (1576, 1582, 1586, etc.), they were again told to leave in 1598. Interveningly, the Republic was admonished by Pope Gregory XIII on May 17, 1581, not to admit Marranos except after careful screening of their orthodox way of life. Nonetheless, some hardy individuals seem to have persisted then and later, until all Jews were shut off in a ghetto in 1660.[8]

Paradoxically, the neighboring duchy of Milan, which had come under Spanish domination, long maintained the Jews in a relatively quiescent state despite the anti-Jewish prejudices of Charles V, Philip II, and their advisers. In 1541, to be sure, Charles outlawed any further residence of Jews in Milan, but he left to the discretion of the governor the matter of whether Jews should be allowed to continue living in the provinces. During the subsequent period of reaction initiated by the Papacy in the 1550s neither Charles nor his son was anxious to follow the lead of their sworn enemy Paul IV. We shall see that the Milanese authorities stoutly resisted papal demands for the confiscation of talmudic and rabbinic works. Although the local inquisitors of Cremona finally prevailed in 1559 and forced a public auto-da-fé which consumed some 10,000 Hebrew books, the local Hebrew press was not prevented from continuing its remarkable output of important Hebrew publications during the following eight years. Early in 1558, the Milanese authorities had actually guaranteed the provincial Jews of the duchy peaceful sojourn and pursuit of business for the following twelve years. Jewish visitors were admitted to the capital for a three-day stay, or longer with the permission of the *capitano di giustizia*. The Jewish position was made slightly more secure by the struggle of the Milanese population against the introduction of a Spanish-type Inquisition attempted by Philip II in 1563. Although himself a native of Milan, Pope Pius IV yielded to Spanish pressure and appointed Bishop Cervantes of Messina inquisitor-general of the new institution. Ultimately, however, the numerous petitions addressed to him, the king, and the twenty-four-year-old Cardinal Carlo Borromeo (the pope's nephew and secretary of state), supported by loud rumblings of a popular revolt, prevailed, and on September 21, 1563, Pius promised to abstain from "innovations." Nonetheless the provincial synods of the

Milanese archdiocese, meeting under Borromeo's chairmanship in 1568, 1579, and 1582, adopted sharply anti-Jewish resolutions. In a lengthy declaration, *De Judaeis,* they not only repeated the traditional segregationist postulates requiring the ghetto, the badge, nonemployment of Christian servants by Jews and of Jews by Christians in public office or for medical consultation, but also demanded that Hebrew not be used in business documents and that Jews sell their houses located near churches within a month, not trade on Sundays or Christian holidays, and not serve as marriage brokers for Christians. Conversions were also to be stimulated by all means at the Church's disposal.[9]

It is small wonder, then, that the 1558 privilege was not renewed at its expiration in 1569. But in their application for renewal the Jews argued that their presence in the country and their moneylending had accrued to the advantage of the local population, the Spanish garrison, and the Treasury. After prolonged deliberations the Senate approved the principle of toleration in 1577, although it suggested a number of restrictions on Jewish rights. Interveningly Jews had been allowed to stay without formal authorization, and a new five-year permit was granted them in 1573. They were doubtless supported by such local lords as Countess Caterina Branca Stampa and Francesco da Trezzo, who thus wished to safeguard their share in the Jewish revenue of the duchy, granted them by reiterated privileges of 1522, 1536, and 1555. In the meantime only 7,500 of the 16,000 lire loaned by the Jewish bankers to the royal Chamber in 1555 had been repaid. Together with a new loan of 5,000 scudi, negotiated in 1558, and the accrued interest, the debt rose to about 32,000 scudi in 1594.[10]

As a result, the anti-Jewish faction found itself thwarted by the resistance of the Spanish officials. True, the capital, formerly one of the largest and most affluent cities of Europe (Milan's population was still estimated at some 250,000 at that time), continued to refuse admission to Jews. But considerable communities persisted in Cremona, Alessandria, Lodi, and Pavia, notwithstanding successive attempts by some city councils to secure their banishment. The Spanish-controlled administration even protected Jews against scurrilous literary attacks, such as a pamphlet distributed in 1576 in Cremona, which read in part:

People of Cremona! Do not fail to bend every effort so that the Jewish dogs may be expelled from this blessed city; otherwise you will be ruined. If only you knew the great blasphemies which these impious Jewish dogs utter against our Saviour, Jesus Christ, the least blasphemy of which would suffice to bring about the ruination of ten, even a thousand, cities, if it were not for the goodness of the supreme God, who has mercy on us Christians! Yet He who continually takes care of us should be similarly treated by us in defense of His honor. If you will not do it, you will witness the wrath of His divine majesty descend upon us. Woe, woe, woe unto him who will contradict it!

After a close investigation, stimulated by a Jewish offer of 100 scudi to any informer, the authorities identified the anonymous writer as Cesare della Porta and punished him accordingly. The extraordinary tolerance of the Milanese authorities toward Jews is doubly remarkable, as during that period Milan's archbishop was the well-known leader of the Counter Reformation Carlo Borromeo (later canonized), and as among the instigators of anti-Jewish actions were such prominent converts as Sixtus of Siena and Vittorio Eliano, grandson of the grammarian Elijah Levita. Possibly, Milanese Jewry was aided by the disrepute into which the local Inquisition had fallen. According to the visitatorial report submitted to Philip II by Luis de Castilla in 1583, the Holy Office in Milan was more interested in financial gain than in "fraternal correction" of souls. Its malfeasance was exemplified by an inquisitor nicknamed "Fra Scelere" (Brother Villain), whom Pius V had had to condemn to galley servitude for his numerous crimes.[11]

In the long run, nevertheless, the Jewish position in the duchy became untenable. The growing Spanish influence under the regime of Governors Carlos de Aragón, duke of Terranova (1583–92), and Juan Fernández de Velasco, constable of Castile (1592–1600), greatly weakened the local population's insistence on the preservation of its traditional "liberties." On their part, the Spanish authorities—even Fernández de Velasco, who was personally quite friendly to Jews—were ready to sacrifice their Jewish taxpayers to the popular clamor. The reaction was particularly vehement in the four cities which resented the discriminatory practice forcing them alone to tolerate Jews. This dichotomy became even more pronounced after Philip II had finally issued, on

December 31, 1590, a general decree banishing all Jews. Originally scheduled for the middle of 1591, the exodus was constantly delayed, not so much because of the effectiveness of the arguments advanced by Simone Cohen Sacerdote of Alessandria, the envoy dispatched by the Jewries of the duchy to the Court of Madrid, as because of the Treasury's inability to repay its accumulated debts to the Jewish bankers, and the ensuing controversy among the major cities. Milan and many other localities refused to contribute their share, claiming that, since they had no Jews, they stood to benefit little from the latter's elimination. The four cities, on the other hand, even Pavia and Cremona, which had long agitated for the expulsion, were unwilling to assume this heavy fiscal burden alone. To remove this obstacle an anti-Jewish leader, Bartolommeo Carranza, argued that, by having ceased to pay their special taxes in 1559, the Jews had incurred a debt to the Treasury which fully canceled their outstanding loans. Ultimately, nearly all Jews had to leave the duchy in 1597, just as their coreligionists had long before left the other Spanish dependencies. Despite Carranza's argument, Philip II's order to all debtors to satisfy their Jewish creditors in full before their departure seems to have applied also to the Treasury itself. In fact, we have some evidence that the exiles were provided with funds by the government, which later led to disputes among the three Jewish deputies charged with the allocation of these funds. The rejoicing of the anti-Jewish population did not last long, however. Within a short time the absence of Jewish bankers made itself severely felt. After the sporadic reappearance of several individuals, Jews as a group were formally readmitted to the duchy in 1633.[12]

The sixteenth century thus ended with the further diminution of the Italian territory legitimately inhabited by Jews. However, there were certain areas which now admitted them for the first time. In 1588, for instance, Trieste made its first compact with Jewish bankers. From that time on, Italian Jewish life proceeded much more peacefully, except when Jews became embroiled, together with their Christian neighbors, in some international complications. We shall see that, as a result of the great power rivalries during the Thirty Years' War, Jews were ousted from Mantua in 1630, but they were speedily readmitted. In general, Italy thus followed the behavioral patterns developed by the medieval "part-of-nationality" states. Basically intolerant of the Jewish minority, many Italian principalities and cities pursued conflicting and self-contradictory policies which for the most part resulted in the elimination of Jews, permanently or for a time. At the end of the sixteenth century most Jews on the Peninsula remained concentrated in the States of the Church, with their French provinces and international aspirations; the Venetian Republic, with its shrinking but still substantial non-Italian colonial possessions; and Piedmont, which shared its regime with predominantly French Savoy. Nor was it accidental that the latest northeastern expansion took the Jews to Trieste and other areas which increasingly came under the influence of the Austrian Habsburgs.[13]

LEGAL STATUS QUO

Just as the nationalist determinants shaping Judeo-Christian relations were little affected by the Counter Reformation, the legal position of Jews living in Catholic lands reflected shifting juridical emphases, rather than changes in fundamental principles. Even in the Pontifical States the old polarity between the Church's basic principles of toleration and large-scale discrimination plus segregation continued unabated. As in earlier periods, some popes accentuated the element of toleration, whereas others—and this was the prevailing mood generated by the Catholic Restoration— stressed both discrimination and segregation, lending them at times more extreme forms than had manifested themselves in the medieval period.

Protection of Jewish life and limb was still upheld, however, at least in legal theory. Following the Roman governor's proclamation of 1566, which imposed a penalty of flogging for any molestation of Jews, a Florentine decree of 1567 placed such assaults under a fine of five gold scudi or physical punishment up to twelve lashes. Protective provisions of this kind became doubly necessary during public festivities, since a wedding or the birth of a child in a ducal family, for instance, gave exuberant youth an excuse to "have fun" at the expense of Jews. The riots against the Jews in Mantua on the occasion of Guglielmo's wedding with Eleanor of

Austria in 1561, again at her giving birth to a child six years later, and at other festive events in 1609 and 1611 had many serious ramifications. While attacking the Jewish quarter on the first of these occasions, the rioters took care of destroying writs of indebtedness, thus hoping to get rid of their debts. The disturbances of 1609 and 1611 came a few years after the enactment (in 1602) of a specific Mantuan ordinance forbidding such excesses. At the same time, the authorities had to be careful in meting out punishment to rioters lest their actions serve to inflame the anti-Jewish passions of the rest of the population. This happened, indeed, in 1582 in Cremona when the courts condemned to death a Christian murderer of a Jew; they merely added fuel to the growing agitation for the expulsion of all Jews. On the other hand, Jews in Mantua, as in Rome and elsewhere, sometimes benefited from general amnesties for past or future transgressions, except for such major crimes as homicide or *lèse-majesté*. Such amnesties, often combined with the renewal of existing privileges, usually had to be heavily paid for by the Jewish communities. They had become necessary because of the frequent miscarriage of justice by general courts handling Jewish defendants, and were particularly frequent in Mantua, where they were granted successively in 1608, 1611, 1613, 1615, and after.[14]

Rulers also frequently tried to curb incendiary sermons. At first, to be sure, they quite cordially treated an extremely popular rabble-rousing preacher, Bartolommeo Cambi da Salutio (or Salutivo), whose addresses endangered the very survival of the Jewish community of Mantua. But when he also began attacking the regime itself, they reacted vigorously. Venice and Ferrara refused to admit him altogether. He was finally denounced to Rome. Initially, Clement VIII greatly sympathized with the preacher, whose eloquent appeals to vast audiences, often numbering thousands of enthusiastic listeners, were likely to stimulate the Catholic revival. In two letters addressed to the duke and duchess of Mantua on August 30, 1602, the pope spoke of the Jews, "who are indeed intolerable," and pointed out that the preacher had helped "remedy the abuses and the insolence of the Jews and the continuous injuries they cause to Your Majesty particularly by their constant excessive familiarity with Christians." Yet when the Curia ultimately ascertained Bartolommeo's rather shady past, it decided to shut him up in a Roman monastery with a strict injunction to hold his peace.[15]

In civic rights, too, the status of the Jews underwent but relatively minor modifications. Jews could still be spoken of even in official documents, as *cives,* enjoying basically the same rights as other citizens except where the law established specific disabilities. This designation, of course, did not connote equality of rights of the type achieved in the modern era. As in the Middle Ages proper, the Italian states of the Reformation era often embraced different forms of citizenship in the same localities. Nor did the term necessarily imply real equality before the law, since most Jews essentially lived under a law of their own. This ambiguity readily lent itself to various interpretations involving legal and economic discrimination, but at the same time it enabled the Jewish communities to enjoy that comprehensive autonomy which they so highly cherished. It was also possible for individuals to reach a high social standing and even to be counted among the nobles. Prominent leaders like Yehudah Messer Leon, Elijah da Fermo, Mordecai da Modena, and Joseph da Fano were officially described as noblemen in contemporary documents. Duke Ercole II of Ferrara granted, in 1543, special letters patent to Abraham Menahem b. Isaac Norsi as a *gentilhuomo* belonging to the "altri nobili della nostra famiglia." Many other members of the Norsi or Norsa family and a number of other Jewish leaders likewise claimed this rank, particularly when they were entrusted with diplomatic missions. The lengths to which some Italian Jews were ready to go in international affairs is illustrated by the three Mantuans—among them the famous dramatist and theatrical expert Leone da Sommi—who, after the death of Stephen Báthory in 1586, tried to arrange for the election of their own prince, Guglielmo Gonzaga, or his son Vincenzo, to the throne of Poland. This was a semipatriotic, semibusiness venture, as is attested by a remarkable extant partnership contract in Hebrew between the three men. They obligated themselves

as faithful partners to endeavor with all possible means to achieve the goal that on the throne of Poland be placed our lord the Duke, or his highness the son, may he live. This agreement is made under the express and repeated condition that all the good which God will bestow upon us in this enterprise, as well as all the expenses on one or the other side shall be shared alike; similarly each man shall derive equal benefits. For we have bound ourselves by a strong tie to work on this undertaking faithfully and righteously and not to divulge anything about it to any person in the world, except to those to whom it must be revealed in order to secure their help in bringing it to successful completion.

Evidently, the three partners acted in consultation with the duke, whose archive has preserved this agreement, together with an Italian translation. Of course, the project failed and a Swedish prince was elected instead and was crowned in 1587 as Poland's King Sigismund III.[16]

Most unusual were the developments under the House of Este. From the beginning that liberal dynasty readily admitted Jewish immigrants, including exiles from Spain and Portugal. Ferrara, especially, became a major haven of refuge for Marranos; Doña Gracia Mendesia went there when she had to leave the Low Countries because of inquisitorial suspicions. Among its permanent residents were members of the Abravanel family who, because they had never denied their Jewishness, did not run afoul of the Inquisition; also such distinguished Spanish Jewish writers as the poet Solomon Usque and the apologist-historian Samuel Usque. A Spanish translation of the Bible likewise made its appearance. Among the outstanding financiers was Don Samuel Abravanel and his wife, Doña Benvenida, who had joined the forced exodus of Jews from Naples in 1541 and settled in Ferrara. So anxious were the Este dukes to attract and keep their Jews that, in 1550, Mosè Halafe had to deposit 100 gold scudi as a bond that he would stay in Ferrara to the end of his life. About that time Duke Ercole II gave Salomon de Ripa a letter of recommendation to the duke of Milan, designating Salomon as a "Jewish friend of mine [ebreo mio familiare]." He also empowered Salomon "to negotiate with Jewish merchants from Bohemia, or from another nation, who might wish to come together with their families in order to live and trade in the Este possessions." In his decree of 1550, moreover, the duke promised to safeguard the rights of Jewish slaveowners by providing, contrary to the ecclesiastical postulates going back to antiquity, that even after adopting the Christian faith slaves could secure freedom only after full compensation was paid to their masters. In defiance of Paul IV, Ercole also confirmed, on December 23, 1555, the rights of the "Portuguese" refugees from Ancona. Three years later he gave an evasive answer to the pope's request, transmitted by Cardinal Antonio Michele Ghislieri, that he expel all Marranos from his dominion. In 1571, when a ship carrying 300 Jews to Salonica was captured by the Venetian navy, his son, Alphonso II, extended full hospitality to the captives in Ferrara.[17]

Nor did the dukes budge from their open-door policy toward Jewish immigration from both turbulent Germany and the Iberian Peninsula during the Thirty Years' War and after. A ducal decree of 1652 declared that the new Jewish arrivals "are wealthy and well-connected people, able to introduce trades and commerce of quality from which one may expect to benefit sufficiently during the present times when trade has greatly declined." The administration also adhered to the pledge it had given in the 1550 general safe-conduct, that Jews "shall be treated as citizens." After the loss of Ferrara in 1597, Duke Cesare upheld this status in Modena and other localities still under the Este regime. Only with respect to Reggio had there existed a long-standing regulation that the implementation of Jewish equality was to be left to the local government's discretion. Although the decree specified that this was but a temporary (per hora) limitation, it was repeated as late as 1730. Yet, with typical inconsistency, another decree extended to Reggio Jewry rights of citizenship until December 7, 1661. While "citizenship" did not prevent the enactment of specific disabilities affecting Jews, nor even unequal treatment of the privileged "Portuguese" Jews as compared with their other coreligionists (this situation, resulting in the different fiscal burdens borne by these groups, generated much intracommunal friction), the rights of Jewish subjects of the Este dynasty continued to contrast favorably with those of most other Italian Jews.[18]

This contrast became immediately marked when the entire duchy of Ferrara was lost to the Este dynasty upon the death of Alphonso II. Invoking a technicality and astutely playing the diplomatic game, Clement VIII incorporated the duchy, as a former papal fief, into the States of the Church (November 22, 1597).

Not surprisingly, many Jews voluntarily departed from Ferrara and its environs for the more hospitable parts of the state. One émigré, Moisè Alatino, explained his unwillingness to continue living in Ferrara, where he felt as if he were "dwelling in another country and another world with its constant flow and ebb of innovations." This feeling was shared by many non-Jewish contemporaries, particularly by courtiers of the House of Este. One of them commented: "Thus passes the glory of the world now that there is no longer any duke in Ferrara, nor princes, nor music, nor singers." With much exaggeration a contemporary writer claimed that 20,000 inhabitants left Ferrara together with Duke Cesare (the population loss is estimated by recent scholars at only 1,800 persons). But there is no question that many Jews left. It appears that Ferrara's Jewish population, which had amounted to some 2,000 souls in 1590 (in addition to about 200 Marranos), decreased to 1,530 persons eleven years later.[19]

To be sure, this was a period of general population decline in many parts of Italy. Normally the Jews in the city of Ferrara would have considerably increased in number in the subsequent decades, because the new papal regime soon introduced Pius V's restrictive system and, in 1639, forced the Jews of the entire duchy to leave the provincial communities and to live exclusively in the three major centers of Ferrara, Lugo, and Cento. As a result the community of Lugo, which ever since the thirteenth century had embraced a small Jewish settlement, now grew rapidly. In 1639 it had 606 Jews, or some 10 percent of the population; among them members of the distinguished Del Vecchio and Da Fano families. Cento remained quite small, but one of its families, named Israeli (later D'Israeli), in 1748 furnished an émigré to England whose grandson was to become a famous British empire builder. The papal regime followed in other areas the example set in Rome by Paul IV and his successors, forbade Jews to acquire real estate, and established a ghetto in Ferrara in 1624 and in Lugo in 1635–39. In 1599 Jews were even ordered to dispose of the immovables they had long owned; this liquidation was completed in the relatively brief span of three years. Under these adverse circumstances all three communities continued to decline in number, affluence, and cultural creativity. By 1703 Lugo's Jewish population was reduced to 242 souls, fully a quarter of whom lived on charity. Even Ferrara's 328 Jewish families had to support 72 persons without any other means of subsistence. Nonetheless, they were still better off than their coreligionists of the papal capital.[20]

Nothing in these developments was wholly unexpected. Just as the Jewish communities which remained under the regime of the House of Este continued their careers along patterns developed during the Renaissance, those who came under the reign of the Counter Reformation popes basically shared the discriminatory treatment accorded to their coreligionists in the other Pontifical States. In contrast, the Jews of Tuscany were subjected to wholly contradictory policies pursued by the same regime in different areas. We recall that Cosimo I had yielded to papal pressure and expelled the Jews from the Tuscan provinces. Only Florence and Siena were allowed to retain Jewish communities; these were to be segregated in ghettos, while the government refused admission to refugees from the States of the Church. It was Cosimo himself, however, who had earlier pointed the way to a partial reorientation of the governmental attitude toward Jewish immigrants, a policy fully developed by his successor, Ferdinand I (1587–1609).

Quite early in his reign Cosimo realized that the commercial relations between Tuscany and the eastern Mediterranean would greatly benefit by the mediation of Levantine Jewish traders. Pisa, in particular, had long maintained an intensive trade with the Middle East. But the rapid expansion of the Ottoman Empire, and the new role played by Levantine Jews in its foreign relations, mercantile as well as political, made it advisable for Tuscany to attract some Jewish merchants for permanent settlement in its cities. After preliminary steps in 1547–48, Cosimo, acting on the advice of Jacob b. Samuel Abravanel, issued on June 16, 1551, a formal invitation to eastern Jews to settle in his duchy under very favorable conditions. Although the progress of this new arrangement was greatly impeded by the reactionary measures taken in 1570–71 in consonance with the papal demands, the idea remained in the minds of the grand duke and his successor. Finally, on July 10, 1593, Ferdinand I issued his renowned charter, named in popular parlance *La Livornina,* in which he established the cities of Leghorn and Pisa as free ports for trade with the Middle

East. Addressed to "Spaniards, Portuguese, Greeks, Germans, Italians, Hebrews, Turks, Moors, Armenians, Persians, and others," the charter had principally former Marranos in mind, to whom it assured immunity against any inquisitorial proceedings for past transgressions. This pledge clearly meant that the Marranos would never be prosecuted for reverting to the Jewish faith when they lived under Muslim rule. Among other favorable provisions were not only commercial privileges, such as freedom from customs duties for all imported goods, permission to travel freely through the country, and relatively moderate taxes, but also the absence of the usual restrictions relating to segregated quarters and the wearing of badges. Jews were even allowed to bear arms in public and to appear in horse-drawn carriages with their own coachmen. Their community, called the Portuguese "nation," was given more extensive autonomy than that usually granted to other Italian Jewish communities. It was entitled to admit Jewish newcomers at its discretion and thus automatically confer upon them Tuscan residence rights. Similar treatment was accorded in 1595 to Italian and German Jewish settlers as well, but the "Portuguese" Jews retained their uncontested supremacy and were even able to prevent the erection of synagogues of non-Sephardic rituals. In time all of these groups became thoroughly "italianized," while their majority proudly displayed their Jewish identity.[21]

This undertaking had a phenomenal success. At first Leghorn was a dependency of Pisa, but it soon outstripped its venerable neighbor and became one of the main foci of international trade in the Mediterranean world. The Jewish population, which had numbered only a hundred-odd souls in the late 1500s, increased to well over a thousand in 1650, whereas the Pisan community barely embraced five hundred persons at that time. A similar rapid increase took place in the ratio of Jews to Leghorn's general population. While in the four decades from 1560 to 1601 the city's civilian inhabitants had increased from 563 to 3,780, their number grew to 9,034 in 1622, to some 12,000 in 1642, and to over 20,000 in 1689. The corresponding Jewish figures are little more than 114 in 1601, 711 in 1622, 1,175 in 1642, and 5,000 (?) in 1689. About one-third of the leading Leghorn merchants were

Jews, probably exceeding the proportion of any other ethnic group. Their influence was greatest in exchanges with the Muslim countries, including North Africa, where a colony of "Gorni" (Leghornese) Jews was soon established in Tunisia. Jews also introduced many industries into the city, among the early leaders being Meir di Gabriele Magino, the inventor whose career in Rome had been cut short by the anti-Jewish reaction under Clement VIII. Within a century the Leghorn community belonged to the chief economic and cultural centers of Italian Jewry. It even developed, in a relatively short time, a peculiar Judeo-Italian dialect of its own, to which a considerable number of extant sonnets composed by local poets bear vivid testimony. At the same time many members kept up their Portuguese speech in the form their ancestors had known in Portugal. As a result, idioms and terms long obsolete in the homeland have been a living ingredient of the dialect spoken and written by Leghorn's Ponentine Jewish residents in recent generations. (This phenomenon, duplicated in the Castilian survivals in the Ladino language of Balkan Jewry, had long before been anticipated by the Babylonian Jews, who, all through the Parthian and early Sassanian periods, had continued to use some of the Persian loan words their ancestors had learned under the Achaemenid regime, words which had interveningly gone into oblivion among the Persians themselves.) The high standing of some new settlers in the intellectual sphere as well was demonstrated by such eminent New Christian doctors as Antonio de Fonseca and Estevão Rodrigues de Castro, who taught at the famous university of neighboring Pisa, while Antonio Dias Pinto was invited in 1609 to lecture on canon law there. Ironically, after brief service as a judge on the ecclesiastical tribunal in Florence, Dias moved to Venice, where he openly professed Judaism.[22]

NORTHERN HEGEMONY

Under the stimulus of the Counter Reformation the center of gravity of Italian Jewry thus continued to move northward. The communities of the States of the Church, which earlier in the century had inherited the mantle of leadership from Sicilian and

Neapolitan Jewry, were now reduced to two: Rome and Ancona, of which only the former participated more fully in the communal and cultural evolution of peninsular Jewry. Their place was now increasingly taken by the Jewries of the Venetian Republic, the duchy of Mantua, and the newly expanding possessions of the House of Savoy.

Leghorn's fantastic rise, in particular, invited emulation. Even Piedmont, one of Italy's most backward states, which had felt little of the impact of the new humanist economy and culture, in 1648 tried to establish a free port in Villefranche (Villafranca), in the vicinity of Nice. Although the favorable provisions of the decree were whittled down four years later, the "Portuguese" Jews who settled there on its terms were legally and economically better off than the "old" Jews of Nice. The same held true of some arrivals from North-African Oran in 1669. The ensuing friction among the various groups made communal cooperation rather difficult. Ultimately, in 1697, the city council protested against what it considered excessive privileges granted to the Jewish merchants. Yet, several years before (in 1691), when the government of Savoy surrendered the city to invading French troops, it felt impelled to insert into the act of surrender a provision reading: "The present treaty shall also comprise the Jews residing in this city under privileges accorded to them by His Highness. They shall live in the same manner as hitherto, on the basis of their privileges and without injury to their interests." Despite that governmental solicitude, however, for purely economic reasons the Jewries of Nice and Villefranche became but miniature replicas of their Tuscan prototype.[23]

Until 1648, however, all Piedmontese and Savoyard Jews lived under essentially medieval conditions. The country, which in the first half of the sixteenth century had been a major battleground between the Habsburg and Valois armies, regained its independence under the energetic rulers of the House of Savoy, Emmanuel Philibert (1553–80), and his son, Charles Emmanuel I, "the Great" (1580–1630). This dynasty now embarked upon its historic career, which two centuries later made it the chief protagonist of Italian unification.

Although Emmanuel Philibert, a nephew of Emperor Charles

V, still was in command of the Spanish armies in Flanders, he confirmed his father's privileges for Piedmontese Jewry soon after his accession to the throne (July 9, 1555). Five years later, to be sure, upon his return home, he canceled these privileges and ordered all Jews to leave. But this may have been only a stratagem of the kind frequently employed by rulers to extort from the Jews a substantial contribution to the Treasury. After negotiations with Jewish leaders he issued new privileges in 1561 and 1564. Without formally revoking the 1430 statute of Amadeus VIII, the duke also extended considerable privileges to new settlers in Nice in 1571, and in Turin and other Piedmontese communities in 1572. He was prompted to do so by his urgent need of funds, which his impoverished country was unable to supply. Moreover, he and his son embarked on a major program of introducing trade and industry into their backward possessions. Learning from his experiences in Antwerp, Emmanuel Philibert hoped to enlist the help of Jewish moneylenders and merchants. He may also have been influenced by a number of Jewish personal friends both in Antwerp and in Turin, as well as by his wife, Marguerite de Valois, a sister of the fairly tolerant King Henry II of France. The duchess seems to have been sufficiently friendly to Jews to merit, on her demise in 1576, a mournful dirge composed in her honor in four languages by Azariah de' Rossi, often styled "the father of Jewish historical criticism." [24]

Of course, this policy ran counter to the wishes of the Papacy, even after the death of Pius V on May 1, 1572. Learning about the duke's pro-Jewish measures, Gregory XIII's secretary of state, Tolomeo Galli, on June 1, 1573, instructed the departing nuncio, Vicenzo Lauro, to protest against them. He wrote:

It has come to the notice of our Master that His Highness is on the point of admitting and introducing into his states those Hebrews and Marranos who may wish to come. He is conceding to them some privileges, about which information has reached His Holiness, which are found to be so far from what one might expect from the goodness and prudence of His Highness that one cannot believe them to be true. [The nuncio should therefore advise the Duke] that the admission of these worst of people is like nurturing a serpent in one's bosom and an agent likely in a short time to spread license among the people, subversion against the states, and a fire which is not easily extinguished.

In the accompanying memorandum Galli pointed out the most objectionable of the privileges, such as the permission for Jews not to wear badges; the granting of impunity to Marranos, which would cause many of them to return to Judaism; the prohibition banning the conversion of Jewish minors under the age of fifteen or of slaves without the payment of full compensation to their owners. The papal secretary was irked by the similar toleration which was to be extended to Turks, Moors, and Persians, as well as by the duke's claim that the Jewish privileges were modeled after similar enactments by earlier popes. The papal intervention (continued by Lauro's successor, Nuncio Girolamo dei Federicis) had little effect, despite the nuncio's warnings that the admission of Marranos might strengthen the heretical influences which, owing to the continued presence of numerous Waldenses in the provinces, constituted a real threat to the progress of the Counter Reformation. Emmanuel Philibert unflinchingly adhered to his policy of admitting Jews, in return for their substantial fiscal contributions. He doubtless was also influenced by Don Joseph Nasi's startling rise to eminence in Constantinople. In his correspondence with the duke of Naxos, Emmanuel Philibert flatteringly reminded Don Joseph of their warm friendship when they both lived in Flanders.[25]

At first the Jews reacted rather hesitantly to the duke's invitation. They doubtless remembered his 1560 decree of expulsion, which was averted only by their huge payments to the Treasury. They also may have learned that, in his exchanges with the papal nuncios, the duke used such lame excuses as that he did not know which of his Jewish contrahents had been New Christians in Portugal—a matter which could be ascertained by an inquiry addressed to the Lisbon Inquisition, an inquiry which Emmanuel Philibert ultimately had to make. His successor, Charles Emmanuel I, was forced to issue a new decree of expulsion for all relapsed *conversos*. However, neither duke took such intolerant moves too literally and many Jewish bankers were allowed unperturbedly to pursue their careers. These policies were essentially dictated by the dukes' interest in stimulating the economic growth and increasing the revenue of the country, both promoted by Emmanuel Philibert's far-reaching monetary reform of 1562. In view of the small number of ineffective *monti di pietà* in the country, the opening of Jewish banks was a genuine economic necessity. It also doubtless was in cooperation with the ducal regime that the various cardinal camerlingos issued, in behalf of Gregory XIII, Sixtus V, and Clement VIII, a whole series of special privileges for individual Jewish bankers to engage in moneylending in various Piedmontese localities (1584–1611). One privilege, granted a Jewish moneylender in Asti in 1603, extended to him one of the then usual absolutions for all crimes and transgressions, "even grave and outrageous, provided they do not relate to matters condemned by the Holy Office." Charles Emmanuel completely disregarded the inquisitorial order issued by Bishop Martinengo of Nice on December 9, 1605, in which Jews were equated with heretics and blasphemers. The result was that Turin, in particular, which in 1563 had been declared the country's capital, soon attracted some 600–700 Jewish settlers. By 1624 there were no less than 100 Jewish banking firms distributed over the major cities, as well as the countryside, of the Piedmontese-Savoyard state, which by that time ranked among the largest in Italy. Moreover, among the newly added territories was the marquisate of Monferrato, where Jews had lived for some time under the benevolent regime of the Gonzaga dynasty. In 1576 no fewer than 48 Jewish banking houses were authorized to do business in Monferrato. Fifteen firms were established in the main city of Casale, the Jewish community of which was able in 1595 to erect a synagogue, often praised as the most beautiful Jewish house of worship in Italy. The liberal treatment of Jews was continued under the rather precarious domination of the House of Savoy, secured after the two wars of 1612 and 1627. To protect the rights of the Jews in the whole realm a conservator was appointed from among the higher dignitaries of the state. Imitating similar officers serving in France before the expulsions of the fourteenth and fifteenth centuries, this official was to safeguard the rights of Jews as spelled out in the *capitoli,* which were decennially renewed until the era of the French Revolution. In practice, the conservator was usually selected from among three candidates designated by the Jewish communities. Jews reciprocated by paying many ordinary and extraordinary taxes and by extending substantial loans to the government.[26]

As long as it was under Gonzaga rule, Monferrato shared the vicissitudes of Mantuan Jewry. We recall that during the Renaissance era the duchy of Mantua had become one of the great centers of Jewish culture and of Jewish contributions to the arts and sciences, particularly medicine and music. Legally, the community still largely depended on the privileges extended to its bankers in the fourteenth and fifteenth centuries, but from 1511 on the ducal decrees mention, with increasing frequency, the Jewish community (*università*), which included many individuals engaged in other occupations. Yet, despite the competition of a *monte di pietà,* the Jewish bankers retained their influence, especially under the regime of Duke Federico (1519–40). While objections were voiced to the large number of Jewish banking firms, and their total was frequently reduced by law, many moneylenders settled in the city's immediate vicinity, as well as in the rest of the duchy, and effectively competed with their coreligionists in the capital. One also heard frequent complaints about the high rates of interest, which induced the regents for Duke Francesco, then a minor, to outlaw Jewish banking completely in 1547. That this decree was issued by Queen Mother Margarita and the generally friendly Cardinal Ercole Gonzaga made it appear doubly ominous. Yet before long the banks were allowed to resume operations; only their maximum rate of interest was reduced in 1557 from 25 percent to 17.5 percent. But so indispensable had the Jewish moneylenders become to the duchy's economy that the dukes sought and obtained special papal licenses for their Jewish bankers (in 1546 from Paul III and in 1585 from Sixtus V); the number of Jewish banking firms throughout the duchy before very long increased to twenty-eight. Federico also used Jews for diplomatic missions. In some cases the duke provided these envoys with warmly phrased safe-conducts. In 1521, for example, he referred to Isaac Norsi, son of that Daniel Norsi who had become a victim of the plot connected with the *Donna della Vittoria,* as *civis et familiaris noster delectus* (citizen and Our cherished friend).[27]

Anti-Jewish currents generated by the Counter Reformation, however, also made themselves felt in the duchy of Mantua. At first the new duke, Guglielmo (1550–87; during the first eight years of his minority the country was governed by a regency), resisted various pressures from the Counter Reformation popes, and even admitted many refugees expelled from the Pontifical States in 1569. But he yielded to the persuasion of Gregory XIII's legate in 1576 and introduced into the Mantuan legislation many provisions of Paul IV's anti-Jewish bull, *Cum nimis absurdum.* Characteristically, with manifold excuses, he omitted certain crucial disabilities. He argued, for instance, that a prohibition against Jews trading in grain was unnecessary, since such trade, even by Christians, required a governmental license. Similarly the regulation of Jewish moneylending depended on special *capitoli,* contracted with individual bankers. However, Guglielmo accepted the principle that Jews should not own real estate, and he inserted many segregationist provisions of the new canon law into his decree. But unlike the authorities of the Pontifical States, the Mantuan administration either delayed, under various subterfuges, the application of the new restrictions or greatly weaked them by numerous exceptions. This system continued under Guglielmo's successor, Vincenzo I (1587–1612). His pro-Jewish stance provoked Clement VIII to declare to Vincenzo's envoy in September 1602, "We are waiting to hear that His Highness had begun to put restrictions on the Jews and to bridle this rabble [*canaglia*] as it deserves and is proper, and are sure that His Highness will not fail in his promise." The duke yielded and imposed many restrictions upon the Jews; he expanded these further in 1601 when he renewed the decree of 1576, and finally laid the foundation for the establishment of a formal ghetto in 1612. There also were frequent anti-Jewish riots, and the police had considerable difficulty in repressing them. In 1623, Duke Ferdinand (1612–26) threatened to expel the Jews altogether, although the terminal date of the renewed *capitoli* still was three years off. He was placated by the payment of a substantial sum, probably the main objective of the threat. At the same time, intergroup relations were so intimate that sex relations between Jews and Christians had to be placed under a fine of up to 25 scudi, rather than under the traditional sanction of capital punishment. The constant reiteration of the new segregationist regulations, including one forbidding Jews to teach Gentile pupils music and dancing, demonstrates their relative ineffectiveness.[28]

Nevertheless, popular outbreaks, alternating with legislative restrictions and administrative chicaneries, were sufficiently frequent to undermine Mantuan Jewry's feeling of security and to weaken its once broad cultural creativity. But at the beginning of the seventeenth century the community still was a focus of rabbinic learning and communal initiative, which extended far beyond the duchy's boundaries. Mantuan Jews succeeded in obtaining from the Church special licenses for the first printing of the *Zohar* (1558) and the reprinting of the Maimonidean Code (1572). We also recall their leadership in trying to reverse the old papal outlawry of the Talmud and to secure from Sixtus V a permit to reprint this rabbinic classic after the deletion of certain incriminated passages. If in 1630 Mantua became the scene of a major anti-Jewish massacre and expulsion, this was primarily the effect of political struggles over the succession to the dukedom in the midst of the great international conflagration of the Thirty Years' War. This tragic turning point in the history of Mantuan Jewry will be treated here in connection with the general impact of that war on the Jews of central Europe.[29]

In contrast, Mantua's great neighbor, the Venetian Republic, after the stormy episode of 1571–73, allowed the Jews to return to their generally favorable pre-Lepanto status. The Republic's financial situation had greatly deteriorated as a result of its vast war expenditures, which were felt with redoubled force because of the government's attempt to amortize the new indebtedness in but seven years (1577–84). Two costly fires in the magnificent palace of the doges in 1574 and 1577, and the severe pestilence of 1575–77, which is said to have caused the death of 50,000 people, or between one-quarter and one-third of the city's population, added to the Treasury's tremendous burdens. The situation was further aggravated by the return of many Venetian officials and merchants from Cyprus, now permanently occupied by Turkey, despite the League's victory at Lepanto. These returning "colonists," often many years away from home, could not easily be absorbed by the shrinking economy of the mother country. Moreover, the spirit of commercial enterprise of the once-famed merchant class of Venice and other Italian cities now betrayed signs of incipient psychological alienation, which was to cause a visitor to comment a century later, "The commerce of Venice is far from being in a flourishing state for various reasons. . . . There are high customs duties on merchandise. Persons of quality consider commerce below their dignity; when merchants become rich and able to enter truly big business they leave it for the most part and with their money insinuate themselves into the nobility." [30]

Under these circumstances, attracting Jewish merchants from the Levant, as well as from the West, became an imperative necessity. Like other mercantile emporia Venice had long accommodated numerous residents and visitors from other lands, including "heretical" Holland and England. In a well-known sonnet, Giordano Bruno sang the city's praises as the "new ark of Noah" and "the world's marvel." Moderation in Jewish policies, too, was clearly a postulate of the age; it was to prove particularly helpful in the resumption of friendly relations with the Porte, one of the main concerns of the Republic's international policies. The Ottoman Empire, on its part, greatly encouraged Jewish mediation. In its decree of June 2, 1541, the Venetian Senate had conceded that "the largest part of the merchandise arriving from Romania [the eastern Mediterranean], as far as one can see, is transported and is in the hands of traveling Levantine Jewish merchants." The Turkish attitude is well exemplified by the following letter of recommendation, written by Sultan Suleiman the Magnificent to the doge in 1564 on behalf of Alvaro Mendes' family. The sultan requested the Venetian authorities to provide Alvaro Mendes' father and his family with a boat and escort to conduct them safely to Dubrovnik (Ragusa), from where they would be able easily to move across the Ottoman frontier and reach the Turkish capital. Although Alvaro, known in Constantinople under his Jewish name Solomon ibn Ya'ish, may have been a relative of Don Joseph Nasi, he was far more sympathetic to Venice than was the duke of Naxos.[31]

As a result the Jewish population of the Venetian capital, as well as of the provinces, grew by leaps and bounds. We recall that the first Jews to settle in Venice proper came there as a result of the war between the City of the Lagoons and the League of Cambrai in 1509. By 1586 their number had increased to some 1,700, and it is said to have risen further to almost 6,000 by 1638 (according to the doubtless exaggerating reports by the contemporary Venetian rabbi Simone [Simḥah b. Isaac] Luzzatto). The Jewish community was divided into three "nations": the old German and Italian settlers, who ever since 1516 were concentrated in the so-called *ghetto nuovo,* and the newer groups of Levantine and Ponentine Jews, who from 1541 on resided in the *ghetto vecchio.* In 1633 a new wave of arrivals from other Italo-German communities was assigned additional space in a quarter called the *ghetto nuovissimo* after the community had guaranteed the settlement there of at least 20 new Jewish families within a year. Remarkably, Jews of Italian origin were but a minority within that interterritorial agglomeration, in which each group tried to maintain its independent congregational structure. In 1636 Leon da Modena, the versatile rabbi of the "Italian" community, and his associates felt prompted to issue a formal invitation to the numerous visitors from other parts of Italy to attend services in their synagogue. They pointed out that "at the time our synagogue was founded the initiators intended not only to provide a place where the Italian residents of our city would be able to pray according to the rite of our forefathers but also to satisfy the desire of transients from other Italian regions to have a synagogue of their own rite." They ordered the sexton to ask all such new arrivals who might come to his notice fully to participate in the congregational services, to be called to the Torah, and to arrange to hold family celebrations such as weddings and circumcisions there. All that for a fee of a quarter of a ducat. The rights of all these groups of Jewish residents were defined in decennially renewable *capitoli.* The renewals were no longer much in doubt, but they lent the government an additional leverage for extorting from the Jews special payments and forced loans. At the same time the Jewish community had to continue maintaining the *banchi del ghetto,* which, by extending loans to the needy Christian population at nominal rates of interest (only gradually increased to 10 percent), made the establishment of a *monte di pietà* unnecessary.[32]

These "ghetto banks," to be sure, were of direct concern only to the Jewish moneylenders, recruited almost exclusively from the Italo-German group. Yet the Levantine and Ponentine members were obliged to contribute to their upkeep, although they themselves were forbidden to engage in banking. Instead they were granted extensive privileges in international and wholesale trade, in both of which they played a disproportionately large role. To underscore the difference between them and the majority of their less privileged coreligionists they were placed under the supervision of the highly influential office of the five *Savi di mercanzia,* a governmental organ the history of which, observes Heinrich Kretschmayr, "is almost tantamount to the history of Venetian commerce." In their aforementioned negotiations with Solomon Ashkenazi in 1574, the Venetian authorities sought to establish a method of liberating Christian slaves in Turkey and Muslim slaves in Italian hands. These negotiations may have aimed at an immediate exchange of prisoners of war, as well as at some mutual accommodation regarding captives turned slaves by pirates in "peacetime." Through Ashkenazi the Venetians also hoped to persuade the Porte not to object to the castles recently erected by them on the Dalmatian-Turkish frontier, claiming that these structures were serving as mere dwellings for some noblemen and had no military importance. Shortly thereafter, in 1577–82, a Jewish merchant, Daniele Rodriguez, established at his own expense a free port in Split (Spalato) on the Dalmatian coast, which then was under Venetian control. This free port, which Rodriguez, appointed its "consul," provided not only with adequate harbor facilities but also with hospitals and coffee houses, led to his financial ruination, but it remained a permanently valuable link in the Venetian maritime network. Replacing Durazzo and competing with Dubrovnik (Ragusa), it long helped the Republic to maintain its undisputed hegemony over the entire Adriatic Sea. In general, a safe-conduct of 1589 promised the Levantine and Ponentine Jews full protection against molestation from any quarter and stated that "they may navigate [the seas] as they do now without being obliged to pay any impost larger than that they are now paying or than that which may be paid by our subjects in the future." Culturally and intellectually, too, the "western" Jews made significant contributions to the Venetian civilization, which in the late sixteenth and seventeenth centuries was in gradual retreat from the heights it had achieved during the Renaissance. Side by side with Jews, many of whom had previously been New Christians, lived Marranos genuinely professing Christianity. Although expelled from Venice in 1497 and again in 1550, a considerable number of New Christians persevered in both the city and the provinces, from time to time becoming the objects of inquisitorial curiosity.[33]

Among the communities of the *terra ferma* those of Padua and Verona assumed increasing significance. Despite the establishment of a *monte di pietà* in Padua in 1491 the city at first maintained as many as thirty Jewish banks. But after moneylending on interest outside the reorganized *monte* was outlawed in 1547, most Jews turned to handicrafts and general merchandising. However, both these occupations were of a more local character than in Venice and, hence, they largely remained in the hands of Jews of German origin. Because of its famed medical school, Padua also attracted Jewish students from various lands, including Poland-Lithuania. Notwithstanding occasional manifestations of popular hostility, the legal status of the Jews remained relatively favorable. Except for 1571, the year of a major pestilence, the Paduan community maintained a steady growth in both numbers and affluence until the great plague of 1631, when it lost about two-thirds of its members. Verona, on the other hand, which during the eight years of Habsburg occupation (1509–1517) had witnessed the nearly total elimination of its small Jewish community, readmitted Jews in increasing numbers throughout the late sixteenth and seventeenth centuries. Here, too, the majority of Jews turned to petty commerce—they soon owned twenty open shops in the city—after the enactment of strict anti-usury laws in 1548 and 1578. The growth of the Veronese community was likewise stunted in 1631, when only 300 of the 721 Jewish residents survived the plague. The city nevertheless continued to function for a time as a significant center of Jewish culture. It was there, for example, that Isaac (Fernando) Cardoso, formerly a distinguished Marrano physician and writer in Madrid, wrote his *Las Excelencias y calunias de los Hebreos* (published in 1679), a jewel of Jewish apologetic literature. Nor was he the only former New Christian who had publicly reverted to Judaism in Verona. In general, relapsed Marranos seem to have been less frequently disturbed by the local Inquisition in the Venetian provinces than in the capital.[34]

FINANCIAL RAISON D'ETAT

The replacement of the decaying Byzantine Empire and the Mameluk states by the powerful and expanding Ottoman Empire, combined with the rising naval and piratical strength of the North-African corsairs, created an entirely novel situation for Italy's mercantile states. At the same time, the discovery of the New World and the growing importance of the Atlantic trade had begun to shift the center of gravity of world commerce from the Mediterranean and the Indian Ocean to the Atlantic, enhancing the significance of the great western foci of Seville and Lisbon, Bordeaux and Antwerp, Amsterdam and London. Like the other builders of the modern European states, the sixteenth-century Italian rulers of the brand of Cosimo I and Ferdinand I de' Medici in Florence, Emmanuel Philibert and Charles Emmanuel in Piedmont-Savoy, and the successive doges of Venice readily pursued the policies of the now dominant *raison d'état* in the economic, as well as the political, sphere. This situation also dictated, as we have just seen, some reorientation in the now outworn traditional treatment of Jews.

Clearly, the new economic realities militated against the adoption, by most Italian principalities and republics, of the occupational restrictions imposed upon Roman Jewry by the papal bull *Cum nimis absurdum* of 1555. One state after another began adopting mercantilist policies designed to increase both domestic production and international exchange; many performed important pioneering services in the early stages of modern capitalism. These trends did not create a favorable climate for the continued adherence to partially obsolete, ecclesiastically oriented business ethics and the economic segregation of non-Catholics. One of the major casualties of the changed economic system was the canonical doctrine of the "just price," especially in international trade. Here, and frequently also in domestic commerce, the domination of the ever larger and more complex cartels made prices independent of "legitimate" margins above costs. While in many cases powerful mercantile combines sharply reduced competition and kept Jewish traders out of various markets, in some instances they stimulated cooperation that transcended national and denominational boundaries.

Needless to say, there also were many vested interests trying to uphold the established order, including the keeping of Jews at arms' length. Interested parties could make maritime journeys extremely perilous for Jews. Always exposed to attacks by pirates, Jewish passengers were doubly endangered now because of the division of the Mediterranean world between the Ottoman Empire and the West, a division which increased suspicions against Jewish travelers. In a characteristic inquiry addressed to Gregory XIII in 1578, the grand master of the Maltese Order, John Levesque, reported the capture of two Jews who, sailing from Tripoli on a Venetian ship, had been stranded in Malta. He argued that they should be treated as slaves because "they are more hostile to our religion than the very Turks." In the long run, nevertheless, Italy's obvious economic decline in relation to her Atlantic competitors caused many a regime to adopt more progressive policies and to overrule objections to change.[35]

If, in matters relating to the states' self-interest, few Italian rulers were ready to follow the lead of the Church blindly, many powerful local groups were still arrayed on the side of the papal prohibitions and included them in their local legislation. In some areas ownership of real estate was either restricted or entirely forbidden to Jews simply because Christian landlords wished to reserve that prerogative for themselves. On the other hand, Jews often succeeded in extending the permission to trade in *strazzaria* (secondhand goods), in which local aristocrats were personally interested as both sellers and purchasers, to include many items manufactured by themselves. Even in communities under strong papal influence they were able to engage in wholesale and petty trade and to enter various crafts. In 1588 Duke Vincenzo Gonzaga of Mantua expressly confirmed the Jews' right to trade in grain, textiles, and clothing, as well as to engage in gold- and silversmithery. These freedoms were reconfirmed by Vincenzo's successors. As usual, individuals were given special privileges. For instance, one

Lioncino Sermoneta, who supplied the Gonzaga court with meat, was granted a special travel permit in 1570 to acquire cattle and fowl anywhere in the duchy. Nor did Mantuan Jewish craftsmen encounter any serious legal difficulties. On two occasions, to be sure, the craft guilds of Mantua sued their Jewish competitors before the courts; once, curiously, because some Jews had refused to become guild members. But, as the plaintiffs themselves pointed out, five other Jews had joined their respective guilds and subjected themselves to the statutory restrictions imposed upon all members.[36]

In most cases the rulers, even if personally unsympathetic, protected Jewish businessmen and artisans. Jealous Venice, too, bent upon promoting trade with both the Levant and the West, had endowed, as we recall, the "Levantine" and "Ponentine" Jews with more extensive privileges than those granted to the majority of the older Jewish settlers. Not only were the former to be protected in peacetime, but, as the *capitoli* renewed on September 26, 1647, expressly provided, "on the occasion of a war with any prince no merchant shall be detained, his merchandise seized, or his family disturbed in any way . . . but they shall all be preserved in their aforementioned state of security." An incident of 1559 illustrates particularly well the length to which the Republic was prepared to go in safeguarding the rights of its Jewish (and Marrano) traders. In the piratical jungle which comprised much of the Mediterranean trade, Jews were often victimized as "infidels" by both Christian and Muslim corsairs. Acting upon the assumption that Jewish property could be confiscated with impunity, a Spanish naval squadron in August 1559 forced the Venetian ship *Massona*, out of Alexandria, to land in Syracuse, Sicily, and to unload there all merchandise belonging to Jews. In reprisal, the Venetians decided two months later to capture some of Philip II's frigates and, as a sign of contempt, to throw their flags into the sea. Similarly, in the 1551 agreement between Cosimo I and Servadio "the Greek" about the admission of Levantine Jews to Florence, the Jews were specifically authorized in the case of war with the Ottoman Empire "freely to depart from Our aforementioned Dominion together with all your possessions and wares to whichever place you may wish, provided you will have first satisfied your creditors with respect to all debts you may have contracted in Our State or with Our subjects in any other locality." At the same time Cosimo requested the rulers of all lands through which these prospective immigrants had to travel before reaching their Florentine destination "to recognize you [the Jews] as Our favorite persons, to be kind and helpful to you in any matter. Every favor and courtesy extended to you will be considered as a gracious deed rendered to Us and be kept in grateful remembrance for any occasion in which We might be able to reciprocate with a similar favor." Nor did the Medicean grand dukes hesitate to breach their own segregationist policies with respect to their Jewish subjects in Florence and Siena by inviting Levantine Jews to settle freely in any section of their free port of Leghorn. The popes themselves invoked economic need as justification for keeping Jews in Rome, Ancona, and Avignon after expelling them from other parts of the Pontifical States. Sixtus V, one of the ablest administrators on the papal throne, openly readmitted Jewish traders to the whole realm.[37]

The important role played by Jews in supplying foodstuffs was dramatically illustrated in 1608–1609 during one of the recurrent Mantuan famines. Instead of negotiating with individual Jewish merchants, Duke Vincenzo imposed upon the community at large the obligation to supply the entire population with grain. The community entrusted this task to a committee of five Jewish businessmen who, after spending 54,600 Mantuan lire from the communal treasury, acquitted themselves so well that in the end the duke was left in possession of 650 sacks of surplus grain. Of course, the community was now ordered to repurchase that surplus from the duke and to distribute it among its own members.[38]

Even less successful was the attempt of the Counter Reformation to put "teeth" into the old canonical prohibition against Jewish doctors attending Christian patients. True, the popes, who had themselves previously employed a number of Jewish court physicians, now were more scrupulous in adhering to that prohibition. On the question of whether Jews should be allowed to graduate from medical schools, some Counter Reformation popes and canon jurists adopted a hard line. In 1618 when Roman Jews applied to the Inquisition for permission to obtain doctorates "in grammar and other sciences" and pointed out that they had long been able to secure medical degrees, Pope Paul V denied their request and stated that the older practice had been illegal. He ordered the University of Rome thenceforth to refuse admission to Jewish candidates for doctorates in medicine. Yet the practice continued unabated, especially in Padua and Siena. Here even Pope Urban VIII joined the grand duke of Tuscany in 1639 in granting a pertinent dispensation for Guglielmo, scion of the famous Mantuan medical family Portaleone. A similar papal dispensation was granted to another Portaleone in 1655. However, even when formally licensed, Jewish physicians often had to overcome certain handicaps arising from their nonadmission to local medical societies. In most cases such exclusion did not have to be expressly stated; as in the case of artisan guilds, it was the incidental effect of the religious character of these associations. The medical society of Vicenza, without any direct reference to Jews, included in its statute of 1555 many pious Catholic declarations to which no conscientious Jew could subscribe; for instance, the statement that the statute had been adopted "for the praise and glory of the omnipotent God, the sublime Virgin Mary, and the Saints Leontius and Carpophorius, erstwhile physicians and patrons of this magnificent city." Nor could a Jewish doctor readily fulfill the requirement, adopted in 1563, that all members participate in the Corpus Christi procession, or else either send a torch-bearing substitute or pay a fine of 1 ducat.[39]

Typical of many princely concessions was the license issued by Duke Emmanuel Philibert of Piedmont on June 10, 1561 (a year after the proclamation and revocation of his decree banishing all Jews from the country), to Leon, son of Emmanuel, doctor of medicine and philosophy. Leon was granted permission "to live in any section of Our states, together with his whole family, funds, and possessions, to exercise his profession there and to do all that appertains to his said doctoral degree; he may freely extend medical help to any caller." The duke also ordered the local authorities to conform with this license "without any contradiction if they esteem Our grace." Marrano physicians, too, were able to carry on their professional activities, except perhaps for Amatus Lusitanus, whose presence had become too conspicuous, both because of his professional eminence and because he had resided in Ancona at the time when the Marrano community was struck down by Paul IV. The Venetian Republic was particularly accommodating. Elijah (Filotheo) Montalto, although known to have been born in Castello Branco, Portugal, two generations after the forced conversion of all Portuguese Jews in 1497, achieved so great an international reputation through his medical practice in Venice that he was invited to Paris by the queen, Marie de Médicis. In a letter dated May 6, 1613, he was called a "nobleman" and a "councilor and physician in ordinary of the Queen." In Verona, Isaac (Fernando) Cardoso could not only undisturbedly pursue his extensive medical practice but also devote much of his time to the composition of his apologia for Judaism and his comprehensive scientific-philosophic work, the *Philosophia libera,* published in Venice, 1673.[40]

Jews also benefited at times from the widespread quest for industrial self-sufficiency, stimulated by the teachings of Niccolò Machiavelli and other political thinkers. This passion sometimes affected even smaller localities. With a constant growth in population and urban concentration, agricultural production proved to be a decreasing source of livelihood for the masses. A telling example is offered by the relatively small municipality of Legnago, in the vicinity of Verona. Incorporated into the Venetian Republic and serving it as a fortress, Legnago suffered severely from the wars ravaging northern Italy during most of the sixteenth and early seventeenth centuries. In order to counteract the pauperization of its residents, the city sought to establish within its territory an effective textile industry. At first it decided to encourage its own citizens to go into the production of woolens, and supplied them with the necessary buildings and equipment. When this experiment ended in dismal failure in 1566, the municipality concluded, on March 14, 1604, an agreement with the Jewish brothers Donà and Abraham, sons of Donato of Finale di Modena, to introduce the manufacture of both woolen and silk goods into the city. But they had to provide the necessary facilities at their own expense. Although Modena had remained under the domination of the tolerant Este family, the example of Ferrara, so easily taken over but a few years earlier by the then antagonistic Papacy, caused consternation among the Jews of the entire duchy. Many were now persuaded that they might fare better under the Venetian regime. Despite their inexperience in the production of textiles, Donà and Abraham were ready to try their luck under the very favorable terms offered them by the Legnago *condotta*. They were to be allowed, simultaneously, to lend money at the annual interest rate of 12 percent and with fairly liberal provisions for their handling of pledges. They also were to enjoy a monopoly in both their industrial and their banking enterprises. Articles 9 and 10 of the *capitoli* unequivocally stated that

for the duration of the said *condotta* [which, subject to certain conditions, was to run for eighteen years and could then be renewed] no other person, of whatever rank or condition he may be, shall be able to manufacture cloth of any kind in this land and territory except the said Hebrews and their agents. For the duration of the said *condotta* no other Hebrew shall be allowed to come and live in this land, except the said Donà and Abraham, together with their children and their issue, their agents, factors, and household help.

Furthermore, they were also to be free to bring their goods in without paying customs duties and were not to be subject to any municipal imposts or billeting of soldiers from the garrison of the fortress. In practice, however, these high expectations ended in total frustration on both sides. A combination of inexperience and limited funds prevented the manufacturing establishment from getting off the ground. After the expiration of the original eighteen-year term, the *capitoli* were not renewed and, perhaps even before their termination, the Jews had left for more promising parts.[41]

In the larger cities, on the other hand, Jews often had an uphill struggle in entering industrial occupations against the vested interests of powerful guilds. Doubtless many were now forced to seek new outlets for their enterprising abilities, because their traditional money trade could not support their growing number, especially since Jewish bankers now were adversely affected by the spread of the *monti di pietà* and the renewed papal drive against Jewish "usury." At the same time the credit system was increasingly becoming the lifeblood of the new political and economic expansion and helped to alleviate the distress of large occupational groups ground under the relentless wheels of change. Typical of the new attitude is the aforementioned assertion of the Spanish crown prince, Philip (soon thereafter King Philip II), in a letter to his father at a militarily critical moment in 1554, that in war "nothing can be accomplished without money and credit." Despite the ensuing ambivalence of the Catholic attitude to loans on interest, there was a disconcertingly large outcropping of anti-usury pamphlets, for the most part with an anti-Jewish slant, such as those by François Hotman and Sisto de' Medici. In his apologetic treatise, published in 1638, Simone (Simḥah) Luzzatto did not try to justify usury on moral grounds, but rather on those of economic necessity. He quoted to that effect Tacitus' observation about the equally reprehensible trade of astrologers and magicians which "in our city will always be outlawed, and yet always practiced." Were the Jews totally to abstain from moneylending, they would only reduce the amount of credit available, forcing the interest rates charged by Christian lenders to rise higher and higher at the expense of the borrowers. Most Venetian Jews, Luzzatto insisted, preferred to engage in legitimate commerce, for which, under the impact of circumstances, they had developed a special aptitude. "That is why we see that wherever Jews have lived, commerce has flourished." On the other hand, nearly a century earlier (in 1559), in explaining his treatise on the Jewish laws of banking and interest, Yeḥiel Nissim da Pisa, himself both a scholar and a banker, wrote, "Since moneylending had become the common vocation of the [Jewish] people and the chief source of their livelihood [in Italy], it became necessary [for me] to compose a short treatise that would, in the best possible fashion, include in it all the laws of interest." [42]

Sometimes Jews still were specifically invited to settle in order to provide credit for the needy population. Even if not clearly spelled out, the resources and know-how of Jewish moneylenders doubtless played a considerable role in the readmission of Jews to Venice after 1509. They partially helped to fill a gap created by the grave crisis in Venetian banking during the first half of the sixteenth century. Similarly, in their effort to raise the economic level of Savoy and Piedmont, the dukes did not hesitate in the 1570s forcefully to stand up to the Papacy in behalf of their Jewish moneylenders. Later on, popes themselves readily cooperated and, beginning in 1584, issued numerous permits for provincial bankers; one of these permits, dated October 12, 1599, explicitly ordered a local count and a baron to obey its provisions. This apparent inconsistency, moreover, was fully in line with the Papacy's growing recognition of the changing economic realities. After founding the Banco di Spirito in Rome in 1605, Paul V had to allow this new deposit bank to charge interest for its loans, although this was still done surrepititiously and was not formally approved until 1684. Similarly, the *monti di pietà* were now customarily charging some interest under one guise or another. As late as 1670 Charles Emmanuel II entered in a memorandum the following characteristic remark: "The Duke of Florence is dead, and, since his successor does not love Jews, upon whom he imposes taxes, one ought to send the Morena to induce some of the richest among them to establish their residences in the port of Villafranca." While the main purpose of that initiative was to promote Piedmont-Savoy's international trade in its competition with Leghorn, the new settlers were apparently to be encouraged to engage in credit transactions as well.[43]

In the long run, nevertheless, new pressures, combined with the old resentments on the part of the masses of debtors, tended to diminish the role of bankers versus that of merchants and craftsmen within the Jewish community. This transition became outwardly marked as more and more privileges were addressed to the community (*università*) as a whole, rather than to individual banking families. Rates of interest likewise steadily declined, in legal theory and in practice, from the lofty heights they had reached in the Late Middle Ages. The experience of Modena Jewry probably was fairly typical. In 1527 the *capitoli* provided that Jews could charge 4 denari per lira a month in loans of 10 lire or less, 5 denari per lira for larger loans, and 6 denari per lira in loans of any size to nonresidents. If adhered to, this provision established maximum interest rates of 20, 25, and 30 percent, respectively. But in 1579 a uniform maximum rate of 20 percent was enacted. It was further lowered to 18 percent in 1631. Moreover, the accumulation of capital necessary for lucrative investment became increasingly difficult in the face of the mounting economic stringency and governmental exactions. At times Jewish bankers surreptitiously borrowed funds from their archrival, the *monte di pietà*, by pledging pawns with it through Christian intermediaries. This practice called forth a 1611 ordinance in Mirandola threatening such middlemen with the forfeiture of the pawns and the immediate forced repayment of the entire loan to the *monte*. The combined effect of these manifold pressures was a growing diversification of Jewish occupations at the expense of banking, which became less and less remunerative.[44]

TIGHTER SEGREGATION

A major byproduct of the Catholic Restoration was a renewed emphasis on the old ecclesiastical postulate for keeping Jews and Christians sharply apart. Notwithstanding the close social contacts between the two denominations developed during the Renaissance, the Papacy now encountered little resistance to its energetic campaign to establish the first formal ghettos in the States of the Church. Most Jews, to be sure, had been living in fairly concentrated settlements even where the law had not required it. But wherever a new Jewish quarter was legally set aside, many non-Jews had to be relocated in other sections of the city, while the relatively few Jews scattered through other quarters had to be resettled in their assigned street. At times new houses had to be built, while older dwellings remained unoccupied; gates and, occasionally, walls had to be erected, and other measures taken entailing great expense, which neither the governments nor the Jews were eager to defray. Yet on principle there was relatively little opposition.

Occasionally, segments of the local population vociferously agitated for such segregation, partly under incitation by zealous preachers and partly to satisfy the personal interests of individual burghers. For example, the *podestà* of Modena, Andrea Cadebo, found it quite profitable to sell his house to the Jewish community. Others hoped to collect higher rentals from the new Jewish tenants, although in most places rent control laws were speedily enacted. In Mantua, after the Jews moved into the ghetto in 1612, the rents were actually lowered by one-third, the duke taking cognizance of the vast expenses otherwise incurred by the community. Priorities also had to be given to established shopkeepers; new stores could be opened only when space became available. Like dwellings, shops were generally handed down from generation to generation and their selling prices varied with supply and demand. On the other hand, Christian residents and even institutions such as churches, monasteries, or *monti di pietà* were as a rule transferred out of the ghetto area before the Jews moved in. Fires, which were generally extremely destructive and often engulfed entire cities, large and small, also were a major menace to the ghetto inhabitants. Grateful to the Lord for averting such a calamity in 1765, the Jews of Padua thenceforth celebrated an annual *Purim del Fuoco*.[45]

Needless to say, Jews were rarely assigned desirable locations. Only where a considerable number of Jews had lived for a long time in a certain district, was it often found more convenient to establish a Jewish quarter there by exchanging the Christian inhabitants with the relatively few Jews scattered over other sections of the city. In Rome, for example, the new ghetto proclaimed by Paul IV in 1555 was concentrated in the area inhabited by Jews, among others, from ancient times. However, if the Jewish community was relatively young and an entirely new quarter had to be found for it, the tendency was to select some low-cost slum district, which the Jews would be forced to improve and which, at the same time, would underscore Jewish inferiority. Even in Florence, where the newly established Jewish quarter was located near the center of the city in a section once inhabited by patricians, the area had by 1571 become run-down, largely populated by delinquents and prostitutes. To remind the Jews permanently of their "infidelity," Cosimo I placed an inscription on one of the ghetto gates which stressed the stiff-neckedness of the inhabitants and their segregation from the society of Christians, although it also pointed out that the grand duke had "not wished to eject them." Here and in other cities, moreover, the rulers reserved for themselves the right to grant exceptions to favorite individuals and families. In Mantua, for example, Duke Vincenzo in August 1611 permitted the banker Moses Bonaventura and his son, Mordecai, to continue living in their bank building outside the ghetto and even to hold divine services there. They also could entertain Jewish visitors for up to six days at a time. This banking family could not make use of the privilege, however, because after Vincenzo's demise his son, Francesco II, revoked all exceptions and forced the Bonaventuras to join their coreligionists then moving into the new quarter. Nor did the Dutch Jew Pinchas Netto apparently have any success with a petition he made for redress of an obvious wrong: In 1665 he had introduced into Reggio, under the joint protection of the duke and Cardinal D'Este, the manufacture of silk shoes along English lines. When the ghetto was established in that city in 1671 he pleaded in vain that his work would be hampered seriously by removal to a locality which did not offer the "required amount of light." Elsewhere, too, individual exceptions, so dear to arbitrary rulers for centuries, now diminished in number. In the long run, many Jews themselves preferred to move into their own quarter, where they could live among their coreligionists and enjoy the ghetto's increasing cultural amenities; some may also have felt more secure there against individual assaults.[46]

It is a widespread misconception that the formal ghetto was essentially a medieval institution. We recall that such formal establishments, under severe legal sanctions, began to be instituted throughout Castile and Aragon, as well as in some German cities, only during the fifteenth century. In Italy, the ghetto in the technical sense really was the product of the early modern period. Apart from the resolution adopted by the Venetian Senate in 1516, which was in so far exceptional as it related simultaneously to the admission of Jews to semipermanent residence and to their seclusion in a separate quarter, the segregationist movement did not start until Paul IV's bull *Cum nimis absurdum,* of 1555. The papal cities of Bologna and Ancona followed suit in 1556, and, for specific reasons mentioned above, Florence emulated that example fifteen years later. Other cities proceeded with varying degrees of caution. Even when the duchy of Ferrara was reincorporated into the Pontifical States in 1598, the ghetto walls were not erected until 1624 in the capital, and 1639 in Lugo and Cento, in connection with the concentration there of Jewish subjects expelled from the Ferrara countryside. Remarkably, in the remaining provinces of the Este dynasty Jewish quarters were independently established in Mirandola as early as 1602 (as a result of an inflammatory sermon by the Capuchin friar Bartolommeo Cambi da Salutio), in Modena in 1638, and in Reggio in 1671. However, the ghettos of Finale and Correggio were not erected until 1736 and 1779, respectively. In the Venetian Republic, Italy's pioneer in that form of legal segregation, the authorities allowed Jews to live among non-Jews in Verona until 1600, in Padua until 1603, in Rovigo until 1613, and in Conegliano until 1675. The dukes of Piedmont-Savoy were quite slow in executing the pertinent papal demand, although some legislative attempts in this direction dated back to 1425 and formed part of Amadeo VIII's basic decree governing Jewish life in the duchy since 1430. Turin did not fully enforce the ghetto until 1679, while the Jewish communities of Vercelli, Casale Monferrato, Acqui, and Moncalvo were not compelled to move into special quarters until 1724–32. Evidently, legally imposed segregation had become a greater necessity under the Counter Reformation, with its sharp reversal of the rapprochement between Jews and Christians during the preceding Renaissance, than it had ever been in the Middle Ages proper, when more or less automatic, if incomplete, separation corresponded more closely to the prevailing social and psychological realities.[47]

Among the propelling forces for the establishment of the ghetto were the Christian neighbors' greed and envy. We recall the Modena *podestà's* admission that he had obtained a substantial gain from the sale of one of his houses in the newly established Jewish quarter, as well as the complaint of the Paduan city council of 1541 that some Jews, "not content with their accustomed location together with other Jews, had the audacity to rent houses among Christians in the most beautiful sections of town to the offense of our Lord God and to little honor for the city." When, sixty years later, following the general fashion of the day, the council decided to establish a formal ghetto in Padua, it allowed the Jews to make proposals about its location and boundaries. To prevent rent gouging it also provided that if Christian houseowners of the quarter and their new tenants could not agree on proper rentals, the city rectors would set the amounts in an equitable manner. But in the end the landlords were immediately allowed to raise the rents by 33 percent over and above what they had theretofore received. In a few cases competitive interests were so strong that, for instance, the Modena artisans, led by the guild of silk weavers, actually offered to defray the large expenses of relocating Jews into, and Christians out of, the ghetto. As a rule, however, the agitators for segregation fell back, genuinely or hypocritically, upon the old demands of canon law and claimed that, as enemies of Christ, Jews should always have lived apart from faithful Christians. It was their duty, therefore, to pay the heavy costs of remodeling old structures, adding such new buildings as synagogues and baths, erecting walls and gates, and compensating the Christian tenants for moving to other locations. For the most part, the authorities followed that policy. Jews facing an overpowering alliance of the rulers, the Church, and vested interests, could at most engage in delaying actions. As Anselmo del Banco (Asher Meshullam)—the Jewish negotiator who tried unsuccessfully to forestall the establishment of the Venetian ghetto and subsequently to reduce the communal taxes—had exclaimed when he surrendered to the state's exorbitant demands, "When will conflicts with power, power comes out uppermost." [48]

A by-product of ghetto legislation was the increasing ease with which the governments could control the admission of Jewish settlers. Although in earlier years the distinctive badge, wherever strictly enforced, made new Jewish arrivals readily recognizable, in many areas enforcement was rather lax and numerous unlicensed individuals found it none too difficult to infiltrate into cities without being instantly identified. Now, it devolved upon the Jewish community leadership itself closely to supervise immigration into the ghettos and to clear each new person's right of settlement with the proper authorities.

This obligation was not altogether unwelcome to the Jewish elders. Certain xenophobic manifestations had long been apparent in various Jewish communities, especially where competition by newcomers threatened to undermine the livelihood of important segments of the existing population. Soon after the establishment of the Mantuan ghetto in 1612, the communal board appointed a Committee of three elders to be in charge of all "outsiders who came, or wish to come, to live here in Mantua." On July 14, 1617, this Committee was authorized to petition the duke to prohibit further Jewish immigration, even from the duchy's provinces, because new arrivals would aggravate the crowded conditions in the ghetto and give the local Jews a bad name among their Christian neighbors. The Committee was even empowered to ask for the expulsion of all settlers of the preceding two years. On their part the rabbis were to excommunicate all transgressors, as well as individuals seeking special ducal exemptions without the consent of the community. As a result, the communal board was authorized by the government in 1624 to expel alien Jews with the aid of the Mantuan police. Five years later another local ordinance, approved by the duke, forbade the Mantuan Jews to accommodate "foreign" Jews at their homes or to rent them housing without a special ducal permit. In practice, to be sure, here and elsewhere, such restrictions were sometimes circumvented by individual negotiations with either ducal or Jewish authorities. Wealthy or learned would-be settlers were, as a rule, able to overcome the legal obstacles with relative ease. But the masses of poor and unskilled were more or less successfully kept away—a measure which sometimes appeared indispensable for the sheer survival of the existing community. In most ghettos the shortage of living space greatly intensified the struggle for the few locations still available and reinforced the already powerful communal controls. This situation thus helped more and more to convert the early modern Jewish community into a miniature "state within the state." Ironically, this development was unwittingly promoted by the increasingly authoritarian "enlightened absolutism," which was otherwise generally bent on curtailing local autonomy.[49]

Under these circumstances the Jewish leaders generally resisted the establishment of ghettos less fiercely than they contested, collectively or individually, the wearing of distinguishing marks. In the 1516 negotiations with Venice, they certainly voiced their preference for living in the city proper, rather than in the mainland suburb of Mestre. Although their representative, Anselmo del Banco, suggested placing the ghetto in the choice residential section of Murano, any location within the city was clearly far less exposed to enemy attack than Mestre, as was shown by the Jews' disastrous experiences during the war with the League of Cambrai seven years before. Characteristically, some Jewish communities themselves enjoyed living a sheltered existence. At least in Verona, about twenty years after the ghetto's establishment in 1600, the Jews proclaimed an annual festival in commemoration of the event. That *Purim Verona* was celebrated every year with the recitation of a poem composed by a local rabbi, Mordecai Bassano, and appropriate sermons. As late as 1765, but three decades before the city's occupation by the French Revolutionary army, the speaker on that occasion, Rabbi Menaḥem Navarra, exclaimed, "On that day the Lord brought out the children of Israel from the midst of the Gentiles and performed miracles for us. That is why we celebrate this great festival as a permanent and eternal memorial never to be forgotten, and we assemble to give thanks to His great name, may He be blessed, for He has done wonders for us." To extol the virtues of segregation, this well-educated rabbi quoted passages from the philosophic works of Aristotle and Maimonides, as well as from the Talmud and Midrash. In another connection we shall see how well territorial separation fit into the general pattern of Jewish corporate life during the medieval and early modern periods.[50]

Other segregationist measures were likewise pushed now with renewed vigor. Ever since the Fourth Lateran Council of 1215, the Church universal had been in the forefront of the struggle for the imposition of a Jewish badge, but in practice distinguishing marks had often been allowed to go into disuse. The municipality of Reggio nell'Emilia had even formally declared in 1437–38 that "Jews may walk through the city without a sign." In Mantua, too, a public announcement of 1509 freed the Jews from wearing badges "until further notice," because "soldiers annoy Jews wearing distinguishing marks." With the new religious enthusiasm generated by the Counter Reformation, however, the Church and its local organs opened a regular campaign to stimulate the renewal of old regulations and, wherever needed, the enactment of new ones. Even relatively liberal Mantua now tightened its provisions concerning Jewish badges in several decrees establishing regular tariffs of penalties for each transgression (they ranged from ten to thirty scudi according to an ordinance of 1577). For more effective enforcement, the authorities promised informers a share of one-third of the fine. Florence, too, insisted, in 1567, that Jews wear badges, Cosimo's secretary being told by the auditor, Francesco Vinta, that distinguishing marks were

convenient not only for the glory and honor of the Christian faith but also in order to serve as an example and good guidance for the faithful that he who lives outside the flock of Jesus Christ and obstinately walks to his eternal damnation, as does the Jew, should be differentiated by some outward sign from Christians. Just as he is intrinsically contrary to, and an enemy of, truth, he should also appear and be recognized as such externally.

This renewed drive produced immediate results throughout Italy, although in time the laxity of local officials and the Jews' growing aversion to this increasingly derogatory, costly, and sometimes perilous form of discrimination encouraged frequent evasions. The new Jewish settlers in Leghorn enjoyed, from the outset, a general exemption from that unpleasant duty. In its campaign to dissuade Duke Emmanuel Philibert from attracting Jews, including former Marranos, to Piedmont-Savoy, Spanish diplomacy emphasized the dangers of the absence of visible segregation. In his report to Philip II of December 12, 1572, the Milan governor Luis de Requesens, *commendador mayor* of Castile, insisted that "one of the matters which the duke concedes to them [the Jewish arrivals] and which appears to me highly unreasonable is that they may walk without a badge," for this concession would enable visitors from Spain and other countries to conceal their Jewish identity. Nonetheless, in many areas "privileged" Jewish bankers and others secured special exemptions. The very reiteration of the decrees concerning badges, for instance in Mantua, shows their ineffectiveness against the Jews' passive resistance. In contrast, the oath *more judaico* had become a relatively minor issue. The procedure, purified of its harshest folkloristic accretions, had been so firmly established and the formulas so well defined in the preceding generations that they apparently underwent very little change during the Counter Reformation era. With but few alterations they lasted well into the nineteenth century and were not immediately suspended even by the French emancipatory legislation.[51]

Segregation in daily life was likewise made more exacting. A Roman inquisitorial decree of 1598 simply stated that "Christians attending Jewish circumcisions, accepting breakfasts [*ientacula*] or unleavened bread, serving in the homes of Jews, conversing with them in a familiar vein, or discussing matters of faith with them shall be punished, together with those very Jews, by the Holy Office." This decree was renewed in 1628 (1629) with an additional clause warning against any interference with its execution. Jews were also often reminded that they must not employ Christian servants even for the performance of tasks prohibited to themselves on the Sabbath. The decree, promulgated on March 1, 1576, by Duke Guglielmo I in Mantua after the visit of a papal legate well summarized the numerous segregationist provisions adopted in various Italian states under the stimulus of Paul IV's bull *Cum nimis absurdum*. In keeping with the times, Jews and Christians were forbidden in many cities to exchange lessons in Latin or grammar, though there was no mention of Jews teaching Hebrew to Christians, perhaps because the Church recognized the necessity of using Jewish instructors in this field. Interfaith dancing and music lessons were prohibited, as was Jewish marriage-brokerage for Christians. Representative of the new segregationist drive was the proclamation issued by the Spanish governor of the duchy of Milan, Gabriele de la Cueva, duke of Albuquerque, on April 27, 1570:

In the cities, lands, and places of the said state [Milan] where Hebrews live, many Christians with little zeal for the honor of our Lord God, but rather to the greatest scandal of His holy faith, have ventured to visit parties and balls held in the houses of the said Jews, and to dance at those parties. . . . [Hence it is ordered] that any Christian found at a party held by Jews in their homes, or one who dances with a Jewess, shall incur the penalty of three lashes for the first time; be condemned to the galley for three years the second time; and for life on the third occasion. These penalties shall be carried out irreducibly against the disobedient.

However, all this was more or less *vieux jeu* in Judeo-Christian relations and wholly depended on the law-enforcement agencies, whose zeal abated again in the following generations. From the outset, moreover, practice differed widely from state to state, even locality to locality and, as before, many a hardship was mitigated by a properly timed douceur.[52]

Characteristically, there was relatively little emphasis on the old penalty of capital punishment for a Jew who had sexual relations with a Christian woman, possibly because that ultimate sanction had never been formally reduced. In contrast with Renaissance Italy, however, where such relations had become more frequent and the culprits, if prosecuted at all, were usually subjected only to moderate fines, the religious zeal generated by the Counter Reformation led both to greater moral restraint and to more stringent separation between the two faiths. In the Este possessions, for example, where Ercole I had in 1473 reduced the monetary fine for Jewish bankers apprehended in the act, later ordinances prohibited fornication even among Christians, under the sanction of galley slavery and a large fine of 500 gold scudi. These sharp penalties were repeated in an ordinance of 1686, but they had to be reduced in 1715 to 50 scudi, 5 lashes, and the obligation to marry the lady. Since for Jewish paramours such marriage was illegal, the ordinance gave much leeway to judges by providing that "the penalty shall consist of flogging, galley slavery, or even death." If few executions are recorded in Italy at that late date, the possibility that a puritanical judge, or one acting under the pressure of an excited populace, would impose the extreme penalty doubtless served as an effective deterrent. This contingency was enhanced by the hypocrisy often attached to the obscure domain of sex relations. Prostitution was so much taken for granted in Rome that in 1601 no less than 604 prostitutes were officially counted there in a population of 109,729. Their number almost doubled to 1,148, by 1650, while the total population had increased to only 126,192. Yet occasionally a member of that oldest profession was subjected to public flagellation. In 1628, when a condemned woman was on the point of being flogged, it sufficed for a passer-by to identify her as a Jewess for her to be burned alive. The mere threat of capital punishment, moreover, could well be used for monetary extortion. In 1538, the *podestà* of Reggio was led on a donkey through the streets of the city because of his part in a conspiracy against an amorous Jew. A Christian lady had arranged to have her Jewish suitor apprehended at her home by her "irate" husband, accompanied by the *podestà* and two assistants. The wealthy Jew got away by leaving with the lady a gold belt he had promised her, and by appeasing the husband and the officials with a gift of 400 scudi.[53]

OVERWEENING INQUISITION

Sex offenses and other breaches in the wall of Judeo-Christian segregation were added to the jurisdiction of the Holy Office as part of a general intensification of inquisitorial trials—a major facet, indeed, of the Counter Reformation. Clearly, the new drive toward religious conformity also had political implications. It has been said that the protest voiced by Machiavelli against the existing political structures had its counterpart in the religious protests of leading reformers such as Bernardino Ochino and Pietro Paolo Vergerio. Similarly, the Catholic Restoration implied as much the preservation of the established sociopolitical order as that of the established Church.

The Counter Reformation was aided in Italy by the growth of centralized absolutism in many states and the nationalist revulsion against the Germans, now viewed as the major foreign invaders. The intense anti-Teutonism among the Italian people discouraged many thoughtful individuals from following in Luther's footsteps and weakened their resistance to inquisitorial encroachments. Some, like a character in one of Matteo Bandello's novels, readily repeated the cliché that the tragic sack of Rome by the imperial troops in 1527 had been the work of "Lutherans, Marranos, and Jews." The ensuing expansion and strengthening of the authority of the Holy Office also had serious effects on Jewish communal and religious autonomy. The large-scale burning of rabbinic works and the renewed insistence that Jews be allowed no more than one synagogue in any locality—combined with the destruction or confiscation of synagogues and cemeteries abandoned by exiles, even if temporary—often played havoc with the Jewish way of life. In Venice the government resented the extensive use of bans by Jewish authorities and outlawed it completely in 1581, and again in 1606. In 1593 the Roman Inquisition, riding roughshod over religious scruples which had been deferred to even by Roman emperors before and after 313 c.e., ordered Jews summoned before the authorities to appear on the Sabbath. However, these more or less arbitrary infringements merely confirmed the general rule that the Catholic Restoration respected the traditional Jewish self-government in religious matters. More representative, therefore, of the Church's regnant policy was Clement VIII's renewal, after Ferrara was taken over from the Este dynasty in 1597–98, of the extensive judicial privileges theretofore enjoyed by the local Jews.[54]

The papal Inquisition now spread its tentacles to the rest of Italy, often defying the opposition of local regimes insistent upon their own sovereign prerogatives. In Spain and, to a lesser extent, in Portugal, the Holy Office largely served as a governmental agency, designed to promote royal absolutism and bureaucratic centralization, whereas in Italy, outside the Pontifical States, it was essentially a foreign institution, controlled by the international Papacy and often manned by foreign citizens. Moreover, here the religious deviations arising from the Protestant Reformation affected mainly individuals, rather than organized groups, and were so divergent in their ideologies that they hardly constituted a serious menace to Catholic conformity.

In Tuscany, for example, the religious controversies, quite extensive in the Middle Ages, received strong impetus through the reformatory work of Girolamo Savonarola and the liberalizing spirit of Humanism. Neither of these movements was aimed at undermining Catholic fundamentals; nonetheless, they, too, were submerged in the wave of intolerance engendered by the Counter Reformation. At the same time, not only was Tuscan Jewry shut up in the ghettos of Florence and Siena, but, since the country remained open to the incursions of Iberian Marranos, who outwardly appeared to be professing Catholics, these settlers became fit objects of prosecution by inquisitorial courts. Jurists like Francesco Vinta and Lelio Torelli argued in 1557 that the Inquisition had no jurisdiction over Jews, who could not be accused of Christian heterodoxy and hence were to be prosecuted only by secular authorities for any offenses they might have committed against the Christian faith. But they admitted that Marranos properly came under ecclesiastical control. So did such rabbinic works as had been condemned in 1553. The Spanish Inquisition, too, often stretched out its rapacious fingers toward Iberian refugees who had found shelter under the grand dukes of Tuscany. From documents preserved in the Inquisitorial Archives of Toledo, Haim

Beinart has shown that in 1629 the Madrid Inquisition had collected evidence against two secret Judaizers who had settled in Pisa, which, as a free port, was supposed to offer a safe haven to all new settlers. But the Spanish tribunal seems not to have expected to punish the "culprits" effectively unless they fell into the trap set for them in Seville, which they were said to have visited frequently on business. In fact, in *La Livornina* of 1593, addressed to foreign merchants, including Jews and Marranos, Grand Duke Ferdinand II had solemnly declared that for its duration "there shall be no inquisition, search, denunciation, or accusation against you or your families, even if in the past you lived, outside Our possessions, in the manner or under the name of Christians." This overt departure from the generally pursued ecclesiastical policies was strictly adhered to by the Tuscan administration. In 1730, when Jacob Gutierrez Penha, a recent arrival, was arrested by an overzealous inquisitor, his wife, Leah, successfully appealed to the Florentine authorities and he was immediately released.[55]

Growing popular piety and the enthusiastic drive to purify Catholic life of many shortcomings attacked by the reformers began affecting also the Church's attitude toward recent converts to Christianity. This contrast to the earlier indulgence is well illustrated by events in Siena and Ferrara two centuries apart. In 1438 and 1472 one Jacob Dattali, condemned for a variety of crimes (including theft, attempted rape of a Jewish minor, and cohabitation with Christian prostitutes), was allowed to go scot-free after accepting conversion. The Sienese *podestà* and court justified acquittal by arguing that, through his baptism, Jacob "had been reborn and hence had become a new man and ceased to be Jacob the Jew." In 1605, on the contrary, a Ferrara Jew, sentenced to galley servitude for counterfeiting [*pro falsitate*], was allowed to undergo conversion with his family, "but without delaying his penalty." Another Jew, who in 1635 had destroyed a picture of the Virgin, was handed over for execution by the secular arm, despite his baptism together with his entire family. Similarly, when four Roman Jews, condemned in 1607 for different crimes, turned Christian, they were not automatically released; they had to appeal directly to the pope for a pardon, pointing out to him that his forbearance might encourage some of their former coreligionists to accept conversion. Regrettably, the papal reply is not recorded.[56]

In Lombardy the problem of New Christians was complicated after 1535 by the Spanish domination. On the one hand, the royal officials sought to promote Catholic conformity with all means at their disposal. On the other hand, their very ardor inspired fears in the local population that the new regime might try to install in Milan an Inquisition after Spanish models. In his report to Pius V, even Cardinal Carlo Borromeo stressed those widespread suspicions that such an institution might be established "not so much because of religious zeal as for the interests of the State and the greed of one or another minister or councilor who in this way might be able to enrich himself from the fortunes of nobles and burghers." For the Jewish residents this threat was even more direct. Since their communities included members of Iberian origin, rumors about the cruel methods employed by the Holy Office in Spain must have created deep anxiety. Certainly, the Jews' old privileges were now seriously imperiled. During the fifteenth century Jews of many Lombard cities had acquired from Francesco Sforza and other dukes or municipal councils privileges which included specific provisions against inquisitorial prosecutions. A typical decree, issued by Philip Maria Visconti in 1435 and confirmed by the municipality of Novara in 1447, included the clause "that no ecclesiastical person nor any inquisitor or executor shall be able, or be allowed, in any way to inject himself into any negotiations or deeds performed by Hebrews or any of their persons." Torture, too, had been specifically forbidden by a Milanese ordinance in 1396, although its practice had become too ingrained in most criminal courts to be totally eliminated. Occasionally, we even hear of Jews, like one named Manno, who allegedly tried to convert Christians to Judaism, an allegation probably referring principally to relapsing converts. Curiously, under the very noses of the Spanish rulers a few Marranos for a while prospered in Milan without being directly subject to inquisitorial reprisals.[57]

Yet here, too, there was a sharp reaction. As in Rome the persecutions began with the burning of Jewish books. Under Julius III the Roman Inquisition informed other Italian states that the pope threatened capital punishment for Jews refusing to deliver their rabbinic works. A typical letter, dated September 16, 1553, notified the authorities of Milan:

We are unable to tolerate, as indeed we must not, nor conceal the blasphemies and impiety against the Lord God and human mores which the divine goodness has revealed to us manifested in the books of Jews they call the Talmud. These books contain many errors against the very law of Moses, the honor of the Lord God, and human beings. We have examined them with great care in the presence of their rabbis and found them full of crimes, examples of which we are submitting to your Excellency in the enclosed copy. We have, therefore, condemned and burned them publicly and forbidden them by strong edicts. Before God we request the same from all Christian princes.

The grand-inquisitor, Cardinal Michele Ghislieri, went even further with respect to Cremona, which was then developing into a major center of Hebrew printing. Having heard that a Cremona publisher had issued a new edition of the Talmud, he addressed, on December 11, 1557, a sharp letter to the Senate of Milan asking it to investigate that rumor. If true, the Senate was not only to destroy the forbidden books but also to see to it that the transgressors be duly punished according to the papal decree. This letter set in motion a protracted investigation and a rather tedious correspondence over the following two years. Although an inquiry by the *podestà* of Cremona showed that the city's only printer of Hebrew books, Vincentius, roundly denied printing any talmudic texts, and stated that for many years past no other printer in the city had been able to issue such texts, the matter did not come to rest. With the help of converts (among them Vittorio Eliano, grandson of Elijah Levita), the local inquisitors indiscriminately seized a large number of Hebrew books and long refused to part with them. The Jewish community protested the seizure of books previously permitted them by the local administration, a confiscation which also violated its long-established privileges. The Milanese Senate conceded the legitimacy of this complaint and, in a lengthy report to the governor of the duchy, dated January 23, 1559, it argued, among other matters, that many of the newly condemned books "not only contained nothing against the [Christian] religion, but did not even deal with subjects related to religion. On the contrary, they were of great service to students of various disciplines." At the same time the Senate also remonstrated against the confiscation of vernacular Bibles produced by some thirty local printers; the suppression of these works would cause severe financial losses to the publishers and would deprive women and other uneducated persons of access to Scripture. Ultimately, the inquisitors were forced to return to the Jews books which demonstrably had not been placed on the papal Index (even the comprehensive Index issued by Paul IV in 1559), but they destroyed all Hebrew books having any more or less direct relationship with talmudic literature. The Holy Office was abetted in this move by the local priests who, appealing to the masses over the heads of their rulers, incited the populace to expel the "Jewish dogs," or else face ruin because of the blasphemies against Christ contained in the Talmud. "Their slightest blasphemy would suffice to ruin ten cities." [58]

This upsurge of inquisitorial prying augured badly for the few Marranos who had found their way into Lombardy. In his original letter to the Milanese Senate of December 11, 1557, Ghislieri complained of having heard that "a very large number of men popularly called Marranos, whom our most holy lord [Paul IV] had caused to be ejected from the city of Ancona," had found their way into Milan. "I most urgently exhort your lordships to take care that this pest be expelled from the city, as was done by the most illustrious and prudent duke of Urbino. Nor shall you tolerate that it persist in any other localities of the duchy of Milan." The grand-inquisitor made no distinction here between New Christians who genuinely professed Christianity and those who lived as secret Jews. Such wholesale condemnation opened the gate to prosecution of professing Jews, too, particularly if they were of Iberian origin. In vain did the Senate contend that no Marranos had settled in the duchy. It invoked the testimony of the *podestà* of Cremona based on questioning not only Vittorio Eliano but also two Jewish leaders, who enumerated to him independently the names of all their coreligionists in the city. Likewise independently each had assured him that for at least the past four years no Marrano had been seen in Cremona. All these vicissitudes ended in 1597, when, all Jews of whatever origin were expelled from the duchy.[59]

In contrast to the community in Milan, Mantuan Jewry seems

to have experienced few difficulties with the Inquisition. To be sure, a Holy Office functioned in the city as early as the thirteenth century. In 1486, and again in 1492, Francesco Gonzaga ordered the secular authorities to lend a helping hand to the local inquisitor "in accordance with the canonical sanctions and the statute of Mantua." Alarmed by the spread of Protestantism, even the fairly liberal Cardinal Ercole Gonzaga sponsored a series of trials, some of which led to the burning of the exhumed bodies of deceased heretics. Other "culprits" were put to flight, including Francesco Stancari, who founded a little sect of his own in Germany. Three heretics were burned alive in 1568. This happened after Ercole's death, however. We also recall the cardinal's friendly relations with some Mantuan Jewish leaders, especially during the sessions of the Council of Trent. Doubtless under his influence, the authorities in 1558 allowed the printing of the *Zohar,* although their imprimatur may have been owing in part to the belief of some humanists that they had found in that kabbalistic classic evidence for the truth of Christian doctrines. More significantly, even after inquisitorial activities intensified during the pontificate of Pius V, the Mantuan Inquisitor Giovanni Battista da Milano in 1572 authorized several Paduan Jews to publish and sell Maimonides' Code with Joseph Karo's commentary thereon. Nor do we hear of any prosecution of local Marranos during the Counter Reformation era. Yet, only a few New Christians seem to have settled in the city. Perhaps the spectacular burning there of the brilliant and widely revered Solomon Molkho in 1532 served as a strong warning for other Marranos. Since Mantua's trade was mainly oriented toward the Empire and the Italian mainland, rather than toward the Mediterranean harbors, the city attracted fewer Levantine and Ponentine settlers. The Jewish majority, consisting of Ashkenazic Jews, may also have evinced less sympathy for the New Christians, whose orthodoxy and rabbinic learning it, not unjustifiedly, held in rather low esteem now, several generations after the Iberian expulsions. Being largely in control of the admission of new Jewish settlers, the elders may indeed have felt that the new arrivals might give the entire community a "bad name" among its Christian neighbors, a fear which, as we recall, strengthened their xenophobia.[60]

Mantua seems to have been an exception, however. A report submitted to Pope Pius IV in 1564 concerning Portuguese developments boldly asserted that "there is no city in Italy where there are no Portuguese Marranos, fugitives of the Portuguese Inquisition. Being able as Christians to engage in any kind of business, many become rich, whereupon they emigrate to Turkey, where they inform the Turks about anything happening here. . . . This has been the state of affairs from the time they were converted to Christianity until today." Ever since Paul IV the Papacy had abandoned the more liberal interpretation once given by Paul III to the status of Marranos. It had reverted to the older position of canon jurists that a convert, once baptized without "absolute" force, had to profess Christianity to the end of his life. In the case of the Portuguese Marranos there was no question that all Jews living in Portugal in 1498 had been forcibly converted, though not necessarily through a *vis absoluta* in the technical sense. At least some of them or their offspring may have neglected to go through the ceremony of baptism. Paul IV, however, overruled all such considerations. In his edict of April 30, 1556, he declared that all judaizing New Christians were to be treated as apostates and punished accordingly,

notwithstanding their persistent negation under torture that they had been baptized, had ever lived as Christians, performed Christian works, or partaken of any ecclesiastical sacraments. For it has become obvious and clear to the Holy Faith and it is accepted that, for some sixty years, no Hebrews would have been allowed to dwell in Lusitania or Portugal unless they were baptized and lived as Christians.

From the standpoint of canon law and this official papal interpretation Paul IV's view now permanently prevailed. The only proof of guilt an inquisitor needed was that the particular New Christian defendant had been practicing certain Jewish rites. Even the fairly tolerant Gregory XIII, as we recall, in 1580 induced Alphonso II of still liberal Ferrara indiscriminately to expel all Marranos from his duchy.[61]

Paul III's more liberal view was to find an eloquent, if not wholly effective, champion in Paolo Sarpi, on whom the Venetian authorities were to lean heavily in their momentous dispute with Pope Paul V. Bent on upholding the sovereignty of their Republic, they long tried to limit the independent authority of inquisitorial tribunals. While their frequent complaints that these courts were manned almost exclusively by foreigners went unheeded, the doge and his associates insisted that every major move by the Holy Office require the cooperation of secular officials.

Under these circumstances the Marrano colony grew rather freely, subject only to the frequent general political and military changes characteristic of Venice's international relations. Even the two expulsions of Marranos in 1497 and 1550, adopted by the Senate with a vote of 119:36 (with 5 abstentions) and of 146:25 (with 29 abstentions), respectively, were engendered more by secular than by religious interests. True, the authorities borrowed from ecclesiastical terminology when they spoke, on November 13, 1497, of some Marranos having used "sinister and detestable methods" to gain admission to the Republic. They also claimed that the New Christians "in possession of abundant funds, and greedy for personal advancement, do not hesitate to commit many wrongs to the universal damage and injury of this city and its very faithful people." The Senate resolution of July 8, 1550, likewise referred to these settlers as "an infidel people, without religion, and wholly inimical to our Lord God" and stated that expulsion had become necessary so "that this contagious sort of people be kept away from our state." The Marranos were told to leave all the Venetian possessions within two months, under the sanction of the confiscation of all their property and two years of galley servitude. The same penalty was to be imposed upon all unlawfully returning exiles and upon all nobles, burghers, and other subjects hiding or otherwise helping such delinquents to evade the law. Informers were promised a third of the yield of confiscations. Soon, however, the authorities were swamped with protests from merchants doing business with Marranos, both resident and foreign, whose converso identity, they claimed, they were in no position to ascertain. The government had to undertake, therefore, the difficult task of identifying each suspected trader as a Marrano. It also had to extend departure time of the prospective exiles for an additional six months, and exempt all nonresident New Christians from the original ukase. The enforcement of the 1550 decree was, in fact, so lax that, as early as July 6, 1555, Domenico Morosini, Venetian ambassador to Rome, was induced by the Roman Inquisition to complain to his Council of Ten that, "according to certain indications, there are in Venice many Christians who have returned to Judaism to the injury of Our Saviour Jesus Christ. When one was incarcerated, certain agents of [foreign] princes intervened in his favor." The Council paid little heed to this complaint, although it had more readily submitted to Carafa's earlier outlawry of rabbinic books, which had actually had specific Venetian antecedents. The ensuing destruction of valuable Hebrew books and manuscripts was the more severe a blow to Jewish culture, as Venice had theretofore been the world's major center of Hebrew printing. Even if the publishers and printers were predominantly Christian and included many members of the city's patrician families, the editors and proofreaders were, for the most part, Jewish scholars.[62]

However, the rulers soon recognized that the resulting material losses to the Republic and its trade were greater than it could afford during that period of recession in its international commerce. By 1580 they were ready to admit Marrano refugees from Ferrara openly, though they knew that they would incur the displeasure of Gregory XIII, the initiator of the Ferrara exodus. Venice was now also prepared to defend its sovereignty in the religious sphere more vigorously. It refused, in particular, to grant to the Inquisition, which was generally despised by the otherwise rather conforming population, the wholly autonomous authority to which it aspired. The Venetian courts argued that they could not relinquish their authority over cases which involved inheritance laws. In fact, in a remarkable case, reported in a lengthy dispatch to Rome by the papal nuncio Alberto Bolognetti (1578–81), one Giovanni Ribiera, son of a Portuguese Christian merchant in Venice, married "a noble Jewish woman, a relative of Giovanni Miches [Don Joseph Nasi], a most favorite person among the Turks." He moved to the ghetto and lived there with her publicly in a legitimate union, promising her that as soon as he settled his affairs he would emigrate as a professing Jew to Turkey. His father, Gaspar, approved of the marriage and in writing promised 3,000 scudi to his daughter-in-law. Before long, however, Giovanni died and his widow sued Gaspar for the pledged amount. This litigation led to a lengthy inquisitorial investigation of Gaspar Ribiera as a Judaizer; at the time of Bolognetti's report, the inquiry had not yet been concluded. In the same dispatch the nuncio also mentioned that some Venetian Jews had been accused of having purchased a number of Moorish children transported from Arabia to Aleppo and of having converted them to Judaism. The defendants denied that allegation and argued that these children were their own offspring by Moorish women, a contention supported by the presence of quite a few Moors among the inhabitants of the Venetian ghetto. In neither case, it appears, did the Venetian secular authorities take an active part in the prosecution. Nor did the Serenissima hesitate to tolerate individual heretics and others considered undesirable by the Church, including Pietro Aretino and Giordano Bruno. (Bruno's subsequent burning at the stake in Rome is vividly described in an inquisitorial document of February 17, 1600.) Neither did the Venetian authorities prevent professors of the University of Padua from spreading Averroist teachings which, readily expounded in the more broad-minded age of the Renaissance, were now outlawed by the ecclesiastical censors. On February 11, 1558, a Jesuit, Benedetto Palmio, wrote to Diego Laynez that "this Paduan territory is full of heretics," a statement which cannot be checked against the local inquisitorial archives, long since destroyed. According to Bolognetti, the Venetian authorities defended their noninvolvement by stressing Padua's autonomous rights, as well as their fear to offend the German people.[63]

Finally, this divergence led to an open break with the Papacy in 1606–1607. During the subsequent politicoreligious conflict, the friar Paolo Sarpi defended the Republic's position in speeches and pamphlets, and sharply denounced the entire approach of the Inquisition. Among other matters he argued against any form of forced conversion. In the case of a child baptized in 1615 without the consent of her mother (a prostitute), he seemed inclined to accept the argument that baptism, even if performed wrongly, "is a more pious deed and a greater favor and reverence to the holy faith" and hence that the girl should not be returned to her mother, who would bring her up as a Jewess; however, he contended that Marranos, who had never willingly adhered to Christianity, had the right to give up a religion imposed upon them by force. In his stress on the primacy of secular courts to pass judgment on religious transgressions against Christianity by Jews and other infidels, Sarpi also claimed that

in 1581 Pope Gregory XIII issued a bull against the Jews in which he subjected them, as well as other infidels, to the jurisdiction of the Inquisition in ten cases. These were so widely drawn that, if the bull had been observed, no infidel could reside or trade in a Christian land. Although printed, the bull was promulgated and accepted in but a few localities. Moreover, Popes Sixtus V and Clement VIII, paying no heed to it, granted safe-conducts to Marranos in the city of Ancona. . . . In short . . . the office of the Inquisition has been instituted against heresy, and it is incorrect to extend [its authority] to other transgressions.

Abandoned by her allies, to be sure, Venice was forced to her knees by a papal interdict in 1607, and the government now had to give more leeway to the inquisitorial courts. Nevertheless, lacking prestige among the population and deprived of firm backing by governmental authorities, the Holy Office proved quite ineffective in the City of the Lagoons. If during the half century of 1550–1600 it had prosecuted altogether 20 persons, only half that number were tried during the following one hundred and twenty years. In its instructions of June 1, 1621, to the new nuncio Paolo Emilio Zacchia, the Roman Curia admitted that the papal victory over Venice had had few enduring effects, and complained of the dangers arising from "the commerce of heretics and schismatics who are much too freely admitted to the city." Indeed, all along many distinguished Marrano merchants and scholars had lived in Venice, as well as in Padua and Verona, without serious interference. By 1651 a cleric complained that among the inhabitants of the Venetian ghetto were "many Portuguese wearing red hats [the mark of a Jew] who had served as Christian priests in Portugal." In short, the Republic's political and economic self-interest gained precedence over its otherwise well-attested quest for Catholic conformity.[64]

Similarly, in Piedmont-Savoy the government was protective of the incoming New Christians. In 1572 three or four Portuguese families were expressly allowed to settle in Turin, the government arguing with the papal nuncio that this permission was not sinful. When two of his Jewish bankers were imprisoned on their journey from Ferrara, Duke Emmanuel Philibert of Piedmont speedily obtained their release. Although eight years later his successor, Charles Emmanuel I, expelled all "Portuguese" (with some exceptions) from his country, the relatively few Marranos who subsequently lived in Piedmont-Savoy seemed to have suffered little from the local Inquisition. In other parts of Italy, too, prosecutions were relatively rare and affected Jewish books more than persons. Here and there contemporary documents recall the presence of "Portuguese" who had allegedly lived as Jews in their home country. For instance, an undated record of Urbino under the reign of Duke Francesco Maria II della Rovere (1574–1631) mentions the presence of such individuals, but there is no indication of real burnings of "Judaizers" in seventeenth-century Italy.[65]

Remarkably, even Naples, which had expelled all Jews and Marranos in 1541 was not completely devoid of judaizing tendencies. We learn, for example, of the return to Naples in 1543 of two students from Padua who, having been inspired by some of the sympathizers of Reform among their teachers, allegedly tried to spread heresies in their native city. We are also told that they visited there a Spaniard, Juan de Villafranca (d. 1545), who

negated the invocation of saints, purgatory, confession, and the authority of popes, generally maintaining Lutheran opinions; he also denied the presence of our Lord Christ in the most sacred sacrament of the altar. Ultimately, he became an Anabaptist, rejected the divinity of our Saviour, Jesus Christ, and repudiated part of the Gospel of St. John and those of other evangelists attesting Christ's divinity.

One suspects that Villafranca may have been a first-generation New Christian or have been influenced by Jewish or New Christian friends who lived in Naples before the expulsion. More remarkably, in 1571 twelve Catalan ladies were made to retract their judaizing beliefs in a public ceremony held in front of the Naples Cathedral. In the following year a provincial synod meeting in Lanciano, under the chairmanship of Archbishop Antonio Rodriguez, resolved "that Christians should not receive Jews [or New Christians] in their homes, eat with them, or serve them; nor shall those Jews enter the Church of Santa Maria, except when sermons are preached." Nor did the religious zeal of the local clergy spare Jewish visitors to Lanciano fairs. On July 20, 1613, the episcopal vicar-general, accompanied by several priests, suddenly arrested six Anconitan Jewish merchants while they were attending a Sabbath service in the local synagogue [schola]. According to the Jewish complaint, the vicar also seized some books which had always been placed there "for the common use of all Jews." Apparently the merchants were released and were enabled to attend to their business at the fair.[66]

All this inquisitorial activity against Judaizers in Italy was but a side show, however. The main efforts were concentrated on extirpating all forms of Protestant heresies, which, because of their very diversity and relative lack of appeal to the Italian national tradition, affected small groups, rather than masses of the population. If, by combining fine humanistic training with great religious fervor, some "heretics" played a greater historic role than might appear from the number of their followers, many were forced to leave the country; they became important Reform leaders in Zurich, Basel, Geneva, Strasbourg, Holland, and particularly Poland-Lithuania. We shall see that they had a strong impact also on the destinies of the rapidly growing Polish Jewish community.

NEW MISSIONARY EFFORTS

Concomitant with this struggle against the Protestant reformers was a revitalized Catholic mission among Jews, Muslims, and others. Not only were new missionary tracts of all kinds written and widely distributed among the Jewish masses, often with the aid of Jewish converts, but a vast polemical literature against the teachings of Judaism now reached, by means of the printing presses, unprecedented circulation. Fino Fini's *Flagellum in Judaeos* was published by his son in Venice in 1538, some nineteen years after the author's death. The Jewish convert to Christianity Giulio Cesare Misuracchi published his "Reasonings for the Advent of the Messiah against Jewish Obduracy and Stubbornness" in Orvieto in 1629, while Ignazio Landriani's "Demonstration against Hebrews and Heretics," regarding the divinity of Christ, appeared in Milan in 1641. Few novel ideas or arguments were presented in this literature. Most authors simply borrowed weapons long before assembled in the armory of medieval oral and literary controversies. Even the thirteenth-century classic the *Pugio fidei* by Raymond Martini was now popularized, especially under the influence of the writings by Porchetus de Salvaticis and Petrus Galatinus. Remarkably, the most important apologist of the early seventeenth century, Tommaso Campanella, who had debated religious issues with Protestants but, beginning in 1610, evinced special interest in the conversion of Jews and Muslims, was not wholly accepted in the more conservative Catholic circles. Although his treatise *Per la conversione degli Ebrei*, part of a larger work, *Quod reminiscentur*, was completed in 1618, its publication was delayed by the papal Curia until 1630, because some of its philosophic teachings deviated from the official doctrine. Nor were the Italian reformers any more averse to propagandizing their faith among Jews than were their northern confreres. Even extremists like the visionary Leone Nardi (or Giovanni Leonardi), living as an émigré in Switzerland, who repudiated both Catholics and Evangelicals as equally desirous to bring about the death of the Church, that "saintly and honest Susanna who refuses to fornicate with them," did not hesitate to publish in Basel, in 1553, a comprehensive tract against Islam and Judaism. He contended that not only Jews but also Muslims had misunderstood their own Scriptures because they had failed to see in them the confirmation of the advent of Christ.[67]

On their part Jews were now far more reluctant to reply in kind than they had been in the Middle Ages. Printing presses could be readily supervised, even suppressed, by alert censors; whereas individual copyists, usually scattered over a wide area, had been financially less dependent on the sizable distribution of any particular work. When the prolific Leon da Modena composed, among numerous other works, a Hebrew reply to Christian controversialists under the title *Magen ve-Hereb* (Shield and Sword), he was so fearful of inquisitorial reprisals that he never had it printed. (Not until 1960 did Shlomo Simonsohn issue it in the Hebrew original.) So terrorized were many Italian Jewish authors in the era of the Catholic Restoration that Leon, after composing his classic treatise on Jewish rituals, which was clearly devoid of any anti-

Christian animus, denounced himself to the Venetian Inquisition in order to obtain formal clearance for his book. His *Riti* secured, indeed, a surprisingly wide circulation in the Christian world, not only in its Italian original but also in early French and English translations.[68]

Of course, in that highly articulate age filled with religiopolitical tensions, polemics could be written on almost any subject and did not necessarily pursue immediately practical aims; they may have served merely to satisfy their authors' literary ambitions, sometimes verging on graphomania. A large segment of the controversialist literature, though outwardly addressed to Jews and Muslims, may have been essentially an exercise in literary skill and ingenuity, or been intended to fortify the faith of wavering Catholics. Tommaso Campanella, for instance, called by a recent writer "the philosopher of the Catholic Restoration," never tried to propagate his faith among the infidels in a Muslim country, nor did he preach to Jewish audiences. His tracts were evidently addressed principally to like-minded Christians. Written in the customarily vituperative style of contemporary polemics, they could only have discouraged Jewish or Muslim readers. Certainly, Muslims would not have acquiesced to the comparison of Mohammed with a pig, in the opening page of Campanella's anti-Islamic treatise. But such invectives greatly appealed to the crude tastes of the religiously intolerant mass of Christian readers of the time.[69]

Far more effective in gaining proselytes were the financial and administrative measures adopted by the Church. Here, too, the Catholic Restoration merely had to reinforce methods long used in the medieval propagation of the faith, and to refine them in certain details appropriate for the new age. As before, prospective converts were accommodated in houses of catechumens wherever such existed; but they were protected in their property and inheritance rights much more extensively than in the Middle Ages. Alexander VII, for instance, provided in 1659 that converts who became priests, and hence were unable to stay married even if their wives were also baptized, were not obliged to return the latter's dowries or wedding presents. Some municipalities were more generous and gave new converts substantial subsidies to start their new life. In Padua several gifts of 50 ducats each are recorded dur-

ing the first half of the seventeenth century. In time, however, as
the financial condition of the city deteriorated and perhaps the
number of converts increased, the city elders were far less magnanimous. When a Jewish woman was baptized in 1673, she received
no donation. In contrast, the 1622 baptism of Derea, daughter of
Simone Mantua of the founding family of the small Jewish community in San Daniele di Friuli, so impressed the city fathers that
they gave her no less than 200 ducats. To encourage conversions
further the system of obligatory attendance at Christian sermons
now spread to many Italian cities outside the Pontifical States.
Canon law also emphasized the one-sided character of acceptable
conversions, those of Jews to Islam, or vice versa, being strictly
prohibited. Jews purchasing Turkish prisoners and manumitting
them on the condition that they would adopt Judaism were to be
severely punished.[70]

Most annoying to Jews was the new interpretation of the old canonical outlawry of forced conversions, particularly of children.
The Papacy and the Roman Inquisition now decided that children aged seven and over might be admitted to baptism at their
own discretion, if they were considered mentally mature enough
to be capable of committing a felony (*doli capaces;* 1638). To add
insult to injury, parents of minors converted without their consent
were obliged to pay for the childrens' support. Going further,
some zealous laymen time and again took the law into their own
hands and baptized younger Jewish boys and girls without their
parents' approval. Although such acts were a clear violation of
canon law, the new interpretation tried to legitimize them after
the act. In Modena a Christian surgeon and a nurse, attending a
sick Jewish child, persuaded the father to bring them water in
order to alleviate the child's fever. While applying the water to
the child's forehead the surgeon mumbled the baptismal formula
under his breath. Informed of this action, a priest had the child
snatched from the parental home; it was never returned to its parents despite vigorous protests by the community. Lawless acts of
this kind had occurred in the Middle Ages, too, but they now became far more frequent; they aggravated the Jewish feeling of insecurity even in relatively tolerant communities like Modena. At
the same time, the Italian Church could not wholly escape the ra-

cist influences emanating from the Iberian Peninsula. Contrary to the long-established canonical equality of converts and born Christians, an inquisitorial decree of 1611 provided that "men of Jewish ancestry shall not be admitted to the office of canons in cathedral churches, dignities in chapters, and benefices having charge of human souls." Little did the inquisitors realize how much they were thereby impeding the Church's chief aim of promoting conversions.[71]

Among all the discriminatory measures taken by the Papacy, the burning of the Talmud made the deepest and most lasting impression upon the Jews. Using the numerical equivalence of the year [5]314 (1553–54) and *Shaddai,* the Hebrew designation of the Almighty, some writers applied to that year the biblical sentences "For the Almighty hath dealt very bitterly with me" (Ruth 1:20) and "The Almighty shall be among thy foes [*be-ṣarekha*]" (Job 22:25). Some contemporaries not only composed dirges on this sad event but, like Menaḥem Abraham b. Jacob ha-Kohen Rapa of Porto, thereafter commemorated it by an annual fast day, "for that day was as mournful as that of the burning of our Lord's House." Another contemporary, Mattatiah b. Solomon Delacrut, who succeeded in escaping from Italy to Poland, entered into his hitherto unpublished Book of Reminiscences the following reference to the auto-da-fé:

In the metropolis of Venice they burned more than one thousand books of the complete Talmud, apart from five hundred copies of *Alfasi* and other works without end, both new and old. . . . I have succeeded in salvaging my books, which happened to be within my reach, from the turmoil and have brought them with God's help to my place of refuge, the city of Brest [Brześć] in the land of Rus, where I have established my residence. . . . I have decided to record in writing what I have learned there from my teachers and from the books which the Lord salvaged for me . . . so that they may serve as a reminder for me in the days of my old age.

Another author, Yehudah b. Samuel Lerma, had the shattering experience of seeing the entire edition of 1,500 copies of his newly printed Commentary on the Sayings of the Fathers—a book which dealt with ethical, rather than religiously controversial, problems —seized and consigned to the flames. Undaunted, he began writing it anew. After completing three chapters, he chanced on a copy salvaged from the fire by some Gentiles and he rejoiced at finding that his new version was an improvement upon the original text.[72]

Nor was this new manifestation of literary intolerance a merely temporary outburst. We recall that for years thereafter some anti-Jewish popes and inquisitors relentlessly pursued the suppression of rabbinic literature in Cremona, Venice, and other centers of Jewish learning. As late as 1629 Cardinal Desiderio Scaglia referred to pontifical letters demanding the destruction of copies of the Talmud found in Recanati, an old but now greatly weakened focus of rabbinic and kabbalistic studies. The cardinal wrote, doubtless with some exaggeration, that 10,000 copies of the Talmud and other outlawed rabbinic works had been assembled and marked for destruction. All Italian Jewry was thus forced to make grave intellectual and educational adjustments in order to pursue its traditional studies without the aid of these basic texts.[73]

VITALITY WITHOUT ALARM

Viewed in its totality the Counter Reformation slowed down, checked, and even completely reversed certain earlier trends of Italian Jewish history. The revived Catholic enthusiasm interfered with the growing integration of the Jewish communities into Italian life during the Renaissance era. The burning of Jewish books had a profound psychological effect on both Jews and Christians, who but a short time before had observed some of the same Hebrew works enjoying quite a vogue among Christian Hebraists. The Jewish losses of entire libraries, collections often accumulated over several generations of patient acquisition, were staggering. Most significantly, the Papacy for the first time resorted to the expedient of banishing Jews from its Italian provinces. Elsewhere in Italy, the establishment of formal ghettos, under the impact of the papal example and often on ecclesiastical initiative, graphically underscored the new segregation. On the other hand, outside the Pontifical States and Tuscany, seclusion in ghettos was not accompanied by the elimination of the Jews from the countryside. We must realize, moreover, that separate Jewish quarters had for a long time been a normal feature of Jewish life and that in most areas the majority of Jews preferred to concentrate in Jewish streets without any governmental compulsion.

Not even the powerful Catholic drive to suppress heresy seriously affected Italian Jewish life. True, at some autos-da-fé a number of Marranos "sanctified the name of the Lord"; most dramatically in Ancona in 1556. However, these bloody persecutions were quite sporadic. While the Inquisition caused many New Christians to live dangerously, its main concern was to uproot the Protestant movements, a task which, aided by the genuine upsurge of Catholic piety, it rapidly accomplished. The occasional imitation of Spanish racialist practices and the withholding of higher ecclesiastical dignities from New Christians were, in fact, exceptions confirming the rule that converts from Judaism were generally welcomed by Italy's Christian society and rather speedily assimilated. In certain areas, such as Leghorn, the Venetian Republic, and the duchy of Piedmont-Savoy, even secret Jews lived more or less undisturbed in the late sixteenth and early seventeenth centuries.

At the same time we must not overlook the constant anguish and sufferings of the Jewish masses. Regrettably, the man of the Jewish street was no more articulate than his compeer living in a Christian quarter. Niccolò Rodolico has rightly observed that the story of the grandeur of early modern Italian civilization readily overlooks "the most unhappy life of the people at large. . . . Famines and epidemics, new terrible diseases heaped upon the old" were the constant accompaniment of life for the downtrodden masses. The chasm separating the upper from the lower classes grew ever deeper. "One [man] negotiates a loan of 100,000 florins, while the poor die of hunger," observed a Florentine chronicler in 1496. This contrast was doubly manifest a century or two later. In the Jewish case, such gaps were partly bridged by the existing strong communal controls and the people's inner solidarity in the face of an indiscriminate persecution of its members of all classes. Nevertheless, the ordinary Jews must have been affected by the discriminatory legislation even more severely than their wealthier and more learned coreligionists. We recall the complaint of the Roman elders that the large majority of their community were dependent on charity. But this very charitableness of the Jews, which expressed itself through the work of numerous philanthropic societies as well as the community at large and exceeded in effectiveness the social welfare operations under the control of the Church—there was little other public welfare available—created many psychological compensations for both givers and recipients. These facets of life were conducive to instilling in many Jews a pride in their heritage and greatly contributed to Jewish survival.[74]

Perhaps the most remarkable feature of Italian Jewish life during the early modern period was the people's great inner vitality, which helped it overcome most difficulties. Its ever-present powers of resurgence and self-renewal are clearly attested by its numerical growth notwithstanding the losses inflicted by voluntary and forced conversions, recurrent pestilences, and the endless hardships occasioned by forced migrations. True, as a result of the numerous expulsions, the total area of Jewish settlement shrank considerably during the sixteenth century, and it was allowed to expand but little in the following more stable decades. But in the communities which tolerated Jews, their number constantly increased, at a rate usually exceeding that of the Gentile population. This growth can be accounted for only partially by immigration from other parts of Italy, from Germany, and the Iberian lands.

A few illustrations will suffice: The Roman community, which had numbered some 3,000 souls at the time of its transfer to the ghetto in 1555, rose to about 4,500 a century later, and continued to grow despite the disproportionately large loss of 1,600 members (amounting to some 11 percent of all the dead in the city) during the pestilence of 1656, and the constant drain by conversions. If it be true that between 1634 and 1790 no less than 2,430 Jewish residents of the papal capital changed their faith, that high ratio may well have been equaled, if not exceeded, during the preceding eight decades of more passionate Counter Reformation and conversionist activity. By way of contrast, far more tolerant Ferrara is said to have witnessed only 94 conversions during the seventy years before the city's integration into the Papal States. In Venice, fairly reliable government statistics reveal the presence of only 902 Jews in a total population of 158,067 in 1552. The number of Jews rose to 1,694 in a diminished total population of 148,640 inhabitants in 1586, to increase again, after an intermediate decline, to 2,414 in a total of 98,244 in 1632. The last ratio doubtless was distorted by the great loss of lives from the severe pestilence of 1630, a loss which in the case of Jews probably was made up during the following two years by the large-scale immigration from Venetian provinces, and particularly from Mantua, whence the Jews were temporarily expelled in 1630. Subsequently, both the general and the Jewish population recovered, allegedly reaching a total of 4,870 Jews in a population of 158,722 in 1655. The Jews' numerical growth in Mantua was no less spectacular. The Jewish population, estimated in 1500 at no more than 200 (within a total of some 32,000 inhabitants) in the city and 100 in the provinces, increased ninety-one years later to 1,591 Jewish "mouths," that is, persons over three years of age considered consumers of grain, in the city (in a total population of 50,000) and to 253 "mouths" in the provinces. By the time the Mantuan Jews moved into the ghetto in 1610–12 their number had further increased to 2,325 persons in the city (in a generally stationary population) and to between 500 and 700 Jews in the provinces. Writing in 1638, Simone Luzzatto, a careful observer, estimated the entire Jewish population in Italy at 25,000, probably a slight understatement. These data, the significance of which will become clearer in our general review of Jewish social life during that period, testify to the great resilience of Italian Jewry in that era of severe persecutions.[75]

The economic and intellectual consequences of the Counter Reformation upon Italian Jewry were nevertheless far-reaching. True, the general crisis of the Italian economy paralleled, rather than resulted from, the new religious conservatism. Forces beyond the control of the religious leaders gradually shifted the centers of European economic life from the old Mediterranean emporia to the upsurging maritime powers of Holland and England. But Italy's adherence to certain outworn economic principles, even if they had been quite innovative in their Renaissance heyday, now proved to be a retarding influence. In Jewish life, too, a quiescent pause, a stabilization of sixteenth-century economic achievements, replaced the earlier dynamic upswing. Even among the leading Jewish moneylenders of the Venetian Republic or the Grand

Duchy of Tuscany, there were few bankers to rival the House of Da Pisa of the early sixteenth century. Only the opening of new avenues of trade by the Sephardic immigrants to Venice and Leghorn prevented these communities from stagnating economically like the Jewry of Rome, the largest among them.

Intellectually, Italian Jewry in the Counter Reformation era likewise lost much of its élan of the preceding century. On the Christian side, the deep interest of many Renaissance leaders in Hebrew letters now gave way to a more restrained, if not altogether negative, appraisal of the Jewish heritage. We recall that, under the impact of the Council of Trent and such eminent Catholic thinkers as the Cardinals Borromeo and Bellarmine, even biblical studies were carefully delimited, lest they weaken in the slightest the supreme authority of the Vulgate. Personal exchanges between Jewish and Christian scholars became less frequent and intimate. If the Jewish masses continued increasingly to absorb elements of Italian speech and culture, this was essentially the result of the inevitable time lag between the impact of the cultural revolution of the Renaissance on the leading Jewish minds and its gradual penetration into the broader circles of the population. On the top levels of Jewish intellectual endeavor, however, there was a pronounced return to the more traditional Jewish domains of rabbinic and kabbalistic learning. To be sure, individual Jewish artists and musicians continued to flourish in the seventeenth century, but their number and influence among their coreligionists greatly declined. For example, Jewish historiography, which had suddenly flowered in the sixteenth century under the leadership of such historians as Azariah de' Rossi, now reverted largely to the more traditional, medieval type of chronicling. These aspects of cultural reorientation will be more fully analyzed in later chapters. But the most important fact of the crucial transformations of the century of 1550–1650 was that the Italian Jewish body politic, despite the numerous wounds inflicted upon it by antagonistic popes and rulers, had remained a basically intact and healthy community looking forward to a brighter future.

LXI

IMPERIAL TURMOIL

EVELOPMENTS in the Holy Roman Empire during the reassertion of Catholic power at first appeared even more threatening to the Jews than the parallel trends in Italy. Rather than immediately benefiting from the internecine struggle between the Christian sects, the German Jews could have sensed that the religious peace proclaimed by the Diet of Augsburg in 1555, with its tacit recognition of the principle *Cujus regio, ejus religio,* might undermine the very basis of their existence. Although the statesmen assembled in Augsburg did not have Jews in mind, not even to the extent of excluding them from that mutual accommodation as they tried to exclude the Calvinists, the principle that any ruler could impose his personal religious preference on all his subjects could easily have led to the total withdrawal of toleration from Jews. On the Protestant side such withdrawal had indeed been anticipated, as we recall, by the leading Lutheran electors of Saxony and Brandenburg, whose example was soon followed by the Calvinist rulers of the Palatinate. Total exclusion of Jews had its counterparts in the somewhat more sporadic actions by the Wittelsbach and other Catholic princes. If consistently applied, the new principle would surely have led to the refusal of all governments to tolerate religious minorities—and the Jews had long been the minority par excellence.

It was fortunate for German Jewry that the Augsburg compromise was almost immediately disregarded in most German states. The Catholic Restoration, given form by the Council of Trent and the remarkably effective ideological propaganda and educational reforms of the Jesuit Order through such outstanding leaders as St. Peter Canisius, was rapidly gaining ground in many German areas. Its advances strengthened the hands of the Habsburg emperors, who had been, relatively speaking, the most dependable protectors of imperial Jewry. While the broadly international character of Charles V's regime had been transformed during the more German-oriented reigns of Ferdinand I and his successors, the Habsburg rulers had to take into consideration the multinational character of their hereditary possessions. Ever since 1526, moreover, their rule over the largest and most affluent parts of their realm, in Bohemia, Moravia, Silesia, and the parts of Hungary which they salvaged from the Ottoman occupation, depended to a large extent on the good will of the Estates, which, for a long time, had to be placated with extensive concessions to regional autonomy. The Estates may as a rule have been unfriendly to Jews. Yet they injected into the domestic administration of the Habsburg rulers in the hereditary lands, and indirectly also in the Empire, consideration for the varying needs and attitudes of heterogeneous ethnic elements, which precluded any clear-cut, consistent intolerance. Simultaneously, the rise of the new capitalistic order —spearheaded especially by such maritime centers as Hamburg— combined with the growing need for financing and equipping the standing armies, played into the hands of at least a select group of Jewish entrepreneurs. In time, these new trends were bound to color also the government's treatment of the Jewish communities at large.

HABSBURG POSSESSIONS

In the German states, even more than in Italy, the Catholic Restoration became embroiled in local political and military conflicts. Of decisive importance was that the Holy Roman emperors remained pious Catholics, even if occasionally a prince, like the later Maximilian II, revealed a certain fondness for Protestant teachings. Equally important was that the Electoral College retained its Catholic majority after the deposition of the Lutheran sympathizer Archbishop Hermann V von Wied of Cologne in 1547 and the pro-Calvinist Archbishop Gebhard II Truchsess of that city in 1587. Together with the three archbishops-electors, the Habsburgs, as kings of Bohemia, were assured of a permanent Catholic majority of four out of seven electors, although to underscore imperial independence the emperors now refrained from being crowned by popes. The second half of the sixteenth century saw a constant ebb and flow of Catholic advances against Protestantism. On balance, however, the Catholic Restoration, often aided by Spanish troops from the neighboring Netherlands, was making slow but steady progress, until the final test of strength during the Thirty Years' War.

In their attempt to eradicate Protestantism, the Habsburg monarchs viewed the Jewish question from contradictory angles. Though unavoidably affected by the deepening spirit of religious intolerance, they could not dispense with Jewish fiscal contributions to the conduct of their wars with both the Turks and their domestic foes. As a group neutral in the struggle between the Christian denominations and wholly dependent on royal good will, Jews could actually appear to be the most loyal segment of the population. That is why even outright decrees of banishment were rarely carried out, and protracted negotiations with the royal authorities usually enabled Jews to postpone and ultimately to defeat such extreme measures.

In the Austrian provinces, too, from which Jews had been formally expelled in the fifteenth century, individual traders, physicians, and artists began reappearing in increasing numbers. In 1528 and 1536 Ferdinand I regulated the conditions under which foreign Jews might stay in Vienna and elsewhere, and also referred "to the domestic and resident Jews who are the possession of the royal Chamber." Using strongly anti-Jewish verbiage, the king insisted that Jews be distinguished by badges; refrain from trade, craftsmanship, and moneychanging; and, in Vienna, reside solely in two houses especially assigned to them. The king acted under constant pressure from the Vienna burghers, who resented Jewish competition, and, more broadly, from the Lower Austrian Estates, which nurtured a long-standing animosity toward the Jews. In their typically anti-Jewish petition of 1546 the Estates contended:

There are not a few persons of the Jewish persuasion in this country, including the city of Vienna. They do business alongside the Christians, as do those of Günss and Eisenstadt where they serve a good-for-nothing [böser] clientele. Many Jews live in the countryside and on the frontier, where they engage in intelligence service, high treason, and other misdeeds in favor of the Turks.

The Estates saw as the only remedy the total elimination of Jews, supplemented by provisions that any Jew seized thereafter would be punished "in his body and life," as would those responsible for his infiltration. In 1521 Charles V, then at the beginning of his reign in the Holy Roman Empire, yielded to such remonstrations. His successor, Ferdinand I, however, proved less pliable. A confirmed absolutist and Catholic, like his "Catholic" grandfather and namesake, Ferdinand resented the self-assertive aspirations and Protestant sympathies of many burghers. In 1522 he condemned the mayor of Vienna, Martin Siebenbürger, to death, although the election of that proud leader of the Viennese bourgeoisie had but a year earlier been approved by Charles. Together with seven other "conspirators," Siebenbürger was executed in Vienna's public square. By 1550 the religious conflicts had reached such dimensions that no Corpus Christi processions could be held in the capital, and the University's Theological Faculty had to suspend all classes because of the absence of students. In 1556, when the Austrian Protestants demanded that the provisions of the Augsburg Peace of 1555 be extended to their churches, the king refused outright, arguing that he, too, must obey his religious conscience. His assertion of royal supremacy also moderated his treatment of Jews. Yet Ferdinand did not dare wholly to antagonize the Estates, since he badly needed their good will in voting new taxes and subsidies to prosecute his recurrent wars with the Turks.[1]

As a result, Ferdinand steered a middle course. He admitted individual Jews whom he considered useful to the state, and discouraged the settlement of others. Yet in view of his dependence on the cooperation of the Estates, he issued in 1543–46 several decrees banishing Jews from all of Lower Austria, as well as Moravia. Because of the close relationship between the two provinces, he explained in 1546, the expulsion from but one of them would have been meaningless. The enforcement of these decrees lacked vigor, however, and Ferdinand himself issued, in 1551, the aforementioned detailed ordinance concerning Jewish apparel. Three years later there followed another decree of banishment from Lower Austria, with the special reservation that Jews prepared to adopt Christianity should "receive all Our good will [Gnade] and all Our Christian subjects should treat them with the Christian love and benevolence due them." But almost immediately the king began to grant extensions until 1556 and 1557. In 1560 the government itself inquired about the presence of Jews even in such smaller communities as Zistersdorf, Wolkersdorf, Marchegg, and Eisenstadt. Finally, Ferdinand's son and successor, Maximilian II (1564–76), found in 1565 that the authorities had so completely disregarded his father's decree of banishment that he had to renew it formally.[2]

Nevertheless, Maximilian showed still less perseverance in implementing the intolerant order than had his father. In general, he was a much weaker and more complex person; one, moreover, deeply torn between his private predilection for Protestantism and his sense of dynastic duty to promote the Catholic Restoration in his hereditary possessions and in the Empire. Charming and gifted (he spoke several languages, including Czech and some Hungarian), he was aptly characterized by the Venetian ambassador as a perfect courtier, rather than a vigorous ruler. It is small wonder that, despite his rhetorical declarations alleging that great harm was caused by Jews particularly to the countryfolk, he did not press for the execution of his 1565 decree. In 1567, and again in 1568, he merely issued ordinances against Jewish usury, while in 1569 he prohibited foreign Jews from engaging in trade in his country without first securing a special license. But he emphasized that local Jews required no such permission. Finally, in 1571 and 1572 Maximilian decided to concentrate all Viennese Jews in the heart of the city, rather than in a suburb. In this way he hoped to keep them under closer surveillance and to control the influx of foreign Jews more effectively. True, in 1572 he also issued another decree of expulsion. But about two months later he informed the Estates that he had extended to the Jews a period of grace for their departure. At the same time the authorities, in an ordinance issued sometime during the 1570s, reemphasized the Jews' obligation to wear distinguishing marks and added the sanction that the garments of any Jew found walking in the street without a badge be confiscated on the spot and half their value turned over to the informer. In view of these governmental vacillations some officials became completely baffled. On June 27, 1564, Handgraf Christof Zoppl vom Haus, who was in charge of supervising all commercial transactions in the city, inquired of his superiors how he was to treat some foreign Jews who had brought horses from Poland, Bohemia, Moravia, and Hungary (the case attests their widespread international trade) and were prepared to bring in more. He considered such imports and corresponding exports, as well as the revenue resulting from customs duties and tolls, very valuable, but he was not sure whether Jews were to be allowed to do any business in Vienna. We do not know the reply of the Lower Austrian Chamber, but it probably pursued the same hard line it took seven years later in roundly denying the right of a particular individual to trade in the Habsburg hereditary possessions, although his imperial passport expressly stated that he was "under Our and the Empire's protection." [3]

Some of these inconsistencies may be explained by the very small number of Jews. In 1571, when the authorities discussed the establishment of a special Jew Inn (*Judenherberge*) in Vienna, they considered accommodations for only seven Jewish families then licensed to stay in the city. Even so, the house in the Himmelpfortgasse, assigned to them and the family of a Christian superintendent, proved to be too small, and before long they had to be transferred to a new quarter, in what was later to be named the Leopoldstadt. Moreover, behind the laxity in enforcement and the numerous official extensions loomed such stubborn economic realities as had been expressed by Ferdinand himself in his decree of April 23, 1554:

> In the course of their business they [the Jews] have incurred great debts with a number of Christian subjects, debts which they could not speedily repay without evident and final ruin. On the other hand, Our Christian subjects are also committed to do many things on their behalf which, during these difficult times, would likewise be extremely burdensome for them quickly to perform and to meet their obligations. In addition, they partially own their houses, vineyards, and adjoining lands, which they could not convert into money in so short a time without great hardship and difficulty.

Clearly, a few years did not suffice to resolve such a complex situation, and several subsequent extensions appeared wholly justified. More importantly, the Treasury, then badly in need of cash to finance the wars and the ever-expanding bureaucracy, could not afford to dispense with the disproportionately large Jewish revenue. Only the prevailing high rates of interest enabled the Jews to recoup a part of the heavy imposts they paid. For instance, Emperor Rudolph II himself had to pay 25 percent for a loan he contracted with the Jew Menssl (possibly identical with Mordecai b. Gerson Menzel, assassinated in the 1580s). And this arrangement was considered a concession to the emperor, since the prevailing rates then ranged from 30 to 50 percent.[4]

Intimidating Jewish residents with threats of expulsion became a regular fiscal stratagem of the Austrian authorities under the weak regime of Rudolph II (1576–1612). In 1599 Archduke Matthias, who was to serve as the real monarch from 1607 on although he was not crowned emperor until after Rudolph's death in 1612, demanded from the Jews 15,000, or at least 10,000, florins immediately, threatening them with banishment if they refused. They argued in vain that, consisting of only thirty-one families who had already made war contributions of 9,260 florins and had lent the government an additional 8,000 florins, they were able to offer merely a one-florin capitation tax. In the following year Matthias instructed the Court Chamber again to "invite" the Jews to make another contribution of 20,000, or at least 10,000, florins under the same threat of expulsion. Against pleas of poverty the Treasury agents argued that the Jewish merchants had made huge profits in their trade in velvet and silk and could well afford the new impost. This enormous fiscal pressure on the Jewish taxpayers can be explained only by the Treasury's deplorable shortages, as noted by the keen-witted Venetian ambassador Zuan (Giovanni) Michele in 1564. The military expenditures, especially, were extremely burdensome. Michele wrote:

Everyone knows that, if he did not receive his pay, a German son would not serve his father. All of them, whether princes or private persons, are so mercenary that, if anyone will pay and maintain them, not only will they serve him against their own nation and prince, but, one may dare say, one brother will serve against another.

Jews were, of course, the most defenseless victims of that system. Although the reiterated threats of expulsion were probably intended merely to tighten the screws on resisters, the total number of Jewish families in 1601 is said to have declined from 31 to 12 (embracing 77 persons), according to a detailed, though doubtless incomplete, enumeration submitted by the Court Chamber to Archduke Matthias. It rose again to 44 families by 1614. The small number of Jews recorded in 1601 did not prevent an eager official of the Court Chamber from preparing, two years later, a draft for a report to the emperor which asserted that "Jews have so greatly increased in number that today almost a quarter of the city is said to be inhabited by them." Probably as a result of such highly inflated rumors, the Vienna community was subjected to another detailed review; this census was ordered in 1611 by Matthias (II), who had interveningly ascended the throne of Austria and Hungary and would later assume those of Bohemia and the Empire. "We desire," the king wrote to the Lower Austrian Estates, "that you should describe each and every Jew in Vienna, together with his wife, children, and employees, and that you should inquire from each about his doings, business, and conduct, as well as under whose protection he lives." [5]

Regrettably, the available documentation does not show the extent to which the struggle between the officially sponsored Counter Reformation and the large Protestant segment of the population affected these royal policies. There is no question that the emigration of Protestants from the country, among them some wealthy burghers, left many commercial and fiscal gaps which the government may have sought to fill by others, including Jews. At times anti-Protestant regulations went further than the restrictions imposed upon Jews. For example, the validity of wills was denied to Protestant testators but recognized in the case of Jews; Richard Matt has shown that, as a result, the extant testaments by known Protestants avoid mentioning the writer's faith.[6]

All during that period the law divided the Austrian Jews into three categories: the "court-privileged" (hofbefreite), the foreigners, and the "common" Jewish residents. Persons of the first category, already called "court Jews" (Hofjuden) in some documents, enjoyed high privileges which placed them almost on a par with the nobility. They could travel freely, accompany the royal Court on its journeys, and, in return for special taxes, were free from all local imposts and customs duties. Probably most galling to the Vienna burghers was the complete exemption of these Jews from the authority of the city council and their subjection to the direct control of the marshal of the Court. Time and again the city unsuccessfully tried to alter that situation. The city council had more jurisdiction over the foreign "visitors," many of whom had settled down to a prolonged residence. The "common" Jews lived for the most part as employees, real or fictitious, of their privileged coreligionists, although many engaged in trade on their own account. Despite the constant ebb and flow caused by the partially effective decrees of expulsion and the arrival of new settlers, this tiny Viennese group succeeded in establishing a more or less functional Jewish community and in preserving for it a fair degree of continuity. Small and insecure as it was, this community was able to maintain a cemetery and two rented places of worship, in addition to a private chapel owned from 1603 on by its leader Samuel Phoebus b. Moses Aaron Lemml (Theomim), surnamed Veit Munk, who after his demise in 1616 was extolled on his tombstone as a great "benefactor who accommodated visitors and took care of all their needs." Another outstanding citizen was R. Manoah Hendl b. Shemariah, author of a Hebrew commentary on Baḥya ibn Paquda's *Duties of the Heart* and of other works. On July 3, 1611, shortly before his death, Manoaḥ seems to have arranged a preventive divorce between a childless couple so that, in case of the anticipated death of the then hopelessly ill husband, the wife would not be dependent on a levir. This divorce, followed by the husband's recovery and rather complicated negotiations, created a stir in Jewish juristic circles in many communities.[7]

Vienna's increasingly self-assertive Jewry now sought to secure from the emperor a series of protective regulations going beyond the mere act of toleration. In their petition to Archduke Matthias of May 21, 1601, the elders not only demanded that Jewish visitors be made to contribute to the upkeep of the cemetery and the "synagogues," since these served the strangers as well as the local population, but they also daringly argued that in litigations between Jews and Gentiles the parties be made to repair to Jewish courts, "so as not to trouble your Highness or the subordinate authorities." The elders also pointed out that the existing system in which creditors had to keep unredeemed pledges for many years—for instance, pawned clothing, which often depreciated to less than half the value of the loan—worked to the disadvantage of both lender and borrower. They suggested that, like most other localities, Vienna should allow creditors to dispose of pledges after a year and a day. Remarkably, the community did not fear to raise this issue, notwithstanding repeated governmental prohibitions of usury in any form (the latest anti-usury ordinances aimed specifically at Jews had been promulgated in 1582 and 1592). In stating a negative opinion on this petition the royal officials characteristically failed to refer to the recent Austrian decrees, but rather emphasized the resolution passed by the imperial Diet of Augsburg in 1530, which had outlawed Jewish usury throughout the Empire. They also repeated the old clichés about the Jewish "enemies of Christ and blasphemers"; insisted that Judeo-Christian litigations be adjudicated exclusively by the municipal courts; and demanded that, as fellow beneficiaries, Jews be made to contribute their share to the maintenance of artillery and other equipment installed for the city's defenses. No immediate decision by the emperor is recorded, but in 1617 the city secured an imperial ordinance granting it exclusive judicial authority over newly admitted Jews. In other instances, too, some higher Austrian officials were anything but friendly to Jews. Yet they insisted on preserving the royal prerogatives; and on one occasion they severely censured the Vienna city council for arbitrarily closing some Jewish shops. They spoke in this connection of the city elders' "immodesty" in arrogating to themselves such power. The vicissitudes of the renascent Viennese community have been described here at some length because the community's proximity to, and close relationship with, the Court enabled the handful of Viennese Jews to play a wholly disproportionate role in the affairs of the entire Jewish population under the Habsburg dynasty.[8]

BOHEMIAN CROWN

More far-reaching were the developments in the larger and more numerous Bohemian and Moravian Jewish communities, which, though decimated by the expulsion of 1542, tenaciously clung to the temporary extensions of their right of sojourn. Although no longer living in that state of tranquillity described by Bohuslav Hassenstein (Hašištensky) von Lobkowicz in his letter of April 22, 1497, to King Vladislav ("The Jewish people, lowliest settlers among the Christian nations, are attacked by no one"), the Jews seemed to have weathered the storm by 1546. Certainly, the few Jews who had survived the expulsion, largely because they had failed to obey the order and had remained in the country illegally (apart from the few privileged individuals officially permitted to remain behind to settle their and their coreligionists' affairs), had every reason not to display their religious identity publicly.

Yet an official 1546 list of Prague Jews, their families, and servants, preserved in the archives of the Bohemian provincial government, enumerated 976 persons, "apart from the children of fourteen persons serving at the hospital and those who have not yet shown their licenses." This list included both Jews living on the basis of official permits of one kind or another and those who resided in the city without *gleity* (licenses). However, the enmity of the population and the Diet continued, while Ferdinand I began to feel that the disadvantages of maintaining Jews against the vociferous public opposition outweighed the advantages. In pursuing his absolutist aims, he had to proceed gingerly against the Estates which wished to maintain their traditional independence. Their attitude to the Bohemian king had long been epitomized in the adage: "You are our king, we are your masters." This time the issue of the Jews' purported disloyalty in the war with the Turks was replaced with renewed and intensified rumors that they were smuggling much silver and currency out of the country, thereby sapping the strength of the economy and the government. As early as 1547 the king ordered the Bohemian Chamber (Treasury) to forbid Jews to export any silver whatsoever. In 1556 this prohibition was extended to all subjects, whereas the Jews were specifically ordered not to melt any gold, but rather to deliver all gold and silver produced in Bohemia to the royal mints in Prague, Kuttenberg (Kutna Hora), or Joachimsthal (Jachymov). A few months later the king's son, Archduke Ferdinand, reported that Jews had failed to obey that ordinance and suggested that, since they were engaged in extensive counterfeiting of coins as well, they be expelled from the country. This suggestion was the more menacing as it came from the same archduke who, but four years earlier, had urged a local official not to banish the Jews from the city of Teplitz (Teplice). The city councils of the three Prague municipalities soon echoed Ferdinand's demand and argued, more broadly, that the Jews were responsible for the general decline of the Christian burghers' business. At the same time, well-informed about the emperor's fiscal concerns, they requested that their city not be burdened with making up the deficiency created by the absence of Jewish taxpayers.[9]

Once again Ferdinand yielded and, on August 27, 1557, issued another decree of expulsion ordering the Jews to leave within a year, though this time the Moravian Diet refused to follow suit. Vigorous Jewish resistance led to the usual extensions, and in 1559 Ferdinand allowed the prospective exiles to leave behind ten selected representatives to supervise the liquidation of Jewish loans and debts. But he added, "Should some Jew or Jewess with spouse and children smuggle himself into the lands of Bohemia, Moravia, the Two Silesias, or Lusatia in order to stay there for a shorter or longer period of time, or else to remain there, he should be arrested and severely punished in his person and property." The king's fiscal motivations in allowing the few Jews to remain were obvious to all, and Jews might well have echoed the exclamation of Pastor Johannes Mathesius of Joachimsthal. Speculating on why the government tolerated members of the Lutheran clergy like himself, Mathesius wrote with a sigh: "Perhaps Plutus is our patron." With respect to the extension of 1560, the court preacher, Bishop Urban of Gurk, took up the problem of Hebrew books in Jewish possession and suggested to Archduke Ferdinand the following procedure:

You should demand from the Jews the submission of their books, have them examined by learned persons who understand the matter and are familiar with the language. The latter should expurgate and correct whatever blasphemies are found therein against our holy Christian faith and religion. In this way their [the Jews'] children, who (as we are told) must learn such blasphemies from their childhood, would be removed [from such indoctrination]. Secondly, Your Highness should order them earnestly, under the sanction of the loss of limb and life, to proclaim publicly in their synagogues that any person, man or woman, young or old, wishing to attend Christian sermons may do so without any difficulty and without their trying to prevent it by their ban. Thirdly, if thenceforth someone among them should desire to accept the Christian baptism and faith, he must not be persecuted on this score, disinherited, or made insecure in any other fashion.

In these reservations one clearly senses the impact of the Counter Reformation. To be sure, the censorship of Jewish books, ordered by Ferdinand again in 1561, was mitigated here to expurgation, rather than burning—a policy which, as we have seen, Archbishop Anton Brus of Prague was shortly thereafter to promote, evidently with the emperor's concurrence, at the Tridentine Council. Nor was attendance at missionary sermons compulsory. Although the newly established Jesuit Order engaged in extensive proselytizing, the number of Jewish converts seems to have remained very small. When, in 1562, the Society asked the government for a refund of 120 thalers spent on the maintenance of two baptized Jewish boys, the emperor ordered the Bohemian Chamber to refund only 70 florins.[10]

Mere extensions were but palliatives, however. They kept the Bohemian Jews in a state of constant tension, which accrued neither to their nor to the emperor's benefit. Yet it was widely believed that Ferdinand was unable to revoke the decree of banishment and even had to repeat it formally on March 24, 1561, because he had purportedly taken an oath to rid his country of Jews. He felt free only to grant them temporary extensions. Hence he resisted pro-Jewish intercessions like those of the Bohemian nobles assembled at the Diet of 1561. The nobles had good reasons to favor the retention of Jews in the country, many of whom not only served as their bankers and intermediaries but also often bought up most of their agricultural produce for immediate cash or on short-term installment plans, and in turn supplied them with a variety of goods, including some manufactured by Jewish craftsmen. The Bohemian landlords found the Jews doubly useful, in fact, because of the latter's general defenselessness. For example, when a Prague Jewish butcher failed to pay Baron Johann Czernin an amount due on April 23, 1642, the baron asked, on August 10, the Jewish elders of Prague to force the butcher to pay. Otherwise, he threatened, he would seize any Jewish merchant traveling through his territory to Linz, confiscate his wares, and sell them up to the full amount of his claim. In contrast, a Prague Jewish businesswoman named Peprle found it extremely difficult to collect a debt owed her by the widow of a noble landowner. In 1631 Peprle had delivered black cloth and other merchandise for the elaborate funeral of the deceased landlord, the widow signing a note promising immediate payment of more than 400 florins. Since the deceased had left behind many debts, however, his estate went into receivership. Peprle tried in vain to secure payment, notwithstanding her reiterated pleas that she and her orphaned children lived in great penury. Even successive court orders to the receivers to meet this obligation, which enjoyed legal priority, proved of no avail. Only after ten years did the landlord's brother, Count Wilhelm Slawata, partially respond to Peprle's urgent requests. While denying any personal responsibility, he advanced her 100 florins (or about a quarter of the amount due) "out of compassion." The extant documents record no further payments. It is small wonder, then, that the landlords viewed with dismay the prospect of losing such profitable business connections.[11]

Ferdinand's son, Maximilian, who was crowned king of Bohemia in 1562, still in his father's lifetime, likewise advocated moderation. At his coronation the new king was paid homage by the Jewish community in a ceremony similar to that performed for his father upon entry as the newly crowned Holy Roman emperor four years before. The participation of a colorful Jewish group with its scrolls of law and other paraphernalia created quite a sensation among the onlookers and was widely commented on by the contemporary chroniclers. We are further told that Ferdinand decided not to enforce his 1557 decree only after a Prague Jewish printer, Mordecai Ṣemaḥ, son of Gerson Katz, traveled to Rome in 1563 and secured from Pius IV a dispensation from the king's alleged oath. This story may be apocryphal, but we know that on August 31, 1563, the papal secretary of state informed the nuncio in Vienna, Zaccaria Delfino, that some Prague Jews had intervened with Pius IV and that the pope had been moved by mercy to intercede for the people in whose behalf the Church was offering prayers. It was left to the nuncio's discretion, however, how he wished to discuss this matter with the emperor so as neither to offend him nor to detract from the dignity of the pope. Evidently, the nuncio spoke to Ferdinand, who had earlier listened to Bishop Urban's suggestion that he follow Paul IV's lead in censoring Hebrew books and now responded to the more tolerant spirit prevailing at the papal See under Pius IV. The Prague Jews seemingly were so grateful for being allowed to remain, on however temporary a basis, that when Ferdinand died in 1564 one of their intellectual leaders, the historian David Gans, called him "a pious and God-fearing man who did justice and charity in the land." True, such laudatory statements need not always be taken at their face value. Hebrew writers of the period were keenly aware that their books might subsequently be cited, especially by malevolent apostates, as proof of Jewish disloyalty. At a time when Bohemian Jewry was constantly living under the cloud of suspicion of harboring pro-Turkish sentiments, Jewish authors must have been doubly circumspect. In addition, Jews in Bohemia, as elsewhere, permanently included in their Sabbath and holiday liturgy prayers for the welfare of their rulers; and, in connection with the conspiracy allegedly hatched at the large Jewish Council of Frankfort in 1603 (about which more will be said below), they offered such a *laudatio* as evidence of their staunch loyalty to the emperor. Yet Gans would have toned down his encomium or omitted it altogether if he had felt that Ferdinand had been hostile to his people.[12]

Maximilian II partially reversed his father's policies. Although strongly influenced by Spanish culture and political ideas (after marrying his Spanish cousin Maria, he spent two years in an influential post at the Court of his brother-in-law Philip II), he was sufficiently independent to evince certain pro-Protestant sympathies. In the Bohemian lands, moreover, he faced a large popular majority opposed to Catholicism. Even the papal nuncio estimated the number of Catholics in Bohemia at only 304,000, in a population which seems to have exceeded 3,000,000 souls. With respect to Jews, on April 4, 1567, Maximilian formally authorized those still living in Bohemia to remain and engage in trade there. He also slightly relaxed the stringent admission policies for Jews settling in the possessions of feudal lords. For example, Adam II of Neuhaus (Jindrichov Hradec, 1565–96) attracted to the area under his control Jews beyond the statutory maximum of four families, long observed there. Yet under pressure from interested parties the emperor peremptorily barred Jews from the mining cities, not only because, according to reports, they were exploiting the local population, but also because they allegedly smuggled ores mined in the Sudeten Mountains out of the country. Nor did he interfere with the burning, in 1568, of two Jewish martyrs, Israel b. Isaiah, of the distinguished rabbinic family of Horowitz, and Israel's son-in-law, Moses b. Joel—apparently in connection with a rather obscure Blood Accusation in the small town of Strakonitz.[13]

Maximilian's son Rudolph II, though generally rather erratic and intolerant of Protestantism, treated his Jewish subjects more benevolently. As early as February 14, 1577, he issued a major privilege for Bohemian Jewry. Echoing King Vladislav's privilege of 1510, he even included the pledge that "they would never be expelled from Prague or the Bohemian Crown." Understandably, this reversal of recent policies encountered much public resistance, and a Prague merchant, Hans Folk, published a sharply anti-Jewish pamphlet. As in most other Central-European cities the artisan guilds often formed the vanguard of the anti-Jewish forces. Even more than the merchants, they constantly complained that the Jews undersold them in the markets. They were particularly irate at the Jewish secondhand-clothing dealers—as well as at the pawnbrokers disposing of pledges of defaulting debtors—for offering them "unfair" competition. Successive protests, especially by the Prague guilds of furriers and tailors, kept the royal administration busy devising methods of mutual accommodation during the last third of the sixteenth century. Often contradictory and impractical, these compromises usually proved to be of brief duration. Consumers greatly benefited from the lower prices charged by the Jews, and at the same time from the legal safeguards against untrammeled profiteering by Jewish, but not by Christian, traders during that period of severe inflation generated by the unsettled conditions in the country. On their part, the central and local authorities followed the imperial decrees rather closely and merely quibbled over implementation. Even the Bohemian Diets, now convoked less frequently and mainly in response to royal wishes for ever-new war taxes, debated the Jewish question chiefly from the standpoint of Jewish fiscal contributions. There was much haggling on all sides, and on one occasion Rudolph, trying to make the Jewish taxpayers more compliant, resorted to the old threat of banishing them all, in disregard of his own earlier anti-expulsion pledge. He also consistently kept the Jews out of the mining cities. Nonetheless, in 1611, shortly before his death, he formally renewed all Jewish privileges, including those which guaranteed a large measure of Jewish communal autonomy. Despite these weather-vane policies, Jews were now able to breathe more freely; they acquired houses, vineyards, and other property, engaged in large-scale trade in gold and silver, and almost monopolized the manufacture of jewelry. Among the Jewish goldsmiths of that period Joseph de Cervi (Hirsch) received a noteworthy privilege from the emperor on March 16, 1577. It allowed him to pursue his time-honored Jewish craft in the city of Prague, as well as in the royal castle, "without hindrance by the head of the guild . . . or by the Prague Jews." On the other hand, Rudolph himself turned in 1596 against Jews who had failed to join the Goldsmiths' Guild (the so-called *Staller*), and threatened them with imprisonment unless they pledged themselves to work for some employee of the Court or for a Prague master artisan.[14]

Their strong communal organization proved of immeasurable assistance to Jews in their struggle for survival in the Czech lands; it endured despite endless internal squabbles and external bureaucratic interference. As elsewhere, the local authorities often attempted to arrogate to themselves greater powers of supervision over internal Jewish affairs than had been granted to them by the royal legislation. In its report of October 5, 1538, the Bohemian Chamber complained of the existing "excessive" Jewish autonomy while it advocated the appropriation by the state of a tax of 200 Schock theretofore paid by the community to the city of Prague. The Chamber actually suggested for royal consideration the possibility of totally eliminating the Prague Jewry. On the other hand, the Bohemian Jews lived so precariously, under the constant specter of expulsion, and were so dependent on the good will of officials, that they put up little resistance to infringements of their self-government. They allowed royal officials to prescribe in great detail their mode of electing communal elders and to make the outcome dependent in each case on royal confirmation. We must bear in mind, however, that the official documents present a one-sided picture of the regulations, which the bureaucracy tried, but often failed, to enforce. For the actual situation we must consult the contemporary Hebrew letters, of which unfortunately not too many are extant. However, perusal of the writings of R. Yehudah Loew (Liwa) b. Bezalel (known in Jewish folklore as "der hohe Rabbi Loew") shows that, on the whole, the communal leadership unperturbedly pursued its traditional course and even contemplated major educational and other reforms without consulting the government. Doubtless feeling that in the constant crises it had to face, the community needed encouragement and comfort, rather than scolding and censure—the stock in trade of most homilists—R. Yehudah Loew sometimes spoke glowingly of its fortitude in adversity. In a famous sermon of 1573 he compared the government's alternate expulsions and readmissions of Jews to quarrels between fickle lovers who separate and reunite as the spirit moves them.[15]

In time such analogies sounded less incongruous, as the Jews with truly amazing speed recovered from their depressed condition under Ferdinand I. Like Austria's *hofbefreite Juden,* some wealthy Prague Jewish merchants enjoyed a privileged position in Bohemia. One of them, Mordecai (Markus) Meisel (Meysel, 1528–1601), left a permanent imprint upon the Prague community. About a decade before his death, his contemporary David Gans praised him as "one of the pillars of the synagogue, a leading philanthropist, and father of the poor." He not only built the famous synagogue in Prague which has borne his name ever since but also paid for paving the whole Jewish quarter, erected a bathhouse and hospital-hostel *(heqdesh)* for the poor, annually married off at least two impecunious Jewish girls, and kept his house open to the poor at all times. He advanced funds to struggling craftsmen and merchants; in one case up to 800 thalers. His benefactions extended to Poland, where the community of Poznań had then suffered from a devastating fire; he gave or lent it 20,000 florins. He also helped support the indigent of the Holy Land. At the same time he maintained excellent relations with the government. In the special privilege Rudolph II granted him on December 22, 1593 the ruler emphasized:

Since Markus Meysel has always and everywhere made efforts, to the extent of his power and ability, to assist His Imperial Majesty and the whole kingdom of Bohemia with money and other services, and since neither in these services nor otherwise has he shown himself guilty of any dishonest or dishonorable action, His Imperial Majesty graciously consents to take the said Markus Meysel and his wife, together with the possessions of both, under his all-highest personal, imperial, and royal protection, and to extend over them his all-highest protective hand. He also graciously ordains that in case it should happen that some evildoer of the Christian faith, obviously because of ill will or vengeance, should invent some accusation against him, Markus Meysel, no one shall seize Meysel's person or property, but his case shall immediately be referred to His Imperial Majesty's personal knowledge. In the absence of His Imperial Majesty the matter shall be submitted to the governor of the kingdom of Bohemia. His Imperial Majesty will then, together with the highest government officials and royal councilors, subject the matter to most careful scrutiny, and order that everything be adjusted with all possible thoroughness and justice.

The privilege also included a provision that Meisel would not be forced to accept any communal office against his will. Five years later, at Meisel's request, supported by some of the highest court officials, Rudolph II granted him another privilege, which went into greater detail, including the right to display in his newly erected synagogue "the flag of King David" similar to that still visible in their "ancient house of worship," doubtless referring to the shield of David or hexagram displayed in the famous *Altneuschule*. In addition to spelling out a series of commercial advantages, this decree also granted Meisel the right to make free testamentary provisions concerning his estate.[16]

Little did the aging Jewish merchant suspect that, upon his demise but three years later (1601), the authorities, led by an unscrupulous councilor, Philipp Lang, would completely disregard both his testament (dated March 1–2, 1601) and the imperial pledge, and confiscate the entire estate, most of which had been left to various relatives in legacies ranging up to 10,000 florins. According to a contemporary record, the Bohemian Chamber received amounts totaling no less than 516,250 florins in cash—an enormous sum in those days. To justify the confiscation, the imperial attorneys had submitted, on May 5, 1601, a long memorandum, primarily arguing that, since Meisel had died childless, his property automatically reverted to his royal overlord. According to King Vladislav's ordinance, testamentary freedom could be granted only to members of the nobility, not to Jews, who are not vassals but captives of Your Majesty, as king of Bohemia. They live here by the grace of Your Majesty and under Your license, possessing none of the rights and privileges, granted to the lords, gentry, and other Estates. For this reason they cannot bequeath their possessions by will, nor enjoy royal privileges to this effect, but rather when they die their property remains intestate and, if they are childless, these possessions do not fall to their wives, but rather to the government of Your Majesty as king of Bohemia. It remains, therefore, in the discretion of Your Majesty to issue, according to Your own will, a gracious order thereon.

As to the contrary specific privilege of 1598, the attorneys contended that many of its paragraphs ran counter to Bohemian law because the emperor had failed to consult the Estates. These legalistic cavilers thus did not hesitate to invalidate a royal enactment, so long as they thereby secured Meisel's extensive possessions for the Crown. Perhaps encouraged by this act of rapacity, as well as by the absence from the scene of any really influential Jewish spokesman, the burgomaster and the council of the Old City of Prague argued, in their lengthy memorandum of April 1, 1602, for the expulsion of the Jews from Bohemia. But the government paid no heed to this request. In time the imperial circles tried to assuage their bad conscience about the expropriation, and, in subsequent years, began restoring houses and other property from Meisel's estate to his legatees or their heirs. This process extended over almost the entire seventeenth century, but of course a great deal remained permanently under the control of the royal Treasury.[17]

Somewhat different was the privilege extended in 1599 to the brothers Samuel and Jacob Bassevi who, together with their families and employees, were granted the freedom of the entire Holy Roman Empire. They were to be allowed to travel and do business in any of its territories without being subject to any court other than that of the emperor himself or an official designated by him. The imperial authorities were ordered to extend help to the Bassevi brothers also with respect to their business dealings outside the Empire. Still another Jew who had frequent access to Rudolph and his entourage was the aforementioned Prague rabbi Yehudah Loew b. Bezalel (1531–1609), a distinguished moralist and educational reformer, about whom Jewish folklore was to spin many legends. One of these linked the emperor with the rabbi in the alleged creation of a *golem*—a story which made quite a career in later German literature.[18]

In contrast to this relaxation of political pressures on the Bohemian Jews, the Catholic clergy intensified its missionary and segregationist efforts, with the redoubled zeal stimulated by the Counter Reformation, although its progress in Bohemia was impeded by the powerful Hussite underground, buttressed by Czech national feeling. On the other hand, Lutheranism, too, had become an important instrument of the progressive Germanization of Prague and other cities. Some of the fervor of the early religious debates may have died down. The observation made in 1489 by Bohuslav Hassenstein (Hašištensky) von Lobkowicz was not quite so true a century later: "Everywhere people debate matters of faith. Old and young, men and women, expound Scripture, which they had never studied before. As soon as a new sect emerges, it immediately gains adherents. So great is the zest for innovations." Nonetheless, the missionary activities of the Jesuits and other champions of the Catholic Restoration—strongly supported by the royal officials for political as well as religious reasons—affected Jews, though to a lesser extent than Protestants. In fact, the sharp nationalistic frictions between Czechs and Germans helped to reduce the anti-Jewish feelings which had characterized the earlier, monolithic Czech nationalism. Religiously, however, the Prague archdiocesan synod, meeting in September 1605, passed a stringent resolution reading:

In order to reduce the occasions for the spiritual damage which usually arises from excessive contacts and commerce of the faithful with Jews, we prohibit Christians from entering the latter's synagogues at banquets, weddings, or festive days; from playing or dancing with them; and from being their servants. Nor shall Christian women be allowed to serve under any contract as nurses in Jewish homes. Neither shall parents send their sons and daughters to Jews for instruction in any liberal or other arts. No clerics or laymen shall deposit money with any Jew for the purpose of a gainful loan or deposit.

At the same time, the synod adopted safeguards lest Jews be too readily admitted to baptism without proper preparation. It also warned the clergy not to allow, "what has been discovered as occasionally happening," that a Jew be baptized twice. Anti-Jewish publications, in prose and in poetry, likewise continued to make their appearance; among them an interesting Czech satire on Jewish physicians. Nevertheless, compared with the mid-century persecutions, Jewish life in Bohemia proceeded with relative smoothness and tranquillity. There is no evidence, for example, that the government itself actively promoted Jew-baiting. In 1570, when the Jewish convert Elchanan Paulus applied to the emperor for a subsidy toward the publication of two anti-Jewish pamphlets which he had dedicated to Archdukes Ernst and Maximilian, his petition seems to have been refused, even in relatively conversionist Vienna. Only occasionally did the rulers yield to local pressures, as in 1595 when Rudolph II forbade the Jews of Prague to become surgeons, furriers, or tailors; we recall, without lasting effect. In general, the number of Jews increased rapidly, and the communities were able to resume their intellectual activities on a high plane. Before long the Prague rabbinate included, besides Yehudah Loew b. Bezalel, such luminaries in rabbinic homiletics and ethics as Solomon Ephraim Lentshits (Łęczyca) and Isaiah Horowitz. They were later joined by the youthful Yom Ṭob Lipmann Heller.[19]

The same held true, to a lesser extent, for Moravia, but not for Silesia. In both these provinces the divided sovereignties greatly impeded any concerted action. In the course of the fifteenth century Jews had been effectively eliminated from most Moravian cities: Iglau (Jihlava) in 1426; Brünn (Brno), Olmütz (Olomouc), Znaim (Znojmo), Mährisch-Neustadt (Unicov), and others in 1454–55. The loss of residential rights in Olmütz must have been particularly painful, since the city was speedily becoming the political, economic, and ecclesiastical center of the entire province. While the Jews found shelter in some of the neighboring hamlets and villages under the protection of feudal lords, their status remained extremely precarious. To counteract the designs of their enemies, some Jews enlisted the aid of the leading Bohemian aristocrat Wilhelm von Pernstein und Helfenstein. In a remarkable contract of 1490, Von Pernstein promised the Jewish leader Meyer, in return for a lifetime annual payment of 50 Hungarian florins, guaranteed by nine other Jewish elders, "not to refuse to give them advice and to do them good whenever they [the Jews] would appeal to him, so long as it would not involve action against the lord God or the country." This last reservation was not to be interpreted too strictly, since the *Obersthofmeister* of the realm was known to be a man of broadly tolerant religious convictions. (He supposedly declared on one occasion: "I believe with the Romans [Catholics], I side with the Utraquists, and I die with the Brethren.") When King Vladislav took over the duchy of Troppau (Opava) in 1500, he stipulated that Jews should be allowed to remain in the places where they happened to be at that time. But his successor, Louis, was forced to yield in 1523 to the demands of the local burghers, and banished the Jews. Other expulsions occurred in Hradisch in 1514 and in Neutitschein (Nový Jičín) and Sternberg in 1562. In addition the Moravian Jews were affected by the general decrees of expulsion issued by Ferdinand I for the Bohemian Crown in 1542 and 1557. The hostility of the local population also came to the fore in isolated attacks on Jews. The royal decree of expulsion of 1557, which had set in motion a large number of Jewish refugees in various lands of the Bohemian Crown, offered a welcome opportunity to numerous Moravian and other hoodlums to assail the wretched wanderers and thus give vent to their pent-up hatreds and their avidity for loot. Ferdinand I's decree of April 14, 1559, specifically addressed to Moravia, Silesia, and Lusatia, and demanding free passage for these sufferers, was observed in its breach. Finally, Polish Jewry, with the support of its king, joined its Bohemian coreligionists in a petition, addressed to the Habsburg authorities on February 25, 1560, asking for effective protection of the displaced persons and severe punishment of their assailants.[20]

Under these circumstances the Jews' vitality and their success in retaining toeholds in many smaller localities is truly amazing. Some communities were able to maintain a measure of continuity; among them Prossnitz (Prostějov) and Kremsier (Kroměříž). On one occasion in 1535 the Kremsier elders were even able to intercede in behalf of coreligionists in Silesian Jägerndorf (Krnov), threatened with expulsion because of an unfounded accusation, and secured for them a fairly protective decree from Ferdinand I. As late as 1593, the Moravian Diet meeting at Brünn (Brno) provided, however, that Jews spending a night in any of the royal cities without permission of the city council might be arrested by the municipal authorities and severely punished. This situation began changing only under the pressures of the Thirty Years' War.[21]

The intolerant decrees of Ferdinand I achieved full validity in Silesia, too, while their subsequent modifications and revocations often encountered even stiffer local resistance there than elsewhere in the Bohemian lands. The anti-Jewish sentiments of both the princes and the other Estates came clearly to the fore in their resolution of 1558, in which they demanded the total elimination of Jews, who "are infidels, stiff-necked, stubborn, hating the name of Christians, betraying Christianity to the Turks, persecuting the local subjects, exploiting them, and taking away their possessions." Similar sentiments were expressed in the princely Estate in 1538, 1545, 1559, 1560, 1561, and again every year from 1580 to 1586. In 1563, three leading Silesian cities, Kosel, Glogau (Glogow), and Oppeln (Opole), sought guarantees from the government that "no Jew will forevermore remain, dwell, or arrive *in* the city, *before* the city, or anywhere *near* the city." This antagonism persisted under Rudolph II. In reply to the insistent demands for expulsion, the emperor instructed his officials to investigate the matter. On July 12, 1581, he wrote:

Since the Jews regularly pay the tax imposed on them and in former days the revenue from Jews was often pledged by emperors [for loans], one ought to give serious consideration as to whether their banishment should be carried into effect. The commissioners should carefully negotiate thereon with the princes and the Estates and ascertain whether they insist on the implementation of their demands.

The princes stubbornly adhered to their position and even suggested that the small Jewish revenue which would be lost could easily be made up by the Christian taxpayers (July 21). Willy-nilly, on March 26, 1582, Rudolph ordered all Jews to leave Silesia, under the sanction of total confiscation of their property, and allowed them thenceforth to pursue their trade only at open fairs. This concession was doubtless made out of fear of Polish reprisals against Silesian businessmen visiting neighboring Polish cities. The silence of the princes in their subsequent assemblies with respect to most localities seems to confirm the disappearance of Jews from almost all Silesian cities, except where they happened to be favored by local potentates, as in Oberglogau (Upper Glogow) and Zülz (Biala). Here the repeated remonstrations of the princes, and even the emperor's confirmation of the decree of expulsion in 1592, proved of no avail. Elsewhere, however, especially in Breslau (Wrocław) only a few transients, for the most part visitors to fairs, maintained some sort of continuum of Jewish life.[22]

Individual exceptions made by the emperor or a local lord often extended not only to members of the beneficiary's family but also to persons in his employ, be it for business or religious reasons. In this fashion there evolved a dangerous dependence of entire communities on the privileges extended to individual members, who were thus able at their discretion to grant or withhold residence permits from the other Jews. We have here a repetition of the Italian conditions of the fifteenth century, when many communities depended entirely on the *condottas* negotiated by the cities with individual Jewish bankers. But this time moneylending played a relatively minor role, whereas general trade, frequently involving government contracts, became the foundation of much of Jewish communal as well as economic life.

HUNGARY

Even more stormy was the career of Hungarian Jewry, whose tragic vicissitudes had begun long before the catastrophic battle at Mohács in 1526. Its impoverishment was clearly demonstrated in 1524, when, despite strong fiscal pressures, the total royal revenue from the Jewish taxpayers amounted to only 1,600 florins. The Jewish population in the major cities numbered only 11,400 souls; a few thousand more may have been scattered through the smaller towns and the countryside. In their growing xenophobia the burghers vigorously agitated against Jews, as well as against some foreigners. In 1524, for example, the city council of Ödenburg (Sopron) forbade Jews to bathe in the municipal bath. According to the famous Venetian diarist Marino Sanuto, in 1525 the Hungarians staged uprisings all over the country against the German, Spanish, and Italian courtiers employed by King Louis II and Queen Beatrice, and also pillaged Jewish houses. Among these was the mansion of a Spanish Jewish convert, renamed Imre (Emerich) Szerencsés (Fortunatus), who served as the king's fiscal adviser and assistant treasurer. He is said to have been a brother of the Castilian "chief rabbi" Abraham Seneor. Unlike his brother, he refused to adopt Christianity in 1492 and went into exile; but he later submitted to baptism, although he seems to have secretly continued to observe Jewish rites.[23]

Szerencsés' services were the more urgently needed in the mid-1520s as the financial stringency of the country was becoming ever more alarming. The great landowners enjoyed practically complete tax immunity, and the entire fiscal burden rested upon the middle class, particularly the Jews. Since under the menace of an approaching Turkish invasion the fiscal disarray became nearly total, the royal Treasury frequently had to resort to the time-honored expedient of reducing the silver content of coins. In 1521 Chancellor Szálkai tried to explain to the assembled Estates the necessity of another such devaluation, which then proceeded apace with Szerencsés' technical help, while the real culprits were the magnates and the bishops, with their disastrous financial policies. In the preparation of the country's defenses against the Turks, Szerencsés alone succeeded in manning a number of ships with troops and equipping them with adequate weapons; yet he was accused by the Estates of "an evil life and evil currency manipulation," and they demanded his death by burning. The nobles actually sent sixty and, later, one hundred and twenty delegates to the king demanding the deposition of the assistant treasurer who, it may be noted, despite his conversion was generally called a "Jew" also in official documents. He was indeed imprisoned by the king. At the same time the populace again gave vent to its pent-up hatred of all Jews. In Buda the Jewish quarter was sacked; it was saved from total ruin only by the nobles who, together with the army, carried out the royal order to stop the riot.[24]

Szerencsés' imprisonment did not last long, however. In fact, the Estates themselves, prompted by Palatin Stephen (István) Werbőczy, seriously considered transferring to him the farming of all Hungarian copper mines, theretofore in the hands of agents of the famous Augsburg banking firm, the Fuggers. Although the proposal was rejected, the debate revealed Jacob Fugger's ruthless profiteering at public expense, an exploitation facilitated by the cooperation of his Hungarian partner, Ján Thurzo, the king's chief financial adviser. But he was too powerful a financier to be repressed even by the consensus of the Hungarian Estates. Suffice it to quote his letter of 1523 to Charles V, in which he wrote:

Your Imperial Majesty doubtless knows how much I and my cousins have hitherto been inclined humbly to serve the House of Austria for its benefit and welfare. For this reason we have agreed with Your Imperial Majesty's ancestor, the late Emperor Maximilian, to do His Majesty a favor and try to secure the Roman Crown for Your Royal Majesty. We have done it in cooperation with several princes who have placed their entire confidence and faith in me and perhaps in no one else; we have also for this purpose advanced a large sum of money to Your Majesty's commissioners. . . . It is also generally known and quite obvious that Your Imperial Majesty could not have secured the Roman Crown without my help; I can prove it by autograph documents written by Your Majesty's commissioners. In all that I have not pursued any selfish aims. Had I deserted the House of Habsburg and wished to promote the French interests I would have gained much money and property, which was indeed offered to me.

Certainly, neither Szerencsés nor any other Jewish or converted financier of the period would have dared to write such a letter to the most powerful monarch in Christendom. Yet, the Hungarian Estates' verbal attacks on Fugger were neither so vehement nor so effective as were those on the "Jewish" councilor of King Louis II.[25]

During the sanguinary Turkish invasion which followed, the Jews suffered even more severely than most of their compatriots. When the Turkish army approached the capital, Buda's Jewry staunchly helped to defend the city's fortifications. As a result, Turkish artillery bombarded the Jewish quarter and destroyed many houses. After conquering the city, the Turks are said to have staged a blood bath among the Jews. According to several chroniclers, whose reports differ only in details, the Turkish commanders divided the Jewish population into three groups: men between twenty and forty years of age; men above forty; and men below twenty, women, and small children. The third group were carried away into captivity, whereas most of the adult males, allegedly 3,500 in number, were mercilessly slaughtered. These facts and figures doubtless are vastly exaggerated. The Turkish chronicler Ibrahim Pechevi, himself a native Hungarian and eyewitness of many events he describes, tells us that Suleiman the Magnificent carried several thousand skilled Jewish and Christian artisans away to Turkey, and settled them in many Turkish cities, such as Galata and Salonica. He thus wisely sought to increase the productive capacity of his country. But it appears that some of the Turkish invaders took bloody vengeance on the Jews for their defense of the city (as conversely did the Christian conquerors of Buda in 1686), underscoring the falsehood of the widespread accusations that Jews connived with the Turks in the sixteenth century. Most Buda captives doubtless were ransomed by their Turkish coreligionists. Later joined by voluntary expatriates from Hungary, they introduced another cultural ingredient into that vast melting pot of the populous middle-eastern Jewish communities, dominated by the Iberian exiles. (For instance, the renowned community of Safed, Palestine, included in 1555–56 a distinct group of 12 Hungarian Jewish families.) Later, too, during their recurrent campaigns in Hungary the Turkish soldiers committed many atrocities against Jews and other civilians. In Buda itself, a chronicler informs us, on the renewal of hostilities in 1542, the Turk, "the hereditary enemy of all Christians who keeps neither promise nor faith," assembled the local Jews in the Buda Jewish cemetery, "where they were all mowed down and slaughtered like cattle." Recurrent tragedies of this kind did not prevent the Hungarian population from holding the Jews responsible for its army's defeats. In 1526, in immediate reaction to the battle of Mohács, the Diet of Stuhlweissenburg (Székesfehérvár) banished all Jews from the country. Similarly Ferdinand, who because of an older treaty became King Louis' heir, likewise blamed the success of the Turkish invasion upon the Jews. Shortly after his accession to the Hungarian throne he is reported to have issued a general decree "that Jews be immediately expelled from every region, city, and town of this kingdom." In 1544, in conjunction with similar measures taken in his Bohemian possessions, Ferdinand repeated his decree of expulsion for Hungary. He ordered the local authorities "at this moment and at the sight of this rescript to remove them [the Jews] from the areas under your control and from the whole country." This time he made an exception, however, for the Jews of Eisenstadt (Kismarton) and the frontier fortress of Günss (Köszeg, famed for its stand against the Turks in 1532). Another decree of banishment was issued by Maximilian II in 1576. While the very repetition of these intolerant decrees testifies to their partial ineffectiveness (in Stuhlweissenburg itself a Jewish quarter is recorded in 1546), the number of Jews in Hungary must have been greatly reduced, out of proportion to the decline of the total population. As late as 1623 Ferdinand II, to explain a restriction allowing Jews to come to Pressburg as moneychangers and collectors but not as mercantile entrepreneurs, argued that the constitution of the kingdom did not permit the permanent settlement of Jews. This was, of course, a distortion invoked only to justify his wholly arbitrary occupational discrimination.[26]

Among the cities most affected by the early decrees of banishment were Buda, Ödenburg, and Pressburg (Pozsony, Bratislava). The Buda community, however, showed an extraordinary resilience. Decimated as it was by the two Turkish onslaughts and the expulsions of 1526 and 1544, it gradually rebuilt its shattered remains. According to a Turkish census preserved in Vienna, the community numbered in 1547 no less than 75 old-time taxpayers and 25 new arrivals. Fourteen years later the city was incorporated into the Ottoman Empire, and during the following century of Turkish rule it enjoyed the benefits of Turkish toleration, though it soon also shared the gradual decline in the Empire's economic prosperity. As a result, the Austrian reconquest in 1686 found no more than 25 houses in the Jewish street, with a population of approximately the same size as in 1547. On its part, the Ödenburg community, perhaps to forestall the execution of the 1526 decree of banishment, claimed that it had been established in ancient times, possibly as early as the reign of Emperor Tiberius, the original founder of the city, which was called Scarbantia by the Romans. In any case there is no doubt that both the synagogue and the Jewish cemetery had existed for many generations before the battle at Mohács, although the 1526 document's reference to six-hundred-year-old Jewish tombstones probably is exaggerated. Nonetheless the Ödenburg Jews were ruthlessly uprooted, their synagogue and cemetery expropriated, and the tombstones later used for building purposes. We have the testimony of a local stonemason that, in 1539, he took four carloads of stones, needed for the completion of the Church of St. Michael, from the former Jewish burial ground. As elsewhere, to be sure, the exclusionist policy was not consistently carried out. From the outset there arose serious complications when the burghers had to compensate the Jewish exiles for the houses appropriated from them. Moreover, from time to time individual Jews began to reappear in the city. In 1529 some burghers complained of the presence of a Jewish moneylender, echoing a similar complaint voiced three years earlier. In 1541 the Jews had to be forbidden to bring cloth and other goods to the city; the ordinance laid special emphasis on the prohibition of Jewish peddling, allegedly because of the numerous frauds committed by peddlers, to the injury of their "simpleton" customers.[27]

Similar inconsistencies also occurred in Pressburg. Here Jews were able to evade the prescribed banishment to some extent by settling in an area surrounding the city's castle which, being under the direct authority of the governor, was regarded as located outside the city limits. A decree of 1540, harking back to an ordinance issued by Matthias I Hunyadi in 1464 (in turn based upon a provision enacted in 1291 by Andrew III), admitted that originally the Jews had enjoyed "equal liberties with the burghers." It nevertheless insisted that the city no longer be open to Jewish traders. In Pressburg, too, the old synagogue and cemetery were expropriated; a few of the tombstones have only recently been recovered from the various buildings into which they had been immured. But with their usual tenacity the Jews, living outside the walls of the city but allowed to visit it for business in the daytime, succeeded in speedily rebuilding their community as an effective organ of group survival.[28]

Ferdinand himself did not hesitate to make exceptions in favor of Jewish individuals whom he considered useful to the Crown. For example, he issued a special privilege to Abraham "the Jew," son of Imre Szerencés, allowing him to settle in Eisenstadt (Kismarton) and to enjoy there all the rights granted the other Jews of the city. Evidently, Abraham either had reverted to Judaism or had never followed his father into the new faith. In any case, like his father, whose financial ingenuity with respect to the management of both public finance and private business was extolled by the Venetian diarist Marino Sanuto, Abraham undoubtedly possessed enough funds to make his presence in Eisenstadt highly welcome. Ferdinand also had to consider the specific interests of the Esterhazy (Eszterházy) family, who as lords of the Eisenstadt district subsequently pursued a rather consistent, tolerant policy and attracted numerous Jewish settlers. They ultimately helped to convert Eisenstadt into a major focus of Jewish life and learning.[29]

Of course, the Esterhazys were not wholly disinterested. In their lengthy Jewish privilege of 1627, for example, they evinced more concern for their own prerogatives than for Jewish rights. Most of the twenty-two articles of that decree were bent on ensuring that Jews would report to the government any important happening in their community. They were particularly obliged to notify the authorities about the arrival of Jewish visitors, who as a rule were forbidden to spend more than three days in the city, under the severe fine of 6 ducats. Only a few of these transients were to be admitted to permanent residence, allegedly because they formed a health hazard. On the other hand, neither were the local Jews to settle elsewhere without notifying the authorities. The community also had to inform the officials of any misdeeds which came to its attention, whether committed by Jews or by non-Jews. Most remarkably, Jews had to let the administration know of all important family events in their midst, such as marriages. While allowed to trade freely, they were to keep the authorities fully informed about their imports of wines and their moneylending (at moderate interest rates). They were also told to treat their Christian clients with respect and reverently to greet all Christian acquaintances on the streets. Jews not only were forbidden to acquire suspected stolen objects but were ordered to report their suspicions to the police. They had to keep their houses clean, as well as sweep their street, particularly before any Corpus Christi procession. Only one article referred to their autonomy: "When a Jew sues another Jew, the hearing is to take place in the presence of the rabbinical judge and his jurors in the community house." But they were not to adjudicate litigations against Christians; on the contrary, they were to assist the Christian judges and burghers in any lawsuits in which the latter might be involved. These provisions were to be enforced by the unequal penalties of 5 and 15 florins, respectively. Yet, compared with the situation in other areas, the Jews' general condition was fairly tolerable in Eisenstadt and the six adjoining communities, which under the name of *Sheva' qehillot* (seven communities) were to play a prominent role in all-Hungarian Jewish affairs in the eighteenth and early ninteenth centuries.[30]

Fortunately for the Hungarian Jews the initially intolerant Habsburg regime extended over only a small part of the country. Most of Hungary, including the capital, was soon occupied by the Ottoman armies, and remained under Turkish suzerainty until after the unsuccessful second siege of Vienna by the Turks in 1683. Despite their early clashes Jews and Turks began to get along with one another on friendly terms. From time to time individual Hungarian Jews served as agents of Turkish pashas. Others engaged in business with Christian countries, particularly with Poland and the lands of the Bohemian Crown. On one occasion in 1600, we are told, some Salonican Jews appeared before Emperor Rudolph II, claiming that they were empowered to negotiate a peace treaty between Austria and the sultan. According to the Hungarian historian Miklós Istvánffy, the emperor should have executed them for that fraud (perhaps also because they were presumed as former Marranos to have apostasized from the Christian faith), but he was satisfied with condemning them to life imprisonment. Their alleged adventurous scheme, though lacking confirmation from any other source and at first glance highly dubious, need not be completely ruled out. The startling diplomatic successes of Don Joseph Nasi and Solomon Ashkenazi, and possible rumors about the aforementioned plan of some Mantuan Jews to place a Gonzaga prince on the Polish throne, may well have inspired some Salonican dreamers to try to arrange a peace treaty between sultan and emperor, the two great potentates representing the Muslim and Christian worlds.[31]

Habsburg ambivalence in the treatment of Jews, so frequently demonstrated in the Austrian and Bohemian provinces, was doubly evident in the dynasty's generally cautious religious policy in its embattled Hungarian possessions. Here Protestantism, both Lutheran and Calvinist, spread quite early and rapidly, as did its radical wings of Anabaptists, Unitarians, and Socinians. A large segment of the nobility followed the new sects, and the Catholic administration did not dare to suppress religious dissent even to the moderate extent it had at first attempted in the Habsburg hereditary possessions. In fact, in 1563 Ferdinand had to give a formal pledge to treat "Arians and Antitrinitarians" kindly. The decree added: "In order to induce Jews and Anabaptists the sooner to immigrate into the realm, help bear the burdens, and pay the dues, His Imperial Majesty has graciously admitted them, as desired by the native population." While we do not have exact data concerning the amount of Jewish taxation, a decree of 1593, later included in the *Corpus iuris hungarici,* ordered the Jews to pay a capitation tax of 20 dinars, and the Anabaptists one of 12, while Walachians and other eastern, principally Greek Orthodox, settlers, were to be treated like the local peasants. Another document of the same year, referring to Nyitra (Nitra, Neutra), enumerates in detail the local Jewish population (amounting to 131 persons), which contributed a total of 26 florins and 20 dinars.[32]

Equally important were the Jewish contributions to the country's commerce. Although the limited extant documentation includes many accusations of Jewish malpractices and usury, Jews performed a necessary function, not only as moneylenders but also as landlords' agents, importers of cloth, and exporters of the country's agricultural produce. To be sure, they often antagonized business rivals. In 1598 the Pressburg burghers complained to Emperor Rudolph about the Jews' alleged unfair competition and secured from him, on April 12, a broad privilege which, among other provisions, forbade "the Bohemian and Moravian traders, as well as the Jews, to engage in any smuggling, private and petty trade, or the [retail] sale of cloth or linen by ells during fairs anywhere in the realm." This privilege was renewed in 1635 by Ferdinand II, and three years later by Ferdinand III. Yet it probably had no lasting effect. Apart from the local Jews, Polish Jewish traders frequently visited Hungary, despite certain difficulties arising from the monetary disparity. On one occasion King Sigismund I of Poland rejected Ferdinand I's suggestion that Polish Jewish merchants increase the importation of goods from Hungary, pointing out that two-way transactions would be difficult, "since no Hungarian coins, except gold coins, are accepted in Our dominions" (1534). In 1624 two Jews of Brody complained to the authorities of repeated chicaneries to which they and their merchandise were exposed at the hands of a despotic local lord in Vyhel. However, these difficulties did not seriously impede the trade between the two countries. As the Jewish community of Vienna grew in number and affluence, its business relations with the neighboring Hungarian cities and gentry increased appreciably. Some of the wealthy Viennese court Jews, in particular, figure prominently in the manifold transactions recorded in the documents of the early decades of the seventeenth century extant in the archive of the Batthyány family. The court Jews Moses and Jacob Löbel (with their wives, Bella and Rebecca), Jacob Schlesinger, and others frequently extended loans to Adam Batthyány and other members of that leading aristocratic clan.[33]

The Batthyány family archive furnishes valuable data on non-banking services performed by Jews. In 1622–23 a Jewish agent informed Count Ferenc Batthyány that he had considerable difficulty in acquiring 1,000 barrels of salt, which he could not ship out of Vienna, probably because of the shortages created by the great war. For the same reason, the agent complained, cloth which used to cost 1 florin per ell now fetched 3 to 4 florins. His problems were further increased by the presence of different coins in circulation. Jews may also have helped the Batthyánys in their extensive exportation of cattle to neighboring Austria. Curiously, in writing to the Vienna court Jew Moses Löb and later to his widow, Bella, Count Ferenc addressed them as "Lieber Judt" and "Libe Jüdin Lebin," which probably reveals a certain degree of familiarity between the count and his Jewish bankers. On another occasion we find a Jew serving as the agent of a bishop. Among the foreign Jewish traders one might also mention the Frankfort resident Alexander vom Korb; his suit filed against a Pressburg burgher in 1618 was dismissed by the Pressburg court, however.[34]

As early as the 1560s some Jews supplied silver utensils to Count Nicholas zu Salm and other grandees of the realm, as well as to Queen Maria. In 1560–61 payments were recorded to Jewish glaziers (*fenestripares*) of Bavaria and Moravia. Occasionally we even hear of foreign Jews contributing to the local cultural evolution. In 1572, for instance, one Jacob de Anselmis, doctor of philosophy and medicine, arrived from Italy with his wife and family, although he apparently merely stopped over in Hungary on his way to Poland. It is possible that some Jews also supplied learned Hungarians with such scholarly tracts as a Hebrew grammar and works by Josephus and Philo. These books are mentioned in documents of 1587 and 1592. In short, despite the various regimes' alternating fits of tolerance and persecution, the Jews maintained a sufficiently firm foothold in many West-Hungarian cities to play an increasing role in the country's economy and culture after the reunification of the provinces under the Habsburgs in the late seventeenth century.[35]

All along, treatment of the small Jewish community in one of these provinces, Transylvania, was less consistently harsh. To begin with, the sovereignty over this region was disputed between the Habsburgs and the local governors, beginning with John Zápolya, who after Mohács declared himself independent king of Transylvania. Habsburg control was not fully reestablished here until the end of the seventeenth century. Zápolya's successors, moreover, vacillated between Catholicism and Calvinism, while the masses of the population, which included a large German ("Saxon") segment, tended to join other Protestant sects. The Jews, who, according to their own traditions, had settled there in remote antiquity but had almost vanished in the Late Middle Ages, now began to figure more prominently in the socioeconomic life of the country.

Mutual toleration was facilitated by the heterogeneity of the population and the absence of a clearly dominant majority. These factors led the Transylvanian Diet of Thorenburg (Tórda, Turda) to order, in 1556, the confiscation of the property of the Catholic Church for use in education. By 1568 another Thorenburg Diet actually proclaimed the free practice of religion by Catholics, Calvinists, Lutherans, and Unitarians. While Catholicism was still being officially declared as the regnant faith in the enactments of the Habsburg overlords between 1548 and 1563, religious freedom for the various Christian denominations was confirmed by the distinguished prince of Transylvania Stephen (István) Báthory (1571–86), who also played a great international role as the century's most celebrated king of Poland-Lithuania. It was under his regime that Jews were first specifically mentioned in a resolution of the Diet of Klausenburg (Kolozsvár, Cluj), which somewhat obliquely stated that Greeks and Jews "should not engage in trade in places other than those specially assigned to them for residence." As far as the Jews were concerned this resolution, if carried out, would have restricted their commerce to the city of Karlsburg (Gyulafehérvár, formerly Alba Julia), located on the border between Turkey and Transylvania. Yet, in his anti-Protestant crusade, the Jesuit István (Stephen) Szántó did not hesitate to include the Jews among the alleged enemies of Catholicism and the government. In 1577 he wrote to Báthory:

Among the leading men who follow Your Majesty's Court, there are prominent heretics infected by the ferment of the Sacramentarians and [Anti-] Trinitarians. They not only with intolerable audacity blaspheme, deride, and heap unheard-of contumely upon the divine majesty in sacred places, but they also inflict no slight ignominy upon Your Royal Majesty. . . . There used to be an old custom in the Catholic Church, still diligently observed in orthodox areas, to exclude Jews, pagans, heretics, and catechumens from the sacrifice of the Mass, lest our *sacra* be treated with contempt and ridicule, and lest, against the Lord's precepts, pearls be cast before the swine.

He also complained that "with Jewish obstinacy" the heretics had hardened their hearts against all Catholic missionary efforts. But his plea evidently had little effect on the humane prince.[36]

Nonetheless, the toleration of the relatively few Jews living in Transylvania remained quite precarious. Even after an Ottoman intervention, when Stephen Bacskay (1604–1606) proclaimed the general principle of religious liberty, he left the implementation entirely to the discretion of the individual lords. It was not until the reign of another distinguished Transylvanian ruler, Gabriel (Gábor) Bethlen (1613–29), that Jewish residence permits were formally extended to all fortified cities (1627–28). This despite the fact that the Counter Reformation was making steady progress and some Christian sects, like the Unitarians, were severely persecuted. After his election in 1618 even Ferdinand II had to swear to appoint judges without regard to their faith. Bethlen actually invited Jews from Turkey to his Transylvanian realm. Inspired by a Jewish physician from Constantinople named Szasza, Bethlen authorized his envoy Nicholas Toldalaghy to bring some Turkish Jews back to Hungary with him. He declared: "Those Jews who wish to come shall receive Our letter of assurance and come with you, and once face to face with Us, if they like the conditions, We shall take such care of them as their situation may require. It does not matter if they bring expensive cattle with them, there will be buyers for them." Unfortunately for the Jews, Bethlen's ambitions to utilize the turbulence of the Thirty Years' War to expand his controls over the Habsburg Hungarian possessions failed to materialize. But his regime largely opened Transylvania to Jewish settlement, which survived the more restrictive policies of George (György) I Rákóczy (1629–48) into the era of reunification after 1683.[37]

These conditions also made it possible for the important Sabbatarian sect to arise. Founded in 1588 by Andreas Eössy, this judaizing sect observed many Jewish laws, including all holidays, and particularly stressed the observance of the Sabbath on Saturday. Although severely persecuted by Gabriel Bethlen and George Rákóczy, the sect survived into modern times, until its remnant of some thirty families formally adopted full-fledged Judaism in 1868.[38]

At Hungary's southwestern periphery, the areas later known as Croatia and Slavonia likewise became a battleground between the Habsburgs and the sultans. In fact, the Habsburg administration established here the so-called Austrian Military Border, whose soldier-farmers, endowed with numerous privileges and tax immunities, were not only Austria's most loyal defenders against the Turks but also remained staunch Catholics, fiercely resisting the inroads of Protestant teachings. Under the harsh conditions of a permanent military administration, little leeway was given to Jewish settlers. Hence the chief Jewish community of the region, located in Zagreb (Agram), which had flourished in the fourteenth and fifteenth centuries, now gradually withered away, not to be revived until the reestablishment of more peaceful conditions after the Austrian expansion in the early eighteenth century. Even then only a few Jews were able to settle in Zemun (Semlin). When in 1758 the military governor Baron Philip Levin von Beck suggested the admission of some Jewish traders to Bjelovar in order to lower the prices of uniforms for the local soldier-citizens, he encountered the resistance of the Diet and was roundly refused by the intolerant Empress Maria Theresa. Even when in 1775 Joseph II proposed to his mother the settlement of Jewish families in Croatia as a means of stimulating the stagnant economy of the Military Border, Maria Theresa rejected the proposal on religious grounds. It was not until the middle of the nineteenth century that Jews were enabled to return to Croatia in significant numbers.[39]

DISINTEGRATING EMPIRE

Preoccupied as they were with Jewish residents of their hereditary possessions and Hungary, the Habsburg emperors made only occasional use of their imperial prerogatives to protect Jews elsewhere in the Empire. Charles V's successors were not oblivious of his efforts to strengthen the central government and to utilize, for that purpose, the imperial authority over the Jewish "serfs of the Chamber." As we recall, both Maximilian II and Rudolph II (in 1561 and 1577, respectively) formally confirmed the all-German privilege granted by Charles to the Jews on April 3, 1544. They had, needless to say, no power to enforce their will in the major electorates and principalities. Without an imperial army or imperial finances under their control, they had to rely exclusively on the financial and military strength of their own lands, a strength which was frittered away in foreign wars and domestic squabbles. With respect to Jews, on whose collaboration in the domains of public finance and military supplies they now increasingly depended, the emperors maintained a measure of control only over the imperial cities and some bishoprics. There Jews now continued to live under a combination of local and imperial privileges.[40]

If, as we recall, the theory of imperial overlordship could be used by government attorneys to impair the validity of Mordecai (Markus) Meisel's testament, it also could be invoked to protect Jews. In his decree of September 14, 1571, addressed to those parts of Alsace which were under special Habsburg overlordship and to the rest of Germany, Maximilian II demanded that Jewish rights and privileges previously granted by emperors, popes, and Church councils be fully upheld.

They [the Jews] shall remain in the Empire without any obstacles and enjoy all the rights extended to them. They shall freely and securely travel and trade anywhere in the Holy Empire; their persons, possessions, and property shall be protected against attacks and arrests; and they shall not be burdened with extraordinary imposts in either war or peacetime, in cities or in the countryside. All this under a penalty of 40 gold marks, half of which is to fall to the imperial Chamber and the other half to Jewry.

Maximilian also intervened in individual cases. In 1574, after the aforementioned execution of the mintmaster Lippold in Berlin on charges of sorcery and poisoning the deceased elector of Brandenburg, the emperor was approached by Lippold's widow, who had received a mere 1,000 thalers from the very large estate left behind by her husband. This amount was not sufficient to maintain herself and her nine minor children. Maximilian felt prompted to write an urgent letter to the new Elector John George (February 10, 1574), but received a lengthy evasive reply two months later. In fact, as we recall, the rest of Brandenburg Jewry had intervingly been ordered to leave the country immediately. Nevertheless, other Jews continued appealing to the emperors for redress of local wrongs. Time and again they invoked the imperial privileges and occasionally asked for imperial intervention to prevent local Jew-baiting officials from violating them. In 1570 Maximilian exhorted the imperial officials throughout Germany to aid the Jews of Frankfort in collecting the debts due them. A broader imperial edict issued for Frankfort Jewry in 1612 also served other communities in defense of their rights. The Jews of the Swabian county of Burgau in 1618 pathetically asked for protection "so that this small rejected group may be able to live in constant peace and security under the wings of the Roman eagle." The request was supported by a written recommendation from a high churchman, Cardinal Franz Dietrichstein, archbishop of Olmütz. In compliance, the emperor confirmed the Jewish rights not only in Burgau but also in nearby Neuburg, Thannhausen, Hieben, Pinzwangau,

Ichenhausen, and Pfersten (August 27, 1618). The wealthy court Jews of Vienna and Prague, too, from time to time intervened in behalf of their coreligionists elsewhere. On one such occasion (in June, 1598) the community of Prague asked Rudolph II to intercede in behalf of three Jews imprisoned in the distant city of Emden. We do not know, however, whether their appeal met with success.[41]

Events in the relatively small town of Memmingen were typical of developments in many parts of Germany. Throughout the sixteenth century the city itself proved inhospitable to Jews. But it could not prevent the petty lords of the neighboring communities from admitting individual Jewish businessmen and from enabling them to trade with, and lend money to, the city residents as well. The number of settlers involved was very small. A census conducted in 1541 found a total of 40 Jewish families in 11 localities. Even assuming that some persons were overlooked, an average of about 4–5 families per locality must have been approximately correct. Moreover, some burghers helped the Jewish moneylenders by formally appearing as the creditors and collecting installments from the debtors—of course, for a share in the profits. Unable to cope with this situation, Memmingen induced a number of neighboring townships to join it in 1541 in an appeal to Charles V. The emperor complied with their request and, on July 14, 1541, issued a privilege (ironically named *Die Judenfreiheit* here, as were similar privileges for the cities of Nördlingen and Ulm of the same year) forbidding Jews to extend loans to local Christians. Imperial inconsistency was demonstrated, however, when six days later Charles himself issued a protective decree in favor of the Jews throughout the Empire. Ten years later Memmingen complained again to both emperor and Diet about the outrageous effects of Jewish usury. It obtained formal redress when the Augsburg Diet of 1551 resolved for the whole country:

Henceforth Jews shall not be allowed to have a deed of indebtedness written except before a constituted authority, although they ought not to be prevented from taking part in honest transactions and trade at open free fairs and markets. Should they nevertheless secure deeds other than those composed in the presence of the authorities, such deeds shall be declared null and void and no judge shall recognize them. Nor shall any Christian henceforth purchase from a Jew any claim against another Christian, nor shall any Jewish creditor cede his claim to a Christian, under the sanction of the loss of such a claim.

Even this imperial resolution did not resolve the Memmingen difficulties, however, and in 1571 the city had to secure a renewal of its 1541 privilege from Maximilian II.[42]

More or less similar provisions were later obtained by the bishopric of Strasbourg in 1575, that of Worms in 1584, the archbishopric of Treves in 1618, and others. But economic factors proved stronger than the law. In the very year 1571 the combination of a pestilence and bad crops created great food shortages, so that prices often trebled and the population sorely needed credit to tide it over the emergency. The consequent increase in borrowing from Jews and some ensuing litigations so aroused the Memmingen council that, in 1574, it ordered the police to arrest any Jew found in the city. In 1575, finally, it appealed to the *Reichskammergericht* (the Empire's Supreme Court) for redress. This tribunal, established in 1495 and partly restructured in the following sixty years, consisted of only twenty-four judges with little assisting personnel and hence found itself increasingly overburdened with lawsuits. It apparently failed to settle the issue, which was resolved only by a compromise between the parties several years later. In the early seventeenth century, on the contrary, it was the turn for the Jews of a neighboring community to complain against some unlawful restrictions imposed upon them by the city elders of Memmingen.[43]

Imperial mastery, to be sure, was not always beneficial to Jews. It almost spelled disaster for many Jewish communities in the aftermath of the German Jewish regional Council convened in Frankfort in 1603. Having attracted sufficient representation from most West-German Jewries, the Council was able to adopt ordinances reminiscent of the medieval Jewish synods—an important step, indeed, in the reconstruction of Jewish communities then slowly recuperating from the successive expulsions of the fifteenth and sixteenth centuries. Unlike its predecessors in the days of Emperors Sigismund, Frederick III, and Maximilian I, this important gathering of Jewish leaders was not primarily devoted to fiscal negotiations with the imperial Treasury. Nor was it, like the 1530

Augsburg assembly convoked by Josel of Rosheim, reacting to hostile moves anticipated from an imperial Diet. Bent upon reorganizing German Jewish community life, the Council was in itself an illustration of the growing strength and self-assertion of German Jewry. Most of its resolutions dealt with the internal management of Jewish affairs; they certainly appeared to be politically innocuous. On the contrary, by threatening with severe penalties Jews trading in counterfeit coins, purchasing stolen goods, or borrowing money from Gentiles with no intention of repaying the loan, the assembly tried to remove some of the most disturbing sources of friction between Jews and their neighbors. Such resolutions should have been acclaimed by the government. Yet three years later, when a learned but unscrupulous Frankfort Jewish butcher, Löb Kraus, who had unsuccessfully tried to blackmail the communal elders, accused the Council delegates of a treasonable plot against the imperial regime, he found ready listeners among the imperial officials.[44]

Kraus' denunciation, supported by many distortions in detail, evoked a sufficiently sympathetic echo in the ever-suspicious imperial Chancery for the emperor to ask the archbishops of Mayence and Cologne to investigate the matter. Although the Jews of Frankfort and Worms had the support of their city councils, which were apprehensive that the imperial investigation might infringe on their own ancient privileges, the accused had to stand trial. Under the guise of seeking the original minutes and resolutions of the assembly the officials dispatched to Frankfort by the two archbishops seized many communal records, closed the synagogue, and placed the entire community in jeopardy. Ultimately, the imperial fiscal (attorney) drew up, doubtless with Kraus' cooperation, a long indictment covering seventy-one charges, to which he later added sixteen more. Some of these points were completely fallacious, as when he accused the Jews of having illicitly erected a second synagogue in Frankfort in defiance of the old canonical and imperial prohibition. On closer examination it turned out that this "synagogue" was but a newly erected bakery which was used for divine services when the influx of Jewish visitors to the city's fairs caused an overflow of worshipers in the existing house of worship. More significant were the charges relating to the Council's first resolutions, which threatened with excommunication Jews repairing to general courts of justice, although these resolutions fully conformed with safeguards for Jewish communal and judicial self-government that dated back to the ancient Roman and Carolingian Empires. Nevertheless, with the growing trend toward royal absolutism, any steps aimed at strengthening communal bonds without special governmental authorization were now viewed with grave suspicion. Other decisions of the Council, aimed at strengthening the power of rabbis and communal elders, could likewise be interpreted as infringements of the undisputed supremacy of the royal bureaucracy.

On their part, the Jews, ably assisted by Christian lawyers supplied by the Frankfort and Worms city councils, submitted extensive, well-documented memoranda, citing the time-honored Jewish privileges and disputing the fiscal's accusations. The entire matter was resolved when Kraus, who had in the meantime transferred his residence to Bonn, made another blackmail attempt through letters, as well as in a personal appearance in Frankfort. He contended that, for a substantial consideration, he could secure the quashing of the prosecution. The elders again refused, but made use of the informer's imprudent steps to reveal his machinations to the city council. Totally disgusted, the council took renewed courage and submitted all the evidence to the emperor himself in 1608. Although our documentation leaves us here, with many questions unanswered, it appears that the two archbishops simply terminated the prosecution, which had dragged on for two years, without issuing a formal sentence. The whole affair might have been completely forgotten in the convulsions of the Thirty Years' War, were it not for the sudden demand of the Cologne archiepiscopal chancery in 1623 that the Frankfort community refund it the costs of the trial, in addition to a fine of 30 gold marks (for the delay?), half of which was to go to the imperial Treasury. For some reason the Mayence archbishopric was not mentioned in this connection. Willy-nilly, the Frankfort Jews paid the demanded sum, and the storm blew over.[45]

On the other hand, in matters affecting the security of Jewish life, Rudolph and Matthias at times took decisive measures. When in 1595 Luther's *On the Jews and Their Lies* was reprinted in

Dortmund and widely circulated in Frankfort and other cities with Protestant majorities, the Frankfort Jews feared its incendiary effects upon the masses. Their complaints to the emperor found a ready response, inasmuch as Rudolph was a determined champion of Catholicism, as well as the sponsor of the Imperial Police Ordinance of 1577, which, even more strictly than the precedent ordinances of 1530 and 1548, gave the imperial bureaucracy a wide range of police powers. The emperor therefore ordered the city council of Frankfort to suppress all copies of the new edition found in any bookstore. On his own initiative he also wrote to the city council of Dortmund, ordering the imprisonment of the publisher and the destruction of his stock. But this intervention may well have added to local resentments and may have helped provoke the decree expelling Jews from Dortmund, promulgated on February 21, 1596. In contrast, the emperor did not suppress similar "subversive" publications in the powerful electorates. There is no record, for instance, of any imperial intervention against the printing and distribution of L. Fabritius' *De schem hamphorasch usu et abusu apud Judaeos orationes duae,* issued in Wittenberg, 1569, which harked back to Luther's sharply anti-Jewish pamphlet of 1543.[46]

FETTMILCH UPRISING AND ITS AFTERMATH

Frankfort Jewry's great sensitivity reflected the growing tensions within the city. On the whole, the municipal authorities pursued a fairly tolerant religious policy. When the Augsburg Peace of 1555, implying the principle *Cujus regio, ejus religio,* came up for discussion at the Frankfort city council, the elders decided that "such an article has little bearing on this honorable city, since every person is free to adhere to any religion." Yet, when the Dutch War of Independence brought to Frankfort many Calvinist refugees from the Low Countries, some of whom possessed advanced skills and considerable capital and thereby helped to enhance the city's position in West-European trade and industry, some Lutheran patricians felt endangered by this influx and succeeded in forcing out most of these superior immigrants to the neighboring cities of

Hanau and Oppenheim. Similarly, the city's attitude to the Council of Trent was extremely mixed.[47]

Jews enjoyed the relative blessings of general toleration, interrupted by occasional fits of persecution and legal restriction. Moderate compared with most other German cities, Frankfort attracted many new Jewish settlers, despite the municipality's efforts to restrict their immigration. Before long the Jewish quarter, established in 1462, began bursting at the seams. This is quite evident from the aforementioned statistics of Jewish houses embraced by that quarter, which showed an increase from 14 houses in 1496 to 197 houses in 1610. No less than 50 buildings had been added during the years 1595–1610. Moreover, because of the growing shortage of land, many taller houses were built. The ghetto population, estimated at a mere 110 persons in 1463, more than doubled to 250 by 1520, and increased further to 900 in 1569, and to 2,200 in 1600. Some Jewish merchants and bankers now began engaging in large-scale business transactions. Although the city, as well as the Jewish community itself, tried to impede local contacts with foreign Jews, the number of Jewish visitors to the growingly important Frankfort fairs increased constantly. One Frankfort Jew, Joseph zum Goldenen Schwan, served as a correspondent for leading German banking firms. On one occasion he provided the firm of Imhof with loans aggregating 100,000 florins, for a commission of but 1 percent in addition to an annual salary. In 1565 he was able to lend 25,000 florins to the House of Fugger. Among his numerous debtors were no lesser princes than the archbishops-electors of Cologne and Treves, the elector palatine, and the landgrave of Hesse. Although he ultimately went bankrupt because of the failure of his borrowers to pay their debts, and ended his life in 1572, after five years in prison, while his case was still pending at court, his firm actually showed 162,238 florins of assets against only 101,935 florins of liabilities. Evidently, his assets were not liquid enough to meet his obligations in cash. Less daring Jewish financiers lent money to the Frankfort city council, though they also engaged in far-flung commercial and financial transactions reaching across the Alps and into the Baltic lands.[48]

At the same time, locally the position of Frankfort Jewry left much to be desired. The patrician council was of divided mind on the Jewish issue. On the one hand, it appreciated the Jews' contributions to the city's economy and treasury. On the other hand, it resented the competition offered by them to the few fellow patricians who were still engaging in trade, rather than living on the revenue of their landed estates or as *rentiers*. From time to time Jews were accused of currency manipulation and the circulation of depreciated coins. Undoubtedly some individuals, both Jewish and non-Jewish, were involved in such unsavory practices, if not in outright counterfeiting—practices made easy by the governments, themselves producing an increasing number of coins with ever greater admixtures of alloys. As a result, the original ratio of 68 kreutzer to one thaler, set by the Diet in 1566, increased by 1619 to 174 kreutzer to a thaler, itself with a diminished silver content. Partly as a result of such currency inflation the cost of living went up some 160 percent in the years 1552–1612, while wages increased by only 30 percent. This meant that real wages had dropped about one-half, causing much misery and deepening the social unrest. It was easily forgotten that the Jewish community itself vigorously combatted such abuses; the Frankfort Jewish Assembly of 1603, severely censured currency manipulations as a serious peril to the Jewish community. Even greater was the dissatisfaction among the masses of petty merchants and artisans. The Jews were theoretically allowed to dispose only of the pledges of defaulting debtors, but were not permitted to sell regular merchandise. Yet the guilds bitterly complained that, among the wares exhibited by the Frankfort Jewish merchants at the fairs were many articles especially manufactured or acquired by them for sale. Although the law forbade them to keep open shops in the city, nothing prevented them from attracting purchasers to their homes, or from engaging in widespread peddling both in the city and in the countryside. While in the rural areas Jewish peddlers filled a major sociocultural need, their trading within the city limits naturally aroused much controversy and led to frequent accusations of unfair competition, charges made by the powerful guilds, which had long been used to the protectionism characteristic of medieval trade and industry.[49]

More important was the inner discord among the various classes of the Christian population itself. The struggle between the artisan groups, which in the fifteenth century had tried to seize the reins of government in many West-German cities, and the entrenched patrician minority created a permanent state of flux in the city's affairs. In the late sixteenth century the patrician-dominated city council generated much further disaffection among the masses by its religious policies. The patricians were confirmed Lutherans, as were the majority of burghers. Though granting dissidents considerable freedom of worship, they denied Catholics and Calvinists any participation in municipal affairs.

At the same time, the Calvinist merchants, some of whom were refugees from the Low Countries, often resented Jewish competition in business. For this reason, rather than drawing together with the other disfranchised minorities, the Calvinists joined the rabble-rousing leader of the artisan guilds, Vincent Fettmilch, and the gifted but unscrupulous lawyer Nicholas Weitz in their attacks on both the city council and the Jews. During the coronation ceremonies for Emperor Matthias in 1612 the insurgents submitted a petition stressing the evils of Jewish usury. They wrote:

Your Imperial Majesty may wish to consider how large are the amounts expended on the maintenance of so many thousands of idle souls, since they cannot live from air. How else do they gain their livelihood than from our sweat and blood? They are our parasites and our leeches who do not stop until they devour the very marrow of our bones and we are turned into beggars.

Subsequently, in their ever more acrimonious accusations against Jews, these ringleaders combined a variety of economic and religious arguments to demand first the curtailment of the Jews' rights and then total expulsion. For example, in their attack on Jewish physicians they wrote, "Physical cure is impossible without the cure of the soul; it is better to be sick by God's will than to be healthy through the use of devilish and other forbidden means. To use Jewish doctors is tantamount to warming snakes in one's bosom and raising wolves in one's house." This is but one of a long series of indictments among the "361 Articles" which the rebel representatives submitted to the city council at the end of 1612. Not surprisingly, one of their leaders republished and widely circulated Luther's *On the Jews and Their Lies,* the distribution of which was apparently not forbidden here by the imperial censorship. Some opponents went so far as to denounce the haughty patrician elders for allegedly favoring Jews over their Christian "subjects." On the whole, however, these outbursts against Jews were both a renewed manifestation of the age-old Jew-baiting proclivities of the artisan groups and a significant phase of the broader social revolution occurring at the height of the city's major economic crisis. Friedrich Bothe, the most assiduous student of the Fettmilch uprising, stresses only the socioeconomic mainspring of the upheaval, however, when he declares: "Economic pressures and social misery were the true causes; the activities of Jews were first considered to be injurious by an already sick economic body." [50]

With the progress of the uprising, which, like many other revolutions, became increasingly radical, the Jewish issue loomed larger and larger. At first the grievances were mainly of a constitutional nature, and the parties who, on December 21, 1612, negotiated a compromise agreement, called the *Bürgervertrag*, thought that they could dispose of the Jewish question in a single article (xxii) among seventy other provisions. But in time the verbal and, finally, physical attacks on Jews overshadowed the internal constitutional problem. During the first phase of the rebellion the imperial cities of Worms, Spires, Strasbourg, Nuremberg, and Ulm tried to play the role of peacemakers in order to forestall an impending imperial intervention, which, under the existing conditions of power, was likely to establish precedents unfavorable to the sovereign claims of all imperial cities. In time, however, they realized the uselessness of their resistance to measures reluctantly taken by the imperial commissioners to restore public order. Quite early, Ulm recommended that the rebel leaders not use force against the Jews, but rather, through various chicaneries, make their life in Frankfort so unbearable that they would voluntarily depart.

In this fashion the popular uprising, of which the Jews were to become the principal victims, assumed ever greater dimensions. In the course of four years (1612–16), the artisans not only secured due representation on the council but for a while gained full control over the city. At the same time the opposing legalistic in-

terpretations concerning Jewish status, as argued in juristic memoranda prepared on both sides, revealed the ambiguity of this status
in all imperial cities. Fettmilch, Weitz, and their associates laid
particular stress upon Charles IV's pledge of his Jews to the city in
1349; in their view, the emperor had transferred his entire overlordship over Jews to the municipal government. They claimed
that since then the Jews had become "serfs" of the city, which, as
their undisputed master, could expel them, confiscate their property, and generally do with them whatever it pleased. Even after
the suppression of the revolt, the more moderate leaders (the
"Eighteen") wrote, in their memorandum of February 26, 1615,
that the city had originally "acquired" her Jews from Charles IV
and the archbishop of Mayence in 1349, 1358, and 1372, for 26,000
florins, which in purchasing power were the equivalent of 161,400
florins in 1615. They also contended that the huge increase in the
Jewish population from 2–6 families in 1417–39 to 56 in 1536,
and to 454 families in 1613, had created an intolerable situation.
The Jews and their partisans produced, to the contrary, many
imperial privileges of more recent vintage, including Charles V's
widely publicized privileges of 1530, 1544, and 1551, confirmed by
Maximilian II in 1570 and 1577 and by Matthias himself in 1612,
which showed that the Jews still were under the tutelage of the
emperor.

Irresistibly drawn into this controversy, Matthias delegated
Archbishop Johann Schweickard of Mayence and Landgrave
Louis V of Hesse (a Catholic and a Protestant prince) to adjudicate the issues. Through deputies dispatched to the city on several
occasions the two dignitaries tried to secure an amicable settlement. The populace led by Fettmilch, however, became increasingly unruly, so that the deputies themselves often felt threatened
and intimidated. Ultimately, on August 22, 1614, the mob staged
a mass attack on the Jewish quarter. Since the ghetto was surrounded by a wall, a number of armed Jews took up positions at
the gates and successfully fought off the assailants during the after-
noon and evening. However, during the night another group of
attackers found a weak spot in the wall, breached it, and pene-
trated the Jewish street, pretending to bring assistance to the be-
leaguered Jews. This ruse helped them to persuade the defenders

to lay down their arms, whereupon the gates were opened to the pillagers. In contrast, however, to the mobs that perpetrated the medieval massacres, these assailants were less interested in slaying the Jews than in plundering their homes. They allowed the Jewish community to forgather in the cemetery and there await the final decision of the newly constituted city council. It appears that only two Jews and one assailant lost their lives during the melee. Ultimately, the Jews were ordered to leave the city without delay. This victory of the rabble proved to be very short-lived, however. Matthias soon issued stern orders, placing all ringleaders under an imperial ban, restoring the old city council, and commanding it to proceed with severity against the guilty. Finally, Fettmilch and several others were executed and the Jews were formally recalled to Frankfort. Their return resembled a triumphant procession, accompanied by a guard of Mayence and Hessian soldiers with the blowing of trumpets and with shouts of rejoicing. Fettmilch's house was razed, never to be rebuilt; in its place was erected an obelisk as a reminder of his crimes. Although the city council repeatedly issued strict instructions that objects plundered from the Jewish quarter be restored to their owners, returning Jewish creditors were for a long time plagued by debtors' demands for the restoration of pledges which they no longer possessed. The city helped rebuild the three gates of the ghetto, each of which now displayed an imperial eagle with the inscription: "Protection of the Roman Imperial Majesty and the Holy Empire." The synagogue and many other damaged buildings were likewise restored at the city's expense, despite the objections of many city fathers that innocent taxpayers should not be penalized for the guilty mob. In fact, quite a few burghers had distinguished themselves during the critical moments of the uprising by offering shelter to Jews or their possessions until the return of peace. Individual claims submitted by 262 returning exiles and ranging from 30 to 8,250 florins (the total amounted to 175,919 florins) led to haggling between the city and the Jews over several years, until the Jews finally gave in and accepted partial settlements.[51]

To commemorate these events the Jewish community introduced two fast days (on Elul 27 and Adar 19), followed by a festive celebration of the so-called *Purim vins* (Vincent; Adar 20);

all were observed for many years. More significantly, since the expulsion of the Jews was constitutionally justified by the expiration, in 1614, of their basic, triennially renewable, privilege, a new *Stättigkeit* was promulgated by the emperor in 1616. It included one novel feature: thenceforth the number of Jewish residents was to be limited to 500 families; no more than 12 Jewish couples were to be married, nor more than 6 foreign Jews be admitted to settlement, each year. Otherwise the new text essentially repeated the provisions of the old law; but it significantly omitted the former three-year time limit. Since the new statute had no expiration date, it offered a permanent legal foundation for the Jewish community, down to the French Revolution. In its conclusion, moreover, the decree provided that the oath of loyalty to the city of Frankfort customarily taken by all burghers and journeymen should include the solemn pledge "to leave the entire Jewish community unmolested and uninsulted on and outside the [Jewish] streets and, in case of unexpected further riots or fires, as well as in other similar emergencies, to protect and help defend them [the Jews] against all mishaps." Finally, instead of being issued by the Frankfort city council, the *Stättigkeit* now came forth as an imperial mandate, subject to revocation by the emperor alone. It thus helped greatly to solidify and clarify the Jewish position, although enough ambiguities were carried over into the new statute from the accretion of centuries for pro-Jewish and pro-city jurists to argue the legal status of the Jewish community in Frankfort for a long decade (1814–24) before the Congress of Vienna and the Diet of the Germanic Confederation in the post-Napoleonic era. Only under the pressure of the great European Powers did the city and its Jewry settle the controversy through a compromise agreement in 1824.[52]

The Frankfort revolt spilled over to Worms and other cities. We recall that, at the beginning of the conflict between city and emperor, the Frankfort elders had received moral and legal support from several other imperial cities, although most of these had long before expelled their Jews and hence had no serious Jewish problem of their own. Only Worms had a sizable Jewish community, one which could look back on hundreds of years of distinguished history.

Perhaps because of this long past, the Jewish legal situation in Worms was quite complicated. Besides the emperor and the city, the local bishop traditionally claimed control over the Jews of the city and its environs; this control was more direct than that exercised by the archbishop of Mayence over Frankfort Jewry. A privilege issued by Bishop Emmerich in 1312 indeed still furnished the legal basis for the Worms Jewish community's structure. On the other hand, the municipal council invoked decrees issued by Charles IV in 1347 and 1348, which, as in Frankfort, handed the Jews over to the city. At the same time a noble family of neighboring Dalberg had independent claims on Jews, derived from special grants. As a result, on May 10, 1563, the Jewish community concluded an agreement with the Dalberg Chamber, promising that no Worms Jew would lend money to Dalberg subjects on either real estate or movable pledges and setting a tariff on the fees Jews were to pay for the permits they needed to attend weddings or funerals in Dalberg territory. On its part, the Jewish community kept on record a considerable array of privileges extended to it by emperors, particularly after Charles V had begun his drive for the reestablishment of imperial supremacy over Jews residing outside the powerful electorates and principalities. Charles V's pro-Jewish 1530 privilege for Alsace was confirmed by the Worms council for its Jewry in 1544. The emperor's broader privilege addressed to the entire Holy Roman Empire at the Diet of Spires of that year likewise applied to the city. It curiously concluded with an appeal to all electors, princes, and other authorities to observe it very carefully, under the sanction of the emperor's and the Empire's "severe displeasure" and a fine of 50 gold marks, which was to be equally divided between the imperial Chamber and the Jews. To reinforce that privilege, the Worms Jewish community in 1551 secured from Charles a similar decree specifically addressed to it. Charles' brother Ferdinand I, to be sure, was less friendly and, in 1558, granted the city permission to expel its Jews. However, on the intervention of the Worms bishop, Dietrich, he postponed the implementation of that decree; and in 1562 he fully confirmed Charles' privilege of 1544. Interveningly, perhaps to forestall further imperial interventions, the city itself made a compact with its Jews in 1557, spelling out in considerable detail Jewish rights and disabilities. But this agreement was limited to four years, and at its expiration in 1561 some Worms burghers began agitating for the total withdrawal of toleration from Jews. The latter appealed to Ferdinand, who asked Archbishop Daniel of Mayence, Landgrave Philip of Hesse, and the city council of Strasbourg to investigate the dispute. When the recalcitrant elders paid little heed to the commissioners, the emperor summoned representatives of both parties to his court. Even that move failed to achieve results and, it appears, the matter had to be submitted to the Imperial Supreme Court, the *Reichskammergericht,* where it was still pending decades thereafter. In the meantime, Ferdinand's successors, Maximilian II and Rudolph II, reconfirmed the Jewish privileges in 1566 and 1577, respectively. Ferdinand himself, moreover, in 1559 had ordered all imperial Jewry to pay homage to R. Jacob of Worms as their chief rabbi.[53]

Nevertheless, the revolutionary movement set in motion in Frankfort found imitators in neighboring Worms. Here, too, after an extended internal struggle, the local craft guilds, aided by a clever lawyer, Chemnitzer, succeeded in banishing the Jews. On April 10, 1615, no less than 1,400 Jews are said to have been expelled, in a more orderly fashion than their Frankfort coreligionists. But as early as March 1614, while the trouble was still brewing, Emperor Matthias had demanded from the city a report on the incipient disorders and had ordered the revocation of all "innovations and intolerable aggravations" theretofore instituted against the Jews in defiance of their imperial privileges. He also insisted upon the punishment of all instigators of anti-Jewish riots. On April 23, 1615, at the height of the disturbances, though before news had reached him about the banishment of the Worms Jews, he appointed a new commission, consisting of the bishop of Spires and the count palatine, to try to establish peace. Two weeks later, upon learning of the expulsion as a *fait accompli,* he took sterner measures.

We consider Ourselves [he wrote to the two commissioners] obligated by Our holding the Imperial Office, as well as by Our personal concern, to protect the Jews, Our serfs and those of the Holy Roman Empire's Imperial Chamber, against all violence and the aforementioned illegality [which accrues] to Our and the Empire's detriment. We also must consider the danger emanating therefrom and the bad example and disturbance it may set. We are forced, therefore, to apply appropriate penalties.

He instructed the commissioners to see that the Jews be restored to Worms and to their property, as well as be paid the requisite indemnities. Nonetheless it took another eight months before the exiles returned, with a convoy of imperial soldiers (January 9, 1616). As in Frankfort, this restoration was followed by a new *Stättigkeit*, issued by the emperor on February 22, 1617, which, with certain modifications introduced by Ferdinand III in 1641, was confirmed by all subsequent Holy Roman emperors down to Francis II. However, even this statute did not completely allay the local unrest or reestablish the former friendly relations between the burghers and the small Jewish community—which in 1620 numbered only 113 adult Jews, to increase in the following 22 years to 80 households, or approximately 500 souls. This increase occurred in the midst of the Thirty Years' War, from which both Jews and Christians suffered severely. Real stability was not to come until 1699, ten years after the destruction of the city by the French army. During that decade Worms was slowly rebuilt through the combined efforts of old and new settlers, Christian and Jewish; and the burghers finally conceded, among other matters, that Jews should no longer be styled "serfs." [54]

Less dramatic, but legally no less complicated, was the position of Jews living in other imperial cities, in so far as they were tolerated there at all. After their expulsion from their great medieval centers of learning, they tried to build new communities wherever possible. One of these was the community of Friedberg in Upper Hesse, which played a relatively minor role in all-German Jewish affairs but in the sixteenth and seventeenth centuries gained some significance in the orbit of the Frankfort community. From a total of 16 in 1536, its taxpaying members grew to 107 in 1609. Its status was more dependent on the good will of the emperor and his burgrave than on that of the city council. In 1561, when an Austrian officer killed the communal rabbi, Eliezer Liebmann, in front of the synagogue, the burgrave ordered his execution, despite pleas for mercy by several German princes. The privilege once enacted by Emperor Rudolph I in 1275 remained the fountainhead of all subsequent regulations; it was formally renewed by Charles V in 1544. During the so-called War of Liberation of the Protestant League, led by Duke (Elector) Maurice of Saxony, in alliance with Henry II of France, against Charles V, Friedberg Jewry was subjected to severe reprisals for its allegiance to the emperor. In his dispatch of July 23, 1552, to Maurice, Margrave Albert of Brandenburg reported that he had delivered the Jews of Friedberg to one of the allied generals "with the right to impose contributions on them and to deal with them as he pleases." In consequence, the Friedberg community offered to pay 12,000 florins. Ultimately, however, it delivered only 3,000 florins. Although unwittingly drawn into the investigation of the Frankfort Council of 1603, at which it had participated, the Friedberg community suffered no ill aftereffects. Its privilege was, in fact, reconfirmed by Matthias in 1612 and by later emperors down to 1707. Somewhat similar were the developments in the neighboring community of Hanau, another participant in the Frankfort Assembly, although at that time it embraced only 10 Jewish families. In the critical years of the Fettmilch uprising, Hanau could actually serve as a haven of refuge for many Jewish exiles from Frankfort. On the other hand, the imperial city of Wetzlar was given a freer hand by the emperors in dealing with its Jewish inhabitants. The city took its responsibilities, as well as authority, quite seriously, and, when in 1552, the Jews of Wetzlar, like those of Friedberg, had to pay the Protestant commanders a contribution of 3,000 florins, the city council enabled the community to borrow 2,000 florins from Christian burghers under the city's guarantee. This action was taken but eight years after a threatened expulsion of all Jews. Thenceforth the status of the local community was regulated primarily by city statutes, including a basic *Stättigkeit* of 1626 which was renewed, with but minor modifications, in 1726.[55]

ECCLESIASTICAL DOMAINS

Such defiance of imperial mandates by Frankfort and Worms— and especially the disregard of Matthias' comprehensive confirmation, shortly after his accession to the throne, of all earlier Jewish privileges (August 11, 1612)—inspired fear in many other Jewish

communities that they might suddenly be uprooted by mob violence. This was particularly the case in the numerous towns located within bishoprics, whose sovereigns often lacked the military
and bureaucratic resources of the ever more absolutist secular
princes. The Jews of the abbey of Fulda, for similar reasons, appealed directly to the emperor, in October 1614, for protection
against anticipated popular outbreaks. Touching on the most controversial constitutional issue, they argued that Emperor Henry
VII's original donation of the Fulda Jews to the abbot related
only to the transfer of the fiscal revenue from Jews, and not to the
legal and political controls, which remained with the imperial office. Their anxieties proved unfounded, however. Abbot Johann
Bernhard of Fulda, who some five months before (May 21) had issued a new regulation concerning Jews, adhered to it strictly and
prevented any anti-Jewish outbreaks in the territories under his
authority. The first three articles of that privilege merely provided
that no foreign Jews should settle anywhere in the abbey without
the abbot's permission, but no such license was required for persons marrying native Jews, scholars attending a local academy, or
religious personnel needed by the community. Jews were not to
discuss the Gospels or blaspheme against Jesus, nor accept church
objects and arms as pledges for loans. Only the concluding article
(xvi) contained the menacing reservation that the abbot might in
the future enlarge or reduce these rights, and even totally eliminate Jews from the abbey. Evidently, it was against such an even-
tuality that Jews sought imperial safeguards. This was, indeed, the
bearing of the more general decree issued by Matthias on August
27, 1618, in which he sweepingly declared that in the Empire no
domain where Jews had been living and possessed synagogues
should have the authority to remove them or to curtail their rights
without the prior knowledge and consent of the reigning emperor.
This decree was specifically addressed to several cities in central
Germany, but its message was clearly intended for the whole
Empire.[56]

Apart from their weak powers of enforcement, these imperial
decrees suffered from their excessive insistence on the preservation
of the *status quo*. They did not apply to areas which had previously expelled Jews. Some cities, moreover, managed to secure

imperial privileges reaffirming and even expanding their older intolerant laws. Even Charles V, who generally tried to uphold broad imperial prerogatives, conceded to the city of Ulm in 1541 "a privilege against the Jews and their contracts with Ulm burghers and subjects." This privilege aimed, in particular, at preventing outside Jews, including those from some neighboring localities controlled by lesser lords (they had long been excluded from the city itself), from lending money on interest to Ulm residents and from summoning them before "foreign" courts. As usual, Ferdinand went further and, at the Diet of Augsburg of 1559, granted the Ulm burghers the right to declare null and void any contractual clauses in which Ulm residents pledged not to invoke the city's anti-Jewish safeguards. He further sharpened these provisions in another privilege of 1561. To insure compliance by both the Jews and the Gentile population of Ulm's environs, the city dispatched to the neighboring townships and hamlets officials who, aided by local authorities, read this imperial privilege to the assembled Jewish residents and enjoined its observance, under manifold threats. This performance was repeated ten years later, when the city secured a renewal of its privileges from Maximilian II.[57]

No less inconsistent were the various episcopal regimes. In no case did the intolerant spirit generated by the Counter Reformation as such seem deeply to influence the archbishops or bishops in their treatment of Jews. On the contrary, it appears that, at the turn of the sixteenth century, there was a certain relaxation of the anti-Jewish animus which, in the preceding generations, had communicated itself to the bishops from their burgher-dominated capitals. On the whole, the survival of Jews in these areas after the recurrent expulsions during the fifteenth and early sixteenth centuries was owing more to the relative forebearance of the bishops and the cathedral chapters than to the secular authorities. And here, as elsewhere, the self-interest of petty lords, who controlled numerous enclaves within the various dioceses, contributed to the continued, or renewed, settlement of small numbers of Jews.

Most important were the developments in the three archiepiscopal electorates, Cologne, Mayence, and Treves, which set the tone for the entire Catholic hierarchy in Germany. As we recall, the Jews were peremptorily eliminated from the city of Cologne in

1424. Many had survived, however, in the lesser towns of the electorate, particularly the important community of Deutz near the capital. Remarkably, even a Wittelsbach prince exercising authority in Cologne did not quite follow the rigidly intolerant example set by his relatives in his Bavarian homeland. The Jewish ordinance issued by Archbishop-Elector Ernst (1583–1612) in 1599 was quite moderate, partly because, during his protracted war against his predecessor and rival, Gebhard Truchsess von Waldburg (1577–84), some Jews had proved helpful to him personally, as well as to the electorate's Treasury and economy. According to the new decree, admittedly enacted over the objections of the electoral Estates, Jews, though still excluded from the city of Cologne itself, could live scattered throughout the provinces on the basis of specific licenses (*Geleite*). They could lend money on movables, but not on church implements, stolen goods, arms, or agricultural tools, nor on real estate. If pledges were not redeemed within two years, they had to be sold at public auction under court supervision. Interest, set at 3 hellers per thaler a week, could not be compounded. In general, Jews were not supposed to own landed property or engage in any commerce or craft, except that of glaziers, of whom there apparently had long been a shortage. Jewish businessmen were further ordered to keep their ledgers in German, rather than in Hebrew or Yiddish, and carefully to enter there all income and expenses, so as to make them readily available for court inspection. The ordinance also included less usual provisions; for example, that in wartime Jews should stand guard in their respective localities under the command of princely or municipal officers. On the other hand, the decree emphasized a number of sharply segregationist provisions, allegedly because Jews were making fun of Christians and the Christian religion. Curiously, however, in contrast to his three immediate predecessors, Elector Ernst did not avail himself of the ancient privilege of having Jews extend to him an interest-free uncallable loan, but he imposed upon them a rather heavy property tax. Ernst's successor, Ferdinand (1612–50), first tried to get rid of Jews unlicensed by him who lived in the possessions of the petty lords, in so far as they had no electoral licenses, but he confirmed the 1599 ordinance in 1614 and it remained in force for many generations thereafter. All along, the city of Cologne as such still refused to admit Jews, except needed professionals like the veterinarian David and later visiting Jewish doctors from Deutz and Mühlheim.[58]

Cologne also opened its gates wide to New Christians, especially those coming from the Low Countries, then in the throes of the Dutch War of Independence. The Mendes family had quite early maintained some contacts with Cologne, as well as with the neighboring spa of Aix-la-Chapelle. But in 1566 members of the Pires and Nunes families settled in Cologne. Other arrivals included several prominent merchants belonging to the interrelated families of Ximenes, Rodrigues d'Evora, and Alvares Caldeira. A few returned to Antwerp when conditions there temporarily improved, for, as one of them expressed it, "the population here [in Cologne] is uncultured [ruda] and the city has little trade nor, it seems, will it have much in the future." But quite a few reappeared in Cologne in 1576. Some of them remained faithful Christians, but others secretly professed Judaism in the city; a few reverted to the Jewish faith publicly after transferring their residence to Hamburg. These merchants, with their far-flung commercial relations with the Iberian Peninsula, the New World, and the Far East, helped to reestablish some of Cologne's mercantile glory which, because of the gradual shift of world trade from the Mediterranean to the Atlantic, had begun losing its medieval brilliance.[59]

Politically and ecclesiastically the archbishop-elector of Mayence still maintained a nominal primacy in Germany's Catholic episcopate. But his real power had sharply declined after the rise of the great secular principalities, both Catholic and Protestant. Nevertheless, for the Jews it was important to establish at least a toehold both in the city of Mayence, from which they had been expelled several times during the fifteenth century, and in the provinces. To be sure, the territorial ordinance of the Rhenish district (Rheingauer Landesordnung) of 1579 had in theory denied the right of settlement to any Jews for the whole area. Yet some individuals began reappearing, both as residents and as visitors. In a memor book started in 1598, no less than 24 entries record the death of communal members in the years 1583–1600. The aforementioned Worms physician Joseph Beyfus, who had received his medical degree from the renowned University of Padua, was apparently allowed to practice in Mayence during his brief stay there in 1602–1603. The community began growing, however, only with the influx of refugees from the disturbances in Frankfort and Worms in 1612–16. Half a century later (in 1662), Elector John Philip felt obliged to establish a new Jewish quarter, "because Mayence Jewry had too greatly increased in number, and had thereby reduced both the livelihood and the dwelling space of the burghers, giving rise to many complaints." He also proclaimed that no more than twenty licenses be granted for Jewish families to stay in the city, whereas all the others were to move to some other locality "willing to tolerate them." [60]

Jews had begun reappearing in the electorate of Treves at the beginning of the sixteenth century, particularly in the cities of Koblenz and Boppard. As early as 1512 and 1518, two and three Jewish families were recorded, respectively, in privileges given them by Elector Richard for settlement in Lützel-Koblenz and Koblenz. A 1610 entry in the Koblenz memor book mentions the physician Saul Benjamin as head of the community. In 1547, 34 Jewish families received a similar residence permit from the elector for Boppard and neighboring localities. Eight years later they were even allowed to appoint a rabbi. True, in 1580 Elector Jacob von Eltz, in consonance with the renewed Rheingau ordinance, formally expelled all Jews from the electorate, but he made exceptions for certain individuals provided with a special license. His successor, Johann, freely extended such licenses to Jewish merchants from Egypt and Syria, hoping thereby to extend Treves' commerce with the Middle East, as well as to enrich his Treasury with customs duties. Perhaps the anti-Jewish fervor among both the clergy and the populace was deflected by the widespread witch-hunting hysteria which at that time took on extraordinary dimensions in the Treves area and cost the lives of many innocent women. Yet as late as August 14, 1663, the archbishop-elector had to warn his subjects not to interfere with the Jews' access to Sauerbrunnen and public pastures, nor to hinder them in the acquisition of kindling wood. In a new *Judenordnung* of 1681 the elector specifically authorized Jews freely to engage in wholesale trade, but they were to be allowed to keep retail shops open only if these did not compete with the Christian guilds. Elsewhere, however, the Rhenish ordinance found fairly general compliance: Jews were expelled, from Dortmund in 1596 for instance, and the city of Spires even forbade its burghers in 1603 to engage in trade with foreign Jews.[61]

Of the lesser bishoprics we need but mention here the noteworthy developments in the three more northerly dioceses of Halberstadt, Essen, Hildesheim, and their three counterparts in the south: Bamberg, Augsburg, and Würzburg. Even during the period of total exclusion, individual Jews began reappearing in Halberstadt. For instance, in 1517 Cardinal Albert admitted a Jewish physician named Jacob, particularly well known for his skill in curing (*Franzosencur*) the newly spreading, much-dreaded disease of syphilis. The cardinal wrote: "As we heard that the said Jew was expert and renowned in medicine, we did not wish to deny him to our subjects struck by the malady." B. H. Auerbach may not be wrong in suggesting that the cardinal himself required the treatment. On the other hand, when another Jew, appearing in the records in 1538, had supposedly purchased a gilded silver monstrance stolen from a church in Erxleben, it was suggested to the cardinal that he withdraw his toleration from all Jews—probably with no tangible results. In any case, the community was allowed to grow substantially in the second half of the sixteenth century, particularly after the influx of refugees from Nordhausen in 1551. However, after 1566, when the city came under the control of the duchy of Brunswick, its ruler, Henry Julius, in an outburst of intolerance issued three successive decrees of banishment, in 1590, 1591, and 1594. Not only were the Jews told to leave within a very short period, for the most part set at two months, but the decree of 1591 specified

that no Jew whatever shall be tolerated any longer in Our land. Their bodies, possessions, and goods will no longer enjoy Our protection and security, so that anyone will be allowed to attack and insult them. They shall totally avoid Our territory, nor even pass through it, but if their journeys lead them to this area they shall travel around [rather than through] Our land and territory.

In 1594, however, Henry Julius himself made exceptions for Jewish visitors to fairs, though he still prohibited them from spending more than two nights in any locality. During that period of legally proclaimed insecurity a number of Jews were really mugged and even murdered, according to the local memor book. On the other hand, some Jews took comfort in the fact that, because of the preceding expulsions, they had been spared the devastation caused by a severe pestilence of 1596–97, which had killed about one-third of Halberstadt's population. They even reflected that, had they still resided in the city, some enemies might have revived the medieval accusation of Jewish poisoning of wells. Curiously, however, under the influence of a Jewish leader, Jacob b. Israel Naphtali, Henry Julius himself changed his policy and, in 1606, issued a number of residence licenses to Jews. Yet, the local populace disliked the new arrivals and, in 1621, staged an uprising, also aimed at Christian moneylenders, and set fire to Jacob's home and the synagogue built by him. But it was unable permanently to eliminate the Jewish community, which was destined to play a significant role in the subsequent evolution of German Jewish culture.[62]

It should also be noted that, in its gradual evolution toward the nineteenth-century *Rechtsstaat,* the early modern German state no longer completely subjected its Jewish residents to the rulers' whims. Some Jews were able not only to "lobby" but also to stand up and fight for their rights. For example, in contrast to the usually arbitrary treatment of Jews by other governments, then still meekly accepted by most victims, Nordhausen found in the self-assertive Jew Joachim Ferber a relentless opponent. He sued the city council before the *Reichskammergericht* for illegally expelling him and his brother-in-law Elkan, since their ancestors had lived there from time immemorial. Thereupon the tribunal issued an urgent summons to the city either to show cause for its decree within thirty-six days or else to allow the plaintiff and his family to reside there without interference. Characteristically, this summons was issued in the name of Charles V on September 28, 1551, barely four months after his original approval of the Nordhausen decree of expulsion. In its reply the council argued not only that, in accordance with the imperial mandate, it had the right to banish its Jews, but also that Ferber had personally been guilty of a serious blasphemy against Jesus. In a conversation with a Christian carpenter employed by him in the fall of 1550, he had allegedly stated, "Your Jesus, also a carpenter, was an unruly student in Jerusalem; his misdeeds rightly induced the authorities to impose upon him the deserved punishment." The lawsuit, in which the neighboring count of Hochstein and the duke of Brunswick also became involved, ended in a compromise: the city allowed Ferber, who had in the meantime settled in Hochstein-controlled territory, to visit the city on legitimate business whenever needed. In fact, the city itself in 1577 condemned an imperial judge for having used "intemperate language" against Ferber and threatened to kill him.[63]

In Essen Jews depended on the combined good will of the city and the abbey. In 1545 they were forced to leave the area, on orders of Abbess Sibylla von Montfort. Not until 1578 was a Jew, Godtschalckh, readmitted by the then ruling Abbess Elisabeth von Sayn, for a period of fourteen years, after he had proved that he had a general imperial license for himself and his family. Other Jews followed, and their number gradually increased, as is evidenced by the growing Jewish revenue recorded in the local archives. To be sure, Jews were forbidden to engage in any "honorable commerce, craft, or burghers' livelihood," but were confined to moneylending under strictly regulated conditions. In contrast to several extant individual licenses which allowed their holders to live and trade according to custom and to charge interest of 4 hellers per thaler weekly, the general "Jew Ordinance" issued by the city in 1598 concentrated on enumerating a variety of restrictions. Emphasizing that the imperial Police Ordinance of 1577 had granted all regional and local rulers the discretion to decide whether and under which conditions they wished to tolerate Jews, the city provided, among other matters, that Jews must not buy any merchandise before the burghers had satisfied their needs, under a penalty of 3 gold florins for each transgression; that they must not serve as middlemen for Christian lenders, under the penalty of arrest of both the lenders and the Jews; and that they must return stolen objects to their owners without compensation, even if they acquired them in good faith either through purchase or as pledges for loans. These and other sharply discriminatory regulations remained in force for a century and were substantially reconfirmed by the abbey in 1695, after it had reasserted its control over the revenue from local Jews in a conflict which lasted nearly a quarter of a century (1662–86). Nonetheless the Jewish community of Essen made slow but steady progress until the outbreak of the Thirty Years' War.[64]

In the bishopric of Hildesheim, too, the enforcement of the decree of expulsion of 1457, followed by the destruction of the synagogue and Jewish cemetery, was gradually relaxed for the benefit of certain favored individuals. From the outset a number of Jews were able to remain in some adjacent communities, despite the solemn promise of the episcopal chapter never to tolerate them in the entire diocese. In fact, the city of Hildesheim itself violated that promise in 1529 when it admitted to residence the "Long" Michael who had distinguished himself as a soldier. Subsequently, one Leifmann was granted residence rights so that he might instruct the local Protestant clergy in the Hebrew language. In time a few more Jews settled in both the city and its environs, as is still attested by a number of extant Hebrew inscriptions dating back to the sixteenth century. When in 1595 the city attempted again to banish the small Jewish community, it was sued by the Jews before the Imperial Supreme Court and the emperor himself. This lawsuit was settled by an agreement dated March 4, 1601, whereby the Jews were formally readmitted to the city, where in 1609 they successfully weathered the accusation that they had brought with them the plague which was decimating the city's population. However, relations with non-Jewish neighbors still remained rather tense. As late as 1738 the city council had to send a guard to one of the frequent theatrical performances staged during Carnival, to prevent the schoolboys from molesting and insulting Jews.[65]

Inconsistency also marked the policies of the Bamberg bishops toward their Jewish subjects. The banishment of Jews in 1478 was followed by readmission of numerous individuals. Subsequent expulsions—even if formulated in drastic fashion like the decree issued in 1515 by Bishop Georg von Limburg, which actually forbade Jews even to pass through the bishopric—remained ineffective. This was particularly the case of the decrees of 1565, 1566, 1585, 1589. The comprehensive ordinance of 1593 was frequently repeated in later years, no less than six times in the course of the quarter century from 1687 to 1713 alone. In each case a number of Jews departed, but a good many others remained, for the most part after bribing the officials in charge. One such functionary was publicly reprimanded in 1585, and four years later the bishop found it necessary to remind his subordinates that, through their behavior, they jeopardized the reputation of the entire bishopric. At the same time many individuals who were forced to leave often suffered from attack on the road, so that three months after issuing his 1593 decree of banishment Bishop Neidthart von Thüngen specifically had to forbid highway assaults on exiles, under severe penalties. Yet compared with the neighboring Bavarian areas Jewish life in Bamberg succeeded in maintaining a modicum of continuity.[66]

In contrast, Augsburg was among the more persistently intolerant bishoprics. Probably more than any other city serving as a frequent locale of the Imperial Diets, it tried to reduce the freedom of movement of the occasional Jewish visitors to the parliamentary sessions. It required the intervention of the hereditary marshal of the Empire, Count von Pappenheim, who was in charge of arrangements, to persuade the city elders not to refuse admission to these Jews. Even when a formal agreement with all cities playing host to Diet sessions was signed in March 1584, there were renewed controversies, which had to be settled by another compact thirty years later. The marshal retained full jurisdiction over all Jewish visitors, who were to stay in the Diet cities only when the king or his commissioners were present at the sessions, to live only in quarters assigned to them by the respective city, and to refrain from appearing in public after dark, except in urgent cases, and then only if they were accompanied by a Christian guard. Obviously, the Diets attracted many influential citizens, including Jews, who found these assemblies convenient for establishing or renewing contacts with leading statesmen. One such likely "lobbyist," the prominent Jewish banker Michel of Derenburg, inadvertently offended Count von Pappenheim. According to the story, told at length by Burgomaster Bartholomäus Sastrow, Michel regularly appeared on the Augsburg streets in 1548 clad in luxurious attire with gold chains around his neck, riding on well-accoutered horses, and accompanied by ten or twelve liveried Jewish servants. On one occasion he was met by Count von Pappenheim, who in his nearsightedness thought that he had encountered one of the high dignitaries of the Empire, and paid Michel his obeisance. Quickly recognizing his error, instead of blaming himself, the marshal exclaimed, "May God's elements dishonor you, you old blackguard Jew!" Yet it was doubtless owing to the marshal's general moderation that, according to the records kept at the Imperial Chancery, one Isaac of Mantua was condemned to a relatively minor fine of 10 florins for the "capital crime" of intercourse with a Christian woman, while another Jew, Gump von Schwakhausen, had to pay 8 thalers for allegedly spreading malicious and libelous rumors. On other occasions, the city of Augsburg not only strictly forbade Jews in 1540 to enter for even a brief visit, but it also prohibited its burghers from admitting Jews to their own landed estates outside the city limits. It doubtless was this decree which inspired the local shoemaker-chronicler-poet Clemens Jäger (a protégé of Konrad Peutinger) to describe the achievements of the city fathers glowingly. In his history of Augsburg, composed in poetic prose in 1541, he extolled the great patience with which they had succeeded in eliminating two major evils from the city's life: the Jews and the Catholic clergy. Nonetheless the city council had to renew the 1540 prohibition within six years—a clear sign that there had been intervening violations. In 1569 the council sent a delegation to Archduke Ferdinand of Austria to seek, through him, the expulsion of Jews from the minor locality of Pfersee. Four years later the city caused the insertion into the electoral capitulations of the new Catholic bishop, Egolf von Knowingen, of a special episcopal pledge to expel the few Jews remaining in his entire diocese (for instance, in the town of Oberhausen) and to admit no others; but it achieved complete success only within the city limits, where it possessed full authority.[67]

In Würzburg, another formerly important Jewish community in central Germany, Jews had suffered from a decree of expulsion from the entire bishopric in 1453. However, this decree was never fully carried out. Other Jews began to resettle in the city and its environs in increasing numbers. As a result, the city council complained to the bishop in 1556 that Jews were gradually penetrating all quarters; they allegedly numbered then no less than 300 souls. The council demanded total banishment. The bishop procrastinated, but finally in 1559 Emperor Ferdinand gave him permission to expel the Jews within one to three years. On May 16, 1561, all the Jews in the bishopric were indeed ordered to leave within two months. Although this decree, too, was not fully implemented, since, for instance, the Von Thüngen counts protected the Jews in their small territory, the city no longer tolerated any Jewish residents. In fact, in 1575 Bishop Julius Echter suggested to the cathedral chapter that, because many pious poor Christians had been found dead on the streets during the winter, a new hospital be erected on the former Jewish cemetery. Jewish exiles protested to the emperor against the desecration of their old "house of eternity," but without avail.[68]

SECULAR PRINCIPALITIES

Complying with the provisions of the Police Ordinance of 1577, the Habsburg emperors as a rule refrained from interfering with the wishes of the ecclesiastical princes. Only occasionally did they evince concern for the fate of their Jewish "serfs." Needless to say, their occasional involvement did not stem from their Counter Reformation ideology, which, if anything, promoted religious intolerance, but rather from their efforts to maintain whatever vestiges of control were left to them outside their hereditary possessions. At the most, their Catholic bias may have made them more determined to intervene in behalf of Jews in such predominantly Lutheran cities as Frankfort or Worms. Lacking imperial ambitions, Germany's other Catholic princes were inclined to give freer rein to their personal biases and princely interests in the Jewish question as well.

Some Catholic rulers, like those of the next largest Catholic country, Bavaria, disposed of the matter simply by joining their Protestant compeers in expelling the Jews. On the instigation of the Estates, Duke Albert V (1550–79) issued in 1551 (1553) a decree of banishment which, he emphasized, was promulgated with the "gracious consent of his Roman Imperial Majesty." Generally easy-going, a lover of the arts and a builder of monumental structures, the duke fell deeper and deeper into debt and became increasingly dependent on the Estates' voting new taxes for him. He also took seriously his father's testamentary injunction "not to deviate from the Catholic Church, nor to allow any such deviations in his duchy." Personally, too, he detested Lutheranism. On one occasion he pointed out to the Estates that "among those who boast of the Augsburg Confession, there are ten different and conflicting interpretations of several major articles of faith, wherefore they accuse one another of heresy in public and in print." He thus became the outstanding champion of the Counter Reformation among the German princes. He also took his anti-Jewish decree very seriously and, with his characteristic combination of diplomatic skill and persistency, saw to it that it was enforced. Thenceforth any Jew wishing to enter the country was to secure a special safe-conduct, for which he was to pay a fee calculated per mile of his journey, in addition to the usual tolls for his wares. During his sojourn in the duchy he was to engage in no business and to depart as speedily as possible. Otherwise he was to be punished both bodily and by a fine. More, no Bavarian was to enter any contractual relationship with Jews abroad. In 1566 the duke actually obtained permission from the emperor to nullify all contracts between "foreign" Jews and his subjects, a permission which was renewed in 1571, 1577, and 1580. These provisions were repeated verbatim in the Police Ordinance of 1616.[69]

Bavaria was not a monolithic entity, however. The three major bishoprics of Bamberg, Augsburg, and Würzburg were not the only ecclesiastical possessions which formed deep enclaves in the electorate. Ratisbon, for instance, continued to pay conflicting loyalties to its city council, the bishop, and the emperor, as well as to the Bavarian duke and later elector. While Jews were peremptorily kept out of the city itself after 1519, the Jewish settlement in the suburb of Stadtamhof created frequent complications. In 1533 the Ratisbon city council complained that some of the burghers had "looked with contempt at, and violated" the existing prohibition against borrowing money from Jews or doing any other business with them. It now threatened the offenders with severe physical and other penalties, extending to the borrowers but a very brief period of grace for the redemption of their pledges. It mattered little that the Jewish moneylenders conducted their business honorably. A year before, an arrested Christian thief had confessed that he had stolen a number of silver objects from the archbishops of Mayence and Magdeburg, then visiting the city to attend the sessions of the Diet. But when he had tried to pledge them with a Jew in Stadtamhof for 12 florins, the moneylender had refused to accept that pledge and later testified against the defendant. The thief was thereupon forced to take a solemn oath never to appear in Ratisbon or anywhere within the confines of the bishoprics of Mayence, Magdeburg, and Halberstadt. Another source of dissension arose from the city's obligation, assumed after the expulsion of 1519, to compensate the imperial Treasury for its loss of Jewish revenue by an annual payment of over 357 florins, which lent itself to frequent reassignment to other beneficiaries. Around 1543, when the question was raised as to whether Jews should be readmitted to residence in the city, the elders protested vigorously to the emperor. They argued that the expulsion had been occasioned by the ruinous Jewish competition with the local burghers and that even then, almost a quarter of a century after the departure of the Jews, the city still owed much money on the obligations (totaling 60,000 florins) which it had had to assume toward various creditors of the former Jewish community. Still another crisis arose in 1549, when the Bavarian duke planned to raise Stadtamhof to the status of an independent city. The Ratisbon city council protested that the newly elevated town would perpetuate the trade relations between its Jews and the inhabitants of Ratisbon, and pointed out that, interveningly, that suburb had considerably increased its populated area because it had attracted more and more Jews seeking to partake of that trade. Several decades thereafter, however, Ratisbon's intolerance paid off, in the elders' view, when many Jews left Stadtamhof, partly because of both cities' economic decline. But this was a high price for Ratisbon to pay for the realization of its exclusivist designs.[70]

Many other enclaves likewise forced the Bavarian dukes to share their sovereignty with lesser secular lords and municipalities. Although because of the new changes in international trade Nuremberg had lost much of its economic and political eminence, the city's elders tried staunchly to uphold their intolerant policy toward Jews after the expulsion of 1498. They could not prevent the neighboring city of Fürth from developing a major new Jewish community, however. Its beginnings date back to 1528 when two Jews, Mendel Perman and Uriel Wolff, received from the Margrave of Ansbach permission to settle there. They were followed by many, among them, the wealthy banker Michel of Derenburg, whom we have encountered in Brandenburg and other states. His yearly contributions (400 florins, amplified by 100 thalers each from his two Jewish associates), made him as welcome a settler to the Ansbach lords as they had to other German rulers. Later the bishop of Bamberg allowed three Jewish families to establish residence on a piece of land in Fürth belonging to the provost of his cathedral. Thenceforth the margraves and the bishops competed in attracting Jews to Fürth, although both frequently made intolerant motions in their other possessions. We recall that in 1565, 1585, and 1593, the Bamberg bishops repeatedly issued decrees banishing Jews from the bishopric, but apparently neither they nor their subordinates took these decrees very seriously. On the other hand, neighboring Nuremberg consistently agitated for the exclusion of Jews from Fürth. In 1573, the city even obtained from Maximilian II an imperial decree which, glibly repeating the city's anti-Jewish accusations, tried to reinforce the municipal prohibitions against Jewish trade in Nuremberg, a practice often engaged in by the nearby Fürth Jews. Transgressors were threatened by the emperor with "Our and the Empire's serious displeasure and penalty" and a heavy fine of 40 gold marks, to be equally divided between the Imperial Chamber and the Nuremberg city treasury. Nevertheless the community of Fürth continued to grow in the face of occasionally antagonistic Ansbach legislation. A local chronicler contended, with evident exaggeration, that in the forty years preceding 1617 the Jews of Fürth had increased from 2 to 1,500 souls. Before long, Fürth became a leading Jewish cultural center, to some extent inheriting the prestige of the medieval Bavarian communities of Nuremberg, Augsburg, and Ratisbon.[71]

Remarkably, Margrave George the Pious, who authorized the foundation of the Fürth community in 1526, had a decade earlier begun his rule over all of Ansbach-Bayreuth with an anti-Jewish decree. After he and his brother Casimir had seized the reins of government from their deposed father, they ordered all Jews to leave their possessions, and threatened to refuse assistance to Jewish moneylenders in collecting loans from defaulting Christian debtors (April 26, 1414). By this concession the young margraves hoped to gain the good will of the Estates, which had long agitated for the expulsion of Jews. However, they simultaneously enjoined their subjects from committing any acts of violence against the departing exiles. Most extraordinarily, when a group of Jews were attacked by a mob in the hamlet of Hof and despoiled of their goods, the rulers ordered their Treasury to pay the victims an indemnity of 150 florins (May 21, 1516). Nor did the later legislation follow a simple pattern. Despite repeated decrees of banishment a number of Jews remained in various localities under the protection of local nobles. One Gottfried, claiming to have studied medicine in Padua, succeeded in settling in Hof in 1582 and attracted a considerable local clientele. It took his Christian competitor four years to persuade the authorities that Gottfried was an impostor and that he deserved to be placed behind bars. In 1611 the new margrave, Christian, finally yielded to the entreaties of the Estates and peremptorily banished the Jews; but he soon had second thoughts and used a subterfuge to avoid the appearance of breaking his word. He simply ceded his Jews to his wife Maria, who, not bound by her husband's pledge, issued a general license for the Jews to stay on under her protection. Characteristically, in her decree of June 16, 1611, she argued that, while the burghers complained of Jewish competition, "the majority of the common people of the land preferred the Jews to remain, for they find it much easier to secure a loan from Jewish lenders than from their friends, or other Christians." We indeed possess a remarkable license issued by the margravine for a Jew in Baiersdorf and certified by three Jewish witnesses signing in Hebrew. Maria disregarded even the censure of her spiritual adviser; and the Jews remained to face, with their neighbors, both the devastation and the new opportunities offered by the Thirty Years' War.[72]

These minor details are given here at some length to illustrate the oppressive pettiness and insecurity of the life of the numerous tiny Jewish communities in the Holy Roman Empire in the decades preceding the great war. They attest time and again the truly amazing perseverance and adaptability of a small minority under adverse circumstances. Relying exclusively on their own spiritual and physical resources, the vast majority of German Jewry resisted the great temptation to give up their seemingly endless struggle by the easy step of conversion to the dominant faith.

Much less needs to be added here to what was said in the last volume about the Jews in Germany's Protestant lands. In his apologetic treatise about the Jews of Venice, Simone Luzzatto in 1638 pointed out an important difference between the Catholic and Protestant countries. He stated: "Jews, for the most part, do not settle in countries which have separated from the Roman Church. It is a matter of common knowledge that in many of its principles the Jewish people leans more toward the Roman Church than toward these countries' opinions, for the Jews believe that many passages in Scripture cannot be fully understood without the aid of tradition." This may have been an overstatement by an apologist who wished to flatter his own Catholic rulers, but in essence it reflected the contemporary reality. Only a very small number of Jews at that time continued to live, or settled anew, in Protestant areas, except for the burgeoning Dutch center. Having been expelled from the major Protestant states and cities in the sixteenth century, but few Jews survived in Protestant principalities, under extremely precarious conditions. In Hesse, for example, even Landgrave Philip's relatively moderate legislation of 1539 offered them few opportunities for earning a living. Typical of the existing conditions is the 1559 petition of a Jewish physician in Giessen. The doctor wrote that he had been forced to give up his medical practice after a local preacher had proclaimed that any Christian dealing with him would be damned and had vowed to withhold communion from such "sinners." He had subsequently tried to enter commerce, but had been stopped by the merchant guild, which had him heavily fined. He therefore asked the government for permission to engage in moneylending, since the need for credit remained very urgent. Legally, there was no change in the status of Hessian Jewry under George I (1567–96) and Louis V (1596–1626). But many minor chicaneries were codified in a new ordinance issued in 1629 by George II (1626–61). Curiously, the greatest emphasis was now laid upon the religious disparity, in which the Lutheran legislator followed completely in the footsteps of the Counter Reformation popes. He instituted a quest for Jewish books, to ascertain whether they were "not opposed to the Christian faith." He warned the Jews not to instigate converts to relapse, while Christians were to abstain from attending Jewish ceremonies, such as circumcisions. Neither were the Jews spared the agonies of forced attendance at missionary sermons, for instance in Giessen in 1643, though such sermons proved no more successful there than in Catholic countries. Some of the economic regulations also were sharpened.[73]

In the Rhenish Palatinate the Calvinist rulers remained totally exclusivist. The outlawry of Jewish settlement "for all time" by Frederick III in 1575 continued unabated under his successors Louis VI (1576–83), John Casimir (1583–92), Frederick IV (1592–1610), and Frederick V (1610–32). The religious coloring of their entire legislation is well illustrated by John Casimir's lengthy decree of 1589. Here the elector-palatine felt it necessary to explain the peculiar provision that the few Jews allowed to pass through the state had to secure a "living safe-conduct," that is, a personal escort to accompany them from one frontier to the other (of course, they had to pay for both the written and the living safe-conducts). He declared that he hoped that such passages would "turn so sour" for the Jews that, dependent as their Worms community was on free access through Hesse, they would be induced to abandon that city, which lay outside the Palatinate's jurisdiction. At the same time John Casimir felt that he had to expostulate for permitting Jewish travel at all. He claimed that "the opinion is widespread among theologians that Jews should not be refused such passes, both because they are God's creatures and because they are more closely related to Christ by the flesh than we are; they may someday secure the Divine grace." And this was the prince who, in the name of religious freedom, actively supported the uprising against Philip II in the Spanish Netherlands. Other Protestant princes were even more implacable. We recall that in 1591, when Duke Henry Julius of Brunswick banished the Jews from his duchy (which then also controlled Halberstadt), he publicly declared that thenceforth everyone would be allowed "to attack and insult them." Such outbursts did not prevent him from doing business with Jews, however, which explains both his change of mind concerning their admission to Halberstadt in 1606 and his letter of recommendation for the Prague Jewess Johanka Meyslin in 1612. Nor did the southerwestern principalities of Württemberg and Baden relax their intolerant policies toward Jews. Stimulated by their increasingly "enlightened" but politically less and less self-reliant bourgeoisie, the predominantly Protestant imperial cities, too, apart from Frankfort and Worms, insisted upon keeping their gates shut to Jews.[74]

Similar conditions existed in other German regions, Catholic and Protestant. It would be too tiresome to recite still other series of decrees of expulsion, their greater or lesser degree of enforcement, the transfer of Jewish settlements from larger to smaller localities, and the refusal of most Jews thus harassed to surrender their faith. Of course, a substantial number of exiles left for more hospitable regions, particularly in Poland and Lithuania. However, before long, as we shall see, a silver lining appeared in the early seventeenth century, when such northwestern cities as Hamburg and Glückstadt began opening their gates to New Christians.

CONFLICTING TRENDS

On its face the latter part of the sixteenth century merely continued the anti-Jewish tendencies which had manifested themselves in Germany during the preceding generations and had reached a climax in the expulsions from Brandenburg, Saxony, Ratisbon, and Rothenburg. By stimulating general religious intolerance the Counter Reformation actually seemed to increase the venom of anti-Jewish agitation. Nonetheless, it was precisely in the countries where the Catholic Restoration was most successful, as in the Habsburg possessions under Rudolph II and his successors, that there was a gradual improvement of Jewish status. This was particularly the case in the lands of the Bohemian Crown, with their ethnically and denominationally heterogeneous population, which now accommodated the largest segment of imperial Jewry. At the same time, the second largest Catholic principality, that of Bavaria, under the Wittelsbach dynasty, for the first time effectively eliminated Jews from its territories, although it could not quite prevent the ecclesiastical and lay lords of its numerous enclaves from extending toleration to Jews. Characteristically, the very Catholic bishops, who seemingly marched in the vanguard of the Catholic Restoration, pursued a more moderate policy toward their Jewish subjects than did some of their secular confreres.

In the meantime Jewish economic restratification was making steady progress. The more sharply the government outlawed Jewish moneylending on interest, the more the Jews turned to other occupations, now opening up to them because of their growing dispersal through many hamlets and villages. Peddling, which had played a relatively minor part in the medieval Jewish economy, partly because of the insecurity of roads and the economic self-sufficiency of many manorial estates, now furnished a livelihood to an increasing number of small-town Jews. As elsewhere, peddlers not only contributed to the distribution of manufactured products from the cities but also were effective agents of communication between diverse localities, which sometimes differed greatly in customs, outlook, and even speech. In the smaller settlements Jews also were less likely to encounter resistance by organized Christian guilds to their engaging in crafts and petty trade. As cattle dealers and grain merchants, too, they began performing an increasingly significant role in the rural economy *qua* buyers and sellers. Jewish doctors, now appeared in smaller localities which had long been deprived of medical care. In all these areas many Jews performed truly pioneering services, in some respects reverting to the original functions performed by their ancestors in the early medieval civilization.

Even in moneylending there was a considerable change in attitude. On the one hand, the greater permissiveness toward charging interest, which was gaining acceptance not only in Calvinist but also in Lutheran and Catholic circles, operated to the Jews' detriment. An increasing number of Christian lenders now collected interest more or less openly. From the Fuggers and Welsers down to the local petty bankers Christians could extend loans to both governments and private citizens with less opprobrium than in the medieval period. As a result, Jews faced an ever larger group of competitors, and became wholly expendable even in certain areas which had theretofore depended primarily on Jewish

credit. At the same time, Jewish "usury" could no longer be cate-
gorically condemned. For the first time voices were heard like that
of the Ingolstadt cleric who, in a tract published in 1590, wrote:

How could the Jews have caused so much suffering and misery with
their usury, money trade, and their other financial and commercial
trickery if the Christians had not helped them everywhere? The Christians did so because they were too lazy to work, indulged in excessive
luxury in dress and other waste which made them dependent on the
often much sought-after Jews. Some Christians themselves have actually taken part in these usurious transactions. Yet, they accuse the
Jews alone and do not say, as would be right, *mea maxima culpa,* my
own guilt is heaviest.

The poet Pamphilus Gengenbach, generally no friend of Jews,
nevertheless presents in his dramatic poem "The Plaint of Various
Classes" a Jewish spokesman bitterly bemoaning the sharp discrimination practiced by Christians against Jews, which leaves
them only usury as a legitimate avenue for earning a living. Another poet, Johann Balthasar Schupp, blames usury on the all-too-
human weakness of "hardness of heart" which prevents people
from extending the much-needed credit to fellow men free of
charge.[75]

Such soul-searching, to be sure, was not common. Nonetheless
with the growth of law consciousness, owing in part to the reception of Roman law and the rise of a large class of lawyers, legal redress became less difficult for Jews than in earlier generations.
Needless to say, many arbitrary acts were still committed by both
officials and private citizens against helpless Jews. The increasing
presence of lawyers on municipal councils and in the state bureaucracies at times proved harmful to Jews, as was the case in
Frankfort and Worms in the critical years of the Fettmilch revolt.
Jurists schooled in the Code of Justinian could no more escape the
impact of its anti-Jewish orientation than they and other human-
istically educated persons could completely dispel the impression
made upon them by Tacitus' Jew-baiting descriptions. Yet the assistance of a sympathetic lawyer was immeasurably helpful to
Josel of Rosheim in his legal battle against the intolerant measures taken by the city of Colmar. Certainly, it had seldom happened before that a government felt sufficiently responsible to in-

demnify Jewish victims of assaults, as occurred in Bayreuth in 1516. Nor could an individual Jew have quite so easily forced his government, by protracted lawsuits before a supreme court, to reach a compromise solution, as did Joachim Ferber of Nordhausen.[76]

The growing absolutism among the various governments also promoted the preservation of law and order. Although here and there we still hear of local anti-Jewish skirmishes or attacks on Jewish refugees during their wanderings, such incidents became relatively rare. Certainly, Jew-baiters no longer tried to settle their differences with Jews by large-scale massacres similar to those of the thirteenth and fourteenth centuries. Not even the Fettmilch rebels shed much Jewish blood; they concentrated mainly on pillaging Jewish homes and on forcing Jews out of their city. The occasional emergence of influential Jewish bankers and merchants— for instance Michel of Derenburg, Joseph zum Goldenen Schwan, and the Prague leaders—also appeared as harbingers of a new era. But before these trends could come to full fruition, the Jews, like the rest of the population, had to sustain the turmoil of the Thirty Years' War.

THIRTY YEARS' WAR

I RRECONCILABLE internal and external conflicts finally drove Germany to a test of strength which turned out to be one of the greatest wars in modern European history. Ever since 1667, when Samuel Pufendorf in his memorable work *De statu imperii Germanici* gave that armed conflict, with its various phases, the name of a Thirty Years' War, scholars have speculated on its causes. The immediate cause was obvious to all. As often happens in history it was a relatively minor episode—the march, on May 23, 1618, of some 100 armed rebels on the Prague castle—which served as the tinder for the great conflagration. Their act of defiance in the famous defenestration of two imperial councilors and their secretary (without loss of life) set in motion a chain of events which led to an attempt by the Bohemian Estates to sever their relations with the Habsburg dynasty. But the more fundamental causes were, as is frequently the case in major conflicts, a combination of manifold factors, economic, political, sociocultural, and religious.

One may debate the question as to whether the Holy Roman Empire was going through an economic depression at the beginning of the seventeenth century, but there is no question that large masses of the population suffered much want. In the very Austrian provinces there soon broke out a peasant revolt reminiscent, in part, of the outbreaks of 1525. The growing inflation, causing a constant rise in the cost of living, deeply affected the sizable class of salaried personnel and *rentiers*. It was nurtured, as we shall see, by the increasingly unscrupulous currency manipulations on the part of various governments which flooded the country with ever more depreciated coins. According to the imperial mintmaster, Bartholomäus Albrecht, in 1606 no less than 5,000 different coins circulated in Germany, baffling to all but the most astute moneychangers. The gradual shift of the center of world trade to the countries bordering on the Atlantic Ocean likewise left behind a trail of dislocated merchants and craftsmen, even though it opened new opportunities for alert and enterprising businessmen. Equally important was the intensive drive of the princes to suppress the old "liberties" of the several Estates, with their numerous subdivisions, and to replace them with a more efficient bureaucratic machinery under absolute rulers. Emperor Ferdinand II (1619–37), in particular, who in many ways resembled his relative Philip II of Spain, laid the foundation for a fairly centralized Austrian regime, although he came too late into the arena of history to extend similar controls over the Empire as a whole. Understandably, the affected classes, particularly the nobles and the burghers, were not willing to submit to this transformation without resistance.

Above all, however, loomed the religious issue. The Catholic Restoration brought forth a new generation of southern Germans, especially in the Austrian provinces and Bavaria, imbued with real Catholic piety and dreaming of a return to true Catholicism in almost millenarian terms. Even Ferdinand himself, though primarily a level-headed statesman and administrator, had moments of genuine religious enthusiasm almost comparable in mood to Loyola's "Spiritual Exercises." Combining this religious dedication with his absolutist proclivities, he was prepared to listen to advisers who preached the importance of religious conformity as a cement for the state's political unity. Although Matthias' chief adviser, Cardinal Melchior Khlesel, suffered immediate disgrace and arrest after Ferdinand's accession to power, the Counter Reformation ideas long propagated by him still found eager listeners in the Court's influential circles. Asked in 1604 by Rudolph II and the then Archduke Matthias to render an opinion on the grievances submitted by Austria's Lutheran nobility, the future cardinal had this to say:

Your Majesty knows that, according to all religions, the subjects' blood is being required from the hands of the authorities. Therefore, every high religious officer devoted to his religion must seek to establish a single faith in his country so that all may profit and be blessed. However, when one renders such concessions that they lead untold souls who otherwise might have been blessed to eternal damnation, the only alternative to diminishing Your Majesty's future responsibilities is to revoke those concessions which generate so much evil.

While neither Rudolph nor Matthias had been able or willing to adopt such an intolerant policy, Ferdinand had shown, when he ruled over only Styria and Carinthia, that forcible suppression of religious dissent was indeed attainable.[1]

Religious intolerance thus came to dominate the clash of arms during the great War. True, at the outset the Catholic Charles Emmanuel of Savoy-Piedmont, who had accounts to settle with the Spanish Habsburgs in neighboring Milan, sent Count Ernst von Mansfeld, a typically unprincipled *condottiere,* with 2,000 men to help the Protestant rebels against their Austrian rulers. On the other hand, the Lutheran Elector John George of Saxony sided with the Austrians against the rebellious Czechs and, especially, their newly elected Calvinist king (John George detested Calvinism as much as Catholicism). Yet the first years of the War assumed the aspect of a primarily religious conflict, between German Catholicism and German Protestantism. Only in time did the political self-interest of the various states overshadow the religious issue, and Europe witnessed the strange spectacle of a great Catholic power, France, led by a cardinal of the Roman Church, Armand Jean du Plessis de Richelieu, allied with the Protestant princes of Germany and the ardently Protestant Swedish king, Gustavus II Adolphus, against the Catholic princes, led by the Austrian and Spanish Habsburgs. Even the Roman Curia's attitude to the War began to be colored by its desire to maintain papal independence from Habsburg dictation. Nonetheless, on the battlefields the War was still largely a religious struggle between Catholics and Protestants, and the soldiery of either side often felt free to massacre and plunder the "heretical" or "papist" civilian populations.

In this respect the Jews were somewhat better off. Not being directly involved in the religious controversy, they could play a relatively neutral role. Some statesmen and commanding generals of the opposing armies, particularly Emperors Ferdinand II and Ferdinand III (1637–57), realized the value of preserving that segment in the population which, being removed from the ideological struggle, could help to maintain some continuity in their countries' economic life. For this reason a contemporary Jewish writer, Yuspa (Joseph) Nördlinger Hahn, could write in the middle of the War:

We have seen with our own eyes and heard with our own ears that the living God is among us and performs miracles for us at all times. We have seen that quite obviously, particularly with regard to the soldiers who for many years past have traversed our cities and villages. . . . They behaved well toward our people, much better than toward the uncircumcised, to whom they caused much injury. At times Gentiles of certain localities secreted away their possessions in Jewish houses. [We also remember] the miracles which happened to those upon whom the wrath of their enemies had descended so that they wished to carry them away as captives but had failed. Also to those who have been easily saved with God's help, for the most part without any ransom or with small amounts paid for their redemption. . . . Were I to record on paper what I and my friends know [about God's miracles in our days], the scroll would not suffice to contain it.

Clearly, this was an overstatement by a moralist seeking to convey an unduly optimistic lesson to his coreligionists. We shall see that in that very year of 1630, when Hahn's book was completed, the important community of Mantua was totally uprooted as a result of the military clashes in northern Italy, and was but partially restored in the following year. On the whole, however, Jews suffered more from ruthless warfare than from religious persecution specifically aimed at them.[2]

INCIPIENT INVOLVEMENT

Such a neutral role could not easily be maintained. At the very outset of the War the Jews of Prague, for instance, took action which might have brought them much grief. When in 1619 the Protestant-dominated Estates elected as king of Bohemia Elector Frederick of the Palatinate (nicknamed the "Winter King" because of the short duration of his reign), in opposition to the Habsburg Ferdinand II, whom they had two years earlier recognized as king of Bohemia under Emperor Matthias, the Prague Jewish community's elders followed established precedents. They were unable formally to participate in the welcoming ceremonies for the new king because the city elders had deliberately assigned to them exclusively the task of serving as fire watchers throughout the city, so that the Christian population might wholeheartedly rejoice in the arrival of their new sovereign. Yet they were later able to pay homage to Frederick and offer him precious gifts. Subsequently, under enormous pressure, they even contributed some 50,000 florins to his Treasury, which had been faced by a mutiny of the soldiers because their wages were in arrears. It required all the self-control of Ferdinand and his associates, who recognized the enforced nature of such gifts and contributions, not to impose any reprisals on the community. On the contrary, shortly before the battle of the White Mountain the emperor in two letters dated October 5, 1620, instructed the commanding general and head of the Catholic League, Duke Maximilian of Bavaria, then marching into Bohemia, to extend to Jews the same protection as to Catholics, for, he claimed, almost all of them had more or less openly allied themselves with the imperial party. The emperor must also have heard of Jews who helped out Catholics in difficulty. In 1619, for instance, two Jesuits had found themselves suddenly surrounded by soldiers and in real danger, but they were saved by one Lazarus Aaron of the town of Lichtenstadt, "who not only received and harbored them in a hospitable fashion but also dressed them in his own clothing, gave them horses, personally accompanied them toward Kupferberg into Bamberg territory, and thus saved them." Of course, Jews had to accept many wartime orders from local authorities, such as that of Prague's Old City to serve as a fire brigade in the event of hostilities between Frederick and Ferdinand, and also to place four saddled horsemen at the City Hall's disposal. But Ferdinand's initial order, upon his entry into Prague and the departure of the "Winter King," helped to stave off the impending disaster. The Austrian general, Count Karl Bonaventura Bouquoy, was instructed to place a guard in the Jewish quarter. This unexpected escape from imminent danger so impressed the community that its distinguished spiritual leader, Isaiah Horowitz, author of one of the famed classics in Hebrew ethical literature, proclaimed that the day (Marḥeshvan 14, 5381– November 10, 1620) should be a permanent memorial day annually celebrated by prayers and rejoicing. Two new liturgical pieces were composed by a younger rabbi, Yom Ṭob Lipmann Heller, who was later to achieve equally great renown as a jurist and commentator. For more than a century, that Purim-like celebration was observed in the Prague synagogues, including the one then recently founded by Mordecai Meisel.[3]

After the momentous battle of the White Mountain, conditions in Bohemia slowly returned more or less to normal. Yet the intervening changes created a considerable void in the population. At first the Utraquist Party, the main residuum of the Hussite Reformation, now in power, severely persecuted the Catholics. Many of the latter, especially among the upper bourgeoisie, sought refuge in neighboring Catholic countries. After November 5, 1620, on the other hand, a sharp repression of Protestantism by the reestablished Habsburg regime began. Not only were all persons suspected of having taken part in the uprising severely prosecuted, but the Catholic reaction was so severe that many Protestants of all denominations had to flee the country. As a result, the old Czech aristocracy was decimated, its vast estates were largely confiscated, and a new nobility, often recruited from the imperial bureaucracy, took its place.

Prague's depopulation created a vast housing surplus. Confiscations added to the supply of real estate thrown onto the market. Naturally this gave the Jews, among others, many opportunities to acquire new houses, particularly in the vicinity of their former habitations. Not surprisingly, the availability of Jewish purchasers made houses located near the Jewish quarter more readily salable than those situated in other parts of the three-borough city. Ultimately, the Jewish quarter grew to become a regular Jewish town, which came to be called the *Judenstadt*. Among the newly acquired houses was the palatial mansion (valued at more than 5,000 florins) of Samuel Bassevi, about whom more will be said below. Most of the houses, however, like those of the rest of Prague, were extremely humble. At least according to the relatively judicious English traveler Fynes Moryson, who in 1591–97 traversed Germany five times, the vast majority of Prague houses were very primitive. After briefly describing, in 1591, "a little City of the Jewes, compassed with wals," and the New and the Old Cities, he observed:

So as Prague consists of three Cities, all compassed with wals, yet is nothing lesse than strong, and except the stinch of the streetes drive backe the Turkes, or they meet them in the open field, there is small hope in the fortifications thereof. The streetes are filthy, there be divers large market places; the building of some houses is of freestone, but the most part are of timber and clay, and are built with little beauty or Art, the walles being all of whole trees as they come out of the woods, the which with the barke are laid so rudely, as they may on both sides be seen.

Nonetheless the increase in Jewish real estate generated all the more opposition on the part of the city elders and churchmen, as the new Jewish owners refused to pay the municipal imposts and church tithes theretofore collected from the former owners. Jews argued that they had to defray all the expenses of their own quasi-municipal administration, in addition to the heavy Jewish taxes they paid to the government. On their part the Christian city elders complained to the Bohemian Chamber in 1623 that the Jews had acquired no less than 150 houses—indubitably a gross exaggeration, since in the official real estate records covering the period of 1621–65 only 40 houses were registered as having come into Jewish possession between 1621 and 1648. This list may be incomplete, however. In any case the Bohemian governor, Prince Karl von Liechtenstein, rejected the city's complaint, specifically stressing that Jews had done much to provide the government with the sinews of war.[4]

Remarkably, during the ups and downs of the revolutionary movement of 1618–20, the Bohemian Jews appeared to be the safest segment of the population, because they could keep aloof from the religious strife among their compatriots. In the early period some of their Catholic neighbors placed precious objects in Jewish custody so as to insure them against pillage by the Protestant rulers and fellow burghers. After the reversal in the power struggle it was the turn of the Protestant burghers to seek refuge for their persons and property in Jewish houses. Needless to say, the occupying garrisons had their share in looting property, especially of absentee owners. Not surprisingly, some of the plundered objects were offered to Jews for purchase or as pledges for loans. The new administration severely forbade such "fencing," but at times Jewish traders or moneylenders, who in the past could not be too discriminating with respect to the origin of objects offered by their clientele, may have innocently violated the prohibition. One such case created a widespread sensation. In 1621 a Jewish merchant had acquired, perhaps in good faith, some damask curtains stolen from the palace of the new governor, Prince Liechtenstein. When

the purchaser learned about the provenance of the curtains he voluntarily deposited them, as had long been the custom, with the
communal authorities for ultimate restoration to the owner. However, Albrecht Waldstein, later renowned as the great General
Albrecht von Wallenstein, did not let the matter rest. Serving as
military governor of the unruly Bohemian city, Waldstein threatened to execute the communal beadle ("door-knocker"), Ḥanokh
b. Moses Altschul. In his Reminiscences Ḥanokh later emphasized
that Waldstein was "very quick in passing death sentences and
that many soldiers [plunderers] had been hanged during his regime." Waldstein thus forced the community to reveal the purchaser's name. He finally "compromised" by imposing on the "culprits" a huge fine of 10,000 florins, necessarily defrayed by the
communal treasury. To add insult to injury Waldstein, himself a
fairly recent Catholic neophyte, turned the money over to a Jesuit
foundation for the support of Jewish converts. However, there
were so few converts to support that, some forty years later, the
foundation concentrated on helping sons of Prague's Catholic patricians. It still functioned, under another guise, in the nineteenth
century.[5]

More important were the Jewish contributions to the Austrian
Treasury and armed forces. For a time the Jews' function largely
consisted not only in paying taxes and advancing loans but also in
helping the government to get the necessary silver for minting new
coins, with increasing admixtures of alloys. This was the period of
the so-called *Kipper und Wipper* (clippers and counterfeiters), in
which the participation of private individuals was far overshadowed by that of the governments themselves. The duke of tiny
Brunswick-Wolfenbüttel is said to have operated not less than 32
legal mints for depreciated coins. In the short period of some two
years the silver content of the Prague mark declined by stages so
that coins originally valued at 19 florins and 37 kreuzers were now
considered equal to 78 florins and 2 kreuzers. Some persons
claimed that one could obtain from one old-time mark anywhere
between 85 and 110 florins. Jews had long played a considerable
role as moneychangers because of their expertise in ascertaining
the silver content of each coin. Now they also served as suppliers
of silver and even as outright minters.[6]

Among the Prague Jews, Jacob b. Samuel Bassevi (1570–1634;

popularly called Jacob Schmieles) played a leading role in the currency manipulations; he worked hand in hand with Prince Liechtenstein and Waldstein. Ultimately, in 1622, a consortium of businessmen, headed by Hans de Witte, secured from the Court Chamber a monopoly in the acquisition of older, purer coins, which had been minted in Bohemia, Moravia, and Lower Austria before 1620, so that their silver content could be extracted for use in cheaper coins. Of the fourteen members of the consortium, the best known are, next to De Witte, Liechtenstein, and Waldstein, Count Paul Michna, a leading general and secretary of the royal court, and Bassevi. The Jewish banker's contribution to the work of this group was so outstanding that, within a month of its formation, he was raised by the emperor to the rank of imperial nobility, with the title Ritter von Treuenburg, and assigned a coat of arms adorned with jewels. With this elevation went a number of privileges, including the right to lend money on landed estates; the freedom to trade in any kind of merchandise and to reside in any locality, including many Bohemian cities from which other Jews were officially barred; and immunity from all sorts of municipal taxes and tolls. Bassevi even secured the privilege of being judged exclusively by the marshal of the royal court rather than by any ordinary tribunal. Needless to say, the manipulations of the consortium created much ill will among the population, particularly among the numerous speculators, the inevitable losers in the devaluation which necessarily followed the rampaging inflation. When the day of reckoning came and a new, stable currency began to be issued in December 1623, the existing coins were devalued by 87.7 percent. This so-called *Münz-Calada* was tantamount to declaring state bankruptcy, the greatest in the history of Austria before the First World War and the ensuing dissolution of the Austrian Empire. As usual it was the Jew, Bassevi, who was principally blamed for the bad repute of the new coins, which were speedily nicknamed *schmieles thalers*. Not unexpectedly, Bassevi's financial operations increased the popular antagonism to Jews, long a primary target for denunciations on this score. As early as 1604, a Lower Rhenish assembly had complained that "one had to permit the wretched Jews and some egotistical merchant-financiers who control the monetary system to bring it to such a state that any private person is able at his discretion to intrude into the high royal privilege of issuing currency. As a result the various coins change their value from hour to hour." In 1609 a pamphleteer asked: "Is it not a sin and a shame that Jews are the minters of Germany?" A woodcut of *circa* 1620 presents Jews and Gentiles busy in collecting and melting coins, all under the supervision of the devil clad in Jewish garb. In the end, Bassevi fell from imperial grace; although temporarily saved from complete ruin by his friend Wallenstein, he lived out his life in obscurity, somewhat more fortunate than his protector (then serving as the chief commander of the Catholic armies), whose life was cut short by an assassin.[7]

In comparison with the developments in Prague even provincial Bohemian Jewry was, at first, affected to but a slight extent by the War. Because of the cautious policy of the Protestant leaders in Moravia and Silesia, the provinces were not invaded by the Habsburg armies, and for a while conditions remained rather unchanged. This was also true of Silesian Jewry, although the sizable community of Hotzenplotz (Osoblaha), which in 1616 embraced 135 families, was forced by a Protestant general in 1618 to contribute the sum of 1,000 thalers in two hours, while the rest of the city paid only 2,000 thalers. Soon thereafter, in the critical years of 1622–24, one Manasse (Moses ben Manish) of Hotzenplotz played a considerable role in supplying silver to several Silesian mints. Like his predecessor, Isaac Meyer of Prague in 1546, he was frequently persecuted by various local authorities, and saved only by the direct intervention of the Habsburg Archduke Charles. However, his career was abruptly terminated in 1624, when he was condemned to death by hanging. Endowed with a powerful constitution, he survived being suspended in Jewish fashion with his head down for four hours. Simultaneously bitten by two ferocious dogs hanged together with him, he saved himself by accepting baptism, which was performed with considerable fanfare. But, on the first occasion, he escaped to Poland and reverted to Judaism. Yet, though aided by a powerful Polish official, his and his son's efforts to regain some of his confiscated possessions, were unavailing. On the other hand, the Jewish community of Hotzenplotz, in accordance with its privileges of 1570–77, confirmed in 1616 (and reconfirmed in 1678), insisted on its independence in the subsequent calamities, and often refused to share in the city's burdens. Only in 1642, after prolonged negotiations, did it consent that its members would either, like the burghers, personally perform guard duties, or pay for guards placed in front of Jewish houses. Another compromise of 1659 settled an even more protracted controversy over the Jewish share in the debts contracted by the city during the War. In contrast, Vienna, which now increasingly became the heart of the Empire, was from the outset considered by the Bohemian rebels and their allies an important military target. There they hoped to find, in the substantial Protestant segment of the nobility, helpers to overthrow the centralized regime and to replace it with a sort of confederation of more or less independent states, essentially run by the Estates under a nominal sovereign. The Protestant army actually occupied Upper Austria, which in addition suffered from a serious peasant uprising. At this point Ferdinand, who had been elected emperor in August 1619 by the unanimous vote of the Protestant, as well as Catholic, electors, found an effective ally in Duke Maximilian of Bavaria, under whose command the Austrian army threw back the rebels and reestablished the emperor's control.[8]

From the onset of the Bohemian revolution Vienna Jews were called upon, under severe threats, to pay increasing amounts in taxes. On January 11, 1619, Emperor Matthias ordered his commissioners to see to it that the Viennese community, which had shortly before delivered 3,000 florins, should within fourteen days pay an additional 30,000 to 35,000 florins. The Jews pleaded inability to deliver any additional funds, "for even a well from which too much water is drawn finally runs dry." By June the new ruler, Ferdinand, ordered his commissioners to point out to the Jews the menace of an enemy invasion and to force them to contribute 18,000 to 20,000 florins, under the threat of cancellation of all their liberties and immediate expulsion. After promising to pay a total of 10,000 florins, the Jews secured from the commissioners a pledge that they would intercede with the emperor for a renewal of all their privileges (June 12–17, 1619). Nonetheless, three months later the emperor again demanded from the Jews a "loan" of 30,000 to 35,000 florins for the suppression of the disturbances in Bohemia. Shortly thereafter Archduke Leopold, the rather ruthless governor of Vienna, simultaneously serving as bishop of both Passau and Strasbourg, found a new method of squeezing money out of the relatively small Jewish community: he threatened to billet soldiers in its homes. Under the conditions of that time, billeting was tantamount to a formal license for pillaging. As usual, the Jews compromised and in April 1620 paid an unspecified amount for the acquisition of horses for the artillery. Another effective threat was used soon thereafter: the Jews were told that, unless they made another substantial contribution, their synagogue and their more important stores would be closed down. Nor were the few Jewish bankers in the city freed from the obligation to cooperate with the governmentally controlled monetary ventures. On August 21, 1620, the Lower Austrian Chamber was ordered to force them to discontinue exporting any coins, yet on July 19, 1621, the same Chamber was instructed to make them distribute coins of smaller denominations than theretofore, under the sanction of severe penalties. Finally, on January 10, 1622, the Jews of Vienna were granted, against the payment of 76,000 florins, the exclusive right, to last for six days (February 10–16), to issue coins and convert the so-called Spires' silver into currency, without further accounting. Two months later the Treasury actually attested that, between March 24, 1621, and February 16, 1622, the Jews had administered the monetary transactions according to instructions, "faithfully and honorably." It was in this rather friendly atmosphere that the Jewish community applied for a permit to construct a synagogue in lieu of the two existing small places of worship in private houses. The community felt that such a new building would give it a permanent social and religious center, independent of the whims of non-Jewish landlords. The negotiations had been proceeding slowly but favorably when, for reasons to be discussed below, the entire community was transferred to a new quarter in 1624.[9]

Less is to be said about the early stages of the War in their effect upon the Jews of Hungary. True, the Transylvanian ruler, Gabriel (Gábor) Bethlen, used the embarrassment created for the Habsburgs by the Bohemian revolt and Ferdinand's initially uncertain accession to the throne, to attack Austria's Hungarian possessions. But his great ambitions remained unfulfilled, and ultimately he had to be satisfied with a slight increase of his territorial domain, and the title of prince of the Empire. True, like the other inhabitants, Hungarian Jews in the territories overrun by Bethlen's army suffered severely. But there was no basic change in their economic pursuits, their legal status, or their cultural life; at least not in the first Austro-Bohemian phase of the great European drama.[10]

EUROPEAN RAMIFICATIONS

By 1624 the first phase of the War, centered around Bohemia and the Palatinate, seemed to draw to a successful conclusion for the Habsburg and Catholic cause. But the victors' extravagant hopes were speedily deflated. After the defeat of Count Mansfeld's Protestant army at Stadtlohn on August 9, 1623, the commanding general of the Catholic League, Johann Tserclaes von Tilly, somewhat rashly voiced his conviction that the Protestant "forces would not be able to stage an early recovery and resume their resistance." He did not quite realize the extent of involvement of the other European powers in this internecine struggle between the Germans. In the following years Danish, Swedish, and French troops successively appeared in increasing numbers on the German scene. The Peace Treaty of Prague of 1635, to be sure, in part nurtured by the growing concern of German nationalists at the sight of the foreign troops, tried to put an end to the hostilities, but it proved to be an ephemeral pause in the ruinous encounters, which, in the main, continued to be fought on German soil. The numerous peace feelers of the early 1640s interfered little with the bloody and ruinous campaigns, until sheer exhaustion forced the belligerents to reach a settlement in the Treaties of Westphalia in 1648.

In essence the Thirty Years' War remained a preeminently German war. After Stadtlohn, Tilly had tried in vain to persuade the emperor and his allies to invade Holland, "for so long as these rebels are not extirpated, the Holy Roman Empire will not enjoy a secure peace." As a result, whatever battles were fought by the Dutch and the Spaniards on the high seas and between the latter and the French in northern Italy were essentially a continuation of their separate long-time conflicts, and only indirectly, if importantly, contributed to the final outcome of the Catholic-Protestant confrontation in the Empire. Certainly, the staggering losses of the civilian population and the ensuing exhaustion of all German parties far overshadowed the comparable effects of the War on other European societies. In the case of Jews, the great drama unfolded itself almost entirely within the confines of the Empire; the few other encounters on land or sea took place on the periphery of Jewish settlements. In so far as they had an impact on some Jews in such outlying districts as Brazil, they will be mentioned in later chapters. But here we need concern ourselves only with the military and sociopolitical struggles in and over Germany.[11]

Growing Catholic self-assertion in the early stages of the War made itself immediately felt among Jews in the centers of Catholic power: Vienna and Prague. Despite his general friendliness to Jews and his growing utilization of Jewish skills and capital for the prosecution of the conflict, Ferdinand II now emphasized more than before certain anti-Jewish elements of the Catholic tradition. In a decree of December 6, 1624, he assigned a special quarter to the Jews of his imperial capital. True, this was done with the Jews' full collaboration. Reminiscing later about his rabbinical leadership of the Vienna community during that period, Yom Ṭob Lipmann Heller boasted that "it is generally known that I issued fine and appropriate ordinances there, so that they [the Vienna Jews] became one community. Before that time they had lived scattered among the Gentiles, not as a group together, until our lord, the emperor, assigned to them a special location outside the city." The designated area was sufficiently large to accommodate the growing Jewish population, and during the half century of the ghetto's existence it did not develop the usual characteristics of an overcrowded slum. Nor were the sanitary conditions, despite the high mortality rate among children and child-bearing women, any worse than those prevailing in the Christian community or in other cities. In general, the government tried to avoid the appearance of hostility toward the Jewish subjects. In his decree establishing the new Jewish quarter in *Der untere Werd* (later part of the well-known Viennese district Leopoldstadt) Ferdinand merely emphasized the practical aspects of this measure, supposedly taken because of the city's overpopulation. He thus removed any implication offensive to Jews. He also inserted numerous protective provisions for the security of the inhabitants and against their being overcharged by the quarter's former house owners or by parish priests seeking to maintain their previous income. But a month later the emperor proceeded with another expulsion of unlicensed Jewish residents. Whatever his motives may have been, the new ghetto did indeed fulfill one of the major segregationist demands of the Counter Reformation popes.[12]

Another manifestation of the regime's readiness to comply with these demands was the introduction, in 1630, of conversionist sermons, to be compulsorily attended by Jewish residents of Vienna. The guiding spirit behind this regulation was the bishop of Vienna, Cardinal Melchior Khlesel, who, interveningly restored to the emperor's graces, had resumed his vigorous leadership of the Austrian Counter Reformation. After allegedly advocating the total expulsion of Jews, which was roundly rejected, he rejoiced on hearing, shortly before his death (September 18, 1630), that the emperor had decided to order the Jews to attend missionary discourses. To cite the Court Chancery's report of March 12, the cardinal had wished thereby to place at the emperor's disposal a method of serving the divine will:

Just as Your Imperial Majesty endeavors with God's help zealously to promote the holy Catholic religion and to convert the heretics to it, so You may remember to bring the Jews, too, to the true recognition of the Christian faith. The cardinal likewise considers himself obligated to do his share in this matter and considers it a subject most worthy of careful deliberation. For this purpose he has called together several theologians, especially from among the fathers of the Society of Jesus, who offered to present within a short time a preacher familiar with the Hebrew language in order to initiate this work.

Khlesel also promised to write to Rome and ask the papal Curia to designate additional qualified personnel for this service. With the emperor's approval the authorities commanded the Jewish community thenceforth regularly to send two hundred Jews and Jewesses, including up to forty adolescents aged fifteen to twenty, to attend and listen carefully to these sermons. Special guards were to prevent the audience from falling asleep or leaving before the completion of the services, while absenteeism was to be punished by progressively heavier fines. In contrast to the usual procedure in Rome and other localities, however, the Viennese churchmen considered it improper to have Jews meet in a church. They therefore arranged to hold these sessions in the auditorium of the University, although special precautions had to be taken there against frivolous insults by students, since youthful attacks on Jews had become rather commonplace throughout the Holy Roman Empire. Such assaults seem to have become doubly frequent now, perhaps in response to the growing violence characteristic of the protracted War and from the ensuing loosening of public and private morals. Time and again the government had to order the University authorities to punish the guilty. In more severe instances, such as the knifing of an innocent Jewish passerby, it took direct punitive action. Even more remarkably, the 1624 ghetto decree for the first time officially freed the licensed Jewish residents of Vienna from the obligation to wear badges.[13]

Jews resisted fiercely. We hear of practically no conversions to Christianity in Vienna and of very few in the much larger community of Prague. The Jewish elders must have found it doubly galling when, after the loss of a member by apostasy, they had formally to release him from all communal obligations. Wherever possible, families tried hard to dissuade straying members from thus completely severing their ties with relatives and friends; in some cases they induced converts to return to the fold, in defiance of the canonical prohibition. In 1635, after the archbishop of Prague had personally administered baptism to the daughter of one Löbl Pasca, the young woman suddenly disappeared, and a search through the Jewish quarter proved unsuccessful. Thereupon the police arrested her father and accused him of having caused her relapse. Another convert, Ferdinand Franz Engelsberger, at first succeeded in persuading his family to accept baptism. But soon thereafter his wife and children, apparently stricken with remorse, escaped from Prague and, with the aid of unnamed Jewish friends, found their way to Poland, where they reverted to Judaism. In this case their abettors seem not to have been apprehended, the Prague inquisitorial searches evidently being far less effective than similar pursuits on the Iberian Peninsula.[14]

The revival of medieval heresy hunting by the Counter Reformation also brought forth renewed attacks on alleged Jewish literary polemics against Christianity. These denunciations gave rise to the *cause célèbre* of 1629–30 involving R. Yom Ṭob Lipmann b. Nathan Heller. This distinguished scholar—author of many rabbinic works, including the *Tosefot Yom Ṭob* (Yom Ṭob's Supplements), a famous commentary on the Mishnah still widely used today—had returned in 1627 from Vienna to Prague to serve as chief rabbi and head of the Academy. Two years later he was denounced by some of his quarrelsome Prague coreligionists for allegedly having blasphemed against Christianity in his twin super-commentaries (colorfully called "Royal Dainties" and "Delightful Bread") on Asher b. Yeḥiel's classic halakhic work on the Talmud. According to his own dramatic description, Heller and the lay leaders of the community learned with dismay that Ferdinand II had ordered him to be brought in chains to Vienna for trial. The elders protested to the Prague authorities that, as soon as the news about the imprisonment of their spiritual leader would spread, the populace would assume that "Jews had rebelled against the emperor, a rumor which would cause the Jews of every town to be maltreated." By further arguing that the ensuing scandal would be injurious to the emperor's own interests, they secured from the governor of Bohemia permission for the rabbi to travel to Vienna on his own and to stand trial there. In listing the rabbi's purported blasphemies the prosecution cited statements in his works extolling the merits of the Talmud, while he should have known that this work had long been condemned by the Church. All his explanations were rejected, and Heller was in mortal danger, but he was finally released from prison after promising to pay the huge fine of 10,000 florins. He was deprived of his rabbinic post in Prague and forbidden to serve in a similar capacity in any Habsburg community. (He emigrated to Poland where, as the widely revered rabbi of Cracow, he died in 1654.) Possibly in a delayed reaction to this incident the famous Jewish printing presses in Prague and smaller establishments in the provinces were shut down by a decree of 1630. They were not reopened until three years later.[15]

Perhaps the most noteworthy aspect of the Heller affair was that the emperor refrained from drawing any conclusions affecting the rest of Jewry. Neither the community of Prague nor that of Vienna suffered any retribution. Here again it was not Ferdinand II's sense of justice alone which accounted for his restraint, but rather his recognition of the signal services rendered him by a number of court Jews and their agents throughout the country. To facilitate the work of these Jewish agents and army contractors, his son and successor, Ferdinand III, reiterated as late as January 12, 1645, that "if one or another [Viennese] Jew wishes to follow Our Imperial camp with his trade" he should be treated on a par with Christian merchants and should be made to pay tolls by land or water in exactly the same amount as his Christian compeers. The Jews of Prague had even earlier (August 12, 1627) received the right of freely visiting any fair in Bohemia or Silesia on the same basis as the Christian merchants. The decree specifically forbade the authorities to charge Jews higher tolls than were customary in each locality or in any other way to interfere with their legitimate business. More significantly, Jews were given the general right to engage in any craft and to train for it without obstacles. This privilege was further expanded in a long, solemn document, dated June 30, 1628, which placed any violation of these provisions under the severe penalty of 30 marks gold. These decrees are doubly remarkable, as they ran counter to a solemn promise the emperor had made shortly before to the burghers of the Old City of Prague. In response to the burghers' complaints against the undue expansion of the Jewish quarter in the preceding years, Ferdinand II had given, on April 8, 1627, a guarantee that Jews would not be allowed "to sell, transfer, give, or pledge" any of the houses they had acquired after the victory at the White Mountain, except to Christians. The decree of August 12, on the contrary, expressly confirmed the unrestricted Jewish rights of ownership to the so-called Liechtenstein houses. These rights were reconfirmed by Ferdinand III in his privilege of April 8, 1648, and were honored in practice.[16]

ECONOMIC POLICIES

Such imperial inconsistencies also characterized the Habsburg economic policies with respect to Jews, since the imperial officials could not completely disregard the burghers' perpetual hostility to their Jewish protégés. In a petition to the emperor of 1637(?), the mayor and city council of Vienna once again demanded the banishment of all Jews to a radius of at least three leagues from the city. Among their major grievances they listed the following: unfair Jewish competition, specifically the practice of securing business ahead of Christians by awaiting the arrival of visitors to the city in the inns; Jewish malfeasance in the exchange of currency and the smuggling of inferior coins into the city; the overcrowding of Jewish houses, which often accommodated 30–50 persons in a tiny building, creating serious health hazards for all the city's inhabitants; the Jews' continued blasphemies against Christianity and the contempt they often demonstrated against religious processions and other *venerabilia* of the Christian faith. The burghers did not hesitate to refer, at least in passing, though evidently with little conviction, to the Jews' "formerly described evil deeds of poisoning the wells and utter desecration of the holy host." True, Ferdinand III dismissed these accusations and, on November 5, 1638, issued a new "patent" of protection for the Viennese Jews. But there were other occasions on which, like his father, he yielded to the manifold pressures from burghers and churchmen and issued a variety of anti-Jewish regulations. On the other hand, the vagaries of imperial legislation sometimes operated in the Jews' favor. According to the general Land Ordinance of 1623, Jews were supposed to return stolen objects pledged with them to the owners without compensation. When the Jewish moneylenders argued, however, that this law would enable fraudulent debtors to borrow money from the bankers through third persons and subsequently reclaim the pledges as belonging to them, without indemnifying the creditors, the authorities reversed themselves and in 1627 ordered full indemnification to Jewish lenders in good faith. Similar contradictions crept into the government's mediating efforts between the monopolistic demands of the Christian artisan and merchant guilds and the Jews' drive to secure relief from the existing severe restraints on their trade and industry. While the burghers always invoked their older privileges, often carried down for generations from the controlled medieval economic systems, the Jews plausibly demonstrated that, through their crafts and trade, aimed at a greater turnover at less profit per unit, they had made many lower-priced articles available to the masses for the first time. On the whole, the relatively small Jewish community of Vienna could largely acquiesce in the industrial restrictions placed on them, but the more numerous Jews of Prague and other Bohemian cities had to fight hard for maintaining, and if possible enlarging, their industrial opportunities, without which they would not have been able to earn even substandard incomes.[17]

Most alarming to the Jews was the dichotomy between the general prohibition of usury by canon law and their own vital interest in moneylending, buttressed by the growing demand for credit on the part of both the productive and the needy segments of the population. This dichotomy was sharpened now by the reinvigorated religious zeal of the Counter Reformation. In 1627 the Court Chamber submitted to the emperor a report on its deliberations for some time past concerning the advisability of an outright prohibition of usury in all forms, which it had decided would be to "Your Majesty's great detriment and prejudice." It claimed that usurious contracts were constantly being entered into by members of all classes, including persons of high social standing, and that Jews especially were charging 27 percent interest and more, instead of the 6 percent which an imperial rescript had theretofore declared permissible. The Chamber suggested a careful investigation of how this evil could best be eliminated. It must have realized the complexities of these problems, which had been aired as recently as the 1580s and 1590s by the Lower Austrian Estates. The grievances voiced by the anti-usury forces had at that time prompted a number of restrictive acts, which were almost immediately disregarded in practice. They were thrown into complete limbo under the impact of the inflationary trends and shortages of capital created by the Thirty Years' War. Because of its deep roots in the Catholic tradition, however, the outlawry of all usury greatly appealed to Ferdinand II, who now renewed the old prohibition, with all its severe sanctions, in a decree dated September 11, 1628.[18]

Touched to the quick, the Jews reacted vigorously. In a lengthy petition addressed to the Lower Austrian authorities sometime in 1629, their elders emphasized that even before the imperial decree had been issued the Vienna community had proclaimed a ban on all Jewish lenders charging more than 10 percent interest. They intimated that fewer Jews would dare to violate such a communal ban than to break an imperial law. At the same time, the few exceptional offenders would by no means be discouraged by a reduction of the permissible interest rate to 6 percent. More fundamentally, the Jewish leaders pointed out differences between Jewish and Christian moneylending. While Christians as a rule lent hundreds of florins or more over terms of a year or longer and demanded expensive pledges like jewelry or other precious objects, Jews for the most part served the broader masses of the population with short-term loans of a few florins, accepted any kind of second-hand clothing or household goods as pawns, and permitted the borrowers to repay the loans at any time. Hence, the Vienna elders reasoned, Jews ought to be allowed to charge a higher rate of interest for such costly transactions. Moreover, they pointed out:

We are tolerated only by the grace of Christians, and as human beings must make a living. Yet we are not allowed to learn and exercise any craft under whatever name; nor are we admitted to any office or dignity; and we are precluded from the purchase of fields, vineyards, mills, and other landed possessions of any kind. . . . We are allowed only to trade in open shops and to lend money on "Jewish interest." In addition, everyone knows that our assets are very small and that if a Jew were to lend a total of 100 florins or so at a low rate of interest he would hardly be able to maintain his own person, not to speak of a wife and children. It is also a matter of common knowledge that a Jew must contribute [to the government] from property valued at 100 florins as much as a Christian does from one estimated at 1,000 florins.

For these reasons, the petitioners argued, the Papacy had permitted the Jews of Rome to charge 20 percent per annum. Some such arrangement in the case of Viennese Jews was likewise fully justified. Whether or not this petition proved cogent enough for the imperial authorities formally to abrogate or modify their legal restrictions, Jews continued to lend money at relatively high rates of interest in both the Austrian provinces and those of the Bohemian Crown. In fact, this issue was to play a certain role in the extended discussions preliminary to the expulsion of the Jews from Vienna in 1670. Interveningly, however, these and other factors propelled more and more Jews out of the sphere of moneylending into that of general merchandising and, in Bohemia particularly, into the various handicrafts.[19]

In this way Jews were able to continue making their major, badly needed contributions to the imperial Treasury. In 1627 Bohemian Jewry arranged for a lump-sum annual payment of 40,000 florins. This was a moderate sum compared, for instance, with the sudden assessment of 240,000 florins demanded from the Jews in 1623. However, the 40,000 total now regularly expected was frequently augmented by independent imposts levied by the Diet, special wartime "contributions" demanded in such emergencies as the occupation of Prague by the Saxon troops and their withdrawal in 1632, and a variety of local taxes imposed on the lesser communities by their respective lords. Some taxes, or parts thereof, were paid in kind, as in 1645, when the Jewish community delivered 3,000 soldiers' uniforms with shirts and shoes valued at 28,744 florins and 42 kreuzer. There also were poll taxes on all men over twenty and, in lesser amounts, on Jewish boys between 10 and 20 years of age as well as real estate taxes on houses. Owners of Jewish houses in Prague paid about four times as much as the average taxes assessed on non-Jewish real estate. For better exploitation of its Jewish resources the administration twice (in 1627 and 1635) attempted to conduct a census of the Jewish population, but never succeeded in completing the count. It had to fall back on estimates, variously offered by the government and the Jewish elders. In the end it usually was some negotiated settlement which established the cash sum or the equivalent in kind which was to be paid. Extorting money from the Jews often turned into a battle of wits. At times Treasury officials "borrowed" money or precious objects from wealthy Jews, allegedly for the benefit of the Crown. For instance, in 1581 the imperial paymaster Joan Medori received from Mordecai Meisel 2,000 thalers in cash, and some silver utensils supposedly for use in the emperor's kitchen "and in the Netherlands." This loan was to bear interest at the rate of a penny per thaler a week, or some 20 percent per annum. But the banker soon complained that he had received neither interest nor payments on the principal, while he himself was paying interest on his debts. More remarkably, two years earlier the clerks at the Bohemian Chamber and Accounting Office had reported to the emperor that Meisel lent 1,000 florins on the security of a borrower's landed estate. Arguing that mortgages on rural estates were legally barred to Jews, the officials suggested that the loan be confiscated and distributed among themselves.[20]

In Vienna, with its much smaller Jewish population, the amounts were likewise subject to more or less arbitrary settlements. Here, too, the imposts were sometimes paid in kind. For example, in 1624 the War Paymaster, Peter Sutter, was ordered to collect from the Viennese community the cloth offered in part-payment of the 20,000 florins which it was supposed to contribute. A year later several imperial councilors called upon the Jews to make a "voluntary" donation of 10,000 florins for the maintenance of the *Stadtquardi* (municipal guard). The Jewish elders expostulated that they had but recently contributed 36,000 thalers and 6,000 florins to the Treasury, while the houses in the new quarter had cost them 39,000 florins. Together with the erection of a wall for better protection and other expenses, these outlays had plunged the community into great debt and precluded the advance of any further funds. But ultimately, the Jews had to agree to contribute 3,000 florins for the upkeep of the guard. Such bargaining continued in the following years; it usually ended in some sort of compromise, the Jews always delivering disproportionately high per capita amounts to the Treasury. It may be noted, however, that, though a variety of pressures were employed, the government no longer used the outworn threat of expulsion. Of course, the absence of such threats did not guarantee the Jews absolute security, as they were to learn to their chagrin in 1670. Even the much larger and more deeply rooted Prague community was to face the menace of total banishment under the "enlightened absolutism" of Maria Theresa in 1744. Yet Viennese Jews now had a certain feeling of stability, which enabled them to plan ahead at least for some years to come. This strengthening of their backbone, in the ultimate sense, also accrued to the benefit of the imperial Treasury, which, even at that late date, still referred to a somewhat modified version of Jewish Chamber serfdom. On December 10, 1669, for instance, the Court Chancery informed the Bohemian administration that "His Imperial Majesty has clearly indicated before, that he considers Jewry a Chamber possession belonging to the prince; hence it should be taxed beyond its present tribute." [21]

Characteristically, in order to collect more revenue from Jews, the government had to reinforce the internal Jewish communal controls, exercised in part by the leading financiers. Ferdinand II readily conceded in 1632 to the small Jewish community of Vienna the right to maintain a prison of its own similar to those erected in Prague and elsewhere. As was usual in that period, the general privilege was quickly circumscribed by special immunities for favored individuals, but in 1635 Ferdinand had to retrace his steps and revoke most such exemptions. That some authoritarian elders abused their power and, in the actual tax collections, tried to shift the main burden from their own class to the less privileged groups, was to be expected. Occasionally, even the imperial authorities had to intervene against such abuses, as in a decree of May 2, 1629, when Ferdinand prohibited the elders and the rabbi of Prague from excessively burdening their poorer constituents.[22]

Not surprisingly, the hostile burghers of Vienna used every opportunity, including that of a change on the throne, to secure new restrictions of Jewish rights. No sooner did Ferdinand II pass away (in 1637) than the burghers submitted a petition to the new monarch, Ferdinand III, referring to commercial privileges they had long enjoyed and adding, "Were such rights really granted only to burghers, they would be quite well off. But Vienna now includes many foreign residents, both Jewish and Christian, who are exempted from the burghers' burdens and take their bread away." The burghers requested the total banishment of Jews from Vienna, if not from the entire country, with the proviso that the exiles never be allowed to approach within three leagues of the city. The new emperor, who generally followed in his father's footsteps, paid no heed to this petition, however.[23]

Understandably, the frequent defeats of the imperial armies, after rather easy initial successes, to some extent also undermined the emperor's authority in his hereditary possessions. His own commanders sometimes pursued arbitrary courses of action against the central government's expressed will. In the case of Jews this was particularly true of the outlying provinces, where the general legal situation was less clear and there was plenty of room for maneuvering and arbitrary decision by self-seeking generals.

A good illustration is offered by the conditions in Silesia. Long before ousted from most counties and cities, and for special reasons kept merely in Hotzenplotz (Osoblaha), Glogau, and Zülz, the Jews lived there under the protection of local potentates, aided and abetted by the emperor, but against the oft-repeated wishes of local assemblies of princes and cities. During the first half of the seventeenth century this constant tug of war greatly complicated the life of these two small communities and enormously increased their fiscal burdens. Partly under pressure from neighboring Poland, to be sure, the assembly of the Estates of 1601, was induced to open up all other Silesian cities to Jewish merchants during fairs, in return for a special impost of 100 ducats. But through a sleight of hand this single payment, which was supposed to guarantee the Jews a degree of commercial freedom for nine years, was converted into an annual tax of 100 florins, and in the 1620s was raised to 200 florins. More significantly, Ferdinand II's aforementioned imperial privilege of August 12, 1627, for all Bohemian and Silesian Jews and its confirmation of June 30, 1628, were effectively sabotaged by the local authorities. For instance, the provision that Jews be allowed freely to travel and trade, and pay only the same tolls as Christian merchants, was almost totally ignored. An assembly of Silesian princes, meeting in October 1628, to all intents and purposes denied the validity of these imperial decrees because they ran counter to the old anti-Jewish privileges enjoyed by the local powers. In overt defiance, the princes, bishops, and cities in the following years frequently demanded the total exclusion of Jews from Silesia, or at least the further curtailment of their commercial rights. The exigencies of the War, which sometimes made Jewish suppliers indispensable, on occasion played into the hands of Jew-baiters. To defend Silesia against the approaching Swedes, the high command of the Austrian army decided to convert Glogau into a major fortress. Count Raimondo Montecuccoli, later famous as a general and military theorist, thereupon ordered the demolition of no fewer than 486 houses, including the entire Jewish quarter, to make room for strong fortifications. A Jewish petition to the emperor on November 14, 1631, for the reassignment of a new and somewhat roomier locale in the vicinity of the castle brought forth no immediate response. Even Albrecht Wallenstein, who had interveningly become the lord of Glogau, gave the Jews only an evasive answer, actually intimating that he had grave doubts about tolerating them in the fortress at all (October 30, 1633). There is no way of telling whether the generalissimo, then in a highly indecisive frame of mind, really meant to implement his threat, or whether he merely intended to use it to force some further payments out of the Glogau Jews. Only after Wallenstein's death four months later and the restoration of direct imperial controls, were the Jews able to resume negotiations with the city and the imperial authorities. They reestablished their quarter in 1637, but were to enjoy neither security nor peace. In the new agreement with them the city entered the reservation that it was not thereby forfeiting the earlier privilege *de non amplius recipiendis Judaeis* (expressly disavowed by Ferdinand II in 1623). Many negotiations, moreover, had an aura of unreality as long as the city was occupied by enemy forces. This was often the case. In fact, the Swedes did not finally depart until 1650, two years after the Peace of Westphalia.[24]

Interveningly, only a few feudal landlords, such as Count Georg Christoph Proskowski, owner of Zülz, effectively resisted these hostile pressures. On the other hand, Burgrave Karl Hannibal zu Dohna, commander of the imperial forces and ruthless exponent of the Silesian Counter Reformation, extorted exorbitant amounts from the few Jews of the entire region. Protesting representatives of the Zülz Jewish community were thrown into prison, the emperor himself but mildly restraining the ardor of his commander. True, the Jews were better off in one respect than their Lutheran compatriots, who were made forcibly to abjure their faith. The lengthy formula of their oath of abjuration started with the declaration: "I, a poor, miserable sinner, confess to you, Oh priests, that for many years I have partaken of the damnable, godless Lutheran teachings and have lived in grave error. . . . I now repudiate and deny that abominable error and damned doctrine for the present and for evermore." Members of other Protestant denominations were treated even more harshly. Yet the few Jews who were formally tolerated and allowed to dwell in Silesia and publicly to profess their ancestral faith lived in a state of permanent insecurity; the good will of the imperial office did not always suffice to overcome the innumerable difficulties placed in their path by the local authorities.[25]

Silesian Jewry thus suffered with the rest of the population the ravages of the War, aggravated by the prevailing methods of warfare. Some commanders, including the famous general Albrecht Wenzel Eusebius von Wallenstein (formerly Waldstein), who, in a meteoric career, became duke of Friedland and Mecklenburg and even could dream of unifying Germany, nominally under the emperor but effectively under his own control, were hardly distinguishable from freebooters. Twice Wallenstein had to raise armies on his own. Consisting largely of mercenaries recruited from the riffraff of various German lands, these forces lived off the territories they occupied and engaged in large-scale plunder. Wallenstein's simple motto was: "War must nourish war."

Jews, reputedly wealthy and as a group least able to resist encroachments, were preferred targets. In his famous agreement of April 13, 1632, before assuming the supreme command of all Habsburg armies, Wallenstein had stipulated among other matters that he would have a completely free hand in confiscating property in conquered territories and in granting (or withdrawing) pardons and safe-conducts to individuals of his choice. In time, the duke of Friedland matured into the leading German figure of the Thirty Years' War, which he remained until the tragic denouement of his extremely complicated intrigues (their ramifications may have overtaxed even his great intelligence) finally led to his dismissal by the emperor and his assassination in 1634. At the beginning of his career in Prague, we recall, he had evinced little sympathy for Jews. But during the last years of his life he learned to appreciate the services of Jewish financiers and army contractors such as Jacob Bassevi. After Jacob's disgrace and arrest in

1631, owing largely to internal Jewish squabbles, Wallenstein offered him shelter at his own headquarters in the Bohemian city of Gitschin (Jičín). Like many other Bohemian Jewish settlements, that of Gitschin sustained severe losses. The city's postwar administrator, Baron Rudolf von Teuffenbach, justified his pro-Jewish decree of 1651 by stating that he "had learned on good authority that, during the turbulent war period, the Jews had suffered many privations and oppressions, had often been robbed of all their possessions through enemy action, and yet had supplied the soldiery with all sorts of merchandise and groceries, as much as they possibly could." Bassevi's Jewish enemies pursued him even after his release from prison and his settlement in Gitschin under Wallenstein's protection. In fact, in August 1633 Wallenstein had to order the Gitschin Jews to leave his friend in peace. However, Bassevi's days of glory had passed and there is no evidence that he significantly contributed to the duke of Friedland's levy of a large army, exaggeratedly estimated at 100,000 men, during the crucial years of 1632–34. Certainly, Bassevi's share, if any, in this vast enterprise lagged far behind that of his former collaborator, Hans de Witte. In both Gitschin and Böhmisch Leipa (Česká Lipa), moreover, the Austrian commander-in-chief extended the Jews' trading rights, obviously because he expected some benefits therefrom for his armed forces. He was quoted as saying: "I gladly hear that the Jew wishes to do business in Gitschin; let him do so," and allegedly even advanced some funds to Jewish traders. In short, Wallenstein was enough of a dreamer, as well as a far-sighted realist, for us to assume that, if his lofty expectations had come true, he might have initiated some far-reaching amelioration of the status of all German Jewry.[26]

RESIDUA OF IMPERIAL AUTHORITY

After 1625, when the Bohemia-Palatinate phase of the great War had drawn to a close, Scandinavian, French, and Spanish armies began traversing the territories of the Holy Roman Empire from one end to the other. Now the Jews residing in other parts of Germany, who had largely escaped the brunt of the hostilities during the early years, were unavoidably drawn into the vortex of the ever-changing fortunes of the War. With the rest of the civilian population, though they were ideologically more "neutral," they became the victims of an increasingly complex war machine.

Wallenstein, generally considered the father of the Austrian standing army, which during the following generations became the mainstay of Habsburg power, further refined the new methods of warfare, which had been gradually developed by the Italian *condottieri* and other mercenaries. He and other leading generals of the period (including Tilly) conducted their campaigns almost as semiprivate enterprises for profit, and often succeeded in amassing great fortunes. There was little difference in this respect between native and foreign military leaders, except perhaps that foreign generals had even fewer compunctions about the ultimate effects of their exploitation on the economy of the occupied territories. Nor was there much distinction between Catholic and Protestant commanders, although, as has been shown, Protestants (including Protestant converts to Catholicism like Wallenstein) proved to be more efficient business managers than born Catholics. In this respect the Protestants have been compared with the Jewish army contractors, whose prowess in organizing supply lines for the armies, as well as in securing intelligence services, often elicited praise from field commanders. The same Lazarus Aron of Bohemian Lichtenstadt who in 1619 had saved two Jesuit fathers from a hostile populace and safely conducted them to the bishopric of Bamberg, continued serving the imperial cause with much dedication and skill. In 1633–34 he received several enthusiastic testimonial letters from the leading Austrian generals, Count Matthias Gallas, Duke Ottavio Piccolomini, and Field Marshal Count Rudolf Colloredo. He was praised for providing the Habsburg forces both with much needed supplies and with warnings about approaching enemy armies. They emphasized that he did it at great peril to his life—he had indeed lost a brother through enemy reprisal—and, as emphasized by Piccolomini, "without any profit whatsoever." Not surprisingly, he became a thorn in the flesh to the Protestants, and Elector George I of Saxony placed the high prize of 10,000 ducats on his capture.[27]

More generally, however, as the most defenseless group in the population, Jews became easy prey for these organized despoliations. We are best informed about the conditions in the growing and affluent Jewish community of Frankfort. Strategically located at important crossroads, the city was time and again seized by the contending forces and made to pay heavily for its alleged part in the preceding hostilities. As early as June 3, 1622, Count Ernst von Mansfeld, commander-in-chief of the Protestant armies, demanded from the Frankfort Jews, under dire threats, a large "loan" of 100,000 florins. Despite all the help the Lutheran-controlled city extended to its Jewry, the Jewish elders had to promise to pay the general's intermediary 10,000 thalers. In the meantime, Duke Christian of Brunswick, then marching to unite his troops with those under Mansfeld's command, insisted, through an emissary, that the city of Frankfort place at his disposal transportation across the Main for his forces. At the same time he tried to exact a contribution of 30,000 thalers from the Frankfort Jews, "for, according to military law, they are to be considered legitimate prizes in such warlike expeditions." This concept could have arisen only from ignorance of the existing laws, an ignorance compounded by the widespread popular assumption of general Jewish rightlessness. The fact that this was a clear juridical misconception would not have spared the Jews much agony. What was said about Mansfeld applied to other commanders as well: "Defeated in every encounter with the Imperialists, he could still draw recruits by the promise of loot his name carried." However, in this case the Frankfort city council vigorously protested, claiming that it had long held its Jewry under the city's protection. While those negotiations were still under way, the Jews put off paying the 10,000 thalers promised to Mansfeld until the arrival of the imperial army under Tilly, which on June 20, in the battle of Höchst, decidedly defeated Brunswick's troops and forced Mansfeld to withdraw. Yet the mere readiness of the Jews to reach a compromise with the Protestant general was now held against them by the imperial officers, who used this alleged "betrayal" as a means of pressuring them into paying the supposed "loan" of 10,000 thalers to the imperial chest as a war contribution. On order of Archduke Leopold, Ferdinand's brother, the commandant of Worms went so far as to imprison a Frankfort Jew who was visiting Worms, sequester all amounts owed by Worms inhabitants to Frankfort

Jews, and generally impede the latter's commercial transactions. These efforts were cut short only by Ferdinand II's decree of September 4, 1623, which ordered the cessation of all such harassment and the return of all sequestered property to the rightful Jewish owners. The emperor also commended the Frankfort city council for its endeavors to protect the Jews.[28]

As a matter of fact, the Frankfort city fathers' well-meaning contention that the local Jews lived under exclusive municipal protection was, during those very years, the subject of a protracted controversy between the city and the emperor. This controversy hinged on the legal implications of Emperor Charles IV's original mortgage of the Frankfort Jews in exchange for the city's "loan" in 1356. As a result of Emperor Matthias' intervention in the Fettmilch uprising, it was he who, through his commissioners, enacted in 1616, as we recall, the new *Stättigkeit* as the fundamental law for the reconstituted Jewish community. Now Ferdinand raised the problem of the Jews owing him both a coronation tax (which they had indeed paid to Sigismund, Frederick III, and other emperors) and the capitation tax known as the Golden Penny (instituted by Louis the Bavarian). Similar demands had earlier been advanced by Rudolph II in 1583 and Matthias in 1617. They had been rejected by the city, however, with reference to a 1511 verdict of the Imperial Supreme Court that the Frankfort Jews were not obliged to make any contributions to the imperial Chamber. But this did not deter the imperial agents, or the military commanders of the Catholic forces during the various campaigns, from insisting that Frankfort Jewry now extend special financial aid to the imperial war effort. Most significantly, the emperor's representatives now raised with the city council the issue of a possible "redemption" by the Empire of its fourteenth-century "pledge." In 1625 they ordered the council to submit a complete record of its administration of Jewish affairs during the quarter millennium of 1356–1625, including the original documents relating to that pledge. Ferdinand's fiscal advisers thus hoped to prove that the city had collected from the local Jews in rentals and other revenues much more than the Treasury had owed it according to the original contract. In support of this contention Matthias Maximilian Norbertin, a converted Jew, in 1629 calculated that only twenty-two Jewish houses had originally been pledged by Charles IV, for a loan of 22,000 florins, but that subsequently the city had collected taxes from several hundred Jewish households, including those of very wealthy businessmen. Hence, Norbertin argued, Ferdinand had the right to demand not only the restitution of all Frankfort Jews to his direct sovereignty but also the repayment of the illegitimately collected surpluses. None of this was taken very seriously as a practical matter, but it served to increase the pressure upon the city to make larger contributions from its own budget, and to weaken its resistance to excessive imperial demands upon the resources of its Jewish inhabitants.[29]

Not that the Frankfort city council was especially partial to Jews. In a basic reversal of medieval nomenclature, it now definitely refused to classify Jews as burghers, calling them only "protected members" (*Schutzgenossen*). This Frankfort usage contrasted with the practice in Hesse-Kassel, where, as late as 1655, Jews were still invoking their rights as "free Roman persons and burghers." Jews were also called *cives Romani* by the juridically well-informed poet Matthias Abele von Lilienberg. Apart from this terminological downgrading of Jews, the Frankfort city council strictly applied the Jewish statute of 1616 which had limited the size of the total Jewish population to 500 households and the annual quota of marriages to 12, of which no more than 6 could be entered into with foreign residents. At the same time, however, it resisted the pressures of many interested parties, including local craftsmen and physicians, further to restrict Jewish competition in their respective areas, and protected the Jewish community in its other basic rights. It did so not for altruistic reasons but mainly because of the financial benefits it derived from Jewish trade and banking and because it feared imperial intervention against any overtly intolerant act.[30]

Preservation of Jewish fiscal integrity for the city's benefit became the more necessary as the municipal expenditures for defense and the upkeep of the garrisons of the various occupying powers grew by leaps and bounds. The Jewish military contributions to the city treasury, which had totaled 5,200 florins in the four years 1620–23, ranged annually from a maximum of 14,800 in 1635 to a minimum of 3,604 florins in 1642. In addition Jews paid 665–849 florins a year in lieu of guard duty, while, to save funds, they ceased paying the tax for fortifications and instead personally built the ramparts for their quarter. It is small wonder, then, that the city defended its Jews against the demands of Protestant generals, even after 1631, when it had capitulated to the Swedish army—although it could not prevent its new "ally" from imposing on the Jewish community a tax of 2,000–3,000 thalers for horses, carriages, and other equipment. However, when in that year the Swedish general, Count Alban von Brandenstein, suddenly demanded from Frankfort Jewry the payment within twenty-four hours of the huge sum of 100,000 florins, the city council threatened to appeal directly to the chancellor, Count Axel Gustafsson Oxenstierna, which caused the general speedily to desist. Together with other Estates, representatives of the city also successfully resisted the imposition upon all imperial Jewry of an annual per capita tax of one florin for the maintenance and reform of the *Reichskammergericht*. Although adopted by the Imperial Diet at Frankfort in 1644, this impost was defeated by the staunch resistance of princes, nobles, and free cities, despite the Diet's argument that a more efficient supreme court would prove of great assistance to the Jews themselves.[31]

As soon as the War was over, however, the imperial administration renewed its claims on the Frankfort Jews, demanding from them the payment of no less than 30,000–40,000 thalers. Once more the city vigorously protested. In his discussion with the imperial official Count Kunz, the Frankfort representative Jeremias Pistorious roundly denied the legal contention that Jews were under the direct (*immediat*) control of the emperor. He argued that "if the Jews, living as protected persons and inhabitants of Frankfort, were to be removed from the city's jurisdiction, absolutely considered imperial subjects, and thus universally recognized, the same would apply also to the Jews of the electorates and the other estates of the Empire. They would become direct (*immediat*) subjects of the emperor, and the territorial lords would no longer be able to impose upon them any further contributions." In his interesting report thereon of June 9, 1649, Pistorious summarized his argument by calling such a concept of Jewish status *unbesonene imaginationes* (ill-considered fantasies).[32]

Conversely, whims of military commanders could sometimes prove helpful to Jews against hostile city administrations. To the east of Frankfort the imperial city of Schweinfurt (later part of Bavaria) had ever since 1555 peremptorily barred Jews from residence or even occasional visits. In 1637 it fined a burgher 10 thalers because he had offered overnight hospitality to a Jew, and it punished others for dealing with Jews by confiscating the goods involved. Yet when, in that very year, the mayor ordered the arrest of a Jewish transient who was apparently performing useful services for the local garrison, he was informed by the commander that, unless the Jew were immediately released, soldiers would be ordered to break into the prison, set the Jew free, and place the mayor behind bars. Similarly, after the occupation of the city of Heilbronn (in the vicinity of Heidelberg) by French troops, Major General La Varenne found it useful to employ a Jew, Aaron, in the handling of commercial drafts and other matters. Without much ado he overruled, in 1647, the city's objection to being thus forced to tolerate a Jewish resident. Invoking its old privileges and claiming that, in 1642, it had admitted a few Jews from neighboring Neckarsulm for only eight days because of a threatening military attack, the Heilbronn council made strenuous efforts to banish Aaron. But La Varenne replied, "Although this may well be the city's usage and privilege, we are now in the middle of a war and such matters need not be considered. It is his superiors' will that the Jew be allowed to stay there; privileges here, privileges there, the Jew handles bills of exchange better than a Christian." [33]

One of the difficulties confronting all citizens, including Jews, was the frequent billeting of soldiers in private homes before and after battles, particularly during the relatively peaceful winter months. Always extremely burdensome, billeting led to additional complications in Jewish homes because of the differences in modes of living between "guests" and "hosts" and the soldiers' frequent anti-Jewish feelings. Wherever possible, therefore, Jews tried to evade that responsibility, for the most part at a high price.

For example, in 1627 the Jewry of Schnaittach secured from the burgrave of the neighboring fortress of Rothenberg a privilege enabling it "to reach an agreement with the officers" concerning lodgings during their passage. At the same time it was to be "spared from other billeting demands, under whatever name they might appear. . . . In case of dangerous troop movements, they [the Jews] will be allowed, together with their wives and children, to stay in our fortress of Rothenberg as long as it may be necessary." The reason here given, that the Jews of Schnaittach had legitimate grievances against the "ranting and drunken" soldiers, applied with equal force to other communities. Needless to say, the Rothenberg burgraves were not wholly disinterested. Shortly thereafter, Lieutenant Colonel Wolf Christoph von Leoprechting, during nearly four years of command in the fortress (1632–35), extorted so much money from the Schnaittach Jewish community for his private purse, that the government subsequently sued his heirs for repayment of the excess yield of that "woolshearing," as Leoprechting himself had called his financial transactions. The lawsuit proceeded very slowly; not until 1671 were the first witnesses heard. By that time only four of the original Jewish taxpayers were still alive. Unable to marshal sufficient evidence, the prosecution finally dropped the lawsuit in 1683, almost half a century after the event. One may perhaps understand, therefore, the admittedly slanted remark of another fortress commander (in Giessen, 1622–23), who expressed the wish that 25,000 Jews lived in his fortress.[34]

In Worms, only Emperor Ferdinand II's direct intervention in 1636 prevented the imperial commanders from imposing upon the Jewish community both payments in kind and billeting. The emperor referred to a petition of the Vienna communal elders stating that Worms Jewry had "suffered much from the continued warlike upheavals and other exactions and pressures, wherefore it had reached a state of great poverty and penury. Nevertheless, during the last six months, it had in part maintained the two regiments stationed in Worms." Ferdinand ordered, therefore, that the Jews, being under imperial protection, should be "totally exempted from billeting and other war-connected pressures and that . . . they be freed from any arbitrary executions, monetary imposts, or forced deliveries of large or small cattle, horses, carriages, grain, or other foodstuffs." Upon Ferdinand's demise, to be sure, the city tried once again to exact from the Jews manifold contributions. But the new emperor refused to yield any part of his imperial prerogative. The outcome was a new *Stättigkeit* for Worms Jewry, dated November 8, 1641, and published on April 5, 1642, which spelled out the Jews' rights and duties in even greater detail than the two earlier enactments. At the request of the Worms city council, a copy of the *Stättigkeit,* now extant in the Frankfort Municipal Archive, was designated an *Interim Judenordnung,* with a notation stating: "against which the city of Worms had entered a most humble remonstration because it contained various points extremely prejudicial to the city's traditional rights and liberties; it was imposed upon the city during the disturbances of the Thirty Years' War. It [the city] has solemnly reaffirmed its rights as an imperial estate." Yet this statute retained its validity as the basic constitution of Worms Jewry and it was reconfirmed by each subsequent monarch down to Francis II, the last Holy Roman emperor. Interveningly, other reasons against billeting were advanced by the Frankfort Jews. On one occasion, in 1636, they claimed that the 180 houses in the Jewish quarter were too small and overcrowded to accommodate any additional inmates. Two years later they argued, on the contrary, that, because of the departure of many Jews, some of their houses had been uninhabited for a long time and hence were so badly neglected that they were not fit for habitation. Both contentions were partially true. At the beginning of the War, as we shall see, Frankfort's Jewish population rapidly increased, overtaxing all existing housing facilities; later, as a result of the subsequent population decline, many houses stood empty, indeed.[35]

The unsettled conditions in the country also opened the gates to a variety of criminals. Regular gangs of robbers and marauding soldiers attacked businessmen and other travelers with increasing frequency, making all travel extremely hazardous. A sharp imperial patent of March 6, 1638, trying to stem the crime wave proved only partially effective. New opportunities also beckoned to adventurers and confidence men—often at the expense of the defenseless Jews. For example, a Lieutenant Colonel Immel suddenly appeared in 1641 in Frankfort as the emperor's representative. Denouncing both the city and its Jewry for having conspired with the French and furnished them with food, munitions, and even recruits, he demanded from the Jewish community an indemnity of 30,000 thalers. On investigation it turned out that the entire "conspiracy" consisted in nine Jewish horse dealers having sold horses in 1640 to Weimar and French officers without inquiring into their identity—a procedure long followed in commercial circles. The affair ended, after prolonged negotiations by the city's envoys in Vienna, with Immel's discharge from the army, and his quiet departure, almost escape, from Frankfort. The prolonged War and the ever-alternating victories and defeats of the contending parties opened vast opportunities for officials, real and pretended, to exact payments from innocent civilians under one guise or another. Finally the various states started to circulate blacklists of convicted document forgers and others.[36]

All through the War, moreover, Jews still suffered from the traditional animosities. Perhaps the most remarkable accusation was hurled at them in Hanau, a city which was generally more liberal than neighboring Frankfort toward both Jews and Dutch Calvinist refugees. Formally readmitted by Count Philip Louis II in 1603, Jews began pursuing their commercial careers and building their synagogues and schools in relative peace. But negotiations conducted with the count in 1606–1609 in behalf of some Venetian Marranos for permission to settle in the city broke down, because the New Christians, technically considered "renegades" from Christianity, could not obtain an imperial safe-conduct for themselves and their possessions. The public, however, still nurtured its deep-seated feelings of hostility toward the relatively few Jews in its midst. In 1617, when three Jews sentenced to hanging for robbery and theft were comforted on their way to the gallows by two rabbis, this act of mercy evoked much adverse comment among the local Christians. (This event also seems to be reflected in a moving Yiddish folksong of the period.) During the War the Jews were held responsible not just for one or another specific shortage or enemy attack but for the War itself and all its hardships. According to a 1627 communication from the Vienna elders to the emperor, the Jews of Hanau were exposed to real danger if they dared to appear in the streets on Sundays, because of the unceasing flow of incendiary sermons by the local clergy.

These preachers do not fail to attack the Jews in all their public sermons and homilies. They claim that the present War (because of
God's anger) has come about because the Jews are tolerated in Hanau
and in other localities of the Holy Roman Empire.

Ferdinand II immediately requested Count Philip Moritz of
Hanau to protect the local Jews in the enjoyment of their accustomed privileges and particularly to prevent riots by the common
people, such as occurred elsewhere "in these dangerous times."
Needless to say, this imperial order did not prevent the Austrian
general, Lamboy, from bombarding Hanau in 1636 and destroying its Jewish quarter, including the synagogue. In other localities,
Jews were occasionally held responsible for the spread of the pest.
This accusation was originally voiced, in 1609, by Hildesheim
against its thirty Jewish families, formally admitted to the city in
1601 by a special compact which had ended in a protracted jurisdictional controversy between bishop and city. Although the
emperor also became involved, this controversy was still pending
before the Empire's Supreme Court during the War. While no
further clarification could be obtained during the confused conditions of the War, the Jewish population more than doubled. In
Nuremberg, on the contrary, the burghers so bitterly opposed the
admission of Jews that, in the midst of a major military campaign,
the city council adamantly refused to grant even temporary shelter to some Jewish refugees. In 1627–28, it twice restated its old
prohibition against the Christian population's engaging in any
trade with Jews whatsoever.[37]

RAVAGES OF WAR

It goes without saying that Jews suffered along with other inhabitants from the destruction of life and property occasioned by
the War. The misfortunes which befell the synagogue of the then
rising community of Fürth were fairly typical. Severely damaged
by the Protestant general Count Mansfeld in 1621, this house of
worship was soon thereafter used as a prison for Count Tilly's
marauding soldiers, and in 1635 was turned into a horse stable by
the occupying Croatian soldiery. Conditions in the smaller com-

munities, open to plundering by the marching armies, often became so intolerable that many provincial Jews had to seek refuge
in neighboring larger towns, where they were rarely received with
open arms. An incident in the town of Höchstadt in the bishopric
of Bamberg well illustrates the general situation in Germany. In
1631 a number of Jews left the smaller hamlets because, to cite the
report of the city council of Bamberg of September 5, 1639, "the
soldiery was particularly interested in those localities where Jews
lived, so that they might despoil them of their possessions." Yet in
1632, when a suburb of Höchstadt was overrun by the Swedes, and
the episcopal official (*Amtmann*) of Höchstadt admitted some Jewish refugees into the castle for more effective protection, he and
his wife were sharply reprimanded by the bishop for their failure
to secure the prior consent of their superiors. Apart from telling
the official to pay careful heed to the orders of the military commander, the bishop wrote:

You will secretly and with all diligence inquire [concerning the Jewish
refugees]. In so far as such will be found in our government house or
in the city, you shall pick out all the men and hand them over to Colonel von Salis so that he may bring them here as prisoners and deliver
them to us. The women and children, together with all their movable
possessions, you shall lock up in a building, the gate and other exits of
which shall be provided with constant guards. Nothing of the slightest,
whether in letters, closed trunks, or other sealed objects, shall be allowed to be carried into or out of the building without being opened.
Whatever material of this kind you will find you shall keep in good
custody and prove your good discretion so that you shall not be subject
to suspicion. You will also obediently report the progress [of this
investigation] to Us from time to time.

This storm seems to have blown over after the Jews paid a substantial indemnity. But the Catholic party continued accusing the
Jews throughout the bishopric of espionage in favor of the Swedes
—ironically, the very foes from whom many of them had run away.
Moreover, because of the confusion arising from the movement of
the Jewish population, which now included both licensed and unlicensed Jews, the new prince-bishop Melchior Otto in 1642 decreed that all of them be indiscriminately expelled. This order
was more a stratagem than an expression of serious intent; it enabled the new regime to restore closer governmental controls over

the bishopric's Jewish settlements, which ever since 1619 had established an over-all communal organization under a single chief rabbi.[38]

Some cities maintained their anti-Jewish stance more adamantly, however, even in the face of the wartime emergency. Nordhausen, for example, had in 1591 rejected a tempting offer from a Jew, Jacob, of neighboring Elrich, who had sought admission for his four Jewish brothers-in-law, in return for an immediate payment of 600 thalers and an annual tax of 100 thalers. The newcomers were also to lend money to the local citizens at the moderate interest rate of 15–25 percent. Having admitted no Jews before 1618, the city severely censured those of its burghers who, at the beginning of the War, offered even a single night's shelter to Jewish visitors. Nor did it heed the request of the duke of Brunswick-Lüneburg to admit certain Jews of Elrich living under his protection, although in a sharp note of March 2, 1620, he had threatened Nordhausen with severe reprisals if it denied his request. When in 1630 three Jews took up residence in the city, they and their Christian hosts were told to evacuate the premises within a month, under the severe sanction of 20 gold florins.[39]

Increased lawlessness likewise made Jewish life in the war period very difficult. Riots against moneylenders, both Christian and Jewish, increased in number. In a disturbance of this kind in Halberstadt in 1621 the synagogue, erected earlier in the century by the philanthropist Israel b. Jacob Naphtali, went up in flames, together with its library and communal archive. For the following thirty years the community was forced to perform its services in a private house under the leadership of a R. Simmlein, who was praised in the local memor book as an effective defender of Jewish rights, a task he had at times performed under great personal danger. He was apparently successful in negotiating with both the Protestant Swedes and the Catholic bishop, Leopold Wilhelm, a Habsburg archduke. Beginning in 1633, when the Estates clamored for the expulsion of the Jews, the Swedish governor, Ludwig von Anhalt, procrastinated and finally consented to eliminate those individuals who could not prove having received formal writs of protection. On his part, Leopold Wilhelm actually extended new licenses to eight Jewish families—for a substantial fee.

Halberstadt thus became a relative oasis for Jews, whose number increased to such an extent by 1641 that the community's circumcisers were able to organize an association of their own. In contrast, their coreligionists in the Margraviate of Bayreuth complained that, because of the wartime disturbances, no Jew dared to show his face outside his house, still less to pursue his business or collect instalments on debts due him. Such a condition, they pathetically exclaimed, had never existed since the creation of the world and, if it were to continue without change, all Jews of the country would become beggars. While we may discount the obvious exaggerations in this plaintive response to Margravine Maria's unprecedented demand that Jews replace the worn-out horses on her vast estates with new animals, it does reflect the widespread inability of many Jews, as well as non-Jews, to earn a living. There was no exaggeration at all in the plea of inability to pay by the Jews of the small Bavarian community of Georgesmünd. Because they were unable to raise even the ordinary fees for protection, all but two of them had to leave their homes. The expatriates joined the growing number of Jewish migrants from one German territory to another, quite a few of whom departed for "greener pastures" in Holland.[40]

It is small wonder, then, that the Jews, like the rest of the population, rejoiced when an occupying army, Catholic or Protestant, left their city. The story of Bingen on the Rhine is quite typical. While Mayence itself did not tolerate any Jews, neighboring Bingen, sometime before 1580, readmitted them under such favorable conditions that they could form a regular community and appoint a rabbi, who soon served as the spiritual leader for the Jews of the entire Mayence region. No less than three Bingen delegates were able to attend the famous Frankfort Synod of 1603. The great War attracted further refugees. But in 1636 the city council, on orders from the archiepiscopal Chapter, expelled all unlicensed Jews and severely restricted the commercial rights of the few licensed families. In 1640 the council, on its own initiative, asked the Mayence Chapter to reduce the number of protected Jewish families from the 6 or 7 theretofore authorized to but 3 or 4. This request was probably refused, and the community continued to function without hindrance. When the Austro-Spanish troops evacuated

Mayence in 1643, and the city celebrated its liberation with a public procession, the Jews happily commemorated the event by displaying on their synagogue ark a curtain with the inscription *Ve-natati shalom ba-areṣ* (And I will give peace in the land; Lev. 26:6). This rejoicing was, of course, premature. Before long the city underwent another forcible occupation, this time by the French. In his aforementioned autobiographical sketch, Judah Mehler, now rabbi of Bingen, commented: "No one was free from the services they [the French] demanded and from the heavy yoke they imposed upon all the inhabitants of this city. They behaved in this fashion in all localities they occupied, and this system lasted until finally the Lord brought about peace among the states."[41]

Hunger, as well as the bombardment of cities, decimated the civilian population, at times causing as many losses among noncombatants as among soldiers, whose number was always relatively small. Gustavus Adolphus' initial army which swept through the Holy Roman Empire may have consisted of no more than 15,000 men, later to increase to some 40,000. Few Jews participated in direct belligerent actions. To be sure, as early as 1582 a Geneva writer, De Condolle, suggested that Jews be made "to serve as soldiers, since they would cost nothing." Sometime thereafter a poet named Riederer urged the Jews to fight in Hungary against the Turks, sarcastically assuring them that their race would not thereby suffer decline. Although the few recorded Jewish combatants, for example, those in the Swedish army in 1633 and among the Saxon troops in 1635, ended as converts, professing Jews must have sustained considerable losses in their work on fortifications and firefighting, two tasks regularly assigned to them, as in Prague. In 1624, in the midst of raging hostilities, Ferdinand II took special note of the services rendered the Austrian army by Josef Pinkherle of Gorizia, Moses and Jacob Marburger of Gradisca, and Ventura Parente of Trieste, services similar to those performed by their ancestors during the War of the League of Cambrai one hundred and fifteen years before. He mentioned pro-Jewish decrees by Maximilian I in 1509, Ferdinand I in 1526, and their successors, and emphasized that these four Jews had demonstrated "their unstinted loyalty by offering with unsparing devotion their bodies, possessions, and blood in the struggle against Our enemy." The following list of casualties in the final battle over the Bohemian capital, in July 1648, between the Swedish general Hans Christoph Königsmark and the city's defenders, led by students and abetted by Jews, is highly informative. Apart from more than 100 fatalities among the Swedish soldiers, the burghers of the Old City lost 80 dead; those of the New City, 22; students, 13; the clergy, 2; and Jews, 22. This last number was in addition to many other casualties the Jews sustained while extinguishing fires and working on fortifications. Fortunately for all these groups, hostilities immediately ceased when news about the conclusion of the Peace Treaties of Westphalia reached the combatants. The Jewry of Prague thus escaped the tragedy of another enemy occupation, but the provincial communities suffered severely. According to the contemporary Prague scribe Yehudah Leb b. Joshua, many Jewish settlements, including those of Tabor, Brandeis, Kolin, and Jungbunzlau (Mladá Boleslav), were attacked by both the Swedish soldiery and the peasants. The imperial "defenders" did not behave much better—all this while in Osnabrück and Münster the diplomats continued haggling for years over some minute details of the peace terms.[42]

Among the main killers of both soldiers and civilians were the frequent epidemics, particularly typhoid fever, syphilis, and bubonic plague, which repeatedly struck the populations from Spain to Poland in the 1620s and 1630s. The city of Spires was afflicted three times during the War (in 1625, 1632, and 1635–38). Italy is said to have lost one-third of its population in those decades, mainly from contagious diseases. Of course, Jews suffered along with their neighbors, although it is barely possible that their ritualistically imposed, relatively hygienic way of life may have slightly counteracted the spread of communicable diseases among them. At least in Mantua, where the combined impact of the siege and the pest in 1629–30 apparently reduced the city's population from some 50,000 to but 7,000, the Jews seem to have lost only about a third of their number before the expulsion of 1630, about which more will be said below. Of course, the loss of one-third of any population was not easily recovered under the dismal socioeconomic conditions of the seventeenth century, with the prevailing small surpluses of births over deaths even in peacetime. Some Jewish families, like that of Theomin in Fürth and elsewhere, sustained irretrievable losses in the pest years of 1620 and after. In Prague the great pestilence of 1639 likewise deeply affected the entire community. Of 65 persons who had participated at a meeting in 1636, only 9 were still alive three years later. The number of Jewish tombstones dating from 1639 also is disproportionately large. True, we no longer hear denunciations alleging that the poisoning of wells by Jews was the main cause of the spread of epidemics. Germany had by that time become scientifically too sophisticated to accept such an obvious fabrication, just as the intervening dogmatic controversies between Catholics and Protestants concerning the Eucharist had all but obliterated accusations of Jewish desecration of the host. Despite climactic tensions, there also were relatively few blood libels, although pertinent literary discussions could not be wholly silenced. Yet Jew-baiters were by no means deterred from searching for new, more rational, explanations of the Jews' responsibility for pestilences. In cities as far apart as Vienna and Mantua, their enemies imputed to Jewish traders the responsibility for spreading the epidemics by their alleged purchases of contaminated secondhand clothing from soldier-pillagers for sale to the Christian public.[43]

Only exceptionally, however, did such folk suspicions lead to direct persecution of Jews. The most flagrant case occurred in Mantua (the accusation there is given credence even by a modern historian like Selwyn Brinton). The conflict between partisans of Austria and France over the succession to the ducal throne led to the city's occupation by imperial troops, followed by extensive murder and pillage in the Jewish quarter and by a formal decree expelling all Jews in 1630. Here the cupidity of the imperial commanders was combined with a wish to punish the Jews for their financial assistance to the French-sponsored Duke Charles of Nevers and for their active participation in the defense of the city during its prolonged siege. On July 28, 1630, Colonel Dietrich Stein ruthlessly announced to the Jewish communal leaders that all Jews must depart from the city within three days and leave behind all their possessions, except three florins per person. Any Jew thereafter found in Mantua would be executed. Some 1,600 Jews—their original number had been cut in half by the pest, war, and emigration—hurriedly departed, some under a military escort provided by the Austrians. The "protection" given by the soldiers turned out to be more disastrous than the anticipated perils of the journey, however. On urgent representations by Mantuan Jewish envoys, supported by the influential court Jews in his entourage, Emperor Ferdinand II, then attending a Diet at Ratisbon, revoked the decree of expulsion on September 2, 1630, and ordered the restoration of both the exiles and their property to their former status. But such restitution was effectively sabotaged by the field commanders, who claimed that much of the yield of the confiscated property had been spent on the soldiers' wages. As a result, not all refugees returned to the city. Although it vigorously embarked on the task of reconstructing the ghetto ruins, the surviving community, reduced to one-third of its earlier size, thenceforth remained but a shadow of its glorious former self of the era of the Gonzaga dukes.[44]

On the whole, however, imperial Jewry may have sustained fewer population losses than its Christian neighbors. It is generally assumed that the Thirty Years' War brought about a catastrophic decline of Germany's population, which was reduced from a total between 17,000,000 and 25,000,000 in 1618 at least one-third by the end of the War. While Jewish population data of that period are extremely limited, we know that, according to the municipal records, the number of Jewish households in Frankfort had increased from 370 in 1618 to 409 in 1624; it gradually shrank to 285 in 1639, but slightly recovered to a total of 329 in 1648. Multiplying this figure by approximately 5.4 (as appears justified by the census figures of 1703), Isidor Kracauer has estimated Frankfort's total Jewish population at 1,998 in 1618; 2,209 in 1624; 1,539 in 1639; and 1,777 in 1648. In addition there were temporary settlers of all kinds, but their number was never large. If these estimates are correct, the Jewish population over the thirty-year span of 1618–48 declined by only some 11 percent. Prague, occupied by a hostile army only in 1632, attracted many refugees from the war-ravaged provincial communities. Hence the speedily enlarged "Jewish city" in 1638 accommodated, according to an official though not quite reliable census, no less than 7,815 Jews—

indeed far more than any other city in the Empire. Reduced by about one-half during the pestilence of the following year, the community seems to have fully recovered its strength after a decade or two. In Vienna, which had not suffered enemy occupation, the situation was equally favorable. At the establishment of the new ghetto in 1625, the Jewish houses totaled 15, the families, 130. We do not have the precise breakdown for the year 1648, but at the time of their expulsion from Vienna in 1670, the Jews numbered some 500 families, occupying 132 houses. (The decline of the average number of families per house from about 8.7 to about 3.9 may have been owing to the slowness of construction of new houses before the hurried transfer of Viennese Jewry to its new quarter in the *unterer Werd,* a deficiency remedied in the following years.) Of course, neither Frankfort, Prague, nor Vienna had communities quite typical of German Jewry as a whole. At the other extreme one might mention the great decline of the Jewish population in Silesian Glogau (Glogow). Numbering some 600 persons in 1625, the Glogau community was reduced six years later to but 200 souls, a figure confirmed in 1638 by an official report, which explained the decline by the Jews' great losses from both war and pestilence.[45]

The War also set in motion a reversal of the trend of the preceding decades, when a great many urban Jews had settled in hamlets and villages under the domination of lesser lords. Now, with regular armies, as well as bands of marauders, traversing the length and breadth of Germany, many Jewish and non-Jewish villagers and small-town dwellers sought the somewhat greater security offered by major walled cities. It stands to reason, therefore, that the Jewish population suffered a much sharper decline than is indicated by the Frankfort, Prague, and Vienna statistics. Hence total Jewish demographic losses may not have been much smaller than those estimated for the entire German population.

Economically, too, some communities suffered irreparable damage. To cite the example of Frankfort again, where our information is more reliable and detailed, the reiterated complaints of the community give a vivid picture of deep impoverishment. Even if we discount some of the pathetic descriptions as attempts to secure relief from inordinately heavy taxation, they could not be completely devoid of reality, since they were addressed to well-informed city elders. In 1639, for instance, the Jewish representatives wrote:

Those Jews who trusted strangers [by extending them loans] on bonds, have been ruined together with their insolvent debtors. They have often been reduced to beggary and, unable to sustain the pains of hunger with their wives and children, they have been driven out to Poland and other foreign localities. The others who heretofore engaged in trade with merchants and local burghers—may God have mercy on them—have experienced the same misery and destitution because the tradesmen have generally been ruined by highway robbery, plunder, and the stoppage of all commerce. Some of them have become insolvent, while the local fairs have been totally neglected. . . . At the same time we must support a great many [sixty] widows, as well as over eighty destitute and crippled men; to these we must add their children.

This decline is also illustrated by the diminishing revenue from Jewish taxes—notwithstanding the terrific pressures exerted by the municipality and the occupying forces—as shown by the figures preserved in the Frankfort Municipal Archive concerning the returns from the so-called *Quartier, Wacht, und Schanzengeld* (the tax in lieu of billeting soldiers, standing guard, and building fortifications). According to a list covering the years 1634–54, the city initially expected to collect the large amount of 300 thalers weekly from the Jewish community. But as early as 1635 apparently no payments were made between January and April, and the amounts deposited in May, June, July, November, and December totaled slightly less than 4,000 florins, or less than a third of the annual assessment of 15,600 thalers. In constant renegotiations, the assessments were frequently altered, until the revenue dwindled to as little as 4,880 florins in 1642, and 3,600 florins in 1646. Of course, these direct payments were only part of the fiscal burdens borne by the community, which, according to the archival data compiled by Isidor Kracauer, in the years 1634–48 contributed more than 131,500 florins to the city's total revenue of about 1,863,450 florins.[46]

As was the case among non-Jews, the general impoverishment of the Jewish population did not prevent a few alert and lucky individuals from amassing moderate fortunes in the midst of the general turmoil. Nor is there any way of estimating whether the losses sustained by German Jewry as a whole equaled those suffered by the German population at large. But the general change in the Jews' legal status, however slow and imperceptible at first, probably enabled them to recover their economic strength somewhat more speedily than the majority of the population—although recent investigations have in fact tended to lower our estimates of the permanence of Germany's over-all economic decline.

SILVER LINING

Notwithstanding great individual suffering, serious loss of life and property, and the uprooting of many smaller settlements which had served as havens of refuge for countless families ejected from their age-old habitats in the larger cities, the Thirty Years' War in some respects marked a favorable turning point in the destiny of German Jewry. Events in northwest Germany appeared particularly promising. Without long premeditation, the imperial city of Hamburg and the neighboring towns of Altona, Wandsbek, and Glückstadt, then mainly under the control of the kings of Denmark, pioneered by admitting Jews, particularly of Sephardic origin, under novel legal conditions. Keen observers of the contemporary scene could even then have realized that these happenings were harbingers of a new era. Forward-looking rulers of the northwestern areas were forced to reorient their economic policies by the phenomenal rise of the Atlantic trade, the control over which was gradually slipping away from the great Iberian powers to Holland, England, and France.

Here the Marranos formed the entering wedge. Because they outwardly appeared to be Christians, they encountered less difficulty in penetrating many formerly xenophobic German regions, which now enjoyed greater freedom of action because the declining Hanseatic League no longer could enforce its protectionist policies on all member states. The League's former leader, Lübeck, stubbornly persevering in its hidebound traditional attitudes, began to fall behind the upsurging commercial emporium of Hamburg in a way that affected Jews, too. As late as 1658, 1660, 1668, and 1671 Lübeck repeatedly threatened any Jew found in its territory with immediate arrest and speedy expulsion; only in

1677 did it leave a loophole for authorizing a few individuals to spend an occasional night in the city. The Lübeck Senate was particularly prone to listen to complaints like that of the local Gold- and Silversmiths' Guild, which claimed in its petition of March 23, 1658, that "many Jews and other riffraff have smuggled themselves into this good city. One can see them almost daily running through the streets and peddling their impure silver, gold, and other objects, while buying up other silver [of better quality]." This complaint attributed to the Jews responsibility for the operation of "Gresham's law." But going beyond the usual grievances voiced by guilds against "interlopers," it greatly impressed the authorities. In view of the high appreciation of precious metals in that growingly mercantilistic era, it implied that Jews were directly contributing to the city's impoverishment through their illicit trade in precious metals. Rulers and public alike had also become extremely sensitive about currency manipulation since the *Kipper und Wipper* era earlier in the century, which had caused even the more liberal Austrian and Hamburg regimes to distrust such Jews as Jacob Bassevi and Alvaro Dinis. But while Hamburg was ready completely to rehabilitate Dinis, as we shall presently see, the Lübeck authorities unquestioningly accepted rumors of alleged misdeeds by unnamed Jewish individuals and blamed the supposed crimes on the entire Jewish community. Even more recklessly, as late as 1691 the Lübeck artisans insisted that, if Jews were admitted to residence in the city, "their smell would destroy man and beast." [47]

However, Lübeck's intolerant policies no longer served as a model for the rest of the decaying Hanseatic alliance, the decline of which was greatly accelerated by the Thirty Years' War and the rise of the Scandinavian kingdoms. The weakness of the League was clearly demonstrated in the ineffectual gathering of representatives from eleven Hanseatic cities in Lübeck in 1628. In the meantime, some New Christian merchants residing in Antwerp had, as we recall, established themselves temporarily in Cologne. Other Marranos found their way into Mannheim. But these inland centers held less promise for full-scale development of international trade than the port of Hamburg, which, as early as 1597, was called by the physicist Johannes Bökel "the most flourishing emporium of all Germany." Hence some of the "Flemish" traders, like Ferdinand Ximenes, left Cologne for Hamburg, in the records of which Iberian names appear with increasing frequency from the 1580s on. These newcomers followed in the footsteps of the English Merchant Adventurers. Many Iberian arrivals, whether of Old or New Christian stock (Ximenes among the latter), undoubtedly were good Christians. But others were secret Jews who had escaped the clutches of the Inquisition. Their number increased substantially during the decade of 1601–1610, when the government of Philip III temporarily liberalized its emigration policies for New Christians in both Spain and Portugal and, in 1604, even extended a "general pardon" to them. Since Hamburg was very anxious at that time to expand its commercial relations with the Iberian Peninsula and was to send a trade delegation to Spain in 1606, its Senate became apprehensive lest the "Portuguese" merchants, some of whom served as agents of prominent Spanish firms, place serious obstacles in its merchants' path. It therefore listened sympathetically, in 1605, to the plea of some Portuguese merchants that they be left alone in matters of religion. True, many New Christian settlers tried to conceal their allegiance to Judaism, especially if for business reasons they found it necessary to pay occasional visits to their home country. Their coreligionists themselves looked with disfavor upon such visits, which endangered not only the persons concerned but also the entire community. Any member seized by the Inquisition was likely, under torture, to implicate a number of fellow Marranos, even if he was not an outright informer (as were Hector Mendes Bravo in 1617, Gaspar Bocarro in 1641, and Diego de Lima in 1644). Ultimately, in 1658, the Hamburg community placed such trips under a religious censure by providing that, for two years after their return, the travelers would not be called to the Torah nor be allowed to perform any other synagogue function.[48]

Concealment of Judaism was facilitated by the growingly cosmopolitan character of the Hamburg business community, which resulted from the settlement in the city of diverse ethnic merchant groups. The Dutch and the English had actually preceded the Portuguese in helping to revamp the economy of the old Hanseatic city. The first Jewish settlers were not recognized as such; they came simply as "Portuguese" traders. However, modern scholars have been able to ascertain that, by 1595, the Portuguese residents embraced at least a dozen families more or less certainly identifiable as professing Jews, although such identification has been greatly impeded by the diversity of names under which many individuals appear in the records. Numerous new arrivals bore separate Iberian and Hebrew names, the former used in commercial transactions and political negotiations, the latter in communal and religious activities. In addition, few scribes, official or private, bothered to make sure of the correct spelling of names, but reproduced them phonetically, at times inconsistently in the same document. For one example, Alvaro Dinis, mentioned here in several connections, had the Hebrew name of Samuel Hyac or Yaḥya. He evidently belonged to the well-known Ibn Yaḥya family, which had played a considerable role in Portuguese Jewish affairs before the Expulsion. Contemporary scribes called him Alvaro, Alberto, or Albertus, Dinis, Din(n)iz, Denis, Deniz, Dionys (Dionis), Dionysius, or even Albrecht de Nies, or Albertus de Nyes.[49]

At first, the forward-looking Hamburg Senate tried to overcome the opposition of the more conservative burghers by denying, in 1604, that these Portuguese settlers were Jewish. Soon, however, the issue could no longer be side-tracked, since from 1604 to 1607 these "foreigners" paid the city some 10,000 marks in customs duties alone. In 1608, possibly on Jewish initiative, negotiations were instituted with the intent to legalize the newcomers' status as Jews. In an extant memorandum the "Portuguese nation" was reported as offering the Senate an unspecified payment for the city's defense, above and beyond the taxes and duties which its members were to pay on a par with the Dutch colony.

In addition the nation asks that it be given the freedom which is granted it in Holland, namely, that in matters of religion it be allowed to use its own discretion, for which it hopes to answer before God Himself. It should be subject to no inquiry on that score, nor should anyone molest it. Moreover, the nation obligates itself, as heretofore, to conduct itself quietly and restrainedly, not to engage in any religious disputations, nor to prevent anyone who wishes to adhere to, and confess our [the Christian] religion [from doing so], and still less to persuade one of ours to their religion.

The Portuguese finally requested that they be given permission to bury their dead freely at a place designated by themselves. This privilege was necessary because in the past a special tax had had to be paid when persons were buried outside the municipal cemetery (as well as when baptisms or marriages were performed under other than municipal auspices), the tax being in lieu of the service charge which would otherwise have been collected by the city. At first the burghers' reaction was not favorable, but after further negotiations a detailed agreement was drawn up, on February 19, 1612, which met most of the demands of the new community, then already numbering some 150 souls. This agreement was limited to five years, but it was regularly renewed thereafter.[50]

Before taking this decisive step the Hamburg Senate had to overcome much opposition from the burghers, some of whom feared that their share in the city's increasing trade with the Iberian Peninsula would be adversely affected by Jewish competition. As usual, the burghers supplemented these economic reasons with religious arguments. To assure itself of the legitimacy of admitting Jews, the Senate secured formal opinions from the Protestant Theological Faculties of Jena, Leipzig, Frankfort on the Oder, and Giessen. All of these answered in the affirmative, emphasizing the fact that, according to the constitution of the Holy Roman Empire, each ruler was at liberty to allow the settlement of Jews, "provided they would live quietly and unobtrusively." The faculties also pointed out that Jews had indeed been admitted to many German principalities and cities; only the faculty of Jena suggested that the Jews be forbidden to circumcise Christians or to employ Christian servants and be made to attend Christian sermons. Needless to say, these "authoritative" counsels were neither literally followed by the Senate, nor did they completely silence the opposition, lay or clerical.[51]

Religious freedom, to be sure, was far from complete. The intransigence of Hamburg's Lutheran clergy was shown by its attitude to the Dutch Calvinists, who were not only prevented from forming a congregation of their own but, as late as 1603, despite the intercession of the Dutch Estates General, were even refused permission to organize a local congregation around the Calvinist church in neighboring Altona. Hamburg's Portuguese Jews, too, could at best hold services only in private homes. When one such dwelling was assigned for regular Jewish worship, the local clergy sharply assailed the act in 1617. Nevertheless private services were continued in that house, and another meeting place was added ten years later. Before long a third congregation functioned in the city, somewhat along the lines of the Amsterdam congregations of that period. These groups enjoyed a large measure of communal self-government, which contrasted sharply with the repression still practiced by the government against the Catholic minority. This contrast actually caused some international complications during the Thirty Years' War. After several futile attempts to secure permission to hold Catholic services in a private home, the Dominican friar Dominicus Janssen appealed to Emperor Ferdinand II and Generalissimo Tilly, then at the height of his power after his victories over the Danes and their Protestant allies. Emperor and general responded quickly and, in their notes to the Senate of Hamburg, protested against the anti-Catholic discrimination, since both the English and the Jews were allowed to worship God freely in their fashion. However, rather than granting the Catholics the requested freedom of worship, the Senate decided to curtail the privilege theretofore extended to Jews. But this senatorial narrow-mindedness little affected the progressive building up of the Jewish communal institutions.[52]

From the outset, however, the conservative burghers were apprehensive that liberal privileges might attract an excessive number of Marranos to the city. Hence detailed lists of settlers had to be submitted to the authorities. Today these lists furnish scholars with unusually dependable information about the origins of the Portuguese settlement, which, together with that founded by immigrants from other German areas and Poland, was destined to grow into the largest Jewish community in Germany in the eighteenth century. As early as 1646 the Senate estimated the Portuguese Jewish population at 100 families, while seventeen years later Count Galeazzo Gualdo Priorato, councilor of ex-queen Christina of Sweden, raised this estimate to 120 families, in addition to some 40-50 families of Ashkenazic Jews. This growth, accelerated in the following century, was not surprising, since

Hamburg as a whole began to be extolled by its admirers as the largest city in the Empire. More remarkably, the burghers' sustained opposition did not prevail even to the extent of forcing the Jews to live in a quarter of their own. To be sure, the compact of 1612 and its subsequent renewals did contain this provision (cited from Article 15 of the renewal of 1650): "They [the Jews] should own no houses in their own names in the city. They should also endeavor as much as possible to reside closely together in one or another place in the *Enge* and its adjoining streets, where most of them now live." But this never became a formal legal requirement. If most Jews lived in the proximity of their private places of worship, this was a matter of choice rather than legal enforcement. For the most part they were deeply interested in their community, which, among its other functions, assiduously cultivated several charitable institutions, a matter of major importance to all Jewish immigrant communities.[53]

The Jewish community's growth was further accelerated by its combination with the neighboring settlements of Altona and Wandsbek to form a single *qehillah qedoshah* (holy community), bearing the Hebrew abbreviation AHU (or AHW). Altona, newly established as an important trading center by its lords, the counts of Schaumburg (Schauenburg), attracted mainly Ashkenazic settlers, although as early as 1611, even before reaching the final agreement with the Hamburg authorities, the Hamburg "Portuguese" acquired a plot of land there suitable for a cemetery. Among the signers of the contract for the cemetery was Alvaro Dinis, who, because of his currency manipulations, got into difficulties with both the Hamburg and the Altona authorities and had to leave temporarily. Yet he was later readmitted to both cities and, in 1644, received an award of 200 thalers from the Hamburg Senate for his distinguished mediating services between their city and the Danish government. Many other Portuguese residents of Hamburg used Altona as a temporary domicile or place of refuge, also after it came under Danish-Holstein rule. A regular Portuguese communal organization was not to be established there until 1703, however. On the other hand, beginning in 1627, a number of German Jews settled in Hamburg. In 1644 some Altona families, escaping from the Swedish invaders, found shelter in the larger free city. Despite reiterated demands by the burghers that these Jews be banished, Hamburg, like Altona, harbored a growing Ashkenazic community, augmented by refugees from the Thirty Years' War throughout Germany and from the catastrophic results of the Cossack massacres and the Muscovite and Swedish wars with Poland in 1648–56. Despite the aversion evinced by the Portuguese Jews toward their German coreligionists (*Tudescos*), whom they tried for a while to keep at arm's length from Hamburg proper, the wealthy Portuguese merchants charitably supported the Ashkenazic refugees. A remarkable entry in the communal minute book of Sivan 2, 5416 (May 25, 1656), starts by saying: "Since our unfortunate coreligionists, forced by war and cruelty, had to leave Poland and regrettably have been exposed more and more to oppression, persecution, and misery, it is absolutely necessary to deal mercifully with them, as has been done on many previous occasions." When the communal treasury became overtaxed, the elders called together a general assembly of members to raise additional voluntary contributions. Before long the German community, too, began to flourish economically and culturally. The Altona segment, after 1641 authorized by the new Danish administration to establish both a synagogue and a cemetery, assumed the leadership of the entire tri-city community. It shared with Wandsbek, in particular, the benefits of the relatively friendly Danish regime, which, among other advantages, offered the Jews a fairly large market, not only in Schleswig-Holstein and Denmark but for a time also in Norway and beyond.[54]

Apart from the competition thus offered Hamburg by the Jews in Altona and Wandsbek, Christian IV of Denmark opened a new competitive establishment in Glückstadt. The king, himself no mean princely entrepreneur, as were Duke Julius of Brunswick-Lüneburg and King Gustav Vasa of Sweden, quite early made strenuous efforts to attract Portuguese New Christians and other important foreign merchant groups to Glückstadt, which beginning in 1617 he tried to develop into a major trading center. It had an ice-free harbor, and therefore appeared to be superior to Hamburg and other Hanseatic ports which became icebound during the winter. Once again it was Alvaro Dinis who made the necessary arrangements. The city had begun attracting numerous

Portuguese and other Jews (a list dated Easter 1623 named 8 Portuguese merchants and 6 craftsmen who had already lived in the city from one-half to three years) when Christian IV's unfortunate entry into the Thirty Years' War cut short its promising development. Damaged by a flood in 1625, Glückstadt was subjected to a five-months' siege in 1628. Even the Peace Treaty of Lübeck of 1629, though generally unfavorable to Denmark, brought major improvement to Glückstadt. The king, following a suggestion by Dinis—whom Christian IV addressed as "the honorable Albertus Dinnis, Our former mintmaster, burgher of Glückstadt, and Our dear faithful [subject]"—issued a formal invitation to Portuguese and other merchants to settle in Glückstadt. He had this proclamation announced in Emden, Hamburg, Holland, France, Portugal, Spain, and elsewhere. Apart from greatly extending the rights of the city as a whole, with special reference to the various foreign groups settled in it, he endowed the Portuguese Jewish community with a special privilege, dated June 19, 1630, which, claiming to be but a renewal of older provisions, formally safeguarded the Jews' civil and religious rights, going beyond anything known in the German communities of the period. The Portuguese were allowed to engage in any trade or craft of their choice; could own real estate throughout the city; were free from special taxes or obligations, including billeting in war or peace; and paid only the customary burghers' dues. They also were permitted to build synagogues and schools, send their children to general schools in order to learn Greek and Latin, and practice medicine freely among both Jews and Gentiles. Characteristically, the formula of their oath was changed to eliminate those magic and folkloristic accretions which had made the oath *more judaico* so objectionable to modern Jews. The Jewish party or witness merely had to place his hand upon an open Bible and state: "I swear by God the Almighty who has created heaven and earth, and His Holy word, as truly as He may help me to attain salvation and eternal life." The 1630 privilege was renewed in 1648, extended for another ten years in 1655, and for another twenty-five years in 1664.[55]

Once again, however, Denmark's wars with Sweden underscored Glückstadt's vulnerability to foreign entanglements and its ultimate inability to compete with Hamburg. Time and again the larger Portuguese community had to come to the aid of its weaker sister. In a characteristic letter of 1656 the Hamburg elders wrote:

The *Parnassim* [elders] of Geluquestate [Glückstadt] have on several occasions addressed themselves to our Board and described their present plight. It is almost impossible for them to maintain their community, wherefore they have requested our aid and assistance. . . . Since our predecessors have in the past expended considerable funds to help maintain that community, and lest the latter, God forbid, go under, which would accrue to the detriment of the liberty of our nation here, in our nearest neighbor [Altona], and elsewhere, the Board has decided to help it out in this emergency to the full extent possible.

As a first step the Hamburg elders, through a substantial salary increase, persuaded Yehudah Carmy, Glückstadt's spiritual leader, to stay at his post. In words and deeds the Hamburg community thus clearly indicated that it considered such relief action in part as insurance for itself. On more than one occasion, indeed, imperiled individuals found it highly advantageous to have a nearby haven of refuge until they could straighten out some of their tangled affairs. The importance of such insurance diminished in time, however, and Glückstadt's tiny community merely lingered on in the shadow of its larger neighbor. The same held true for the smaller and largely ephemeral Jewish settlements in neighboring Emden or Stade. The latter's ruler, Archbishop Johann Friedrich of Bremen, had actually lodged in 1615 with the Hamburg Senate a formal protest against the imposition of a "Jewish" license fee on his court Jew Salomon Herscheider, a physician. He threatened, by way of reprisal, to discontinue the free passage theretofore granted through his territory to Hamburg's Portuguese Jews, and to place them on an equal footing with their "German" coreligionists. This archiepiscopal threat, following the old adage: "If you beat my Jews, I beat yours," must have reminded the Senate that but a few years before it had used the specter of Stade's competition as a weapon to silence the burghers' opposition to its 1612 agreement with the Portuguese Jews. In any case, the mere flirting by high dignitaries of state and Church with the idea of inviting the Portuguese Jews to settle and endowing them with favorable privileges demonstrated the altered position of this new Jewish element in German society.[56]

In contrast, Hamburg suffered relatively little from the armed clashes of the Thirty Years' War. As a result, it greatly benefited from its uninterrupted trade and the inflationary profits it derived from sales to more deeply involved neighbors; it also required relatively few loans during the entire war period. If few Jewish bankers appear among the city's creditors, this may have been owing to apprehensions concerning eventual repayment (Jewish financiers had learned from bitter experience about the unreliability of politically powerful debtors), and their likely preference to extend such loans through the Hamburg Bank, in which they had invested considerable funds.[57]

NEW BEHAVIORAL PATTERNS

It was, indeed, a different breed of Jews which now appeared on the German scene. The New Christian leaders, often brought up in a Christian environment and used to the luxurious ways of living of wealthy Spaniards and Portuguese, behaved like their opposite numbers among the upper reaches of the Old Christian bourgeoisie. They lived in mansions, whether or not formally registered in the city records as owned by them, surrounded by a retinue of servants and business employees. In public they often appeared in colorful and costly attire, the very splendor of which aroused much antagonism and called forth certain antiluxury ordinances from both the municipality and their own community. As late as 1686, and again in 1709, the Hamburg Senate had to warn them in printed decrees against displaying swords and other arms while appearing at the Stock Exchange—a display generally discouraged by their own community as early as 1658. Some of their leading families actually claimed blood relationships with high-ranking Spanish and Portuguese nobles. The family ties between the Hamburg Abendanas and the Portuguese Mendes de Brito, or between the Teixeiras and the marquis de Sampayo (São Payo), could not easily be controverted. Two members of the Abas family in Hamburg were independently raised to the rank of nobility by Emperor Matthias in 1614 for the distinguished services they had rendered to the imperial Crown. Some of these men served as the accredited agents of foreign monarchs, including the kings of Portugal (after 1640), Denmark, and Sweden. Gabriel Gomez of Glückstadt was described by the high-sounding titles of "Commissioner of Finance, General Factor and Court Steward" of the king of Denmark in a document of 1664 recording his acquisition of the estate of Herzhorn from the king for the substantial sum of 29,890 thalers.[58]

Moreover, from the outset the Hamburg community included a number of distinguished scholars and poets. One temporary resident, Uriel (Gabriel) da Costa (1590–1647), could boast both of noble ancestry and of original views in religious philosophy. Among the several doctors of repute, Rodrigo de Castro and his sons were outstanding; even the generally antagonistic city council of Hamburg felt obliged to make an exception in De Castro's favor by allowing him to buy a house in his own name. Another physician, Jacob Rosales (Manuel Bocarro Francês), had distinguished himself in Portugal as a physician and a poet. However, his poem on the future of Portugal, published in 1624, although dedicated to the king of both Spain and Portugal, really betrayed Sebastianist tendencies and aimed at the restoration of Portugal's independence. These irredentist leanings, as well as his Jewish ancestry, ultimately forced him to emigrate. In Hamburg he joined the Jewish community, practiced medicine (among his patients were the crown prince of Denmark and the empresses Maria Anna and Eleanora), and ultimately served as the resident diplomatic representative of Spain. In this capacity he claimed to have advanced 15,000 ducats of his own to hire mercenaries for the Spanish army. Nonetheless his equivocal religious position led to some questioning of his character. He was called an "impious apostate" by his brother, Gaspar of Cochin, who in 1641 appeared as a defendant before the Lisbon Inquisition. Yet in two decrees of the same year Emperor Ferdinand III conferred upon him the dignity of the "small palatinate" and freed him "from the blemish of Jewish ancestry." These diplomas were handed to Rosales by the Spanish envoy. In 1649 the three Hanseatic cities of Hamburg, Lübeck, and Gdańsk (Danzig) gave him a prize of 100 Hungarian ducats for his mediating services in their favor during the peace negotiations. Nonetheless, his ambiguous diplomatic activities and his disagreements with the Jewish communal leaders forced him to leave Hamburg and to settle in Leghorn. He died in 1662 on his way from Leghorn to Florence, where he was to attend the gravely ill duchess of Strozzi. There also lived in Hamburg historians, rabbis, and talmudic scholars. Even a speculator and lobbyist like Alvaro Dinis did not hesitate to indulge in literary exercises. In 1629 he published a collection of thirty addresses— although comparing him to Joseph Penso de la Vega, the Jewish poet-historian and banker of Antwerp and Amsterdam, seems hardly justified.[59]

Among the outstanding Jewish families in Hamburg was that of Diego Teixeira de Sampayo, or São Payo, and his son Manuel (called in Hebrew Abraham and Isaac Ḥayyim Senior, respectively). Born in 1581 in Lisbon, Diego-Abraham had a long and checkered career before he settled in Hamburg in 1646, toward the end of the Thirty Years' War. In the following year he and his son were circumcised, and they later became pillars of the Sephardic community of Hamburg. In fact, according to a communal list of taxpayers in 1656, "Abraõ senior Teixeira" contributed 660 marks, and "Ishach seneor" 240 marks, whereas none of the other contributions exceeded 96 marks. The majority paid 12 marks or less. Not surprisingly, the far-flung financial, commercial, and diplomatic relations of the Teixeira firm whetted the appetites of the Habsburg administration. Although Diego had in 1643 received from the Spanish authorities in Antwerp a confirmation of his noble status and his relationship to the Sampayo family, the Austrian government addressed to the city of Hamburg a formal *démarche* on December 6, 1648, which read in part:

A foreigner named Diego Gery [Teixeira] has heretofore lived in Antörff [Antwerp] as surveyor of public debts in the service of his Royal Majesty of Spain. He conducted himself there as a Catholic Christian, attended Catholic services, confessions, and communions, and behaved in everything as a faithful adherent of the Catholic Church. Afterwards he moved to Cologne, where he likewise claimed to be a Catholic. But after transferring two years later to Hamburg, where he at first also appeared to be a Christian, in his advanced age, and undoubtedly under the prompting of Satan, he irritatingly denied the saving faith of Christ in the quiet week of Good Friday of 1647. He decided to leave the Christian Catholic religion and to profess accursed Judaism. He did not hesitate to have an old rabbi circumcise both him and his two sons (one of whom was illegitimate).

According to the Austrian note, Teixeira had also persuaded his Christian-born wife and a Christian virgin of Antwerp to adopt Judaism. In complete secrecy the Austrian representative now urged the Hamburg Senate to arrest Teixeira, hand him over to the imperial fiscal under an indictment for the crime of *laesae majestatis divinae,* and sequester all his possessions and accounts. But the Hamburg authorities refused to cooperate. They argued that Teixeira, like many other Spanish and Portuguese Jews, had openly settled in the city as a Jew, and that circumcisions in advanced age had frequently occurred. The Sentate also intimated that, if it took punitive action against Teixeira, it would frighten the other Portuguese Jews, who might leave the city, to the detriment of its commerce and finances. The Austrian authorities did not relent, however, in their efforts to seize the sizable Teixeira family funds (at one time estimated at 800,000 florins), and they intermittently pressed their claims even after Diego's death in 1666. The matter was not completely disposed of until 1670 when Manuel, aided by friendly Austrian representatives, settled with Emperor Leopold I's envoy Johann Gabriel Selb by endorsing a note for 10,249,700 silver maravedis and paying an additional 3,000 thalers to the emperor (plus 18,000 thalers to Selb personally for his mediating services). In the meantime, however, the Teixeiras had unperturbedly pursued their mercantile and banking careers; entertained ex-queen Christina of Sweden and other Swedish and Danish dignitaries, as well as various German princes, in their beautiful mansion; and contributed much to the continued rise of Hamburg as a commercial and financial center which rivaled Amsterdam and London. When Manuel Teixeira decided to move to Amsterdam in 1698, after a renewed conflict between the burghers and the Senate over the Jewish status, the Hamburg Stock Exchange received a severe jolt. According to one of Hamburg's leading councilors, Manuel was the main pillar of the Exchange, which had no member "equaling him in honesty and assets." [60]

Most importantly, these new arrivals performed economic functions for state and society which greatly differed from what the German public had expected from its older Jewish compatriots. Even before settling in the northwestern German cities, many Sephardic merchants and industrialists had entered the mainstream of the Commercial Revolution; they were able to bring with them now the necessary skills and capital. Among the first Portuguese settlers in Glückstadt was Gonsalvo Lopes Coutinho, who quite early established a sugar refinery, an oil mill, and a soap factory. Other Jewish industrialists erected saltworks and a tannery. In their money trade they generally shunned the customary petty loans on pledges, and rather entered the realm of high finance, negotiating loans with governments and leading merchants. They were usually satisfied with relatively low interest rates of 12 percent or less, in part because they had at their disposal ample funds from Iberian relatives and friends happy to remove capital from the reach of greedy inquisitors. No less than 40 Jewish families were involved in the foundation of the Hamburg Bank in 1619. Stimulated by the currency fluctuations of the period, the founders of that institution modeled it after the Bank of Amsterdam; it was the first such public institution in the area. Jews also played a great role in international trade, even with such outlying areas as Brazil and the Azores. While neither the clergy nor the populace reacted speedily enough to alter their traditional deprecation of all Jews, even they could not avoid noticing the changed social structure, personal behavior, and friendly social relationships with Christian neighbors of the new arrivals, whose very Jewishness had often but gradually unfolded. In their enlightened self-interest princes and statesmen frequently were quicker to realize the benefits to themselves and their countries from this new type of Jewish immigration. In time there emerged something approaching a rivalry between them as to who would strike the first or better bargain with these eager new settlers. In his famous negotiations with Oliver Cromwell in 1655–56, Menasseh ben Israel could actually point to Hamburg and its liberal legislation as an example worthy of emulation by any regime interested in enhancing the wealth of its country.[61]

Of course, the Jews of Hamburg were only doing what their coreligionists accomplished on a much larger scale in Amsterdam, and what others, still operating under their enforced New Christian disguise, had been achieving in Antwerp, Rouen, Bordeaux, and London. In this respect, too, the Thirty Years' War greatly accelerated the dominant trends. Its very territorial readjustments led to the incorporation of some older German communities, as well as some new Marrano settlements, into states more deeply influenced by the new economic and ideological trends. In the Empire proper the growth of Brandenburg under the "Great Elector" Frederick William (1640–88) opened up that forward-looking country to Jewish resettlement after a century of rigid exclusion. Also, by adding to the possessions of Brandenburg such adjacent territories as the bishopric of Halberstadt, the Treaties of Westphalia brought about a fundamental change in the position of these new subjects. Soon thereafter, this territory was to become the kingdom of Prussia, the major princely power in the Empire, second only to that of the Habsburgs.[62]

Similarly, when the emperor saw himself forced, as a result of the War, to cede his scattered Alsatian possessions, the very cradle of the Habsburg dynasty, to victorious France, he paved the way for the early occupation of the entire region by the French troops under Louis XIV and for its integration into the French monarchy. Alsatian Jewry now began sharing to some extent the fruits of the glorious evolution which was to elevate eighteenth-century France into a position of military, political, and cultural leadership of Western civilization. In neighboring Lorraine, the entry of French troops, followed by annexation to France, also marked a basic change in the destinies of the local Jewries. On his visit to Metz in 1632 (the city had been under French rule for eighty years), Louis XIII emphasized the great contributions made by Jews to the French war effort through the matériel and funds they had supplied to the garrison of that fortress, and particularly through the equipment they had furnished to officers of the detachment located in their quarter. Because of these services the king now renewed the significant privileges previously granted to the Jews of Metz, revealing that he had had a complete change of heart in the seventeen years since 1615, when he had wished to eliminate all Jewish settlements from his realm. Even in Avignon, relatively neutral and not ravaged by the War, Jews felt its effects; they were now drawn into such services as guarding the city gates. In their report to Rome of 1645, the Avignon consuls described these services as aimed at staving off the plague and also as involving

errands which one must daily perform in connection with the passage of many soldiers and vagrants who try to smuggle themselves into our city under the pretext of wishing to buy some merchandise of little value or to speak to certain persons. . . . Too many of this kind of people have been found here during the last two years, [a development] which was largely caused by the recent relaxation of the demands placed in this respect upon the Jews.

But all these incidents were merely phases in the transformation of Jewish status in western Europe which accompanied the Resettlement era, a transformation generally accelerated by the impact of the prolonged War, as will be seen in the next volume.[63]

TOWARD LIBERTY OF CONSCIENCE

Undoubtedly the most important result of the crosscurrents of the War and the ensuing peace treaties was the major, if still quite hesitant, step taken by the powers toward ensuring a measure of religious freedom under international guarantees. True, religious toleration, based upon the recognition of each individual's right to believe and worship in his own way, had been sporadically preached during the entire Renaissance era. But both the masses and the powers that were still continued firmly to believe in religious conformity as a mainstay of the existing social order.

The enormous destruction engendered by the victories and defeats of both coalitions arrayed in the conflict, and the ultimate conviction that neither side would emerge totally victorious, made them realize that only by safeguarding the rights of their respective religious minorities could they secure a lasting peace. This was indeed the greatest historic achievement of the 1648 treaties of Osnabrück and Münster in Westphalia. It was facilitated by the basic changes in the character of the War which became manifest during the three decades. At its inception it appeared to be purely religious, although Bohemian nationalism and other sociopolitical rivalries inherent in the chaotic structure of the Holy Roman Empire loomed very large behind the denominational façade. The masses of the population doubtless believed to the very end that they were fighting for religious ideals. But in reality the religious issue was increasingly overshadowed by the perennial imperialist conflicts, so that Catholic France, domestically intolerant of its own Huguenot minority, became the champion of the Protestant powers in their stuggle against the Catholic Habsburgs and their allies. Machiavelism, formally frowned upon by Christian ethics (*The Prince* had been placed on the papal Index by Paul IV and was generally rejected by Jesuit, as well as Calvinist, spokesmen), and its doctrine of the *raison d'état,* became the keynote of international relations.

Understandably, political interests also predominated in the peace treaties. Most of the provisions spelled out in great detail the territorial changes in favor of the non-German powers, France and Sweden. Within the Empire, too, the territories of secular princes grew at the expense of numerous bishoprics, now secularized, and free cities. Only 61 *Reichsstädte* remained to form an independent section of the imperial Diet, alongside of 8 (instead of the former 7) electors, and 69 religious and 96 secular princes. The lesser states strove to secure ever greater independence from the imperial overlordship, the treaties giving them the right to pursue independent foreign policies and even to conclude alliances with foreign states. The qualification that such alliances must not violate the oath of fealty which each prince had to render to the emperor had become rather meaningless in the light of a century-old tradition of Protestant states' open defiance of the imperial power, with the aid of its foreign enemies.

Together with these political transformations, however, a decisive attempt was made to establish a *modus vivendi* between the conflicting German denominations. The following provisions of the Franco-Austrian treaty of Münster indicate the extent to which mutual toleration was now guaranteed by the signatories of that and the other treaties:

It was further resolved that subjects adhering to the Augsburg Confession under Catholic rulers, as well as Catholic subjects of Estates professing the Augsburg Confession, who during the year 1624 could publicly or privately exercise their religion; also those who, after the proclamation of peace, will in the future profess or adopt a faith different from that of their ruler, will all be tolerated in a friendly fashion. They will not be hindered in dedicating themselves in free conscience to their private religious services at home without outside investigation and disturbance. Nor shall they be prevented from participating wherever and as often as they may wish in public divine services in their neighborhoods, and from entrusting their children's education to foreign schools of their faith or to private teachers in their homes. However, such inhabitants, vassals, and subjects shall otherwise fulfill all their obligations [to their respective states] with due allegiance and submission, and not give rise to any disturbances.

Whether the subjects profess the Catholic or the Augsburg Confession, they shall nowhere be subject to contemptuous treatment on account of their religion, nor shall they be excluded from the community of merchants, craftsmen, or guilds, from inheritances, legacies, hospitals, nursing homes, arms, or other rights and businesses; still less shall they be kept away from public cemeteries or honorable burials.

The treaties also provided for complete equality among the states, that of Osnabrück with Sweden stating expressly: "What is right for one party, should also be right for the other party." In fact, the treaties went so far as to abandon the majority principle in favor of "parity" in matters of faith. Thenceforth in religiously controversial matters the Protestants and Catholics at the Diet, regardless of their number, were to vote separately (according to the principle of *itio in partes*), and only a consensus of both parties could produce a valid vote.[64]

This was, of course, a far cry from complete equality of rights for individuals. Jews, in particular, were nowhere mentioned in the treaties. Nor did the Jewish question come up for serious discussion during the prolonged negotiations, which, originally proposed in 1641, started at the end of 1644 and went on for nearly four years while thousands of soldiers and civilians fell victim to the continued hostilities. From the outset the negotiations were conducted by parties, belonging to two distinct bodies of Catholics and Protestants, who tried to reach some accommodation to end the War but who otherwise were utterly uninterested in establishing the general principle of liberty of conscience for other denominations as well. The negotiators made concessions for diverse religious groups whose presence in the Empire was a long-established fact, rather than for individuals seeking to commune with the

Deity according to the dictates of their own conscience. The emphasis was also laid on the behavior of the individual states, whose absolute sovereignty had to be somewhat curtailed by the enforced recognition that religious disparity may not be completely outlawed, but which otherwise emerged, if anything, even more fully in control of their domestic affairs than before. Under the circumstances, Jewish leaders of the time rightly abstained from raising the Jewish issue before the assembled peace conference. The chances are that even if mid-sevententh-century German Jewry had had a spokesman as effective as Josel of Rosheim had been a century earlier, he would have considered it the better part of wisdom not to bring up the Jewish question before what undoubtedly would have been a rather unfriendly audience.[65]

Nor were even the limited religious freedoms promised by the treaties fully accepted by the more extreme exponents of the various faiths. Going beyond its reaction to the Religious Peace of Augsburg of 1555, the Papacy immediately protested against the Westphalian pledges of mutual toleration. Innocent X, echoing warnings sounded from Westphalia by the papal nuncio Fabio Chigi as early as November 1647, wrote a breve, *Zelo domus Dei* (dated back to November 20, 1648, though not issued until August 20, 1650), which roundly repudiated the treaties. He paid no heed to the concession to Catholics in the Osnabrück provision that any future controversies about interpretation should be adjusted in the spirit of the new pact, in perpetuity or "until by God's grace there would be mutual agreement about the religion itself." To conservative Catholics this clause meant nothing less than the hope of an ultimate restoration of the undisputed dominance of the Church universal. Moreover, the Jesuit Johannes Vervaux, father confessor of the new Bavarian "Elector" Maximilian, voiced the reservation widely shared in Catholic circles, that "any such obligation [as that included in the peace treaties] remains valid only so long as it may be fulfilled without sin. Toleration of heresy becomes a sin as soon as, under changed circumstances, there is no longer a need for such toleration." Even the Venetian ambassador, Alvise Contarini, who served as an influential go-between during the negotiations in Münster, explained the papal protest as intended "to leave the door open for the recovery of what they had lost as soon as the prospects for their arms are propitious." [66]

Nonetheless, the treaties marked a step in the right direction. No longer was the religious adherence of an individual the preeminent criterion for his rights of citizenship. Although the new provisions applied expressly to Catholics and Lutherans—and, to a lesser extent, to Calvinists and other Protestants—it was not too difficult to extend them to Jews, as well as to enlarge their scope to other areas. Generations passed before this broadened principle and its application became dominant in Western civilization. But there is little doubt that, without the deadlock generated by the Thirty Years' War, the adoption of general religious freedom would have been considerably delayed.

EFFECTS OF THE WAR ON JEWISH STATUS

Even the keenest Jewish observers of the period could hardly have envisaged that the Thirty Years' War would prove to be such an important turning point in the destinies of German Jewry. True, many scholars writing in the war- and depression-weary 1930s repeated the then popular slogan that "wars never solved anything" and applied it also to the Thirty Years' War. For example, in 1939 Cicely Veronica Wedgwood sweepingly dismissed this protracted conflict: "The war solved no problem. Its effects, both immediate and indirect, were either negative or disastrous. Morally subversive, economically destructive, socially degrading, confused in its causes, devious in its course, futile in its result, it is the outstanding example in European history of meaningless conflict." [67]

This is a decided misreading of history. Of course, the same results might in the long run have been obtained, without bloodshed and wholesale destruction of property, by the slow unfolding of the basic social factors then operating in European society. But Karl Marx's designation of revolutions as "locomotives of history" applies with equal force to wars, which as a rule have greatly accelerated the process of social change, although at a very high price. On many occasions the sociopolitical fabric has included many conflicting forces which have balanced one another in strength, and only the violence of war or revolution could tip the scale in one or another direction.

It must have been a novel realization to Jews living during the Wars of Religion that they no longer were the most persecuted religious minority. Yuspa Hahn, as we recall, could not suppress his wonderment over this turn of affairs, which he piously attributed to the will of Providence. In the very early stages of the great conflict in Bohemia, a leading aristocrat, Wilhelm von Lobkowitz, tried to salvage some precious objects by concealing them in Prague's Jewish quarter. That he was not altogether successful and that the Habsburg authorities, upon receiving information from secret agents or individual citizens, made the Jews deliver seventeen boxes of gold and silver objects belonging to him and other "rebels," did not alter the fact that Jewish depositaries were thought to be more immune from attack. The Austrian authorities themselves had to enlist the cooperation of the Prague rabbinate, which, under a formal ban, ordered its coreligionists to hand over to the police all property secreted with them. Even after the War (ca. 1662) the son of the unfortunate Winter King was advised to entrust his funds for safekeeping to Frankfort Jews, with whom they would be "as safe as in Heaven." This was indeed a complete reversal of conditions in the Middle Ages, when the deposit of precious objects in churches or monasteries had seemed to offer maximum security, whereas placing money or jewelry in Jewish hands had appeared quite risky.[68]

Obviously, Jews suffered some serious reverses as a result of the War. While we have no adequate statistics on Germany's Jewish population at the beginning and the middle of the seventeenth century (the above-cited data for Frankfort, Prague, and Vienna are too fragmentary to allow any safe generalization), it is quite possible that the Jews lost fewer lives in war casualties and pestilences than the Christians. In any case, the numerical decline of the Jewish population, doubtless partly due to emigration to Holland, was made up soon after 1648 by the stream of immigrants from pogrom- and war-ravaged Poland and Lithuania. However, there simultaneously occurred a more permanent demographic shift, from rural districts to the cities, reversing the trend which characterized the progressive Jewish dispersal over the German countryside following the expulsions from the cities in the fifteenth and early sixteenth centuries. We have seen that many Jewish refugees from villages and hamlets found at least temporary shelter in neighboring towns and cities. Some of the provisional admissions turned out to be unexpectedly permanent, and relatively few refugees seem to have returned to their old rural habitats. This was a significant and, in the long run, favorable reversal. With the growing role of urban civilization in modern society, this progressive reurbanization of German Jewry put the Jews a step ahead of their neighbors in the momentous evolution of the new order.[69]

With the almost total debacle of imperial overlordship, to be sure, the Jews lost their traditional protection against outbursts of total intolerance. The secularization of many bishoprics likewise weakened an element of the German power structure which tried to maintain, at least partially, the traditional canonical equilibrium between toleration of and discrimination against the Jews. However, both imperial and episcopal protection had proved increasingly uncertain in the storms of anti-Jewish agitation of the Reformation era, the Habsburgs themselves paving the way with many expulsions, actual or threatened, of Jews from Austria and Bohemia. On the other hand, during the War there occurred a highly significant, albeit tentative, reorientation of some Protestant rulers toward acceptance of Jewish subjects. While the intolerant teachings of Luther, Bucer, and Calvin largely determined the policies of Protestant states in the first decades after 1517, and the total intolerance initiated by the elector of Saxony in 1536 was much emulated by later Protestant princes and city councils, the early seventeenth century witnessed a meaningful turnabout. Under the leadership of the Protestant States-General in Holland, King Christian IV of Denmark, and the Hamburg Senate, the readmission of Jews, under vastly improved privileges, became a watchword of the age. Soon the "Great Elector" of Brandenburg (later Prussia) set the tone for many Protestant princes in Germany. Before long even in Saxony, the citadel of Lutheran intransigence, voices were heard, like that of the noble author of the *Cours de la Pologne,* which advocated the admission of Jews, although these men entertained vastly exaggerated hopes about the economic benefits which would immediately accrue to the state from such admission.[70]

Quite apart from such exaggerated expectations, the practical lessons of the War were not lost on the rulers of the postwar era. Statesmen and generals had discovered that Jewish bankers, merchants, and contractors could prove very useful in the building up of their resources. Werner Sombart's oft-quoted declaration, that the German prince and the German court Jew during the early modern period marched shoulder to shoulder in erecting the modern German state, is clearly an overstatement. Yet it contains a kernel of truth: Jewish capital and managerial skills proved increasingly helpful to the modern state in its domestic, as well as foreign, policies. This factor had manifested itself on many occasions during the Thirty Years' War. Together with the general military and political deadlock and the enforced mutual toleration of Catholics and Protestants, these new sociopolitical and religious facts of life were bound deeply to affect also the relations between the Jews and the majority peoples. They enabled many Jewish capitalists and their agents, with their long repressed energies, to seize new opportunities, just as the conflicts between Spain and the other maritime powers made possible the Jews' resettlement in Holland and England and the rise of Jewish communities in the New World. These deeply interrelated factors, reinforced by the novel intellectual trends in European and Jewish society, helped to begin a new epoch in Jewish history.

NOTES

ABBREVIATIONS

Abrahams Mem. Vol.	Jewish Studies in Memory of Israel Abrahams. New York, 1927.
AFP	Archivum fratrum praedicatorum
AHDE	Anuario de historia del derecho español
AHDL	Archives d'histoire doctrinale et littéraire du moyen âge
AHP	Archivum historiae pontificiae
AHR	American Historical Review
AHSI	Archivum historicum Societatis Iesu
AJHQ	American Jewish Historical Quarterly
AKKR	Archiv für katholisches Kirchenrecht
Annales ESC	Annales Economies, Sociétés, Civilisations
ARG	Archiv für Reformationsgeschichte
AS	Archivio storico (with identifying name, Lombardo, Siciliano, etc.)
ASI	Archivio storico italiano
ASPN	Archivio storico per le provincie napoletane
b.	ben or bar (son)
Bab.	Babylonian Talmud (identified by the respective tractates)
BAE	Biblioteca de autores españoles
Baer Jub. Vol.	Sefer Yobel le-Yitzhak Baer (Yitzhak Baer Jubilee Volume), Jerusalem, 1960.
BAH	Boletín de la Real Academia de la Historia, Madrid
BEC	Bibliothèque de l'Ecole des Chartes
BEP	Bulletin des études portugaises
BH	Bulletin hispanique
BHR	Bibliothèque d'Humanisme et Renaissance
BJRL	Bulletin of the John Rylands Library
BMGJW	Bijdragen en Mededeelingen der Genootschap voor de Joodsche Wetenschap in Nederland
BNYPL	Bulletin of the New York Public Library
BSHPF	Bulletin of the Société de l'histoire du protestantisme français
CH	Church History
CHE	Cuadernos de historia de España
EcHR	Economic History Review
E. 'E.	Eben ha 'Ezer
EHR	English Historical Review
Festschrift Schäfer	Forschungen und Versuche zur Geschichte des Mittel-

alters und der Neuzeit. Festschrift Dietrich Schäfer. Jena, 1910

Festschrift Steinschneider   Festschrift zum achtzigsten Geburtstag Moritz Steinschneider's. Leipzig, 1896.

Freidus Mem. Vol.   Studies in Jewish Bibliography and Related Subjects in Memory of Abraham Solomon Freidus (1867–1923). New York, 1929.

GS   Gesammelte Schriften

HAHR   Hispanic American Historical Review
HJ   Historia Judaica
HJB   Historisches Jahrbuch
Homenaje Millás   Homenaje a Millás-Vallicrosa. 2 vols. Barcelona, 1954–56.
HTR   Harvard Theological Review
HUCA   Hebrew Union College Annual
HZ   Historische Zeitschrift

JAOS   Journal of the American Oriental Society
JFF   Jüdische Familien-Forschung
JGJCR   Jahrbuch der Gesellschaft für Geschichte der Juden in der Čechoslovakischen Republik
JHI   Journal of the History of Ideas
JJLG   Jahrbuch der Jüdisch-Literarischen Gesellschaft, Frankfurt a. M.
JJS   Journal of Jewish Studies
JNOS   Jahrbücher für Nationalökonomie und Statistik
JQR   Jewish Quarterly Review (new series, unless otherwise stated)
JSS   Jewish Social Studies

KA   Korrespondenzblatt . . . Akademie für die Wissenschaft des Judentums
KS   Kirjath Sepher, Quarterly Bibliographical Review

MGH   Monumenta Germaniae Historica
MGWJ   Monatsschrift für Geschichte und Wissenschaft des Judentums
MHJ   Monumenta Hungariae Judaica (Magyar-Zsidó Oklevéltár)
MHSJ   Monumenta historica Societatis Jesu
MIOG   Mitteilungen des Instituts für österreichische Geschichtsforschung
MZS   Magyar-Zsidó Szemle (Hungarian Jewish Review)

NRS   Nuova rivista storica

PAAJR   Proceedings of the American Academy for Jewish Research
PAJHS   Publications of the American Jewish Historical Society

Philippson Festschrift	Beiträge zur Geschichte der deutschen Juden. Festschrift . . . Martin Philippson. Leipzig, 1916.
PL	Patrologiae cursus completus, series Latina, ed. by J. P. Migne
QFIA	Quellen und Forschungen aus italienischen Archiven und Bibliotheken
RABM	Revista de Archivos, Bibliotecas y Museos
RAM	Revue d'ascétique et de mystique
RBPH	Revue belge de philologie et d'histoire
REJ	Revue des études juives
Resp.	Responsa, or *She'elot u-teshubot*
RH	Revue historique
RHE	Revue d'histoire ecclésiastique
RHPR	Revue d'histoire et de philosophie religieuses
RI	Rivista israelitica
RMI	Rassegna mensile di Israel
RQH	Revue des questions historiques
RSCI	Rivista di storia della Chiesa in Italia
RSI	Rivista storica italiana
SB	Sitzungsberichte der Akademie der Wissenschaften (identified by city: e.g., SB Berlin, Heidelberg, Vienna).
SZG	Schweizerische Zeitschrift für Geschichte
TG	Tijdschrift voor Geschiedenis
TJHSE	Transactions of the Jewish Historical Society of England
VSW	Vierteljahrsschrift für Sozial- und Wirtschaftsgeschichte
ZBL	Zeitschrift für bayerische Landesgeschichte
ZDMG	Zeitschrift der Deutschen Morgenländischen Gesellschaft
ZGJD	Zeitschrift für Geschichte der Juden in Deutschland
ZGJT	Zeitschrift für die Geschichte der Juden in der Tschechoslowakei
ZGW	Zeitschrift für Geschichtswissenschaft
ZHB	Zeitschrift für hebräische Bibliographie
ZKG	Zeitschrift für Kirchengeschichte
ZRG	Zeitschrift der Savigny-Stiftung für Rechtsgeschichte

NOTES

CHAPTER LIX: CATHOLIC REFORM

1. See the pertinent discussions by E. W. Zeeden, "Zur Periodisierung und Terminologie des Zeitalters der Reformation und Gegenreformation," *Geschichte in Wissenschaft und Unterricht*, VII, 433–37; R. García Villoslada, "La Contrareforma. Su nombre y su concépto histórico" in *Saggi storici intorno al papato (Miscellanea historiae pontificiae*, XXI), pp. 189–242; P. Prodi, "Riforma cattolica e contrariforma" in *Nuove questioni di storia moderna*, I, 357–418; *infra*, n. 45; and, on the history of the respective terms, H. Jedin's *Katholische Reformation oder Gegenreformation?*. See also E. Iserloh, J. Glazik, and H. Jedin, *Reformation, Katholische Reform und Gegenreformation;* and P. G. Camaiani, "Interpretazioni della Riforma cattolica e della Contrariforma," *Grande Antologia filosofica*, VI, 329–490.

2. See H. Finke, ed., *Acta Concilii Constantiensis;* L. R. Loomis, *The Council of Constance: the Unification of the Church*, ed. and annotated by J. H. Mundy and K. M. Woody; U. Frommerz, *Johannes von Segovia als Geschichtsschreiber des Konzils von Basel;* M. Simonsohn, *Die Kirchliche Judengesetzgebung im Zeitalter der Reformkonzilien von Konstanz und Basel;* J. Gill, *The Council of Florence;* idem, *Eugenius IV, Pope of Christian Union;* J. Décarreaux, *L'Union des Églises au concile de Ferrare-Florence, 1438–1439;* A. Domíngues de Sousa Costa, "Canonistarum doctrina de Judaeis et Saracenis tempore Concilii Constantiensis," *Antonianum*, XL, 3–70, esp. pp. 9 ff., 32 ff.; and *supra*, Vol. XI, pp. 193 ff., 379 f. nn. 1 and 3. The ambiguous relationships of Catholic powers to the expansion of the Ottoman Empire are well illustrated by such monographs as F. Babinger's "Kaiser Maximilians I. 'geheime Praktiken' mit den Osmanen (1510–11)," *Südost-Forschungen*, XV, 201–236; R. B. Merriman's biography of *Suleiman the Magnificent, 1520–1566;* H. Pfeffermann, *Die Zusammenarbeit der Renaissancepäpste mit den Türken*, with a Foreword by F. Blanke; and, more generally, R. Schwoebel, *The Shadow of the Crescent: the Renaissance Image of the Turk (1453–1517);* S. N. Fisher, *The Foreign Relations of Turkey 1481–1512;* and S. A. Fischer-Galati, *Ottoman Imperialism and German Protestantism, 1521–1555*.

That the demands for Church reform had in part been stimulated by specifically anti-Jewish developments, such as the massacres of 1348 and the accompanying marches of the Flagellants, has rightly been stressed by H. Tüchle in his *Kirchengeschichte Schwabens*, II, 45 ff. On the impact of the Great Western Schism and the conciliar crisis on the rise of the *converso* class in Spain and the latter's contribution to reformatory trends see L. Suárez Fernández, *Castilla, el Cisma y la crisis conciliar*. Other Jewish aspects of these movements have frequently been mentioned in my earlier volumes and need not be repeated here. The specific references will be more easily located after the publication of an Index Volume which is expected to cover the material on the entire period from 1200 to 1650.

3. See esp. F. Pericoli, "L'Abolizione della feudalità negli Stati della Chiesa," *Rivista araldica*, LIV, 110–16; G. Garrani, *Il Carattere bancario e l'evoluzione strutturale dei primigenii Monti di pietà*; A. Dauphin-Meunier, *L'Église en face du capitalisme;* and *supra*, Chap. LVII, nn. 32–33; and Vols. IX, pp. 51 ff., 265 nn. 60–61; X, pp. 272 ff.; XII, pp. 167 f., 325 nn. 41–42, etc.

4. V. H. H. Green, *Luther and the Reformation,* esp. p. 9; Girolamo Aleandro, *Die Depeschen des Nuntius Aleander vom Wormser Reichstage, 1521,* trans. by P. Kalkoff, pp. 18 f. (though the text refers to "merchants of Moorish descent," Aleandro doubtless had Marranos in mind); Charles V's letter to Pope Leo X of 1519; and other data cited *supra*, Chaps. LVII, nn. 28–29; and LVIII, nn. 12–13; and *infra*, n. 17; Archbishop Silíceo's statement of 1547, cited by A. A. Sicroff in his *Les Controverses des statuts de "pureté de sang" en Espagne du XVe au XVIIe siècle,* p. 111. See also *infra*, n. 17; and such monographs as M. Gachard, ed., *Correspondance de Charles V et d'Adrian VI;* D. Gnoli, *La Roma di Leon X;* and J. Sambuc, "Documents sur les procès (1533) de Jean de Roma, inquisiteur. Étude analytique du manuscrit J. 851 des Archives Nationales," *BSHPF*, CIX, 180–95.

5. J. Beumer, "Suffizienz und Insuffizienz der Heil. Schrift nach Kard. Thomas de Vio Cajetan," *Gregorianum*, XLV, 816–24; G. Hennig, *Cajetan und Luther. Ein historischer Beitrag zur Begegnung von Thomismus und Reformation;* V. Baroni, *La Contre-Réforme devant la Bible; la question biblique;* H. Mackensen, "The Diplomatic Role of Gasparo Cardinal Contarini at the Colloquy of Ratisbon of 1541," *CH*, XXVII, 312–37. In his communication of April 17, 1546, to Cardinal Christopher Madruzzo, Bishop Jacob Nacchianti of Chioggia reported about a dispute among the Spanish delegates to the Council of Trent concerning the permissibility of using vernacular translations of the Bible. According to the bishop, Don Diego Hurtado de Mendoza, Charles V's envoy to Venice and Trent, argued that the opposition to the existing Spanish translations at home had arisen because the current Bibles had been prepared largely by Marranos but that this negative attitude ought not to be generalized for all countries. See G. Buschbell, *Reformation und Inquisition in Italien um die Mitte des XVI. Jahrhunderts*, pp. 294 f. No. 59; P. Prodi, "Riforma cattolica," *Nuove questioni di storia moderna,* I, 378 ff. On the differences of opinion, on this and other scores, between laymen and the clergy, see C. Dionisotti, "Chierici e laici nella letteratura italiana del primo Cinquecento," *Problemi di vita religiosa in Italia nel Cinquecento,* in the *Atti* of the Convegno di storia della Chiesa in Italia (1958), pp. 167–85. See also A. Sacconi, *Ercole Gonzaga e la riforme pretridentina della diocesi di Mantova;* and other studies reviewed by G. Ritter in his "Wegbahner eines 'aufgeklärten' Christentums im 16. Jahrhundert. Bericht über neuere italienische Forschungen," *ARG*, XXXVII, 268–89; and *infra*, n. 18; Chap. LX. Of course, Catholic theology also tried to maintain its medieval continuity during the Renaissance and the Counter Reformation. Many bridges were built even by monastic orders such as the Augustinians, which Egidio da Viterbo for a time served as general and which furnished several important spiritual leaders to both the Reformation and the Counter Reformation. On the medieval antecedents of that role, see R. Arbesmann, *Der Augustinereremitenorden und der Beginn der humanistischen Bewegung* (reprinted from *Augustiniana*, XIV–XV). That medieval heritage has also been analyzed, from another angle, on the example of Gabriel Biel, by H. A. Oberman in *The Harvest of*

Medieval Theology. Gabriel Biel and Late Medieval Nominalism (with the comments thereon by F. Clark in "A New Appraisal of Late-Medieval Theology," *Gregorianum*, XLVI, 732–65); and in other writings examined by the same author in "Theologie des späten Mittelalters. Stand und Aufgaben der Forschung," *Theologische Literatur-Zeitung*, XCI, 401–416.

6. Johann Maier von Eck (of Egg) himself collected many earlier anti-Lutheran pamphlets in his five-volume work, *Opera contra Ludderum* (this spelling had occasionally been used by Luther himself in his early years), published in 1530–35. On his unblushing affirmation of the blood libel, see his *Ains Judenbüechlins Verlegung; darin ain Christ gantzer Christenhait zu Schmach will es geschehe den Juden Unrecht in Bezichtigung der Christen Kinder Mordt* of 1541; and the older but still useful biography by T. Wiedemann, *Dr. Johann Eck, Professor der Theologie an der Universität Ingolstadt*, esp. pp. 330 ff., 636 ff. The tremendous impact on Catholic historiography of Johannes Cochlaeus' (Dobeneck's) biography of Luther, published after the latter's death in 1549, has been fully documented by A. Herte in *Das Katholische Lutherbild im Bann der Lutherkommentare des Cochläus*. See also M. Spahn's list of the numerous other works by this early opponent of Luther in his *Johannes Cochlaeus. Ein Lebensbild aus der Zeit der Kirchenspaltung;* and on the twentieth-century Catholic reactions to the German reformer, R. Stauffer's survey, *Luther as Seen by the Catholics*, or in its more expressive French edition, *Le Catholicisme à la découverte de Luther. L'évolution des recherches catholiques sur Luther de 1904 au 2ᵐᵉ Concile de Vatican* (beginning with Heinrich Denifle's and Hartmann Grisar's comprehensive works about Luther).

7. H. Bernard-Maître, "Un Grand serviteur du Portugal en France. Diogo de Gouveia l'Ancien et le Collège Sainte-Barbe de Paris (1520–1548)," *BEP*, n.s. XV, 57 ff.; Paul III's bull *Regimini militantis ecclesiae* of September 27, 1540, in *Bullarium romanum*, VI, 303 ff. No. xxxiii, with its analysis and additional data by P. Tacchi Venturi in his *Storia della Compagnia di Gesù in Italia*, I, Part 2, pp. 179 ff. No. 50; Loyola's letter to Joannes Alphonso de Polanco of February or March 1547 in *MHSJ, Monumenta Ignatiana*, 1st ser. *Epistolae et instructiones*, I, 458 f. No. 152; in W. J. Young's slightly different English trans. of Loyola's *Letters*, p. 114. The biographical literature on Loyola is enormous. Beginning with his autobiography, *Acta quaedam*, in *MHSJ, Monumenta Ignatiana*, 4th ser., *Scripta de Sancto Ignatio*, I, 31–98; *The Testament of Ignatius Loyola, Being "Sundry Acts of Our Father Ignatius, under God, the First Founder of the Society of Jesus, Taken Down from the Saint's Own Lips by Luis Gonzalez*," English trans. by E. M. Rix, with a Foreword by G. Tyrell and a Biographical Appendix by H. Thurston (there also are well-documented French and German translations of this report on Loyola's pilgrim years), his life and works were enthusiastically described by his close associate Joannes Alphonso de Polanco in *Vita Ignatii Loiolae et rerum Societatis Jesu historia*, reprinted in *MHSJ, Historia Societatis Jesu*, and by many others. See the mutually complementary bibliographies by J. Juambelz, "Bibliografía sobre la vida de San Ignacio de Loyola, 1900–1950," *Razón y fé*, CLIII, 351–99 (401); J. F. Gilmont and P. Daman, *Bibliographie ignatienne (1894–1957). Classement méthodique;* "Homenaje bibliográfico a San Ignacio de Loyola en el IV Centenario de su muerte (1556–1956)," *Bibliografía Hispánica*, XV, 198–212 (this anonymous writer lists

fifty interesting publications of 1599–1905 from an unnamed private collection); H. Becher, "Ignatius von Loyola im Licht der gegenwärtigen Forschung," *Scholastik*, XXXII, 206–220; and *infra*, n. 16. See also Pedro de Ribadeneira, *Historia de la Contrareforma*, with an Intro. and Notes by E. Rey (includes biographies of Loyola, Laynez, Salmerón, and Borgia); and the fine selection of sources, bibliographies, and secondary literature by L. Willaert in Vol. XVIII of A. Fliche *et al.*, eds., *Histoire de l'Église*, pp. 130 ff., 450.

8. L. Cristiani in A. Fliche *et al.*, *Histoire de l'Église*, XVII, 296; J. A. de Polanco's *Vita Ignatii* in *MHSJ*, *Historia Societatis Jesu*, VI, 231 No. 818, with the editor's note thereon; and P. M. Baumgarten, *Ordenszucht und Ordensstrafrecht. Beiträge zur Geschichte der Gesellschaft Jesu in Spanien*, Vol. I (Untersuchungen zur Geschichte und Kultur des sechzehnten und siebzehnten Jahrhunderts, Parts 7–9), pp. 103 ff., and *passim*. Here and in his "Kritische Bemerkungen zum elften, zwölften und dreizehnten Band von Pastors Papstgeschichte," *ZKG*, XLVIII, 421, 430, Baumgarten decidedly exaggerates when he claims that "innumerable Jewish progeny at that time flooded all the Jesuit provinces of the Iberian Peninsula." One must distinguish between the headquarters in Rome, which practiced no discrimination, and the Iberian provinces, where the requirement of *limpieza* was stressed with increasing vigor. In the case of Luis Molina, adduced by Baumgarten, we have Molina's own claim that he was of "pure" (*limpio*) descent and was merely being confused with members of a New Christian family by the same name. See P. Browe, "Die Kirchenrechtliche Stellung der getauften Juden und ihrer Nachkommen," *AKKR*, CXXI, 185 n. 2; and *supra*, Chap. LVI, nn. 29 and 36. But Browe goes to the other extreme in underestimating the Marrano role in the early stages of the Jesuit Order. See *infra*, nn. 9–10. Of course, the case of Giovanni Battista Eliano was different in so far as, before his conversion, he had been not a Marrano but a professing Jew of German descent. On the various steps leading up to his conversion; his entry into the Society of Jesus in 1551; Loyola's great friendliness toward him after his arrival in Rome in 1552, when he assumed the name of Romano; the first mention of his name as Eliano in 1577; his role in the censorship of Hebrew books; and his subsequent troubles with the Jews of Alexandria, see his *Autobiography*, dated January 24, 1588 ("on the day of St. Paul's conversion" specified in his own hand), and an additional document, ed. by J. C. Sola in his "El P. Juan Bautista Eliano: un documento autobiográfico inédito," *AHSI*, IV, 291–321, esp. pp. 295 ff., 299 ff., 303 n. 31; and I. Sonne's comments on Eliano's *Autobiography* in his Hebrew rendition of several excerpts therefrom in *Mi-Pavlo ha-rebi'i*, pp. 150 ff.; *infra*, nn. 29 and 34.

9. See Laynez' Memorandum (*Commentarius*) addressed to Catherine de Médicis in 1562 and reproduced in *MHSJ*, *Lainii Monumenta: Epistolae et acta*, VIII, 775 ff., 780; his visitatorial tour in Sicily recorded *ibid.*, I, 279 f.; his address reproduced in *Concilii Tridentini Acta*, VI, ed. by S. Ehses (in the collection, ed. by S. Merkle *et al.*, IX), pp. 94 ff.; and, more generally, H. Grisar, ed., *Iacobi Lainez Disputationes Tridentinae*, esp. I, 399 ff. App.; C. J. Hefele *et al.*, *Histoire des conciles*, IX, Part 2, pp. 892 f. and *passim*; X, Part 1, pp. 474 ff. (cf. *Index*); J. Ruppert's monograph, *De programmate secundi praepositi generalis Societatis Jesu reformationem Papatui per Concilium generale imponere temptantis*. See also the recent debate thereon between G. Alberigo in *Lo Sviluppo della dottrina sui poteri nella Chiesa universale*.

Momenti essenziali tra il XVI e il XIX secolo; and W. Bertrams in his "Notae aliquae quoad opus recenter editum de potestate Episcoporum in Ecclesiam universalem," *Gregorianum,* XLVI, 343–54; G. Philippart, "Visiteurs, commissaires et inspecteurs de la Compagnie de Jésus de 1540 à 1615, Part I: 1540–1572," *AHSI,* XXXVII, 3–128 (referring also to numerous other organizational contributions by Laynez and Polanco); C. S. Sullivan, *The Formulation of the Tridentine Doctrine of Merit,* stressing, in particular, Laynez' contribution to the repudiation of Double Justice (pp. 47 ff.); *infra,* nn. 13–14; and, more generally, the interesting Marxist interpretation of "The Council of Trent and the Jesuits" by K. Piwarski in his *Szkice z dziejów papiectwa* (Sketches from the History of the Papacy), pp. 45–97. On Laynez' Jewish descent, see A. E. Palacín, *Nuevas investigaciones histórico-genealógicas referentes al M. R. P. P. Diego Lainez y su distinguida familia de Almazán y de Matute;* P. Browe, "Die Kirchenrechtliche Stellung," *AKKR,* CXXI, 181 ff.; and the literature listed *infra,* n. 13. However, the contemporary allusions to Laynez' purported candidacy for the papal see consist of mere hearsay; on the other hand, P. M. Baumgarten's denial (see *supra,* n. 8) of that candidacy because it is not mentioned in L. Pastor's detailed description of the election of Pius IV, is a weak *argumentum a silentio.*

There seems to be no question, however, concerning Loyola's own Castilian ancestry. See, for instance, F. Arocena, "El Abuelo materno de San Ignacio," *AHSI,* XXV, 7–14; and D. de Arecitio, "Nuevos datos sobre el abuelo materno de San Ignacio de Loyola," *ibid.,* XXVI, 218–29. On the nearly total absence of Jews from the entire Basque province of Guipúzcoa, stressed by Loyola himself, see *supra,* Chap. LVI, n. 31.

Remarkably, in his acute characterization of Polanco included in the thumbnail sketches he made of nine associates for Loyola (*ca.* 1545), Laynez spoke of the future secretary as "a native of Burgos, of a wealthy family and a noble father," but did not refer to his New Christian parentage. See L. Lukács, "Le Catalogue-modèle du Père Laínez (1545)," *AHSI,* XXVI, 57–66, esp. pp. 64 f. No. 2 (with the facsimile of Laynez' autograph). See also C. Englander, *Ignatius von Loyola und Johannes von Polanco. Der Ordensstifter und sein Sekretär;* Loyola's instructions at Polanco's appointment as secretary-general of the Order in 1547, published by M. Scaduto in "Uno Scritto ignaziano. Il 'Del Officio del secretario' del 1547," *AHSI,* XXIX, 305–328; and F. Roustang, "Sur le rôle de Polanco dans la rédaction des *Constitutiones S. J.,*" *Revue d'ascétique et de mystique,* XLII, 193–202. These constitutions, as published with a Foreword by Polanco in 1559, remained authoritative for generations. According to Francesco Sacchini, all subsequent editions were suppressed, "lest anything be added to these constitutions that Ignatius had not edited." See A. Backer *et al.,* eds., *Bibliothèque de la Compagnie de Jésus,* new ed. by C. Sommervogel, VI, 945. On the impact of biblical institutions on some of these constitutional provisions, see M. A. Fiorito, "Alianza bíblica y regla religiosa. Estudio histórico-salvífico de las constituciones de la Compañía de Jesús," *Stromata,* XXI, 291–324; and, more generally, several *Conferenze commemorative* on the four-hundredth anniversary of the foundation of the Society of Jesus, delivered in 1941 at the Pontifical Gregorian University in Rome, and published under the title *La Compagnia di Gesù e le scienze sacre.*

10. See A. Astrain, *Historia de la Compañía de Jesús en la Asistencia de España,* esp. III, 573 ff.; and Baumgarten's remarks cited *supra,* n. 8. The Jewish preacher

praised by Bruno was plausibly identified by M. Liber as the converted missionary to the Jews Joseph Sarfati (Andrea del Monte). See Liber's "Montaigne à Rome," *REJ*, LV, 114 f., referring to L. Auvray's publication of notes by the contemporary friar Guillaume Cotin in "Giordano Bruno à Paris d'après le témoignage d'un contemporain (1585–1586)," *Mémoires* of the Société de l'histoire de Paris et de l'Île-de-France, XXVII, 288–301, esp. pp. 291 f. n. 2; and *infra*, n. 43. See also G. Cozzi, "Un Documento sulla crisi della 'Sacra Lega.' Le Confidenze del Padre Francisco Toledo all'avogadore di comun Nicolò Barbarigo (ottobre 1572)," *Archivio Veneto*, 5th ser., LXVII, 76–96, esp. pp. 79 f., 93 ff.; and *infra*, Chap. LX, n. 6.

11. Paul III's bull, *Illius, qui pro Dominici* of February 19, 1543, in *Bullarium romanum*, VI, 353 ff. No. xlvi; Don Giovanni da Torano's denunciation, reported by Joannes Alphonso de Polanco in his *Vita Ignatii Loiolae et rerum Societatis Jesu historia* (includes *Chronicon Societatis Jesu*), III, 25 No. 40, with the editor's note thereon, and analyzed in detail by P. Tacchi Venturi in his *Storia della Compagnia di Gesù in Italia*, I, Part 2, pp. 20 f., 273 ff. No. 73; II, Part 2, p. 266 n. 4. See also Loyola's letter to Francis Xavier of 1543–44 in *MHSJ, Monumenta Ignatiana Epistolae*, I, 267 f. No. 70 (shedding light on his attitude to the conversion of Jews and the establishment of the House of Catechumens); P. Dudon, *St. Ignatius of Loyola*, English trans. from the French by W. J. Young, pp. 386 ff.; and J. Brodrick's studies, *Saint Ignatius Loyola: the Pilgrim Years; The Origin of the Jesuits;* and *The Progress of the Jesuits*. On the houses of catechumens in Rome and elsewhere, see *infra*, n. 24.

12. Ignatius de Loyola, *MHSJ, Monumenta Ignatiana, Epistolae et instructiones*, I, 336 No. 100; V, 335 No. 3646; VIII, 446 No. 5198; Pedro de Ribadeneira, "Dicta et facta S. Ignatii collecta," *ibid.*, 4th ser. I, 398 f. No. 32; in *Obras escogidas*, ed. by V. de la Fuente; J. J. Brodrick, "St. Ignatius Loyola and the Jews," *The Bridge*, IV, 294–309; P. Browe, "Die Kirchenrechtliche Stellung," *AKKR*, CXXI, 182 f. On the Toledan statute and its wide repercussions see *supra*, n. 4; and Chap. LVI, nn. 29 ff.; and, with special reference to the school of Juan de Ávila, J. M. de Buck, "Le Bienhereux Juan de Avila et les Jésuites espagnols," *Nouvelle Revue théologique*, LIII, 596–611, 674–84, esp. pp. 681 f. We shall see (*infra*, Chap. LXV) that, after Portugal regained her independence in 1640, the Portuguese Jesuits were to play an important role in mitigating their country's general policies of *limpieza*. See also the data supplied by E. Rey, "San Ignacio de Loyola y el problema de los 'Cristianos Nuevos,'" *Razón y fé*, CLIII, 173–204; Ignatius de Loyola, *Obras completas. Edición manual*, transcribed with introductions and notes by I. Iparraguirre (includes his *Autobiografía*, ed. and annotated by C. de Dalmasses); M. Quera, "San Ignacio, legislador del la Compañía de Jesús," *Estudios eclesiásticos*, XXX, 363–90; P. de Leturia, *Estudios Ignacianos*, rev. by I. Iparraguirre (these essays are particularly valuable for the light they shed on the environmental factors in Loyola's life); and H. Rahner's stimulating collection of essays assembled in his *Ignatius von Loyola als Mensch und Theologe*.

13. See Jerome (Hieronymus) Nadal, *MHSJ, Epistolae Nadal*, IV, 98 ff. No. 25, 109 ff. No. 5, 133 ff. No. 15, 729 ff. Supplementum 1; Pedro de Ribadeneira's *Vida del Padre Maestro Diego Lainez*, in *Obras escogidas*, ed. by V. de la Fuente, pp. 119 ff., 136 ff.; Nicholas Alonso Bobadilla in *MHSJ, Monumenta Bobadillae*, 184

No. 111 n. 4; the letter of the Toledan province and Francesco Sacchini's reply of 1622 in *MHSJ, Lainii Monumenta*, VIII, 831 ff. Nos. 77–78. It may be noted that, perhaps because of his Majorcan Old Christian ancestry, Nadal did not hesitate to evince considerable interest in Hebrew letters and even to engage in friendly exchanges with Avignonese rabbis. He himself had tasted the bitter fruits of suspicion when he almost lost his life as an alleged Spanish spy and on another occasion, when he was maltreated by a soldier as "a dog of a Jew." See F. Secret, "Notes sur les Juifs d'Avignon," *REJ*, CXXII, 180 ff.; and G. Codina Mir, "La Ordenación y el doctorado en teología de Jerónimo Nadal en Aviñon (1537–1538)," *AHSI*, XXXVI, 247–51. All the same, Nadal on another occasion extolled, in sentimental rhetoric, the purely Christian ancestry and surroundings of St. Ignatius in his native province of Guipúzcoa. See his "Apologia pro Exercitiis S. P. Ignatii" in *MHSJ, Epistolae Nadal*, IV, 825 f. Supplementum 25; and *supra*, n. 9.

The relations between the Society and the Spanish Inquisition became further strained in 1561, when Laynez and his associates resisted the inquisitors' prohibition against Spanish pupils studying in Rome and the insistence that all New Christians return from the papal capital to their home localities. Although backed by a royal decree of 1559, these extreme demands remained unfulfilled. See J. I. Tellechea Idígoras, "Un Percance inquisitorial desconocido (1561). Los jesuitas y la real pragmática de Felipe II de 1559," *AHSI*, XXXIV, 79–85. Needless to say, Laynez was a devout Christian who went to considerable lengths in abetting the conversion of Jews. At one Jew's baptismal ceremony in 1541, performed by Alphonso Salmerón, a fellow-Jesuit and later a colleague in the leadership of the Trent Council, Laynez delivered the sermon. See Loyola's letter to Peter Faber of September 20, 1541, in *MHSJ, Monumenta Ignatiana, Epistolae*, I, 181 ff. No. 33; Joannes Alphonso de Polanco's *Chronicon Societatis Jesu* in his *Vita Ignatii*, I, 109 f.; and, more generally, E. Rey, "San Ignacio," *Razón y fé*, CLIII, 180 f.; idem, "Dimensión de Diego Lainez (Cuarto centenario de su muerte, 1565–1965)," *ibid.*, CLXXII, 437–54. See also *supra*, n. 9; the comprehensive studies by F. Cereceda, *Diego Lainez en la Europa religiosa de su tiempo, 1512–1565*, esp. pp. 4 ff., 10 n. 1; and by M. Scaduto, *Storia della Compagnia di Gesù in Italia, III: L'epoca di Giacomo Lainez. Il governo (1556–1565)*; with R. [García] Villoslada's comments thereon in his "Lainez e su tiempo," *Razón y fé*, CLXX, 125–30; as well as several other biographical studies listed by them; by L. Lukács in "Le Catalogue-modèle," *AHSI*, XXVI, 57 n. 2; and by J. A. Pérez-Rioja in "Una Bibliografía en torno al P. Diego Lainez," *Celtiberia*, XV, 213–43. This issue, dedicated to the fourth centenary of Laynez' death, also includes other interesting essays on the life and outlook of this important Jesuit leader.

14. A. Astrain, *Historia de la Compañía de Jesús en . . . España*, III, 6 f., also citing the Vatican Archives; H. Ramière, *Compendium Instituti Societatis Iesu, praepositorum generalium responsis et auctorum sententiis illustratum*, ed. by J. Besson, pp. 46 f.; J. B. Sägmüller, *Die Papstwahlen und die Staaten von 1442 bis 1555;* C. Hollis, "The Jesuits Before and After Their Suppression," *History Today*, XVIII, 180–87; and the literature cited *infra*, n. 15. The saintly Francisco Borgia (who, in contrast to the much more talented Laynez, was later canonized by the Church) was a scion of the well-known Spanish family of Old Christian stock. Yet he seems to have evinced no animosity toward his New Christian colleagues and, quite apart from the exigencies of Jesuit discipline, apparently was an admirer of

both of his extraordinary predecessors. This may perhaps be deduced from the two orations he delivered shortly before and after his election as general on July 2, 1565. See C. de Dalmases, "Sancti Francisci Borgiae orationes in Congregatione generali secunda, 28. iunii et 3. septembris 1565," *AHSI*, XXXIV, 86–95; and, more generally, P. Suau's biography, *Saint François de Borgia (1510–1572)*, esp. II, 97 ff., 100 f., 284 (showing that he entered nothing in his journal about the election, except that on June 23, 1565, two days after the opening session, he had asked for the pope's blessing, and that he referred to July 2, the day of the election, as "the day of my cross"; but there is no indication of the anti-Polanco campaign).

Since ascertainment of one's "pure" ancestry required thorough investigation, it stimulated the members to spy upon one another, as well as upon prospective novices, a practice which became fairly widespread during Acquaviva's regime. This was one of the defects of the Society's organization, complained of by the distinguished political thinker Juan de Mariana, who claimed that, as a result, the Society's archives might eventually cast a shadow on the ancestry of every Jesuit. See his *Discurso de las enfermedades de la Compañía;* and, more generally, G. Lewy's *Constitutionalism and Statecraft during the Golden Age of Spain: a Study of the Political Philosophy of Juan de Mariana, S. J.*, esp. p. 32.

15. Paul III's bulls, *Cupientes Judaeos* of March 21, 1542; *Illius, qui pro dominici* of February 19, 1543, in *Bullarium romanum*, VI, 336 f. No. xli, 353 ff. No. xlvi; H. Vogelstein and P. Rieger, *Geschichte der Juden in Rom*, II, 62 ff.; A. Bea, "La Compagnia di Gesù e gli studi biblici," in *La Compagnia di Gesù e le scienze sacre. Conferenze commemorative,* held in 1941 at the Gregorian University in Rome, pp. 115–43; F. Secret, "Les Jésuites et le kabbalisme chrétien à la Renaissance," *BHR*, XX, 542–55. It may be noted that, despite the recruitment of most early leaders from Spain and the presence even in Rome of Spanish national churches, Loyola and his associates thought primarily in international terms and placed their Society wholly in the service of the international Papacy. See J. Fernández Alonso, "Las Iglesias nacionales de España in Roma. Sus orígenes," *Anthologica annua*, IV, 9–96; and R. García Villoslada, *Ignacio de Loyola. Un Español al servicio del Pontificado.*

16. S. Simonsohn, *Toledot ha-Yehudim be-dukhsut Mantovah* (History of the Jews in the Duchy of Mantua), I, 20 f. The entire problem of the attitude of the Society of Jesus to Jews and Judaism still awaits careful and comprehensive analysis. See, for the time being, the following studies by members of the Society of Jesus: L. Koch, "Jesuiten und Juden," *Stimmen der Zeit*, CIX, 435–52; J. Cardoso, "San Ignacio de Loyola y los Judíos," *Mensajero del Corazón de Jesús*, XV, 674–80; E. Rey, "San Ignacio," *Razón y fé*, CLIII, 173–204; and, for the later period, R. G. Brüggemann and G. Spellenberg, "Die Gesellschaft Jesu und die Juden. Eine Betrachtung über die Folgen des jesuitischen Antijudaismus," *Werkhefte katholischer Laien*, XV, 47–60. Of course, the material is exceedingly plentiful and widely scattered. But pertinent researches are greatly facilitated now by the availability of such bibliographical aids as L. Polgár's *Bibliography of the History of the Society of Jesus;* and his annual reviews of the "Bibliographia de historia Societatis Jesu" published in *AHSI;* J. Juambelz's *Index bibliographicus Societatis Jesu*, Vols. I–IV, for the years 1938–50; and the studies listed *supra*, n. 7. There also is much unpublished material still available in the public archives as well as in those of the

Society's headquarters in Rome and the numerous provincial collections throughout the world. See A. Guglieri Navarro, *Documentos de la Compañía de Jesús en el Archivo Historico Nacional,* with an Intro. by F. Mateos; G. Teschitel, "L'Organizazione dell'Archivio Generale della Compagnia di Gesù," *Rassegna degli Archivi di Stato,* XXII, 189–96; and his historical review of "Das Generalarchiv der Gesellschaft Jesu in Rom," *Römische Historische Mitteilungen,* IV, 247–54.

17. G. Müller, "Zur Vorgeschichte des Tridentinums. Karl V. und das Konzil während des Pontifikates Clemens' VII," *ZKG,* LXXIV, 83–108; Fridericus Nausea (Gran, 1480–1552), *Miscellanearum libri VIII,* v.15; Girolamo Aleandro (1480–1542), *De convocando concilio sententia,* both reproduced by V. Schweitzer *et al.,* in their ed. of *Concilii Tridentini Tractatuum pars prior completens tractatus a Leonis X temporibus usque ad translationem Concilii conscriptos,* I, 119 ff., 412; S. Ehses, ed., *Concilii Tridentini Acta,* I, 534 f. with reference to Neh. 8:6; V, 594 f. No. 304 (a continuation of S. Merkle's ed. of the Council's *Diaria;* these vols. are numbered IV and VIII of the series, respectively; see below); *Decretum de justificatione,* Intro. Arts. 1–2 and canons 1–2 in H. J. D. Denzinger, comp., *Enchiridion symbolorum definitionum et declarationum de rebus fidei et morum,* 21st–23d ed., rev. by C. Bannwart and J. B. Umberg, pp. 284 f., 295; in the English trans. by R. S. Deferrari, entitled *The Sources of Catholic Dogma,* pp. 248 f., 259; and H. J. Schroeder, ed., *Canons and Decrees of the Council of Trent. Original Text with English Translation,* pp. 29 ff. (English), 308 ff. (Latin). Nausea's general outlook on the state of the Church is briefly analyzed by H. Gollob in "Der Wiener Bischof Friedrich Nausea und die Weltanschauungskrise des 16. Jahrhunderts," *Wiener Geschichtsblätter,* XXII, 139–44. On Aleandro, who according to Luther was himself a New Christian, see P. Kalkoff, *Aleander gegen Luther. Studien zu ungedruckten Aktenstücken aus Aleanders Nachlass;* J. Paquier's biography, *L'Humanisme et la réforme: Jérôme Aléandre;* F. Gaeta, *Un Nunzio pontificio a Venezia nel Cinquecento (Girolamo Aleandro);* G. Müller, "Zum Verständnis Aleanders," *Theologische Literaturzeitung,* LXXXIX, 525–36 (taking a mediating position between Kalkoff's total rejection and Paquier's great admiration); *supra,* n. 4. At the same time Oleastro dared to espouse at the Council the somewhat radical view that the Vulgate did not fully reproduce the original meaning of the Bible. This was in consonance with the attitude of Cardinal Ximénez much more than with that of the Council majority, interveningly become far more inflexible. See A. Vilela, "Un Exegeta português do Concilio de Trento: Oleastro—No IV Centenario da sua morte (1563–1963)," *Brotéria,* LXXVIII, 16–28; R. E. McNally, "The Council of Trent and Vernacular Bibles," *Theological Studies* (Woodstock, Md.), XXVII, 204–227; and R. Daunis, "Schrift und Tradition in Trient und in der modernen römisch-katholischen Theologie," *Kerygma und Dogma,* XIII, 132–58, 184–200.

Needless to say, other Council members shared the hope of converting Jews, and at times expressed it by baptizing Jewish catechumens in public ceremonies at the gate of the Trent cathedral. According to contemporary diarists, on at least two occasions the delegates themselves served as godfathers. The baptismal ceremony on Holy Saturday, April 10, 1563, was particularly impressive. It involved three adult converts (over twenty-five years of age) who received the names of Peter, Antonius, and Paul. The officiating bishop was Paul of Braga, while the envoys of the emperor (as king of Hungary) and of the kings of France and Portugal participated as godfathers. See the mutually complementary reports by Ludovico Boudoin de

Brancis Firmani in *Diaria*, reproduced in S. Merkle's ed. of *Concilii Tridentini Diaria*, 2d impression, II, 566 (his designation of the three converts as *tres Hebraeos Lusitanos* can refer only to descendants of Portuguese exiles) and by Bishop Nicholas Psalmaeus in his *Fragmenta de Concilio Tridentino, ibid.*, p. 836.

18. S. Ehses, ed., *Concilii Tridentini Acta*, V (in the collection ed. by S. Merkle *et al.*, VIII), pp. 328 ff. No. 229, 788 n. 4; J. Šušta, *Die Römische Kurie und das Konzil von Trient unter Pius IV*, III, 236 ff. No. 65; M. Stern, *Urkundliche Beiträge über die Stellung der Päpste zu den Juden*, I, 135 f. Nos. 128–30. Cardinal Ercole Gonzaga's early humanistic interest and his friendly relations with such Jewish authors as Jacob Mantino are well illustrated by the latter's dedication to him of a Latin translation of Averroës' *Epitome Metaphisicae*, Bologna, 1523. See D. Kaufmann, "Jacob Mantino," *REJ*, XXVII, 35 f., 221 ff. No. i.2. Ercole had also engaged in intensive reformatory activities in Mantua as well as at the Council. Moreover, from the outset he must have agreed with his nephew Francesco Gonzaga that one could not expect the Protestants to send delegates to the Council, as was planned by its leaders, if their writings were placed on an Index before their arrival. See G. Drei's ed. of "La Corrispondenza del card. Ercole Gonzaga, presidente del Concilio di Trento (1562–1563)," *AS per le provincie Parmense*, XVII, 185–242; XVIII, 30–143, esp. XVII, 201, 203 f.; and the Milan dissertations by G. Baraldi, *Il Cardinale Ercole Gonzaga (1505–1563)*; and A. Saccani, *Ercole Gonzaga e la riforma pretridentina della diocesi di Mantova*. See also H. Jedin's succinct sketch, "Kardinal Ercole Gonzaga, der Sohn der Isabella d'Este," in his *Kirche des Glaubens, Kirche der Geschichte. Ausgewählte Aufsätze und Vorträge*, I, 195–205.

19. See *supra*, Vol. IX, pp. 63 ff., 270 f. nn. 11 ff.; and *infra*, n. 26. Although there is no dearth of documentary information about Archbishop Anton Brus von Müglitz' activities at the Council, his role in the censorship of Jewish books is uncertain. See S. Steinherz, ed., *Briefe des Prager Erzbischofs Anton Brus von Müglitz 1562–1563*, esp. pp. 12, 14 f., 102, 137 f.; T. Sickel, ed., *Zur Geschichte des Concils von Trient. Aktenstücke aus österreichischen Archiven*, esp. pp. 268 f., 647 f.; H. Reusch, *Der Index der verbotenen Bücher. Ein Beitrag zur Kirchen- und Literaturgeschichte*, I, 45 ff., 258 ff., 312 ff., 320 f.; G. Wolf, *Das Tridentinische Concil und der Talmud*, esp. p. 11; G. Bondy and F. Dworský, *Zur Geschichte*, I, 481 f. No. 655. On Brus' earlier activities in Vienna see R. Till, "Antonius Brus von Müglitz, 1558–1563, Bischof von Wien," *Wiener Geschichtsblätter*, XIX [LXXIX], 258–69. See also H. Graetz's brief survey, "Die Schicksale des Talmud im Verlaufe der Geschichte," *MGWJ*, XXXIV, 529–41. However, Graetz's suggestion that the Prague community's letter to Brus, written in correct Latin, must have been composed by Mordecai Ṣemaḥ, a member of the Prague community who in 1561 had been sent by it to Pope Pius IV (pp. 534 f. n. 1), was rightly denied by G. Wolf in his "Notiz [zu den Schicksalen des Talmud]," *ibid.*, XXXV, 94–96. Wolf not only pointed out that many documents submitted to the authorities by Jewish communities were composed with the aid of Christian scribes but also questioned the historicity of Ṣemaḥ's mission to the pope. See *infra*, n. 42 and Chap. LXI, n. 12.

The Prague community's letter of thanks to Brus is dated by both Wolf and Bondy and Dworský to February 16, 1563. Since the text in neither edition gives a date, one wonders whether the editors were not misled by some erroneous entry in the registry, rather than guided by the original letter preserved in the Archiepiscopal Archive in Prague. On that date Brus still was in Trent (he did not come to Prague even for a visit until several weeks later) and the Tridentine discussions of all problems relating to the Index still were very much in flux. If the Prague Jews heard about his report to the emperor of February 3, they would have had little reason to be grateful for the tenor of that report and the enclosed list of "blasphemies" in the Talmud. It is more likely that their letter was presented to the returning archbishop in Prague on the following February 16 (1564). At that time the Jews may indeed have attributed to him as chairman a major share in the Commission's final decision to hand the matter over to the pope, as the Jewish delegates had been instructed to request (see below). It is also possible that interveningly the archbishop had received certain favors from the Jewish "lobbyists" in Trent. We know from his correspondence that he often was in financial straits. Before his departure the Imperial Treasury had promised him a monthly allowance of 600 florins, admitting that this amount would not cover all his expenses and that he would have to supplement it from his income as archbishop. In fact, however, the emperor's chest was so empty that in fifteen months Brus received no more than 2,000 florins and incurred many debts. After the closing session of the Council on December 4, he was unable to depart, and as late as December 27 he was still writing home for money to defray his travel expenses. It is likely, although we have no evidence to that effect, that among his lenders was one or another Mantuan Jew. Be this as it may, Brus, as well as Gonzaga, may indeed have been helpful in preventing the Council from taking the dreaded decision outlawing the Talmud.

Nor do we have any information about what position, if any, was taken during these deliberations by Cardinal Christophoro di Madruzzo, who, as archbishop of Trent, served as official host to the Council. Certainly, his personal attitude to Hebrew letters was friendly. It was he who had granted the Jews of neighboring Riva di Trento the privilege of establishing a Hebrew press, which in the preceding few years (1558–62) had published an impressive array of thirty-four rabbinic works, including Maimonides' *Commentary* on the Mishnah and Mordecai b. Hillel ha-Kohen's *Sefer Mordekhai*. He doubtless also was in contact with R. Joseph Ottolenghi, the leading promoter of Hebrew printing both there and in Cremona. See E. Carmoly, *Annalen der hebräischen Typographie von Riva di Trento (1558–62)*, 2d ed.; and J. Bloch, "Hebrew Printing in Riva di Trento," *BNYPL*, XXXVII, 755–69; idem, "A Hitherto Unrecorded Hebrew Publication in Riva di Trento," *JQR*, XXVI, 128–32 (referring to *Parashiot*, a collection of sections of Pentateuchal lessons read in synagogues on Mondays and Thursdays; probably the first printed edition of this type). Because of the absence of Jews from the city for nearly half a century, even the establishment, in 1523, of a *monte di pietà* seems not to have exacerbated the intergroup tensions generated by the local Blood Accusation of 1475. See G. Cortisella, "Il Monte di pietà di Trento," *Studi trentini di scienze storiche*, XLII, 114–25; XLIII, 19–40. See also I. Rogger, "Il Governo spirituale della diocesi di Trento sotto i vescovi Cristoforo (1539–1567) e Ludovico Madruzzo (1567–1600)," *Il Concilio di Trento e la riforma tridentina*, pp. 173–213.

20. M. Stern, *Urkundliche Beiträge*, I, 137 f. Nos. 131–32, with minor corrections by S. Simonsohn in his *Toledot*, I, 303 f.; Pedro González de Mendoza (Gonçales de Mendoça), *Lo Sucedido en el Concilio de Trento*, in S. Merkle's ed. of *Concilii Tridentini Diaria*, II, 706. See also, more broadly, N. López Martínez, "El Cardenal Mendoza y la reforma tridentina en Burgos," in the "Miscellanea commemorativa

del Concilio de Trento (1563–1963)," *Hispania sacra*, XVI, 61–137. The complicated debates at the Index Commission of the Council and its inner divisions are well illustrated by the papal legates' report to Cardinal Carlo Borromeo of July 29, 1563, published from a Vatican archival document by J. Šušta in *Die Römische Kurie und das Konzil von Trient*, IV, 144 ff. No. 32 B. Not surprisingly, the Commission often engaged in political maneuvers. For example, the Jesuits Laynez and Salmerón, who had attended its meetings on some occasions, were not notified of a gathering of several members called together to discuss the writings of Archbishop Bartolomé Carranza. Evidently the influential Spanish faction feared their moderate stand with respect to the alleged "heresies" of the prominent churchman. See Laynez' letters of May 17, 1563, to Francisco Borgia, and of June 7, 1563, to the Castilian provincial Antonio Araoz, in his *Epistolae et acta* (in *MHSJ*, *Lainii Monumenta*, VII, 91 f. No. 1832, 124 ff. No. 1846); and *supra*, Chap. LVI, n. 13. This apprehension was doubtless deepened by Laynez' great influence among the members of the Council, which had manifested itself throughout the debates. It probably also was his prompting, as the prior-general of the Jesuit Order, which induced the Council at its last meeting (December 4, 1563) to resolve that the activities of the Society of Jesus "in the service of God and Church" be approved. See *supra*, nn. 9 and 13; and *infra*, n. 23. See also S. Ehses, "Zur Vorgeschichte des Trienter Index verbotener Bücher," *Erste Vereinsschrift* of the Görresgesellschaft, 1921, pp. 68–83; M. Mortara, "Die Censur hebräischer Bücher in Italien und der *Canon purificationis* (*Sefer ha-Ziqquq*)," German trans. by M. Steinschneider in his *Hebräische Bibliographie*, V, 72–77, 96–101, esp. pp. 74 f., and his editorial postscript, *ibid.*, pp. 125–28.

According to Simonsohn, the documents preserved in Mantua's communal archives mention only the solicitation by communal leaders of financial contributions to the delegates' expenses from both the independent group of local bankers and the provincial communities in the duchy. Apparently no other communities were approached; the sums raised were correspondingly small. In the absence of other data one must conclude that even the rest of Italian Jewry was not too greatly aroused about the possibility of anti-Jewish conciliar decisions. The German communities, perhaps further restrained by their wish to appear neutral in the Catholic-Protestant conflict, appear to have remained fairly passive, except for the Prague letter of thanks after the event.

21. S. Ehses, ed., *Concilii Tridentini Acta*, VI (in the collection ed. by S. Merkle *et al.*, IX), p. 1106, with Ehses's succinct comments thereon, *ibid.*, p. 1104 n. 1; Pius IV's bull *Dominici gregis* of March 24, 1564, in *Bullarium romanum*, VII, 281 ff. No. xliv; *Index librorum prohibitorum cum regulis confectis per patres a Tridentino Synodo delectos*, Venice, 1564 ed., fol. 14b. The indebtedness of this papal Index to the long preliminary work done by the Commission of the Council also lends some justification to the later Jewish contention that the printing and circulation of the Talmud, after the expurgation of disapproved passages, had been authorized by the ecumenical assembly. It was in this vein that the Roman rabbis wrote to their colleagues of Mantua on July 20, 1590, when they solicited contributions for an intervention with Pope Sixtus V to secure the confirmation of that purported conciliar decision. See M. Stern, *Urkundliche Beiträge*, I, 157 f. No. 150; and the less outspoken comment in the continuation of Joseph ha-Kohen's chronicle, cited *infra*, n. 22. Evidently, the rabbis felt that by invoking the growing authority of the

Tridentine Council they could more readily persuade the pope and Christian public opinion to overrule the intervening harsh decrees by Pius V, on which see *infra*, nn. 32–34. See also n. 38. Of course, from the outset, papal control over the Council's deliberations was very strong, despite the reservations suggested by H. Jedin in "Rede- und Stimmfreiheit auf dem Konzil von Trient" in his *Kirche des Glaubens*, II, 160–76; and his "Papst und Konzil. Ihre Beziehungen vor, auf und nach den Trienter Konzil," *ibid.*, pp. 429–40.

To be sure, the "Ten Rules Concerning Forbidden Books" which underlay the discussions at the Council and the papal approbation (see the official text in the *Index* of 1564 and in the *Canones et decreta sacrosancti oecumenici Concilii Tridentini*, pp. 231 ff.) began on a threatening note. Rule I provided that "all books condemned before the year 1515 by the popes or ecumenical councils, but not found in the present Index, should be considered condemned in the same fashion as they had originally been." The original dividing line had been set at the year 1500. See the Rules adopted before November 27, 1563, as reproduced by V. Schweitzer and H. Jedin, in their ed. of *Concilii Tridentini Tractatus* (in S. Merkle's compilation, Vol. XII), pp. 603 ff. No. 94 Doc. xii. Yet the new system of expurgation and change of title seemed sufficient to modify the prohibition whenever there was enough good will on the part of the ecclesiastical authorities. Characteristically, no action at all was taken on the questions raised by the Benedictine abbot Stephanus Catanius Navarensis, member of the Commission, as to whether "good and faithful expositions of the Old Testament by more recent infidel Jews," as well as the "sacred histories" by Philo and Josephus, were likewise to be outlawed. See his Memorandum reproduced *ibid.*, pp. 594 f. No. 94 Doc. vi; and the anonymous *Adnotationes* on the aforementioned Rules, *ibid.*, pp. 606 f. No. 94 Doc. xiii. See also, more generally, the comprehensive study by H. Reusch, *Der Index der verbotenen Bücher*, I, 45 ff.; A. Rotondò, "Nuovi documenti per la storia dell' 'Indice dei libri proibiti' (1572–1638)," *Rinascimento*, XIV, 145–211; A. Leite, "O Indice dos livros proibidos no IV Centenario da sua publicação," *Brotéria*, LXXIX, 437–48; and other literature cited *supra*, Vol. IX, p. 269 n. 9.

22. The continuation of Joseph ha-Kohen's *'Emeq ha-bakha*, p. 138 (with S. D. Luzzatto's note thereon); in Wiener's German trans., p. 112; G. Menestrina, "Gli Ebrei a Trento," *Tridentum*, VI, 304–316, 348–74, 385–411. The text of the *Catechism* of 1566 is quoted here from the *Catechismus ex decreto Concilii Tridentini ad parochos Pii Quinti Pont. Max. iussu editos*, v.1 ff., esp. qu. 11, Leipzig, 1862 ed. (Tauchnitz), pp. 39 ff., 45; and from the English trans. entitled *Catechism of the Council of Trent for Parish Priests*, issued by order of Pope Pius V, trans. by J. A. McHugh and C. J. Callan, pp. 50 ff., 54, 57, 363 ff. (I am indebted to Dr. Edgar Alexander for turning my attention to these passages.) That this catechism did not completely stymie anti-Jewish interpretations is not at all surprising. Suffice it to cite here the Portuguese *Catechismo da douttrina christiã*, issued on order of Mendoza and revised by the archbishop of Braga, 2d ed., Lisbon, 1792. Arranged in a question and answer format, this summary of Catholic doctrine thus describes the ancient events (p. 34): "Q.: Who condemned Him [Jesus] to death?—A.: Pontius Pilate, governor of Judaea, appointed by the Romans.—Q.: Who asked for His death?—A.: The Jews.—Q.: Who delivered Him into the Jews' hands?—A.: Judas, who, being an apostle, turned traitor."

23. Diego (Jacobus) Laynez, *Disputationes tridentinae,* ed. by H. Grisar, II, 227 ff., 320; Grisar, "Die Frage des päpstlichen Primates und des Ursprungs der bischöflichen Gewalt auf dem Tridentinum," *Zeitschrift für katholische Theologie,* VIII, 458–507, 727–84; *supra,* n. 13; the exchange of letters of 1693 between Gottfried Wilhelm Leibniz and Jacques Bénigne Bossuet, esp. Letters xxviii and xxx, in Bossuet's *Oeuvres complètes,* ed. by F. Lachat, XVIII, 184 ff., 206 ff. Of the enormous historical literature on the Tridentine Council, which greatly proliferated after 1609, when Paolo Sarpi first published his hostile description (later issued in N. Brent's English trans. entitled *History of the Council of Trent*), we need but mention here the recent studies by H. Jedin, esp. his comprehensive work, *A History of the Council of Trent,* trans. from the German by E. Graf, Vols. I–II (covers only the preliminaries and the first assembly of 1545–47); the essays ed. by G. Schreiber under the title *Das Weltkonzil von Trient. Sein Werden und Wirken; Il Concilio di Trento e la riforma tridentina (Atti* of the Convegno storico internazionale, Trento, 2–6 settembre 1963), which includes essays by G. Alberigo, "Le Potestà episcopali nei dibattiti tridentini" (I, 1–25); and by M. Roca Cabanellas, "Diego Laynez en la última etapa del Concilio di Trento" (I, 85–114); and the aforementioned (n. 20) special anniversary issue of *Hispania Sacra,* XVI, entirely dedicated to "Miscelanea conmemorativa del Concilio di Trento (1563–1963)," which includes J. I. Tellechea Idígoras's ed. of "Cartas y documentos tridentinos inéditos (1563)," shedding interesting light on a certain sense of insecurity felt by the Spanish delegation with respect to the Council's attitude toward the excesses of the Inquisition (pp. 191–248). Other important documentary studies include S. Tromp's "De duabus editionibus Concilii tridentini," *Gregorianum,* XXXVII, 51–96; XXXVIII, 481–502; XXXIX, 93–129; C. Gutierrez, "Nueva documentación tridentina, 1551–52," *AHP,* I, 179–240; II, 211–50; and particularly E. A. Barletta's *Aspetti della Riforma cattolica e del concilio di Trento. Mostra documentaria.*

See also such pertinent monographs as H. Jedin, *Papal Legate at the Council of Trent, Seripando,* English trans. by F. C. Eckhoff, esp. pp. 268 ff., 283 ff. (the German two-volume original, published a decade earlier, contains many additional footnotes and appendixes omitted in the English version); idem, *Krisis und Abschluss des Trienter Konzils, 1562–63. Ein Rückblick nach vier Jahrhunderten;* G. Alberigo, "Studi e problemi relativi all'applicazione del Concilio di Trento in Italia (1945–1958)," *RSI,* LXX, 239–98; A. Monticone, "L'Applicazione a Roma del Concilio di Trento: I. Le visite del 1564–1566; II. I 'riformatori' e l'Oratorio (1566–1572)," *RSCI,* VII, 225–50; VIII, 23–48; and other publications listed by L. Willaert in A. Fliche's *Historie de l'Église,* XVIII, 44 ff.

24. D. Kaufmann, "Jacob Mantino," *REJ,* XXVII, 34 f., 220 f. No. i.1, 226 No. i.5, 238 No. vii; *supra,* Vol. XI, pp. 102, 331 f. n. 33; A. Berliner, *Aus schweren Zeiten,* p. 8; A. d'Ancona, *Origini del Teatro in Italia. Studi sulle sacre rappresentazioni;* M. Stern, *Urkundliche Beiträge,* pp. 78 ff. No. 78, 82 f. No. 81; "Die Juden im Kirchenstaat und in Toskana," *Allgemeine Zeitung des Judentums,* V, 560 (anonymous); Jacopo (Jacobus) Sadoleto, *Epistolae,* xii.5, in his *Opera omnia quae extant,* II, 7 f. (also *ibid.,* xii.15–17, pp. 29 ff.). Sadoleto's action was approvingly cited some three months later by Cardinal Reginald Pole in a letter to Sadoleto summarized in English in R. Brown's ed. of the *Calendar of State Papers,* Venice, V, 80 f. No. 208. See also other data summarized by H. Vogelstein and P. Rieger in their *Geschichte der Juden in Rom,* II, 60 ff.; and, from other angles, W. Reinhard, *Die Reform in*

der Diözese Carpentras unter den Bischöfen Jacopo Sadoleto, Paolo Sadoleto, Jacopo Sacrati und Francesco Sadoleto, 1517–1596.

Joshua Corcos also successfully negotiated, in 1541–42, an agreement between Rome's Christian and Jewish tailors with respect to the manufacture of "Romanesque" clothing. See Berliner, pp. 9 and 24 (Hebrew text). Nor did the Italian Jews find it difficult to secure papal permits for the transfer of synagogues from one place to another, or even for the erection of new buildings. Such permits were issued, for instance, to the communities of Core [Cori] in 1536 and Mantua in 1540. Despite his ever delicate diplomatic relations with Charles V, Paul III did not hesitate to admit Jewish and Marrano exiles from the Kingdom of Naples in 1541. He particularly favored their settlement in Ancona, which, unforeseen by him, was to become a source of grief to them some fifteen years later. Equally remarkable was the pope's truly humanist interest in the publication of Hebrew books. See Stern, pp. 81 Nos. 79–80, 89 ff. Nos. 89–93, and *passim*. See also Y. N. Pavoncello's notes on "I 'Sefardim' a Roma," *Le Judaïsme sephardi*, XXVII, 1153–61 (mainly relating to events of 1492).

25. S. Ehses, ed., *Concilii Tridentini Acta*, I (in S. Merkle's compilation, IV), pp. 364 ff. No. 276; A. Herculano, *History . . . of the Inquisition in Portugal*, English trans. by J. C. Branner, pp. 603 ff., 616; L. Wadding, *Annales Minorum*, XVI, 114 f.; H. Vogelstein and P. Rieger, *Geschichte der Juden in Rom*, II, 60 ff. On Roman Jewry's vicissitudes created by the new houses of catechumens see A. Milano, "L'Impari lotta della comunità di Roma contro la Casa dei catecumeni," *RMI*, XVI, 355–68. According to a contemporary observer, the conversion of a learned rabbi named Moyses created a great sensation in the papal capital. Calling the new convert "the great chancellor, chief rabbi and interpreter of his law," Ferdinand Montesa informed the bishop of Artois that the latter was supported by the emperor, "for it is the cause of great confusion among all Italian Jews to see their prime rabbi turn Christian together with his six children." See Montesa's letter of February 20, 1549, preserved in a Madrid MS and reproduced in G. Buschbell's ed. of *Concilii Tridentini Epistolae*, II (in S. Merkle's collection, XI), p. 493 n. 2. To be sure, the establishment of the new Roman Inquisition was not aimed primarily at Jews or Marranos, but rather at the growing number of Christian "heretics" with their politically dangerous utopian programs. See A. Stella, "Utopie e velleità insurrezionali dei filoprotestanti italiani (1545–1547)," *BHR*, XXVII, 133–82; and *infra*, Chap. LX. Yet sooner or later Jews, too, were bound to be affected. Before very long, Paul went so far as to employ the aforementioned subterfuge of approving the Toledan statute of "purity of blood" without going through the routine of having it sanctioned by the *Rota* and published in the regular way. See *supra*, Chap. LVI, n. 35; and the numerous passages in A. A. Sicroff's *Les Controverses*, listed in the Index, p. 310 *s.v.* Paul III. But in these matters Paul merely followed well-established precedents for dealing differently with Iberian affairs than with those relating to the Papal States.

The foundation and evolution of the Roman *monte di pietà* are described by M. Tosi in *Il Sacro Monte di Pietà di Roma e le sue amministrazioni (1539–1874)*. True, the earlier popes—including Innocent VIII in 1488, Julius II in 1506, and Leo X in 1515—had, over the objections of some Dominicans, given their seal of approval to the Franciscan idea of a charitable loan bank. See the collection of *Bolle e provisioni per il sacro Monte di pietà in Bologna*, published in Bologna, 1580–1623; and *supra*,

Vols. IX, pp. 51 ff., 265 nn. 60–61; X, p. 417 n. 53; XII, pp. 167 ff., 325 nn. 41–42. Yet the timing of the establishment of such a *monte,* as well as that of the Houses of Catechumens in Rome, is related to the incipient Catholic Restoration.

These vacillating policies were but partly owing to Paul's old age, which also made him fall asleep at inappropriate moments; for instance, during Bishop Balthasar de Limpo's inflammatory speech. With respect to other aspects of his administration, see H. Jedin's pertinent characterizations of several popes in his "Spätleistungen und Altersdefekte in der Papstgeschichte" (1964), reproduced in his *Kirche des Glaubens,* pp. 293–304.

26. M. Stern, *Urkundliche Beiträge,* pp. 95 ff. No. 99, 98 ff. Nos. 100 ff.; *supra,* Vol. IX, pp. 15 ff., 70, 247 f. nn. 14–16, 273 n. 20; Chap. LVI, n. 47. Andreas Masius' letter to Cardinal Sebastiano Pighini in *Acta* of the Mannheim Academia Theodoro-Palatina, VII, 344. Masius' autograph Hebrew letter to Johann Albert Widmanstetter and some of his other learned correspondence with Cornelius Adelkind and the Roman Hebrew scholars were published by J. Perles in his *Beiträge,* pp. 203 ff. See also, more generally, M. Lossen's ed. of *Briefe von Andreas Masius und seinen Freunden, 1538–1573;* and H. de Vocht's brief biographical sketch of "Andreas Masius (1514–1573)" in *Miscellanea Giovanni Mercati,* IV, 425–41, esp. pp. 433 ff. On Guillaume Postel's eyewitness account of the Roman auto-da-fé, see *supra,* Chap. LVII, n. 6.

27. Moses b. Jacob Ḥagiz, *Mishnat ḥakhamim* (The Lore of the Wise; a theological tract), Altona-Wandsbek, 1733, fol. 120b Nos. 628–29, also reproduced by I. Sonne in his *Mi-Pavlo ha-rebi'i,* p. 109 App. i item 7; and other data assembled by A. Yaari in "The Burning of the Talmud in Italy: On the Four-Hundredth Anniversary of the Decree" (Hebrew), reprinted in his *Meḥqere sefer* (Studies in Hebrew Booklore), pp. 198–234. On the Avignon developments see Ponce Cogordan's letter of March 22, 1555, to Ignatius of Loyola, seeking clarification and also asking for a list of the books burned in Rome and the objections raised against them by the convert Alessandro Franceschi (formerly Ḥananel) da Foligno, in *MHSJ, Monumenta Ignatiana, Epistolae mixtae,* IV, 570 f. No. 941; F. Secret, "Notes sur les Juifs d'Avignon," *REJ,* CXXII, 182 (also furnishing bibliographical data on the identity and work of Ḥananel da Foligno; p. 183 n. 3). The destruction of many copies of the Talmud throughout Italy is further illustrated by the data analyzed *infra,* Chap. LX, *passim.*

Not surprisingly, some rabbis, harking back to the old Jewish tradition of self-accusation, blamed the destruction of the precious Hebrew books on the Jews' own neglect and disparagement of talmudic literature. In his *Livyat ḥen* (Chaplet of Grace; a Hebrew grammar), published in Mantua in 1557, Immanuel b. Yekutiel Benevento commented: "There is no question that the Talmud was burned only because of the sins of those who ridiculed it and because many of the ignoramuses who prided themselves . . . on their knowledge of the false opinions and views of philosophers spoke evil about the sages of the Talmud" (fol. 109a). This was but one of many censures conservative leaders aimed at the rapprochement between Renaissance Jewish scholars and Christian humanists and the former's growing interest in general philosophic studies at the expense of the traditional concentration on talmudic learning. See other examples cited by M. A. Shulvass in his

Ḥayye ha-Yehudim be-Italiah, pp. 181, 199. These internal struggles within the Italian Jewish communities will be discussed in later chapters.

28. J. Schröteler, *Das Elternrecht in der katholischen theologischen Auseinandersetzung*, pp. 255 ff.; C. Fedeli, *Un Singolare documento pontificio riguardante l'Università di Pisa* (1554); and other sources cited in H. Vogelstein and P. Rieger's *Geschichte*, II, 144 ff.

29. See A. Z. Schwarz, ed., "Letters Concerning the Confiscation of Books in 1553" (Hebrew), *'Alim*, II, 49–52; and other sources reproduced and carefully analyzed by A. Yaari in his *Meḥqere sefer*, pp. 228 ff., and by I. Sonne in his *Mi-Pavlo ha-rebi'i*, pp. 99 ff., App. i, including an excerpt from the contemporary *Iggeret ha-nissim* (Epistle on Miracles), prepared for Rome's Jewish community in commemoration of its "miraculous" redemption from the blood libel. See the text in D. Kaufmann's "Délivrance des Juifs de Rome en l'année 1555," *REJ*, IV, 94 ff. But Sonne goes too far in drawing, however cautiously, a line between the judgment about Marcellus by contemporary well-trained historians and that by other Jewish writers. Generally, the pope's short-lived initiatives, as well as his complex character, were subject to diverse interpretations even by much closer observers. The appraisals by Jewish outsiders could be based only on unverifiable rumors about the pope's intentions, rather than on his positive actions. Nor do we learn about his personal responses to the materials which he had accumulated in earlier years in his private collection (now in the Florentine Archives) and which included a discussion as to "whether it is expedient to abolish the Hebrew commentaries," a "defense of Jewish books," and an "accusation of Jewish books." See G. Buschbell's ed. of *Concilii Tridentini Epistolae*, I (Merkle, X), p. xxiii; II (XI), pp. 423 f. No. 387, etc.; and *supra*, n. 25. On Joseph of Arli, see also A. Marx, "Rabbi Joseph of Arli as Teacher and Head of an Academy of Siena" in *Louis Ginzberg Jub. Vol.*, Hebrew section, pp. 271–304.

30. See the biographical sketch of Paul IV by Onuphrius Panvinius, cited by S. Merkle in his ed. of *Concilii Tridentini Diaria*, II, 271 f. n. 1; Girolamo (Hieronymus) Seripando, *De Tridentino Concilio Commentarii, ibid.*, p. 405; M. Scaduto, "Lainez e l'Indice de 1559," *AHSI*, XXIV, 332; I. S. Révah, "Un Document sur l'application de l'Index de Paul IV: l'instruction de février 1559," *Annali* of the Istituto Universitario Orientale of the University of Naples, II, 79–82; P. Paschini, *Lezioni di storia ecclesiastica*, new ed., esp. III, 304 f.; idem, *San Gaetano Thiene, Gian Pietro Carafa e le origini dei chierici regolari teatini*, esp. pp. 28 ff., 37, 100 f. Carafa's antiheretical zeal came to the fore in the memorandum he submitted on October 4, 1532, to Pope Clement VII, in which he described the unsatisfactory religious situation in Venice. Without referring directly to Marranos—he mentioned only three Christian heretics by name—Carafa suggested that the pope sharply repudiate all "apostates" and exercise control over books published and circulated in the City of the Lagoons, as well as institute major internal reforms in the Church. See his "De Lutherorum haeresi reprimenda et ecclesia reformanda ad Clementem VII," reproduced by V. Schweitzer in his ed. of *Concilii Tridentini Tractatus*, I (*Concilium Tridentinum*, ed. by S. Merkle *et al.*, XII), 67–77, esp. pp. 69 ff. See also such recently published letters as those ed. by C. Matz, "An Unpub-

lished Letter of Gian Pietro Carafa," *Regnum Dei,* XXII, 158–66; and by V. Meysztowicz in "Epistola Pauli IV P. M. ad Bonam reginam Poloniae," *Antemurale,* XI, 23–24; and, more generally, G. M. Monti's *Ricerche sul Papa Paolo IV Carafa,* esp. pp. 9 ff., 28 ff., 53; and his succinct "profile" of "Papa Paolo IV" (1928), reprinted in his *Studi sulla Riforma cattolica e sul Papato nei secoli XVI-XVII.* Paul IV's religious zeal was often overshadowed by political considerations, even personal animosities, however. Despite his early admiration for Ferdinand the Catholic, he developed a lifelong hatred of Ferdinand's Habsburg grandsons. He considered placing Emperor Ferdinand I under a ban, not because the latter had agreed to the Augsburg Treaty of 1555 pledging mutual nonbelligerency among German Catholic and Protestant princes, against which the pope himself had lodged no formal protest, but rather because, after Charles V's abdication, Ferdinand had allowed himself to be crowned Roman emperor without papal approval. See J. Grisar, "Die Stellung der Päpste zum Reichstag und Religionsfrieden von Augsburg, 1555," *Stimmen der Zeit,* CLVI, 454 f. See also Conte F. Cristofori, ed., *Il Pontificato di Paolo IV ed i Caraffa suoi nepoti,* Vol. I. On the missionary aspects of Christian kabbalism, see *supra,* Chap. LVII, nn. 15 ff. The internal Jewish reaction to this aspect of the mystic lore and its connection with the outlawry of the Talmud will be analyzed in a later chapter.

31. Paul IV's bull *Cum nimis absurdum* of July 14, 1555, in *Bullarium romanum,* VI, 498 ff. No. iv; Joseph ha-Kohen, *'Emeq ha-bakha,* pp. 116 ff.; in Wiener's German trans., pp. 93 ff.; Gedaliah ibn Yaḥya, *Shalshelet ha-qabbalah* (Chain of Tradition; a world chronicle), Venice 1587 ed., fol. 117ab.

32. David Ascoli, *Apologia hebraeorum,* 1599, in *La Galleria di Minerva,* III, 268; H. Vogelstein and P. Rieger, *Geschichte,* II, 151 ff.; *supra,* Vols. IX, pp. 32 ff., 255 f. nn. 34–38; XI, pp. 87 ff., 324 ff. nn. 15–24, etc.

33. See D. R. Ancel, "L'Activité réformatrice de Paul IV," *RQH,* LXXXVI, 97 ff.; M. Radin's analysis of "A Charter of Privileges of the Jews in Ancona of the Year 1535," *JQR,* IV, 225–48 (although addressed to certain German Jews and at first limited to five years, this decree had a more general and lasting application); Julius III's decree of December 3, 1553, in M. Stern's *Urkundliche Beiträge,* I, 108 ff. No. 106; other sources cited *supra,* Chap. LVI, nn. 66 ff.; Bishop Balthasar de Limpo's active participation at the Council of Trent, as evidenced in the numerous entries in the Index to S. Merkle's ed. of *Concilii Tridentini Diaria,* I, 914 *s.v.* Portnensis (Lusitanus) episcopus; and J. de Castro's comprehensive review of *Portugal no Concilio de Trento,* esp. IV, 177; V, 224; VI, 122 ff. See also *supra,* n. 25; H. Rosenberg, "Alcuni documenti riguardanti i Marrani portoghesi in Ancona," *RMI,* 2d ser. X, 306-323, esp. pp. 319 ff. Doc. 1; and, more broadly, C. Ciavarini's *Memorie storiche degli Israeliti in Ancona,* 2d ed.; and M. Natalucci's *Ancona attraverso i secoli,* esp. Vol. II.

34. M. Stern, *Urkundliche Beiträge,* I, 108 ff. Nos. 106 and 111; Bernardino Navagero's report, cited by C. Feroso (M. Maroni) in "Di alcuni Ebrei portoghesi giustiziati in Ancona sotto Paolo IV," *AS per le Marche,* I, 696 ff.; Joseph b. David ibn Leb, *Resp.,* Jerusalem, 1957–60 ed., II, No. 54; R. Perugini, "L'Inquisition romaine," *REJ,* III, 95 f. Nos. 2 and 3 (includes a 1578 confirmation of Portico's

decree); and *supra*, n. 30. In the various modern discussions of Paul IV's reversal (see I. Sonne, *Mi-Pavlo ha-rebi'i*, pp. 30 ff. nn. 3–4), his return to the orthodox interpretation of the pertinent canonical provisions, from which Paul III had deviated, has not been given sufficient weight.

35. With respect to the Ancona auto-da-fé we do not depend only on partially extant inquisitorial records; we also possess several elegies written by contemporary Hebrew poets. This material is readily available in the excerpts published by S. Bernfeld in his *Sefer ha-Dema'ot*, II, 320 ff. See also other sources, reproduced by I. Sonne in the Appendix to his *Mi-Pavlo ha-rebi'i*, pp. 95 ff.; or cited by C. Roth in his *The House of Nasi: Doña Gracia*. Some of these elegies were recited for generations thereafter at divine services on the Ninth of Ab in Ancona and Pesaro. See D. Kaufmann, "Les Martyrs d'Ancône," *REJ*, XI, 149–56; idem, "Les 24 martyrs d'Ancône," *ibid.*, XXXI, 222–30 (also in its German original in his *GS*, II, 292–95); idem, "Deux lettres nouvelles des Marranes de Pesaro aux Levantins touchant l'interruption des affaires avec Ancône," *ibid.*, pp. 231–39; the report by Abraham Joseph Shelomo Graziano in Kaufmann's "Délivrance des Juifs de Rome en l'année 1555 (Marcello II—Paul IV—Les Martyrs d'Ancône—Mort de Caraffa)," *REJ*, IV, 96 f.; H. Rosenberg, "Elégie de Mordekhaï ben Yehouda di Blanes sur les 24 martyrs d'Ancône," *ibid.*, XC, 166–68; and other poems listed by I. Davidson in his *Oṣar ha-shirah ve-ha-piyyuṭ* (Thesaurus of Mediaeval Hebrew Poetry), I, 79, No. 1711. In the light of such overwhelming evidence, it is truly amazing to find an Italian scholar, Cesare Gariboldi, completely denying the historicity of *Un Asserto auto da fé nel pontificato di Paolo IV*. This is an example of historical skepticism pushed to ludicrous extremes for apologetic reasons.

36. The Anconitan Council's letter is cited from the local archives by C. Feroso (Maroni) in his "Di alcuni Ebrei" *AS per le Marche*, I, 693 f. Understandably, the epistle of the Jewish exiles in Pesaro was couched in pathetic but ambiguous terms in case it fell into inappropriate hands (the rest was to be communicated in person by the messenger, Yehudah Faraj). It was published, together with a subsequent letter written in Turkey, by D. Kaufmann in "Les Marranes de Pesaro et les représailles des Juifs levantins contre la ville d'Ancône," *REJ*, XVI, 61–72 (also in the German original, but without the documentation, in his *GS*, II, 285–91). As a matter of fact, half a year before the auto-da-fé and the ensuing boycott (in December 1555) the Ancona city council had asked its envoy in Rome to appeal to the papal authorities for the transfer of all inquisitorial proceedings to Macerata. It contended that the public tortures administered to defendants in Ancona were terrifying many oriental merchants and causing much damage to the city. See H. Rosenberg, "Alcuni documenti," *RMI*, 2d ser. X, 314 f.

37. Bernardino Navagero's dispatch of June 22, 1557, in his *Giornale delle lettere . . . al Senato Veneto*, cited by C. Feroso in his "Di alcuni Ebrei," *AS per le Marche*, I, 691; and by B. Croce in *Un Calvinista italiano. Il Marchese di Vico Galeazzo Carracciolo*, pp. 34 f.; and *supra*, Chap. LVI, n. 44. The sultan's *démarche* with the pope was first reproduced by G. Ruscelli in his *Lettere di Principi*, I, 177 f., while Paul IV's reply was edited, from a MS copy extant in Grenoble, by P. Grunebaum in "Un Épisode de l'histoire des Juifs d'Ancône," *REJ*, XXVIII, 142 f. See also H. Rosenberg's "Alcuni documenti," *RMI*, 2d ser. X, 321 ff. Docs. 2–3, reproducing the

Italian texts of the protest of March 5, 1556, transmitted by the French dragoman in the name of Rustem Pasha, and of the Sultan's letter of April 1556, both addressed to the elders of Ancona.

38. See A. Arce, "Espionaje e última aventura de José Nasí (1569–1574)," *Sefarad*, XIII, 257–86, esp. pp. 266 f. In this highly colored article, the author accuses Don Joseph, a Turkish councilor, of anti-Spanish espionage, but in the same breath praises the Greek-Orthodox patriarch of Constantinople for his pro-Spanish spying, which clearly was a betrayal of his Ottoman fatherland.

39. The rabbinic correspondence of the period is found particularly in the following volumes of responsa: Joseph b. David ibn Leb, II, No. 54, Jerusalem, 1960 ed., pp. 147 f.; Moses b. Joseph di Trani (the Elder), I, Venice, 1629 ed., fols. 112 f. No. 237; Joshua Soncino, *Naḥlah li-Yehoshu'a* (Joshua's Heritage; Responsa), Constantinople, 1731 ed., fols. 44b f. Nos. 39–40; Samuel b. Moses di Medina, IV, No. 59. On the events in Ferrara and Da Fano's work see D. Kaufmann in "Les Martyrs d'Ancône," *REJ*, XI, 150 f. See also, more generally, the story as retold by C. Roth in *The House of Nasi: Doña Gracia*, pp. 134–75; and by I. Sonne in his *Mi-Pavlo ha-rebi'i, passim*. Some Turkish leaders conceived the bright idea of placating the duke of Urbino with a gift of 20,000 ducats, lest he carry out severe reprisals against the Marrano exiles for their failure to fulfill their promise. But the disunited Turkish communities failed to raise the requisite amount. See Soncino, *Naḥlah li-Yehoshu'a*, fol. 44b No. 39.

40. *Ibid.*; Joseph ha-Kohen, *'Emeq ha-bakha*, pp. 117 ff.; in Wiener's German trans., p. 95; Benjamin Neḥemiah b. Elnathan, *Dibre ha-yamim* (Chronicle), ed. by I. Sonne in his *Mi-Pavlo ha-rebi'i*, pp. 24 f. True, as special pleaders, both Soncino and Joseph ha-Kohen were prone to exaggerate or to understate their respective cases. Soncino was arguing for the discontinuation of the Ancona boycott. The chronicler, on the other hand, was pursuing the general theme of his book, describing the endless sequence of Jewish sufferings; he therefore tended to neglect aspects of Jewish history which did not have a direct bearing on anti-Jewish decrees, massacres, or expulsions. But even discounting these biases, the contemporary recitals clearly attest the persistence of the traditional Jewish outlook on martyrdom. See also my remarks on "Newer Emphases in Jewish History," reprinted in my *History and Jewish Historians*, pp. 90–106.

41. Joseph ha-Kohen, *'Emeq ha-bakha*, pp. 124 f.; in Wiener's German trans., pp. 101 f.; Angelo Massarelli, *Diaria* in S. Merkle's ed. of *Concilii Tridentini Diaria*, II, 270 f., 332 f.; S. Caponetto, "Due relazioni inedite dell'ambasciatore Montino del Monte al Duca di Urbino sugli avvenimenti romani dopo la morte di Paolo IV," *Studia Oliveriana*, I, 25–40, esp. pp. 35 ff. A graphic eyewitness account of these events is also included in Benjamin Neḥemiah b. Elnathan's chronicle, ed. by I. Sonne in his *Mi-Pavlo ha-rebi'i*, pp. 79 ff. See also A. Bastiaanse, "Le Memorie dell'-Almeyden sui papi e cardinali del Seicento basate sulle esperienze personali," *AHP*, IV, 155–95, esp. p. 189.

42. Paul IV's interpretive ordinance, *Bando sopra gli Ebrei* in *Regesti di bandi, editti, notificazioni e provvedimenti diversi relativi alla città di Roma*, ed. by P.

Fedele *et al.;* the acquittal of Giovanni Morone in the congregation held on March 13, 1560, reproduced by S. Ehses in his ed. of *Concilii Tridentini Acta,* V (in S. Merkle's collection Vol. VIII), pp. 11 f. No. 7; Pius IV's bull *Dudum a felicis recordationis* of February 27, 1562, in *Bullarium romanum,* VII, 167 ff. See also L. Pastor, *The History of the Popes,* XIV, 289 ff., 468 ff. Apps. 46–47; M. Radin's analysis of "A Papal Brief of Pius IV," *JQR,* I, 113–21; E. Rodocanachi, *Le Saint-Siège et les Juifs: Le ghetto à Rome,* pp. 177 ff.; *supra,* n. 24; and *infra,* Chap. LXI, n. 12.

43. Pius V's bulls *Romanus pontifex* of April 19, 1566, and *Cum nos nuper* of January 19, 1567, in *Bullarium romanum,* VII, 438 ff. No. x, 514 ff. No. xlii; J. de Laderchi, ed., *Annales ecclesiastici* (a continuation of Caesarius Baronius' [Baronio's] and Odericus Raynaldus' well-known work), *ad* 1566, III (XXXV), 37 ff. Nos. 100–112; M. Schwab, "Une Supplique de la communauté de Rome à Pie V," *REJ,* XXV, 113–16 (this petition, previously published by E. Rodocanachi, evidently stemmed from an individual Christian and not from a Jewish community); M. de Maulde, *Les Juifs dans les états français du Saint-Siège au moyen âge,* pp. 25 n. 2; A. Mercati's well-documented, but a bit slanted, apologia for the inquisitorial proceeding in *I Costituti di Niccolò Franco (1568–1570) dinanzi l'Inquisizione di Roma esistenti nell'Archivio Segreto Vaticano* (Studi e testi, CLXXVIII). The pope's accusation that some Roman Jews professionally engaged in "divination, conjuring, magic arts, and witchcraft" contained a kernel of truth, but he readily overlooked the fact that they had many Christian competitors, including priests. See the allusions thereto in the writings of Pietro Aretino, Lodovico Ariosto, and Benvenuto Cellini, cited *supra,* Vol. XI, pp. 140 f., 354 f. n. 23.

It is small wonder, then, that as papal oppression grew, some such Jewish "sorcerers" tried to predict in 1568–69 how long Pius V, then in his mid-sixties, was going to live. Evidently, they and their clients hoped that his successor would greatly moderate the rigor of his regime. Needless to say, when apprehended, such culprits were severely punished. See the *Avvisi di Roma* of June 12, and July 31, 1568, and July 13, 1569, cited by L. Pastor in *The History of the Popes,* XVII, 334 n. 1. See also other sources cited *ibid.,* pp. 334 ff.; by E. Rodocanachi in *Le Saint-Siège,* pp. 182 ff., 315 ff.; and, more generally, A. de Fuenmayor, *Vida y hechos de Pio V. Pontifice romano . . . con algunos notables successos de la Christiandad del tiempo de su pontificado,* Madrid, 1595, new ed. with an Intro. by L. Riber; and G. Carocci's survey of *Lo Stato della Chiesa nella seconda metà del secolo XVI,* pp. 33 ff.

44. See G. Cozzi, "Un Documento sulla crisi della 'Sacra Lega,'" *Archivio Veneto,* 5th ser. LXVII, 79 f.; *supra,* nn. 10 and 13; the description of the 1566 baptismal rites by the then papal master of ceremonies, Cornelius Firmani di Macerata, reproduced and analyzed by H. Vogelstein and P. Rieger in their *Geschichte,* II, 165 f., 423 ff. App. 16; Pius V's bull *Cum nos nuper* of January 19, 1567, in *Bullarium romanum,* VII, 514 ff. No. xlii; L. Serrano, ed., *Correspondencia diplomática entre España y la Santa Sede durante el pontificado de S. Pio V,* III, 79, 81 f. No. 31, 168 n. 1; L. Pastor, *The History,* XVII, 288 ff., 300 ff., 334 ff.; D. Kaufmann, "Don Joseph Nasi, Founder of Colonies in the Holy Land, and the Community of Cori in the Campagna," *JQR,* II, 291–310, esp. pp. 305 ff.; M. A. Shulvass, *Roma vi-Yerushalayim* (Rome and Jerusalem: a History of the Attitudes of the Jews of Italy toward Palestine), pp. 74 ff. Obviously, the relatively tolerant spirit of the Council

of Trent did not communicate itself to Pius V's regime, but this was not a singular exception. The clergy in general was slow in implementing the conciliar resolutions concerning its way of life. See the careful analysis by A. Monticone of "L'Applicazione a Roma del Concilio di Trento," *RSCI*, VII, 225–50; VIII, 23-48.

Because of its vastly extended range of activity the Roman Inquisition had to enlarge its personnel in an unprecedented fashion. A new committee ("congregation") of four cardinals was appointed to speed up proceedings. Curiously, at times the Holy Office found itself in the awkward position of being unable to recruit enough notaries to certify its numerous documents, although in the years 1549–61 no less than 700 persons qualified to engage in that profession at the Curia. Aside from the old functionaries, these newcomers alone represented more than one percent of the city's total population. See J. Grisar, "Notare und Notariatsarchive im Kirchenstaat des 16. Jahrhunderts," *Mélanges Eugène Tisserant*, IV, 255. Understandably, the growing emigration from the Papal States also created numerous complications in Jewish family life. One such issue arose when the wife of a Bologna Jew refused to follow him to Ferrara in 1567 or 1568, R. Aaron Finzi declaring her guilty of a breach of her marriage contract. See his responsum, excerpted by I. Sonne from a MS in his possession in *Mi-Pavlo ha-rebi'i*, pp. 205 ff.

45. Pius V's bull *Hebraeorum gens sola* of February 26, 1569, in *Bullarium Romanum*, VII, 740 ff. No. cxxiv; Joseph ha-Kohen, '*Emeq ha-bakha*, pp. 130 ff., 138 ff.; in Wiener's German trans., pp. 106, 112 ff.; C. Dejob, "Documents tirés des papiers du Cardinal Sirleto," *REJ*, IX, 85; A. Mossé, *Histoire des Juifs d'Avignon et du Comtat Venaissin*, pp. 82 f.; M. de Maulde, *Les Juifs dans les états français du Saint-Siège*, p. 18 n. 4. De Maulde also mentions the complaint of the city council of Sorgues against an influx of Jews who occupied seven houses, *ibid.*, p. 19 n. 1. The pertinent archival document is not precisely dated, but it seems to relate to the resettlement of Jews in that southern French community after the expulsion of 1569, most likely after Pius V's death in 1572.

46. M. Stern, *Urkundliche Beiträge*, pp. 143 ff. Nos. 134–36; H. Vogelstein and P. Rieger, *Geschichte*, II, 163 ff.; I. Sonne, *Mi-Pavlo ha-rebi'i*, pp. 204 ff., esp. pp. 210 f. No. 3. The story of the exodus of the Jews from the States of the Church has been told, partly in picturesque detail, in two contemporary Hebrew accounts, published respectively by M. A. Shulvass in "A Story of the Misfortunes which Afflicted [the Jews] in Italy," *HUCA*, XXII, Hebrew section, pp. 1–21; and I. Sonne in his "Chapters from a Tract on Expulsions," *ibid.*, pp. 23–44, both with fine explanatory notes. These texts were subsequently republished by Sonne in *Mi-Pavlo*, pp. 181 ff. App. iii. The ensuing Jewish migratory movements affected many Jewish communities in both Italy and the Ottoman Empire and will be mentioned here on various occasions. See also F. Goubau, ed., *Apostolicarum Pii Quinti Pont. Max. Epistolarum libri quinque*, esp. pp. 93 ff. No. xiv; A. de Fuenmayor, *Vida y hechos de Pio V*.

It should be noted, however, that Pius V treated his Christian subjects harshly, too. Contemporary wags claimed that he wanted to convert all of Rome into a monastery. A Capucin friar, Girolamo da Pistoia, vainly tried to influence the pope by pointing out to him that, for each verse in the Bible praising God's justice, one could cite ten verses praising His mercy. See C. Cantù, *Les Hérétiques d'Italie; discours historiques*, French trans. from the Italian *Gli Eretici d'Italia*, II, 410, citing the report of the Venetian ambassador dated April 15, 1570; L. Pastor, *The History*, XVII, 366.

47. See *supra*, Vol. X, pp. 253 f., 412 f. n. 40. The Rome-Ancona agreement of July 12, 1581, reproduced in M. Stern's *Urkundliche Beiträge*, I, 149 ff. No. 139; A. Theiner, ed., *Annales ecclesiastici* (continuation of Baronius, Raynaldus, and Laderchi, only to January 18, 1585) I, 351 No. 63, 529 ff. No. 107; Joseph ha-Kohen, *'Emeq ha-bakha*, p. 134; in M. Wiener's German trans., p. 109; Gregory XIII's bull *Sancta Mater ecclesia* of September 1, 1584, in *Bullarium romanum*, VIII, 487 ff.; G. Bartolocci, *Bibliotheca magna rabbinica*, III, 784; L. Ponnelle and L. Bordet, *St. Filippo Neri and the Roman Society of His Time (1575–1595)*, English trans. by R. F. Kerr, pp. 280, 381 ff.; Andrea del Monte (Joseph Sarfati), *Mebukhat Yehudim* (Confusione de' Giudei) and *Iggeret Shalom* (Lettera di Pace), *passim*. Andrea's frequent attacks on Jews and Judaism, his denunciations of the Jewish community for possessing forbidden Hebrew works, and other hostile acts did not prevent him from occasionally collaborating with the Jewish leaders—for a consideration. In 1562, when the Jewish community needed the text of a 1443 agreement between it (acting in behalf of all Italian Jewry) and the papal administration safeguarding a measure of liturgical freedom in synagogue worship, it was able to secure the original of that important document only through the convert-preacher after a payment of 50 scudi. See A. Berliner, *Geschichte der Juden in Rom*, II, Part 1, pp. 70 ff.; Part 2, pp. 8 f., 19.

In his 1584 decree Gregory made it clear that the missionary sermons ought to be so arranged "that all Jews aged twelve and over should assemble to listen to them in rotation in such a fashion that no less than one-third of their members be present" on every occasion. This became a permanent institution; whenever attendance fell below the required quorum (which was sometimes set in absolute figures, rather than in percentages) the Jewish elders were heavily fined. They had to pay between 25 and 50 gold scudi for each major infraction or 1 scudo per missing listener. Understandably, the Jews frequently resisted; under Benedict XIV (1740–58), the Confraternity of Christian Doctrine complained to the pope that Jewish parents failed to bring with them any offspring below the age of twenty. To this failure, as well as to the inconvenient locality where the sermons were delivered, the writers attributed their grievous lack of success. See A. Zucchi, "Memorie dominicane in Roma," *Memorie dominicane*, LI, 200–205, 255–64, 313–21, esp. pp. 259 ff. On Michel de Montaigne's description of such a performance see the literature listed *supra*, n. 10; Chap. LVI, n. 61; and *infra*, nn. 56–57; also other sources cited by A. Vogelstein and P. Rieger in their *Geschichte*, II, 169 ff. The conditions in Malta, where from 1530 on the Knights Hospitalers vied with the Barbary corsairs in pirating merchant ships and using their passengers and crews as slaves until ransomed, are briefly sketched by C. Roth in "The Jews of Malta," *TJHSE*, XII, 187–251, esp. pp. 212 ff.

Gregory's frequently bitter jurisdictional disputes with Philip II, but partially mitigated by Cardinal Carlo Borromeo's mediating efforts, may have been of some benefit to the Roman Jews. See G. Catalano, *Controversie giurisdizionali tra Chiesa e Stato nell'età di Gregorio XIII e di Filippo II* in *Atti* of the Accademia di scienze . . . di Palermo, 4th ser., XIV, 2; P. Prodi, "San Carlo Borromeo e le trattative tra Gregorio XIII e Filippo II sulla giurisdizione ecclesiastica," *RSCI*, XI, 195–240.

Incidentally, Borromeo, who in 1560, at the age of twenty-one, had been appointed cardinal and secretary of state by his uncle Pius IV, shared the intransigence of Pius V, rather than the moderation of his own uncle. When Pius V issued his stringent anti-Jewish decrees, Borromeo helped to implement them through his influence in other Italian states. He was particularly successful, at least with respect to enforcing the badge, in his native Milan. See the continuation of Joseph ha-Kohen's *'Emeq ha-bakha*, pp. 138 f.; in Wiener's German trans. p. 113. It was his combination of religious zeal with great diplomatic skill which earned Borromeo his later canonization.

48. Gregory XIII's bulls *Alias piae memoriae* of May 31, 1581, and *Antiqua Iudaeorum improbitas* of July 1, 1581, in *Bullarium romanum*, VIII, 371, 378 ff.; I Cor. 5:12; *supra*, Vol. IX, pp. 57, 266 f. n. 3; Chap. LV, n. 1; R. Perugini, "L'Inquisition romaine et les Israélites," *REJ*, III, 94–108; C. Roth, "Joseph Saralvo: a Marrano Martyr at Rome," *Festschrift zu Simon Dubnow's siebzigsten Geburtstag*, ed. by I. Elbogen *et al.*, pp. 180–86; A. Theiner, ed., *Annales ecclesiastici*, III, 308 f.; the continuation of Joseph ha-Kohen's *'Emeq ha-bakha*, p. 147; in M. Wiener's German trans. p. 120. See also other data in L. Pastor, *The History of the Popes*, XIX, 296 ff.; L. Beltrami, *La Roma di Gregorio XIII negli Avvisi alla Corte Sabauda;* D. Orano, *Liberi pensatori bruciati in Roma dal XVI al XVIII secolo;* and *infra*, n. 60.

49. L. Pastor, *The History of the Popes*, XXII, 180 n. 2; Sixtus V's bull *Christiana pietas* of October 22, 1586, in *Bullarium romanum*, VIII, 786 ff. No. lxix, with D. Kaufmann's remarks thereon in "A Letter from the Community of Pesaro to Don Joseph Nassi," *JQR*, [o.s.] IV, 509–12 (this bull, exceptionally, was promulgated in Italian, rather than Latin, probably in order to bring it more readily to the attention of the masses); the continuator of Joseph ha-Kohen in *'Emeq ha-bakha*, p. 155; in Wiener's German trans., p. 127; and other sources cited by H. Vogelstein and P. Rieger in their *Geschichte*, II, 176 ff.

50. L. Pastor, *The History of the Popes*, XXI, 124 ff., 192 ff.; G. Bartolocci, *Bibliotheca magna rabbinica*, IV, 20 ff. It appears that, even before Magino's enterprises came to their full fruition, they withered away under Clement VIII's intolerant policies, the inventor himself moving to Leghorn and later to Lorraine and Württemberg. See E. Hecht, "Notizen," *MGWJ*, X, 276 f.; I. Bloch, "Une Expulsion de Juifs en Alsace au XVIe siècle," *REJ*, XXXI, 75, 88 ff. App. i. In 1587 Sixtus accepted the dedication to him of David b. Isaac de Pomis' distinguished Hebrew-Aramaic dictionary, *Ṣemaḥ David* (The Scion of David), and David perhaps had the pope in mind when he published his *De medico hebreo enarratio apologetica* in the following year.

Sixtus' reversal of his predecessors' policies, including those governing the status of Jews, naturally generated some opposition. In any case, the vigor of his administration clearly put him outside the class of those popes whom H. Jedin placed among the "late bloomers" (his reign at the age of 63 to 68 made him one of the relatively younger popes), rather than among the blunderers because of senility. See Jedin's aforementioned essay, "Spätleistungen," reprinted in his *Kirche des Glaubens*, pp. 293 ff. Nor is it surprising that Sixtus' personality caught the attention of several serious biographers, including Gregorio Leti in his comprehensive *Vita di Sisto V pontifice romano* published in a much enlarged ed. in Amsterdam, 1686 and 1698 (it was translated into English in 1704); and R. Canestrari's *Sisto V*. See also, more generally, G. Carocci's *Lo Stato della Chiesa nella seconda metà del secolo XVI;* and some studies included in P. Paschini's *Lezioni di storia ecclesiastica,* new impression, which relate largely to earlier periods. On the connection between Sixtus' alleged Solomonian judgment and the Shylock figure and the attack by a French pamphleteer on Sixtus, the "rabbi," see *infra,* Chap. LX, n. 42; and Vol. XV.

51. See the fine documentation in M. Stern's *Urkundliche Beiträge,* I, 153 ff. Nos. 141 ff., esp. Nos. 150, 152, 155; and some additional data from Mantuan sources supplied by S. Simonsohn's *Toledot ha-Yehudim be-dukhsut Mantovah* (History of the Jews in the Duchy of Mantua), I, 305 ff. See also M. Mortara, "Die Censur hebräischer Bücher in Italien und der *Canon purificationis (Sefer ha-Ziqquq),*" German trans. by M. Steinschneider, *Hebräische Bibliographie,* V, 72–77, 96–101, 125–28; and W. Popper's Columbia University dissertation, *The Censorship of Hebrew Books,* pp. 66 ff.

52. See the literature listed in the last note. On Sixtus V's sponsorship of a new edition of the Bible, Cardinal Bellarmine's role therein, and the latter's general appreciation of the Hebrew original as transmitted by Jews, see X. M. Bachelet, *Bellarmin et la Bible Sixto-Clémentine. Études et documents inédits;* G. Buschbell, *Selbstbezeugungen des Kardinals Bellarmin. Beiträge zur Bellarminforschung,* pp. 74 ff.; P. M. Baumgarten, *Neue Kunde von alten Bibeln. Mit zahlreichen Beiträgen zur Kultur- und Literaturgeschichte Roms am Ausgange des sechszehnten Jahrhunderts;* and, more generally, V. Baroni's aforementioned Lausanne dissertation, *La Contre-Réforme devant la Bible;* and *infra,* Chap. LX, nn. 1 and 6.

Characteristically, the unnamed memorialist must have known that Alessandro Scipione Renatto, the official censor of the Mantuan Inquisition, had been laboring for a year over the revision of the Hebrew texts (he received for it 20 gold scudi from the Jewish community). At the same time the Jewish delegates had even engaged their sworn enemy Andrea del Monte to collaborate with the original Roman censor, Jacobo Giraldino, in the expurgation of objectionable texts. To the conservative opposition, this was merely another "astute move to lend color" to the secret designs of the rabbis. Moreover, in the three decades since the Ferrara resolution of 1554, the Jewish censors themselves had acquired considerable expertise in deleting from their Hebrew writings passages which might breed ill will among their Christian neighbors. See W. Popper, *The Censorship,* pp. 40 f., 135 f.; and I. Sonne, "Expurgation of Hebrew Books: the Work of Jewish Scholars; a Contribution to the History of the Censorship of Hebrew Books in Italy in the 16th Century," *BNYPL,* XLVI, 975–1015. Riding roughshod over all such considerations, the opposition succeeded in frustrating the Jewish "lobby" by delaying the final papal decision until Sixtus' death.

53. See I. Sonne's persuasive analysis of "Eight Sixteenth-Century Letters from Ferrara" (Hebrew), *Zion,* XVII, 145–56, esp. pp. 151 f. Letter iii; P. M. Baumgarten, "Kritische Bemerkungen zum elften, zwölften und dreizehnten Band von Pastors Papstgeschichte," *ZKG,* XLVIII, 428; Clement VIII's bulls *Cum saepe accidere possit* of February 28, 1592; *Caeca et obdurata* of February 25, 1593 (promulgated on March 13); *Cum Hebraeorum malitia* of February 28, 1593; and *Paterna nostra* of May 25, 1596, in *Bullarium romanum,* IX, 523 ff. No. iv; X, 22 ff. Nos. lv–lvi,

269 ff. No. cxxxii; M. Stern, *Urkundliche Beiträge*, I, 163 ff. Nos. 156–59, 175 No. 161 items 27–28; A Bertolotti, "Les Juifs à Rome au XVIe, XVIIe et XVIIIe siècles. Documents et notices recueillis dans les Archives de Rome," *REJ*, II, 278–89, esp. pp. 279 f., 288 f.; C. Corvisieri, "Compendio dei processi del Santo Uffizio di Roma (da Paolo III a Paolo IV)," *Archivio* of the Società Romana di storia patria, III, 261–90, 449–71; and, more broadly, Bertolotti, *Martiri del libero pensiero e vittime della Santa Inquisizione nei secoli XVI, XVII e XVIII;* H. Reusch, *Der Index der verbotenen Bücher*, I, 49 ff., 333 ff., 339, 534 f.; L. Pastor, *Allgemeine Dekrete der römischen Inquisition*, pp. 50, 52; idem, *The History*, XXIV, 98 ff., 218 ff.

54. R. Perugini, "L'Inquisition romaine et les Israélites," *REJ*, III, 101; L. Ferraris, *Prompta bibliotheca canonica*, III, 300 ff. Nos. 187, 195, 197 ff., 207; E. Rodocanachi, *Le Saint-Siège*, pp. 177 ff., 189 f.; Clement VIII's bull *Cum ex iniuncto* of January 11, 1598, in *Bullarium romanum*, X, 414 f.; J. de Olarra Garmendia and (his widow) M. L. Larramendi, eds., *Correspondencia entre la Nunciatura en España y la Santa Sede durante el reinado de Felipe III (1598–1621)*, II: Años 1602–1605; *infra*, Chap. LXV; H. Höpfel, *Beiträge zur Geschichte der Sixto-Klementinischen Vulgata*, esp. pp. 106 f.; L. Pastor, *The History*, XXIV, 223 f. See also, more generally, E. Pontieri, "Il Papato e la sua funzione morale e politica in Italia durante la preponderanza spagnola," *ASI*, XCVI, Part 2, pp. 64–87. The threat of galley slavery perhaps was to induce Jewish culprits not only to desist from further attempts to interfere with conversions to Christianity but also to seek escape from that dreaded penalty by themselves asking for baptism. In petitioning in 1607 for this alternative, four Jews suggested that their liberation might serve as a good example for other Jews in a similar predicament. See A. Bertolotti in "Les Juifs à Rome," *REJ*, II, 282 f.

This is but one more illustration of the manifold conversionist pressures upon the Italian Jews, which, characteristically, emanated not only from ecclesiastical circles. Even the rather queer, heterodox thinker Francesco Pucci, who in a letter to Gregory XIII had tried to persuade the pope that he possessed "the gift of the Divine Spirit," wrote in 1592 an obviously conversionist letter to some Jews and later inquired as to whether some of these or other Jewish readers had taken it to heart. See D. Cantimori and E. Feist, eds., *Per la storia degli Eretici italiani del secolo XVI in Europa. Testi raccolti*, pp. 111 ff., 168 n. 1.

55. See L. dal Pane, *Lo Stato Pontificio e il movimento riformatore del settecento*. Regrettably, in his standard work on *The History of the Popes*, Ludwig von Pastor furnished few data about Jews under the reigns of the seventeenth-century popes. This lacuna has already been stressed by Paul Maria Baumgarten, who observed that "the rich materials for the history and treatment of Jews under Paul V and Urban VIII have remained almost totally unexplored, although a review of these matters might have been much more significant than many a long-drawn-out discussion of political problems." See his "Kritische Bemerkungen," *ZKG*, XLVIII, 437.

56. P. L. Bruzzone, "Documents sur les Juifs des États Pontificaux," *REJ*, XIX, 131–40, esp. p. 137; M. Stern, *Urkundliche Beiträge*, I, 176 ff. No. 161, items 31, 45, and 63; C. Dejob, "Documents tirés des papiers du Cardinal Sirleto," *REJ*, IX, 78 f. (citing a seventeenth-century MS). The ambiguity of the canonical provisions con-

cerning the conversion of Jewish minors without parental consent had been heightened, rather than clarified, by the lengthy discussion of the question, "Whether children of infidel Jews before reaching puberty may be baptized against their parents' will," in the *Summa summarum,* or the so-called *Summa silvestrina* by the Spanish theologian Silvester Mazzolini de Prierias (da Prierio). According to Johann Friedrich Schulte, an eminent student of the history of canon law, this *Summa* had replaced all earlier works of its kind in the estimation of contemporaries and held undisputed authority to the end of the sixteenth century. See that *Summa,* in the Leiden, 1533 ed.; J. F. Schulte, *Die Quellen des kanonischen Rechts,* II, 455 f.; J. Schröteler, *Das Elternrecht,* pp. 236 ff.; *supra,* Chap. LVII, n. 33; and Vol. IX, pp. 12 ff., 15 ff., 246 ff. nn. 11–16. This attitude of the papal organs, far more equivocal now than it had been in the Middle Ages, encouraged many local churchmen to use a variety of legal subterfuges to convert, more or less underhandedly, Italian Jewish adults and children. See the data assembled in C. Roth's "Forced Baptisms in Italy: a Contribution to the History of Jewish Persecution," *JQR,* XXVII, 117–36; and *infra,* Chap. LX, n. 71.

57. Gregory XIII's bulls *Vices eius* of September 1, 1577; *Sancta Mater ecclesia* of September 1, 1584; those by Sixtus V, *Christiana pietas* of October 22, 1586; and Clement VIII, *Caeca et obdurata* of February 25, 1593, all in *Bullarium romanum,* VIII, 188 ff. No. lxxiii, 487 ff. No. clxx, 786 ff. No. lxix; X, 22 ff. No. lv; A. Zucchi, "Memorie dominicane in Roma. I: Il Predicatore degli Ebrei in Roma," *Memorie domincane, Rivista di Religione,* LI, 200–205; II: "Ragioni della predicazione agli Ebrei," *ibid.,* pp. 255–64; III: I Predicatori domenicani degli Ebrei in Roma," *ibid.,* pp. 313–21; E. Rodocanachi, *Le Saint-Siège,* pp. 272 ff.; A. Milano, "Un Sottile tormento nella vita del ghetto di Roma: La predica coattiva," *RMI,* XVIII, 517–32 (furnishing interesting data also on seventeenth-century Urbino); idem, "L'Impari lotta della communità di Roma contro la Casa dei catecumeni," *ibid.,* XVI, 355–68); Michel de Montaigne, *Journal du voyage en Italie, par la Suisse et l'Allemagne en 1580 et 1581,* ed. with notes by A. d'Ancona, pp. 298 f.; in the English trans. by W. Hazlitt, entitled *Diary of the Journey into Italy,* in Montaigne's *Complete Works,* p. 608; M. Liber, "Montaigne à Rome," *REJ,* LV, 109–118 (suggesting that Andrea del Monte had also impressed Giordano Bruno in 1585–86); C. Dejob, "Documents," *ibid.,* IX, 86 ff.; and *supra,* nn. 10 and 47.

Another outstanding missionary was the well-known papal censor Domenico Hierosolymitano. He not only translated the entire New Testament into Hebrew in three volumes (completed in 1615–17) but also left behind transcripts of many sermons delivered to Jewish audiences in the years 1573–86. To make them more readily usable for literary propaganda among the Jewish masses, he composed these Italian addresses in Hebrew characters. They are still extant among the manuscripts of the Roman House of Catechumens. See G. Sacerdote, comp., "I Codici ebraici della Pia Casa de' Neofiti di Roma," *Atti* of the R. Accademia dei Lincei, 4th ser. X, Part 1 (Memorie), pp. 178 ff. Nos. 32–36. All this sound and fury encountered the staunch resistance of Roman and Avignonese Jewry, however, probably even stauncher now than under the more liberal regimes of the Renaissance popes. See also F. Secret's "Notes sur les Juifs d'Avignon," *REJ,* CXXII, 184 ff.; and on the earlier history of enforced attendance at missionary sermons, see P. Browe, *Die Judenmission im Mittelalter und die Päpste,* pp. 13 ff., 215 ff.; and other data cited *supra,* Vol. IX, pp. 79 ff., 274 ff. nn. 21 ff.

58. J. Grisar, "Francesco Ingoli über die Aufgaben des kommenden Papstes nach dem Tode Urbans VIII (1644)," *AHP*, VI, 289–524; Tommaso Campanella, *La Città del Sole*, Original Text, ed. with Introduction and Documents by E. Solmi; idem, *Per la conversione degli Ebrei*, ed. by R. Amerio, which is but Part 3 of his more comprehensive tripartite missionary treatise, *Quod reminiscentur* (1617–18). (Parts I–II were likewise ed. by Amerio.) See also G. di Napoli's *Tommaso Campanella, filosofo della restaurazione cattolica*. Many other controversial tracts of the period are listed in J. A. Fabricius' *Delectus argumentatorum et syllabus scriptorum qui veritatem religionis Christianae . . . asseruerunt*, pp. 576–663; C. J. Imbonati's *Bibliotheca latino-hebraica;* and, more briefly, F. Vernet's "Juifs (Controverses avec les)," *Dictionnaire de théologie catholique*, VIII, Part 1, esp. cols. 1899 f. See also S. G. Mercati, "Il Trattato contro i Giudei di Taddeo Pelusiota è una falsificazione di Constantino Paleocappa," *Il Bessarione*, XXXIX, 8–14; and *supra*, Vol. IX, pp. 288 ff. n. 4. Not surprisingly, in an undated letter to Del Monte one of his confreres claimed that, in addition to raising certain general objections to the convert's sermons, the Jews had asserted that "they would much rather listen to lectures and instruction by any other Christian." See C. Dejob, "Documents," *REJ*, IX, 87 f.

Relations between the *Congregatio de Propaganda fide* and the Jews have never been analyzed. Much material still is available in its rich archives, as illustrated by its archivist, N. Kowalsky, in his "Inventario dell'Archivio storico della Congregazione 'de Propaganda fide,'" *Neue Zeitschrift für Missionswissenschaft*, XVII, 9–23, 109–117, 191–200. See also the data offered by H. Tüchle in his ed. of *Acta S. C. Propaganda fide Germaniam spectantia* (Die Protokolle der Propaganda-Kongregation zu deutschen Angelegenheiten 1622–1649); and the description of two visits in 1957–1963 by J. B. McGloin in search of materials for the history of the Catholic mission in California, in "The Roman Propaganda Fide Archives: an Overflow and Assessment," *CH*, XXXIII, 84–91.

An interesting eyewitness description of the picturesque baptismal ceremony for a Leghorn Jew in St. Peter's basilica in Rome is offered in the *Journal* of the English visitor Charles Talbot, Duke of Shaftesbury. At that ceremony of 1704 Queen Maria, widow of John Sobieski of Poland, served as godmother, while Pope Clement XI personally performed the ritual. Thereupon the convert assumed the pope's family name, Albani. See A. F. Steuart, "Jews in Rome, 1704," *JQR*, [o.s.] XIX, 398–99; and H. P. Chajes's remarks thereon in his "Rivista delle Riviste," *RI*, IV, 41–43, esp. pp. 42 f. These conversionist efforts were seriously impeded, however, by the continued hostility of many Christians to their new coreligionists. A particularly pathetic case was called to the attention of Cardinal Sirleto in 1584. A Jewess held as a slave in a Christian household was no less harshly treated by her employers after her baptismal ceremony. Made pregnant by a member of the family, she was shipped to Messina, where she was to be sold in the market. The complainant, himself a neophyte, offered the cardinal a financial contribution of his own and also in behalf of other converts so that she might be ransomed. See C. Dejob, "Documents," *REJ*, IX, 81; and, on Sirleto's general administration, G. Denzler's recent Munich dissertation, *Kardinal Guglielmo Sirleto (1514–1595). Leben und Wirken*.

59. The statistical data quoted in the text are supplied by E. Natali in *Il Ghetto di Roma*, p. 245. In his comment thereon (in his *Geschichte*, II, Part 2, pp. 40 f.) A. Berliner mentions a detailed list of converts in the years 1603–1702 which, ac-

cording to the communal register, had once existed in the archive of the Jewish community of Rome. But this document could no longer be located in the early 1890s. Even if Berliner's suggestion be correct that Natali's figures included "Turks" admitted to the House of Catechumens, their number must have been considerably smaller than that of the Jewish converts, since there were but few Muslim residents in the States of the Church. However, the House of Catechumens, which offered a fairly comfortable mode of living to its inmates, may have attracted some renegades from both Islam and Judaism in distant localities.

60. Prospero Farinacci, *Praxis et Theoricae criminalis pars quarta* (also in *Opera omnia*); in the English trans. by R. C. Jenkins entitled *The Law and Practice of the Church of Rome in Cases of Heresy,* esp. p. v; C. Roth, "Joseph Saralvo: a Marrano Martyr at Rome," *Festschrift . . . Simon Dubnow,* pp. 180–86; P. Tamizey de Larroque and J. Dukas, eds., "Lettres inédites écrites à [Nicolas C. F. de] Peiresc par Salomon Azubi, rabbin de Carpentras (1622–23)," *REJ,* XI, 101–125, 252–65; XII, 95–106 (with a note by É. Benamozegh, *ibid.,* XI, 264 f.), esp. XI, 258 ff.; R. Perugini, "L'Inquisition romaine," *REJ,* III, 94–108; A. Berliner, *Aus schweren Zeiten,* pp. 8 ff.; M. Stern, *Urkundliche Beiträge,* I, 178 No. 161 item 54; E. Natali, *Il Ghetto di Roma,* p. 143; A. Bertolotti, *Le Tipografie orientali e gli orientalisti a Roma nei secoli XVI e XVII,* pp. 34 ff., 47 ff.; Gregory XV's bull *Apostolatus officium nobis* of December 30, 1622, in *Bullarium romanum,* XII, 779 f.; F. Secret, "Les Dominicains et la kabbale chrétienne à la Renaissance," *AFP,* XXVII, 319–36.

Some interesting Jewish data are also included in A. Bertolotti's *Martiri del libero pensiero,* esp. pp. 112, 125, with Israel Lévi's notes thereon in his "Revue bibliographique," *REJ,* XXV, 122–43; D. Cantimori, *Eretici italiani nel Cinquecento, ricerche storiche;* D. Orano's *Liberi pensatori bruciati in Roma dal XVI al XVIII secolo* (includes a dramatic description of the difficulties confronting the pre-execution "comforters" of the professing Jew Iacobo di Elia da San Lorenzo, in January 1616; pp. 95 f.; also p. 91).

It is also noteworthy that the Hebrew language still played a considerable role in the Church's defense of its traditional position. Despite the onset of the "Counter Renaissance," which accompanied the Counter Reformation, Pope Paul V insisted in his bull *Apostolicae servitutis* of July 31, 1610, that the monastic schools offer missionaries thorough instruction in Hebrew, as well as in Greek, Latin, and Arabic, in order "to fortify the faithful in their beliefs and charity, to lead the infidels out of the darkness of infidelity, and to free the heretics and sinners from the perversity of error and the bondage of sin." See *Bullarium romanum,* XI, 625 ff. No. clv; with the comments thereon by A. M. Ammann in "Eine Sprachverordnung Papst Pauls V. Ihr Denkmal im Vatikan," *Orientalia christiana periodica,* XXXIII (*Miscellanea iubilaria* of the Pontifical Oriental Institute in Rome), 294–302, thereby also explaining the message conveyed by the painter of two frescoes for the *torre di venti* erected by Gregory XIII. On the general reorientation of Catholic thought, see *supra,* nn. 1 and 5; H. Daniel-Rops, *L'Église de la Renaissance et de la Réforme,* Vols. I, in the English trans. by A. Butler, entitled *The Protestant Reformation;* II, English trans. by J. Warrington, entitled *The Catholic Reformation;* L. Febvre's collection of essays, *Au Coeur religieux du XVIe siècle;* and numerous other studies analyzed by G. Ritter in his "Wegbahner eines 'aufgeklärten' Christentums im 16. Jahrhundert. Bericht über neuere italienische Forschungen," *ARG,* XXXVII, 268–89; and by E. W. Zeeden in his "Zeitalter der europäischen Glaubenskämpfe. Gegenreformation und katholische Reform: ein Forschungsbericht," *Saeculum*, VII, 321–68. Interesting insights are also offered in W. Maurer's aforementioned lectures on *Kirche und Synagoge*.

61. F. Pericoli, "L'Abolizione della feudalità negli Stati della Chiesa," *Rivista araldica*, LIV, 100–116 (with special reference to Pius V's bull *Apostolicae servituti officium* of November 17, 1565); M. Stern, *Urkundliche Beiträge*, I, 177 ff. items 39, 44, 46, and 61. On the Portaleone family and its privileged status as Mantuan court physicians see *supra*, Chap. LVI, n. 47; S. Simonsohn's *Toledot . . . Mantovah*, II, 468 ff.; and the sources cited there. The 1636 decision against Guglielmo Portaleone could not have been made without Urban VIII's approval. It marked, indeed, a certain change at the papal court itself, where fewer Jewish physicians functioned after that date. See G. Marini, *Degli archiatri pontifici*, II, *passim*. It may be noted that the David Kaufmann collection (now at the Budapest Academy) includes a MS entitled *Consulti medici di Guglielmo Porta Leone Mantovano [e] d'altri italiani dal MDLXXXII al MDCLXV*. Because of the early initial date in the title, Simonsohn suggested that the author was not Guglielmo, but his grandfather Abraham. However, these consultations, extending over 83 years, came from several authors and may indeed have been compiled by Guglielmo, who died *ca.* 1683. See M. Weisz, *Katalog der hebräischen Handschriften und Bücher in der Bibliothek des Professors Dr. David Kaufmann*, p. 158 No. 458; Simonsohn, II, 470 f. nn. 204–207. It is somewhat surprising that the application for a papal license preceded by some three years the M. D. degree Guglielmo received from Siena with Urban VIII's approval. See L. Luzzatto, "Appunti storici sulla famiglia Portaleone," *Vessillo israelitico*, VI, 154 ff.

62. P. Farinacci *et al.*, eds., *Sacrae Rotae romanae decisionum recentiorum libri*, IV, Part 2, Nos. 194, 269; A. Berliner, *Geschichte*, II, Part 2, p. 30; M. de Maulde, *Les Juifs dans les états français du Saint-Siège*, p. 45 n. 1; A. Bertolotti, "Les Juifs à Rome," *REJ*, II, 284 f., 289; A. Berliner, *Aus den letzten Tagen*, pp. 21 f.; M. Wischnitzer, *A History of Jewish Crafts and Guilds*, pp. 143 f. Despite these grandiloquent assertions of the *Rota*, one basic economic right was increasingly denied to Jews. While legislation in this area was not backed by the same firm and universal tradition as some of the Church's other discriminatory and segregationist provisions, a decree of 1654 could state without much ado that "Jews may not possess immovable property." See the register of the Roman Inquisition, excerpted by M. Stern in his *Urkundliche Beiträge*, I, 181 No. 161 item 66. This prohibition stemmed essentially from Paul IV's bull of 1555. See *infra*, n. 63.

63. Pius IV's ordinance *Cura, sicut accepimus, non sine* of 1559 in *Bullarium Romanum*, VII, 1 ff.; Diego (Jaime) Laynez, *De usura variisque negotiis mercatorum* in H. Grisar's ed. of his *Disputationes tridentinae*, II, 227 ff.; E. Loevinson, "La Concession des banques de prêts aux Juifs par les papes des seizième et dix-septième siècles. Contribution à l'histoire des finances d'Italie," *REJ*, XCII, 1–30; XCIII, 27–52, 157–78; XCIV, 57–72, 167–83; XCV, 23–43; E. Rodocanachi, *Le Saint-Siège*, pp. 246, 251, 259 ff.; H. Vogelstein and P. Rieger, *Geschichte*, II, 184, 209; V. Franchini, "La Congregazione 'De usuris' in Roma," *Economia*, n.s. VIII, 413–23; A. Bertolotti, "Les Juifs à Rome," *REJ*, II, 284 f., 289; L. Poliakoff's general survey in "La Communauté juive à Rome aux XVIe et XVIIe siècles," *Annales ESC*, XII, Part 1, pp. 119–22 (referring to the considerable amount of Jewish economic

material preserved in extant notarial registers in Rome and citing an anonymous pamphlet *Il Vero stato degli Ebrei in Roma,* published in 1668 probably by a convert, which states that the Roman Jewish community had a floating debt of no less than 250,000 scudi); and, more fully, in *Les "Banchieri" juifs et le Saint-Siège;* and *supra,* Vol. XII, pp. 167 ff., 176 f., 325 nn. 41–42, 330 n. 51. See also M. Venard, "Catholicisme et usure au XVIe siècle," *Revue d'histoire de l'Église de France,* LII, 59–74; and, more generally, such recent analyses as W. Friedberger, *Der Reichtumserwerb im Urteil des Hl. Thomas von Aquin und der Theologen im Zeitalter des Frühkapitalismus;* and G. Barbieri, "L'Etica economica cristiana ed il Concilio di Trento," *Economia e storia* (Milan), XI, 345–455. The gradual evolution of some of the *monti di pietà* into regular banking establishments is well analyzed by G. Garrani in *Il Carattere bancario e l'evoluzione strutturale dei primigenii Monti di pietà. Riflessi della tecnica bancaria antica su quella moderna.*

Side by side with the few wealthy bankers (for instance, one Moisè Misano who is mentioned in 1607 as owning hundreds of precious jewels and stones) lived the large poverty-stricken majority of Roman Jews. See C. Trasselli, "Un Ufficio notarile per gli Ebrei di Roma (secoli XVI e XVII)," *Archivio* of the R. Deputazione romana di storia patria, LX, 231–44, esp. pp. 235 f., 238 f., 243 f. App. (reproducing, among other documents, the text of a 1575 concession to a German Jewish banker, Benjamin Samuel Zadich, to fill a vacancy in the customary group of forty Jewish moneylenders). Interesting sidelights are shed by A. Milano in "The Private Life of a Family of Jewish Bankers at Rome in the Sixteenth Century," *JQR,* XXX, 149–86 (based on notarial records of the Toscano banking family for the years 1614–61; an Italian version of that essay appeared in *RMI,* XIV, 260–67, 303–311, 359–68, 396–406). See also idem, "Ricerche sulle condizioni economiche degli Ebrei a Roma durante la clausura nel ghetto (1555–1848)," *RMI,* V, 445–65, 545–66, 629–50; VI, 52–73, 159–68; M. Tosi, *Il Sacro Monte di Pietà di Roma;* and, more generally, H. Lapeyre, "Banque et crédit en Italie du XVIe au XVIIIe siècle," *Revue d'histoire moderne et contemporaine,* VIII, 211–26; E. Werner, *Pauperes Christi. Studien zu sozial-religiösen Bewegungen im Zeitalter des Reformpapsttums;* and J. Delumeau, *Vie économique et sociale de Rome dans la seconde moitié du XVIe siècle,* esp. I, 214 ff., 281. Nor should we overlook the role played in economic, even more than political, matters by the Roman city council, which sometimes altogether supplanted the papal authorities, particularly in periods of the Papacy's weakness. See the succinct observations by S. Rebecchini in his lecture on *Il 'Magistrato' di Roma dal secolo XII al 1870.*

64. E. Natali, *Il Ghetto di Roma,* I, *passim;* E. Amadei, "Gli Ebrei a Roma," *Capitolium,* VIII, 253–60; the comprehensive *Raccolta di costituzioni pontificie, sentenze, decisioni, voti e pareri concernenti il Gius di Gazagà degli Israeliti sulle case del Già Ghetto di Roma;* A. Baccelli, "Brevi note intorno al carattere del 'Jus di gazagà' in Roma," *Legge,* XXXII, Part 1, pp. 712–20; M. Finzi, "Il Diritto di hazaká," *Festschrift . . . Berliner,* pp. 93–96; U. della Seta's Roman dissertation, *L'Origine e la natura giuridica del diritto di gazzagà* (typescript); V. Campajola, "Il Ghetto di Roma (Studio urbanistico e ambientale)," *Quaderni* of the Istituto di Storia dell'Architettura, 1965, Nos. 67–70; B. Colonna, "Una Gloria di Casa Caetani; l'apertura del ghetto," *Urbis,* 1952, Nos. 9–10, pp. 33–38; and, more generally, A. Milano's comprehensive description of *Il Ghetto di Roma. Illustrazioni storiche;* and *supra,* Vol. IX, pp. 48 f., 263 n. 54, etc. On Toscano's will see A. Milano, "The Private Life," *JQR,* XXX, 149–86, esp. p. 186 App. i. See also F. Gregorovius's dis-

tinguished older *History of the City of Rome in the Middle Ages,* trans. from the 4th German edition by A. Hamilton, particularly the section dealing with *The Ghetto and the Jews of Rome,* trans. by M. Hadas; and the more recent voluminous *Storia di Roma,* published by the Istituto di Studi Romani, which includes Vols. XII: *Roma nel Rinascimento* by P. Paschini; and XIII: *Roma nel Cinquecento* by P. Pecchiai.

On the growth of the Jewish population see J. Delumeau, *Vie économique,* I, 214 ff., 281, giving the data for 1592. The presence of 3,500 Jews in that year contrasts with a figure of 500 at the beginning of the century, and of some 1,750 within a total population of 55,035 enumerated in 1526-27. The general population grew in the seventeenth century to little more than 130,000. See D. Gnoli, "*Descriptio Urbis* o censimento della popolazione di Roma avanti il sacco Borbonico [1526-27]," *Archivio* of the R. Società Romana di storia patria, XVII, 375-520, esp. pp. 384 (quoting from the MS of Marcello Alberini's *Discorso del sacco di Roma*), 496 ff. relating to the district of Santo Angelo; and, for the later period, F. Cerasoli, "Censimento della popolazione di Roma dall'anno 1600 al 1739," *Studi e documenti di storia e diritto,* XII, 169-99 (based upon a MS stemming from the Jesuit Collegio Romano and on other unpublished records), esp. p. 177, where the various ups and downs of the Roman population, ranging from 111,727, to 116,454 in 1623-29, may have reflected inadequacies of enumeration more than actual declines; L. Pastor, *The History,* XXIX, 376; and, more generally, K. J. Beloch, *Bevölkerungsgeschichte Italiens,* II, 8 ff.

An interesting description of Jewish life in the Roman ghetto is offered by A. Milano in "L'Interno di due case private nel ghetto di Roma del seicento," *RMI,* XXIV, 366-78, reproducing, largely from the synagogue archives of the Scòla Nova, a number of documents, including an inventory taken of the estate of one Giacomo Viterbo in 1631. Though a member of a wealthy banking family, Viterbo lived in a two-room apartment, overstuffed with furnishings of all kinds. See also P. L. Bruzzone's "Documents" in *REJ,* XIX, 131-40; and, on the two other communities, C. Ciavarini, *Memorie storiche degli Israeliti in Ancona;* and J. de Dianous, "Les Communautés juives du Comtat Venaissin et de l'état d'Avignon d'après leurs statuts (1490-1790)," summarized in the *Positions des thèses* of the École Nationale des Chartes, 1938, pp. 31-36; idem, "Les Juifs d'Avignon et du Comtat Venaissin de 1490 à 1790," *ibid.,* 1939, pp. 53-59. By analyzing a number of statutes enacted by the communities of the Comtat, those two theses effectively supplement the information given in the broader treatments by L. Bardinet, M. de Maulde, and A. Mossé.

65. M. Stern, *Urkundliche Beiträge,* I, 176 f. No. 161, item 41. It is small wonder that, beginning with Paul IV, the Papacy evinced great sympathy for the movement toward *limpieza* in Spain. See *supra,* n. 14; Chap. LVI, n. 28; and *infra,* Chap. LXV.

CHAPTER LX: ITALIAN CONFORMITY

1. U. Cassuto, *Gli Ebrei a Firenze nell'età di Rinascimento,* pp. 98 ff., 385 f. Apps. xxvii–xxviii; Pius V's statement in D. Mellini's *Ricordi intorno ai costumi, azioni, e governo del serenissimo Gran Duca Cosimo I,* Intro. pp. ix f.; V. Bibl, "Die

Erhebung Herzog Cosimos von Medici zum Grossherzog von Toskana und die kaiserliche Anerkennung (1569–1576)," *Archiv für österreichische Geschichte,* CIII, 1–162; L. Carcereri, *Cosimo Primo Granduca.* Ironically, it was the New Christian Jesuit Francisco de Toledo who, in 1572, was sent by the pope to secure from Maximilian II the confirmation of Cosimo's new title. The emperor at first resisted, but three years later he finally gave his seal of approval. See G. Cozzi, "Un Documento sulla crisi della 'Sacra Lega,'" *Archivio Veneto,* 5th ser. LXVII, 76–96. See also *supra,* Chap. LIX, n. 54; and *infra,* n. 4.

2. S. Caponetto, "Due relazioni inedite dell'ambasciatore Montino del Monte," *Studia Oliveriana,* I, 25 ff.; G. Luzzatto, *I Banchieri ebrei in Urbino nell'età ducale,* esp. pp. 45 f., 55 ff.; U. Cassuto, "La Comunità di Senigaglia attraverso i secoli," *Settimana israelitica* of August 30, 1912. The gradual decline of Pesaro's Jewish population, which was accelerated in the eighteenth and nineteenth centuries, is graphically illustrated by the figures presented by C. Mengarelli in "La Popolazione di Pesaro dal 1628 al 1839," *Rivista internazionale di scienze sociali,* XLII, 668–89, esp. pp. 684 ff. The number given for 1656, to be sure, is somewhat less certain even than the other figures because the records failed to mention infants under three years of age and the author had to estimate their number by comparing the data for 1628. The general deficiencies of the extant documents are also demonstrated by the substantial swings in the years 1668–79. But that Pesaro never again embraced more than 600 Jewish souls seems indubitable.

Nonetheless, because of its relative antiquity and long-time cultural eminence (it had included distinguished scholars and writers, even a Jewish dancing master, in the fifteenth century), Pesaro ranked highest among the Jewish communities of the duchy. As late as 1696, the Roman elders addressed to it a plaintive letter in which they claimed, among other matters, that their community counted only ten wealthy families, contrasting with 6,000 "barefoot and ragged paupers." See O. Kinkeldey, "A Jewish Dancing Master of the Renaissance (Guglielmo Ebreo)," *Freidus Mem. Vol.,* pp. 329–72; and A. Berliner, ed., "A Letter Addressed by the Roman Community to the Elders of Pesaro" (Hebrew), *Qobeṣ 'al yad,* XIX, 68–71. See also the continuation of Joseph ha-Kohen's *'Emeq ha-bakha,* p. 140; in Wiener's German trans., p. 114.

3. The Bolognese proverb, cited with special reference to Cardinal Benedetto Giustiniani's administration by L. Frati in "La Legazione del card. Benedetto Giustiniani a Bologna dal 1606 al 1611," *Giornale ligustico di archeologia,* XIV, 114 f.; L. Pastor, *The History,* XXV, 85; V. Rava, "Gli Ebrei in Bologna," *Educatore israelita,* XX, 237–42, 295–301, 330–36, esp. pp. 330 ff.; and other literature quoted *supra,* Vol. X, p. 420 n. 61. See also B. Schnapper's general observations in his "Storia e sociologia. Uno studio su Bologna," *Studi storici,* VIII, 550–78. To contemporaries, Pius V's decree of banishment appeared doubly unprecedented, since probably neither the Romans nor the Jews remembered the threat of such an expulsion in the days of John XXII (1321–22). As we recall, that threat, if at all serious (the pertinent sources are quite dubious), was quickly averted by the intervention of King Robert of Anjou. See *supra,* Vol. X, pp. 253 f., 412 f. n. 40. On the other hand, Duns Scotus' minority position was kept alive, particularly with reference to the conversion of Jewish children against their parents' will, by jurists such as Ulrich (Udalricus) Zasius and preachers like Bartolommeo Cambi da Salutio,

especially in the latter's much-discussed Mantuan sermon of August 10, 1602. See
F. Sarri, *Il Venerabile Bartolommeo Cambi da Salutio (1557–1617), oratore, mistico,
poeta,* pp. 60 ff., 64 n. 1, 88 ff.; and *infra,* n. 15.

4. E. Cochrane, "The End of the Renaissance in Florence," *BHR,* XXVII, 7–29
(quoting revealing contemporary statements, the self-congratulory tenor of which
shows that the creative era of the Florentine Renaissance was drawing to an end);
U. Cassuto, *Gli Ebrei a Firenze,* pp. 88 ff., 92 ff., 102 ff., 173 ff., 384 ff. Apps. xxvi-
xxviii, xxxi-xli, 409 ff. App. liv; idem, "La Famille des Médicis et les juifs," *REJ,*
LXXVI, 132–45; N. Pavoncello, "Origine e sviluppo della comunità ebraica a Siena,"
Nova Historia, VII, Parts 5 and 6, pp. 31–51; *supra,* n. 1; and *infra,* n. 37. Needless
to say, Cosimo could even less afford to antagonize the pope by admitting Jewish
refugees from the States of the Church or from Urbino. The Jews of Siena petitioning in 1570 for the admission of these unfortunates were told that the state already
had more Jews than was desirable. See Cassuto, *Gli Ebrei,* pp. 104 f.

At the same time, the concessions granted two decades earlier to the Levantine
Jews remained unimpaired. Their commercial usefulness had, indeed, proved so
great that, as we shall see, the grand duchy soon sought to attract many more
easterners to the newly established free ports of Pisa and Leghorn. See *infra,* n. 21;
and, more generally, P. Battara, *La Popolazione di Firenze alla metà del '500;* and
J. Lucas-Debreton, *Daily Life in Florence in the Time of the Medici,* English trans.
by A. L. Sells. Remarkably, neighboring Lucca, once very tolerant toward Jews, now
adamantly refused to admit them. The only concession the city was willing to
grant in 1572 to a few Jewish visitors was a temporary sojourn of no more than
fifteen days. See also the literature listed *supra,* Vol. X, pp. 421 ff. nn. 64–69.

5. N. Porgès, "Élie Capsali et sa chronique de Venise," *REJ,* LXXVII, 20–40;
LXXVIII, 15–34; LXXIX, 28–60, esp. LXXVIII, 16 ff.; Marino Sanuto, *I Diarii
(MCCCCXCVI-MDXXIII),* ed. from a Venice autograph by F. Stefani, R. Fulin
et al., VIII, 262, 314, 376, 548; IX, 281; XXXIX, 55, 98; XLI, 57. See also the stray
incidents recorded by H. Simonsfeld in *Der Fondaco dei Tedeschi in Venedig und
die deutsch-venetianischen Handelsbeziehungen,* with the brief comments thereon by
D. Kaufmann in his "Notes sur l'histoire des Juifs de Venise," *REJ,* XXI, 289–92;
and the more general local descriptions analyzed in the following studies: L. A.
Schiavi, "Gli Ebrei a Venezia e nelle sue colonie. Appunti storici su documenti editi
e inediti," *Nuova Antologia,* CXXXI, 309–333, 485–519; C. Roth, *Venice* (Jewish
Communities Series), pp. 39 ff.; D. Fortis, "Gli Ebrei di Verona. Cenni storici,"
Educatore israelita, XI, 199–203, 301–305, 392–94; XII, 68–70, 110–12, 209–211; N.
Pavoncello, *Gli Ebrei in Verona (dalle origini al secolo XX);* E. Morpurgo, "Notizie
sulle famiglie ebrei esistenti a Padova nel 16° secolo," *Corriere israelitico,* XLVII,
161–65, 193–97, 229–34, 257–60; idem, "L'Università degli Ebrei di Padova nel XVI
secolo," *Bollettino* of the Museo Civico di Padova, XII, 16–25, 65–75; and some other
literature listed *supra,* Vol. X, pp. 430 f. nn. 84–89. Much can be learned about the
position of Jews from the status of another religious minority, the Greeks, who
formed a sizable colony in the City of the Lagoons. Of course, there also were major
differences between the two groups. See G. Fedalto's recent *Ricerche storiche sulla
posizione giuridica ed ecclesiastica dei Greci in Venezia nei secoli XV e XVI,* esp. pp.
70 ff. Of interest also are such more general treatments as M. Brunetti, "Treviso
fedele a Venezia nei giorni di Cambrai. Documenti inediti su Antonio dal Legname,"

Archivio Veneto, 5th ser. XXIII, 56–82; A. Bonardi, "I Padovani ribelli alla Repubblica di Venezia (a. 1509–1530)," *Miscellanea di storia veneta,* 2d ser. VIII, 303–614, esp. p. 328 (neither in his extensive documentation on the postwar trials of the Paduan rebels, suspects, and émigrés, nor in his long list of names in the Appendix does the author refer to Jews); and C. Gini, *Alcune ricerche demografiche sugli Israeliti in Padova.*

6. Joseph ha-Kohen, *'Emeq ha-bakha,* pp. 148 f., 176 f.; in Wiener's German trans., pp. 120 f., 146; C. Roth, *The House of Nasi: the Duke of Naxos,* pp. 138 ff.; H. Kretschmayr, *Geschichte von Venedig,* III, 22, 30 ff., 48 ff., 70 ff., 577 ff.; and *infra,* nn. 34, 37, and 42; M. L. Gentile, "La Battaglia di Lepanto" in *Studi storici in onore di Gioacchino Volpe,* I, 543–55; C. Roth, *Venice,* pp. 84 ff.; and, particularly, M. Diena, "Rabbi Scelomò Ashkenazÿ e la Repubblica di Venezia. Memoria," *Atti* of the Istituto Veneto di scienze, LVI, Part 1, pp. 616–37; G. Cozzi, "Un Documento sulla crisi della 'Sacra Lega,'" *Archivio Veneto,* 5th ser. LXVII, 83 f. n. 4. See also the exaggerating report of the English agent in Paris, Pietro Bizarri (or Bizarro), to Lord William Cecil Burghley on July 7, 1573, in A. J. Crosby, ed., *Calendar of State Papers, Foreign Series of the Reign of Elizabeth, 1572–74,* p. 386 No. 1085. It should be noted, however, that in the midst of the high tension of 1572, the doge did not refuse assistance to a Jewish traveler, Samuel Jacar, who was bringing important letters from Ormuz, Persia, to the emperor. On the background and aftereffects of the Turko-Venetian war, 1571–73, see also L. Serrano, *La Liga de Lepanto entre España, Venezia y la Santa Sede (1570–1573);* A. Tamborra, *Gli Stati italiani, l'Europa e il problema turco dopo Lepanto;* and C. Dionisotti, "La Guerra d'Oriente nella letteratura veneziana del Cinquecento," *Lettere italiane,* XVI, 233–50 (does not refer to any accusations of Jewish treason). The general rivalry between Don Joseph Nasi and Solomon Ashkenazi, their respective diplomatic activities in Poland and elsewhere, and the international repercussions of their internecine conflicts will be discussed more fully in later chapters.

Some communities in the Venetian orbit, however, were destroyed by mob actions, if not by legal fiat. For example, the community of Asolo fell victim to an assault by a company of bandits in 1547. After ten of its members were killed and eight others wounded, the rest fled the inhospitable city and never returned. This event created a considerable sensation and left a permanent impression on local folklore. See C. G. Bernardi, *Pagnan amazza Abràm. La strage degli Ebrei nel 1547 in Asolo e la leggenda del Monforca.*

7. A. Ciscato, *Gli Ebrei in Padova,* pp. 266 ff. Apps. xiv, xv, xvii, xxi; F. Glissenti, *Gli Ebrei nel Bresciano al tempo della dominazione veneta,* esp. pp. 19 ff.; idem, *Nuove ricerche e studi;* A. Gamba, *Gli Ebrei a Brescia nei secoli XV–XVI. Appunti per uno studio storico;* D. Carpi, "Alcune notizie sugli Ebrei a Vicenza (secoli XIV–XVIII)," *Archivio Veneto,* 5th ser. LXVIII, 17–23 (showing that efforts by Jews to establish themselves in the city during the sixteenth and seventeenth centuries, for instance in 1544, were frustrated by the staunch resistance of the local authorities); E. Morpurgo, "Gli Ebrei in Treviso," *Corriere israelitico,* XLVIII, 141–44; 170–72; C. Roth, "La Ricondotta degli Ebrei ponentini. Venezia 1647," *Studi in onore di Gino Luzzatto,* II, 237–44 (also listing texts of similar enactments, published and unpublished, of other dates); *supra,* n. 5; and many of the older sources listed by Morpurgo in his "Bibliografia della storia degli Ebrei nel Veneto," *RI,* VII, 180–

90, 227–32; VIII, 14–29, 68–81, 106–126, 215–29; IX, 49–79, 127–52, 214–30 (incomplete). The two anonymous compilations were published and interpreted by M. A. Shulvass in "A Story of the Misfortunes Which Afflicted [the Jews] in Italy" (Hebrew), *HUCA*, XXII, 1–21; and by I. Sonne in his "Chapters from a Tract on Expulsions" (Hebrew), *ibid.*, pp. 23–44; both subsequently recast and reinterpreted by Sonne in the Appendix to his *Mi-Pavlo ha-rebi'i*, pp. 183 ff.

8. See Joseph ha-Kohen, *'Emeq ha-bakha*, pp. 102, 108 f., 131; in Wiener's German trans., pp. 82, 87 f., 106 f.; P. León Tello's comments thereon in the intro. to her recent Spanish trans. of that work, p. 17 n. 22; M. Stagliano, "Degli Ebrei in Genova," *Giornale ligustico di archeologia*, III, 173–86, 394–415, esp. pp. 179 ff.; G. Musso, "Per la storia degli Ebrei nella Repubblica di Genova tra il Quattro e il Cinquecento," *Miscellanea storica ligure*, III, 102–128, 203–225; idem, "Per la storia degli Ebrei nella seconda metà del Cinquecento," *Scritti in Memoria di Leone Carpi. Saggi sull'Ebraismo italiano*, ed. by Daniel Carpi *et al.*, pp. 101–111. On Bernardino da Feltre, the vigorous anti-Jewish promoter of the *monti di pietà*, see the literature cited *supra*, Vols. IX, pp. 51 ff., 265 nn. 60–61; XI, pp. 414 f. n. 86; XII, p. 325 n. 41, to which add V. Meneghin's *Documenti vari intorno al B. Bernardino Tomitano da Feltre*. No less inconsistent was Genoa's policy with respect to the Jewish badge in the seventeenth century. See Stagliano, pp. 183 f., 394 ff. On the earlier developments, see *supra*, Vol. X, pp. 278, 424 n. 70; and, more generally, J. Heers, *Gênes au XVe siècle, activité économique et problèmes sociaux (1447–1466)*, esp. pp. 257, 263 f., 561 (the author, who carefully reviewed the archival records of the period, attests "the complete absence of Jews. They never appear in either the official documents or in private contracts"); and V. Vitale, *Breviario della storia di Genova. Lineamenti storici ed orientamenti biografici*, esp. I, 173 ff., 300; II, 82.

9. See the extensive data supplied by C. Invernizzi in his "Gli Ebrei a Pavia," *Bollettino* of the Società Pavese di storia patria, V, 191–240, 281–319, esp. pp. 281 ff.; the colored interpretation of these events by E. Rota in "Gli Ebrei e la politica spagnola in Lombardia. I banchi pubblici nel ducato milanese," *ibid.*, VI, 349–82; M. Stern's *Urkundliche Beiträge*, I, 117 ff.; L. Fumi, "L'Inquisizione romana e lo stato di Milano. Saggio di ricerche nell'Archivio di Stato," *AS Lombardo*, XXXVII, Part 1, pp. 299 f., 317 f., 378 ff.; E. Verga, "Il Municipio di Milano e l'Inquisizione di Spagna, 1563," *ibid.*, XXIV, Part 2, pp. 86–127 (includes Pius IV's bull *Quanto Charissimus* and two letters from the municipality, all of August and October 1563; pp. 119 ff.); A. Ratti (later Pope Pius XI), ed., *Acta Ecclesiae Mediolanensis*, I; and other data supplied by M. Bendiscioli in his "Politica, amministrazione e religione nell'età dei Borromei" in the comprehensive and beautifully printed *Storia di Milano*, ed. by G. Treccani degli Alfieri *et al.*, X, 3–350, esp. pp. 143 f., 256 ff., 299 ff. On the burning of rabbinic books in the duchy see *infra*, n. 58. Although the fairly liberal privilege granted on November 20, 1533, for a period of eight years by the last independent duke of Milan, Francesco II Sforza, appears not to have been formally renewed by the Spanish administration, its provisions seem to have been largely observed in the duchy for many years. See S. Simonsohn, "Un Privilegio di Francesco II Sforza agli Ebrei del Ducato di Milano," *Scritti in Memoria di Sally Mayer*, pp. 308–324. See also *infra*, n. 43. Moreover, while insisting on the application of the segregationist and discriminatory postulates of the traditional canon law, Borromeo and the synods also urged Christians not to interfere with the observance

of Jewish festivals and synagogue worship. On the other hand, in 1576 a Rabbi Eliezer of Cremona was arrested on Philip II's order for his alleged attacks on the Christian religion and Christian princes. See also the more detailed researches by C. Bonetti, *Gli Ebrei a Cremona, 1278–1630. Note ed appunti;* I. Bianchi, *Sulle tipografie ebraiche di Cremona nel secolo XVI, col ragguaglio di un salterio ebraico stampato in detta città nel secolo medesimo. Dissertazione storico-critica,* esp. pp. 46 ff.; and *infra*, n. 11. Incidentally, it may be of interest to mention that the Italian term *ragguaglio* may be derived from the Hebrew root *galah*. According to the distinguished sixteenth-century Italian linguist Lodovico Castelvetro, Roman clerics may have overheard Jews of the Roman ghetto using it in some form, and introduced it into the living speech of their Christian compatriots. Although this hypothesis seems to reflect more the passionate interest of Renaissance scholars in Hebrew idioms than an historical fact, it is still seriously entertained by such modern specialists as Carlo Battisti and Giovanni Alessio in their *Dizionario etimologico italiano*, published by the Istituto di Glottologia, V, 3197 f.

10. N. Ferorelli, "Supplica degli Ebrei e pareri del Senato sulla loro permanenza nel Milanese verso la metà del secolo XVI," *Vessillo israelitico*, LXIII, 237–38, 337–39; A. G. [Alessandro Giulini], "Una Dama milanese conservatrice della nazione degli Ebrei nello Stato di Milano," *AS Lombardo*, XLV, 581–82; and other literature listed *supra*, Vol. X, pp. 426 ff. nn. 74–79. Remarkably, in 1558 Philip II even refused to impose a higher tax on the Jewish residents of the duchy as demanded by some local advisers. See also, more generally, L. Bulferetti, "Documenti di storia lombarda dei secoli XVI e XVII negli archivi di Spagna," *AS Lombardo*, LXXXI–LXXXII, 319–70; and L. Papini, *Il Governatore dello Estado di Milano (1535–1706)*, esp. pp. 147 ff.

11. E. Motta, "Pasquinate e censura in Milano nel '500," *AS Lombardo*, XXXVIII, 305–315, esp. pp. 308 f.; A. de Maddalena, "Malcostume e disordine amministrativo nello stato di Milano alla fine del '500," *ibid.*, XC, 261–72, esp. pp. 271 f.; and L. Fumi, "L'Inquisizione romana e lo stato di Milano," *ibid.*, XXXVII, Part 1, pp. 288 ff. It is noteworthy that Philip II resisted the demand of the burghers of Alessandria and Lodi to expel the Jews, although it was supported by the papal nuncio. See the documents preserved in the Spanish archive in Simanca, alluded to by L. Bulferetti in his "Documenti," *ibid.*, LXXXI–LXXXII, 337 No. 408 (2042). According to the testimony submitted by a canon of the Milan Cathedral at the hearings on Borromeo's beatification in Rome, the cardinal during his tenure of office in the archbishopric had been considered "another pope . . . for he had so much power that we had no need to refer to Rome in any matter." See P. Prodi, "Charles Borromée, archevêque de Milan et la Papauté," *RHE*, LXII, 383; M. Bendiscioli, "Politica," in *Storia di Milano*, ed. by G. Treccani degli Alfieri *et al.*, X, esp. pp. 299 ff. Yet the Spanish governors often vigorously resisted Borromeo's encroachments, with the result that one governor was excommunicated by the archbishop. But the ensuing rift between the Church and Philip II was soon healed and the king became Borromeo's ardent admirer, although in the end the archbishop had to relinquish much of his traditional ecclesiastical autonomy and to promise close cooperation with the state authorities. See P. Prodi, "San Carlo Borromeo e le trattative tra Gregorio XIII e Filippo II sulla giurisdizione ecclesiastica," *RSCI*, XI, 195–240, esp. pp. 235 ff. Nos. i–iii; L. Papini, *Il Governatore dello Estado di Milano (1535–1706)*,

pp. 122 ff., 227 *ad* 1596, etc.; and the extensive materials on the two protagonists supplied in such recent publications as A. Sala's *Documenti circa la vita e le gesta di San Carlo Borromeo;* C. Orsenigo, *Life of St. Charles Borromeo,* English trans. by R. Kraus, esp. pp. 154 ff.; and C. Petrie, *Philip II of Spain.*

12. The continuation of Joseph ha-Kohen's *'Emeq ha-bakha,* pp. 158 ff.; in Wiener's German trans., pp. 129 ff.; the essays by Invernizzi, Rota, and Fumi cited *supra,* nn. 9–10; C. Z. Dimitrovsky, "The History of the Jews in the Duchy of Milan before the Expulsion of 1597" (Hebrew), *Talpioth,* VI, 336–45, 708–22 (contributing interesting biographical and social data); idem, "From the History of the Jews in Italy" (Hebrew), *Zion,* XX, 175–81, esp. pp. 179 ff. (on the Jews of Lodi after the expulsion of 1597); C. Bonetti, *Gli Ebrei a Cremona, 1278–1630;* S. Foa, "Gli Ebrei in Alessandria," *RMI,* XXIII, 547–56; XXIV, 121–29, 181–87, 215–20, 320–24, 463–71. In some smaller provincial communities Philip II's order of expulsion was more immediately effective. In Verolanuova, for instance, where the *capitoli* with a Jewish banker had been renewed in 1559, Borromeo's sponsorship of a *monte di pietà* in 1580 helped to remove the main reason for keeping the Jewish settlement. In 1591 the few remaining Jews left the town, and no organized Jewish community existed there ever after. See P. Guerrini, "Gli Ebrei a Verolanuova," *AS Lombardo,* XLV, 549 f. Curiously, during the last stages of negotiation about their exodus from the duchy, the Jews received some protection from the inquisitors of Lodi. Upon Carranza's denunciation, the city authorities seized a number of Hebrew works, but they were immediately censured by the local inquisitor for unlawfully interfering in religious matters, which lay in the exclusive domain of the Inquisition. Ultimately, nevertheless, these books were consigned to the flames on March 17, 1597, evidently as part of the final tragedy of Milanese Jewry. See Joseph ha-Kohen, pp. 158 ff. One wonders what assistance Simone Cohen Sacerdote received in his mission from Joseph Serfatim, Alvaro Mendes' envoy, then in Madrid. See *infra,* Chap. LXIV.

13. See P. Kandler's ed. of the "Capitoli del 1588 con banchieri ebrei per Trieste," *Istria,* III, 174–75. Trieste's Jewish population evidently was too small for the establishment of a formal ghetto before 1684. See R. Curiel, "Le Origini del ghetto di Trieste," *RMI,* VI, 440–72. On the general situation, see also *supra,* Vol. XI, pp. 193 ff.

14. H. Vogelstein and P. Rieger, *Geschichte der Juden in Rom,* II, 164; *supra,* Chap. LIX, nn. 49 and 54; L. Cantini, ed., *Legislazione toscana,* VI, 341; S. Simonsohn, *Toledot ha-Yehudim be-dukhsut Mantovah* (History of the Jews in the Duchy of Mantua), I, 19, 36 f., 92 f.

15. F. Sarri, *Il Venerabile Bartolommeo da Salutio,* pp. 58 ff., 64 ff., 189 ff.; S. Simonsohn, *Toledot,* I, 25 ff.; and *supra,* n. 3. The incident with the Mantuan preacher nevertheless left behind seven Jewish victims. Allegedly having parodied the preacher's delivery, they were condemned for ridiculing the Christian faith as such and were hanged by their feet. See the nearly contemporary woodcut reproduced by Simonsohn, I, 26.

Conditions in Mantua and in the neighboring Venetian possessions were not wholly typical of the entire Peninsula, however. Because of the proximity to the Holy Roman Empire and the ensuing influences of rising Protestantism, there were important modifications in both the method and the extent of the Catholic Restoration. See L. B. Nizzola, "Infiltrazioni protestanti nel Ducato di Mantova (1530–1563)," *Bollettino storico mantovano*, 1956, pp. 102–130, 258–86; with an "Appendice di documenti inediti," *ibid.*, 1957, pp. 205–228. On the general cruelty, combined with some flexibility, in regard to penalties for political crimes of the period see M. E. Wolfgang, "Political Crimes and Punishments in Renaissance Florence," *Journal of Criminal Law and Police Science*, XLIV, 555–81. See also U. Cassuto's article cited *infra*, n. 66. Such anti-Jewish feelings manifested themselves not only in governmental enactments and popular riots but also primarily in the large controversial literature, on which see *infra*, nn. 62–64.

16. See V. Colorni, *Gli Ebrei nel sistema del diritto comune fino alla prima emancipazione*, pp. 34 f.; idem, *Legge ebraica e leggi locali*, pp. 367 ff. Apps. i–ii; C. Roth, "Josef da Fano, il primo ebreo italiano nobile," *RMI*, XIV, 190–94; idem, "A Mantuan Jewish Consortium and the Election to the Throne of Poland in 1587" (Hebrew), *Baer Jub. Vol.*, pp. 291–96 (includes a reconstruction of the badly preserved Hebrew partnership agreement, based on the Italian translation probably submitted to the duke); and Simonsohn, *Toledot*, I, 23 f., 82 f. Simonsohn points out that Joseph da Fano neither was the first Jew raised to the rank of the nobility in Italy nor bore the title of marquis. But one must bear in mind that, just as Italian "citizenship" did not mean the same thing in the sixteenth century as it does in the twentieth, so "nobility" then carried with it but few of the prerogatives of medieval feudal lordship. See also *supra*, Vol. XI, pp. 14 ff., 292 f. nn. 13 ff.; Chap. LVII, n. 30; and this chapter, n. 15.

17. L. Modona, "Les Exilés d'Espagne à Ferrare en 1493," *REJ*, XV, 117–21; A. Milano, "Documenti sui banchieri ebrei a Modena nel secolo XVI," *RMI*, XI, 450–55 (summarizing two newly discovered documents recording *capitoli*—and their renewals in 1527–79—between the dukes and the Jewish bankers; also mentioning the severe punishment inflicted upon one such banker in 1600 until he paid his debt of 20,000 scudi); and particularly, A. Balletti, *Gli Ebrei e gli Estensi*, pp. 75 ff. Of considerable local interest also are such monographs at I. Sonne's ed. of "Eight Sixteenth-Century Letters from Ferrara" (Hebrew), *Zion*, XVII, 145–56 (with noteworthy historical interpretations); and A. Solerti, *Il Terremoto di Ferrara nel 1570* (a description of an earthquake which, among its other effects, inspired Azariah de' Rossi to engage in his momentous literary career in Jewish historiography); S. Sterra, "Un Privilegio di Alfonso II d'Este ad Ebrei," *Scritti sull'ebraismo in memoria di Guido Bedarida*, pp. 271–81 (in addition to the text of a 1587 privilege for two Jewish provincial bankers, the author supplies interesting data on taxes paid by the Jews of Ferrara and on occasional manifestations of popular hostility toward them). See also A. Pesaro, *Memorie storiche sulla Comunità israelitica ferrarese*, esp. pp. 18 ff.; and his *Appendice* thereto; *supra*, Vol. X, pp. 268 ff., 421 n. 62; and, more generally, A. Solerti, *Ferrara e la Corte estense nella seconda metà del secolo decimosesto; I Discorsi di Annibale Romei;* the biographical sketches of *Gli Estensi* by L. Chiappini; and *supra*, Chap. LIX, nn. 46 and 53.

Among the variegated intellectual activities of the Ferrara community, which will be discussed here in their respective contexts, the work performed mainly by Marrano scholars in preparing a new Spanish translation of the Bible is of special interest. It appeared in two different editions in 1553, one for the use of Jews, the other for Christians. See, for instance, M. Morreale's comparative study of "La Biblia de Ferrara y el Pentateuco de Constantinopla," *Oṣar Yehude Sefarad* (*Tesoro de los Judíos Sefardíes*), V, pp. lxxxv–xci; and C. Roth, "The Marrano Press at Ferrara, 1552–1555," *Modern Language Review*, XXXVIII, 307–317.

18. A Balletti, *Gli Ebrei*, pp. 105 ff. According to this author, sometime during the sixteenth century the custom arose of extending to the Jews in the Este possessions *capitoli* of limited duration; this was indeed the prevailing usage in the other Italian states and cities. But apparently no one seriously questioned the renewal of the *capitoli* every ten years.

19. A. Pesaro, *Memorie storiche*, pp. 35 ff.; G. Pardi, *Sulla popolazione del Ferrarese dopo la devoluzione;* L. Pastor, *The History of the Popes*, XXIV, 382 ff., 415 ff.; A. Balletti, *Gli Ebrei*, pp. 79 ff.

20. See G. Volli, "Gli Ebrei a Lugo," *Studi romagnoli*, IV, 143–83, esp. pp. 176 f. App. i (reprinted in *RMI*, XXIII, 65–76, 123–36, 178–85); idem, "La Comunità di Cento e un suo documento inedito del 1776," *RMI*, XVII, 205–209. See also the literature listed *supra*, n. 17; and *infra*, n. 75.

21. U. Cassuto, *Gli Ebrei*, pp. 89 f.; Alfredo Segré, *Ebrei, industria e commercio in Pisa nei secoli XVII e XVIII;* G. (Joseph) Müller, *Documenti sulle relazioni delle città toscane coll'Oriente cristiano e coi Turchi fino all'anno MDXXXI;* and R. Toaff, "Il 'Libro Nuovo' di statuti della Nazione Ebrea di Pisa (1637)," *Scritti sull'ebraismo in memoria di Guido Bedarida*, pp. 227–62 (with a brief historical sketch). The history of the Jews of Leghorn has never received the comprehensive monographic treatment it deserves. For the time being see A. S. Toaff, "Cenni storici sulla comunità ebraica e sulla sinagoga di Livorno," *RMI*, XXI, 355–68, 411–26 (also reprint); G. Bedarida, *Ebrei di Livorno. Tradizioni e gergo in 180 sonetti giudaico-livornesi;* E. Loevinson, "Le Basi giuridiche della comunità israelitica di Livorno (1593–1787)," *Bollettino storico livornese*, I, 203–208; A. Milano, "Le Esequie di un rabbino a Livorno nel seicento," *Annuario di Studi Ebraici*, [III], 65–68 (compares the 1680 funeral conducted with considerable pomp for a Leghorn rabbi with the far more restrained rites for a rabbi of Rome in 1730). On the economic activities of Leghorn Jewry, see, for instance, F. Braudel and R. Romano, *Navires et marchandises à l'entrée du port de Livourne, 1547–1611*, pp. 26–28; and *infra*, n. 37.

22. See C. Roth, "I Marrani di Livorno, Pisa e Firenze," *RMI*, VII, 394–415, esp. p. 411; A. Milano, *Storia degli Ebrei in Italia*, pp. 322 ff.; G. Pardi, *Disegno della storia demografica di Livorno*, pp. 24 ff., 31 ff., 34, 37; G. Bedarida, *Ebrei di Livorno;* G. Tavani, "Appunti sul giudeo-portughese di Livorno," *Annali* of the Istituto Universitario Orientale in Naples, Romance section, I, Part 2, pp. 61–99; *supra*, Vol. II, pp. 206, 405 n. 38; I. Rignano, *La Università israelitica di Livorno e le opere pie da essa amministrate.* See also, more generally, the statistical data, in part restating older historical facts, in the "Bollettino statistico," prepared under the auspices of the Leghorn municipality and appended to various issues of the *Rivista di Livorno;* for instance, IX (1959); G. Vivoli, *Annali di Livorno dalla sua origine sino all'anno di Gesù Cristo 1840*, Vols. I–V; G. G. Guarnieri, *Il Porto di Livorno e la sua funzione economica dalle origini ai tempi nostri; contributo alla storia della*

marina e del commercio d'Italia; idem, *Livorno e la sua elevazione al rango di "città." Studio storico-critico;* M. Baruchello, *Livorno e il suo porto. Origini, caratteristiche e vicende dei traffici livornesi.* Much unpublished material is still available in the local archives, for which we now possess a valuable guide in the publication by the State Archives of B. Casini, ed., *Archivi di Stato di Livorno, Guida-Inventario.*

23. G. B. Borelli, comp., *Editti antichi e nuovi de' sovrani principi de la Real Casa di Savoia,* pp. 1226 ff.; F. A. Duboin, *Raccolta per ordine di materie delle leggi, editti, manifesti, ecc. . . . , pubblicati dal principio dell'anno 1681 sine all' 8 dicembre 1798, sotto il felicissimo dominio della Real Casa di Savoia, in continuazione a quella del Senatore Borelli,* II, 602, 604 ff., 617, 620, 623; J. Decourcelle, *La Condition des Juifs de Nice aux 17e et 18e siècles* (Diss. Aix-en-Provence), pp. 15 ff. Ironically, the city council of Nice was to complain on December 30, 1697, that "the Jews enjoy perfect peace, they are not submitted to forced labor, military service, billeting of troops, nor any other personal services. Since they are unable to own real estate, their usurious rents are not subject to storms, inundations, or devastation." In fact, the inability of Nice Jewry to own land was a relatively recent innovation. What Decourcelle writes about earlier prohibitions (pp. 36 ff.) is based upon conjecture rather than clear-cut evidence.

24. J. Decourcelle, *La Condition,* pp. 25 ff.; V. Emanuel, *Les Juifs de Nice (1400–1860);* J. Bergmann, "Gedichte Asaria de Rossi's," *ZHB,* III, 53–58; my *History and Jewish Historians,* pp. 169, 194. See also the literature listed in the next note; and the detailed *Bibliografia Piemontese-Ligure* (covering more than 8,000 alphabetically arranged entries, Nos. 5,001–13,111).

25. Fausto Fonzi, ed., *Nunziature di Savoia,* Vol. I (15 ottobre 1560–29 giugno 1575), pp. xx n. 3, 477 f. No. 502, 483 f. No. 510; Y. (S.) Foa, "The Conflict between the Princes of Savoy and the Pope concerning the Jewish Bankers from Portugal (1573–1581)" (Hebrew), *Eretz-Israel,* III (1954 = D. M. or Umberto Cassuto Mem. Vol.), 240–43; P. L. Bruzzone, "Les Juifs au Piémont," *REJ,* XIX, 141–46; J. L. Bato, "Herzog Emanuele Filiberto und Don Joseph Nassi," *Sefer ha-Yobel le-Natan Michael Gelber* (Jubilee Volume for N. M. G.), pp. 301–304. One of the documents alluded to by Bruzzone, without a date, even granted a Cuneo Jew the right to take a second wife, because his first remained childless (p. 146). See also A. Segré and P. Egidi's biography of *Emanuele Filiberto,* esp. Vol. II by Egidi; the collection of essays published in 1928, under the title *Emanuele Filiberto,* by a committee in charge of the four-hundredth anniversary celebrations of the duke's birth, with an Intro. by C. Rinaudo, esp. pp. 223 ff., 251 ff., 279 ff., 393 ff.; and other early literature analyzed by C. G. Mor in his "Recenti studi su Emanuele Filiberto," *ASI,* LXXXVII, 77–95.

26. S. Foa, "La Politica economica della Casa Savoia verso gli Ebrei dal secolo XVI fino alla Rivoluzione francese. Il portofranco di Villafranca (Nizza)," *RMI,* XXVII–XXVIII (1961–62); idem, "Banchi e banchieri ebrei nel Piemonte dei secoli scorsi," *ibid.,* XXI, 38–50, 85–97, 127–36, 190–201, 284–97, 325–36, 471–85, 520–35; idem, *Gli Ebrei nel Monferrato nei secoli XVI e XVII;* J. Decourcelle, *La Condition,* p. 18; and, more generally, G. Volino, *Condizione giuridica degli Israeliti*

in Piemonte prima dell'emancipazione; supra, Vol. X, pp. 278 ff., 425 f. nn. 71–73. See also *infra*, n. 40. Emmanuel Philibert also encouraged the settlement of Jewish physicians in his country. As early as June 10, 1561, that is, a year after the intended expulsion of all Jews, he extended a privilege to one Leone di Emanuele, doctor of medicine and philosophy—of whose "virtue, science, learning, experience, and other fine qualities" the duke had been informed—granting him the right to settle together with his family and possessions in any part of Piedmont. Among other doctors, one Leone Ascoli distinguished himself by his service during a pestilence. He attended many patients and even supplied them with drugs free of charge, for which he was praised by Catherine of Spain, the wife of Charles Emmanuel I, and rewarded with a privilege to open a bank in Nice (July 10, 1591). See S. Foa, "Ebrei medici in Piemonte nei secoli XVI e XVII," *RMI*, XIX, 542–51.

27. See V. Colorni, "Prestito ebraico e comunità ebraiche nell'Italia centrale e settentrionale. Con particolare riguardo alla comunità di Mantova," *Rivista di storia del diritto italiano*, VIII, 406–458; E. Castelli, "I Banchi feneratizi ebraici nel Mantovano (1386–1808)," *Atti e memorie* of the Accademia Virgiliana di Mantova, n.s. XXXI, 1–323; G. Amadei and F. Salvadori, *Gli Ebrei ed il loro soggiorna in Mantova. Scienza, storia, statistica;* P. Norsa, *Una Famiglia di banchieri; la famiglia Norsa (1350–1950);* L. Carnevali, *Gli Israeliti a Mantova. Cenni storici;* and, particularly, S. Simonsohn, *Toledot ha-Yehudim be-dukhsut Mantovah*, esp. I, 78 ff., 144 ff.; *supra*, nn. 16 and 26; and Vol. X, pp. 287 ff., 429 f. nn. 82–83. Among the provisions of the privileges was also protection from prosecutions by the Inquisition, even if the bankers should be accused of transgressions against the Christian faith. Moreover, no convert from Judaism was to serve as a witness against any such banker. Simonsohn, I, 82. See also, more generally, G. Coniglio, L. Mazzoldi *et al.*, eds. of the well-documented work *Mantova, La Storia*, with Forewords by M. Bendiscioli and others, esp. Vol. III, pp. 31 ff.; and R. Quazza, *Mantova attraverso i secoli.*

28. S. Simonsohn, *Toledot, passim;* and *supra*, Chap. LVII, n. 20. In 1569 a Mantuan court discussed the problem of the penalties to be imposed upon the culprits in intergroup sex relations. While one judge advocated the death penalty, the majority insisted that no one had ever been executed for that transgression in Mantua. See also A. de Maddalena, *Le Finanze del Ducato di Mantova all'epoca di Guglielmo Gonzaga*, esp. pp. 157 ff. Apps. i–ii, reproducing detailed data regarding the Treasury's revenues and expenditures in 1554 and 1577.

29. M. Stern, *Urkundliche Beiträge*, I, 122 No. 116, 146 No. 137; A. Milano, "Un'Azienda di banchieri e provveditori ebrei alla corte dei Gonzaga Nevers nel Seicento," *RMI*, XXVIII, 181–202 (includes interesting documentary excerpts, for 1543–47 and later years, from a Casale archive); and *infra*, Chap. LXII, n. 39. See also, more generally, C. Roth, *The Jews in the Renaissance, passim;* and M. A. Shulvass, *Ḥayye ha-Yehudim be-Italiah*, pp. 19 f. and *passim;* and, particularly, S. Simonsohn's comprehensive and well-documented *Toledot, passim;* supplemented by such studies as his "Books and Libraries of Mantuan Jews, 1595" (Hebrew), *KS*, XXXVII, 103–122 (list compiled as a result of inquisitorial censorship); and *supra*, Chap. LIX, n. 51.

30. F. M. Misson, *Nouveau voyage d'Italie fait en l'année 1688*, with the Supplement of J. Addison, *Remarques . . . dans son voyage d'Italie*, 5th ed., IV, 53, cited by P. Molmenti in his *Venice: Its Individual Growth from the Earliest Beginnings to the Fall of the Republic*, English trans. by H. F. Brown, III, 39 n. 1; and other data analyzed by H. Kretschmayr in his *Geschichte von Venedig*, Vol. III, *passim*. Many interesting sidelights on the internal political and economic conflicts in Venice during the crucial decades of 1571–1630 are shed by G. Cozzi's comprehensive biography of *Il Doge Nicolò Contarini*, and A. Tenerati's observations thereon in his "A Venise, au début du XVIIe siècle. Autour d'un livre de Gaetano Cozzi," *Annales ESC*, XVI, 780–90.

31. Giordano Bruno's sonnet, *Nuova arca di Noé*, cited in Molmenti's *Venice*, III, 3; C. Roth, "La Ricondotta degli Ebrei ponentini; Venezia 1647," *Studi in onore di Gino Luzzatto*, II, 238 n. 3 (also mentioning that in 1582 the Levantine Jewish merchant Caim Baruch tried to secure a reduction of the customs' duties for his merchandise). Sultan Suleiman's Turkish letter of introduction of 1564 is reproduced from the original, preserved in the Archivio di Stato of Venice, in my forthcoming article, "Solomon ibn Ya'ish and Suleiman the Magnificent," to appear in the *Joshua Finkel Jubilee Volume*. The moderately amicable relations between Venice and the Ottoman Empire in the mid-sixteenth century are reflected in "The Turko-Venetian Treaty of 1540," analyzed by T. F. Jones in the American Historical Association's *Annual Review for 1914*, I, 159–67. On Alvaro Mendes (Solomon ibn Ya'ish) and his important activities for both England and the Ottoman Empire, see esp. L. Wolf, *Jews in Elizabethan England: With Appendix of Documents*, pp. 24 ff.; and other sources cited in my article. Needless to say, there was some opposition to the Venetians' "excessive" friendliness toward the Turks, the hereditary enemies of Christendom. But economic and political needs overcame these scruples, even for such a Christian zealot as Pope Paul IV. See H. Pfeffermann, *Die Zusammenarbeit der Renaissancepäpste mit den Türken*, esp. pp. 1 ff., 210 ff., 229 ff.

32. A. Applebaum, "A Venetian Ordinance of 1636" (Hebrew), *Ha-Zofeh*, XII, 268–70 (publishing the text of the ordinance dated Ve-Adar 3, 5396, or March 10, 1636, adopted by Leon da Modena and some thirty elders); C. Roth, "La Ricondotta degli Ebrei ponentini," *Studi . . . Gino Luzzatto*, II, 240 ff. (reproducing the text of that renewal from "a splendidly-engrossed copy on parchment" preserved in the New York Public Library); *infra*, nn. 33 and 75. Congregational divisions, based largely on the members' different countries of origin, with their diverse rituals—as exemplified in ancient Rome's thirteen synagogues and in early modern Rome's *cinque scuole*, accommodated in one building of the newly erected ghetto—were a characteristic feature of many areas and periods in Jewish history. See my *The Jewish Community, passim*. This phenomenon will be more fully described in a later chapter devoted to the late medieval and early modern communal developments.

33. See G. Cozzi, "Un Documento sulla crisi della 'Sacra Lega,' " *Archivio Veneto*, 5th ser. LXVII, 83 f. n. 4; F. Braudel, *La Méditerranée et le Monde Méditerranéen à l'époque de Philippe II*, pp. 942 ff., 963 ff.; *supra*, nn. 1 and 6; Great Britain, Public Record Office, *Calendar of State Papers*, Foreign, 1572–74, p. 386 (reproducing a

report of July 7, 1573, to Lord William Cecil Burghley); R. Maestro, *L'Attività economica degli Ebrei levantini e ponentini a Venezia dal 1550 al 1700* (typescript); B. Blumenkranz, "Les Juifs dans le commerce maritime de Venise (1592–1609)," *REJ,* CXIX, 143–51; G. Novak, *Židovi u Splitu* (Jews in Split), pp. 12 ff. If we are to accept Blumenkranz's findings, based on an analysis of the records of two Venetian notaries as reproduced and examined by A. Tenenti in his *Naufrages, corsaires et assurances maritimes à Venise 1592–1609,* the role of Jews in the city's maritime commerce during that period was relatively insignificant. Jews appear among those insured to the extent of only about 3.5 percent. Even in shipments to and from Constantinople their share does not exceed 10 percent, while in those to and from Alexandria, Cyprus, etc. it amounts to little more than 1 percent. Only the short-distance trade to Valona and Corfu appears to have been more importantly influenced by Jews. However, these computations, otherwise very valuable, may not accurately reflect the entire situation. Apart from the question of whether the files of the two notaries here analyzed give the total maritime insurances in the city, the Jewish share is based exclusively on identifiable Jewish names. Despite Blumenkranz's valiant efforts, some names may have escaped him. Certainly, some former Marranos, bearing Spanish or Portuguese names, could not be identified as Jews, unless they were known to be such from other sources. Nonetheless, these data effectively warn us against exaggerating the contribution of Jews to the Republic's far-flung maritime trade, at least at the turn of the century.

Of considerable interest also are the autobiographical data supplied by Isaac b. Jacob Levi's *Medabber tahapukhot* (Talking about Perversions; memoirs), ed. by Yehudah (Ludwig) Blau in *Ha-Zofeh,* II, 168–86; III, 45–54, 69–96; Leon (Yehudah Aryeh) da Modena's *Ḥayye Yehudah* (The Life of Judah; an autobiography), ed. with an Intro. and Notes by A. Kahana; his *Briefe und Schriftstücke,* ed. by L. Blau; and his *Resp.,* ed. with an Intro. and Notes by S. Simonsohn. Many interesting data and insights about the situation in Venice in 1638 are supplied by the apologetic work of the Venetian rabbi Simone (Simḥah b. Isaac) Luzzatto in his *Discorso circa il stato de gl'Hebrei et in particolar dimoranti nell'inclita città di Venetia. Et è un appendice al Trattato dell'opinioni e dogmi de gl'Hebrei dall'universal non dissonanti, et de Riti loro più principali,* Venice, 1638 (also in the Hebrew translation by Dan [Dante] Lattes entitled *Ma'amar 'al Yehude Veneṣiah,* with introductions by R. B. Bachi and M. A. Shulvass, ed. by A. Z. Aeścoly). On Luzzatto's population estimates, see *infra,* n. 75. Numerous other sources are analyzed by L. A. Schiavi in "Gli Ebrei in Venezia e nelle sue colonie," *Nuova Antologia,* CXXXI, 309 ff.; C. Roth, *Venice,* esp. pp. 48 ff., 94 ff.; A. Milano, *Storia degli Ebrei,* pp. 276 ff. See also E. Morpurgo's aforementioned "Bibliografia della storia degli Ebrei nel Veneto," *RI,* VII–IX; *supra,* n. 7; and Vol. X, pp. 285 ff., 430 f. nn. 86–88.

34. See the literature listed *supra,* nn. 5–6; and Vol. X, pp. 287, 290 ff., 428 n. 81, 430 nn. 84–85; to which add A. Catalano, " *'Olam hafukh* (The World in Turmoil: a History of the Plague in Padua in the Year 1631)" (Hebrew), ed. by B. (C.) Roth, *Qobeṣ 'al yad,* XIV, 65–101; L. della Torre, "Le Ghetto de Padoue pendant la peste de 1631" (1861), reprinted in his *Scritti sparsi,* II, 300–333; S. Simonsohn, "The Pinkasim [Record Books] of the Jewish Community in Verona" (Hebrew), *KS,* XXXV, 127–36, 250–68; and, more generally, M. Borgherini-Scarabellin, *La Vita privata a Padova del secolo XVI, studio storico documentato ed illustrato.* On Isaac (Fernando) Cardoso and his *Las Excelencias y calunias de los Hebreos,* see Y.

Yerushalmi's *From Spanish Court to Italian Ghetto: Isaac Cardoso, A Study in Seventeenth-Century Marranism and Jewish Apologetics.*

35. M. Stern's *Urkundliche Beiträge*, I, 147 f. No. 138. The papal reply to the Maltese inquiry has apparently not been preserved, but we know from other sources that the Maltese frequently captured Jews and turned them into slaves for sale or ransom. See the examples cited *supra*, Chap. LIX, nn. 47 and 50; M. Benayahu, ed., "R. Shmuel Aboab's Letters to the Palestinian Sages Held Captive in Malta and Messina," *Journal of Maltese Studies*, III, 68–74; and, more generally, B. W. Blouet, *The Story of Malta*, esp. p. 53. On a similar earlier episode on the Italian mainland, see S. Panareo, "Disavventure di Ebrei capitati in Brindisi nel 1547," *Rinascenza salentina*, n.s. III, 26–31. The untrammeled growth of Mediterranean piracy, both Muslim and Christian, became a source of endless tribulations to Venice and other mercantile states; of course, it also greatly affected Jewish travelers. See the numerous illustrations supplied by A. Tenenti in his *Cristoforo da Canal: la Marine vénitienne avant Lépante;* and *infra*, n. 36.

A fuller examination of these new economic trends must be relegated to a later chapter. For the present it will suffice to refer to the following recent studies: A. Dauphin-Meunier, *La Doctrine économique de l'Église;* A. Fanfani, *Catholicism, Protestantism and Capitalism,* English trans. (emphasizing, against Max Weber's well-known thesis, Italy's pre-Reformation contributions to modern capitalism); and other monographs analyzed by him in his "Recenti opinioni sulle origini dell'-economia moderna," *Economia e storia,* II, 245–64 (with special reference to various studies by John Neff); and, more generally, A. Pino-Branca, *La Vita economica degli Stati italiani nei secoli XVI, XVII, XVIII.* See also C. Bauer's *Gesammelte Aufsätze zur Wirtschafts- und Sozialgeschichte;* H. Kellenbenz's stimulating article, "Der Italienische Grosskaufmann und die Renaissance," *VSW,* XLV, 145–67, which have some bearing on Jewish businessmen of the period as well, and A. Norsa's broad observations on "Il Fattore economico nella grandezza e nella decadenza della Repubblica di Venezia," *NRS,* VIII, which apply also to many other Italian territories.

36. The decrees by Dukes Guglielmo and Vincenzo Gonzaga of 1545, 1557–58, 1587, 1590, 1594, etc., are summarized from archival documents by S. Simonsohn in his *Toledot,* I, 190 ff. (also quoting the *Processus Universitatis Hebreorum Mantue contra Artem Sericariorum Mantue*). The extent to which their favorable treatment of Jews was dictated by the strained resources of the Mantuan Treasury is illustrated by A. de Maddalena's aforementioned detailed study of *Le Finanze del Ducato di Mantova all'epoca di Guglielmo Gonzaga.*

37. C. Roth, "La Ricondotta," *Studi . . . Gino Luzzatto,* II, 242; U. Cassuto, *Gli Ebrei,* pp. 173 ff., 409 ff. App. liv; A. Tenenti, *Cristoforo da Canal,* pp. 150 f., 158, 171 nn. 37–38; P. Scrosoppi, "Attività commerciale del porto di Livorno nella prima metà del secolo XVII," *Bollettino storico Livornese,* III, 41–65; G. Cozzi's aforementioned biography of *Il Doge Nicolò Contarini; supra,* nn. 4, 21–22, 33, etc. The admission of Iberian Marrano settlers to Leghorn was later to involve the Tuscan regime in a controversy with Spain. Some ships carrying merchandise belonging to Leghorn Jews were seized in 1694 by the Neapolitan-Sardinian navy, then under the rule of Charles II of Spain, and their cargo was confiscated. Thereupon the Leghorn community persuaded Grand Duke Cosimo III to lodge a protest

in Madrid. The Spanish government not only ordered the release of the goods and their return to the owners but, complying with the grand duke's request, also instructed its naval forces to grant in the future to the possessions of Leghorn Jews, "who are subjects of a friendly prince," the same immunities as were accorded to "the Jews of England and Holland." See A. S. Toaff, "Trattative diplomatiche fra Toscana e Spagna per gli Ebrei di Livorno (1694–95)," *RMI*, XVI (Riccardo Bachi Jub. Vol.), pp. 157–60. See also M. Carmona, "Aspects du capitalisme toscan aux XVIe et XVIIe siècles. Les sociétés en commandite à Florence et à Lucque," *Revue d'histoire moderne et contemporaine*, XI, 81–108. Regrettably, in this "preliminary" study the author omitted many names of businessmen engaged in the *commenda* transactions, and hence it is almost impossible to assess the relative share of Jews in this important branch of trade, in which they had played a considerable role during the Middle Ages. See *supra*, Vols. IV, pp. 200 f., 339 f. n. 64; XII, pp. 104 f., 291 f. n. 39.

Not surprisingly, at times Jewish traders had to overcome the resistance of vested interests among their own coreligionists. For instance, when the Venetian Republic extended to the Ponentine Jews extensive privileges for settlement and trading in Corfu, similar to those they enjoyed in the city of Venice, the island's long-established "Greek" settlers protested vigorously. In reply to their 1611 petition to the doge, the ducal Council recognized, on May 10, the validity of the old privileges held by the local Jews ever since Corfu's annexation in 1376. But in so informing the Corfiote authorities by a pertinent executive order of July 17, the *Pregadi* added this reservation: "Yet it is not intended by this [order] to infringe upon the concessions granted to the foreign Jews, Italian or Ponentine, residing in that island." See the texts, reproduced from a copy long extant in the Jewish Museum in Vienna by J. Steiner in "A Petition of the Jews of Corfu to the Doge of Venice in 1611" (Hebrew), *Zion*, XII, 82–87 (with a Hebrew trans. of the texts by A. Z. Aešcoly). Not unexpectedly, this order did not put an end to the perennial bickering between the two communities. See my "On the History of the Corfu Communities and their Organization" (Hebrew), *Qobeş madda'i* (Studies in Memory of Moses Schorr), ed. by L. Ginzberg and A. Weiss, pp. 25–41 (with documents of the late seventeenth and early eighteenth centuries). See also, more generally, D. Stella, *Commerci e industrie a Venezia nel secolo XVII*.

38. See S. Simonsohn, *Toledot*, I, 198. Local food shortages, even famines, were by no means rare occurrences. Rich Venice herself sometimes had difficulties in securing needed supplies of grain. See A. Stella, "La Crisi economica veneziana della seconda metà del secolo XVI"; and M. Brunetti, "Tre ambasciate annonarie veneziane. Marino (1539–'40), e Sigismondo Cavalli (1559–'60) in Baviera, Marco Ottoboni (1590) a Danziga," *Archivio Veneto*, LXXXVI (5th ser. LVIII–LIX), 17–69, 88–115. Important Jewish grain merchants are also recorded in Reggio nell' Emilia. One of them boasted in 1679 that he supplied the city with thousands upon thousands of sacks of grain. Another was sent by the duke in 1620 on a purchasing mission to acquire fodder in Bavaria. One Benedetto Levi furnished a large quantity of bread to the duke of neighboring Mirandola at the substantial cost of 8,000 scudi (1622). See A. Balletti, *Gli Ebrei e gli Estensi*, p. 165 n. 1. Yet in numerous other localities anti-Jewish economic restrictions affecting trade in foodstuffs were carried down from the Middle Ages to the Emancipation era. See

C. Cattaneo's 1836 analysis of the conditions existing then in his "Ricerche economiche sulle interdizioni imposte dalla legge civile agli Israeliti," *Annali di Giurisprudenza pratica*, XXIII (also reprint).

39. G. Marini, *Degli archiatri pontifici* (the information dries up after Theodor de Sacerdotibus, physician to Julius III in 1550); T. Momigliano, "Un Ebreo professore di medicina all'Università di Perugia nel secolo XVI," *Vessillo israelitico*, LXX, 384–87; M. Mortara, "Un Important document sur la famille des Portaleone," *REJ*, XII, 113–16 (members of this family served the ducal court of Mantua for more than two centuries and secured special licenses from the popes as late as 1591, 1598, 1639, and 1655); Jacopo Pignatelli, *Consultationum canonicarum tomus octavus*, cxliv, Venice, 1722 ed., p. 196, cited by V. Colorni in his "Sull'ammissibilità degli Ebrei alla laurea anteriormente al secolo XIX," *RMI*, XVI (Riccardo Bachi Jub. Vol.), 202–216 (with two documents relating to degrees given in Bologna, 1528, and Pavia, 1563); G. B. Zanazzo, "Lo Statuto dei medici a Vicenza nell'anno 1555. Contributo alla storia della medicina," *Archivio Veneto*, 5th ser. LXXIV, 29–49.

40. S. Foa, "Ebrei medici in Piemonte nei secoli XVI e XVII," *RMI*, XIX, 542–51; B. Trompeo, *Dei Medici e degli archiatri dei Principi della R. Casa di Savoia;* A. Bricchi, *Medici milanesi in tempo di dominazione spagnuola;* H. Friedenwald, "An Italian Holograph Letter of Montalto, Court Physician of Marie de Medicis, and a Second Document Bearing His Signature," *La Bibliofilia*, XLI, 3–7; and other data cited *supra*, Vol. XII, pp. 80 ff., 281 ff. These facts enabled Harry Friedenwald to speak of a general toleration of Jews in sixteenth-century Italy. See his twin essays, "Evidence of Toleration in Sixteenth-Century Italy" (with a translation of Caelio Calganini's oration on the doctorate granted in Ferrara to a Jew named Ruben, published posthumously in 1544); and "Jewish Physicians in Italy: Their Relation to the Papal and Italian States," both reprinted in his *The Jews and Medicine: Essays*, I, 257–62; II, 551–612. On Isaac Cardoso, see *supra*, n. 34.

41. See G. Barbieri's *Ideali economici degli Italiani all'inizio dell'età moderna;* and the text of the Legnago *condotta* of 1604, with the story of its antecedents, published by him in his *Note e documenti di storia economica italiana per l'età medioevale e moderna*, pp. 53 ff., 69 ff., 92 ff. This unsuccessful entry of Jews into Italian textile manufacturing, hampered by such specific local difficulties as the competition from the well-established Veronese craftsmen and the bureaucratic impediments created by the Venetian Signoria, was by no means general, however. Even within the same geographic area some Jews secured a firm foothold in the production of cloth and silk; for instance, in Polesine, Rovigo, and Padua. See R. Cessi, "Alcuni documenti sugli Ebrei nel Polesine durante i secoli XIV e XV," *Atti e Memorie* of the Accademia di scienze of Padua, n.s. XXV, 61 f.; idem, "Gli Ebrei in Rovigo e il commercio della lana (secolo XVIII)" in the *Odone Ravenna Memorial Volume*, pp. 63–82; G. Barbieri, *Note*, pp. 78 f. n. 63; and *supra*, Vol. XII, pp. 53 ff., 270 f. nn. 53–54. See also, more generally, M. Borgherini-Scarabellin, *L'Arte della lana in Padova durante il governo della Repubblica di Venezia, 1405–1797;* and D. Stella, "Les Mouvements longs de l'industrie lainière à Venise aux XVIe et XVIIe siècles," *Annales ESC*, XII, 29–45, explaining the extreme swings in

production, from 1310 pieces manufactured in 1516 to a record output of 26,541 pieces in 1569, and to one of less than 10,000 annually in 1645–47; at the end only about 2,000 a year were produced in 1698–1713.

42. Philip's letter to Charles V of March 17, 1554, in F. de Laiglesia, *Estudios históricos (1515–1555)*, pp. 651 f.; Simone (Simḥah b. Isaac) Luzzatto, *Discorso circa il stato de gl'Hebrei*, iv, xii; in the Hebrew trans. by D. Lattes, pp. 89 ff., 108 ff.; Yeḥiel Nissim da Pisa, *Ma'amar Ḥayye 'Olam* (The Eternal Life; on Laws of Interest), ed. by G. S. Rosenthal under the title *Banking and Finance among Jews in Renaissance Italy*, pp. 9 f. (Hebrew), 40 f. (English); M. Brunetti, "Banche e banchieri veneziani nei 'Diarii' di Marin Sanudo (Garzoni e Lippomano)," *Studi in onore di Gino Luzzatto*, II, 26–47 (illustrating the extent of the Venetian banking crisis on the example of these two leading firms); *supra*, Vol. XII, pp. 159 ff., 320 ff.; and Chap. LVIII, n. 80. To the vast literature on the *monti di pietà* cited in our earlier volumes add more recent publications such as A. Allocati *et al.*, *Tipiche operazioni del Banco della Pietà in alcuni atti notarili dei secoli XVI–XIX;* and M. Abbate, *L'Istituto bancario San Paolo di Torino 1593–1963*, with M. Chiaudano's comments thereon in his "Un Contributo alla storia dei Monti di Pietà e della Banca in Italia. L'Istituto San Paolo di Torino," *ASI*, CXXIV, 250–56. Among the Jew-baiting anti-usury pamphlets see Joannes Annius of Viterbo's *Quaestiones super mutuo judaico et civili et divino iure*, included in *Pro monte pietatis, Consilia sacrorum theologorum et collegiorum Patavii . . . ,* Venice, 1498; Sisto de' Medici, *De foenore judaeorum . . . libri tres*, Venice, 1555; François Hotman, *De usuris libri duo*, Lyons, 1551 and others cited by L. dalle Molle in *Il Contratto di cambio nei moralisti dal secolo XIII alla metà del secolo XVII*, pp. xv ff.

It is not surprising that Shakespeare took an Italian Jewish moneylender as a prototype for the immortal figure of Shylock. From the host of attempted identifications of the Italian model, fictional or real, about which more will be said in Vol. XV, E. Toaff elaborated an interesting suggestion by G. Friedländer that the dramatist was inspired by a rumored bet in 1587 between the Roman Jewish banker Sansone Ceneda and a Christian merchant about the veracity of Francis Drake's reported conquest and devastation of Santo Domingo. In fact, however, it was the Jew Ceneda's pound of flesh which was at stake. According to the Italian chronicler who recorded this event, Sixtus V was so aroused by this inhuman wager that he condemned both bettors to death and was placated only after each paid him a fine of 1,000 scudi—the amount the Jew was to win if his contention proved right. See Toaff's "La Vera fonte del 'Mercato di Venezia' di Shakespeare," *RMI*, XXXII, 161–66; J. R. Marcus, *The Jew in the Medieval World*, pp. 367 ff. No. 76; and *infra*, Chap. LXIV.

Understandably, the constant hammering on the vices of usury by preachers and writers created many moral dilemmas for Christian and Jewish bankers alike. Jews could more easily justify their engaging in this "obnoxious" occupation, since it frequently was the exclusive reason for their toleration by Christian society. Yet even they must often have sought to compensate for their "sins" by a renewed zest for good works, particularly charity and study, although we have no counterpart among the contemporary Jewish writers to the sixteenth-century bishop-novelist Matteo Bandello, who graphically described the deep inner conflicts in the minds of Christian usurers. See his *Tutte le opere*, ed. by F. Flora; the interesting illustrations thereon drawn, on the basis of archival research, from the actual life of a fifteenth-century banker, by G. Barbieri in "L'Usuraio Tomaso Grassi nel racconto Bandelliano e nella documentazione storica," *Studi in onore di Amintore Fanfani*, II, 19–88. See also *infra*, n. 54; and, more generally, Barbieri's *Ideali economici degli Italiani all'inizio dell'età moderna;* the pertinent recent observations in B. Pullan's ed. of *Crisis and Change in the Venetian Economy in the Sixteenth and Seventeenth Centuries;* and such monographs as E. Lattes, *La Libertà delle banche a Venezia dal secolo XIII al XVII . . . con due orationi . . . 1584–1587 dal Senatore veneziano T. Contarini: Ricerche storiche;* G. Luzzatto, "Les Banques publiques de Venise, XVIe–XVIIIe siècles," *History of the Principal Private Banks,* ed. by J. G. van Dillen, pp. 39–73; I. Cervelli, "Intorno alla decadenza di Venezia. Un episodio di storia economica, ovvero un affare mancato," *NRS*, L, 596–642; and other essays analyzed by F. C. Lane in his "Recent Studies on the Economic History of Venice in the XVth and XVIth Centuries," *Journal of Economic History*, XXIII, 312–34.

43. Y. S. Foa, "The Conflict between the Princes of Savoy and the Pope" (Hebrew), *Eretz-Israel,* III (D. M. or Umberto Cassuto Mem. Vol.), 240–43; idem, "Banchi e banchieri ebrei nel Piemonte dei secoli scorsi," *RMI*, XXI; M. Stern, *Urkundliche Beiträge,* I, 154 f. No. 145 (Sixtus V in 1587 authorized the raising of the interest rate by Savoyard Jewish bankers from 15 to 18 percent); E. Loevinson, "La Concession des banques de prêts aux Juifs par les Papes des seizième et dix-septième siècles," *REJ*, XCII–XCV; and, particularly, L. Poliakov, *Les "Banchieri" juifs et le Saint-Siège du XIIIe au XVIIe siècle.* Of considerable interest also are the vicissitudes of a small Jewish community, numbering in 1502 some 40–50 souls, in the Marches on the periphery of the States of the Church, as described by A. Stramigioli in "Gli Ebrei e la vita economica di Osimo nel Cinquecento," *Quaderni storici delle Marche,* III, 43–61. See also *supra*, nn. 23–25; Chap. LIX, nn. 50 and 63; H. Lapeyre's twin essays, "La Banque, les changes et le crédit au XVIe siècle," *Revue d'histoire moderne et contemporaine,* III, 284–97 and "Banque et crédit en Italie du XVIe au XVIIIe siècle," *ibid,* VIII, 211–26, esp. p. 225.

The growing impact of governmental policies on the economic evolution of the Italian and other states during that period had, on the whole, more beneficial than adverse effects on Jewish status. See, for instance, D. F. Dowd's analysis of the "Economic Expansion in Lombardy, 1300–1500: a Study in Political Stimuli to Economic Change," *Journal of Economic History,* XXI, 143–60, which shows how the advantages gained during the fourteenth and fifteenth centuries endured, even under the fiscally oppressive Spanish domination, until about 1620, or through about half the duration of Spanish rule. This factor may also have contributed to the continued toleration of Jews in the Duchy of Milan until 1597, which so sharply contrasted with Spain's intolerance in its other dependencies. See *supra*, nn. 9–12. This interplay of the new political and economic factors in the early modern period will be more fully analyzed in a later chapter.

44. A. Balletti, *Gli Ebrei e gli Estensi,* pp. 69 ff.; and, more generally, Riccardo Bachi, *Israele disperso e ricostruito; pagine di storia e di economia,* esp. pp. 59 ff., 83 ff.; C. Belloni's *Dizionario storico dei banchieri italiani;* and such monographs as are listed in L. Sandri's "Saggio bibliografico di scritti sull'attività bancaria nei secoli XVI e XVII," *Archivi storici delle Aziende di Credito,* I, 405–418.

With the decline of the banking monopoly among Jews the bankers also lost much of their control over the admission of new Jewish settlers. In the early sixteenth century, when the Cremona bankers objected to the opening of a new loan bank by one Aaron di Bassano, they were overruled by the governor, who believed Aaron's pledge to perform "a greater service and be of benefit to the poor in a way which the others might not do." See L. Fumi in *AS Lombardo*, XXXVII, Part 1, p. 293. Such Jewish moneylenders and merchants contributed their share to the still flourishing economy of the city during the sixteenth century and it probably is more than coincidental that, after their final expulsion from the duchy of Milan in 1597, Cremona's prosperity went into a sudden "tail spin." See B. Caizzi, "I Tempi della decadenza economica di Cremona," *Studi in onore di Armando Sapori*, II, 1009–1019. Understandably, the controls over the internal life of the Italian Jews, too, now shifted to the community at large, of which the bankers were only one segment, although they still played a great role everywhere, particularly in Piedmont, as well as in Lombardy during the period of Spanish domination. See E. Rota's data in the *Bollettino* of the Società Pavese di storia patria, VI, 349–82; P. L. Bruzzone, "Les Juifs au Piémont," *REJ*, XIX, 141–46.

45. A. Balletti, *Gli Ebrei e gli Estensi*, pp. 167 ff.; C. Roth, *Venice*, pp. 48 ff., 164 ff.; L. Carnevali, *Il Ghetto di Mantova*, pp. 13 ff.; S. Simonsohn, "The Italian Ghetto and Its Regime" (Hebrew), *Baer Jub. Vol.*, pp. 270–86, esp. pp. 277 ff.; idem, *Toledot*, I, 87 ff.; A. Ciscato, *Gli Ebrei in Padova (1300–1800)*, pp. 86 ff.; *supra*, Vols. IX, 32 ff., 255 f. nn. 34–38; XI, 87 ff., 324 ff. nn. 15–24, esp. n. 20. The community of Verona was less fortunate than that of Padua. As early as 1598 the communal elders complained of a quarter century of frustrations in their negotiations in connection with the establishment of the ghetto. Ultimately, a fire which started there on October 30, 1786, raged for three days before it was brought under control. Five persons lost their lives, many others were injured, while the majority suffered staggering property losses. See D. Fortis, "Gli Ebrei di Verona," *Educatore israelita*, XI–XII, esp. XI, 393; I. Sonne, "Materials for the History of the Jews in Verona" (Hebrew), *Zion*, III, 128 ff. Apart from fires ghettos were also acutely affected by floods and earthquakes, the damage being aggravated by their greater population density. For instance, the Jewish quarter of Modena was half destroyed by the earthquake of 1671, but thirty-three years after its foundation. See Balletti, p. 176.

46. See G. Carocci, *Il Ghetto di Firenze e i suoi ricordi: illustrazione storica;* other monographs by him and other authors cited by U. Cassuto in *Gli Ebrei*, p. 112 n. 2; Cassuto's edition of "I Più antichi capitoli del ghetto di Firenze," *RI*, IX, 203–211; X, 33–40, 71–79; S. Simonsohn, *Toledot*, I, 88 ff.; A. Balletti, *Gli Ebrei*, pp. 182 f. Even after the establishment of a ghetto some of the original street names continued to be used, both by the populace and by contemporary chroniclers, while other streets were renamed after buildings newly erected by the Jews. For example, the Ancona Jewish section included a Via delle Prostitute, in remembrance of some of the preghetto inhabitants, and a Via del Bagno, named for the Jewish bathhouse located there. Other such survivals are cited by A. Milano in his *Storia degli Ebrei*, pp. 535 f.

47. See *supra*, Vols. IX, pp. 32 ff., 255 f. nn. 34–38; XI, pp. 87 ff., 324 ff. nn. 15–24; A. Colombo, *Cenni storici ed amministrativi sulle comunità israelitiche italiane,*

pp. 18, 27, 39; V. Colorni, *Gli Ebrei nel sistema del diritto comune fino alla prima emancipazione*, pp. 54 ff.; idem, "Fatti e figure di storia ebraica mantovana," *RMI*, IX, 217–39, esp. pp. 238 f.; G. Volli's brief survey of "I Ghetti d'Italia," *ibid.*, XV, 22–30; and numerous local studies listed in these works, in A. Milano's *Storia degli Ebrei*, pp. 528 n. 1, 529 n. 1 and his *Bibliotheca historica italo-judaica*, with its *Supplemento 1954–1963*, cf. Index *s.v.* Ghetto. The developments in the Este possessions after the loss of Ferrara are described with adequate documentation by A. Balletti in *Gli Ebrei*, pp. 167 ff. Cesare d'Este's readiness to yield in Mirandola to the pressures of that shady rabble-rouser Bartolommeo Cambi da Salutio offers a telling illustration of how little resistance rulers put up to any agitation in favor of the formation of Jewish ghettos. It seemed like an easy concession to the populace incited by some churchmen and interested parties, since it involved few losses to the Treasury.

48. A. Ciscato, *Gli Ebrei in Padova*, pp. 74 f., 80 f.; A. Balletti, *Gli Ebrei e gli Estensi*, pp. 170 f.; L. A. Schiavi, "Gli Ebrei a Venezia," *Nuova Antologia*, CXXXI, 309–333, 485–519; C. Roth, *Venice*, pp. 45 ff., 57 f.; *supra*, Vol. XI, p. 326 n. 20. It may be noted that, even in the relatively small community of Modena, the expenses connected with the establishment in 1638 of the new quarter for its 53 Jewish families were estimated at over 60,000 lire. Typical of the prevailing hypocrisy in these transactions was the *podesta*'s satisfaction over the completion of this "business . . . through the work and inspiration of the Holy Spirit as proposed by two servants of the Lord living a good and most exemplary life." Balletti, pp. 170 f.

49. See the data summarized from Mantuan records by S. Simonsohn in his *Toledot*, I, 91 n. 71.

50. C. Roth, "La Fête de l'institution du ghetto. Une célébration particulière à Verone," *REJ*, LXXIX, 163–69; I. Sonne, "Materials for the History of the Jews in Verona" (Hebrew), *Zion*, III, 123 ff. The author of the poem undoubtedly was Mordecai b. Jacob Bassano, author of a responsum written in 1606, rather than a later rabbi and namesake, Mordecai b. Samuel Ḥayyim Bassano. On the identity of these two rabbis, see my remarks in "A Communal Conflict in Verona: On the Basis of a Responsum by Rabbi Mordecai Bassano of the End of the Seventeenth Century" (Hebrew), *Sefer ha-Yobel . . . Shemuel Krauss* (Samuel Krauss Jubilee Volume), pp. 217–54. It is possible that the establishment of the ghetto also helped to pacify the Christian population, which thus learned to get along better with its Jewish neighbors. In Conegliano Veneto, where during the sixteenth century (1511, 1522, 1560, and 1567) the city council had constantly petitioned the Venetian authorities to expel the Jews, the establishment of the ghetto in 1637 seems to have marked the beginning of more friendly relations between the two faiths. See F. Luzzatto, "La Comunità ebraica di Conegliano Veneto ed i suoi monumenti," *RMI*, XXII, 34–43, 72–80, 115–25, 178–86, 227–38, 270–78, 313–21, 354–60 (with additional bibliography, p. 360). Many other aspects of that important institution and its impact on the internal life of the Jewish communities will be discussed in a later chapter.

51. A. Balletti, *Gli Ebrei*, pp. 149 ff.; S. Simonsohn, *Toledot*, I, 9 ff., 81 ff., and *passim*; U. Cassuto, *Gli Ebrei a Firenze*, pp. 101 ff.; H. Beinart, "The Settlement of

Jews in the Duchy of Savoy on the Basis of the Privilege of 1572," *Scritti in Memoria di Leone Carpi*, ed. by D. Carpi *et al.*, Hebrew section, pp. 72–118, esp. pp. 95 f. Doc. 13; *supra*, nn. 25–26; Vols. IX, pp. 27 ff., 253 ff. nn. 28–33; XI, pp. 96 ff., 106 ff., 328 ff. nn. 25–43. On the oath *more judaico*, see, for instance, the grand-ducal circulars of 1815 and 1842 in Tuscany, cited by I. E. Rignano in his *Sulla attuale posizione giuridica degli Israeliti in Toscana*, p. 18. See also the formula quoted by Marquardus de Susannis, and other statements of sixteenth- and seventeenth-century jurists on this subject, cited by V. Colorni in his *Legge ebraica e leggi locali*, p. 226 n. 4.

52. See the numerous inquisitorial rescripts chronologically summarized under sixty-eight headings by M. Stern in his *Urkundliche Beiträge*, I, 169 ff. No. 161, esp. p. 175 item 24; S. Simonsohn, *Toledot*, I, 20, 83 f., 92; L. Fumi, "La Inquisizione romana," *AS Lombardo*, XXXVII, Part 1, p. 318. We must realize that a three-year term of galley servitude did not greatly differ from a life term, for few prisoners were able to survive three years of the extreme hardships usually connected with that service. The enormous variety of local regulations and recorded incidents has been, and will be, mentioned here in various connections.

53. See A. Balletti, *Gli Ebrei*, p. 109 n. 2; F. Ceraschi, "Censimento della popolazione di Roma dell'anno 1600 al 1739," *Studi e documenti di storia e diritto*, XII, 174 ff.; E. Natali, *Il Ghetto di Roma*, I, 143. An interesting debate on this subject took place at a Mantuan court in 1569. While one jurist contended that Jews cohabiting with Christians ought to be sentenced to death, another judge pointed out that in Mantua no Jew had ever been executed for this reason. Two other doctors of law suggested that the best penalty would be the cutting off of the culprit's testicles, "a most beautiful spectacle for a carnival." But all these differences of opinion were superseded by the further progress of the Catholic Restoration. In 1577 the death penalty and the confiscation of property were restored as proper deterrents, and their enforcement was entrusted to the more ruthless inquisitorial courts. See S. Simonsohn, *Toledot*, I, 84. Because the employment by Jews of Christian maids and nurses involved the possibility of seductions, prohibitions of such employment were now frequently reiterated in many areas. See M. Stern, *Urkundliche Beiträge*, pp. 174 f. No. 161 items 17–18, also referring to a letter addressed by the Roman Inquisition to that of Parma, which insisted on the exclusive jurisdiction of the Holy Office over these offenses.

54. See A. Stella, "Utopie e velleità insurrezionali dei filoprotestanti italiani (1545–1547)," *BHR*, XXVII, 133–82; P. Amelung, *Das Bild des Deutschen in der Literatur der italienischen Renaissance (1400–1559)*, esp. pp. 85 ff., 117 ff.; L. Cremonte, *Matteo Bandello e i casi vari e miserabili delle sue novelle; supra*, n. 42; the texts of the Venetian ordinances of 1581 and 1606, reproduced by V. Colorni in his *Legge ebraica*, pp. 371 ff. Apps. iv-v; M. Stern, *Urkundliche Beiträge*, I, 173 No. 161 item 13; and M. Roberti's well-documented study, "Privilegi forensi degli Ebrei di Ferrara" in *Atti e Memorie* of the Accademia di scienze of Padua, n.s. XXIII, 155–66.

55. M. B. Becker, "Florentine Politics and the Diffusions of Heresy in the Trecento: a Socio-Economic Inquiry," *Speculum*, XXXIV, 60–75 (showing the strong impact of the changing political constellations, but insisting that a fuller study still is called for); U. Cassuto, *Gli Ebrei a Firenze*, pp. 91 ff., 110 ff., 385 f. Nos.

xxvii–xxviii; H. Beinart, "The Trial of Two Marranos from Portugal, Residents of Pisa" (Hebrew), *Eretz-Israel*, III, 235–39; C. Roth, "I Marrani di Livorno, Pisa e Firenze," *RMI*, VII, 394–415; idem, "I Marrani in Italia: Nuovi documenti," *ibid.*, VIII, 419–43; idem, "Notes sur les Marranes de Livourne," *REJ*, XCI, 1–27; *supra*, nn. 21–22. Despite its general submission to Pius V's intolerant demands, however, even Cosimo I's administration maintained a measure of independence from the Inquisition. In Siena, in particular, where the governor unsuccessfully tried in 1569 to evade the ducal prohibition against the admission of Jewish refugees from the States of the Church, the authorities courageously suppressed the so-called *Croce-signati* (*Compagnia della Croce*), a vigilante group spreading through Italy and organized to protect all officials of the Holy Office against assaults by their numerous enemies. Nor was that group subsequently allowed to pursue its extralegal activities in Siena despite a papal breve in its favor of October 13, 1570. See C. Cantù, *Gli Eretici d'Italia*, II, 452; *Bullarium romanum*, VII, 860; L. Pastor, *The History*, XVII, 297 n. 1.

56. [N.] M[engozzi], "Conversioni [di Ebrei a Siena nel secolo XVI]," *Bollettino senese di storia patria*, XIV, 174–83, esp. p. 182; M. Stern, *Urkundliche Beiträge*, I, 176 ff. No. 161 items 32 and 60; A. Bertolotti, "Gli Ebrei in Roma nei secoli XVI, XVII e XVIII," *Archivio storico, artistico . . . e letterario della città e provincia di Roma*, III, 260–80 (subsequently summarized in *REJ*, II, 278–89). See also such recent monographs as A. d'Adario's "Note di storia della religiosità e della carità dei Fiorentini nel secolo XVI," *ASI*, CXXVI, 61–147 (its documentation, partly derived from archival research, is to be supplied in a forthcoming volume); and *infra*, n. 64.

57. E. Verga, "Il Municipio di Milano e l'Inquisizione di Spagna, 1563," *AS Lombardo*, XXIV, Part 2, pp. 86–127, esp. pp. 91, 112 f.; L. Fumi, "L'Inquisizione romana e lo stato di Milano," *ibid.*, XXXVII, Part 1, pp. 35, 295, 304, 316; C. Canetta, "Gli Ebrei del ducato milanese," *ibid.*, VIII, 632–35; S. Schaerf, "Appunti storici sugli Ebrei della Lombardia," *RMI*, II, [33]–49; and other sources, cited *supra*, nn. 9 ff.; and Vol. X, pp. 281 ff., 426 ff. nn. 74–79. Much additional information may be gleaned also from such local studies as S. Foa's "Gli Ebrei in Alessandria," *RMI*, XXIII–XXV (discussing conditions before Alessandria was taken over by Piedmont). That Spanish political considerations affected the operations of the Milanese Inquisition goes without saying. This was particularly the case after Philip II had wrung from the Papacy the acknowledgment of state controls over the duchy's ecclesiastical jurisdiction. See P. Prodi, "San Carlo Borromeo e le trattative tra Gregorio XIII e Filippo II sulla giurisdizione ecclesiastica," *RSCI*, XI, 195–240. See also C. Marcora, "La Chiesa milanese nel decennio 1550–1560," *Memorie storiche della diocesi di Milano*, VII, 254 ff.

58. L. Fumi, "L'Inquisizione," *AS Lombardo*, XXXVII, Part 1, pp. 35, 295, 304, 316; M. Stern, *Urkundliche Beiträge*, I, 98 ff. No. 100, 102 f. No. 103, 113 ff. Nos. 107–115; E. Rota, "Gli Ebrei e la politica spagnola in Lombardia. I banchi pubblici nel ducato milanese," *Bollettino* of the Società Pavese di storia patria, VI, 349–82, esp. pp. 356 f.; C. Bonetti, *Gli Ebrei a Cremona, 1278–1630;* and other sources listed *supra*, nn. 9 ff.; and Vol. X, p. 427 n. 77. A number of extant Hebrew letters offer many sidelights on the burning of the Talmud and the conflict between the

secular and ecclesiastical authorities; they are analyzed by C. Z. Dimitrovsky in "The History of the Jews in the Duchy of Milan before the Expulsion of 1597" (Hebrew), *Talpioth*, VI, 336–45, 708–722. See also D. Bergamaschi, "Inquisizione e gli heretici a Cremona," *Reale Deputazione Veneta*, 1907, pp. 112 ff.; 1908, pp. 185 ff. The struggle against Christian heresies had antecedents going back to the twelfth century. See J. N. Garvin and J. A. Corbett, eds., *The Summa contra haereticos Ascribed to Praepositinus of Cremona* (d. about 1210). Nonetheless it appears that the enforcement of the inquisitorial decrees remained quite spotty. If Georges Vajda's very tentative identification of the locale of "Une Liste de livres de 1572," ed. by him in *REJ*, CXXIII, 131–39, is correct, it sheds revealing light on the actual practice. This list of Nisan 1, 5332 (March 15, 1572), shows that the library belonging to a lady named Rachel included a number of talmudic tractates—but not a whole set—and rabbinic works, in addition to Bibles, biblical commentaries, philosophic and medical works, but curiously no belles-lettres, poetry, or Kabbalah. But whether this library was located in Cunico, in the province of Alessandria, is rightly questioned by Vajda himself.

59. See the data assembled by M. Stern and L. Fumi, esp. in the passages listed *supra*, n. 58; and, on the general developments leading up to the expulsion of 1597, *supra*, nn. 11–12.

60. M. Stern, *Urkundliche Beiträge*, I, 122 No. 116, 146 No. 137; *supra*, nn. 14–15. See also V. S. Davari, "Cenni storici intorno al Tribunale della Inquisizione in Mantova," *AS Lombardo*, VI, 547–65, 773–800, esp. pp. 556 ff., 562 ff. Nos. 10–12, 774 ff., 797 No. 12; L. B. Nizzola, "Infiltrazioni protestanti nel Ducato di Mantova (1530–1563)," *Bollettino storico mantovano*, 1956, pp. 102–130, 258–86 (from a Padua dissertation). The burning in 1600 of the seventy-seven-year-old Judith Franchetta by the Mantuan Inquisition in the presence of the duke, the duchess, and some ten to twelve thousand onlookers, was exceptional in several respects. She had allegedly—with the aid of three Jews, two of whom had fled before their arrest—bewitched a former Jewess, who had become a nun of the Order of St. Vincent, and caused her to relapse. Evidently, the alleged witchcraft, combined with the attempt at persuading a convert to relapse called for setting an example. See L. Carnevali, *Il Ghetto di Mantova*, pp. 13 f.; S. Simonsohn, *Toledot*, pp. 25, 539.

61. M. Stern, *Urkundliche Beiträge*, I, 117 f. No. 112; *supra*, n. 58. See also J. L. Bato's general sketch of "L'Immigrazione degli Ebrei tedeschi in Italia dal Trecento al Cinquecento," *Scritti in Memoria di Sally Mayer*, pp. 19–34.

62. D. Kaufmann, "Die Vertreibung der Marranen aus Venedig im J. 1550," *JQR*, XIII, 520–32, esp. pp. 525 f.; idem, "Die Verbrennung der talmudischen Literatur in der Republik Venedig," *ibid.*, pp. 533–38; P. Paschini, *Venezia e l'Inquisizione romana da Giulio III a Pio IV*, esp. p. 114 (reproducing in part Morosini's dispatch of 1555). On the competition between the Venetian Hebrew presses and its contribution to the new outlawry of talmudic writings, see *infra*, n. 72; and *supra*, Vol. X, pp. 76 f., 278 f. n. 10; Chap. LIX, nn. 26 and 30. See also F. Venturi's informative review of "Storiografia e problemi intorno alla vita religiosa e spirituale a Venezia nella prima metà del '500," *Studi veneziani*, VIII, 447–80.

63. A. Stella, *Chiesa e stato nelle relazioni dei nunzi pontifici a Venezia. Ricerche sul giurisdizionalismo veneziano dal XVI al XVIII secolo* (Studi e testi, CCXXXIX), which includes Alberto Bolognetti's noteworthy report, esp. pp. 58 ff., 65 ff., 105 ff., 132 ff., 136 f. (Chap. III), 277 ff., 289 f. (Chap. IX); C. Roth, "I Marrani a Venezia," *RMI*, VIII, 232–39, 304–314; idem, "Les Marranes à Venise," *REJ*, LXXXIX, 201–223; B. Brugi, *Gli Scolari dello studio di Padova nel Cinquecento. Con un appendice sugli studenti tedeschi e la S. Inquisizione di Padova*, esp. pp. 80 ff.; D. Orano, *Liberi pensatori bruciati in Roma dal XVI al XVIII secolo*, pp. 88 f. No. lxxvii. See also the literature listed *infra*, n. 64.

In Padua, which had long played a great role in the struggle between Averroists and Anti-Averroists, also resided a number of early reformers, both natives and arrivals from other cities. Outstanding among them was Peter Martyr Vermigli, whose name later became a household word in England. Vermigli, who had acquired some knowledge of Hebrew from a Jew named Isaac in Bologna, in 1556 succeeded Conrad Pellikan as professor of Hebrew in Zurich. All this created vast opportunities for the inquisitors, who must have felt greatly frustrated by the lack of cooperation from the Venetian authorities. See P. O. Kristeller, "Paduan Averroism and Alexandrism in the Light of Recent Studies," *Atti* of the Twelfth International Congress of Philosophy, 1958, pp. 147–55; A. Poppi, "L'Antiaverroismo della scolastica padovana alla fine del secolo XV," *Studia Patavina*, XI, 102–124; A. Martin, "Tentativi di riforma a Padova prima del Concilio di Trento," *RSCI*, III, 66–94; P. McNair, *Peter Martyr in Italy: an Anatomy of Apostasy*, esp. pp. vii, 125 f., 197, 239 ff.

64. Paolo Sarpi, *Discorso dell'origine, forma, leggi, ed uso dell'Ufficio dell'Inquisitione nella città, e dominio di Venetia*, xxiv and xxviii, with his own elaborations thereon, Venice, 1639 ed. (includes an interesting apologetic Preface by the publisher), pp. 12 f., 91 ff., 94 f., 109 ff.; F. Chabod, *La Politica di Paolo Sarpi*; G. Getto's recent biography of *Paolo Sarpi*; C. Vivanti, "In margine a studi recenti sul Sarpi," *RSI*, LXXIX, 1075–94; A. Stella, *Chiesa e stato*, esp. pp. 73 f. (summarizing Zacchia's instructions); B. Cecchetti, *La Repubblica di Venezia e la Corte di Roma nei rapporti della religione*, esp. I, 478 ff.; II, 368 ff., Docs. Nos. xix A–C; and, more generally, F. Albanese, *L'Inquisizione religiosa nella Repubblica di Venezia*. On the reformatory trends in the Venetian Republic see K. Benrath's older, but still very useful, *Geschichte der Reformation in Venedig;* such more recent data as are published by E. Pommier in "La Société vénitienne et la Réforme protestante au XVIe siècle," *Bollettino* of the Istituto di storia della società e dello stato veneziano, I, 3–26; F. Gaeta in his "Documenti da codici Vaticani per la storia della Riforma in Venezia: Appunti e documenti," *Annuario* of the Istituto storico italiano per l'età moderna e contemporanea, VII, 3–53 (reports by the papal nuncio Girolamo Aleander and other early data). See also F. Gaeta, *Un Nunzio pontificio a Venezia nel Cinquecento (Girolamo Aleandro)*, esp. pp. 87 ff.; G. de Luca, *Letteratura di pietà a Venezia del '300 al '600*, ed. by V. Branca; and other recent literature reviewed by F. Venturi in his "Storiografia e problemi," *Studi veneziani*, VIII, 447–80; *supra*, n. 56; and *infra*, n. 66.

65. Y. (S.) Foa, "The Conflict between the Princes of Savoy and the Pope" (Hebrew), *Eretz Israel*, III, 240–43; C. Roth, "I Marrani in Italia: nuovi documenti,"

RMI, VIII, 419–43; idem, "Les Marranes à Venise," *REJ*, LXXXIX, 210 n. 1; A. Stella, "Utopie e velleità insurrezionali dei filoprotestanti italiani," *BHR*, XXVII, 142; and *supra*, nn, 23–24.

66. B. Croce in *La Spagna nella vita italiana*, pp. 235 f.; A. L. Antinori's *Libro di memorie*, MS preserved in the Lanciano Library and cited by C. Marciani in his "Ebrei a Lanciano dal XII al XVIII secolo," *ASPN*, LXXXI, 181 f., and a notarial document reproduced and commented on, *ibid.*, pp. 187 f., 195 f. App. iii. See also P. Lopez, *Riforma cattolica e vita religiosa e culturale a Napoli, dalla fine del Cinquecento ai primi anni del Settecento;* and, more generally, F. Ruffini, *Studi sui riformatori italiani*, ed. by A. Bertola *et al.;* F. C. Church, *The Italian Reformers, 1534–1564;* and particularly the numerous researches by D. Cantimori, including his *Eretici italiani del Cinquecento, ricerche storiche;* and "Studi di storia della Riforma e dell'eresie in Italia e studi sulla storia della vita religiosa nella prima metà del '500 (rapporto fra i due tipi di ricerca)," *Bollettino* of the Società di studi valdesi, No. 102, pp. 29–38. Other studies by this distinguished student of Italian "heresies" are listed by L. Perrini and J. A. Tedeschi in their "Bibliografia degli scritti di Delio Cantimori," *RSI*, LXXIX (Delio Cantimori Memorial Number), pp. 1173–1208.

67. Finus Finus (Fini), *Flagellum in Judaeos ex sacris scripturis excerptum*, ed. by D. Finus, Venice, 1538; Giulio Cesare Misuracchi, *Ragionamenti della venuta del Messia contro la durezza e ostinazione ebraica*, Orvieto, 1629; Ignazio Landriani, *Virginis partus ejusque filii Emmanuel divinitatis et humanitatis scripturalis dissertatio atque demonstratio adversus Hebraeos et haereticos*, Milan, 1641; F. Secret, "Notes pour une histoire du Pugio fidei à la Renaissance," *Sefarad*, XX, 401–407; Melchior Palontrotti, *Disputa del cristiano con l'ebreo*, Rome, 1647; Tommaso Campanella, *Per la conversione degli Ebrei* and *Legazioni ai Maomettani (Quod reminiscentur*, III–IV), ed. by R. Amerio; idem, *Lettere*, ed. by V. Spampanato; *infra*, n. 69; and other polemical tracts published in the sixteenth and seventeenth centuries and listed by F. Vernet in his article, "Juifs (Controverses avec les)," *Dictionnaire de théologie catholique*, VIII, Part 1, cols. 1899 ff. See also S. G. Mercati, "Il Trattato contro i Giudei di Taddeo Pelusiota è una falsificazione di Constantino Paleocappa," *Il Bessarione*, XXXIX, 8–14; and *supra*, Vol. IX, pp. 99 ff., 287 ff. On Leone Nardi, see D. Cantimori's *Eretici italiani*, pp. 166 ff. To encourage conversions some neophytes, like Andrea del Monte, published their controversial tracts in Hebrew. See *supra*, Chap. LIX, nn. 47 and 56–57. Another baptized Jew, Giovanni Battista Jonas, converted in 1625, in 1658 issued a Hebrew version of Cardinal Robert Francis Bellarmine's *Small Catechism* with numerous rabbinic quotations, and followed it up ten years later with a Hebrew translation of the Gospels.

68. Leon da Modena, *Magen ve-Ḥereb* (Shield and Sword, or Clipeus et gladius: Leonis Mutinensis Tractatus antichristianus), ed. by S. Simonsohn; and, more generally, Simonsohn's *Leon da Modena: a Monograph Based on Hitherto Unpublished MSS.* (typescript). Here is also listed the vast bibliography which has accumulated over the years on this intriguing personality who will reappear in these pages on many occasions.

69. See G. di Napoli, *Tommaso Campanella, filosofo della restaurazione cattolica;* R. Amerio's biography of *Campanella;* his recent editions of other Campanella writ-

ings, partly cited *supra*, n. 67; and works listed in L. Firpo's *Bibliografia degli scritti di Tommaso Campanella*. See also the threefold aims of the linguistic training prescribed for missionaries in Paul V's bull cited *supra*, Chap. LIX, n. 60. Although frequently at odds with the papal bureaucracy, Campanella, as both poet and philosopher, exerted considerable influence on the intelligentsia in Italy and abroad. Apart from the special tract he devoted to the conversion of Jews, the numerous scattered references, overt and oblique, to Jews and Judaism in his prolific writings would deserve monographic treatment. The anti-Jewish attitude of such influential writers during the heyday of the Catholic Restoration carried over into the "Enlightenment era" of the eighteenth century, which generally affected Italy less than either France or England. See U. Cassuto's succinct observations on "L'Antisemitismo settecentesco," *Il Vessillo israelitico*, LV, 613–17, 671–77.

70. See M. Stern, *Urkundliche Beiträge*, I, 178 ff. No. 161, items 53, 62–63, and 65; A. Ciscato, *Gli Ebrei in Padova*, pp. 148 f.; F. Luzzatto, *Cronache storiche della Università degli Ebrei di San Daniele del Friuli: Cenni sulla storia degli Ebrei del Friuli*, pp. 51 f. At the same time the divided Mediterranean world offered venturesome individuals many opportunities to play both ends against the middle. One Moses Israel adopted Christianity in 1624, then reverted to Judaism in Salonica, and subsequently returned to Italy, where he was rebaptized twice. He was finally condemned to a seven-year galley term. See C. Roth, "Forced Baptisms in Italy: a Contribution to the History of Jewish Persecution," *JQR*, XXVII, 117–36, esp. pp. 118, 120, reprinted with some revisions in the recent collection of his *Gleanings. Essays in Jewish History, Letters and Art*, pp. 240–63, esp. pp. 241 f., 243 f.; and *supra*, Chap. LIX, nn. 56 ff.

71. A. Balletti, *Gli Ebrei*, pp. 189 ff. (citing from archival records many cases of illegal conversions); [N.] M[engozzi], "Conversioni [di Ebrei a Siena]," *Bollettino senese di storia patria*, XIV, 174–83. The issue of both forced conversions and the baptism of children without parental permission loomed very large during the early modern period. In principle canon law remained firm in prohibiting the use of force. However, violations were so frequent that in 1593 Levantine Jews, before accepting the invitation to settle in Leghorn, insisted that their basic privilege, *La Livornina* (Art. xxvi), spell out specific safeguards against forced baptisms. This guarantee was repeated in 1764. See *supra*, nn. 21–22. The antecedents of the exclusion of Marranos and other persons of Jewish ancestry from higher ecclesiastical offices in Italy and elsewhere, and the frequent opposition thereto, are discussed, with considerable documentation, by P. Browe in "Die Kirchenrechtliche Stellung der getauften Juden und ihrer Nachkommen," *AKKR*, CXXI, 3–22, 165–91. See also *supra*, Chap. LVI, esp. nn. 28–29.

72. Menaḥem Abraham b. Jacob ha-Kohen Rapa of Porto, *Minḥah belulah* (Mingled Meal-Offering: a commentary on the Pentateuch), Verona, 1594 ed., fol. 203b (on Deut. 33:2); Mattatiah b. Solomon Delacrut, *Sefer ha-Zikkaron* (Book of Reminiscences), Bodleian MS excerpted by A. Neubauer in his *Catalogue of the Hebrew Manuscripts in the Bodleian Library*, p. 566 No. 1623; Yehudah b. Samuel Lerma, *Leḥem Yehudah* (Judah's Bread: a commentary on *Abot*), Intro.; and other contemporary sources cited by A. Yaari in his *Serefat ha-Talmud be-Italiah* (The Burning of the Talmud in Italy), pp. 16 ff.; and his *Meḥqere sefer*, pp. 207 ff. Here

are also reprinted five contemporary *qinnot* (dirges) written in commemoration of
that tragic event.

73. The events of 1629 in Recanati are reflected in Cardinal Desiderio Scaglia's
letter of November 21, 1629, to Cardinal Giovanni Battista Pallotta, papal nuncio at
the imperial court; reproduced by D. Calcagni in his *Memorie storiche della città di
Recanati nella Marca d'Ancona*, p. 105. Here the author claims that, contrary to
the original intentions of the ancient sages, the compilers of the Talmud included
in it not only anti-Christian blasphemies "but also precepts and ordinances against
the Law of Moses, against all reason as held by the nations, and against the Law
of Nature." Hence it was right for the authorities of Recanati to burn 10,000 copies
of that work, and many others, including the Commentary on the Pentateuch by
the local rabbi Menaḥem, "which is full of talmudic impieties." Remarkably, in
Scaglia's letter Ludovico Zdekauer also found support for his theory that, on this
occasion, the Inquisition destroyed much of the city's municipal archive which had
theretofore been maintained in very good order. See his *L'Archivio del Comune di
Recanati ed il recente suo ordinamento* (reprinted from *Le Marche illustrate*), p. 10.
This theory is controverted, however, by B. Ghetti in his review of Zdekauer's
study in *Atti e Memorie* of the R. Deputazione di storia patria per le provincie delle
Marche, n.s. II, 475–80. See also *supra*, nn. 11 and 58; and Chap. LIX, nn. 26–27. To
the literature cited there add the data and lists of 1595 supplied by S. Simonsohn
in his "Books and Libraries of Mantuan Jews, 1555" (Hebrew), *KS*, XXXVII, 103–
122.

74. See N. Rodolico, "Popolo e chiesa" (1957), reprinted in his *Saggi di storia
medievale e moderna*, pp. 3–31, esp. pp. 22 f., also citing the observation by the
Florentine chronicler Landucci; and, more generally, S. F. Romano, *Le Classi sociali
in Italia dal medioevo all'età contemporanea*. We must also remember that even
outright slavery had not yet disappeared from Italian life, while various degrees
of serfdom (not villeinage) still lingered in the cities as well as in the countryside.
See C. Verlinden's brief survey of "Schiavitù ed economia nel Mezzogiorno agli
inizi dell'età moderna," *Annali del Mezzogiorno*, published by the University of
Catania, III, 11–38; and such monographs as G. Prunaj, "Notizie e documenti sulla
servitù domestica nel territorio senese (sec. VIII–XVI)," *Bollettino senese*, XLIII,
136–82, 245–98, 398–438.

75. D. Gnoli in his "*Descriptio Urbis*," *Archivio* of the R. Società Romana di
storia patria, XVII, esp. pp. 466 ff. (shows that in 1526–27 Rome embraced 55,035
inhabitants, including 1,750 Jews); F. Cerasoli in *Studi e documenti di storia e
diritto*, XII, 170 n. 2, 174 ff. (Jews not included); H. Vogelstein and P. Rieger,
Geschichte der Juden in Rom, II, 427 f. App. 19 (reproducing, from a Vatican MS,
anonymous notes of the seventeenth century); L. Livi, *Gli Ebrei alla luce della
statistica*, p. 290; Simone (Simḥah) Luzzatto, *Discorso circa il stato de gl'Hebrei*, p.
91 (in D. Lattes's Hebrew translation, *Ma'amar*, pp. 151 ff.); other sources cited by
M. A. Shulvass in "The Jewish Population in Renaissance Italy," reprinted in his
*Between the Rhine and the Bosporus: Studies and Essays in European Jewish
History;* and his *Ḥayye ha-Yehudim be-Italiah*, pp. 2 ff.; A. Contento, "Il Censimento
della popolazione sotto la Repubblica Veneta," *Nuovo Archivio Veneto*, XIX, 5–42,
179–240; XX, 5–96, 172–235; K. J. Beloch, *Bevölkerungsgeschichte Italiens*, II, 9 ff.;

III, 5 ff., 15; D. Beltrami, Storia della popolazione di Venezia dalla fine del secolo XVI alla caduta della Repubblica; S. Simonsohn, Toledot, I, 139 ff. Regrettably, in their fine study "Lo Sviluppo demografico di Verona e della sua provincia dalla fine del secolo XV ai giorni nostri," Metron, VI, Parts 3–4, pp. 56–180, esp. pp. 102 f., J. P. Donnazzolo and M. Saibante were unable to offer statistical data for the Jewish population of Verona before 1738. But the remarkable growth of the community to a total of 933 Jews in that year and about 1,000 in 1751 (to be followed by a gradual decline to 503 in 1911) was fairly typical of many Italian Jewish settlements.

CHAPTER LXI: IMPERIAL TURMOIL

1. A. F. Pribram, ed., Urkunden und Akten zur Geschichte der Juden in Wien, esp. I, xxii ff., 1 ff. No. 1; A. Novotny, "Ein Ringen um ständische Autonomie zur Zeit des erstarkenden Absolutismus. Bemerkungen über Bedeutung und Untergang Dr. Martin Siebenbürgers," MIOG, LXXI, 354–69; T. Wiedemann, Geschichte der Reformation und Gegenreformation im Lande unter der Enns, I, 147 f.; supra, Chap. LVIII, nn. 67–68; and other recent literature reviewed by H. Molitor, "Studien zur katholischen Reform in Deutschland. Ein kritischer Bericht," Römische Quartalschrift, LX, 267–79. See also J. B. Neveux's comprehensive analysis of the Vie spirituelle et vie sociale entre Rhin et Baltique au XVIIᵉ siècle, de J. Arndt à P. J. Spener which, unlike most other publications of this kind, has a chapter on facets of Jewish spiritual and social life (pp. 746–67). On the "Turkish menace" to Vienna and her environs, which culminated in the two renowned sieges of the Austrian capital in 1529 and 1683, as well as on the temporary spread of Protestantism in that entire area, see the noteworthy essays by H. Kretschmayr et al. in the Mitteilungen of the Verein für Geschichte der Stadt Wien, IX–X: Dem Andenken an die erste Türkenbelagerung 1529 gewidmet; numerous other publications listed by W. Sturminger in his Bibliographie und Ikonographie der Türkenbelagerung Wiens, 1529 und 1683 (Veröffentlichungen of the Kommission für neuere Geschichte Österreichs, XLI); J. K. Mayr, "Wiener Protestantengeschichte im 16. und 17. Jahrhundert," Jahrbuch of the Gesellschaft für die Geschichte des Protestantismus in Österreich, LXX, 41–133, esp. pp. 46 ff.; and infra, n. 5.

2. A. F. Pribram, ed., Urkunden, I, 5 ff. Nos. 2–10; M. Grunwald, Vienna, pp. 75 ff. On Ferdinand's probable approval of the moderate stand taken by his envoy to the Council of Trent, see supra, Chap. LIX, nn. 17–18.

3. See Zuan (Giovanni) Michele's report, read at the Venetian Senate's session of July 22, 1564, and reproduced by J. Fiedler, ed., in Relationen der venezianischen Botschafter über Deutschland und Österreich im sechzehnten Jahrhundert, pp. 227 ff., 239 ff.; A. F. Pribram, ed., Urkunden, I, 29 n. 6, 31 ff. Nos. 11–18; II, 554 f.; and, more generally, V. Bibl's biography of Maximilian II., der rätselhafte Kaiser. Ein Zeitbild. Although Bibl's characterization of the emperor's personality and policies led to heated debates among Austrian historians, it does reflect the uneasiness of many contemporaries as well as of modern analysts in evaluating Maximilian's frequently puzzling course of action. See H. Hantsch, Die Geschichte Österreichs, 4th ed. rev., esp. pp. 262, 270 ff., and the literature listed on p. 391.

The confusion arising from the endless flow of enactments, modifications, revocations, and reenactments, was so great that the compiler of the *Codex Austriacus,* published in 1704, found it necessary to list seven decrees of expulsion promulgated in the sixteenth and seventeenth centuries, of which only the last edict, issued in 1669, was actually carried out (pp. 559 ff.). This list was enlarged by thirty-three additional ordinances for or against the sojourn of Jews, dating from 1463 to 1669, by L. Moses in *Die Juden in Niederösterreich (mit besonderer Berücksichtigung des XVII. Jahrhunderts),* pp. 20 ff. The anti-Jewish circles were understandably prone to exaggerate the number of Jewish residents. In their 1546 complaint about the presence of "not a few" Jews in the country, the Lower Austrian Estates probably included some temporary visitors as well. See Pribram, II, 554; I. Schwarz, *Geschichte der Juden in Wien bis zum Jahre 1625,* pp. 49 ff.; and *infra,* n. 5, where more reliable data on the Jewish population are recorded.

4. A. F. Pribram, *Urkunden,* I, 17 f. No. 8, 27 ff. Nos. 15–16; Menzel's epitaph, reproduced by B. Wachstein in *Die Inschriften des alten Judenfriedhofes in Wien,* I, 1 f. No. 1 (the last two letters of the questionable date on the inscription were probably eroded by time); W. Messing, "Beiträge zur Geschichte der Juden in Wien und Niederösterreich im 16. Jahrhundert," *Jahrbuch* (= *Mitteilungen,* n.s.) of the Verein für Geschichte der Stadt Wien, I, 11–49, esp. p. 31. Messing also mentions Jewish services to the Austrian mint. At least in the earlier years one Israel Guttmann, probably from the Moravian town of Prossnitz (Prostějov), was admitted (in 1549) to residence in Vienna because the mintmaster considered him indispensable in the refining of gold and silver. But after several renewals of his annual permit he was forced to leave Vienna in 1557 (p. 35). We have no pertinent records of a later date, but in view of the paucity of existing documentation, we may not rule out the possibility that other Jews rendered similar services to the Austrian mint during the late decades of the sixteenth century. See J. Newald, "Das Österreichische Münzwesen unter den Kaisern Maximilian II., Rudolph II. und Matthias," *Numismatische Zeitschrift,* XVII, 167–416.

However, none of the Jewish financiers compared in wealth or influence with the outstanding Christian burghers of the time. The far-flung activities of one such Viennese businessman (among whose borrowers was Archduke Ernst, Rudolph II's brother), and the rich inventory of his estate, compiled in 1585, are aptly analyzed by R. Steuer in "Ein Blick in das Leben und Wirken eines Finanzmannes des 16. Jahrhunderts, Lorenz Ostermayr und seine Familie," *Jahrbuch für Landeskunde von Niederösterreich,* n.s. XXXI, 267–82; no mention is made here of any business contacts with Jewish traders or moneylenders. Because of the dearth of available sources, we cannot judge whether the attempts of the Vienna burghers to bar the Jews' entry was based principally on the fear that the newcomers might there, as elsewhere, promote a quicker turnover of merchandise by offering it at lower prices. The Vienna merchants still preferred relatively few sales with higher profit margins, although this practice gave rise to many complaints by consumers. Ironically, when wine prices rose unduly, a visitor from Judenburg complained that the Viennese Christian merchant, like "a Jew uncle [*Vetter Jud*] prefers to keep the money, rather than friendship." See F. Tremel, "Der Österreichische Kaufmann im 16. Jahrhundert," *Festschrift Karl Eder,* ed. by H. J. Mezler-Andelbey, pp. 119–40, esp. p. 131 (citing a document from the Graz Archive).

5. A. F. Pribram, *Urkunden*, I, esp. pp. 38 ff. Nos. 22–24, 43 ff. Nos. 27–28; G. Wolf, *Die Juden in der Leopoldstadt ("unterer Werd")* im *17. Jahrhundert in Wien*, pp. 2 ff.; W. Messing, "Beiträge zur Geschichte der Juden in Wien," *Jahrbuch* of the Verein für Geschichte der Stadt Wien, I, 27; Zuan (Giovanni) Michele's aforementioned report (n. 3), pp. 229, 235 f. These and other keen observations by Michele and his confreres in other capitals have been largely borne out by modern investigations. See, for instance, the detailed comments on an earlier report from Vienna by H. Goetz in "Die Finalrelation des venezianischen Gesandten Michele Surriano von 1555," *QFIA*, XLI, 235–322. See the further details on Viennese Jewry's fiscal burdens supplied by W. Messing in his generally unsympathetic analysis (to be expected from any author under the Nazi regime in Vienna) of "Die Kontributionen der Wiener Judenschaft im 17. Jahrhundert," *Jahrbuch* of the Verein für Geschichte der Stadt Wien, III–IV, 11–72 (although his data, based upon extensive research in Lower Austrian archives, are admittedly incomplete, the author tries hard to minimize Austrian Jewry's fiscal contributions in the years 1582–1669; see esp. pp. 16 ff., 19 ff., 68 ff., and the statistical table, pp. 70 f.).

Partly as a result of the governmental inconsistencies we possess such detailed evidence as the enumeration, by name and family members, of almost all of the 12 Jewish families listed in the report of 1601. The drain on the fiscal resources of the monarchy, occasioned by Austria's frequent wars, was so great that in the critical year of 1599 one official, Wolf von Fürth, advised the government both to threaten the Jews with expulsion unless they paid a ransom and to seize the estates of the priests. See G. Wolf, "Actenstücke," *Hebräische Bibliographie*, IV, 19. On the general vagaries of the Austrian administration of that period, see G. von Schwarzenfeld's biography of *Rudolf II., der saturnische Kaiser*.

6. R. Matt, "Die Wiener Protestantische Bürgertestamente von 1578–1627. Eine reformationsgeschichtliche Studie," *Mitteilungen* of the Verein für Geschichte der Stadt Wien, XVII, 1–51, esp. pp. 6, 13 ff. (only about 170 such testaments are preserved out of a total of some 4,000 which are extant from that period); R. Till, "Glaubensspaltung in Wien. Ursachen und Ausmass," *Wiener Geschichtsblätter*, XXI, 1–15; and, more generally, K. Eder, "Reformation und Gegenreformation in Österreich," *Theologisch-praktische Quartalschrift*, C, 13–30; G. Mecenseffy, *Geschichte des Protestantismus in Österreich;* and *supra*, n. 1. See also I. Barea's brief summary of *Vienna: Legend and Reality*, esp. pp. 44 ff.; and numerous other studies listed in G. Gugitz's *Bibliographie zur Geschichte und Stadtkunde von Wien*.

7. B. Wachstein, *Die Inschriften des alten Judenfriedhofes in Wien*, I, 38 ff. No. 46, 56 ff. No. 66, 531. The recovery of a fairly large number of Yiddish letters written in 1619 sheds interesting light on the conditions of the newly reestablished Jewish community in Vienna. They were edited by A. Landau and B. Wachstein under the title *Jüdische Privatbriefe aus dem Jahre 1619*. Of special communal interest are two letters relating to the redemption of a Jewish captive and addressed by Moses b. Isaac, secretary of the Prague Jewish community, to Abraham Flesch, son-in-law of Samuel Phoebus and author of a short Hebrew confessional tract in Vienna (pp. 86 ff. Nos. 43–44). In the customarily flattering salutation, Abraham is addressed as "a potent, erudite, sharp-witted, and highly informed scholar."

8. A. F. Pribram, *Urkunden*, II, 561 ff. The extensive Vienna fortifications, in the main erected in 1540–60 against the ever-threatening Turkish invasions, were fully described by F. W. Weiskern in his *Topographie von Niederösterreich*, III, 104. See the excerpt reproduced by O. Frass in his *Quellenbuch zur österreichischen Geschichte*, II, 61 f. No. 47.

It is unclear, however, to what extent the rise and decline of Bishop Melchior Klesel (Khlesel or Klesl) affected the government's attitude toward Viennese Jewry. At the height of his power, during the years 1611–18, when he was both a cardinal of the Church and the equivalent of a modern prime minister, he undoubtedly exerted great influence on the policies relating to Jews. Yet his deposition, followed by a lengthy trial, did not seem to alter the course of these policies which by that time had assumed a fair degree of stability under Ferdinand II's vigorous regime. See the vast documentation reproduced in the appendices to J. von Hammer-Purgstall's voluminous *Khlesl's, des Cardinals, Director des geheimen Cabinetes Kaisers Mathias, Leben;* A. Kerschbaumer's *Cardinal Klesel, Minister-Präsident unter Kaiser Matthias. Quellenmässig bearbeitet;* J. Rainer's more recent studies of "Der Prozess gegen Kardinal Klesel," *Römische historische Mitteilungen*, V, 35–163; and "Kardinal Melchior Klesl (1552–1630). Vom 'Generalreformator' zum Ausgleichspolitiker," *Römische Quartalschrift*, LIX, 14–38; and *infra*, Chap. LXII, n. 3.

9. Bohuslav Hassenstein (Hašištensky) von Lobkowicz, *Epistolae*, ed. by A. Potuček, pp. 42 ff. No. 49, esp. p. 46; A. von Druffel, *Beiträge zur Reichsgeschichte, 1552* (in *Briefe und Akten zur Geschichte des sechzehnten Jahrhunderts*, II), p. 298 No. 1179; G. Bondy and F. Dworský, eds., *Zur Geschichte der Juden in Böhmen, Mähren und Schlesien*, I, 391 No. 541, 402 ff. Nos. 564–65, 413 ff. Nos. 578–79 and 581; and the 1546 list, which in many cases indicated the occupation of the heads of households, thus shedding interesting light on the economic stratification of Prague Jewry. It was published in a German trans. by G. Wolf in his "Zur Geschichte der Juden in Österreich, I: Verzeichniss der Prager Juden, ihrer Frauen, Kinder und Dienstboten im Jahre 1546," *ZGJD*, [o.s.], I, 177–89. After 1551, however, the administration in all Habsburg possessions may have been more watchful, since, for a time at least, most Jewish subjects were forced, by a decree dated November 10, 1551 (three months after the similar enactment in Austria), to wear the yellow circle on their garments. See Bondy and Dworský, I, 400 ff. No. 562; and T. Jakobovits's well-documented study of "Die Judenabzeichen in Böhmen," *JGJCR*, III, 145–84.

Ferdinand's and his successors' constant vacillations in the treatment of Jews were but a reflection of the great denominational, as well as socioeconomic, conflicts in the lands of the Bohemian Crown. Quite apart from their own dynastic and fiscal ambitions, the more forward-looking Habsburg rulers realized that only the application of more or less absolutist means could overcome the powerful vested interests of the feudal aristocracy and an economically incrusted bourgeoisie. With a dim anticipation of the regnant mercantilist trends of the seventeenth century, they seem to have striven gradually to throw off the shackles of the tradition-bound Estates also in regard to the Jewish question. This subject merits closer investigation. In the meantime see the brief critical surveys, permeated with an anti-Habsburg spirit, by the contemporary Czech scholars F. Kavka, in "Die Habsburger und der böhmische Staat bis zur Mitte des 18. Jahrhunderts," *Historica*,

VIII, 35–64; and A. Klíma, "Mercantilism in the Habsburg Monarchy, with Special Reference to the Bohemian Lands," *ibid.*, XI, 95–119. See also the vague suggestions offered by J. Janaček in his "Zur Entstehung der Habsburgischen Monarchie im Jahre 1526 (Diskussionsbeitrag)," *La Renaissance et la Réformation en Pologne et en Hongrie (1450–1650)*, pp. 425–30, which are more significant as a reflection of the malaise of the contemporary East-Central-European scholars vis-à-vis the puzzling phenomenon of the ease of the Habsburg take-over of the Bohemian and Hungarian lands than as contributions to a positive solution.

10. G. Bondy and F. Dworský, eds., *Zur Geschichte*, I, 421 ff. Nos. 582 ff., 433 f. No. 593, 449 ff. No. 611, 455 No. 620, 460 ff. No. 627, 471 No. 642, 475 f. No. 645. The story of the expulsion of the Jews from Bohemia in 1557, its antecedents and aftermath, have never been told in full and illuminating detail. The late Samuel Steinherz, to whom we owe the fine analysis of the preceding banishment of 1542 (see his aforementioned Hebrew essay in *Zion*, XV) also planned carefully to review the events leading up to the denouements of 1557, but the papers left behind by him included only the first section, as yet unpublished. We have to rely, therefore, primarily on the few documentary materials summarized by Bondy and Dworský, whose general lack of thoroughness has often been pointed out. See *supra*, Vol. X, pp. 335 f. n. 8. These anti-Jewish measures must be considered, moreover, in the context of the ever-growing general religious intolerance, which led to the nearly total suppression of the Bohemian Brethren by the royal decrees of October 5, 1547, and January 20, 1548. Their remnants survived principally in the territories of some of the rather independent feudal lords. See R. Řičan, *Die Böhmischen Brüder; ihr Ursprung und ihre Geschichte*, German trans. from the Czech by B. Poplař, pp. 128 ff.; and, more generally, Č. Zirbt, *Bibliografie české historie*.

This was the tense period in Bohemia's interdenominational relations which resulted in the popular uprising ushering in the Thirty Years' War. The unpopularity of the Jesuit Order in Prague led the Estates to issue in 1618 a decree expelling all Jesuits from the lands of the Bohemian Crown, because "their evil practices against the estates of this realm have given rise to all sorts of pernicious attacks and have thereby disturbed the public order, law, and justice, the land's liberties, and common peace in this Kingdom." See the text reproduced in O. Frass's *Quellenbuch*, II, 107 No. 80. It may be noted that, despite the ill-feeling engendered among the Jews by the Jesuits' missionary activities, a Jew endangered his life, in 1618, to save members of the Society and other priests. See G. Wolf, "Ein Jude rettet Jesuiten und andere katholische Geistliche mit eigener Lebensgefahr. Urkundlich nachgewiesen," *Jahrbuch für Israeliten*, ed. by J. Wertheimer, n.s. VII, 221–27; and *infra*, Chap. LXII, nn. 3, 13, and 27. On later developments, see M. Güdemann, "Jesuiten und Judenkinder um 1693," *MGWJ*, VIII, 365–74.

11. See M. Rachmuth, "Zur Wirtschaftsgeschichte der Prager Juden," *JGJCR*, V, 9–78, esp. pp. 12 f., 23 f., 61 ff. Otherwise Count Slawata proved rather ruthless. In 1650, for instance, he extracted from the Jews of the town of Teltsch (Telč) the promise to pay him an annual tax of 30 florins, under the threat that he would reduce the total number of Jewish residents allowed in the town to three families. See idem, "Zur Geschichte der Juden in Teltsch," *ibid.*, IX, 199–241. Conversely, some magnates lent their surplus cash to Jews of Prague on mutually

satisfactory terms. On these loans and other activities of the so-called landlords' Jews (*Herrenjuden*), see A. Blaschka, "Die Judenschulden im Register des Prager Burggrafenamtes 1497–1500," *JGJCR*, II, 97–119, esp. pp. 111 f., 115 ff. (reproducing the text of Vladislav's 1497 decree in a German trans.); and V. Pešak, "Die Judensteuer in Böhmen in den Jahren 1527–1529," *ibid.*, VII, 1–35, esp. pp. 1 ff., 24 n. 4. In some respects Czernin merely harked back to the old medieval principle that not only Jews but also Christian merchants were responsible for debts incurred by their compatriots. In the Jewish case, there also was the widespread practice of rulers to delegate the task of collecting the amounts due from Jewish taxpayers to their respective communities. See *supra*, Vol. XII, pp. 109 f., 227 ff., 295 n. 45, 353 ff. nn. 37 ff.

12. G. Bondy and F. Dworský, *Zur Geschichte*, I, 451 ff. Nos. 612 ff., 457 f. No. 623, 463 f. No. 629, 479 No. 652, 487 No. 662; David b. Solomon Gans, *Ṣemaḥ David*, Prague, 1592 ed., II, 110b (Frankfort, 1692 ed., II, 74a) *ad* 1564; A. Stein, *Die Geschichte der Juden in Böhmen*, pp. 49 f.; *supra*, Vols. V, pp. 293 f. n. 2; VII, pp. 265 f. n. 48; Chap. LIX, n. 42; and *infra*, n. 44. The story of Ferdinand's oath and the papal dispensation is told with many embellishments in a Hebrew narrative reproduced in S. Bernfeld's *Sefer ha-Dema'ot*, III, 44 ff. In any case, the printer whose journey to Rome had allegedly proved so decisive belonged to the "Gersonide" family, which not only first introduced Hebrew printing into the Holy Roman Empire (in 1512) but also continued to issue Hebrew books, in part under a special imperial license, for almost a century and a half. See S. H. Lieben, "Der Hebräische Buchdruck in Prag im 16. Jahrhundert" in *Die Juden in Prag*, ed. by S. Steinherz, pp. 88–106; and J. Rokycana, "Die Privilegien für Gerson Impressor und seine Söhne," *JGJCR*, V, 439–41, reviewing the three privileges granted, in 1527 to Gerson (Hermann), in 1545 to his son Moses, and in 1598 to Moses' two sons, Solomon and Isaac; also reproducing the text of the last concession. See also *supra*, Chap. LIX, n. 42.

13. A. Theiner, ed., *Annales ecclesiastici*, II, 152; F. Hrejsa, "Die Böhmische Konfession. Entstehung, ihr Wesen und ihre Geschichte mit Benützung archivalischer Quellen," *Jahrbuch* of the Gesellschaft für Geschichte des Protestantismus in Österreich, XXXV, 81–123, esp. pp. 109 ff. (summarizing his larger and more fully documented Czech study on this subject); G. Bondy and F. Dworský, *Zur Geschichte*, I, 508 ff. No. 698 (1567), 515 ff. Nos. 708–720 (1568–69); II, 554 f. No. 766, 560 ff. No. 773 (1577), 621 f. Nos. 826-27 (1583), 821 f. No. 1041 (1611); M. Rachmuth, "Die Juden in Neuhaus," *JGJCR*, III, 185–216; IV, 183–252, esp. III, 188 f.; *supra*, Chap. LVIII, n. 62; H. Horowitz, "Die Familie Horowitz in Prag im 16. Jahrhundert," *ZGJT*, II, 89–105, 225–28; III, 127–31, 221–24, esp. III, 221 ff., plausibly arguing that the tombstone inscription of 1568 relates to the same event in Strakonitz which a late-sixteenth-century Czech chronicler, Daniel Adam of Veleslavin, places in 1504. See Bondy and Dworský, I, 206 No. 323. An interesting archival document of 1570 reveals the wide distribution of Jews throughout Bohemia; this evidently incomplete list of 413 Jewish taxpayers shows that they resided in more than the fourscore localities, here enumerated, and ranged from 1 to 22½ taxpayers per locality (the highest number being in Teplitz-Teplice). Evidently, the frequent references to one-half a taxpayer were to amounts paid, rather than to persons. See Bondy and Dworský, I, 530 No. 729.

14. See the detailed data presented by T. Jakobovits in "Die Jüdischen Zünfte in Prag," *JGJCR*, VIII, 57–145; W. Pillich, "Jüdische Goldschmiede unter Kaiser Rudolf II," *Zeitschrift für Geschichte der Juden*, IV, 79–82 (quoting the decree of March 16, 1577, in a facsimile of an official Czech copy extant in a Prague archive, and in German trans.); and, with special reference to Moravia, B. Heilig, "Die Vorläufer der mährischen Konfektionsindustrie in ihrem Kampf mit den Zünften," *JGJCR*, III, 307–448. The inconclusiveness of the vacillating decisions and edicts issued by the royal administration over decades is well illustrated by the 1682 admission by the Prague Christian guild of furriers that the protests lodged by the guild over the years against Jewish competition had been ineffectual. See also *supra*, Vol. XII, pp. 58, 273 n. 58; M. Wischnitzer, *A History of Jewish Crafts and Guilds*, pp. 152 ff.; and, more generally, Z. Winter, *Řemeslnictvo a živnosti XVI. věku v Čechách* (Crafts and Occupations in the Czech Lands of the Sixteenth Century, 1526–1620); idem, *Český prumysl a obchod v XVI. věku* (Czech Crafts and Industry in the Sixteenth Century); J. Janaček, *Řemeslna výroba v českych městech v 16. stoleti* (Industrial Output in the Bohemian Cities during the Sixteenth Century); J. Marek's counterpart thereto in his "Industrial Output in the Moravian Cities during the Sixteenth Century" (Czech), *Sbornik matice moravské*, LXXXI, 124–54; and other recent literature cited by L. Żytkowicz in his succinct survey of "The Evolution of Crafts in Bohemian Lands and in Poland in the Sixteenth and the Beginning of the Seventeenth Century" (Czech), *Čechoslovensky Časopis Historický*, XIV, 589–607. Of considerable interest also are the more comprehensive reviews of the general urban stratification written by Czech Marxist scholars, including F. Kavka's "Hauptfragen der Städteforschung im 16. Jahrhundert in Böhmen und Mähren," *ZGW*, X, 153–61; and J. Marek's *Společenska struktura morávskych-královskych měst* (The Social Structure of the Royal Cities in Moravia during the Fifteenth and Sixteenth Centuries; with a German summary).

15. F. B. von Buchholtz, *Geschichte der Regierung Ferdinand des Ersten*, IX, 186 f. No. xix; G. Bondy and F. Dworský, *Zur Geschichte*, *passim*; and, on the internal conflicts in 1567–78, see G. Wolf's "Zur Geschichte," *ZGJD*, [o.s.] I, 309 ff.; and, more generally, B. Z. Bokser, *From the World of the Cabbalah; the Philosophy of Rabbi Judah Loew of Prague*; A. Blaschka, "Die Jüdische Gemeinde zu Ausgang des Mittelalters," in *Die Juden in Prag*, ed. by S. Steinherz, pp. 58–87. The Bohemian Chamber's early hostility toward the local Jewish community and its leader Munko came strongly to the fore in its various reports to the emperor in 1532–34. See Bondy and Dworský, I, 274 ff. Nos. 401 ff.; B. Wachstein, "Wer sind die Prager Munk im 16. Jahrhundert?" *ZGJD*, I, 141–51 (argues for the identity of the Munk and Horowitz families); V. Pešak's detailed analysis of "The Story of the Royal Bohemian Chamber of 1527" (Czech), *Sbornik archivu* of the Czech Ministry of the Interior, III; and *infra*, n. 18; and Chap. LXII, n. 3. Additional material relating to various Bohemian localities may be found in the essays assembled in H. Gold's ed. of *Die Juden und Judengemeinden Böhmens in Vergangenheit und Gegenwart*.

16. David Gans, *Ṣemaḥ David*, Prague 1592 ed., I, 65a (Frankfort, 1692 ed., I, 66a); the privileges of 1593 and 1598 reproduced in B. Foges's German trans. of the original Czech documents in D. J. Podiebrad's and his ed. of *Alterthümer der Prager Judenstadt*, pp. 40 ff.; G. Bondy and F. Dworský, *Zur Geschichte*, II, 670 f.

No. 894, 714 ff. No. 929. See also S. H. Lieben, "Frummet Meisel, die ebenbürtige Gattin Mordechai Meisels," *MGWJ*, LXXV, 374–77 (arguing, among other matters, against David Herzog's interpretation of Meisel's will; see *infra*, n. 17). See also S. Hock's *Mishpeḥot Q. Q. Prag* (Die Familien Prags), ed. by D. Kaufmann, pp. 212 f.; A. Kisch, "Das Meiselbanner in Prag," *Allgemeine Zeitung des Judentums*, LXIV, 404–406; Z. Münzer, "Die Altneusynagoge in Prag," *JGJCR*, IV, 63–105 (with excellent illustrations); and, more generally, H. Volavková, *The Synagogue Treasures of Bohemia and Moravia;* numerous art and ceremonial objects left behind by the Bohemian Jewish communities destroyed during the Nazi holocaust, now displayed in "Das Staatliche jüdische Museum in Prag." See the pertinent review by W. Benda in the *Zeitschrift für die Geschichte der Juden*, III, 85–99; and the numerous older monographs listed in O. Muneles and M. Bohatec's *Bibliographical Survey of Jewish Prague*.

17. See A. Kisch, "Das Testament Mardochai Meysels mitgetheilt und nach handschriftlichen Quellen beleuchtet," *Festschrift zum 300 jährigen Jubiläum der Meyselsynagoge;* an analysis of the proceedings concerning the Meisel estate by G. Wolf in his *Kleine historische Schriften*, pp. 180 ff. (also mentioning that in 1614 a pretender named Maaser Sax Meisel appeared before the authorities and claimed to be Mordecai's son, entitled to a portion of the estate in the amount of 80,000 florins; p. 192); Bondy and Dworský, *Zur Geschichte*, II, 750 ff. Nos. 967–69, 759 ff. Nos. 972–73, 770 ff. No. 979, and *passim*. Among the attorneys' arguments were such vague aspersions on Meisel's honesty as that the permission given him to display the flag of King David in his synagogue was obtained by him "in a certain way." Even when Rudolph II ordered the Breslau (Wrocław) Chamber to pay Mordecai Meisel's niece by marriage, Johanka Meyslin, her uncle's legacy of 10,000 florins, the Chamber procrastinated and the lady, styled in the documents a "Court Jewess," had to secure in 1612 the intervention of such important personalities as Archduke Maximilian of Austria and Duke Henry Julius of Brunswick. These intercessions bore some fruit, and a year later another imperial rescript again ordered payment of the 10,000 florins to her. Yet in the end she had to be content with the receipt of but 4,000 florins. See Bondy and Dworský, II, 829 ff. Nos. 1051–52 and 1058, 854 No. 1072; G. Wolf, *Kleine historische Schriften*, p. 192. In any case, these intercessions attest the close relationships frequently existing between influential Jews and some German princes of that period. On Johanka's relationship to Mordecai Meisel, see S. Hock's data in K. Lieben's ed. of *Gal-'Ed. Grabinschriften des Prager israelitischen alten Friedhofs*, pp. 18 f. No. 16.

18. Bondy and Dworský, *Zur Geschichte*, II, 734 ff. No. 948; R. Rosenberg, *Die Golemsage und ihre Verwertung in der deutschen Literatur*. On the Bassevi family, which was to play a great role in general as well as Jewish history, especially during the Thirty Years' War, see J. Jireček, "Jacob Bassevi von Treuenberg" (Czech), *Časopis Musea Českého Králoství*, LVII, 325–30; and the mainly genealogical studies by L. S. Porta, *Chronik der Familie Löwenstein Porta;* idem, "Die Erste Nobilitierung eines deutschen Juden, meines Vorfahren Jakob Bassevi von Treuenberg," *JFF*, I, 12–15 (the claim made here is controverted, however, by Frederick III's conferral of a similar rank on Jacob Loans; see *supra*, Vol. IX, p. 168; Chap. LVII, n. 23). See also the biographical sketch of Jacob Bassevi by S. Hock in K. Lieben's *Gal-'Ed*, pp. 23 ff. No. 28; and *infra*, Chap. LXII, nn. 7 and 26. The

remarkable career of R. Yehudah Loew b. Bezalel (see *supra*, n. 15) will be more fully discussed in later chapters.

19. G. Bondy and F. Dworský, *Zur Geschichte*, II, 741 No. 955, 794 f. No. 1009; G. Wolf, "Actenstücke," *Hebräische Bibliographie*, IV, 19; V, 41; Bohuslav Hassenstein (Hašištensky) von Lobkowicz, *Epistolae*, ed. by A. Potuček; K. Oberdorffer, "Die Reformation in Böhmen und das späte Hussitentum," *Bohemia. Jahrbuch des Collegium Carolinum*, VI, 123–45 (only to 1547); J. Klik's older analysis of the "National Relations in Bohemia from the Hussite Wars to the Battle of the White Mountain" (Czech), *Český Časopis Historický*, XXVII, 8–62, 289–352; XXVIII, 31–73; and the literature cited *supra*, nn. 1 and 7.

20. A. Engel, "Die Ausweisung der Juden aus den königlichen Städten Mährens und ihre Folgen," *JGJCR*, II, 50–96, esp. pp. 66 ff.; G. Bondy and F. Dworský, *Zur Geschichte*, I, 167 ff. No. 285; F. Palacký, *Geschichte von Böhmen*, V, 206 f.; C. d'Elvert, *Zur Geschichte der Juden in Mähren und Oesterr.-Schlesien mit Rücksicht auf Oesterreich-Ungarn überhaupt und die Nachbarländer*, pp. 91 ff. (although poorly organized and often relying on secondary materials, this volume reproduces some important primary documents); W. Müller, *Urkundliche Beiträge zur Geschichte der mährischen Judenschaft im 17. und 18. Jahrhundert*, pp. 11 ff.; J. Kux, *Geschichte der königlichen Hauptstadt Olmütz bis zum Umsturz*; the story of individual communities in H. Gold's ed. of *Die Juden und Judengemeinden Mährens in Vergangenheit und Gegenwart*; A. Frankl-Grün, *Geschichte der Juden in Kremsier mit Rücksicht auf die Nachbargemeinden*. The Jewish petition of 1560 was published, from a text addressed to Bishop Balthasar von Promnitz of Breslau in his capacity as governor (*Oberlandeshauptmann*) of Silesia which is extant in the Breslau Archive, by B. Brilling in "Eine Eingabe der böhmischen Judenheit vom Jahre 1560," *ZGJT*, V, 59–62. Interesting new documentation for the early modern history of Moravian Jewry has been made available by the cultural administration of the Czechoslovak Ministry of Interior in *Morava . . . Katalog* (Moravia: Moravian Entries in the Bohemian Chancery and Chamber, a Catalogue for the Years [1507] 1527–1625 [1750]), compiled in the form of *regesta* by D. Culková-Stuchliková. See, for example, the reference to a litigation between one Moses Kaufman of Ostrau and his brother-in-law Jacob Peer of Cracow, Poland, and another to a controversy between both these Jews and a Christian merchant of Augsburg. These controversies called forth the intervention of Maximilian II on November 20 and 23, 1565, respectively (I, 131 Nos. 847, 849). See also some threescore other entries listed in the Index, pp. 907 f. *s.v.* Židé na Moravě, etc.

21. G. Bondy and F. Dworský, *Zur Geschichte*, I, 297 f. No. 419; M. Brann, *Geschichte der Juden in Schlesien*, pp. 164 ff.; B. Bretholz, "Die Judengemeinde von Ungarisch-Brod und ihr Streit mit dem Grundherrn Wilhelm von Kaunitz, gest. 1655," *JGJCR*, IV, 107–181; and other sources cited by I. Halpern in the Intro. to his ed. of *Taqqanot medinat Mehren* (Constitutiones Congressus Generalis Judaeorum Moraviensium, 1650–1748), pp. x ff.; A. Frankl-Grün, *Geschichte der Juden in Kremsier*, I, 17 ff. Most remarkably, numerous Jewish merchants were able to visit the important fairs in Linz and transact much business there. In fact, Moravian Prossnitz sent 10 merchants, who had their wares weighed 191 times on the official scales, to the Linz fair of 1594. It outshone even Prague with

its 9 visitors and 158 instances of weighing. *In toto* there were 82 Jewish visitors from 22 localities. At another recorded fair the Prossnitz community did even better. It contributed 15 visitors to the total contingent of 49. See V. Kurrein's note, "Aus dem Archiv der Stadt Linz," *JGJCR*, IV, 481–84. These business activities by Moravian Jewish merchants did not prevent nine Christian petty traders of Iglau from petitioning the government in 1576 again to expel the Jews from their city. See C. d'Elvert, *Geschichte und Beschreibung der (königlichen Kreis- und) Bergstadt Iglau in Mähren*, p. 198. See also, more generally, J. Válka, *Hospodárská politika feudálního velkostatku* (Economic Policy of the Great Feudal Domain in Moravia before the Battle of the White Mountain); and J. Marek, *Společenska struktura morávskych-královských měst*. Some new avenues for research on the Jewish status in pre-Mohács days, a status continued in many respects under the Habsburg and Turkish regimes, have been opened by R. Nový's compilation of *Městké knihy v Čechách i na Moravé 1310–1526* (City Custumals in Bohemia and Moravia, 1310–1526).

22. M. Brann, *Geschichte der Juden in Schlesien*, pp. 178 ff., 203 ff.; R. Berndt, *Geschichte der Juden in Gross-Glogau;* I. Rabin, *Die Juden in Zülz* (reprinted from the *Festgabe zur 700-Jahrfeier der Stadt Zülz OS*), pp. 8 ff.; idem, *Vom Rechtskampf der Juden in Schlesien (1582–1713)*, esp. pp. 5 n. 3, 10 ff.; G. Helmrich, *Geschichte der Juden in Liegnitz*, esp. pp. 21 ff.; B. Brilling, "The Resettlement of the Jews in Breslau (Wrocław) in the Seventeenth Century" (Hebrew), *Zion*, XXII, 70–73 (claiming that, except for occasional visitors, Jews did not return to Breslau as residents until 1656); idem, *Geschichte der Juden in Breslau von 1454 bis 1702*, pp. 14 ff. See also, more generally, the recent, comprehensive *Historia Śląska* (History of Silesia: a Collective Work), ed. by K. Maleczyński *et al.;* and G. Lösche, *Zur Gegenreformation in Schlesien, Troppau, Jägerndorf, Leobschütz (Schriften* of the Verein für Reformationsgeschichte, CXVII–XVIII). On the intensive commercial relations between Silesia and Poland, in which the increasingly important Polish Jewish merchant class played a significant role, see M. Wolański's twin studies *Związki handlowe Śląska z Rzeczypospolitą* (Silesia's Commercial Ties with Poland in the Seventeenth Century, with Particular Reference to Breslau) and *Statystyka handlu Śląska z Rzeczypospolitą* (Statistics of Silesia's Trade with Poland in the Seventeenth Century: Tables and Statistical Data); and S. Inglot's succinct survey of "Silesia's Economic Ties with Poland from the Sixteenth to the Beginning of the Eighteenth Century" (Polish), *Annales Silesiae*, I, 137–70; and *infra*, Chap. LXII, nn. 8 and 24–25. The tenuousness of the Jewish position even in Glogau is evidenced by the complaint of the generally favored Jewish merchant Israel Benedict to the emperor in 1597 about "some inhabitants who, against the liberties granted him, inflict upon him all sorts of unpleasantnesses and pressures." He at least secured a remedial order in 1598, protecting him and his trade throughout the Glogau duchy. See Brann, pp. 190 f.

23. See S. (Alexander) Büchler, "Jewish Settlements in Hungary after the Mohács Disaster" (Hungarian), *Magyar Zsidó Szemle*, X, 315–29, 370–87; E. Marton, "The Family Tree of Hungarian Jewry. Outline of the History of the Jewish Settlement in Hungary" in R. L. Braham's ed. of *Hungarian Jewish Studies*, pp. 1–59, esp. pp. 15 f. See also the voluminous work by B. Hóman and G. Szekfü, *Magyar történet* (History of Hungary; the German trans. by H. von Roosz *et al.* entitled *Geschichte*

des ungarischen Mittelalters—covers only the first two vols.); and *supra*, Vol. X, pp. 29 ff., 312 f. nn. 33–35. The assumptions, long accepted by modern scholars, that Szerencsés was of Polish origin and that his former name was Salomon Glück have been plausibly refuted by Büchler.

24. Marino Sanuto, *I Diarii*, XXXIX, *ad* June 14 and 19, 1525; also in the excerpts therefrom reproduced in full with comments in Hungarian by G. Wenzel in the *Magyar Történelmi Tár (Hungarian Historical Journal)*, XIV, XXIV, and XXV, esp. XXV, 328 ff. (also explains that the Jewish quarter in Pest, then an independent suburb of Buda, resembled in location the Giudecca section of Venice); *Monumenta Vaticana historiam regni Hungariae illustrantia (Vaticani Magyar okirattár)*, 2d ser. I, 188 ff.; and P. Ratkoš's comments thereon in "Die Entwertung der ungarischen Kleinmünze in Jahre 1521 und ihre Folgen in der Slovakei bis 1526," *Studia historica slovaca*, I, 30–62, esp. pp. 33 ff.; *MHJ*, V, Part 1, pp. 147 No. 302, 154 f. Nos. 311–12, 156 f. Nos. 316–17, 159 No. 324; J. Bergl, *Geschichte der ungarischen Juden*, pp. 54 ff.; *supra*, Vol. X, pp. 29 f., 312 ff. nn. 33–35. Jews were also threatened from above, by the rulers' arbitrary actions. The extent to which the royal house felt free to dispose of the possessions of its Jewish subjects is well illustrated by Queen Maria's rescript of September 26, 1526. On petition of a Fünfkirchen (Pécs) burgher owing 50 florins to "the perfidious Jew Jose" of Ödenburg, she ordered the creditor to return all pledged silver objects to the burgher without compensation, because the debtor had allegedly sustained great losses in the defense of the country against the Turkish invaders. See *MHJ*, IX, Part 1, p. 82 No. 92. See also J. Schweitzer, *A Pécsi izraelita hitközség története* (History of the Jewish Community of Pécs-Fünfkirchen); and, more generally, L. Makkai's survey, "Die Hauptzüge der wirtschaftlich-sozialen Entwicklung Ungarns im 15.–17. Jahrhundert" in *La Renaissance et la Réformation en Pologne et en Hongrie (Studia Historica*, LIII), pp. 27–46; J. Szücs, "Das Städtewesen in Ungarn im 15.–17. Jahrhundert," *ibid.*, pp. 97–164, esp. pp. 110 f. (showing how backward Hungary was even in the more prosperous days of the mid-fifteenth century when the total property of the Ödenburg taxpayers was estimated at 26,174 florins, as contrasted with the property of the 160 patrician families of Augsburg, which was said to be worth 472,026 florins); and the numerous other publications reviewed by G. Heckerrst in his "Forschungen zur Geschichte des ungarischen Mittelalters in den Jahren 1945–1964," *MIOG*, LXXIII, 366–81.

25. *MHJ*, V, Part 1, p. 159 No. 324; Jacob Fugger's letter to Charles V of 1523 cited in a modern German translation in O. Frass's *Quellenbuch*, II, 58 f. No. 44; J. Vlachovič, "Slovak Copper Boom in World Markets of the Sixteenth and the First Quarter of the Seventeenth Centuries," *Studia historica slovaca*, I, 63–95, esp. pp. 67 f., 69 n. 20, and statistical table on p. 70; J. Bergl, *Geschichte der ungarischen Juden*, pp. 56 f. Frass also reproduces in the same context an excerpt from the chronicle of the Fugger family, completed in 1599, referring to later deals between the House of Fugger and the Habsburg rulers, with special reference to the exploitation of Austrian mines. See also the recent biographies of the leading members of the Fugger firm by G. von Pölnitz, *Jakob Fugger. Kaiser, Kirche und Kapital in der oberdeutschen Renaissance; idem, Die Fugger*, esp. pp. 55 ff., 117 ff.; idem, *Anton Fugger*, Vols. I–II, esp. I, 415 n. 15, 664 f. n. 21, 667 (on certain transactions in copper in which Jews became directly or indi-

rectly involved in 1526–33 and 1635); and, from another angle, R. Carande's *Carlos V y sus banqueros.* Of course, in the far-flung banking and business deals of the House of Fugger, which extended over most of Europe and the then explored parts of the New World, the Hungarian-Slovakian mines played a minor role. In 1546 the Fuggers completely stopped mining the so-called Neusohl copper, though they still sold it in the European market. In view of its grave financial difficulties, however, Hungary could ill afford any diminution of royal revenue from the mines, one of its relatively dependable sources.

26. S. Kohn, "Die Ofener Juden während der Türkenzeit," *Literarische Berichte aus Ungarn,* ed. by P. Hunfaly, IV, 399–413; J. H. Mordtmann, "Zur Kapitulation von Buda im Jahre 1526," *Mitteilungen* of the Ungarisch-Wissenschaftliches In-stitut in Constantinople, 1908, No. 4, p. 6; W. Björkman, *Ofen zur Türkenzeit,* pp. 69 f. with the sources listed there; Marino Sanuto, *I Diarii* (see *supra,* n. 24); J. Newald, "Beiträge zur Geschichte des österreichischen Münzwesens während der Zeit von 1622–1650," *Blätter* of the Verein für Landeskunde von Niederösterreich, n.s. XVI, 117–47; *MHJ,* V, Part 1, pp. 156 No. 316, 164 ff. Nos. 327, 330, and 333–34, 184 No. 372, 213 f. No. 432, 265 f. No. 520; A. (S.) Scheiber, comp., *Magyarországi zsidó feliratok (Corpus inscriptionum Hungariae judaicarum),* p. 356. The 1623 decree is the more remarkable as it was issued by Ferdinand II, who was otherwise rather friendly to his Jewish subjects. Apparently the progress of the Thirty Years' War, then raging for five years, sufficiently threatened the imperial ad-ministration for it to lend a willing ear to accusations of a Jewish conspiracy with the Turks. On the location of Buda's *Zsidó utca* (Jewish street), reestablished by the Jews returning from the exile imposed by Louis I in 1360 but speedily revoked, see A. Kubinyi, "Topographic Growth of Buda up to 1541," *Nouvelles études historiques* (published by the National Commission of Hungarian Historians on the Occasion of the Twelfth International Congress of Historical Sciences), I, 133–57, esp. pp. 141, 145, 155 ff.; and *supra,* Vol. X, pp. 25, 311 n. 28. See also S. (A.) Scheiber's recent study, *Héber Kódexmaradványok magyarországi Kötéstáblákban* (Hebräische Kodexüberreste in ungarländischen Einbandstafeln. Die Buchkultur der ungarischen Juden im Mittelalter; with a German summary), which sheds light on various other aspects of Jewish communal history as well.

The effectiveness of the 1526 decree of expulsion has been disputed. In his "Jewish Settlements in Hungary after the Mohács Disaster" (Hungarian), *Magyar Zsidó Szemle,* X, S. Büchler claimed that the resolution of the Diet of Stuhlweissen-burg (Székesfehérvár) was largely carried out; but other scholars have contended that the failure of John Zápolya (the governor and later king of Transylvania) to ratify the decree interfered with its execution. However, many cities, including Pressburg and Ödenburg, independently expelled their Jews. In 1539 the same fate befell the Jews of Tyrnau (Trnava, Nagyszombat). It appears that in the following decades most Jews survived on Hungarian soil only by finding refuge in the vast possessions of the magnates, which included many smaller towns. See E. Marton's observations in R. L. Braham's ed. of *Hungarian Jewish Studies,* pp. 17 f.

27. *MHJ,* V, Part 1, pp. 66 No. 156, 160 ff. No. 326, 164 f. No. 329, 173 No. 350, 182 f. Nos. 367–68, 186 No. 376, etc.; L. Fekete, "Buda, Pest and Obuda and Their Non-Muslim Civil Population in 1547 and 1686" (Hungarian), in *Tanulmányak Budapest Multjidból* (Studies in the History of Budapest), p. 124; A. Scheiber,

comp., *Magyarországi zsidó feliratok* (*Corpus inscriptionum Hungariae judaicarum*), *passim*, including the German summary, "Ungarländische jüdische Inschriften vom III. Jahrhundert bis 1686," pp. 349 ff.; *supra*, Vols. III, pp. 211 f., 332 f. n. 50; X, pp. 27, 312 ff. n. 33.

28. D. Gross, "Äusserer Verlauf der Geschichte der Juden" in *Die Juden und die Judengemeinde Bratislava in Vergangenheit und Gegenwart*, ed. by H. Gold, pp. 3–10, esp. pp. 4 ff.; S. Bettelheim, "Geschichte der Pressburger Jeschiba," *ibid.*, pp. 61–67; and other essays in that volume; *supra*, n. 26. Not surprisingly, the Pressburg burghers were quite unhappy when they were called upon to make up for the taxes theretofore paid by the exiled Jews. As late as 1568 the government tried to collect some such tax arrears by reminding the burghers of their original pledge—probably without much effect. *MHJ*, V, Part 1, p. 203 No. 416. See also, more generally, J. Szücz, "Das Städtewesen in Ungarn im 15.–17. Jahrhundert" in *La Renaissance et la Réformation*, pp. 97–164, summarizing numerous monographs written by himself and others in this field in recent years.

29. *MHJ*, V, Part 1, pp. 156 f. No. 317, 159 f. No. 325, 276 No. 537; IX, Part 1, p. 81 No. 91; Marino Sanuto, *I Diarii* (see *supra*, n. 24). Other early Jewish settlers in the Eisenstadt region included the prominent Ödenburg moneylender Manusch (Mosheh b. Pesaḥ). We find him in Mattersdorf in 1530 as the issuer of a receipt for the payment of a loan due him from a Christian woman. It may also be noted that Abraham was apparently not Szerencsés' only relative. At least we have the record of litigations over the father's estate between two Christian claimants "on the ground of adoption." Another claim was raised with respect to a marriage gift of 3,000 florins. Two years later we hear of a house, a garden, and a vineyard which Szerencsés had allegedly bequeathed to a church and a hospital. See A. Kubinyi, *Mitteilungen* of the Verein für Geschichte der Stadt Nürnberg, LII, 125 ff.

30. *MHJ*, V, Part 1, p. 174 No. 352; IX, Part 1, pp. 86 ff. Nos. 97–99. Eisenstadt and its environs proved particularly attractive to Hungarian Jewish settlers because of the town's proximity to Vienna with its increasingly affluent, if small and un-organized, Jewish community. But our information about the early stages of these "seven communities" is still very limited. Modern scholarly interest in their past was awakened mainly after 1920, when the Paris Peace Treaties allotted the so-called Burgenland to the new Austrian Republic. By that time, unfortunately, much of the local source material had been irretrievably lost. Only from the late seventeenth century on, does the documentary and epigraphic evidence begin to flow more freely. It found a highly competent investigator in B. Wachstein, whose twin volumes on the subject are, like their counterpart pertaining to Vienna in-scriptions, models of their kind. See his *Die Grabschriften des alten Judenfried-hofes in Eisenstadt* (includes a fine study by S. Wolf about the art-historical aspects of "Die Entwicklung des jüdischen Grabsteines und die Denkmäler des Eisenstädter Friedhofes"); and his *Urkunden und Akten zur Geschichte der Juden in Eisenstadt und den Siebengemeinden*. See also G. Langeder's Vienna disserta-tion, *Die Beziehungen zwischen Juden und Grundherrschaft im Burgenland* (type-script), esp. pp. 26 ff. (likewise principally analyzing the relations between the Jews and the Esterhazy and Batthyány families after 1650); and the comprehensive

Allgemeine Bibliographie des Burgenlandes, esp. Vol. IV: Geschichte, comp. by G. F. Litschauer, also referring to a number of publications of special Jewish interest. See the Index, *s.v.* Juden, and the like.

31. Miklós Istvánffy, *Historia Regni Hungariae post obitum gloriosissimi Matthiae Corvini regis,* I, n. 474, excerpted in *MHJ,* V, Part 1, p. 228 No. 463; and *supra,* Chap. LX, nn. 6 and 16. Istvánffy's observation that the Salonicans' ignorance of the Spanish language was proof positive of their lack of proper credentials is unconvincing. Perhaps he had in mind that, speaking in the Ladino dialect, then still in the early stages of its evolution, these purported envoys were not in sufficient command of the Spanish literary language, which still had many devotees in Austrian court circles of that time. See also, from another angle, L. Elekes, *Die Verbündeten und die Feinde des ungarischen Volkes in den Kämpfen gegen die türkischen Eroberer;* and W. Björkman, *Ofen zur Türkenzeit, vornehmlich nach türkischen Quellen.* The story of Hungarian Jewry under Turkish rule will be more fully analyzed in a later chapter, in connection with the other Jewish communities in the Ottoman Empire.

32. *MHJ,* V, Part 1, pp. 201 No. 413, 221 ff. Nos. 450 ff. The story of the Protestant Reformation and the various sects generated by it in Hungary has often been told. See esp. the older but still useful source compilation by J. Ribini in his *Memorabilia Augustanae confessionis in regno Hungariae;* and monographs on the specific aspects by J. G. Bauhofer, *History of the Protestant Church in Hungary, from the Beginning of the Reformation to 1850, with Reference to Transylvania,* trans. from the German by J. Craig with an Intro. by J. M. Merle d'Aubigné; P. Doumergue, *La Hongrie calviniste;* M. Szlavik, *Die Geschichte des Anabaptismus in Ungarn;* as well as the more recent comprehensive reviews by M. Bucsay, *Geschichte des Protestantismus in Ungarn;* and by C. d'Eszlary, "La Lutte entre le catholicisme et le protestantisme en Hongrie," *BSHPF,* CIX, 6–46. Other literature on religious as well as secular developments in sixteenth- and early seventeenth-century Hungary are currently reviewed in the annual "Bibliographie choisie d'ouvrages d'histoire publiés en Hongrie," published by the Budapest Academy of Sciences in its *Acta historica.* See, for instance, Vol. XIII, pp. 255–88, covering the publications of 1964. However, invaluable as many of these studies are for the general background and the external factors shaping the destinies of Hungarian Jews, their authors rarely take cognizance of developments directly relating to the small, but not unimportant, Jewish segment of the population.

33. *MHJ,* V, Part 1, pp. 188 ff. No. 380, 197 No. 402, 232 ff. Nos. 477–79, 238 ff. Nos. 484–88, 248 ff. Nos. 495–501, 258 f. Nos. 505–509, 269 No. 526, 284 f. No. 546, 294 ff. Nos. 561–63, 315 No. 598, 316 Nos. 601–603; IX, Part 1, pp. 110 ff. Nos. 117–24, 120 ff. Nos. 128–48, etc.; Rudolph II's decree of April 12, 1598, in favor of the burghers of Pressburg, cited by E. Forbát in his "Zur Wirtschaftsgeschichte der Juden," in H. Gold's *Juden . . . Bratislava,* pp. 11–16. See also, more generally, idem, *Die Geschichte des Handels und des Pressburger Handelsstandes im XVIII. Jahrhundert,* which also sheds some light on earlier developments (see the more than two-score entries in the Index, p. 390 *s.v.* Juden); and *supra,* nn. 24–25, 27.

34. See *MHJ,* V, Part 1, pp. 249 No. 496, 259 No. 509; IX, Part 1, pp. 95 f. No. 103, 97 ff. Nos. 106 and 110. These few illustrations of the role played by foreign

Jews in Hungary's international trade merely whet one's appetite for more information. Certainly a detailed monograph on this subject would help to fill an important lacuna in both Hungarian and Jewish history of the period.

35. *MHJ*, V, Part 1, pp. 200 No. 411, 209 No. 444, 220 f. Nos. 447 and 449; IX, Part 1, p. 90 No. 101. The upsurge in interest in Hebraic studies was, of course, an accompaniment first of the Renaissance and subsequently of the Reformation, both of which played an increasing role in Hungary's intellectual life. In time the division of the country into three segments, as well as the harsher attitudes injected into all sociopolitical affairs both by the struggle against the Turkish "infidel" and by the Catholic Restoration, blunted these endeavors. Nonetheless, Christian interest in the Hebrew heritage did not completely die down. See various essays in *La Renaissance et la Réformation en Pologne et en Hongrie, 1450–1650* (*Studia Historica*, LIII), esp. pp. 243 ff., 275 ff., 397 ff.; and T. Kardos's recent *Studi e ricerche umanistiche italo-ungheresi*.

36. B. Hóman and G. Szekfü, *Magyar történet* (History of Hungary), esp. III, 266, 315, 387; IV, 95, 98; in part cited by C. d'Eszlary in "La Lutte," *BSHPF*, CIX, 13 ff., 20 ff.; and D. Kosáry's comprehensive biography of *Etienne Batory, roi de Pologne, prince de Transylvanie*, jointly published by the Polish and Hungarian Academies of Science. While religious toleration was imposed upon the country *pro quiete regni*, as the Thorenburg Diet of 1564 expressed it (Art. 5), it at first did not necessarily mean good treatment of Jews as well. Certainly, they were neither numerous nor powerful enough to disturb the peace if they were denied their rights. In fact, according to a rather equivocal passage by a contemporary writer, dated September 15, 1600, Klausenburg (Koloszvar, Cluj) was the scene of antialien riots. "All Wallachians, Russians [Razen], Jews, Greeks, in so far as they were found to be Weydisch [*weidlich*, or able-bodied?], were mowed down by our people." However, this may have been but an isolated incident in the protracted struggle between Stephen's successor, Sigismund (Zigmond) Báthory (1586–1604), and his Habsburg overlords. According to a contemporary record, the Habsburg commander in 1601 ordered the total destruction of the city of Kronstadt (Brassó, Brasov, now Stalin), described as "filled with various, most sordid sects of Arians, Anabaptists, and Jews," because it had ejected the imperial commissioners and offered refuge to Báthory. See *Quellen zur Geschichte der Stadt Brassó*, V, 309; *MHJ*, V, Part 1, pp. 227 f. Nos. 460 and 465.

37. See M. Weinberger's topographically arranged review of the "Sources to the History of the Jews in Transylvania" (Hungarian), *Jewish Studies in Memory of Michael Guttmann*, ed. by S. Löwinger, pp. 283–96; E. Marton's summary in R. L. Braham's ed. of *Hungarian Jewish Studies*, pp. 22 ff.; and G. Lentz, *Der Aufstand Bacskays und der Wiener Friede*. In the long run, the effect of the Counter Reformation proved to be quite considerable even in Transylvania. At first the government, as well as the Papacy, abstained from appointing Catholic bishops, in order not to antagonize the various dissident sects. In the seventeenth century, however, such restraints were cast aside and a policy of repression was increasingly adopted. See F. Teutsch's complementary studies *Geschichte der Siebenbürger Sachsen*, 3d ed.; and *Geschichte der evangelischen Kirche in Siebenbürgen;* and, more generally, the vast amount of documentary material assembled by S. Szilágyi in his *Monumenta comitialia regni Transylvaniae;* and by F. Wilhelm

and J. Kaltenbrunner, comps., *Quellen zur deutschen Siedlungsgeschichte in Südosteuropa.* Some additional data may be found in Erich Roth's more recent study of "Die Reformation in Siebenbürgen. Ihr Verhältnis zu Wittenberg und der Schweiz, II," *Siebenbürgisches* Archiv, 3d ser. IV. Habsburg influence in this area greatly varied from regime to regime. At times it was much exceeded by that of the Ottoman administration. On the latter, see, for instance, Z. Veselá-Přenosilavá's twin essays "Zur Korrespondenz der Hohen Pforte mit Siebenbürgen (1676–1679)," *Archiv Orientálni*, XXVI, 585–602; and "Contribution aux rapports de la Porte Sublime avec la Transylvanie d'après les documents turcs," *ibid.*, XXXIII, 553–99.

38. See S. Kohn, *Geschichte, Dogmatik und Literatur der Sabbatarier,* German translation from the Hungarian; and *supra,* Chap. LVIII, n. 24. That sect was not limited to Transylvania, but had its counterparts in Bohemia, Poland, and particularly Russia. However, the Transylvanian brand was in some respects more enduring and had certain unique features.

39. See G. Schwarz, "Contributions to the History of the Jews in Croatia in the Eighteenth Century" (Croatian), *Vjesnik hrvatsko-slavonskog . . . Archiva,* III, 185–94; and, more generally, the older but still very informative *Geschichte der österreichischen Militärgrenzen,* by G. Schwicker; R. Kiszling's more recent survey of *Die Kroaten. Der Schicksalsweg eines Südslawenvolkes,* esp. p. 41; and the twin studies by G. E. Rothenberg, *The Austrian Military Border in Croatia: 1522–1747;* and *The Military Border in Croatia, 1740–1881: a Study of an Imperial Institution,* esp. pp. 56 f.

40. See *supra,* Chap. LVIII, n. 82. Charles V's final attempts to unify the Empire under strong imperial authority and his ultimate failure in the face of powerful regional diversities, the princely drive for power, and the sharp denominational divisions are well analyzed by M. Salomies in *Die Pläne Kaiser Karls V. für eine Reichsreform mit Hilfe eines allgemeinen Bundes;* and H. Lutz, *Christianitas afflicta: Europa, das Reich und die päpstliche Politik im Niedergang der Hegemonie Kaiser Karls V. (1552–1556).*

41. G. Bondy and F. Dworský, *Zur Geschichte,* II, 727 ff. No. 939; J. B. König, *Annalen der Juden in den deutschen Staaten, besonders in der Mark Brandenburg,* pp. 66 ff., 77 ff.; G. Wolf, "Zur Geschichte der Juden in Deutschland," *ZGJD,* [o.s.] III, 159–84, esp. pp. 172 ff.; I. Kracauer, *Geschichte der Juden in Frankfurt a. M.,* I, 327 (citing a certified copy of the 1570 decree preserved in the archive of the Jewish community). We shall see that, inadvertently, the city of Emden had about that time played a significant, though indirect, role in Jewish history. Because a stranded shipload of Marranos, headed by Jacob Tirado, decided in 1593 that settling there would hold little promise, they turned to Amsterdam, where they helped to lay the foundations for the famous Jewish community which was to be styled the Dutch Jerusalem. See *infra,* Chap. LXIII. We are not told what connection the Prague Jews had with the three prisoners of Emden (in northwestern Germany), about whose misadventures they had learned only from visitors returning from the Leipzig fair, but it is a testimony to the growing strength of their leadership that they dared to approach the emperor for assistance to so distant a community. Internally, too, such Prague Jews as Meisel had long maintained far-flung relationships with other Jewries. See *supra,* n. 16.

42. J. Miedel, *Die Juden in Memmingen*, pp. 20 ff.; G. Liebe, *Das Judentum in der deutschen Vergangenheit*, pp. 41 f. See also *infra*, n. 56. The peculiar conditions which induced Charles V to issue a similar *Judenfreiheit* for the city of Nordhausen on March 21, 1551, are described by H. Stern in his *Geschichte der Juden in Nordhausen*, pp. 35 ff., also reproducing the text of that privilege, and the gloating report thereon by the city's mayor, Michael Meyenburg. The mayor had previously admitted that he had "never had anything to do with Jews, but had rather hated them as the blasphemers of God." On the unsuccessful protests by Josel of Roheim, in behalf of German Jewry, against the resolution of the Augsburg Diet of 1551, see S. Stern, *Josel von Rosheim*, pp. 199 f. (German), 254 f. (English).

43. J. Miedel and G. Liebe (*supra*, n. 42). The difficulties encountered not only by a Jewish leader like Josel, in his lawsuit against the city of Colmar, but also by the Christian city of Strasbourg, in its dealings with the Imperial Supreme Court in the 1530's were but an adumbration of the far more cumbersome procedures employed by that tribunal in the following decades, when its cumulative case load was growing in geometric progression. See R. Schelp's Tübingen dissertation, *Die Reformationsprozesse der Stadt Strassburg am Reichskammergericht zur Zeit des Schmalkaldischen Bundes 1531–1541. Ein Beitrag zu einem reformationsgeschichtlichen Rechtsproblem; supra*, Chap. LVIII, nn. 77 and 81. Regrettably, the valuable documentary publication of *Urkunden und Akten der Reformationsprozesse am Reichskammergericht, am Kaiserlichen Hofgericht zu Rottweil und an anderen Gerichten*, with a Foreword by R. Smend, Vol. I: Allgemeines 1530–1534, has not yet progressed beyond those years.

44. M. Horovitz, *Die Frankfurter Rabbinerversammlung vom Jahre 1603;* L. Finkelstein, *Jewish Self-Government in the Middle Ages*, pp. 78 ff., 257 ff.; *supra*, Vol. IX, p. 320 n. 37; Chap. LVIII, n. 73. The significant Frankfort resolutions relating to various facets of Jewish religious and communal life will be discussed in later chapters.

45. See "Untertänige gegründete Antwort, Bericht und Ablehnung, mit Beilagen A, B, C, D usw. der gemeinen Jüdischheit zu Frankfurt contra der Röm. Kays. Maj. Fiscalem," and other sources analyzed by M. Stern in "Der Hochverratsprozess gegen die deutschen Juden im Anfange des 17. Jahrhunderts. Ein Stück Rechts- und Culturgeschichte. Nach den Prozessakten, vorzüglich des Frankfurter Stadtarchivs, dargestellt und beleuchtet," *Monatsblätter für Vergangenheit und Gegenwart des Judentums*, 1890–91, pp. 24–39, 80–90, 115–27, 154–62 (incomplete); and the general review of this material in I. Kracauer's *Geschichte der Juden in Frankfurt a. M.*, I, 330 ff. Similar gatherings of Jewish leaders in Frankfort in 1562 and other years aroused far less interest among the imperial bureaucrats. It stands to reason that in 1603, too, had it not been for the denunciations made by the Jewish informer, the authorities would not have looked askance at a gathering of Jewish notables assembled to discuss their own internal affairs. However, once the officials' attention was turned to this manifestation of self-determination, they grew suspicious. On other occasions, however, the imperial administration rather encouraged Jewish communal organs to maintain internal discipline. In 1566 Maximilian II learned from a joint petition of the Swabian communities that some members had refused to obey orders issued by their chief rabbi (*Obrister Raby*), Isaac of Günz-

burg, who for some thirty years had, like his predecessors from time immemorial, officiated as the head of the region's religious establishment. Thereupon the emperor decreed that the Jews throughout the Swabian localities must submit to R. Isaac, who was authorized "in case of disobedience to pronounce bans according to Jewish law and usage." Resisters "would incur the emperor's and the Empire's severe displeasure and be subject to a fine of 10 marks gold." See J. Miedel, *Die Juden in Memmingen*, p. 31.

46. Rudolph II's orders of July 10, and September 7, 1595, cited by I. Kracauer in his *Geschichte*, I, 328 f.; A. Fahne, *Die Grafschaft und freie Reichsstadt Dortmund*, I, 206. On the imperial censorship of that period, see esp. W. Brückner, "Die Gegenreformation im politischen Kampf und die Frankfurter Buchmessen. Die kaiserliche Zensur zwischen 1567 und 1619," *Archiv für Frankfurts Geschichte*, XLVIII, 67–87. Jews may have entertained exaggerated fears concerning the impact of Luther's Jew-baiting pamphlets on potential rioters; as has been pointed out, the practical effect of these works, even after their first publication, was relatively minor. See R. Lewin, *Luthers Stellung zu den Juden*, pp. 100 ff.; and *supra*, Chap. LVIII, n. 26. But in view of what happened two decades later, the Frankfort community may well have felt the tremors of the popular revolt which was then smoldering and which needed but a spark to set it off.

47. G. Pfeiffer, "Der Augsburger Religionsfrieden und die Reichsstädte," *Zeitschrift* of the Historischer Verein für Schwaben, LXI (Forschungen zum Augsburger Gedenkjahr, 955 + 1555 + 1955), 213–321; H. Wolter, "Die Reichsstadt Frankfurt am Main und das Konzil von Trient," *Archiv für mittelrheinische Kirchengeschichte*, XVI, 139–75; F. Bothe, *Beiträge zur Wirtschafts- und Sozialgeschichte der Reichsstadt Frankfurt;* and, more generally, F. Lütge, *Strukturelle und konjunkturelle Wandlungen in der deutschen Wirtschaft vor Ausbruch des Dreissigjährigen Krieges* (SB Munich, 1958, I), criticizing certain preconceived notions regarding the general economic decline before 1618 and emphasizing the population's great adaptability to changing conditions.

48. I. Kracauer, "Die Geschichte der Judengasse in Frankfurt am Main," *Festschrift zur Jahrhundertfeier der Realschule der israelitischen Gemeinde (Philanthropins) zu Frankfurt am Main, 1804–1904*, Part 2, pp. 303–451, esp. pp. 313 ff.; idem, *Geschichte der Juden in Frankfurt a. M.*, I, 309 ff.; A. Dietz, *Stammbuch der Frankfurter Juden. Geschichtliche Mitteilungen über die Frankfurter jüdischen Familien von 1349–1849*, esp. pp. 111 ff.; and, more generally, idem, *Frankfurter Handelsgeschichte*, esp. III, 1 ff., 47 ff.; and, for the later period, IV, 167 ff. The pettiness of the Frankfort shopkeepers with respect to Jewish competition is well illustrated by their petition of 1517. Although only a handful of Jews lived in the city at that time, the small retailers complained that "wherever they [the Jews] sell their wares, our merchandise remains behind. Thus we of necessity are ruined and are expelled from this land." Cited from a Frankfort archival document by Kracauer in his *Geschichte*, I, 322 n. 1. It may also be noted that only some of the West-German cities had special Jewish quarters; among them the ghetto of Frankfort, already prominent for its historic origin, was to play a distinguished role in the seventeenth and eighteenth centuries. However, R. Ya'ir Ḥayyim Bacharach (died in 1702) rightly contrasted the presence of obligatory ghettos in Frankfort,

Worms, and Hanau with their absence in Treves, Mannheim, and Koblenz. See his *Ḥavvot Ya'ir* (Villages of Jair; responsa), Frankfort, 1699 ed., fol. 125a No. 135; D. Kaufmann, "Jair Chayim Bacharach," *JQR*, [o.s.] III, 310 No. 1; Dietz, *Stammbuch*, pp. 434 ff. (with a map of the Frankfort ghetto); *supra*, Vol. XI, pp. 95 f., 327 f. n. 23; and *infra*, n. 52. See also E. Mayer's recent sketches of *Die Frankfurter Juden. Blicke in die Vergangenheit*, esp. p. 19; *supra*, Chap. LVIII, n. 72; and *infra*, Chap. LXII, nn. 26 ff.

49. F. Bothe, *Beiträge*, pp. 73 ff., 97 f.; idem, *Die Entwicklung der direkten Besteuerung in der Reichsstadt Frankfurt bis zur Revolution 1612–1614*, esp. pp. 191 ff., 283 ff.; *supra*, n. 44. The tensions increased as the economic crisis of the early seventeenth century deepened. See H. Mauersberg, *Wirtschafts- und Sozialgeschichte zentral-europäischer Städte in neuerer Zeit. Dargestellt an den Beispielen von Basel, Frankfurt a. M., Hamburg, Hannover und München*; E. J. Hobsbawn, "The General Crisis of the European Economy in the 17th Century," *Past and Present*, Nos. 5, pp. 33–53; and 6, pp. 44–65; H. B. Trevor-Roper, "The General Crisis of the 17th Century," *ibid.*, No. 16, pp. 31–64; and the discussion between these two writers, E. H. Kossman, *et al.*, *ibid.*, No. 18, pp. 8–42.

50. F. Bothe, *Frankfurts wirtschaftlich-soziale Entwicklung vor dem Dreissigjährigen Kriege und der Fettmilchaufstand (1612–1616)*, Vol. II, p. viii and *passim*; *supra*, n. 46. Thanks to the ample documentation available, the story of the Frankfort uprising has been told many times. In addition to Bothe's selection of documentary materials, see particularly the older but still very useful description by G. L. Kriegk in his *Geschichte von Frankfurt am Main in ausgewählten Darstellungen*, pp. 237–417. On the Jewish aspects, too, we have many printed and archival documents, including some stemming from Jewish writers; see the next note.

51. The story of the Fettmilch uprising and its effects upon the Jews was described in a lengthy Hebrew poem, *Amallel geburot* (I Shall Express the Mighty Acts; a variant of Ps. 106:2), by Elḥanan b. Abraham Helin, first inserted into his historic narrative by the continuator of David Gans' *Ṣemaḥ David*, Frankfort, 1692 ed., II, 80b ff.; and subsequently reproduced, among other items, by S. Bernfeld in his *Sefer ha-Dema'ot*, III, 48 ff. (see also I. Davidson's *Oṣar ha-shirah*, I, 261 No. 5720). Numerous other data were analyzed by I. Kracauer in "Die Juden Frankfurts im Fettmilch'schen Aufstand 1612–1618," *ZGJD*, [o.s.] IV, 127–69, 319–65; V, 1–26; ᵳnd, more briefly, in his *Geschichte*, I, 358 ff.; and by A. Freimann and F. Kracauer in their *Frankfort* (Jewish Communities Series), pp. 73 ff.; as well as by F. Bothe in his *Frankfurts wirtschaftlich-soziale Entwicklung*. The pillage of the Jewish quarter, the subsequent exodus of the Jews, and finally the execution of the ringleaders made a tremendous impression on the population. Some artists commemorated these events in various contemporary woodcuts. See the interesting reproductions in J. J. Schudt's *Jüdische Merckwürdigkeiten*, III, 9 ff.; and G. Liebe's *Das Judentum in der deutschen Vergangenheit*, pp. 45 ff. Figs. 35–39.

52. See the illuminating comparison of the *Stättigkeiten*, in their older formulations printed in 1613 and the new text of 1616, in parallel columns in F. Bothe's *Frankfurts wirtschaftlich-soziale Entwicklung*, II, 247 ff., 315 f.; and the fairly

precise graphic representations, dating from 1554 and 1628, of the Frankfort Jewish quarter, offered with a brief intro. by J. Hülsen in his *Zwei Ansichten der Frankfurter Judengasse*. See also my *Die Judenfrage auf dem Wiener Kongress*, pp. 23 ff. and *passim;* I. Kracauer, "Die Geschichte der Judengasse in Frankfurt am Main," *Festschrift* of the Philanthropin, Part 2, pp. 320 ff.; A. Dietz, *Stammbuch der Frankfurter Juden*, pp. 436 ff.

53. H. Boos, *Quellen zur Geschichte der Stadt Worms;* the 1563 compact between the Jewish community and the Dalberg Chamber still extant in the Worms Municipal Archive, under Privilegien Box I D 31; L. Lewysohn, "Kaiserliches Schreiben betreffs der Belästigungen der Wormser Juden durch Einquartierungen und andere Auflagen," *Jahrbuch für die Geschichte der Juden und des Judentums,* II, 377–79 (reproduces Ferdinand II's decree of May 16, 1636); G. Wolf, *Zur Geschichte der Juden in Worms und des deutschen Städtewesens;* S. Rothschild, *Aus Vergangenheit und Gegenwart der Israelitischen Gemeinde Worms*, 6th ed.; and A. Kober's succinct summary in "Die Deutschen Kaiser und die Wormser Juden," *ZGJD*, V, 134–51, esp. pp. 139 ff.

Understandably, the city now harped on Charles IV's "donation" of 1348. During the litigation before the emperor in 1614, the ruler demanded the submission, by the municipal representatives, of the original deed of that gift. Evidently, no copy had been preserved in the imperial archives. Apart from the possibility of textual alterations in such records by interested parties, Worms Jewry must thus have learned to its chagrin, how important it was for it, too, to preserve official documents for centuries. That is why it kept many original decrees in the Jewish communal archive for future use; among them, those issued by Charles V in 1551, Ferdinand I in 1562, Maximilian II in 1566, and Matthias on February 22, 1617. All these documents were still available to Adolf Kober during the preparation of his aforementioned essay in the 1930s. Worms Jewry felt so secure in its rights that in 1612, when a Jewish physician, Joseph Beyfus, was insulted by a Christian neighbor who called him "a knave and traitor," he did not hesitate to sue for libel. The offender was condemned by the court to a prison term. See A. Kober, "Rheinische Judendoktoren, vornehmlich des 17. und 18. Jahrhunderts," *Festschrift* of the Jüdisch-Theologisches . . . Seminar, Breslau, II, 173–236, esp. pp. 179 f., 220 f. App. iv; idem, "Zur Geschichte der jüdischen Ärzte," *MGWJ*, LXXX, 305–312; and *infra*, nn. 54 and 60. See also M. Stern, "Das Copialbuch der jüdischen Gemeinde zu Worms," *ZGJD*, [o.s.] I, 277–80; and the literature mentioned in the next note.

That the legal status of Worms Jewry had already become quite confused in the Middle Ages, emerges clearly from E. Carlebach's analysis in *Die Rechtlichen und sozialen Verhältnisse der jüdischen Gemeinden: Speyer, Worms und Mainz von ihren Anfängen bis zur Mitte des 14. Jahrhunderts*. See also *supra*, Vols. IV, pp. 67 ff., 272 ff. nn. 86–90; IX, pp. 179 ff., 327 f. nn. 51–53 and the literature listed there. It certainly was doubly difficult to disentangle the various strands in the sixteenth and seventeenth centuries. In any case, the final decision was made not on legal but on political and fiscal grounds.

54. G. Wolf, *Zur Geschichte der Juden in Worms*, pp. 16 ff., 56 f. Apps. xiii–xxiii; A. Kober, "Die Deutschen Kaiser," *ZGJD*, V, 141 f.; Benas Levy, *Die Juden in Worms*, pp. 12, 15, 17; Ernst Roth, ed., *Festschrift zur Wiedereinweihung der alten Synagoge zu Worms;* and E. L. Ehrlich's brief summary in his "Geschichte und

Kultur der Juden in den rheinischen Territorialstaaten. Vom Beginn der Neuzeit bis zum Absolutismus," in K. Schilling, ed., *Monumenta Judaica. 2,000 Jahre Geschichte und Kultur der Juden am Rhein* (in connection with the Cologne Exhibition of 1963-64), Vol. I, Handbuch, pp. 242-81, esp. pp. 249 ff. Interveningly Rudolph II had issued a new statute for Worms Jewry in 1604. Its text is not preserved, but from the reference to it in Matthias' *Stättigkeit* of 1617 one may assume that its tenor was as pro-Jewish as that of the later enactment. As usual, such privileges were obtained only after prolonged "lobbying." In 1604 it apparently was the Prague Jew Jakob Fröschel who, with the aid of a Bavarian duchess and others, secured the privilege from the emperor. Fröschel subsequently sued the Worms community for reimbursement of his substantial "expenses" of 4,500 florins; the litigation extended over the years 1604-1608. The court records of this litigation are still extant in the Worms Archive under "Streitigkeiten" Box VI, 5, 75.

Although a bit shorter than its 1616 counterpart in Frankfort, Matthias' 1617 statute for Worms made it absolutely clear that ultimate supremacy rested with the emperor and that the city could never again expel the Jews without imperial approval. The Jewish community was thus able to resume a fairly stable life, interrupted only by general disturbances such as wars and plagues. We are fortunate, indeed, to possess an interesting eyewitness description of the inner life of Worms Jewry in the seventeenth century; it was left behind by one of its local officials, Juspa Schammasch (1608-1678). See I. Holzer, "Aus dem Leben der alten Judengemeinde zu Worms. Nach dem 'Minhagbuch' des Juspa Schammes," *ZGJD*, V, 169-81; and, more generally, E. Keyser, "Worms" in his ed. of *Deutsches Städtebuch. Handbuch städtischer Geschichte*, IV, 3: Rheinland, Pfalz und Saarland, pp. 451 ff., 458; and *infra*, Chap. LXII, n. 32.

The effectiveness of these imperial interventions was generally a sign of the growing absolutist and centralizing tendencies of the Counter Reformation emperors. While after the debacle of Charles V's imperial policies it was too late for the emperors to realize their dream of restoring the imperial authority of Frederick I Barbarossa, they were able to assert a measure of supremacy over the weaker members of the imperial constituency: the free cities. See O. Brunner, "Souveränitätsproblem und Sozialstruktur in den deutschen Reichsstädten der früheren Neuzeit," *VSW*, L, 329-60; and H. Conrad's succinct observations on "Die Verfassungsrechtliche Bedeutung der Reichsstädte im Deutschen Reich (etwa 1500-1806)," *Studium generale* (Berlin), XVI, 493-500.

55. L. Löwenstein, *Blätter für jüdische Geschichte und Literatur*, ed. by him (Supplement to *Der Israelit*), I (1900) and IV (1903); idem, "Das Rabbinat in Hanau nebst Beiträgen zur Geschichte der dortigen Juden," *JJLG*, XIV, 1-84; A. Kober, "Documents Selected from the Pinkas of Friedberg, a Former Free City in Western Germany," *PAAJR*, XVII, 19-59; B. Brilling, "Aus dem Archiv der jüdischen Gemeinde Friedberg. Das Protokollbuch der Friedberger jüdischen Gemeinde," *Wetterauer Geschichtsblätter*, XIV, 97-103 (reproduces in the App. Rafael Kirchheim's description of the "Ermordung eines Rabbiners zu Friedberg im Jahre 1582"); Margrave Albert's report of July 23, 1552, to Duke Maurice of Saxony, and Maurice's reply thereto of July 25, in A. von Druffel's ed. of *Beiträge zur Reichsgeschichte, 1552* (in *Briefe und Akten zur Geschichte des sechzehnten Jahrhunderts mit besonderer Rücksicht auf Bayerns Fürstenhaus*, published by the Munich Academy, II), p. 699 No. 1673; and K. Watz, *Geschichte der jüdischen*

Gemeinde in Wetzlar von ihren Anfängen bis zur Mitte des 19. Jahrhunderts (*1200–1850*), esp. pp. 130 ff., 145 ff. (analyzing the *Stättigkeit* in its 1626 and 1726 formulations). See also E. J. Zimmermann, *Hanauer Chronik . . . Stadt und Land Hanau von den ältesten Zeiten bis zur Gegenwart;* and H. Bott's more recent study of "Stadt und Festung Hanau, nach dem Stockholmer Plan des Joachim Rim vom 8. Januar 1632, etc.," *Hanauer Geschichtsblätter*, XVIII, 182–222; XX, 61–125.

56. See *supra*, n. 46; and, on the developments in Fulda, the data cited by G. Wolf in his "Zur Geschichte der Juden in Deutschland," *ZGJD*, [o.s.] III, 176 ff. No record of Henry VII's donation of Jews to the abbey of Fulda seems to be extant. The first mention known to us of Jews in Fulda dates from 1235, when the city achieved wide notoriety in connection with the slaying of thirty-two Jews allegedly implicated in the murder of a Christian child for medicinal purposes. This affair gave rise to the convocation by Emperor Frederick II of the international congress which exonerated all Jews from the blood libel. See M. Brann *et al.*, *Germania Judaica*, I, 113 f.; and *supra*, Vols. IX, pp. 143 ff., 311 f. nn. 10–11; X, pp. 146 f., 359 n. 32. On the role the 1235 riot may have played in the development of the doctrine of Jewish "serfdom," see the suggestions advanced in my Hebrew essay on " 'Plenitude of Apostolic Powers' and Medieval 'Jewish Serfdom' " in *Baer Jub. Vol.*, pp. 102–124.

57. E. Nübling, *Die Judengemeinden des Mittelalters*, pp. 522 ff. On similar chicaneries, employed by the city of Memmingen, see J. Miedel's circumstantial account in *Die Juden in Memmingen*, esp. pp. 17 ff.; and *supra*, n. 42.

58. Archbishop Ernst's 1599 ordinance and its successor enactments, reproduced in *Sammlung Kurkölnischer Verordnungen*, I, 216 ff. Nos. 92–93; J. J. Scotti's compilation of *Churkölnische, Westfälische und Recklinghausen'sche Landesverordnungen*, I, No. 50; *Gesetz-Sammlung des Erzstiftes Köln*, I, 216–21, 221–44, 702 ff.; E. Weyden, *Geschichte der Juden in Köln am Rhein von den Römerzeiten bis auf die Gegenwart*, pp. 257 ff. Archbishop Ferdinand, likewise a Bavarian prince, spelled out his predecessor's privilege in much greater detail, and it was in this expanded form that the statute served, so to say, as the basic constitution for the Jewries of the archdiocese in the following generations. See W. Kisky, *Die Regesten der Erzbischöfe von Köln*. See also, more generally, C. Brisch, *Geschichte der Juden in Cöln und Umgebung*, esp. II, 100 ff.; A. Kober, *Cologne* (Jewish Communities Series), pp. 130 ff., 142 ff. Though dealing with somewhat later data, idem, "Die Reichsstadt Köln und die Juden in den Jahren 1685–1715. Ein Beitrag zur Geschichte der jüdischen Hoffaktoren," *MGWJ*, LXXV, 412–28, sheds light on the earlier period also. (Kober quotes from unpublished minutes, for instance, the city council's inhuman decision of 1679; p. 413.) To a lesser extent the same holds true for G. Hoffmann's Munich dissertation, *Die Juden im Erzstift Köln im 18. Jahrhundert*. See also the brief summary by E. L. Ehrlich in his "Geschichte und Kultur" in *Monumenta Judaica*, ed. by K. Schilling, I, 242 ff.; and *supra*, Vols. IX, pp. 173 ff., 323 ff. nn. 44–48; XII, pp. 57, 372 f. n. 51.

59. The role of Marranos in sixteenth-century Cologne has for the first time been described by Hermann Kellenbenz, on the basis of numerous archival and

literary sources. See esp. his *Unternehmerkräfte im Hamburger Portugal- und Spanienhandel 1590–1625*, pp. 241 f.; his comprehensive work, *Sephardim an der unteren Elbe;* his briefer sketch, "Die Juden in der Wirtschaftsgeschichte des rheinischen Raumes. Von der Spätantike bis zum Jahre 1648," in K. Schilling's *Monumenta*, I, 199–241, esp. pp. 229 ff.; and, with special reference to Cologne, his "Die Rodrigues d'Evora in Köln," *Portugiesische Forschungen der Görresgesellschaft*, VI, 272–90; and his "Die Geschäfte der Firma Ferdinand Ximenes und Erben des Rui Nunes' in Köln," *Studi in memoria di Corrado Barbagallo*. See also R. von Roesbroeck, "Die Niederländischen Glaubensflüchtlinge in Deutschland und die Anfänge der Stadt Frankenthal," *Blätter für pfälzische Kirchengeschichte*, XXX, 2–28. These Marrano contributions were characteristic of the far-flung activities of that relatively small but highly influential group of merchants in Antwerp, Hamburg, Amsterdam, and other localities, as discussed *supra*, Chap. LVI, nn. 63 ff.; and *infra*, Chap. LXII, nn. 43 ff.; and Vol. XV. As emphasized by H. Kellenbenz, it undoubtedly was owing to these "Portuguese" residents, as well as to other foreign merchants, particularly Italian and Dutch, that the Cologne quotations of prices for foreign drafts were very widely reported in various commercial centers; in Lyons they were regularly published in print, beginning in 1586. See H. Lapeyre, *Une Famille de marchands, les Ruiz*, p. 293; H. Kellenbenz in *Monumenta*, I, 231 f. See also A. H. de Oliveira Marques, "Relações entre Portugal e a Alemanha no século XVI," *Revista da Faculdade de Letras de Lisboa*, 3d ser. IV, esp. p. 49; F. Steinbach, "Relations entre Lyon et le Nord des Pays Rhénans depuis la fin du moyen âge" (1959), reproduced in his *Collectanea. Aufsätze zur Verfassungs-, Sozial- und Wirtschaftsgeschichte, geschichtlichen Landeskunde und Kulturraumforschung*, ed. by F. Petri and G. Droege, pp. 97–101; and H. Thimme, "Der Handel Kölns am Ende des 16. Jahrhunderts und die internationale Zusammensetzung der Kölner Kaufmannschaft," *Westdeutsche Zeitschrift für Geschichte und Kunst*, XXXI, 389 ff.

60. K. A. Schaab, *Diplomatische Geschichte der Juden zu Mainz*, pp. 171 ff., 223 ff.; S. Salfeld, *Bilder aus der Vergangenheit der jüdischen Gemeinde Mainz*, pp. 47 ff.; idem, "Vorboten der Judenemanzipation in Kurmainz," *Judaica* (Hermann Cohen Jub. Vol.), pp. 348 f. In contrast to Cologne, we have no evidence of the settlement of any Marrano families in Mayence. Clearly, the economic opportunities offered by the declining but still influential trade emporium in Cologne were not equaled by the more provincial capital of the primate of Germany, a capital which was commercially overshadowed in its own archdiocese by Frankfort. Yet, a small Marrano settlement is not unlikely, especially if we accept Mayence as the location where one Jacob Israel arranged in 1584 for the printing of a Spanish-Jewish prayerbook (*Maḥzor*) for the New Year and the Day of Atonement. See H. Heidenheimer, "Zur Geschichte und Beurteilung der Juden von XV. bis XIX. Jahrhundert," *MGWJ*, LIII, 1–27, 129–58, 257–68, esp. pp. 151 f. (also tries to refute M. Steinschneider's earlier caustic critique of the identification of Mayence as the printing place). On the few Jewish doctors appearing in the Mayence area, see the two studies by A. Kober cited *supra*, n. 53.

61. J. J. Scotti, *Churtrier'sche Landesverordnungen*, I, No. 162; G. Liebe, "Die Rechtlichen und wirtschaftlichen Zustände der Juden im Erzstift Trier," *Westdeutsche Zeitschrift für Geschichte*, XII, 311–74; idem, *Das Judentum in der*

deutschen Vergangenheit, pp. 33, 41, etc.; S. Salfeld, "Zur Geschichte des Juden-schutzes in Kurmainz," *Philippson Festschrift*, pp. 135–67 (only important here for the medieval background); B. Brilling, "Beiträge zur Geschichte der Juden in Trier," *Trierer Jahrbuch*, IX; F. P. Kahlenberg, "Jüdische Gemeinden am Mit-telrhein," in F. J. Heyen, ed., *Zwischen Rhein und Mosel. Der Kreis St. Goar*, pp. 359–72, esp. p. 365; and other sources cited *supra*, Vol. IX, pp. 325 f. nn. 49–50. See also the summaries by H. Kellenbenz and E. L. Ehrlich in *Monumenta Judaica*, ed. by K. Schilling, I, 225 ff., 254 ff. On Dortmund see A. Fahne, *Die Grafschaft und freie Reichsstadt Dortmund*; R. Maser, *Die Juden der Frei- und Reichsstadt Dortmund und der Grafschaft Mark*, pp. 49 ff.; L. von Winterfeld, *Geschichte der freien Reichs- und Hansestadt Dortmund*, 2d ed., p. 137; and *supra*, n. 46.

In contrast to its great medieval past, the Spires community's humble modern developments have not been treated with the necessary detailed documentation. See E. L. Rapp's more recent "Beiträge zur Geschichte der Juden Speyers im Mittelalter," *Mitteilungen* of the Historischer Verein der Pfalz, LVIII, 150 ff.; other literature cited in E. Keyser's ed. of *Deutsches Städtebuch*, IV, Part 3, pp. 391 f., 409 f.; E. Carlebach, *Die Rechtlichen und sozialen Verhältnisse der jüdischen Gemeinden: Speyer, Worms und Mainz von ihren Anfängen bis zur Mitte des 14. Jahrhunderts*; L. Rothschild's dissertation, *Die Judengemeinden zu Mainz, Speyer und Worms von 1349–1438*; and *supra*, Vol. IX, pp. 326 f. n. 52.

62. B. H. Auerbach, *Geschichte der israelitischen Gemeinde Halberstadt*, esp. pp. 16 ff.; M. Köhler, *Beiträge zur neueren jüdischen Wirtschaftsgeschichte. Die Juden in Halberstadt und Umgebung bis zur Emanzipation*, pp. 4 ff.; M. Wiener, "Geschichte der Juden in der Residenzstadt Hannover, vorzugsweise während des 16. Jahrhunderts," *MGWJ*, X, 287 ff., 295 ff. App. xx; A. Löb, *Die Rechtsverhältnisse der Juden im ehem. Königreich . . . Hannover*, p. 14. On the German memor books and their significance for Jewish history see *supra*, Vol. XI, pp. 416 f. n. 91. It may be noted that some of the provincial communities in the region, such as Derenburg, embraced a number of influential Jewish bankers. One of them, named Löw, appears in the records of the *Reichskammergericht* in Wetzlar during the years 1553–57 as plaintiff against Count Christoph von Mansfeld, Margrave John George of Brandenburg, and Duke Erich of Brunswick-Lüneburg. See Köhler, pp. 4 f. n. 18.

63. H. Stern, *Geschichte der Juden in Nordhausen*, pp. 37 ff., 40 ff.; and *supra*, n. 43. Evidently, both Ferber and the city had realized that litigations pursued to their logical conclusion before the German Supreme Court were endless and costly (see *supra*, n. 43), and preferred to settle their differences out of court.

64. S. Samuel, *Geschichte der Juden in Stadt und Stift Essen bis zur Säkulari-sation des Stifts von 1291–1802*, esp. pp. 29 ff., 90 ff. Apps. Nos. vi–x; and, more generally, K. Ribbeck, *Geschichte der Stadt Essen*, Vol. I (no more appeared). Remarkably, even the relatively small town of Essen found it necessary to shut Jews off in their own quarter. The concluding paragraph (12) of the 1598 decree provided that Jews must not be seen on other streets after six o'clock in winter or after nine o'clock in summer, under a penalty to be set at the discretion of the authorities. These and other restrictions bear out the statement in the preamble that the decree was issued under pressure from the burghers and the city council.

65. See A. Riemer, "Die Juden in niedersächsischen Städten des Mittelalters," *Zeitschrift* of the *Historischer Verein für Niedersachsen*, V, 303–364; VI, 1–57, esp. p. 16; A. Rexhausen, *Die Rechtliche und wirtschaftliche Lage der Juden im Hochstift Hildesheim;* A. Vogeler, "Das Schauspiel in Alt-Hildesheim," *Alt-Hildesheim; eine Zeitschrift für Stadt und Stift Hildesheim*, No. 10, pp. 58–68, esp. p. 67; and, more generally, J. Gebauer, *Geschichte der Stadt Hildesheim;* A. Bertram, *Geschichte des Bistums Hildesheim*. See also *infra*, Chap. LXII, n. 37.

66. A. Eckstein, *Geschichte der Juden im ehemaligen Fürstbistum Bamberg*, esp. pp. 15 ff.; with *Nachträge* thereto, which deal, however, almost exclusively with the 1790s. See also *infra*, n. 71; and, more generally, J. Looshorn's older but very detailed *Geschichte des Bistums Bamberg*, Vols. I–VII. In the bishopric of Bamberg, too, some intolerant decrees were partially frustrated by the presence of numerous enclaves under the authority of local lords. Since these petty masters often found it to their advantage to admit Jewish taxpayers, it was not too difficult for a few Jewish residents to gain entry into the city of Bamberg and other localities under the bishop's jurisdiction. On the other hand, a characteristic remark in the tax records of the episcopal Chamber of 1487–89 succinctly describes the situation in the areas under the suzerainty of the bishop: "Nothing has been received from Jews, for none are here." See Eckstein, p. 14 n. 2. See also some general studies listed in the "Schrifttum zur Geschichte des Bistums und Hochstifts Bamberg sowie der Randgebiete (1964–1966, mit Nachträgen aus früheren Jahren). Besprechungen und Hinweise," *Bericht* of the Historischer Verein . . . Bamberg, CIII, 505–540.

67. See R. Straus, ed., *Urkunden und Aktenstücke zur Geschichte der Juden in Regensburg, 1453–1738*, pp. 448 f. No. 1215; B. Sastrow, *Herkommen, Geburt und Lauff seines ganzen Lebens*, II, ii. 10, ed. by G. C. F. Mohnicke, II, 83 f. (1547–48); M. Freundenthal, "Zur Geschichte des Judenprivilegs Kaiser Maximilians II. auf dem Reichstag zu Augsburg 1566," *ZGJD*, IV, 83–100, esp. pp. 85 f. (mentioning two Jews, Abraham of Fürth and Jakob of Roth, who on April 2, 1566, but three weeks after the issuance of the decree of March 8, secured in Augsburg a certified copy provided with a seal by Count Heinrich von Pappenheim); Clemens Jäger's versified chronicle, reproduced by F. Roth in his 1929 ed. of Jäger's works in K. Hegel's collection of *Die Chroniken der deutschen Städte*, XXXIV, 364; and the triumphant restatement of these intolerant outbursts in E. Gebele's Nazi-oriented *Die Juden in Schwaben*, pp. 11 ff. See also P. Braun, *Geschichte der Bischöfe von Augsburg*, IV, 12; O. Stobbe, *Die Juden in Deutschland*, p. 87.

68. See F. X. Himmelstein, "Die Juden in Franken. Ein Beitrag zur Kirchen- und Rechtsgeschichte Frankens," *Archiv* of the *Historischer Verein von Unterfranken und Aschaffenburg*, XII, 125–88, esp. pp. 142 f.; A. Friedmann, *Bilder aus meiner Heimatgeschichte. Ein Beitrag zur Geschichte und Heimatkunde der Juden in Bayern*, pp. 14 f. See also M. Bohrer's Freiburg dissertation, *Die Juden im Hochstift Würzburg im 16. und am Beginn des 17. Jahrhunderts* (typescript); and D. Weger's Würzburg dissertation, *Die Juden im Hochstift Würzburg während des 17. und 18. Jahrhunderts* (typescript).

69. J. C. von Aretin, *Geschichte der Juden in Baiern*, pp. 49 ff., 61 ff.; *Polizei-Ordnung*, 1616, v.i; K. Brandi, *Deutsche Reformation und Gegenreformation*, II,

47 ff. The Bavarian authorities were quite exacting in the collection of tolls from the Jews passing through the country. When, in 1621, the count palatine of neighboring Neuburg established a number of minting offices and handed their operation over to Jews, the latter were often forced to cross the frontier to some adjacent Bavarian locality. But in each case they had to pay special tolls, which differed from locality to locality but were always very high. In 1676 some of the Jewish exiles from Vienna passed through Bavaria in search of new shelters. In answer to an inquiry the elector ruled that they be made to pay a double toll or more, and that special cases (doubtless referring to reputedly wealthy Jews) be submitted to his personal decision. See S. Tausig, *Geschichte der Juden in Baiern,* pp. 61 ff. On the great diversity of Jewish status in various parts of Bavaria, see A. Friedmann's nostalgic and badly organized, but informative, *Bilder aus meiner Heimatgeschichte;* and the observations, originating from the controversies raging after the First World War, by A. Eckstein in his *Haben die Juden in Bayern ein Heimatsrecht? Eine geschichtswissenschaftliche Untersuchung mit Kriegstatistischen Tabellen,* with a "Geleitwort zur Kriegsstatistik" by A. Werner; and S. Schwarz's recent monograph, *Die Juden in Bayern im Wandel der Zeiten,* particularly valuable for the nineteenth century (with bibliography). Of considerable interest also are some data supplied in R. Baurreiss's comprehensive *Kirchengeschichte Bayerns,* Vols. I–VI, esp. Vol. VI, dealing with the sixteenth century; and other recent literature, listed by M. Renner in his *Bayerische Bibliographie, 1959–1963* (Supplement I to *ZBL* of 1966).

70. R. Straus, ed., *Urkunden und Aktenstücke . . . Regensburg,* pp. 430 No. 1159, 432 Nos. 1165 and 1167, 433 ff. Nos. 1172 and 1176, 441 No. 1196, 446 f. Nos. 1206 and 1211. See also *supra,* nn. 66 and 68; and Chap. LVIII, nn. 42 and 64. Needless to say, the Jews of Stadtamhof had to pay their own taxes. In voting in 1543 a new tax for the imperial forces in the Turkish War, the Diet of Landshut specifically ordered the Jews of that locality, as well as of Kehlheim to contribute 1 florin per person, "man or woman, young or old." *Ibid.,* p. 435 No. 1179. A contemporary chronicler, Leonhart Widmann, before 1538 reminisced that at the time of the 1519 expulsion a Jew named Mosse had warned the Catholic clergy that it would pay heavily for its incitation of the populace against Jews. Now, Widmann claimed, as a result of the Reformation that prediction had indeed been fulfilled. See his *Chronik von Regensburg 1511–43, 1552–55,* ed. by E. von Oefele in K. Hegel's collection of *Die Chroniken der deutschen Städte,* XV, 32, 148, 159; excerpted by Straus, p. 433 No. 1171. See also R. Straus, *Regensburg and Augsburg* (Jewish Communities Series), pp. 46 ff.; H. Kellenbenz, "Bürgertum und Wirtschaft in der Reichsstadt Regensburg," *Blätter für deutsche Landesgeschichte,* XCVIII, 107.

71. A. Eckstein, *Geschichte der Juden im ehemaligen Fürstbistum Bamberg,* pp. 15 ff.; S. Haenle, *Geschichte der Juden im ehemaligen Fürstentum Ansbach,* pp. 44 ff., 217 ff. App. 4, 223 ff.; A. Würfel, *Historische Nachricht von der Judengemeinde in dem Hofmarkt Fürth,* pp. 47 ff., 60 f.; H. Barbeck, *Geschichte der Juden in Nürnberg und Fürth,* pp. 46 ff. Barbeck offers more reliable data on the growth of the Fürth community, which in 1566 embraced four families living under the Bamberg, and one under the Ansbach, jurisdiction, with dependents a total of some 70 persons. Within sixteen years the Jewish population increased to 200 souls.

It is curious that stubbornly anti-Jewish Nuremberg did not mind entrusting to a Jew, Michael of Fürth, the task of detecting poachers on its territory. Ultimately, Michael delivered six men suspected of murder and burglary to the Nuremberg authorities. However, Margrave George Frederick of Ansbach saw therein an infringement of his sovereignty, and after a trial he had Michael executed in 1596. He posted on the culprit's grave a tablet reading: "Michael, Nuremberg Jew, traitor." All appeals by the Nuremberg council to the emperor to order the removal of that tablet, considered insulting to the city's own dignity, proved unavailing. See Haenle, pp. 56 f., citing a Nuremberg archival document.

72. See A. Eckstein's well documented monograph, *Geschichte der Juden im Markgrafentum Bayreuth*, also listing in his Foreword the earlier publications. See esp. pp. 14 ff., 28 ff., 110 f. App. iii. All along, the margraves of Ansbach and Bayreuth argued that the Jews were useful taxpayers for the Treasury, while the Estates pointed to other countries which readily dispensed with such revenue because it hardly compensated them for the disadvantages accruing to the population from the presence of Jews. Occasionally we also hear the standard arguments about Jewish blasphemies and hostility toward Christianity and its founder. But these denunciations often have a hollow sound; they appear as a rather transparent cloak for the burghers' purely competitive motivations.

73. Simone Luzzatto, *Discorso circa il stato*, xviii, fols. 90 f.; in the Hebrew trans., p. 153; R. Bodenheimer, "Beiträge zur Geschichte der Juden in Oberhessen," *ZGJD*, III, 260 ff.; IV, 11 ff. See also E. Milius, ed., *Der Hessische Landkreis Friedberg*, which includes F. Koppel's essay, "Das Kreisgebiet im Gang der Geschichte," pp. 175–210, esp. pp. 193 f.; and, on the political structure of Hesse as a whole, W. Noack's Mayence dissertation, *Landgraf Georg I. von Hessen und die Obergrafschaft Katzenellenbogen (1567–1596)*.

74. L. Löwenstein, *Beiträge zur Geschichte der Juden in Deutschland*, pp. 58 ff.; O. Stobbe, *Die Juden in Deutschland*, p. 16. M. Weinberg's detailed and well-documented review of a number of communities in his *Geschichte der Juden in der Oberpfalz*; R. Overdick's more recent careful analysis of *Die Rechtliche und wirtschaftliche Stellung der Juden in Südwestdeutschland im 15. und 16. Jahrhundert. Dargestellt an den Reichsstädten Konstanz und Esslingen und an der Grafschaft Baden*. See also, more generally, P. Kruger's Munich dissertation, *Die Beziehungen der rheinischen Pfalz zu Westeuropa, 1576–82. Die auswärtigen Beziehungen des Pfalzgrafen Johann Casimir, 1576–82*; and H. F. Liebel's "The Bourgeoisie in Southwestern Germany, 1500–1789," *International Review for Social History*, X, 283–307. Of interest also are H. Klenk's recent review of "Ein sogen. Inquisitionsprozess in Giessen anno 1623," *Mitteilungen* of the Oberhessischer Geschichtsverein, n.s. XLIX-L, 39–60; and, because of the growing dispersal of Jews into rural areas, W. A. Boelcke's "Zur Entwicklung des bäuerlichen Kreditwesens in Württemberg, vom späten Mittelalter bis Anfang des 17. Jahrhunderts," *JNOS*, CLXXVI, 319–58.

75. Quoted by G. Liebe in *Das Judentum*, p. 67; Pamphilus Gengenbach and Johann Balthasar Schupp, cited by O. Frankl in his Vienna thesis, *Der Jude in den deutschen Dichtungen des 15., 16. und 17. Jahrhunderts*, pp. 95 ff. See also K.

Hansen, "Petrus Canisius' Stand on Usury: an Example of Jesuit Tactics in the German Counter-Reformation," *ARG*, LV, 192–203; and, on the views expressed by Luther, Calvin, and their successors, *supra*, Chap. LVIII, nn. 19, 96, and 104.

76. See O. Brunner, "Souveränitätsproblem und Sozialstruktur in den deutschen Reichsstädten der früheren Neuzeit," *VSW*, L, 348 f.; E. L. Etter, *Tacitus in der Geistesgeschichte des 16. und 17. Jahrhunderts;* and, with particular reference to Jews, S. Ettinger's review of "The Beginnings of the Change in the Attitude of the European Society toward the Jews," *Scripta Hierosolymitana* of the Hebrew University in Jerusalem, VII, 193–219.

CHAPTER LXII: THIRTY YEARS' WAR

1. Bishop Melchior Khlesel's memorandum reproduced by J. von Hammer-Purgstal in his *Klesl's, des Cardinals, . . . Leben*, I, 385 No. 166. On the general developments during the Thirty Years' War see the older but still very useful review by A. Gindely in his *Geschichte des dreissigjährigen Krieges;* or in the English trans. by A. Ten Brooks entitled *History of the Thirty Years War* (somewhat abridged but with the addition of an introductory and a concluding chapter by the translator); G. Pagès, *La Guerre de Trente Ans 1618–1648;* and M. Ritter, *Deutsche Geschichte im Zeitalter der Reformation und des dreissigjährigen Krieges.* Some of the vast array of monographs dealing with specific problems, events, and personalities are reviewed in G. Franz's *Der Dreissigjährige Krieg und das Deutsche Volk. Untersuchungen zur Bevölkerungs- und Agrargeschichte*, 3d ed. See also the 1954 critical survey of the diverse approaches to that War's complicated story by J. V. Polišenský in "The Thirty Years' War," *Past and Present*, VI, 31–43; and S. H. Steinberg's succinct observations on "The Thirty Years' War: a New Interpretation," *History*, XXXII, 89–102. Much information can also be gathered from the studies of the Peace Treaty of Westphalia, such as those mentioned *infra*, nn. 64 ff.

While the religious and political conflicts have long been carefully examined, the War's economic background and developments during its long duration have aroused the intense interest of scholars only in recent years. See, for example, F. Lütge, *Strukturelle und konjunkturelle Wandlungen in der deutschen Wirtschaft vor Ausbruch des dreissigjährigen Krieges* (denies that the German economy had been in a state of decline); the debates mentioned *supra*, Chap. LXI, n. 49; M. Hroch and J. Petráč's apt Polish observations on "The European Economy and Politics during the Sixteenth and Seventeenth Centuries. A Crisis or Retrogression?" *Przegląd historyczny*, LV, 1–21; and F. Redlich, "Contributions in the Thirty Years' War," *EHR*, XII, 247–54, analyzing the large-scale imposts upon groups, rather than individuals, which were the mainstay of the War's financing. Of course, Jewish communities were frequent targets of such forced "contributions." Obviously these economic factors also greatly influenced the attitudes of governments, army commanders, and the local population toward Jews. Even the recurrent peasant revolts must now have more directly affected Jewish villagers than had the more important uprisings of the 1520s, because of the intervening progressive dispersal of Jewish settlements into many rural areas. On these peasant commotions see, for instance, F. Stieve, *Der Oberösterreichische Bauernaufstand des*

Jahres 1626, 2d ed.; J. K. Mayr, "Bauernunruhen in Salzburg am Ende des dreissigjährigen Krieges," *Mitteilungen* of the Gesellschaft für die Salzburger Landeskunde, XCI, 1–106.

2. Yuspa (Joseph) b. Phineas Nördlinger Hahn, *Yosif Omeṣ* (With Added Strength; a ritualistic work), Supplement, Frankfort a. M., 1723 ed., fol. 166b. On the author see M. Horovitz, *Frankfurter Rabbinen*, II, 5 ff. Remarkably, there is no comprehensive monograph on the Jews during the Thirty Years' War. We possess only a few specialized articles, which will be mentioned in the following notes. In view of the great variations existing among different localities and the ever-changing military situation, the results of these specialized researches do not lend themselves to easy generalization. However, on the whole, Hahn's observations reflect some benefits derived by Jews from their relative religiopolitical neutrality.

3. Ferdinand's orders to Maximilian of Bavaria cited from a Bavarian archival document by A. Gindely in his *Geschichte des dreissigjährigen Krieges* (the first three vols. of which discuss only the Bohemian uprising of 1618), III, 320 f.; G. Bondy and F. Dworský, *Zur Geschichte der Juden in Böhmen, Mähren und Schlesien*, II, 875 ff. Nos. 1096 and 1099; A. Kisch, "Die Prager Judenstadt während der Schlacht am Weissen Berge," *Allgemeine Zeitung des Judentums*, LVI, 400–403; G. Klemperer, "The Rabbis of Prague: History of the Rabbinate of Prague from the Death of Rabbi Loewe b. Bezalel ('the High Rabbi Loew') to the Present (1609–1879)," *HJ*, XII, 33–66, 143–52; XIII, 55–82, esp. XII, 48 ff. (This essay, originally published in German in instalments in *Pascheles' illustrierter israelitischer Volkskalender*, 1881–84, appeared here in an English trans. by the author's son, C. Klemperer.) The fullest account of the role played by the Prague Jews during the War is given by K. Spiegel in "Die Prager Juden zur Zeit des dreissigjährigen Krieges," *Die Juden in Prag*, ed. by S. Steinherz, pp. 107–186, esp. pp. 107 ff. For the future of Bohemian Jewry it was doubly important that the active part taken by the antagonistic Bohemian Estates in the anti-Habsburg uprising led to a sharp curtailment of their authority by the victorious imperial regime. On their wartime activities see V. Vaněček's recent study of "Les Assemblées d'états en Bohême à l'époque de la révolte d'états en 1618–1620," *Recueils* of the Société Jean Bodin, XXV: Gouvernés et gouvernants, Pt. 4, pp. 239–54; and the more general older literature listed in Č. Zirbt's *Bibliografie české historie*.

Remarkably, in a substantial collection of letters, written predominantly in Yiddish in November 1619 by various Prague Jews and Jewesses to Vienna coreligionists and intercepted by the Austrian police, we find few echoes of the epochal events which took place in Prague. There are only some minor allusions, such as those to a Prague nobleman who escaped to Heidelberg after despoiling a Jew, or to the coronation, "with great honors," of Frederick V, "the Heidelberger," as king of Bohemia on November 4, 1619. Perhaps Jews had learned from experience that letters often fell into the hands of the authorities and were reticent to express any political opinions which might later be held against them. See A. Landau and B. Wachstein, eds., *Jüdische Privatbriefe aus dem Jahre 1619*, esp. pp. 25 f. No. 8B, 91 No. 45A.

4. See V. Vojtíšek, "On the Enlargement of the 'Jewish City' of Prague in the Years 1622–23" (Czech), *Kalendař česko-židowský*, XXXV, 32–95; K. Spiegel, "Die

Prager Juden" in *Die Juden in Prag*, pp. 109 ff.; J. Rokycana, "Die Häuser des Jakob Bassewi von Treuenburg. Neue Quellenforschung," *ZGJT*, I, 253–66; G. Wolf, *Ferdinand II und die Juden;* and the literature listed in the last note. Fyne Moryson's recital in *An Itinerary Containing His Ten yeares of Travell through the Twelve Dominions of Germany, Bohmerland, Sweitzerland, Netherland, Denmarke, Poland, Italy, Turkey, France, England, Scotland, and Ireland*, in the Glasgow 1907–1908 ed., I, 29, was echoed, with far less restraint, by other English travelers of the period. In a 1645 entry in his *Diary* John Evelyn claimed with abandon, "From the report of divers curious and experienced persons I had been assured, there was little more to be seen in the rest of the civil world after Italy, France and the Low Countries, but plain and prodigious barbarism." Cited by I. Hoffmann in her Münster dissertation, *Deutschland im Zeitalter des 30jährigen Krieges. Nach Berichten und Urteilen englischer Augenzeugen*, pp. 19 f., 43. See also M. Popper, "Les Juifs de Prague pendant la Guerre de Trente Ans," *REJ*, XXIX, 127–41; XXX, 79–93 (was to be continued), esp. XXIX, 129 ff.; F. Priebatsch, "Die Judenpolitik des fürstlichen Absolutismus im 17. und 18. Jahrhundert," *Festschrift Schäfer*, pp. 564–651; the older but still indispensable *Geschichte Kaiser Ferdinands II*. by F. Hurter; H. Sturmberger, *Kaiser Ferdinand II. und das Problem des Absolutismus;* and, for other viewpoints, H. Hantsch, *Die Geschichte Österreichs*, 4th ed. rev., I, 332 ff.

5. See the brief autobiographical sketch by Ḥanokh b. Moses Altschul, *Megillat Pure ha-qela'im* (Scroll of the Curtain Purim), ed. by A. Z. Kisch from an autograph copy preserved in the family and annually recited by it on the anniversary of the author's liberation (Tebet 22, 5382–January 5, 1622), in the *Jubelschrift . . . H. Graetz*, Hebrew section, pp. 48–52; and supplemented by archival data in M. Popper, "Les Juifs," *REJ*, XXIX, 139 ff. See also S. Assaf's "*Megillat yuḥasin* (Genealogical Scroll of the Altschul Family)" (Hebrew), *Reshumot*, n.s. IV, 131–43. The extremely complex personality of Albrecht Wallenstein (erroneously called Rudolph in Ḥanokh's "Scroll") has long intrigued distinguished scholars and dramatists. On his changing relationships with Jews and his generally meteoric rise and fall, see the literature cited *infra*, n. 26.

6. See the somewhat colored description in G. Liebe's *Das Judentum in der deutschen Vergangenheit*, pp. 67 ff. which includes reproductions of two satirical woodcuts stressing the Jewish role among the coin clippers and counterfeiters. The use of such satires, both verbal and graphic, was part of the steady rise of political pamphleteering, on which see, for instance, E. A. Beller, *Propaganda in Germany during the Thirty Years War*. Under the circumstances it is almost impossible for us to identify the actual value of particular coins mentioned in the sources of that period. Their silver content, and thereby their convertibility into other currency, changed almost from day to day. Even Jewish jurists had to take cognizance of that instability. See, for instance, Joel b. Samuel Sirkes' *Bayit ḥadash* (Responsa), ed. by E. F. Eisenberg, fol. 7b-d No. 16 (dated 1623). The issue here was that between Sivan 1, 5383, and Ellul 5384 (May 30, 1623, and August 1624) a Reichsthaler's value increased from 7 to 10 florins, and that of a ducat from 10 to 15 florins, and they were expected to go up further. The question was whether the lender must accept payment before the due date in depreciated currency, or hope that stabilization of the currency would make his claim more valuable at the original expiration date of the loan. Another problem was whether a lender who might thus possibly receive

more value than the amount he had lent would be guilty of obtaining a usurious gain. Sirkes answered the latter question in the negative, while he approved a settlement reached by the parties at the advice of the first judge. For our period see esp. C. von Ernst's older essay, "Ueber die Silberwährung Deutschlands im XVI. und XVII. Jahrhundert," *Numismatische Zeitschrift* (Vienna), IV, 136–60; and J. Newald, "Beiträge zur Geschichte des österreichischen Münzwesens während der Zeit von 1622 bis 1650," *Blätter* of the Verein für Landeskunde von Niederösterreich, n.s. XVI, 117–47. For other German regions see, for instance, W. Kratz's valuable study, "Das Geld und sein Wert in der Zeit vom 16.–18. Jahrhundert im Bereich der Stadt Frankfurt und des unteren Erzstiftes Mainz. Eine Anleitung Geldsummen aus dieser Zeit richtig einzuschätzen," *Mainzer Zeitschrift*, LVI–LVII, 191–204. The author's valiant but not very successful efforts to come to grips with this knotty problem are but another testimony to how far we still are from fully evaluating either the changing metallic content or the constant fluctuations in purchasing power of the money in circulation. The Jewish sources of the period, in so far as they mention coins at all, are as a rule more concerned with halakhic implications than with the value of the currency as such.

The ensuing price inflation and shortages of goods created much popular dissatisfaction. According to a contemporary Austrian chronicler, by 1622 an original ducat had increased to 20 florins, a Reichsthaler to 10 florins, and finally "no good money was to be found." Correspondingly, the prices of foodstuffs increased greatly and on many a morning "about 100 persons queued up in front of a grocery to await their bread." See the excerpt quoted in O. Frass's *Quellenbuch zur österreichischen Geschichte*, II, 112 No. 26, also presenting an interesting table of prices for various articles in 1613 and 1623. Another remarkable illustration is offered by the 1625 action of a Jew in Tachau (Tachov). Since no municipal elder had appeared before the emperor in Prague to beg his forgiveness for the city's part in the 1618 uprising, Tachau was placed under a harsh military administrator who temporarily suspended all the city's liberties. But he confirmed the Jewish privileges. When in May 1625 he offered to sell the salt monopoly for 500 Reichsthaler, a Jew bid twice that amount. See J. Schön, *Die Geschichte der Juden in Tachau*, pp. 29 f.

7. The Lower Rhenish resolution of 1604 cited by G. Liebe in *Das Judentum*, p. 68; K. Lieben, ed., *Gal-'Ed*, pp. 25–27; L. S. Porta, "Die Erste Nobilitierung eines deutschen Juden, meines Vorfahren Jakob Bassevi von Treuenberg," *JFF*, I, 12–15; J. Rokycana, "Die Häuser des Jakob Bassewi von Treuenburg," *ZGJT*, I, 253–66; A. Ernstberger, *Hans de Witte, Finanzmann Wallensteins*, esp. pp. 86 ff., which gives a full analysis, in part based on archival documents, of the 1622 consortium, its composition and operations, although Ernstberger, enamored of his subject, unjustifiedly contrasts De Witte's and Bassevi's financial talents to the latter's disadvantage. See also H. Schnee, "Die Nobilitierung der ersten Hoffaktoren. Zur Geschichte des Hofjudentums in Deutschland," *Archiv für Kulturgeschichte*, XLIII, 62–99; idem, *Die Hoffinanz und der moderne Staat. Geschichte und System der Hoffaktoren an deutschen Fürstenhöfen im Zeitalter des Absolutismus*, esp. III, 234 ff. arguing, none too convincingly, that a pious Catholic like Ferdinand would not have raised an unbaptized Jew to the rank of imperial nobility. Jacob Bassevi's possible relationship with an Italian family of the same name, one of whose descendants was the mother of Benjamin Disraeli, is discussed by C. Roth in "Der Ursprung der Familie Bassevi in Prag und Verona," *JFF*, IV, 58–60. It should be

noted, however, that in reality Jews played but a minor role among the *Kipper und Wipper*, whose presence was felt all over Germany. Characteristically, none of the places where rioting against manipulators took place, including Saxony, Brandenburg, and Magdeburg (here 16 persons died and more than 200 were wounded in the uprising), had any Jewish residents at all. See the contemporary report in *Theatrum europeum*, I, 224, cited by H. Jensen, comp., in *Der Dreissigjährige Krieg in Augenzeugenberichten*, p. 118.

Ferdinand was forced by the exigencies of his ever impecunious Treasury to resort to these questionable currency manipulations. The Austrian administration had long been fighting against tremendous odds to keep up with the demands of its far-flung bureaucracy and the necessary defenses against the Ottoman Empire and other foreign enemies. The outbreak of the revolt in Prague found the government financially and militarily unprepared, which accounted for its very slow reaction. In time, the Habsburgs were aided by their allies, as well as by financial subsidies from the Papacy. Starting with some 10,000 florins monthly, the popes gradually raised their contributions to five times that amount or more. According to an official computation extant in the Vatican Archives, in 1619–23 the papal Treasury paid out 399,229 scudi in subsidies to the emperor; 347,405 scudi (or a total of some 1,880,000 florins) to Bavaria and the League. See D. Albrecht, "Zur Finanzierung des dreissigjährigen Krieges. Die Subsidien der Kurie für Kaiser und Liga 1618–1635," *ZBL*, XIX, 534–67 (esp. p. 567 App.); and idem, *Die Deutsche Politik Papst Gregors XV. Die Einwirkung der päpstlichen Diplomatie auf die Politik der Häuser Habsburg und Wittelsbach, 1621–1623*, esp. p. 13 n. 28. Nevertheless, the considerable accretion of funds through the financial manipulations of Hans de Witte, Jacob Bassevi, and their associates was extremely welcome.

On the official coin clipping and its later effects on the Austrian economy, see the valuable older studies by J. Newald, "Die Lange Münze in Österreich," *Numismatische Zeitschrift*, XIII, 88–132; "Beiträge zur Geschichte des österreichischen Münzwesens während der Zeit von 1622 bis 1650," *Blätter* of the Verein für Landeskunde von Niederösterreich, n.s. XVI, 117–47. The high ratio of 1:8 in the currency devaluation also induced the Moravian communities to adopt a resolution readjusting the claims of creditors. Lest the latter be the sole losers, they were to receive one-eighth of their nominal claims plus one-third. This resolution was recorded in a later responsum by David b. Samuel ha-Levi. See the collection *Teshubot geone batrae* (Responsa of Latter-Day Masters), No. 9; and A. J. Frankl-Grün, "The Ordinances of [the Author of] *Ṭure zahab* [R. David b. Samuel ha-Levi]" (Hebrew), *Ha-Zofeh*, III, 188–90. Similar difficulties in Moravia likewise were the subject of rabbinic discussions. See Y. Z. Kahane, "The Province of Moravia in Rabbinic Responsa" (Hebrew), *Sefer ha-Yobel* (Jubilee Volume in Honor of Hanokh Albeck), pp. 253–82, esp. pp. 257 f. No. 6. See also *supra*, n. 6.

8. See B. Brilling's well-documented sketch, "Manasse von Hotzenplotz, der erste jüdische Münzlieferant in Schlesien (1622–1624)," *JGJCR*, VII, 387–98; idem, "Aus den Archivalien der jüdischen Gemeinde Hotzenplotz (Österr. Schlesien)," *Zeitschrift für jüdische Geschichte*, II, 50–57, esp. p. 57 App. (arguing that Manasse's name was really Moses b. Manish); F. Richter and A. Schmidt, "Die Hotzenplotzer Judengemeinde 1334–1848," *Mitteilungen für jüdische Volkskunde*, XIV, No. 37, pp. 29–36. The ebb and flow of the various diplomatic relations, accompanying the changing fortunes of the War, are well illustrated by the extensive data assembled

by W. Goetz in *Die Politik Maximilians I. von Bayern und seiner Verbündeten, 1618–1631;* and by D. Albrecht in *Die Auswärtige Politik Maximilians von Bayern 1618–1635.*

9. A. F. Pribram, *Urkunden und Akten zur Geschichte der Juden in Wien,* I, 50 ff. Nos. 35–51; M. Grunwald, *Vienna,* pp. 83 ff. It may be noted that after the 1623 reversal of the imperial policy concerning currency devaluation, the Vienna Jews were sharply enjoined, on December 22, 1623, not to melt or export any silver, under penalty of the most severe Jewish excommunication, the loss of all their privileges, and other harsh punishments. See Pribram, I, 82 No. 47 ii. The decree establishing the new ghetto was combined with a renewal of the Jewish privileges. At the same time a public announcement sharply ordered the population to refrain from any attacks on Jews, under severe sanctions. See Pribram, I, 88 ff. No. 53 with the notes thereon; and *infra,* n. 12.

10. The developments during the early war years in Hungary have few echoes in the extant sources relating to Jews. Most of the available data, reproduced in *MHJ,* V, Part 1, pp. 258 ff.; IX, Part 1, pp. 98 f. deal largely with common business transactions, possibly indicating that the daily life of the Jewish community was but slightly affected by Bethlen's ambitious ventures. See, however, the brief notes in *MHJ,* V, Part 1, p. 261 No. 515; and, more generally, D. Angyal, "Bethlen Gábor," *RH,* CLVIII, 19–80.

11. See K. Brandi, *Deutsche Reformation und Gegenreformation,* esp. II, 224 f.; and the literature listed *supra,* nn. 1, 4, and 6. The revulsion generated in German nationalist circles by the foreign entanglements, and its ultimate inefficacy in stemming the particularist interests of the opposing parties, is succinctly analyzed in A. Wandruszka's *Reichspatriotismus und Reichspolitik zur Zeit des Prager Friedens von 1635. Eine Studie zur Geschichte des deutschen Nationalbewusstseins.*

12. A. F. Pribram, *Urkunden,* I, 84 ff. Nos. 52–54, 98 ff. Nos. 60–61, with the notes thereon; Yom Ṭob Lipmann b. Nathan Heller, *Megillat Ebah* (Scroll of Hostility; a record of personal sufferings), [ed. by M. Körner with a German trans. by J. H. Miró], *passim;* or in the slightly different version, reproduced from one of the numerous manuscripts attesting the popularity of this work, in A. Kahana's compilation of *Sifrut ha-historiah ha-yisraelit* (An Anthology of Jewish Historical Literature), II, 277–90, esp. p. 279; G. Wolf, *Die Juden in der Leopoldstadt ("unterer Werd")* im *17. Jahrhundert in Wien* (includes a comprehensive list of Jewish taxpayers); and *infra,* n. 45. On Heller's little tract, see I. Halpern's "Bibliography of R. Yom Ṭob Lipmann Heller's Writings" (Hebrew), *KS,* VII, 140–48, esp. pp. 145 f. No. 32, 147 f. No. 35.

The story of the second Viennese ghetto during its relatively brief period of existence from 1625 to 1670 has been fully described by D. Kaufmann in *Die Letzte Vertreibung der Juden aus Wien und Niederösterreich, ihre Vorgeschichte (1525–1670) und ihre Opfer;* and supplemented by important archival data, especially the principal real estate records for those years, by I. Schwarz in *Das Wiener Ghetto, seine Häuser und seine Bewohner.* Further data were supplied by H. Rotter and A. Schwieger in *Das Ghetto in der Wiener Leopoldstadt,* pp. 31 ff.; with some topographical corrections suggested by L. Steiner in his "Irrtümer in der Literatur über den unteren Werd bzw. über die Leopoldstadt," *Wiener Geschichtsblätter*, XXI (LXXXI), 42–49. The interesting agreement between the city and the local hospital on the one hand, and the Jewish community on the other hand, whereby the Jews obligated themselves to pay them 600 and 400 florins, respectively, per year, is reproduced by Pribram, I, 99 ff. No. 61. Connected with the transfer of Jews was the new imperial privilege of March 8, 1625, which appeared in response to a Jewish petition pointing out that the outlay of 30,000 florins for the land alone, in addition to other expenses, such as the necessary erection of a protective wall, had plunged the community deeply into debt. *Ibid.*, pp. 93 ff. No. 56. On the renewed drive by the Counter Reformation popes to segregate the Jews see *supra*, Chaps. LIX, nn. 30 ff.; LX, nn. 45 ff. and *passim*.

13. A. F. Pribram, *Urkunden*, I, 107 ff. No. 68, 136 ff. No. 86, 144 No. 91; *supra*, n. 1. In Prague, where on Khlesel's prompting Jesuit preachers likewise began in 1630 to deliver conversionist sermons to unwilling Jewish audiences, the archbishop at first also raised objections to holding such services in a church without a special papal dispensation. Nonetheless, the meetings were ultimately held in the Church of Maria an der Lake. Because of its limited space the preachers had to be satisfied with a disproportionately small attendance of but 80–100 persons on each Saturday. See K. Spiegel, "Die Prager Juden" in *Die Juden in Prag*, ed. by S. Steinherz, p. 125; J. Prokeš and A. Blaschka, "Der Antisemitismus der Behörden und das Prager Ghetto in nachweissenbergischer Zeit," *JGJCR*, I, 41–262, esp. pp. 58 ff. It should be noted that Khlesel's project had antecedents in Prague: the Jewish convert, Peter Weidner, professor of Hebrew at the University of Vienna and court physician to three emperors, had published, in 1562, *Ein Sermon den Juden in Prag in jrer Synagoge geprediget; dadurch auch etliche Personen zum Christlichen Glauben bekert worden.*

However, these conversionist efforts were even less effective than the far more strenuous Catholicizing and Germanizing pressures exerted by the government on the Czech population. Whatever one thinks about the much-debated problem of whether Lutheranism served as an indirectly Germanizing factor in Prague, there is no question that, as late as 1630, many artisans (for instance, the majority of bakers) were secret Protestants and that, at the end of the War, the total number of Germans did not exceed 3,000 (about the same as the number of Jews) in a total population of some 40,000. See H. Zatscheck, "Aus der Geschichte des Wiener Handwerks während des dreissigjährigen Krieges," *Jahrbuch* of the Verein für Geschichte der Stadt Wien, IX, 28–74; and W. Wostig, "Das Deutschtum Böhmens zwischen Hussitenzeit und dreissigjährigem Krieg," in *Das Sudetendeutschtum. Sein Wesen und Werden im Wandel der Jahrhunderte*, ed. by G. Pirchau *et al.*, 2d ed., pp. 307–388, esp. pp. 333 f., 350; *supra*, Chap. LIX, n. 55.

14. K. Spiegel, "Die Prager Juden," pp. 125 f. The courts may have failed to prosecute Prague Jews for aid in the escape of the Engelsberger family because of Engelsberger's unsavory character. A brief entry of 1642 in the Vienna municipality's minute book obscurely alludes to his being condemned to hanging for a theft committed by him together with two unbaptized Jews. This case was mentioned in connection with a trial for their alleged blasphemy against the crucifix and the host. See M. Steinschneider's brief note, "Todesstrafe für Gotteslästerung," *Hebräische Bibliographie*, XV, 68, citing a report in the *Telegraf* of 1861, No. 50, p. 2330.

15. Yom Ṭob Lipmann Heller, *Megillat Ebah*, ed. by M. Körner (Hebrew and German); in A. Kahana's *Sifrut*, II, 277 ff.; and *supra*, n. 12. The text relating to the rabbi's misadventure is briefly excerpted in the English trans. by L. W. Schwarz in his compilation of *Memoirs of My People Through a Thousand Years*, pp. 68–74. Although Heller was far from poor, he could not afford to pay the 10,000 florins fine. He was aided by Jacob Bassevi and other members of the Prague community. Bassevi not only advanced the first 2,000 florins, which had to be paid immediately, but also helped Heller with the subsequent instalments.

16. Ferdinand III's Jewish privilege of January 12, 1645, reproduced by A. F. Pribram in his *Urkunden*, pp. 145 ff. No. 92; Ferdinand II's Bohemian decree of August 12, 1627, and its confirmation on June 30, 1628, cited in H. Palm and J. Krebs, eds., *Acta publica*, VIII, 118 f., and summarized by K. Spiegel in "Die Prager Juden," p. 129; J. Čelakovsky's ed. of the *Codex juris municipalis regni Bohemiae*, Vol. I: *Privilegia civitatum Pragensium*, pp. 551 ff. No. 312, 578 ff. No. 324. See *supra*, n. 4. To forestall anticipated objections Ferdinand III had already emphasized in his pro-Jewish Vienna decree of 1645 that he had issued it at the request of the Viennese community, but only "after careful deliberation, good counsel, and thorough knowledge." At the same time he entered the reservation "that this and all Our aforementioned gracious concessions and grants are to be understood only as contingent on Our and Our heirs' and successors' discretion; they are subject to revocation at any time." He also intimated that the enforcement of its provisions was to depend on the Jews' good behavior. Pribram, pp. 145, 150.

All this legislation was another sign of the growing absolutism of the Habsburg monarchy, which in those very years of 1627–28 also found expression in Ferdinand's other privileges for Bohemia and Moravia. They were all issued by royal authority, without consultation with the Estates—a phenomenon duplicated time and again on a lesser scale in the various other German states. See F. Kavka, "Die Habsburger und der böhmische Staat," *Historica*, VIII, 55 f.; and F. L. Carsten, "The Causes of Decline of the German Estates" in *Album Helen Maud Camm* (Studies Presented to the International Commission for the History of Representative Government and Parliamentary Institutions, XXIII–XXIV), II, 287–96. The growing role of the army contractors during the Thirty Years' War is analyzed by F. Redlich in *The German Military Enterpriser and His Work Force: a Study in European Economic and Social History* (*VSW*, Beiheft XLVII–XLVIII), esp. I, 157 ff. Needless to say, Jews at first had a rather small share in these undertakings. None of the four sixteenth-century case studies reviewed by Redlich related to Jews (pp. 74 ff.). But in time their influence, like that of the Protestant businessmen (including converts to Catholicism), greatly increased. See also J. G. O. Mentschl, *Österreichische Industrielle und Bankiers*. The thirty biographical sketches here included also describe the careers of such later outstanding Court Jews as the Oppenheimers and the Wertheimers. See also *infra*, n. 19.

17. See Z. Winter, *Dějiny řemesel a obchodu v Čechách v XIV. a v XV. století* (History of Crafts and Industry in Czech Lands in the XIVth and XVth Centuries), esp. pp. 958 ff.; idem, *Řemeslnictvo a živnosti XVI. věku v Čechách* (Crafts and Occupations in the Czech Lands of the Sixteenth Century, 1526–1620); J. Prokeš and A. Blaschka, "Der Antisemitismus der Behörden," *JGJCR*, I, 63 ff.; and other data summarized by M. Wischnitzer in *A History of Jewish Crafts and Guilds*, pp. 152 ff., 302 ff.; and *supra*, Vol. XII, pp. 58, 273 n. 58. In Prague the Christian

guilds vigorously combated the competition of Jewish tailors, furriers, and butchers; they particularly resented the butchers' underselling parts of animals which were ritualistically forbidden to Jewish consumers. All they achieved, however, was to provoke the formation of independent Jewish guilds. The 1628 privilege, specifically allowing Bohemian Jewry to train for, and engage in, various crafts, greatly aroused the Christian guilds. On their appeal, Ferdinand II was at first ready, in 1636, to yield to their demands; but his son and successor submitted the controversy to the Bohemian Supreme Court, which decided in favor of the Jews (1637). In its motivation the court not only stressed the permissiveness of the 1628 decree but also argued on economic grounds that the poorer classes greatly benefited from the lower prices brought about by Jewish competition. See T. Jakobovits, "Die Jüdischen Zünfte in Prag," *JGJCR*, VIII, 70 ff.

It stands to reason that the War particularly stimulated the craft of sword making in which Bohemian Jews had long excelled. Although our documentary evidence antedates 1618, there is no ground for assuming that Jews abandoned this lucrative occupation at a time when the demand for swords was at its height. See Winter, *Dějiny*, p. 410. Dependent as we often are on names alone, however, it is frequently difficult to determine whether a given craftsman was Jewish. For instance, despite his Hebraic name Jacob Isaac Michael, invited in 1607 by Rudolph II to live at the royal castle at Prague and make gilded rapiers at a monthly salary of 10 florins, may not have been a Jew. See Wischnitzer, p. 160. Needless to say, there also were Jewish craftsmen in other Bohemian and Moravian cities. On the latter see esp. H. Flesch, "Urkundliches über jüdische Handwerker in Mähren," *MGWJ*, LXXIV, 197–217. In contrast, the struggling Viennese community included relatively few craftsmen. As late as 1644 the Christian tailors' guild successfully complained to the city council that, contrary to existing laws, Jews not only sold new clothing but also employed workers to sew such garments for sale to the Christian public. The mayor and the city council thereupon threatened the Jews with confiscation of all "contraband" new garments and with the arrest and deportation of their illegal workers. A. F. Pribram, *Urkunden*, I, 143 f. No. 90.

18. A. F. Pribram, *Urkunden*, II, 570 ff. (to No. 65). In his notes thereon Pribram points out that the Lower Austrian authorities had, in 1582, asked for legislation setting the maximum interest rate at 5 percent and threatening transgressors with severe punishment. Pertinent imperial decrees were indeed issued in 1589 and 1593, but they proved totally ineffective. The same was the case with Ferdinand II's "patent" of September 11, 1628, and with its renewal by Leopold I on June 18, 1659. Yet both of these decrees were subsequently included in the *Codex Austriacus* (II, 509 ff.) as a permanent part of the Austrian legislation. See also G. Wolf, *Geschichte der Juden in Wien (1156–1876)*, pp. 42 ff.; and the next note. It was partially in connection with this agitation against usury that Ferdinand II also issued on March 1, 1627, a "mandate" forbidding the farming out of tolls to Jews; this despite his insistence that, according to local usages, the Austrian Jews should pay higher tolls than their neighbors, which was at variance with his express privilege of the same year for Bohemian Jewry. See Pribram, I, 103 f. No. 64, 105 f. Nos. 65 and 67, 123 f. No. 78; and *supra*, n. 16. Yet, the enforcement of the prohibition against the collecting of tolls by Jews likewise left much to be desired. Its ineffectiveness was admitted by the Court Chamber four years later, whereupon the emperor renewed the ban, apparently with no greater success. See G. Wolf, *Geschichte der Juden in Wien*, p. 46.

19. A. F. Pribram, *Urkunden*, I, 197 ff. No. 115; II, 574 ff.; D. Kaufmann, *Die Letzte Vertreibung, passim*. It is noteworthy that the Vienna community failed to mention here Charles V's similar argument for the legitimacy of a higher Jewish interest rate, in his decree of 1544, mentioned *supra*, Chap. LVIII, n. 82. Such a reference to the highly revered emperor would undoubtedly have impressed his descendants on the Habsburg throne. Possibly the Vienna community, but recently revived, had no records of earlier imperial enactments at its disposal. Of course, Jews were not the only moneylenders. At times, they actually borrowed money from Christian competitors. This was particularly the case in loans contracted by the communities, which sought to avoid paying interest under any guise to coreligionists. That is why, for instance, the Prague community acknowledged on June 11, 1620, a substantial debt it owed to one Ladislaw of Schönaich (Šenoch), although its elders signing the note included the leading financier Jacob Bassevi and other bankers. See G. Bondy and F. Dworský, *Zur Geschichte*, II, 877 f. No. 1100.

20. K. Spiegel, "Die Prager Juden," pp. 166 ff.; G. Wolf, "Actenstücke," *Hebräische Bibliographie*, V, 40 f. In some cases a "loan" was undoubtedly used to disguise an intended bribe to an official, no repayment being expected. Such transactions naturally went unrecorded, as doubtless did the majority of legitimate borrowings. Since the Habsburg possessions did not have "chests" of the type of the medieval English *archae* (see *supra*, Vols. IV, pp. 82 f., 204 f., 280 n. 109, 341 nn. 70–71; XII, p. 140, etc.), the fact that a Jew lent money to a Christian came to the attention of courts and other authorities only in cases of litigation, disposition of estates, and the like. And probably but a minor fraction of these cases happen to have left behind any record which would be still extant today in one or another archive. Hence efforts to compute the total expenditures of Jews for the benefit of the state and its bureaucracy appear quite hopeless.

21. A. F. Pribram, *Urkunden*, I, 83 No. 48, 96 No. 57, 103 No. 63, etc.; D. Kaufmann, *Die Letzte Vertreibung*, p. 12 n. 4. On the earlier development and interpretation of "Jewish serfdom" under the Empire, see *supra*, Vol. XI, pp. 4 ff. A good, but probably incomplete, tabulation of the more formal Jewish fiscal contributions to the Austrian Treasury during the period of 1619–70 is found in M. Grunwald's biography of *Samuel Oppenheimer und sein Kreis (Ein Kapitel aus der Finanzgeschichte Österreichs)*, pp. 20 ff. An example of the bargaining relating not only to outright taxes but also to more or less forced loans is furnished by the negotiations between Jacob Berchtold, councilor of the Court Chamber, and the Jewish community of Vienna at the beginning of 1632. On January 2, Berchtold, who also played a leading role in the fiscal negotiations with Bohemian Jewry, was ordered to demand a loan of 20,000 florins from the Jews. Five days later he reduced the amount to 10,000 florins. Arguing that they were unable to raise such a sum, the Jews offered 5,500 florins instead. In the end they were ordered by the emperor, on January 13, to deliver 6,000 florins; one half immediately in cash and the other half within three or four weeks. Pribram, I, 112 f. No. 70.

22. See G. Wolf, *Ferdinand II.*, pp. 49 ff. No. 9; Pribram, *Urkunden*, I, 113 ff. Nos. 72, 74, and 76. The authorities had more frequent occasion to intervene in favor of both Jewish self-government and the poorer classes in Prague and in other localities of the Bohemian Crown. But even there, interventions by rulers, mainly interested in getting their spoils, were for the most part halfhearted and ineffective.

The fuller story of Jewish communal life and its relations with the Austrian and Bohemian authorities will be narrated in a later chapter.

23. A. F. Pribram, *Urkunden*, I, 131 ff. No. 82. The nostalgic petition of the Vienna burghers ignored the basic changes in the European economy—and the many accompanying psychological transformations—which had taken place during the preceding century. The Vienna merchants were prone to blame Jewish competition for what really was the result of a deep internal crisis, with its far-reaching political effects. "The century of the merchant," observes Ferdinand Tremel, "ends in Austria at the time of the Schmalkaldic War, to be replaced by the century of the nobleman." See "Der Österreichische Kaufmann im 16. Jahrhundert," *Festschrift Karl Eder*, ed. by H. J. Mezler-Andelbey, p. 135; and his succinct survey of "Die Österreichische Wirtschaft zwischen 1620 und 1740," *Österreich in Geschichte und Literatur*, V, 166–81.

24. See *supra*, n. 16; M. Brann, *Geschichte der Juden in Schlesien*, pp. 211 ff. Some of the intolerance of the Silesian Estates may be traced back to the sufferings brought on the whole population by the war-caused inflation, which in Silesia generated not only popular riots against Jews but general xenophobia. The Breslau burghers demanded in 1634 that in the future all Dutch, English, and other foreign merchants be made to pay a double, the Jews a triple, toll on all their merchandise. See J. Krebs, *Rat und Zünfte der Stadt Breslau in den schlimmsten Zeiten des 30jährigen Krieges*, p. 86; and other data supplied by B. Brilling in his "Breslauer Messgäste. Jüdische Messe- und Marktbesucher im 17. Jahrhundert," *JFF*, VI, 315–18; VIII, 506–509; IX, 517–29; XI, 678–84, and, more broadly, in his *Geschichte der Juden in Breslau von 1454 bis 1702*, esp. pp. 16 ff.

25. See the careful analyses by I. Rabin in his *Vom Rechtskampf der Juden in Schlesien (1582–1713)*, esp. pp. 20 ff.; idem, *Die Juden in Zülz*; and, more generally, J. Chrząszcz (Chrzonz), *Geschichte der Stadt Zülz in Oberschlesien* (of which the Rabin essay forms an appendix, pp. 117 ff.); and the sources listed *supra*, n. 24. Harsh and often arbitrary rule by local commanders is also illustrated by the conditions in the provincial Bohemian community of Tachau (Tachov) after the battle of the White Mountain. Here Colonel Johann Philip Hussmann, baron of Remedy und Riolsburg, forcibly converted the local Protestants and ruled the entire district with an iron hand. Jews suffered mainly from his arbitrarily imposed taxes. In 1629 he also restricted the rights of the Jewish butchers and tanners in order to appease the two Christian guilds. See J. Schön, *Die Geschichte der Juden in Tachau*, pp. 29 ff., also mentioning the characteristic text of a local toll ordinance reading: "For a horse or a cow, 1 kreuzer; for a fat pig, 2 kreuzers; for a Jew, 3 kreuzers."

26. E. Hoffmann, "Wallenstein's Stellung zu den Juden. Ein Gedenkblatt zum dreihundertsten Todestage des Generalissimus," *ZGJT*, IV, 1–5; idem, *Geschichte der Juden in Reichenberg* (discussing especially Wallenstein's privilege for a Friedland Jew); and J. Jirčak, "Beiträge zur Geschichte der Jitschiner Juden im siebzehnten und achtzehnten Jahrhundert," trans. from the Czech by A. Blaschka, *JGJCR*, V, 137–56, esp. p. 155 n. 7; A. Salz, *Wallenstein als Merkantilist* (reprinted from *Mitteilungen* of the Verein für die Geschichte der Deutschen in Böhmen,

XLVII, 433–61), pp. 7 ff.; and A. Ernstbergers' aforementioned biographical sketch, *Hans de Witte, Finanzmann Wallensteins*. It is possible, though we have no evidence to this effect, that Witte and Bassevi collaborated again in some minting of coins for Wallenstein, though on a lesser scale than they had for the emperor a decade earlier. See A. Meyer, "Albrecht von Wallenstein (Waldstein), Herzog von Friedland, und seine Münzen," *Numismatische Zeitschrift*, XVII, 417–522.

Of the vast general literature available on Wallenstein, immortalized in German letters by Friedrich von Schiller's famous trilogy, see H. Hallwich, ed., *Briefe und Akten zur Geschichte Wallenstein's (1630–1634)*, with P. Suvanto's recent analysis of that crucial period in his *Wallenstein und seine Anhänger am Wiener Hof zur Zeit des zweiten Generalats, 1631–1634;* and the full-length, well-documented studies by J. Pekař, *Valdštejn 1630–1634*, 2d ed. revised; or *Wallenstein 1630 bis 1634. Tragödie einer Verschwörung*, in the further revised German translation by himself (with assistants); and by H. von Srbik, *Wallenstein Ende. Ursachen, Verlauf und Folgen der Katastrophe*, 2d ed. enlarged and revised (posthumously prepared by Taras von Borodajkewycz). See also A. E. J. Hollaender, "Some English Documents on the End of Wallenstein," *BJRL*, XL, 358–90 (confirming that the generalissimo had placed at the head of his peace proposals one reading: "To let the exercise of Religion be free"; pp. 363 f.); G. Wagner's more recent popular biography, *Wallenstein, der böhmische Condottiere;* J. Polišenský, "Zur Problematik des dreissig-jährigen Krieges und der Wallensteinfrage," *Aus 500 Jahren deutscher tschechoslo-wakischer Geschichte*, ed. by K. Obermann and J. Polišenský, pp. 99–135; and other literature listed by H. Hantsch in *Die Geschichte Österreichs*, 4th ed. rev., I, 396 f. Of interest also are E. Beladiez's Spanish materials analyzed in his *España y el Sacro Imperio Romano Germánico, Wallenstein, 1583–1634;* and, from another angle, the older but still valuable review of *Die Wallensteinfrage in der Geschichte und im Drama* by P. Schweizer.

27. See G. Wolf, "Ein Jude rettet Jesuiten," *Jahrbuch für Israeliten*, ed. by J. Wertheimer, n.s. VII, 221–27 (includes three documents); idem, "Zur Geschichte der Juden in Deutschland," *ZGJD*, [o.s.] III, 159–84, esp. pp. 171 f.; idem, *Ferdinand II, passim;* and *supra*, nn. 7 and 16. Needless to say, justified as is Fritz Redlich's theory of the preponderance of Protestants and Jews among the princely entrepreneurs, there were always some exceptions. In fact, one of the earliest examples of such a ruler in Germany was the Wittelsbach Duke Ernst of Bavaria in the first half of the sixteenth century. See F. S. Strauss, "Herzog Ernst von Bayern (1500–1560), ein süddeutscher fürstlicher Unternehmer des 16. Jahrhunderts," *Mitteilungen* of the Gesellschaft für Salzburger Landeskunde, CI, 269–84. Other Jewish army suppliers are recorded to the end of the War. For example, Colloredo was involved in an-other such deal on June 20, 1648, when, together with Wilhelm von Kollowrat, he contracted with two Jews, Moyses Tschorsch and Löbl Kassowitz for the delivery of 1,481 riding boots, 481 pistols for 3.25 thalers apiece, and 1,381 rifles for 4 florins each. See G. Wolf, "Actenstücke," *Hebräische Bibliographie*, V, 42.

28. J. [I.] Kracauer, "Histoire d'un prêt forcé demandé à la communauté des Juifs de Francfort en 1622–1623," *REJ*, XV, 99–108; idem, "Beiträge zur Geschichte der Frankfurter Juden im dreissigjährigen Krieg," *ZGJD*, [o.s.] III, 130–58, 337–72; IV, 18–28, esp. III, 362 ff.; idem, *Geschichte der Juden in Frankfurt a. M.*, II. 1 ff.; R. J. G. Concannon, "The Third Enemy: The Role of Epidemics in the Thirty

Years' War," *Journal of World History*, X, 501. The affair of the 10,000 thalers was not completely settled by Ferdinand's decree, however. As late as 1631 an imperial colonel demanded, through an intermediary, the payment of that sum, plus a high penalty, from the Frankfort Jews, which they naturally refused. See Kracauer in *REJ*, XV, 108. Remarkably, during all these controversies Tilly himself, good businessman though he was, did not pursue any direct action against the Frankfort Jews; he was satisfied with relatively small contributions, such as twenty-five horses and some equipment for his artillery.

29. See the literature listed in the last note; G. Wolf, *Ferdinand II, passim; supra*, Vol. XII, pp. 209, 217 f., 344 f. n. 13, 350 n. 25. Needless to say, in his calculations Norbertin paid little attention to the great decline in the florin's purchasing power, even deterioration in the coins' metallic content, which had taken place since the mid-fourteenth century. On the changes in value since 1500 alone, see W. Kratz's computations in "Das Geld und sein Wert in der Zeit vom 16.–18. Jahrhundert im Bereich der Stadt Frankfurt und des unteren Erzstiftes Mainz," *Mainzer Zeitschrift*, LVI–LVII, 191–204. Moreover, a glance at a similar study by E. Waschinski, *Währung, Preisentwicklung und Kaufkraft des Geldes in Schleswig-Holstein von 1226 bis 1864*, will show how great were the regional diversities among the German states in this matter.

30. *Sammlung hessischer Landesordnungen*, II, 339 ff.; Matthias Abele von Lilienberg cited by H. Fehr in *Das Recht in der Dichtung* (Part II of his *Kunst und Recht*), pp. 383 f., 541; [R. Hallo *et al.*], *Geschichte der jüdischen Gemeinde Kassel unter Berücksichtigung der Hessen-Kasseler Gesamtjudenheit*, Vol. I, p. 84 n. 30; A. Cohn's Marburg dissertation, *Beiträge zur Geschichte der Juden in Hessen-Kassel im 17. und 18. Jahrhundert*, Part 1: Staat und Umwelt in ihrem Verhältnis zu den Juden; I. Kracauer, "Beiträge" in *ZGJD*, [o.s.] III, 362 ff.; IV, 18 ff. See also, more generally, G. Landauer, "Zur Geschichte der Judenrechtswissenschaft," *ibid.*, n.s. II, 255–61; and E. Remann's Breslau dissertation, *Die Jüdische Sonderrechtsstellung in der Rechtswissensschaft des XVI.–XIX. Jahrhunderts* (typescript); and *supra*, Vol. XI, pp. 14 ff., 292 f. nn. 13 ff.

31. I. Kracauer in *ZGJD*, [o.s.] III–IV, *passim*; idem, *Geschichte der Juden in Frankfurt a. M.*, pp. 14 ff. See, however, the divergent figures cited *infra*, n. 46. Kracauer also points out that, because of the changing fortunes of the War, imperial prestige had sunk very low. The vigorous reassertion of the emperor's supremacy during the Fettmilch rebellion was now replaced by timorous negotiations, which enabled both the city and the Jews of Frankfort to make only more or less voluntary contributions to the imperial Treasury, rather than meekly acceding to the imperial agents' excessive demands. Nonetheless, the city's expenditures during the war years grew very rapidly, and it was owing only to the city fathers' thrift and prudent management that, despite its expenses of some 1,640,000 florins for the unkeep of its armed forces, 1,100,000 florins for war contributions, and 400,000 for fortifications, its public debt increased from 1620 to 1650 from about 1,000,000 to only 1,300,000 florins. See A. Dietz, *Frankfurter Handelsgeschichte*, IV, 17.

32. See the text preserved in the Frankfurter Stadtarchiv, Ugb D 14 P Lit. H; and other documents, including an imperial rescript of July 10, 1649, expressing an

ungnädiges Auffallen (unwelcome surprise) over a memorial submitted to the emperor on this matter. Subsequently the city's intercession was solicited by a lengthy Jewish petition, read at the Senate on July 29. Perhaps in reaction thereto, a draft of the city's letter to the emperor (in which the deletions are as interesting as the text finally proposed) was prepared but, according to a notation on it, was "not sent because the Jews have on their own quietly reached an agreement with the [imperial] commissioner." See the documents included in the fascicle Ugb 14 P Lit. L-N, etc.; and, more generally, H. Conrad's succinct analysis of "Die Verfassungsrechtliche Bedeutung der Reichsstädte im Deutschen Reich (etwa 1500–1806)," *Studium generale,* XVI, 493–500.

33. S. Stein, *Geschichte der Juden in Schweinfurt,* pp. 44 ff., 52; La Varenne's reply to Heilbronn's protest cited from the municipal archive by O. Mayer in *Die Geschichte der Juden in Heilbronn: Festschrift zum 50 jährigen Bestehen der Synagoge in Heilbronn,* pp. 44 f. See also Dürr, "Die Juden in Heilbronn im dreissigjährigen Krieg. Ein Beitrag zur Sozialgeschichte jener Zeit," *Württembergische Vierteljahrshefte für Landesgeschichte,* II, 76–79, showing that, after La Varenne's departure in 1649, the city again tried to get rid of all Jews, including Aaron, but that this time it was stymied by Aaron's suit against it before the Empire's Supreme Court.

Another example of an admission of Jews enforced by wartime conditions is offered by the margraviate of Baden-Durlach. Although Margrave George Frederick, in his testament of November 17, 1615, had solemnly enjoined his successors "in all eternity" not to admit Jews, so as "to avoid our Saviour's wrath and inescapable punishment," one Jew, Jacob Ettlinger, was entrusted in 1636 with the farming of the salt monopoly in the area for 100 thalers a year. Another Jew is recorded as having lived in Durlach from 1645 to 1652. See J. A. Zehntner, "Zur Geschichte der Juden in der Markgrafschaft Baden-Durlach," *Zeitschrift für die Geschichte des Oberrheins,* LI, 385–436, 636–90; LIV, 29–65, 547–610, esp. LI, 401 ff.

34. M. Weinberg in his *Geschichte der Juden in der Oberpfalz,* Part III: Der Bezirk Rothenberg, pp. 20 ff., 23 f.; C. Glaser, *Beiträge zur Geschichte der Stadt Grünberg im Grossherzogthum Hessen nach den städtischen Urkunden und anderen Quellen (Archiv für Hessische Geschichte,* n.s. Supplementband I), pp. 115 ff. So well known was the Jews' aversion to the billeting of soldiers in their homes—for many centuries they had indeed secured exemptions from this duty from various governments—that a mere threat thereof was an effective way of coercing them. In 1631, when the margrave of Bayreuth was ordered to pay a large "contribution" for the upkeep of the imperial troops stationed in his land, he forced the dozen Jewish households of Baiersdorf to lend him 3,000 thalers, by threatening to place a company of imperial soldiers in their homes. The Jews of neighboring Kotzau added to that "loan" an additional 1,000 florins. See A. Eckstein, *Geschichte der Juden im Markgrafentum Bayreuth,* p. 34; and *infra,* n. 35. On the other hand, exemption from billeting and from personal military service was advanced by the Bohemian authorities, in the "opinion" they rendered in 1645 to the emperor, as a reason why the Jewish petition for a one-year moratorium on all their debts should be rejected. See J. Prokeš and A. Blaschka, "Der Antisemitismus der Behörden," *JGJCR,* I, 90 f. nn. 38–39. See also M. Weinberg, *Geschichte,* Part V: Herzogtum Sulzbach, pp. 7 f., telling the fairly typical story of a robbery committed in 1622 on a Jew in the duchy of Sulzbach by soldiers under the command of Count Mansfeld, and the

ensuing jurisdictional conflict between the courts of two neighboring localities under different overlords. It required great effort for the Jewish victim to prove that the stolen property was legitimately his. See also *supra*, n. 28.

35. Ferdinand II's order to the commander of Worms on May 17, 1636, reproduced from the Foreign Office Archive in Vienna by G. Wolf in his *Ferdinand II und die Juden*, pp. 62 f. No. xiii; and from a somewhat different Yiddish version, then still extant in Worms, by L. Lewysohn in his "Kaiserliches Schreiben betreffs der Belästigungen der Wormser Juden durch Einquartierungen und andere Auflagen," *Jahrbuch für die Geschichte der Juden und des Judentums*, II, 377–79 (the figure here given of some 40,000 florins previously expended by Worms Jewry is definitely closer to reality than the 35 florins mentioned earlier); G. Wolf, *Zur Geschichte der Juden in Worms und des deutschen Städtewesens*, pp. 22 f., 78 ff. App. xxv; the MS copy of the Worms decree of November 28, 1641, in the Frankfurter Stadtarchiv, Ugb D7 U; *infra*, n. 40; and, particularly, the data assembled and carefully analyzed by I. Kracauer in his "Beiträge zur Geschichte der Frankfurter Juden," *ZGJD*, [o.s.] III–IV; and idem, *Geschichte der Juden in Frankfurt a. M.*, II, 1 ff. Earlier instances of heavy Jewish contributions to various wars were cited *supra*, Vol. XII, pp. 216 f., 349 f. nn. 23–24.

36. A. Dietz, *Frankfurter Handelsgeschichte*, pp. 15 ff.; I. Kracauer, "Beiträge," *ZGJD*, [o.s.] IV, 20 f.; and, more generally, A. Friese, "Urkundenfälscher und Hochstapler des 17. Jahrhunderts in Mainfranken," *Mainfränkisches Jahrbuch*, VIII, 242–68; and A. Ernstberger, *Abenteurer des dreissigjährigen Krieges. Zur Kulturgeschichte der Zeit* (presenting two vivid biographical sketches of two adventurers, Stephan Karl and Hans Jakob Behaim of Nuremberg).

37. G. Wolf, *Ferdinand II*, pp. 10 f., 46 No. vi; the literature on Hildesheim Jewry, cited *supra*, Chap. LXI, n. 65; F. Priebatsch, "Die Judenpolitik des fürstlichen Absolutismus," *Festschrift Schäfer*, p. 594; A. Rexhausen's Münster dissertation, *Die Rechtliche und wirtschaftliche Lage der Juden im Hochstift Hildesheim*, pp. 50 ff.; H. Barbeck, *Geschichte der Juden in Nürnberg und Fürth*, p. 68. On the pest and famine which afflicted many parts of Germany in the years 1632–37, see esp. A. Dietz, *Frankfurter Handelsgeschichte*, IV, 8 ff.; and *infra*, n. 43. See also L. Löwenstein, "Das Rabbinat in Hanau nebst Beiträgen zur Geschichte der dortigen Juden," *JJLG*, XIV, 1–84, esp. pp. 5 ff., 46 ff. Apps. 2–3; and S. Seeligman's remarks thereon in "The Marrano Problem from the Economic Standpoint" (Dutch), *BMGJW*, III, 126 f. On the sufferings of Hanau Jewry during the 1636 siege by imperial troops, see the graphic description by the community's rabbi, Judah Mehler (1609–1659), the first of three rabbis bearing this name, in his autobiographical sketch, published by P. Bloch in "Ein Vielbegehrter Rabbiner des Rheingaues, Juda Mehler Reutlingen," *Philippson Festschrift*, pp. 114–34, esp. pp. 125 f. (Hebrew). In contrast to the Hanau clergy, the Cathedral Chapter of Treves intervened in 1635 in favor of the Jews of Koblenz. On learning of sanguinary disorders perpetrated by some imperial detachments in the area, the Chapter appealed to the Habsburg commanders to protect the small Jewish community in that Rhenish city. See F. P. Kahlenberg, "Jüdische Gemeinden am Mittelrhein," in F. J. Heyen's ed. of *Zwischen Rhein und Mosel*, p. 366. See *supra*, Chap. LXI, n. 61.

38. H. Barbeck, *Geschichte der Juden in Nürnberg und Fürth*, pp. 60 f.; A. Eckstein, *Geschichte der Juden in ehemaligen Fürstbistum Bamberg*, pp. 17 ff., 51, 62 f. The fact that during the stormy war years the Jewish communities of the Bamberg bishopric were able to respond creatively to the recurrent emergencies by building up their regional community was another testimony to their inner vitality. This is doubly remarkable, for the individual settlers lived under the protection of different sovereigns and possessed varying privileges, granted them by either the prince-bishop or by one or another of the petty lords. Their communal superstructure necessarily reflected that division: the central committee often operated in two chambers in matters relating to the two groups, but acted in unison in questions of common concern. These and other diverse forms of Jewish intercommunal cooperation will be analyzed in a later chapter.

39. H. Stern, *Geschichte der Juden in Nordhausen*, pp. 47 ff. In some areas the uncompromising attitude of the anti-Jewish inhabitants was actually abetted by the conquerors. As late as 1650 the Swedish Chancellor Axel Oxenstierna is said to have forbidden the northeastern city of Elbing to admit Jews, although a Jewish quarter was recorded there in 1440 and the city was under Polish influence. See S. Neufeld, "Geschichte der jüdischen Gemeinde Elbing," *Zeitschrift für jüdische Geschichte*, II, 1–11, citing a hitherto unpublished MS of Pastor W. Rupson's *Annales Elbigienses*, p. 314. For this and other reasons many other German cities were first settled, or resettled, by Jews after the Westphalian Treaties. See, for instance, H. H. Hasselmann's recent monograph on *Die Stellung der Juden in Schaumburg-Lippe von 1648 bis zur Emanzipation*.

40. B. H. Auerbach, *Geschichte der israelitischen Gemeinde Halberstadt*, pp. 21 ff.; A. Eckstein, *Geschichte der Juden im Markgrafentum Bayreuth*, pp. 33 ff. The following list of Jewish house owners in the several communities of the margraviate of Bayreuth in 1619 attests both the Jewish population's smallness and its ability to survive under the most adverse conditions: Baiersdorf, 9; Uehlfeld, 4; Uttenreuth, 3; Bruck, 6; Diespeck, 1; Dormitz, 3. See *ibid.*, p. 33 n. 1. The Jews' enemies, as usual, greatly exaggerated their numbers, as when a church superintendent claimed, in a memorandum to the margravine, that the little town of Ober-Kotzau alone had admitted 150 Jews. On the general Jewish migrations of the period see the illustrations assembled by M. Ginsburger in his "Wandernde Juden zur Zeit des dreissigjährigen Krieges," *Jahrbuch* of the Gesellschaft für die Geschichte der Israeliten in Elsass-Lothringen, 1917, pp. 11–27. These data, based upon the revenue rolls of 1620–51 recording payments of the Jewish personal tolls collected from each entrant, and preserved in the Colmar district archive, are quite informative about the places of origin of the migrants. This is basically true despite the frequent negligence of collectors omitting small tolls or none received from beggars and occasional practical jokes by the wanderers when they listed such nonexistent localities as Hanwna, Schickershausen, or Schodtenweisich (consisting of corrupted Hebrew words to connote Flattery, House of Drunkards, and I Know a Stupid One) as their prior residences. The new German Jewish settlements in Holland in the 1630s and after, will be discussed *infra*, Chap. LXIII.

41. R. Grünfeld, *Zur Geschichte der Juden in Bingen am Rhein. Festschrift*, pp. 15 ff.; L. Löwenstein, *Geschichte der Juden in der Kurpfalz*, p. 61; Judah Mehler's

autobiographical sketch published by P. Bloch in the *Philippson Festschrift*, pp. 118 (German), 127 (Hebrew). On the varying attitudes of the French commanders, which depended entirely on their changing military needs or personal whims, see *supra*, n. 33; and *infra*, n. 63.

42. G. Wolf, *Ferdinand II*, p. 39 ff. App. iv; Yehudah Leb b. Joshua Sofer, *Milḥamah be-shalom* (War in Peace; an autobiographical record), reprinted in *Bikkure ha-'ittim*, 5584 (1824); the analysis thereof by S. H. Lieben in his "Kriegstage der Prager Judenstadt (1648)," in *Das Jüdische Prag. Eine Sammelschrift*, published by the *Selbstwehr*, pp. 44-45; K. Spiegel, "Die Prager Juden" in *Die Juden in Prag*, pp. 117, 121 ff.; J. J. Schudt, *Jüdische Merckwürdigkeiten*, I, 320 ff.; IV, 217; F. Priebatsch, "Die Judenpolitik des fürstlichen Absolutismus," *Festschrift Schäfer*, p. 614. The story of the final efforts of the Swedish army to conquer Prague (which, among other acts of violence, led to the bombardment of the outlying Jewish cemetery, forcing the Jews to bury their dead at its entrance), including some references to the Jewish role in the city's defense, is found in Johann Norbert Zatočil von Löwenbruk's "Tagebuch der Belagerung Prags durch die Schweden im Jahre 1648," excerpted in a German trans. by J. Ritter von Rittersberg in the *Monatsschrift* of the Gesellschaft des Vaterländischen Museums in Böhmen, I, No. 4 (April 1827), pp. 24-42; No. 6 (June 1827), pp. 19-40; and by M. M. in his "Beiträge zur Geschichte der Belagerung der königlichen Hauptstadt Prag durch die Schweden im Jahre 1648," *ibid.*, I, No. 11 (November 1827); II, No. 6 (June 1828); and No. 10 (October 1828). In general, however, Jews aided the military campaigns of the German armies and their allies—on both sides, but particularly on that of the emperor—for the most part through their contributions to military logistics and intelligence and by providing supplies and credit. See E. Sander's somewhat Nazi-colored "Die Juden und das deutsche Heerwesen," *Deutsches Archiv für Landes- und Volksforschung*, VI, 632-46; VII, 317-50 (mainly interesting in his second instalment, dealing with the period after 1648); and F. Redlich, "Military Entrepreneurship and the Credit System in the 16th and 17th Century," *Kyklos*, X, 186-93 (with special reference to A. Ernstberger's aforementioned monograph on *Hans de Witte*; see *supra*, n. 7). This role of the imperial and princely court Jews was to assume ever greater dimensions in the decades following the Thirty Years' War. Hence the fuller treatment of this subject must be left to a future volume.

43. E. Keyser, ed., *Deutsches Städtebuch*, IV, Part 3, p. 66; M. Stern, ed., "Fürther Memorbuch," *Festschrift A. Berliner*, Hebrew section, pp. 113-30, esp. p. 123 n. 3; K. Spiegel, "Die Prager Juden," pp. 120 f.; and the literature relating to Mantua listed in the next note. See also R. J. G. Concannon's succinct observations on "The Third Enemy: the Role of Epidemics in the Thirty Years' War," *Journal of World History*, X, 500-511. On the earlier effects of pestilences on Jews see *supra*, Vols. XI, pp. 159 ff., 268 ff., 365 ff. nn. 47 ff., 417 ff. nn. 94 f.; and XII, pp. 25 f., 257 f. n. 23.

44. Most of our information about the tragic events in Mantua comes from a contemporary Hebrew writer, Abraham b. Isaac Massaran, in his chronicle entitled *Sefer ha-Galut ve-ha-Pedut* (Book of Exile and Redemption, in which Are Described the Events of the Mantuan War and the Pestilence which Ravaged It during the

Siege, the Story of Its Conquest by the Army of Emperor Ferdinand II, the Exile which Afflicted the Jews from these Circumstances; the Catastrophe which Befell Them, and the Method of Their Redemption), Venice, 1634; in the Italian trans. by G. Calò, entitled, "La Cronaca mantovana di Abramo Massarani" in *RMI*, XII, 363–77, with frequent reference to works by Romolo Quazza. See esp. Quazza's *La Guerra per la Successione di Mantova e del Monferrato (1628–1631)*. A native of Mantua, Massaran happened to be away during part of that period, but he collected reliable information from eye-witnesses, in addition to the facts he had been able personally to observe. See also S. Simonsohn's *Toledot ha-Yehudim be-dukhsut Mantovah*, I, 34 ff. One must not assume, however, that all Mantuan Christians were Jew-baiters. Massaran himself describes the dramatic rescue of his teacher, R. Mazzal Shalit, by a Christian friend who removed him from the midst of a howling mob and concealed him in his home. See also, more generally, C. d'Arco, *Studi intorno al municipio di Mantova*, IV, 46 ff.; and S. Brinton, *The Gonzaga—Lords of Mantua*, pp. 215 ff., 227 ff.

45. J. (I.) Kracauer, "Beiträge," ZGJD, [o.s.] III, 130 ff.; J. Prokeš and A. Blaschka, "Der Antisemitismus der Behörden," *JGJCR*, I, 68 f.; M. Grunwald, *Vienna*, p. 88; H. Palm and J. Krebs's ed. of *Acta publica*, V, 345; I. Rabin, *Vom Rechtskampf*, p. 37 n. 1; *supra*, nn. 4, 12, and 43; and Vol. XII, pp. 4 ff. On the Jewish and city-wide demographic changes in Frankfort during the seventeenth century, see also *supra*, Chap. LVIII, n. 78; J. Unna, *Statistik der Frankfurter Juden bis zum Jahre 1866*; and, more generally, W. Gley's data in his "Grundriss und Wachstum der Stadt Frankfurt am Main," *Festschrift* . . . of the Verein für Geographie und Statistik zu Frankfurt am Main, pp. 89 ff., 98 f. We must bear in mind that rapid population shifts were characteristic of the entire war period. It has been estimated, for instance, that while three Thuringian counties lost 66, 73, and 87 percent of their respective populations in the three decades of 1631–59, three other counties gained by 78 to 125 percent. Even more was the loss of life in Württemberg, which is estimated to have had a population of 400,000 in 1618, and of only 48,000 thirty years later. See S. H. Steinberg in "The Thirty Years' War," *History*, XXXII, 100 n. 8; and, particularly, R. Mols's *Introduction à la démographie historique des villes d'Europe du XIVe au XVIIIe siècle*, esp. II, 441 ff., 470 ff.; III, 183 ff. (with a good bibliography; II, 470 f. n. 3).

46. I. Kracauer, "Beiträge," ZGJD, [o.s.] III, 337 ff.; IV, 18 ff.; idem, *Geschichte*, II, 15, 30 f.; "Verzeichniss was die Juden allhie von Quartier und Schanzengeld erlegt und [ge]zalt haven," MS in the Frankfurter Stadtarchiv UGB D 14 ad H No. K3. The figures presented by Kracauer (p. 15) doubtless stem from a different archival computation, but they, too, show the substantial decline in Jewish revenue. See *supra*, n. 31. Because of the generally disturbed conditions Jewish and non-Jewish businessmen alike must have found their trading seriously hampered by growing delays in the receipt of amounts due them. During the crucial years of 1632–38 the city of Frankfort itself was often unable to meet its obligations on time. See A. Dietz, *Frankfurter Handelsgeschichte*, IV, 17. More remarkably, the Viennese Jewish merchants Paul Krembser and Abraham Wundts, who had supplied the imperial Court with groceries at the price of 3,526 florins, had to wait five years for payment. See G. Wolf, "Actenstücke," *Hebräische Bibliographie*, IV, 42. These examples can easily be multiplied. Delays of this kind must have been doubly irksome to Jewish

merchants, whose livelihood was often based on quick turnover with lower profit margins, since very few of them commanded resources in excess of 10,000 florins. See F. Priebatsch, "Die Judenpolitik," *Festschrift Schäfer,* p. 598.

As to the general situation, it may be noted that, after reviewing the century-long controversy on the extent to which the War caused a sudden disastrous decline in Germany's population and economy or merely accelerated declining trends of the preceding decades, T. K. Rabb reached the conclusion that "at best, the Thirty Years' War started a general decline [in lieu of regional variations] that had not previously existed; at worst, it replaced prosperity with disaster." See "The Effects of the Thirty Years' War on the German Economy," *Journal of Modern History,* XXXIV, 40–51.

47. S. Carlebach, *Geschichte der Juden in Lübeck und Moisling,* pp. 5 ff.; and *infra,* nn. 48, 54, 55, and 61. The role of Jews in the officially legalized coin clipping throughout the Holy Roman Empire has never been fully investigated. It stands to reason that, as financiers with vast international contacts, some Jews could prove extremely useful in supplying the scarce precious metals, which the mainly Iberian recipients of the American silver mines were rigidly husbanding for themselves, as well as in widely circulating the debased coins. However, they often ran into difficulties with the rulers, who at that time developed a variety of entrepreneurial interests of their own, and the entrenched mintmasters. Although they had a long tradition of helping to coin and exchange European currencies, Jews (other than Bassevi) do not seem to have played a prominent role in the *Kipper und Wipper* period. Nonetheless, they were readily blamed for the monetary instability, which at times made itself severely felt in the Lübeck-Hamburg-Holstein region. Our information becomes more detailed for the eighteenth century. At that time this system of garnering quick profits was employed with far greater moderation, however. See, for instance, F. Redlich, "Jewish Enterprise and Prussian Coinage in the Eighteenth Century," in *Explorations in Entrepreneurial History,* III, 161–81; idem, "Der Deutsche fürstliche Unternehmer—eine typische Erscheinung des 16. Jahrhunderts," *Tradition,* III, 17–32, 98–112; and the atypical data supplied by F. Priebatsch in "Die Judenpolitik des fürstlichen Absolutismus," *Festschrift Schäfer,* pp. 573 ff. See also *supra,* nn. 6–7. Despite the availability now of a fairly comprehensive literature on the court Jews (see *supra,* n. 7; and Chap. LXI, nn. 17–18), information about their activities in this area during the first half of the seventeenth century still is extremely limited.

48. K. Lamprecht, *Deutsche Geschichte,* 5th ed., V, Part 2, p. 495; L. Löwenstein, *Geschichte der Juden in der Kurpfalz,* p. 79; *supra,* Chap. LXI, n. 59. A graphic description of the final decay of the once formidable Hanse is offered by K. Pagel in *Die Hanse,* pp. 343 ff. Since 1898, when A. Feilchenfeld published his essay on "Anfang und Blüthezeit der Portugiesengemeinde in Hamburg" in *Zeitschrift* of the Verein für Hamburgische Geschichte, X, 199–240 (see also *infra,* n. 49), much research has gone into the story of the settlement of Jews in Hamburg. A major step forward was made by M. Grunwald's *Portugiesengräber auf deutscher Erde;* and his *Hamburgs deutsche Juden bis zur Auflösung der Dreigemeinden 1811.* Although a bit unsystematic, his data are still extremely useful today. Important documentary additions have been made by C. Roth in his "Neue Kunde von der Marranengemeinde in Hamburg," *ZGJD,* II, 228–36 (analyzing the names recorded

in the denunciations made by Hector Mendes Bravo in 1617 and by Diego de Lima in 1644 before the Lisbon Inquisition); and by A. Cassuto in his "Neue Funde zur ältesten Geschichte der portugiesischen Juden in Hamburg," ibid., III, 58–72; as well as his "Zur Bibliographie und Geschichte der portugiesischen Juden in Hamburg," MGWJ, LXXVI, 213–16 (attributing a rare apologetic treatise of 1612 to Ishac, son of the physician Rodrigo de Castro).

This ever richer accumulation of significant data has more recently been crowned by H. Kellenbenz's comprehensive study, Sephardim an der unteren Elbe, ihre wirtschaftliche und politische Bedeutung vom Ende des 16. bis zum Beginn des 18. Jahrhunderts, which, based upon extensive archival researches, has yielded particularly valuable information on the political and economic developments. It is to be read together with the same author's monographs, Unternehmerkräfte im Hamburger Portugal- und Spanienhandel, 1590–1625; "Der Brasilienhandel der Hamburger 'Portugiesen' zu Ende des 16. und in der ersten Hälfte des 17. Jahrhunderts," Portugiesische Forschungen der Görresgesellschaft, I, 316–39; and "Hamburger Wirtschaftsbeziehungen zu den Azoren im 17. Jahrhundert," ibid., II, 277–97. Nonetheless, some of the older investigations, such as R. Ehrenberg's Zur Geschichte der Hamburger Handlung im 16. Jahrhundert, still merit careful consideration. In all these developments the Thirty Years' War exerted both a retarding and a stimulating influence in different areas. See M. Hroch's succinct remarks on "Der Dreissigjährige Krieg und die europäischen Handelsbeziehungen," Wissenschaftliche Zeitschrift of the Ernst Moritz Arndt University of Greifswald, Gesellschafts- und Sprachwissenschaftliche Reihe, XII, 533–43.

49. See the various entries in the Index to H. Kellenbenz's Sephardim, p. 561 s.v. Dinis, and his observations, p. 28; as well as M. Grunwald's earlier remarks, in his Portugiesengräber, pp. 151 ff. Understandably, the local authorities were from the outset confronted with problems arising from the denominational divisions among the incoming merchant groups. Long before dealing with the question of the permissibility of Jewish public worship, for instance, they had to allow the English settlers to hold prayer meetings according to the Anglican rite. See M. Möring, "Die Englische Kirche in Hamburg und die Merchant Adventurers," Hamburgische Geschichts- und Heimatsblätter, XX, 93–112. The Marrano, and later the professedly Jewish, merchants helped to develop Hamburg's international trade with both the old and the new centers of Jewish life, including Amsterdam, Antwerp, London, and Bordeaux. See, for example, J. Fayard, "Note sur le trafic maritime entre Bordeaux et Hambourg à la fin du XVIIᵉ siècle," Annales du Midi, LXXIX, 219–28; and infra, Vol. XV. Nor were the commercial relations between these new Jewish communities devoid of religious complications. For instance, the question of whether supervision over Bordeaux wines was adequate to satisfy the ritual requirements of Hamburg's Jewish consumers was later to give rise to a protracted controversy between the two Jewries. See my The Jewish Community, II, 163 f.; III, 159 n. 42; and A. Hertzberg, The French Enlightenment, p. 87 n. 20.

50. The text of the 1612 agreement is reproduced in J. Klefeker, ed., Sammlung hamburgischer Gesetze und Verfassungen, II, 312 ff.; and G. Ziegra's Sammlung von Urkunden . . . und dergleichen mehr als eine Grundlage zur hamburgischen Kirchenhistorie. See also Hartwig Levy's Hamburg dissertation, Die Entwicklung der Rechtsstellung der Hamburger Juden, esp. pp. 8 ff.

51. See Hartwig Levy, *Die Entwicklung der Rechtsstellung*, p. 11. Of considerable interest also are the opinions rendered by other university faculties with respect to the more specific question of whether Jews should be permitted to maintain synagogues. This question was raised in 1647 by the city of Minden, which had long tolerated the existence of a Jewish house of worship and, in 1624, had tried merely to restrict it to "one of such a character that they [Jews] should be able to offer prayers and hold services there without noise and offense to the Christian community, as has hitherto been the case." It appears that the five families legally protected in Minden in 1641 and after were able to maintain such a locale and to furnish it with the necessary quorum of ten adult males. Yet six years later, on the occasion of the renewal of their license, the city council decided to secure opinions on the subject from the Juridical and Theological Faculties of Wittenberg and the Juridical Faculty of Helmstadt. The two former faculties replied in the affirmative; their lengthy memorandum suggested no further restrictions. The Helmstadt Faculty, too, approved the continued maintenance of the existing synagogue, but argued that, if no Jewish house of worship had existed in Minden before, no *new* synagogue could legally be erected. Remarkably, it was this generally more liberal Protestant Faculty which fell back on the ancient Catholic canonical prohibition of new synagogues, although it must have known that this restriction had been disregarded in countless cases. See M. Krieg, "Die Juden in der Stadt Minden bis zum Stadtreglement von 1723," *Westfälische Zeitschrift*, XCIII, Part 2, pp. 113–96, esp. pp. 118 f., 142 f.

These quibbles lost much of their significance soon thereafter, however, when, as a result of the Peace Treaties of Westphalia, Minden lost her independence and, like Halberstadt, was incorporated into Brandenburg, then ruled by the "Great Elector" Frederick William. See *infra*, n. 62; and, on the general role of the universities in the contemporary religious controversies, see G. A. Benrath, "Die Universität der Reformationszeit," *ARG*, LVII, 32–51 (pointing out that in the period of 1560–1648 the theological and law faculties grew in prestige as the religious controversies became more heated and the burgeoning absolutist bureaucracies needed more and more juridically trained recruits; pp. 47 ff.); and *supra*, Chap. LVII, n. 29. Remarkably, at that late date some juridical faculties were still being used by public authorities as courts of appeal in individual cases. Some intricate problems of alleged swindles committed by a Marburg Jew, Isaac, were submitted in 1666 to the local juridical faculty for its authoritative opinion. See G. Pätzold, *Die Marburger Juristenfakultät als Spruchkollegium*, pp. 161 ff. App. xiii.

52. R. van Roesbroeck, "Die Niederlassung von Flamen und Wallonen in Hamburg (1567–1615). Ein Überblick," *Zeitschrift* of the Verein für hamburgische Geschichte, XLIX–L, 53–76; J. S. da Silva Rosa, *Geschiedenis der Portugeesche Joden te Amsterdam 1593–1925*, pp. 14 ff.; M. Grunwald, *Portugiesengräber*, passim; H. Kellenbenz, *Sephardim*, pp. 37 ff. Among the outstanding clerical opponents of the Jews was Johannes Müller, pastor of St. Peter's Church. Apart from his frequent harangues from the pulpit against Jews and Judaism, he published a pamphlet in 1644 under the telling title *Judaismus oder Judentumb / das ist ausführlicher Bericht von des Jüdischen Volkes Unglauben / Blindheit und Verstockung*. See also, more generally, W. Jensen, *Die Hamburgische Kirche und ihre Geistlichen seit der Reformation*.

53. M. Grunwald, *Hamburgs deutsche Juden bis zur Auflösung der Dreigemeinden 1811;* Galeazzo Gualdo Priorato's report in his *Relationi de' governi e stati delle città imperiali* . . . *di Colonia*, etc., Bologna, 1664, excerpted by Hudtwalcker in "Des Grafen Galeazzo Gualdo Priorato Beschreibung von Hamburg im Jahre 1663," *Zeitschrift* of the Verein für Hamburgische Geschichte, III, 140–56, esp. p. 151. Obviously, even the 600 Portuguese Jews of 1663 formed but a tiny minority in the city's population, which at that time embraced over 60,000 souls. See H. Weczerka, "Bevölkerungszahlen der Hansestädte (insbesondere Danzigs) nach H[enryk] Samsonowicz," *Hansische Geschichtsblätter*, LXXXII, 69–86, esp. pp. 76 ff., with reference to Samsonowicz's "Problems of Historical Demography in the Hanse Region in the XIV–XVth Centuries" (Polish), *Zapiski historyczne*, XXVIII, 523–54.

54. See M. Grunwald, *Hamburgs deutsche Juden*, *passim;* the text reproduced in his *Portugiesengräber*, p. 53. On some occasions, however, the Hamburg Portuguese denied their support to a distant Ashkenazic group, as in 1652 when the elders rejected the plea of a representative of an unnamed Moravian community for a subsidy toward the building of a synagogue. Of course, like other Jews, the Hamburg Sephardim also evinced deep interest in the affairs of Palestinian Jewry and, before long, became emotionally involved in Shabbetai Zevi's messianic movement. See B. Brilling, "Die Frühesten Beziehungen der Juden Hamburgs zu Palästina," *JJLG*, XXI, 19–38; and the pertinent entries in the communal minute book, excerpted in German trans. by J. C[assuto] in his "Aus dem ältesten Protokollbuch der Portugiesisch-Jüdischen Gemeinde in Hamburg. Uebersetzung und Anmerkungen," *ibid.*, VI, 1–54; VII, 159–210; VIII, 227–90; IX, 318–66; X, 225–95; XI, 1–76; XIII, 55–118, esp. VI, 31; XI, 5 ff.

Not surprisingly, in time the Ashkenazic Jews greatly outnumbered their Sephardic brethren and became the mainstay of the tri-city community. On the history of this German community see A. Feilchenfeld, "Die Älteste Geschichte der deutschen Juden in Hamburg," *MGWJ*, XLIII, 271–82, 322–28, 370–81; M. M. Haarbleicher, *Zwei Epochen aus der Geschichte der Deutsch-Israelitischen Gemeinde in Hamburg;* M. Grunwald, *Hamburgs deutsche Juden* (both mainly for the period after 1650); E. (Y.) Duckesz, *Zur Geschichte und Genealogie der ersten Familien der Hochdeutschen Israeliten-Gemeinden in Hamburg-Altona;* idem, *Chachme AHW. Biographien und Grabsteininschriften der Dajanim, Autoren und der sonstigen hervorragenden Männer der drei Gemeinden Altona, Hamburg, Wandsbek* (in Hebrew, with an abridged German trans. by S. Goldschmidt). The exclusive attitudes evolving among Sephardim and Ashkenazim, which assumed much more extreme forms in northwestern Europe than in the Mediterranean lands or the New World, will be analyzed in later chapters. For the time being, reference need be made only to H. J. Zimmels, *Ashkenazim and Sephardim: Their Relations, Differences, and Problems as Reflected in the Rabbinical Responsa.*

55. See M. Grunwald, *Portugiesengräber*, pp. 128 ff.; H. Kellenbenz, *Sephardim*, pp. 61 ff.; A. Cassuto, "Die Portugiesischen Juden in Glückstadt," *JJLG*, XXI, 287–317 (also listing in the Appendix the names recorded on the local tombstones, reproducing some inscriptions and commenting on them); and, more generally, D. Detlefsen, "Die Städtische Entwicklung Glückstadts unter Christian IV," *Zeitschrift* of the Gesellschaft für Schleswig-Holsteinische Geschichte, XXXVI, 191–256; and J. P. Jacobson, "Glückstadt als religiöse Freistatt," *Heimatbuch des Kreises Stein-*

burg, II, 220–49. Remarkably, the term "Portuguese" was used here not only as a synonym for "Jew," as in Italy and France, but also a synonym for the Jewish faith. In the original record of the royal invitation to foreign merchants to settle in Glückstadt we read: "If there is anyone wishing to establish himself in Glückstadt, be he of whatever religion, Portuguese, Catholic, Mennonite, or Calvinist . . . he shall live under the protection of his Majesty, the King, and dwell as a privileged person for twenty years free from all imposts." See D. Detlefsen, *Geschichte der holsteinschen Erbmarschen,* II, 189; Grunwald, *Portugiesengräber,* p. 128 n. 3; and *supra,* Chap. LVI, nn. 59–61.

Understandably, the Glückstadt Jews were so overjoyed by the conclusion of the Peace Treaty of Lübeck in 1629 that they issued a coin with the Hebrew Tetragrammaton imprinted on it; this coin came to be called by their neighbors the "Hebrew" coin. It may also have been connected with some sort of regulation which restricted the duty of billeting soldiers, otherwise imposed upon all inhabitants during hostilities, to the Lutheran burghers. At least this is Detlefsen's interpretation of a somewhat ambiguous application submitted by the burghers in 1631, and of the pertinent royal decree of November 30, 1645. See *Zeitschrift,* XXXVI, 227 f., 248. See also, more generally, K. Asmussen's twin essays, "Die Politischen, wirtschaftlichen und militärischen Pläne Christians IV. als Anlass zur Gründung Glückstadts," and "Die Gründung Glückstadts und ihre Baugeschichte," in *Glückstadt im Wandel der Zeiten,* published by the municipality of Glückstadt, Vol. I, pp. 31–33 and 33–41, respectively.

56. M. Grunwald, *Portugiesengräber,* pp. 9 f., 133 f. On the Jewish community of Emden, see *ibid.,* pp. 142 ff.; A. Cassuto, "Über portugiesische Juden in Emden," *JFF,* V, 173–75. The archbishop of Bremen also effectively employed Herscheider for his currency manipulations, conducted along the lines followed on a larger scale by Alvaro Dinis. In cooperation with his brother-in-law Paul Dirichsen (also known as Paulo de Millão, Moses Abensur, etc.), Dinis participated in the production and distribution of coins not only for the archbishop but also for the counts of Schaumburg, the original lords of Altona and Glückstadt; their successor, the king of Denmark; and Duke Francis II of Saxe-Lauenburg. But, as we saw, Dinis later turned to other less risky, and in the long run less objectionable, business pursuits. See the detailed review in H. Kellenbenz, *Sephardim,* pp. 214 ff. with the sources cited there; and *supra,* n. 49.

57. J. F. Voigt, "Die Anleihen der Stadt Hamburg während der Jahre 1601 bis 1650," *Zeitschrift* of the Verein für Hamburgische Geschichte, XVII, 129–253; H. Kellenbenz, "Hamburg und die französisch-schwedische Zusammenarbeit im 30-jährigen Krieg," *ibid.,* XLIX–L, 83–107. See also H.-D. Loose, *Hamburg und Christian IV. von Dänemark im dreissigjährigen Kriege. Ein Beitrag zur Geschichte der hamburgischen Reichsunmittelbarkeit.* On the Hamburg Bank, see *infra,* n. 61.

58. H. Kellenbenz, *Sephardim,* pp. 35, 338 ff.; and his brief communication, "Tradiciones nobiliarias de los grupos sefardíes," summarized by J. M. Hassán in his report on "El Simposio de estudios sefardíes," *Sefarad,* XXIV, 333.

59. M. Kayserling, "Zur Geschichte der jüdischen Ärzte. Die Familie de Castro," *MGWJ,* VIII, 161–70, 330–39; IX, 92–98; Uriel da Costa, *Exemplar humanae vitae*

in *Die Schriften des Uriel da Costa*, ed. by C. Gebhardt. On the Rosales-Bocarro family, see H. Kellenbenz, "Dr. Jakob Rosales," *Zeitschrift für Religions- und Geistesgeschichte*, VIII, 345–54; idem, *Sephardim*, pp. 338 ff.; P. A. d'Azevedo, "O Bocarro Francês e os Judeus de Cochim e Hamburgo," *Archivo histórico portuguêz*, VIII, 15–20, 185–98; and I. S. Révah, "Une Famille de nouveaux chrétiens: les Bocarro Francês," *REJ*, CXVI, 73–83. See also *infra*, Chap. LXIII. Despite his brief sojourn in Hamburg, Da Costa found a worthy opponent in the local scholar Samuel da Silva. The stir caused by Da Costa's oral denial of the immortality of the soul in 1616, which had resulted in his being placed under a ban by the Amsterdam community, called forth Da Silva's reply in 1623 under the title *Tratado da immortalidade del alma*. It appeared a year before Da Costa's own *Examen dos Tradicõens Phariseas conferidas con a Ley escrita*, which contained a counterattack on Da Silva, called a "falso calumniador." These controversies and other significant contributions made by Hamburg Portuguese Jews to science and literature will be discussed in various other contexts.

60. M. Grunwald, *Portugiesengräber*, pp. 36, 123 f.; H. Kellenbenz, *Sephardim*, pp. 163 ff., 278 ff., 385 ff., and *passim*. Of the relatively large literature on the Teixeira clan see T. R. Valck-Lucassen, "The Teixeira Family in the Dutch Book of Nobility" (Dutch), *Maandblad* of the Genealogisch-heraldiek Genootschap de Nederlandsche Leeuw, XXXVI, 121 ff.; XXXVII, 138 ff.; A. Cassuto, "Die Familie des Dom Diego Senior Teixeira de Sampayo (teilweise alten Aufzeichnungen entnommen)," *JFF*, V, 115–17; R. Silbergleit, "Manuel Teixeira," *ibid.*, pp. 117–18; M. Grunwald, "Le Procès de l'Inquisition contre Diego et Manoel Teixeira," *REJ*, LIX, 239–47; and H. Kellenbenz, "Diego und Manoel Teixeira und ihr Hamburger Unternehmen," *VSW*, XLII, 289–352. In his brief note, Silbergleit reports interesting anecdotes about a Christian preacher who was so impressed with Manuel Teixeira's carriage and liveried coachmen that he bowed deeply to the unknown dignitary inside until he learned to his chagrin that the passenger was a Jew; and about Teixeira's being entertained at a meal by a general who served him a delicious-tasting fish. To the disappointment of the general's chef (perhaps of Teixeira, too) the fish turned out to be of a variety ritually forbidden to Jews. On his father's typically Jewish legacies for the redemption of captives and the marrying off of impecunious girls, see A. Cassuto's brief additional note, "Aus den Testamenten des Abraham Senior Teixeira (Nach einer in dem Besitz des Verfassers befindlichen unbeglaubigten portugiesischen Handschrift)," *JFF*, VIII, 419–20.

61. See H. Kellenbenz's essays cited *supra*, n. 48; H. Gonsiorowski's Hamburg dissertation, *Die Berufe der Juden Hamburgs von der Einwanderung bis zur Emanzipation*; L. Wolf, ed., *Menasseh ben Israel's Mission to Oliver Cromwell. Being a Reprint of the Pamphlets published by Menasseh ben Israel to Promote the Re-admission of the Jews to England, 1649–56*, pp. 88 f.; and other data presented by M. Grunwald and H. Kellenbenz, *passim*. On the Jewish businessmen involved in the foundation and early evolution of the Hamburg Bank (1619–23), see the names listed by H. Reils in his "Beiträge zur ältesten Geschichte der Juden in Hamburg. Aus den Acten des Ministerial-Archivs," *Zeitschrift* of the Verein für Hamburgische Geschichte, II, 380 n.; and, more generally, H. Sieveking, "Die Hamburger Bank" in *History of the Principal Public Banks, Accompanied by Extensive Bibliographies of the History of Banking and Credit in Eleven European Countries*, ed. by J. G.

van Dillen, pp. 125–60. Even the German Jews of Hamburg followed the example of their Portuguese coreligionists in keeping rates of interest at a moderate level. At least in 1648, when the representatives of the burghers demanded from the Senate the expulsion of all German Jews and their replacement by a *Lummert* (Lombard or Loan Bank), the Senate replied that such institutions usually "charged between 24 and 30 percent, which would be of help to no one." See M. Grunwald, *Portugiesengräber*, p. 8 n. 2.

62. See F. Wagner's Münster dissertation, *Die Säkularisation des Bistums Halberstadt und seine Einverleibung in den Brandenburgisch-Preussischen Staat 1648–50*, esp. pp. 49 f.; M. Köhler, *Beiträge zur neueren jüdischen Wirtschaftsgeschichte*, pp. 8 ff., 63 ff.; B. H. Auerbach, *Geschichte der israelitischen Gemeinde Halberstadt*, pp. 23 ff.; S. Stern, *Der Preussische Staat und die Juden*, Part 1: Die Zeit des Grossen Kurfürsten und Friedrichs I., esp. I, Part 2, pp. 92 ff. No. 104 (the text of Frederick William's decree of May 1, 1650, granting a general license to the Jews of Halberstadt). It may be noted that that era, once greatly extolled in the German historical literature, has lost much of its attraction in recent years. See G. Heinrich's remarks in his "Forschungen zur Geschichte der Mark Brandenburg. Ein Literaturbericht über die Jahre 1941–1956," *Jahrbuch für die Geschichte Mittel- und Ostdeutschlands*, IX–X, 375 ff.

63. R. Clément, *La Condition des Juifs de Metz*, pp. 33 f., 260 ff. No. xv; J. Bauer, "Cinq lettres des consuls d'Avignon," *REJ*, LIII, 274 f. No. iii. See also *supra*, n. 31. Since the effects of French rule over Metz and the other communities of Alsace and Lorraine can be understood only in connection with developments in the rest of France and were to make themselves fully felt only after the Peace Treaties of Westphalia, an analysis of these important changes must be reserved for future chapters. In the meantime we need but refer to the brief modern summaries by N. Netter, *Vingt siècles d'histoire d'une communauté juive (Metz et son grand passé)*; and J. Rochette, *Histoire des Juifs d'Alsace des origines à la Révolution*.

64. See the texts of the Osnabrück and Münster treaties ed. in Latin, with a German trans. of selected excerpts by K. Müller in his *Instrumenta Pacis Westphalicae. Die Westfälischen Friedensverträge 1648*, esp. Arts. iv. 34–35, v.i, 48–49, pp. 23f., 41 f. (Latin), 113, 127 f. (German). More comprehensive documentary material was assembled as early as 1734–36 by J. G. von Meiern in his ed. of *Acta Pacis Westphalicae publica oder Westphälische Friedens-Handlungen und Geschichte*. A new effort to issue an up-to-date edition of the *Acta Pacis Westphalicae* was undertaken by M. Braubach and K. Repgen. Volume I of each of three series saw the light of day in 1962–65. Of the vast additional contemporary documentation and still vaster secondary literature, we need but refer here to the selected bibliography listed by F. Dickmann in *Der Westfälische Frieden*, esp. pp. 343 ff., 370 f., 413 ff., with the comments thereon by K. von Raumer in his "Westfälischer Friede," *HZ*, CXCV, 596–613.

Dickmann also points out the sharply divergent nineteenth-century German and French interpretations of the two treaties. The increasingly nationalistic German historians almost unanimously condemned them, whereas their French counterparts tended to echo Voltaire's old characterization that they had symbolized "the glory of France." However the religious factors and libertarian trends, which deeply influenced the negotiations, are somewhat neglected by both Dickmann and his reviewer in their emphasis on the political and constitutional aspects of the treaties. See also the respective presentations made by several French and German historians at an April 1963 colloquium in Münster, published under the title *Forschungen und Studien zur Geschichte des Westfälischen Friedens*. On the complex problem of "parity" and its operation in the German Diet in the following century and a half, see the detailed juridical analyses by L. Weber in *Die Parität der Konfessionen in der Reichsverfassung von den Anfängen der Reformation bis zum Untergang des alten Reiches im Jahre 1806;* and M. Heckel, "Parität," *ZRG*, Kanonistische Abteilung, LXXX, 261–420.

65. See F. Wolff, *Corpus Evangelicorum und Corpus Catholicorum auf dem Westfälischen Friedenskongress. Die Einführung der konfessionellen Ständeverbindungen in die Reichsverfassung;* and R. Dietrich, "Landeskirchenrecht und Gewissensfreiheit in den Verhandlungen des Westfälischen Friedenskongresses," *HZ*, CXCVI, 563–83. It is not surprising, therefore, that in the aftermath of the peace congress, in the endless debates on its decisions on a national or local level, hardly any reference was made to Jews and their status under the novel conditions created by the treaties. See, for one example, A. Ernstberger, "Anklang des Westfälischen Friedens am Nürnberger Reichskonvent 1648–1650," *ZBL*, XXXI, 259–85.

66. Innocent X's breve, *Zelo domus Dei* of November 20, 1648, in *Bullarium romanum*, XV, 603 ff. No. cxvi; Johannes Vervaux's statement cited by K. Brandi in his *Deutsche Reformation und Gegenreformation*, Part 2, p. 297; Alvise Contarini's dispatch of September 26, 1650, reproduced by J. Fiedler in his edition of *Relationen der Botschafter Venedigs über Deutschland und Österreich im 17. Jahrhundert*, I, 293 ff., 334. The changing attitudes of the papal Curia in the last phases of the Thirty Years' War have often been analyzed. See C. C. Eckhardt, *The Papacy and World Affairs as Reflected in Secularization of Politics*, esp. pp. 140 ff., 193 ff.; A. Krause, "Die Auswärtige Politik Urbans VIII. Grundzüge und Wendepunkte," *Mélanges Eugène Tisserant*, Vol. IV (*Studi e testi*, CCXXXIV), pp. 407–452; and, more comprehensively, K. Repgen, *Die Römische Kurie und der Westfälische Friede: Idee und Wirklichkeit des Papstums im 16. und 17. Jahrhundert*, Vols. I–II; idem, "Der Päpstliche Protest gegen den Westfälischen Frieden und die Friedenspolitik Urbans VIII," *HJB*, LXXV, 94–122.

Nor were the Protestant envoys wholly cognizant of the extent to which the peace treaties represented a tacit approval of the secularization of politics. In a memorandum he submitted to the peace conference in 1647, Jacob Lampadius still argued, with reference to biblical precedents, that governments "have the duty to preserve the right cult of the Deity and to steer clear of any false cult and human interpretations of the [true] one." See R. Dietrich, "Landeskirchenrecht und Gewissensfreiheit," *HZ*, CXCVI, 563–83; and, more generally, H. Hansluwka's Vienna dissertation, *Die Religiösen und kirchlichen Fragen im Westfälischen Frieden* (typescript).

In view of the considerable significance attached to the Augsburg Religious Peace of 1555 in both the negotiations and the formulations of the treaties, the views of Catholic and Protestant theologians and jurists on this subject, as well as on the general state and Church relations, exerted much influence on the statesmen assembled in Westphalia. See M. Heckel's twin essays, "Staat und Kirche nach den

Lehren der evangelischen Juristen Deutschlands in der ersten Hälfte des 17. Jahrhunderts," *ZRG,* Kanonistische Abteilung, LXXIII, 117–247; and "Autonomia und Pacis Compositio—Der Augsburger Religionsfriede in der Deutung der Gegenreformation," *ibid.,* LXXVI, 141–248.

67. C. V. Wedgwood, *The Thirty Years' War,* p. 526. See also the literature listed *supra,* n. 1.

68. M. Popper, "Les Juifs de Prague," *REJ,* XXIX, 130 f.; F. Priebatsch, "Die Judenpolitik," *Festschrift Schäfer,* p. 577; *supra,* Vols. IV, pp. 208 f., 344 nn. 76–77; XII, pp. 136 ff., 309 nn. 5–6.

69. The demographic shifts in Germany and Poland and, indirectly, in Western Europe and its overseas dependencies, mightily contributed to the sociopolitical and cultural factors leading up to the ultimate, legally safeguarded, equality of rights. These manifold factors, bringing to fruition many earlier trends but fully shaping up in the mid-seventeenth century and after, will be more fully analyzed in volumes dealing with the Emancipation era.

70. See F. Priebatsch, "Die Judenpolitik," *Festschrift Schäfer,* p. 583; P. Burkhardt, "Die Judenverfolgungen im Kurfürstentum Sachsen von 1536 an," *Theologische Studien und Kritiken,* LXX, 593–98; *supra,* Chap. LXI, *passim.* The changing attitude of Protestant states toward Jews and Judaism began affecting ecclesiastical circles also; it even colored the German liturgy of the time. See the illustrations offered (mainly from the period after 1650) by S. Riemer in his *Philosemitismus im deutschen evangelischen Kirchenlied des Barock* (includes a generally questioning Intro. on "Philosemitismus in der evangelischen Kirche des absoluten Staates?" pp. 7 ff.).